Printing Technology

Fifth Edition

J. Michael Adams, President
Fairleigh Dickinson University

Penny Ann Dolin, Faculty
Arizona State University East

DELMAR
™
THOMSON LEARNING

Australia   Canada   Mexico   Singapore   Spain   United Kingdom   United States

DELMAR

★

THOMSON LEARNING

Printing Technology, Fifth Edition
by
J. Michael Adams and Penny Ann Dolin

Business Unit Director:
Alar Elken

Executive Editor:
Sandy Clark

Acquisitions Editor:
Jim Gish

Developmental Editor:
Jeanne Mesick

Executive Production Manager:
Mary Ellen Black

Project Editor:
Ruth Fisher

Production Coordinator:
Ruth Fisher

Art/Design Coordinator:
Rachel Baker

Executive Marketing Manager:
Maura Theriault

Channel Manager:
Mona Caron

Marketing Manager:
Brian McGrath

Cover Design:
La Verne Abe Harris

Library of Congress Cataloging-in-Publication Data

Adams, J. Michael.
  Printing technology / J. Michael Adams, Penny Ann Dolin.—
5th ed.
    p. cm.
  Includes bibliographical references and index.
  ISBN 0-7668-2232-X (alk. paper) — ISBN 0-7668-2233-8
(instructor's guide : alk. paper)
  1. Printing.   I. Dolin, Penny Ann. II. Title.

Z244 .A515 2002
686.2—dc21

                                         2001017349

NOTICE TO THE READER

The fifth edition of Printing Technology
is lovingly dedicated to the two individuals
who provided the support and encouragement
necessary to complete this revision,
my husband and my daughter,
Ron and Sage Ann Schneider.

—Penny Ann Dolin

Contents

v

Preface

Penny Ann Dolin

Faculty

Arizona State University East

When *Printing Technology* was introduced in 1977, it was one of a new generation of books that dealt with printing as a technology, rather than as merely a process. The decade before had seen a revolution in the printing industry. Computer typesetting had become a commercial reality; presensitized litho plates had been introduced; offset printing had surpassed relief in percentage of sheets printed; web presses had grown in sophistication and acceptance. The first edition of *Printing Technology* covered the priting processes, but it also addressed the printing revolution and offered an introduction to the sophistication of printing.

We are still amazed by and appreciative of the reception of that first edition. Classroom teachers and their students reacted with enthusiasm. Instructors liked the combination of concepts with practice, and students liked the understandable language and contemporary illustrations. The second edition arrived in 1982, and the third came in 1988 as a result of the encouragement of many individuals who offered suggestions for improvement. The third edition was used at nearly every level of graphic arts education—in public, private, and industrial training—and found wide national and international acceptance.

The fourth edition of *Printing Technology* was published in 1996, and at that time the changes that the computer was bringing to the industry seemed revolutionary. It appeared that the computer had entered every aspect of printing, but it was hard to predict just how pervasive it would prove to be and how fast the changes would come.

Preparation of the Fifth Edition

In the past five years the printing industry has continued to face a fundamental restructuring of how it produces its products and conducts its business. Entire job classifications such as pasteup and stripping, have either disappeared or are being rapidly phased out. The Internet has become a dominant force in every aspect of business, and customers producing printed material are also concurrently publishing their information to the World Wide Web. Printers are becoming information managers, with their products having to be repurposed for a variety of different output options. Digital workflows must be understood and embraced for those in the printing industry to stay competitive in the new millennium.

In this fifth edition the challenge has been to introduce technologies that are truly taking hold and proving effective and avoid those that appear with fanfare but fade away quickly. The sections on computer-to-plate and digital printing have been greatly expanded because they are in the process of becoming an integral part of the printing industry. There are estimates today that in just a few years the purchases of digital presses will outnumber those of conventional offset presses. The technologies involved in publishing to the Internet are reviewed as more and more printers are offering web design and production services. New business models involving e-management and data collection have been introduced, and Internet addresses have been added to the list of resources in the Appendix.

The trend in the past decade has been toward consolidation and a blurring of boundaries between what was traditionally considered the purview of prepress and what was considered strictly the printer's domain. Many production components have moved downstream with more and more control residing with the content creator. This has resulted in a printing and publishing industry that is more collaborative in its production processes than it was just a few years ago.

The book is structured such that the reader will first review the historical and traditional processes, because they remain critical to an understanding of where we are today. Basic concepts of traditional prepress are reviewed, but a number of specific procedures have been omitted because they are no longer done, such as process camera work. Four entirely new chapters are devoted to understanding digital terminology and digital prepress concepts. Many chapters have been expanded to reflect changes that will continue to accelerate even as this book goes to press. But even with the myriad changes that are occurring in the graphic arts industry, much of what was contained in the fourth edition still has validity today. For the sound foundation that this classic book evidences throughout, I am completely indebted to the authors who created and continuously improved this book through four editions and the truly revolutionary changes that continue to transform the industry today.

Major Changes and Additions

Chapter 2: Details regarding relief plates have been removed and letterpress specialty applications moved to chapter 17.

Chapters 3, 4 and 6: These chapters are the result of condensing former chapters that detailed traditional production techniques. Although the basic concepts remain, many specific step-by-step procedures have been removed.

Chapter 5: An expanded discussion of color theory and elimination of the step-by-step process of producing color separations in the traditional manner.

Chapters 7 through 10: Completely new chapters covering digital infrastructure terminology and concepts necessary to understand today's digital prepress technology (input, assembly and output).

Chapters 11, 14 and 15: Expanded sections on automation of presses, including a discussion of the CIP3 standard, new developments in gravure and flexography, and a completely revised and expanded section on ink-jet and digital printing.

Chapter 16: A new section on ultraviolet-curing inks.

Chapter 18: An expanded discussion of automated data collection and estimating software, with a completely new section covering the new e-management models being adopted by the printing industry.

Appendixex B and C: Current industry resources have been added, along with information on health and safety issues.

In addition to these changes, new illustrations and photographs have been added throughout. Statistics and updated information have also been added where needed.

Acknowledgments

As in previous editions, many individuals and organizations were critical to the success of the fifth edition of *Printing Technology.* I wish to especially thank the following Arizona State University students whose participation and contributions were invaluable: Daniel Burns, Paul Matthews, Jo Ramirez, and Jennifer Tweedy. In addition, the constant support and encouragement of my fellow faculty and my department chair, Dr. Thomas Schildgen, helped to provide focus and enthusiasm during the course of the revision.

This book would not have been possible without the numerous contributions from members of the graphics arts industry and trade and educational organizations. In particular, I would like to thank the Agfa Corporation for their generosity and willingness to provide resources for this edition. The following companies and organizations must also be recognized for the role they played in making the fifth edition of *Printing Technology* possible.

—Penny Ann Dolin

Contributors to the Fifth Edition

Adobe Systems Incorporated: www.adobe.com
Armotek Industries, Inc.: www.armotek.com
Agfa Corporation:
    www.agfahome.com/publications
American M & M: www.screenprintmachinery.com
AOpen: www.aopenusa.com
Apple Computer, Inc.: www.apple.com
Canto: www.canto.com
Cisco Systems, Inc.: www.cisco.com
Cray Inc.: www.cray.com
Max Daetwyler Inc.: www.daetwyler

DK& A, Inc.: www.dka.com
Douthitt: www.douthittcorp.com
Epson America Inc.: www.epson.com
Flexographic Technical Association:
    www.flexography.org
Fujifilm Graphic Systems: www.fujifilm.com
Gravure Association of America: www.gaa.org
Graphic Arts Technical Foundation: www.gatf.org
Heidelberg USA, Inc.: www.heidelbergusa.com
Heritage Graphics: www.heritagegraphics.com
IBM Corporation: www.ibm.com
Imation Corporation: www.imation.com
Intel Corporation: www.intel.com
Iomega Corporation: www.iomega.com
IPTech Inc.: www.iptech.com
Ironwood Lithographers: www.ironwoodlitho.com
Kodak Polychrome Graphics Incorporated:
    www.kpgraphics.com
Koenig & Bauer AG: www.kba-print.de/de
Komori Corporation: www.komori.com
MAN Roland: www.manroland.com
Marconi Data Systems, Inc. : www.marconi.com
Markzware, Inc.: www.markzware.com
Mega Vision, Inc.: www.mega-vision.com
MicroNet Technology, Inc.:www.micronet.com
Minolta Inc: www.minolta.com
NewerRAM: www.newerram.com
Nikon, Inc.: www.nikon.com
Noosh, Inc.: www.noosh.com
Phase One, Inc.: www.phaseone.com
printCafe Incorporated: www.printcafe.com
Purup–Eskofot A/S: www.purup-eskofot.com
Quad/Graphics: www.qg.com
Quark, Inc.: www.quark.com
R and R Images, Inc.: www.randrimages.com
Rhino Productions, Inc.:
    www.rhinoproductions.com
RISO, Inc.: www.riso.com
Silicon Graphics, Inc.: www.sgi.com
Sir Speedy, Inc.: www.sirspeedy.com

Sun Microsystems: www.sun.com
Tektronix (Division of Xerox):
www.tektronix.xerox.com
University of Pennsylvania
Waterless Printing Association: www.waterless.org
Xeikon America, Inc.: www.xeikon.com
Xerox, Inc.: www.xerox.com
X-Rite, Inc.: www.xrite.com

The author and Delmar Thomson Learning would like to gratefully acknowledge those who served as reviewers for the fifth edition. Their comments and suggestions proved invaluable. Our heartfelt thanks to:

Tom Bates, LaRoche College, Pittsburgh, PA 15237
Dave, Cuatt, Pasadena City College, Pasadena, CA 91106
David Dailey, Eastern KY University, Richmond, KY 40475-3102
Linda Rotschafer, Southeast C C, 8000 "O" Street, Lincoln, NE 68520
Michael Williams, College of the Ozarks, Point Lookout, MO 65726

Contributors to This and Prior Editions
3M Mertle Collection, University of Minnesota
3M Printing & Publishing Systems Division
A.B. Dick Company
Acti Cameras Inc.
Advanced Process Supply/Wisconsin Automated
Agfa Gevaert, Inc.
American Paper Institute, Recycled Paperboard Division
AM International
Apple Computers
Arcata Graphics Company, Fairfield
Art Institute of Chicago
Baumfolder Corporation
Berkey Technical
Beta Screen Corporation
Covalent Systems Corporation
Custom-Bilt Machinery, Inc.
C-Thru Ruler Company
DuPont Crosfield Electronic Imaging
E.I. DuPont DeNours
Enkel Corporation
Environmental Choice Program, Canada

Foster Manufacturing
General Binding Corporation, Northbrook, IL
Gorelick & Associates
Graphic Arts Manufacturing Company
Graphic Arts Technical Foundation
Gravure Association of America
GTI, Graphic Technology Inc.
Hagen Systems Inc.
Heidelberg Eastern
Hewlett-Packard Corporation
IBM Corporation
Indigo America
International Museum of Photography at George Eastman House
Eastman Kodak Company
Kroy, Inc.
LogEtronics Corporation
Macbeth, Division of Kollmorgen Instruments Corporation
Mackenzie & Harris Type
MAN Roland
Mead Paper
Mergenthaler Linotype Company
Morrill Press, Division of Engraph, Inc.
Micro Essential Laboratory, Inc.
Misomex North America, Inc.
Muller-Martini Corporation
NASA
Naz-Dar/KC
NuArc Company, Inc.
Pantone, Inc.
Pearl Pressman Liberty Communications Group
Rachwal Systems
Rockwell Graphic Systems, Rockwell International Corporation
F.P. Rosback Company
Scangraphics
John N. Schaedler, Inc.
Schaefer Machine Company, Inc.
Screen USA, Subsidiary of Dainippon Screen Mfg. Co., Ltd.
Smithsonian Institution
Solna Web USA, Inc.
Southern Gravure Service
Stouffer Graphic Arts Equipment Company
Texet Corporation
Tobias Associates, Inc.
Tourtist Office of Spain
Ulano Corporation, Inc.

University of Pennsylvania
Vandersons Corporation
Videojet Systems International
Western Lithotech
Xerox Corporation
John Britts, Kenneth Dubois and Kevin Fogarty: CANON U.S.A., Inc.
Douglas and George Cauros, Speedway Press, Inc.
Roger Cherry, Macomb CC
Kate Crawford, Sinclair CC
Mark Doyle: Xerox Corporation
Ben Franklin Faux: Buena High School, Sierra Vista, Arizona
Kenneth Fay, HEUFT USA, Inc.
Chuck Finley, Columbus State C.C.
Kenneth Hanulec: Mitsubishi Imaging (MC), Inc.
John Henry, Mitchell Printing Company
Drew Hill and Alex McCombie: Drew Hill Graphic Design Group and New World Media
Ronald Hindmarch: Hilton High School, Hilton, NY
Gary Hinkle, Illinois Central College
Kenneth Hoffman, Michael Kleper, and Jere Rentzel: Rochester Institute of Technology, Rochester, NY
John Kallis, California University of PA
Edward Kelly: 3M Printing and Publishing Systems Division
Dennis Killian, Gregory Shambo, and Keith Fengler: Phillips & Jacobs, Inc.

Kent Kreul, Brayton Brunkhurst, Randy Flynn, and Philip Livingston: Milprint, Inc.
Arthur Lange: Langeraphic
Ling-Hsaia Lee, Central Mich Univ
Nancy and John Leininger: Clemson University, Clemson, South Carolina
Sam Mason: Advanced Color Technology
Andrew Mohr: Eastwood Litho, Inc.
William Mulvey: Geneva High School, Geneva, NY
Arthur Palermo and Jack Williams: Midstate Printing Company
Robert Poormon, Board of Cooperative Education Serives, Mexico, NY
Jesus Rodriguez, Pittsburgh State Univ
Tom Schildgen, Ariz State
Mike Stinnett, Oakland Tech Ctr
Kenneth Swanson: Bowne Business Communications
Janet Zimmer, State University of New York at Oswego
Todd Zimmer, Sealright Corporation, Fulton, NY
State University of New York at Oswego Art Department: Catherine Bebout, Al Bremmer, Cynthia Clabough, Nick D'Innocenzo, Thomas Ecerksley, Donna Fauler, Michael Fox, John Fuller, Paul Garland, Natasha Hopkins, Sewall Oertling, Mindy Ostrow, Barbara Perry, Zabel Sarian, Jon Shishido, Lisa Shortslef, Kate Timm, Helen Zakin, and Richard Zakin

1

The Printing Industry

Historical Background

It is possible to trace the origins of printing to the use of seals to "sign" official documents as early as 255 B.C., during the Han dynasty in

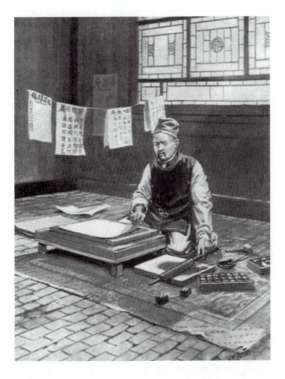

An early Chinese press. The press was a low, flat table solid enough to hold the form in place. The Bettman Archives.

China. A ceramic stamp was pressed into a sheet of moist clay. When dry, the imprint served as a means of certifying the authenticity of the document. When paper was invented, around A.D. 105, the transition to the use of the seal with ink was a natural one.

Early documents and manuscripts were copied and recopied by hand. Frequent copying mistakes were made from one edition to the next; copies often differed significantly from the author's original. Around A.D. 175, the Chinese began the practice of cutting the writings of important scholars into stone. The stones were placed in centers of learning, and students made "rubbings," or copies, on paper from the carvings. The process was faster than hand copying, and all editions were identical to the first.

No one knows when the ideas of the seal and stone rubbings came together, but in China in A.D. 953, under the administration of Fêng Tao, a large-scale block-printing operation was set up to reproduce the Confucian classics. Block prints were generally made from slabs of hard, fine-grained wood that were carved to leave well-defined raised images. The raised portions of the block were inked, paper was laid over the block, and a pad was rubbed across the surface to transfer the ink to the paper.

During the Sung dynasty, around A.D. 1401, a common man named Pi Shêng invented movable type. Building on the ideas of block printing, Shêng cut individual characters into small pieces of clay. The clay was fired to make it hard, and the individual pieces were placed in an iron frame to create the printing form. Because the pieces did not fit together perfectly, they were embedded in a mixture of hot pine resin, wax, and paper ashes. When cold, all the pieces held together perfectly tight, and the form was inked and printed. Reheating the resin mixture loosened the pieces of type so they could be reused. Other materials, including wood, tin, copper, and bronze, were used for the same purpose.

The idea of movable type traveled to neighboring countries. In Korea, in A.D. 1403, King T'aijong ordered that everything within his reach be printed in order to pass on the tradition of information contained in the works. Three hundred thousand pieces of bronze type were cast, and printing began. Less than fifty years later in Northern Germany, Johann Gutenberg worked a similar process, only using the Roman alphabet. His efforts earned him the title "father of printing." It is interesting to speculate if Gutenberg learned of the process from visitors to Asia.

Objectives

After completing this chapter you will be able to:

■ Discuss the evolution of graphic symbols from prehistoric times to the modern alphabet of the present.

■ List the major printing processes and describe the differences between them.

■ List and describe the steps in the printing cycle.

■ Rank the printing industry in terms of number of individual firms, number of employees, and value added.

■ Describe the structure and purpose of each level of a small- to medium-sized printing company.

■ Compare the kinds of services provided by the different types of printing businesses.

■ Describe the different ways to enter, train, and advance in the printing industry.

Introduction

Printing has been identified as the single most significant technological development in the history of the human species. Prior to the invention of printing all information and communication was transmitted verbally. Ideas survived as long as someone could remember the concept. Little information was retained unchanged for more than three generations. Folklore and legend formed the base for all cultures. Before printing it was very difficult

to communicate messages to a large number of people. The oral tradition was limited to small groups and the memory of the speaker.

Printing created the ability to record ideas so they could survive across many generations. It also allowed information to be communicated exactly to any number of people. Once ideas and information were made permanent and everyone had access to them, true science and technological development began.

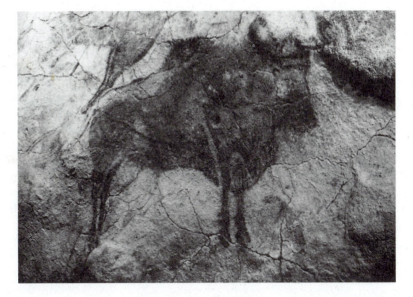

Figure 1.1   An early message. A cave drawing (message made by prehistoric people) in the Altamira caves in Spain. Courtesy of Spanish National Tourist Office, New York.

The foundation, and power, of print is the ability to reproduce graphic symbols and messages in large quantities. Graphic messages are possible because lines can be made into shapes that have meanings to human beings. As early as 35,000 B.C. people were drawing messages on cave walls (figure 1.1). These were probably intended to be temporary messages, but they became permanent. They were simple drawings—merely lines—but they carried meaning to the people of that period: "This is a mammoth," "Oh, what a feast we had," or "We hunted a great hairy beast."

Development of Pictographs

Drawings that carry meaning because they look like real objects are called pictographs (figure 1.2a). Pictographs have a one-to-one relationship with reality. To symbolize one ox (called *aleph*), draw one symbol of an ox. To represent five oxen, draw five ox symbols. It is difficult to use pictographs to communicate complex ideas, such as "I have six oxen—one brown, four white, and one white and brown." It is

impossible to symbolize abstract ideas, such as love or hate, with a pictographic system.

About 1200 B.C., in a small country called Phoenicia (now a part of Syria), a group of traders began to realize the limitations of the pictographic system. They attempted to simplify the picture notations in their account books by streamlining their symbols. But no matter how they drew the lines, *aleph* still symbolized one ox and *beth* still stood for one house (figure 1.2b).

Development of Ideographs

The next step the Phoenicians took was to have drawings symbolize ideas. These drawings are called ideographs. With this system *aleph* became the symbol for food and *beth* represented a dwelling or shelter (figure 1.2c). **Ideographs are simple drawings that symbolize ideas or concepts rather than concrete objects.** They were a vast improvement over pictographs because they could easily represent complex or abstract ideas, but they were still clumsy. The number of symbols in an ideographic system

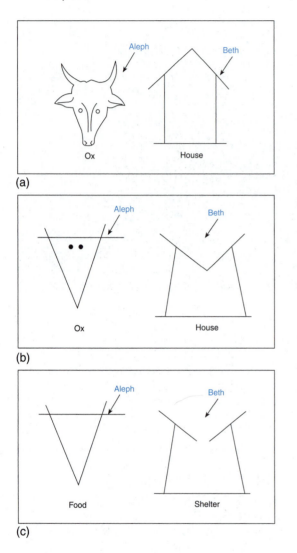

(a)

(b)

(c)

Figure 1.2 **The development of ideographs.**
Pictographs shown here in (a) and (b) were
drawn to represent real objects. They were
gradually simplified to represent general ideas
and became known as ideographs (c).

Development of Phonetic Symbols

By 900 B.C. the Phoenicians had made another
change. Instead of the picture symbolizing the
ox or food, the picture came to represent a
sound. Whenever the readers saw the symbol,
they could make the sound that the symbol
represented. When the symbols were placed
together, whole words could be repeated. This
idea of representing sounds by symbols is
known as a phonetic symbol system and is the
basis for most modern written languages. The
Phoenicians developed 19 such symbols, but
they were traders and were not concerned
with recording all words used in everyday
conversation. We form verbal symbols today
by combining consonants and vowels. The
Phoenician system contained no vowels and
was of little use in recording everyday speech.

By 403 B.C. the Greeks had officially
adopted the Phoenician system after adding
five vowels and changing the names of the letters (figure 1.3). *Aleph* became *alpha* and *beth*
became *beta*, which together form our term *alphabet*.

About one hundred years later, the early
Roman empire borrowed the Greek alphabet
and refined it to meet its needs. The Romans
accepted 13 Greek letters outright, revised 8,
and added *F* and *Q*, for a total of 23—all that
were necessary to write Latin. The Roman system stood firm for nearly twelve centuries.
About 1000 years ago the letter *U* was added
as a rounded *V*, and two *V*s were put together

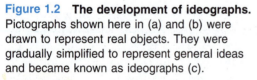

Figure 1.3 **The development of our alphabet.**
Illustrated from top to bottom are the Phoenician
alphabet (900 B.C.), the Greek alphabet (403 B.C.),
and the Roman alphabet (300 B.C.).

can be overwhelming. Most Asian societies,
such as Japan, Korea, and China, still use ideographic symbol systems which contain over
10,000 different characters. It could take a lifetime to learn the meaning of all the symbols.

to form *W*. Five hundred years later the letter *J* was added for a total of 26 letters that form our contemporary Latin alphabet.

There were still some problems with the consistency of rules to be worked out, however. Early Greek and Roman writing was done by scribes—all with different "penmanship." Some wrote from left to right; some wrote from right to left. Combine these differences with the lack of agreement on the use of punctuation marks or spaces between words or sentences, and the whole system could be quite a mess.

It wasn't until movable metal type was introduced by Johann Gutenberg in the mid fifteenth century that any true standard of punctuation or sentence structure was achieved. It took printing technology to stabilize the phonetic symbol system as we know it today. Slight changes have been made, but the basic composition of our alphabet has remained the same from the time of Gutenberg.

Printing Technology

All printing processes reproduce lines and/or dots that form an image. Printing is the process of manufacturing multiple copies of graphic images. Although most people think of printing as putting ink on paper, printing is not limited to any particular materials or inks. The embossing process uses no ink at all, and all shapes and sizes of metals, wood, and plastics are common receivers of printed messages.

Major Printing Processes

The following five major printing processes are used to reproduce graphic images:

- Relief printing
- Intaglio printing
- Screen printing
- Lithographic printing
- Electrostatic printing

Each of these processes is suited for specific applications, such as newspaper, book, package, or textile printing.

Relief Printing

The **relief printing** process includes letterpress printing, flexographic printing, and all other methods of transferring an image from a raised surface (figure 1.4a). Although it was once a major process in the printing industry, letterpress printing has been replaced largely by other printing processes. Most relief printing done today is done with flexography. Flexographic printing is used extensively in the packaging industry for printing on corrugated board, paper cartons, and plastic film. Flexography is also becoming a significant process for printing newspapers, newspaper inserts, catalogs, and directories.

Intaglio Printing

Intaglio printing is the reverse of relief printing. An intaglio image is transferred from a sunken surface (figure 1.4b). Copperplate etching and engraving are two intaglio processes. Industrial intaglio printing is called gravure. Gravure is used for extremely long press runs. Cellophane and aluminum-foil candy bar wrappers are two common packaging materials printed with gravure printing. *Reader's Digest* and *National Geographic* are but two of the many national magazines that are printed with gravure.

Screen Printing

Screen printing transfers an image by allowing ink to pass through openings in a stencil that has been applied to a screen mesh (figure 1.4c). The screen process is sometimes called silk screen printing. Silk is rarely used to hold the stencil industrially, however, because silk is not as durable as industrial screen materi-

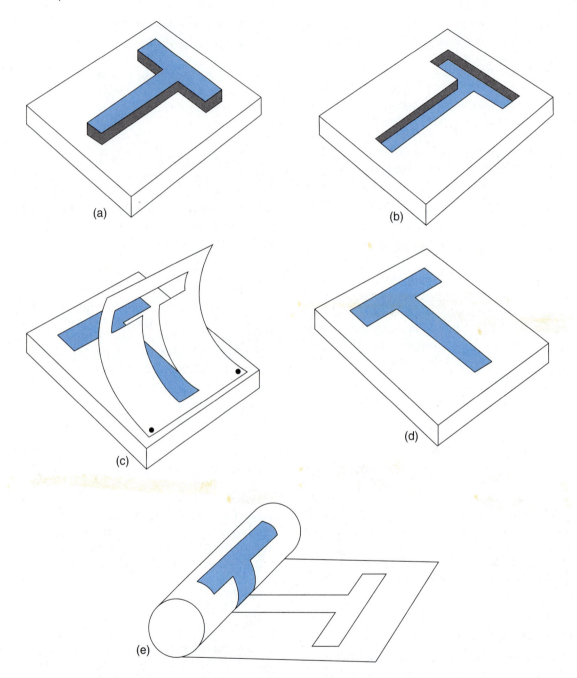

Figure 1.4   Five main printing processes. (a) Relief printing transfers an image from a raised surface. (b) Intaglio printing transfers an image from a sunken surface. (c) Screen printing transfers an image through a stencil. (d) Lithographic printing transfers an image chemically from a flat surface. (e) Electrostatic printing transfers an image using an electrostatic charge.

als. Some of the industrial uses for screen printing include printing on plastic such as round plastic containers, printing large display signs and billboards, and printing on textiles. Another major use for screen printing is in the manufacture of printed circuit boards for electrical/electronic equipment.

Lithography

Lithography as it is known today is a relatively new process, dating from around 1798. A lithographic image is transferred from a flat surface. Certain areas on the surface are chemically treated to accept ink while other areas are left untreated so that they will repel ink. When the surface is inked, the ink remains in the ink-receptive areas, but not in the untreated areas. When a material such as paper contacts the surface, ink is transferred to the paper (figure 1.4d). This process is sometimes called planography, offset lithography, offset, or photo-offset lithography.

Offset lithographic printing is the most widely used printing process in the commercial printing industry. Its major application is for printing on paper; thus it is ideal for printing newspapers, books, magazines, pamphlets, and all other forms of paper publications.

Electrostatic Printing

Electrostatic printing was invented in 1937 by Chester Carlson. It involves creating an image by electrostatically charging areas of a special drum. As a result, the drum attracts a dry or liquid toner. The toner is then transferred and fused to a sheet of paper (figure 1.4e).

Even a decade ago, electrostatic printing would not have been classified as one of the major printing processes. However, today electrostatic reproduction has become a standard part of digital printing. When a "copier" can deliver 6000 or more images that meet or exceed traditional ink density targets in an hour, the copier must be recognized as a printing press.

Although there are several older printing processes, such as collography, which prints from a fragile gelatin emulsion, these five major printing processes account for nearly 99 percent of all work done in the contemporary printing industry.

Printing technology has long been a powerful tool for social change. Edward George Bulwer-Lytton wrote, "The pen is mightier than the sword." But his statement assumes that the ideas the pen recorded are distributed. Without printing, few would read the words, and the pen would be a very weak weapon.

Printers have long been the most influential individuals in the community. Early colonial printers helped to shape our country by reproducing, recording, and distributing the ideas and events of the period. Benjamin Franklin, an early American patriot, was proudest of his role as a printer. After being active in the Revolution, a signer of the Declaration of Independence, a member of the First and Second Continental Congresses, founder of the first American library, an author, an inventor, a publisher, and ambassador to France, he directed that his epitaph should read "B. Franklin, Printer."

Printing Cycle

Since the time of Franklin, the basic cycle of the printing industry has not changed much from the following procedures:

1. Identifying a need
2. Creating an image design
3. Reproducing the image design
4. Distributing the printed message

The printing cycle begins with an identified need. The need might be as simple as the reproduction of a form or as sophisticated as a poster intended to change human attitudes. It could be as ordinary as a package designed to convince a consumer to buy one brand of cereal rather than another. Whatever the need, a graphic design evolves. Special design agencies are often set up whose sole purpose is to sell ideas to clients and work closely with the printer as the design is turned into print.

The function of printing management is to be responsible for creating and controlling the reproduction process. Skilled workers must be employed and an organization created that efficiently and effectively delivers printed products. Once a job is proposed, the most efficient printing process must be identified. Such variables as the type of material to be printed, length of run, number and types of colors, time requirements, desired quality, and customer's cost limitations must all be considered. An estimate must be made for each job. A profit must be made, and yet the estimate must be low enough to attract work in a very competitive market. If the customer approves the estimate, management must schedule the job, arrange to obtain all materials, ensure quality control, and keep track of all phases of production so the job is finished on schedule.

The final test of the cycle is the method of distributing the printed message. Without an audience for the graphic images created by the artist and printer, the printing cycle is useless. Printing is mailed; handed out on busy streets; sold on street corners; and shipped to department stores, corner drugstores, and local newsstands. It is passed out in highway tollbooths, filed in offices, pasted on billboards, carried on placards, or even thumbtacked to poster boards. The purpose of all this activity is to place printed matter in the hands of consumers.

Sequence of Steps in the Printing Processes

The printing industry has historically consisted of shops identified with particular processes, such as relief printing or lithogra-

phy. Craftsmen were trained and then bound by union or guild structure to a particular process. Recently it has become common for a printing establishment to use a variety of printing processes. Regardless of the printing process used, however, there is a sequence of production steps that all printing follows. This sequence consists of the following steps:

- Image design
- Image generation
- Image conversion
- Image assembly
- Image carrier preparation
- Image transfer
- Finishing

The point of a printed product is to meet a need, such as to inform, pursuade, entertain, or convince. The design must fulfill the customer's need. In the **image design** step, sketches and final layouts are made. Design variables such as type style, visual position, type size, balance, and harmony are all considered. After the customer approves the design, the image must be generated and made into a final form. Specifications developed during the image design stage are carefully followed during image generation. Traditionally, image generation was performed by hand, perhaps using photographic techniques. Advances in computer technology, however, have moved most image generation to the computer monitor and keyboard.

Traditionally, printing processes relied to a large degree on photography. Images were converted to transparent film in the **image conversion** step and then photographically transferred to an image carrier during the **image carrier preparation** step. Computers have revolutionized image generation and forever changed the way that image conversion and assembly happen. It is now a digital process happening within software. But no matter how advanced the processes have become, images and pages must still be assembled and prepared for an image carrier, whether film, plate, direct to digital press or prepared for a digital venue like the Internet.

The image must be printed onto a receiver material during the **image transfer** step. **Finishing** is the last step, which combines the printed material into a final finished form that can be delivered to the customer. This may include cutting, perforating, scoring, folding, inserting, stapling, binding, or packaging.

This book is designed to reflect traditional and contemporary printing technology. Letterpress printing is presented first to give a historical overview of the development of modern printing. The discussion of letterpress also introduces new terms and concepts needed to understand the other printing processes. For the same reason, traditional processes, many no longer done, are reviewed to develop a total understanding of the language and techniques that the digital revolution has incorporated. All the steps in the printing sequences for the lithographic and screen processes are examined in detail. The gravure process is discussed only briefly because the complexity of image carrier preparation and image transfer for gravure printing are beyond the scope of this work. Flexography is presented in some depth because it represents a contemporary relief process and is a significant and growing part of the printing industry. Digital printing, both direct imaging presses and toner-based printing, is also discussed briefly to introduce the concepts and technologies involved. This technology is rapidly gaining in importance and presents a challenge to traditional processes that will ultimately forever change the way we approach the craft of printing.

The printing industry is much larger than any one printing process. The printing industry reflects a manufacturing technology. A technology cannot be learned by examining tools or materials. A technology is mastered by understanding concepts. The first six chapters of this text review the traditional prepress procedures and fundamental concepts from which our current technology has evolved. The next four chapters cover the new digital workflow that has become the standard method for prepress and output today. The remaining chapters cover the concepts and technology behind each major printing process and explore the business of the graphic arts industry.

Size and Scope of the Printing Industry

The United States Department of Commerce classifies all industries in the United States by Standard Industrial Classification (SIC) numbers. In this classification system, the printing industry is part of SIC number 27 (Printing and Publishing). Department of Commerce information indicates that the United States printing and publishing industry consists of more than 65,000 individual establishments employing more than 1.5 million people. The number of individual firms has changed in the last decade as mergers and acquisitions have increased, with a greater number of smaller firms under the umbrella of larger organizations. In 1998, industry yearly sales exceeded $146 billion. These figures place printing and publishing among the top five United States industries in terms of number of individual establishments and in terms of number of employees.

Economists use several measures to gauge the importance of an industry in a society's economy. The gross national product (GNP) is a figure that represents the overall annual flow of goods and services in an economy. In the United States, the printing industry is ranked among the top ten contributors to the GNP. "Value added" is a measure of the difference between the cost of raw materials and the final market price of a product. The higher the value-added figure, the more valuable the skills that went into the manufacturing of the product. Again, printing ranks among the top ten contributors to the GNP.

Printing is a major American industry, with significant career opportunities at many levels. Students seeking to enter printing as a career are typically attracted by the technology and the craft associated with the production phase—the smell of the ink; the noise of a large, high-speed press; and the excitement of digital imaging technology. A large portion of this book is concerned with production procedures; however, it must be recognized that production is only one part of this large and complex industry. Perhaps only half of all those employed in printing actually work with the reproduction process. The other half are concerned with management, marketing and sales, accounting, and support services such as supplying equipment, paper, ink, and chemicals and managing the digital infrastructure.

It is important to briefly examine how companies are commonly organized and classified.

Structure of Companies

The printing industry is still dominated by small- to medium-sized companies that employ one to twenty-five people. There are "giants" in the industry that employ many hundreds or thousands of workers, but they account for a very small proportion (perhaps as small as 7 percent) of all the companies involved with the printing trade.

The structure of any printing company depends on many variables, including size, location, physical facilities, type of product, financing method (such as corporation or partnership), and management style. In fact, it is safe to assume that no two printing organizations are structured exactly alike. Figure 1.5 shows a possible structure for a small- to medium-sized company made up of ten to twenty-five employees. In smaller organizations one individual might serve several func-

tions. In larger companies many workers might be assigned to one area.

Board of Directors

The board of directors represents the financial control of the company. The board might own the company or it might be an elected body, as is often the case in large corporations. The president of a company is often a member of the board of directors and acts as the board's representative to carry out its policies. The board defines the scope and purpose of the company, makes or approves major decisions, and monitors financial performance. In our economy profit is the primary driving force for all companies or corporations. The board of directors is responsible to the stockholders for delivery of a maximum return or profit based upon investment.

Management

The president or chief executive officer (CEO) of a company often delegates top-level management of day-to-day operation to a general manager. The office manager coordinates such important tasks as correspondence, record keeping, accounting, payroll, and customer billing. The sales manager is responsible for an important part of the company: managing and directing the sales team that brings customers to the company. Sales representatives contact customers who require printing services and work with skilled estimators who calculate costs. The production manager is responsible for controlling the materials, craftspeople, prepress operators and equipment to deliver a printed product that meets or exceeds customer expectations. Many managerial positions in the printing industry are filled by individuals who have moved up the ranks from the craft or entry level.

Production

The production phase is generally divided into three categories:

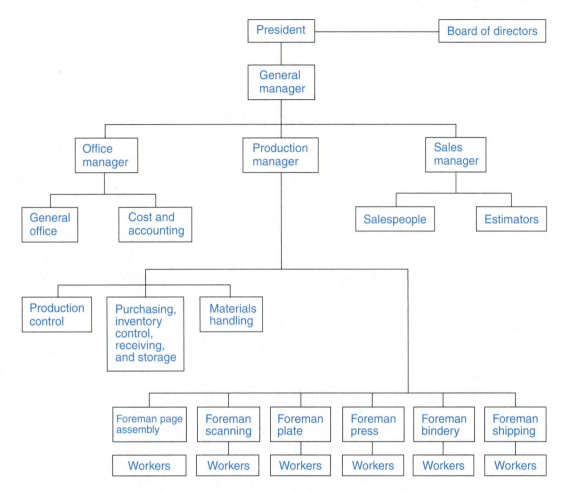

Figure 1.5 **Typical organizational structure of a small- to medium-sized (ten to twenty-five employees) printing company**

■ Production planning
■ Manufacturing
■ Quality assurance

One aspect of planning production is scheduling work efficiently within the limitations of time, equipment, and human skills. People in charge of purchasing, inventory control, and receiving and storage are responsible for the advance ordering of all supplies. Some firms test incoming supplies such as ink, paper, plates, and films to guarantee they meet quality standards. Costly press downtime can be avoided by assuring the quality of the materials used in the printing process. Accurate material handling ensures that supplies are delivered to the correct workstation (such as the camera room or the press room) when needed and that the finished product is removed from the last station on time. Production stations for prepress, plate making, press, bindery, and shipping must be directed by skilled supervisors who work to meet the schedules set by production control. The production itself must be carried out by individuals who are highly skilled in the printing crafts.

Although a worker's skill is not directly related to any form of organization or managerial control, it is important that employees understand the basic organization of their business. The efficiency of an organization directly influences the employment of everyone in the company.

Organization of Printing Services

There are several ways to categorize printing companies. One traditional way is by the kinds of services or produces the companies deliver. With this view, printing organizations can be classified into eight distinct areas:

- Commercial
- Trade shops
- Special purpose
- Quick printing
- In-plant
- Publishing
- Packaging
- Related industries

Commercial Printing

Commercial printing is done by a company that is willing to take on nearly any sort of printing job. Commercial printers can usually handle a large variety of printing jobs, regardless of sheet size, number of ink colors, length of run, or even binding requirements. Typical products produced in a commercial printing shop include small business cards, letterhead stationery, posters, and four-color glossy advertising sheets for mailing. If a commercial printer does not have all of the equipment or skilled staff to perform a whole job, parts of the job, such as die cutting, foil stamp-

ing, or binding, may be subcontracted to trade shops.

Trade Shops

Some companies provide services only to the printing trade. These are called **trade shops**. Not all commercial, special purpose, in-plant, publishing, or packaging companies can afford to own and operate all the equipment necessary to meet their total production requirements. For example, a company might decide not to buy bindery equipment because only a small percentage of its work requires folding, collating, or binding. When the company receives a contract that requires binding, it sends it to a trade shop that specializes in binding.

Special Purpose Printing

Special purpose printing is defined by the limited type of jobs performed by a company. One printer might print only labels. The printer would purchase special equipment and accept orders for only labels. However, the printer would make labels to any size, shape, number of colors, length of run, or purpose. Another printer might specialize in business forms, such as order forms, estimate blanks, filing sheets, school notepaper, or duplicate sales slips. Forms printing is an important area of the printing industry in terms of size and yearly sales. Yet another example of special purpose printing is called *legal* printing. Legal printers are concerned with reproducing pieces such as corporate stock offerings, insurance policies, or financial reports.

Quick Printing

Within the last several years, a **quick printing** sector of the printing industry has grown around the use of electrostatic printing. More commonly known as photocopying, or simply copying, the electrostatic process allows copies to be reproduced without the use of a traditional printing plate press. The explo-

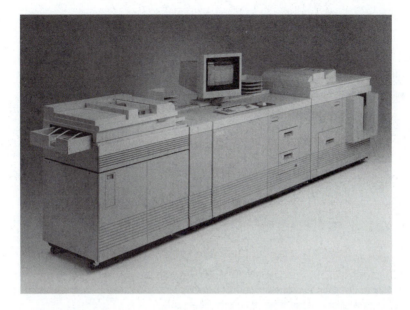

Figure 1.6 **Electrostatic printing.** This unit has a high-resolution digital scanner capable of creating 600 dot-per-inch (dpi) digital masters, which can then be adjusted if needed. The system can print 135 prints per minute at 600 dpi and has optional add-ons capable of binding and outputing booklets.
Courtesy of: Xerox Inc.

sion of quick print shops has revolutionized public access to the reproduction process. Most copy centers offer walk-in services that include copies up to 11 inches × 17 inches or larger, spot (solid) color, full-color images, binding, computer rental time, direct digital copiers, and an array of supplies such as matching envelopes, binders, and presentation folders (figure 1.6). In addition, many quick print shops offer access through the Internet for online ordering and document creation.

In-Plant Printing

In-plant printing is defined as any printing operation that is owned by, and serves the needs of, a single company or corporation. A business might manufacture a variety of products that must each be packaged with an in-struction sheet. Management could decide it is more convenient and cost efficient to set up its own shop to print the instruction sheets rather than to send the job to a commercial printer. The company would then also be able to produce in-house forms, promotion pieces, company letterhead and stationery, time cards, and almost all of its printing needs.

Many in-plant printers use the lithographic process. Equipment manufacturers are currently marketing systems with a platemaker "in line" with a press, collator, and binder. With the *systems* approach, the in-plant printer can enter original copy (such as a typed form) into an automatic direct image platemaking system, select the number of copies to be printed and the preferred binding method, and produce bound copies in a matter of minutes (figure 1.7).

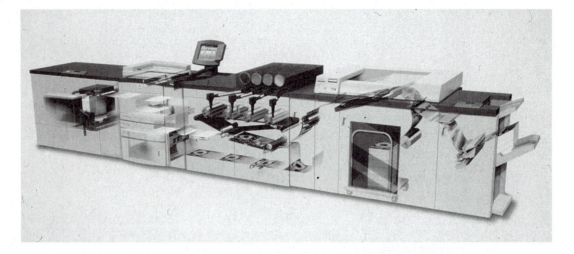

Figure 1.7 **Digital color press.** The DocuColor Digital Color Press allows a company to handle many of its printing needs in-house. This system can print four-color pages at 60 pages per minute (ppm) on a variety of substrates at a cost of less than 10 cents per page.
Courtesy of: Xerox Inc.

Publishing

Another category of printing services that we use nearly every day is **publishing**. Within this category are the thousands of companies that produce daily or weekly newspapers, and the even larger group of companies that produces periodicals, such as *Time* and *Newsweek*, which sell to a national market. Consider also the group of businesses that produces and markets books. The publisher of this book is a private company that produces textbooks. It is important to understand that printers do not usually make decisions to publish a book, CD, or magazine. Printers are rarely the publisher. Publishers, however, require the skills of the printer to manufacture their products.

Package Printing

Hundreds of different containers we use every day are produced by **package printing**. The idea of impulse buying (buying a product on the visual appeal of the package) has skyrocketed the demand for high-quality, multi-color packages that attract the consumer's attention. Package printers decorate and form hundreds of millions of folded paperboard boxes, flexible packages, and corrugated boxes each year. Millions of printed plastic bags are used every day in grocery stores and companies that distribute or package food. Corrugated boxes and thin plastic film are both printed by flexography. Packaging, however, is not restricted to paper or plastic. Think of all the steel and aluminum soft drink and beer containers sold every day. These packages are produced by a special process called *metal decorating*.

Related Industries

The last category of services in the printing industry is called **related industries**. The raw materials of the printer are such things as ink, paper, plates, chemicals, and many other supplies. Printers also use special purpose equipment, such as presses, paper cutters, platemakers, cameras, and light tables, to produce their products. Companies that provide services to printers by either producing or selling these supplies and equipment are called related industries. Other businesses, such as consulting firms and advertising agencies that prepare designs for reproduction, might also perform a service, but they do not make or sell a physical product.

Preparing for a Career in Printing

Viewing the printing industry as made up of commercial, special purpose, quick printing, in-plant, publishing, package printing, trade shops, and related industries is only one way to look at this broad industry. The industry does not stand alone; it is carried by people. There is a need for skilled people power. There are no fixed paths to entering the printing industry, but a few general observations can be made.

Upper-Level Management Preparation

Managerial levels, specifically upper-level positions (see figure 1.5), almost always require a college degree. There are many schools that offer degrees with extensive specialization in printing technology. Printing specialization, however, is not a requirement. Individuals with experience in such areas as art, journalism, engineering, chemistry, physics, research, data processing and computers, sales, marketing, and management are also employed in printing companies.

Middle-Level Management Preparation

Middle-level management, such as section foremen or production control people, and skilled craftspeople enter the industry by a variety of routes. There are trade high schools designed to provide high-school graduates with skills necessary for direct entrance to the industry. Other secondary school programs offer vocational or industrial arts classes combined with a cooperative work experience (where the student spends part of a day in a local printing company and part of the day in school). There are also technical printing programs offered in two-year community colleges that lead to associate degrees.

Craft-Level Preparation

Union membership may influence craft-level entrance to the industry. Printing establishments can be either closed or open shops. A **closed shop** requires union membership. An open shop does not have such a requirement. In an **open shop**, individuals can belong to a union, but they do not have to belong to keep their jobs.

Union Membership

Several craft unions in the United States represent the printing trades. Some reflect only one specific type of skill, such as press operators. Others extend across many craft lines. One advantage of union membership is national negotiating power for wages and benefits. Another advantage of union membership is on-the-job training. In closed union shops trainees generally received on-the-job training through structured apprenticeship programs.

Nonunion Organizations

Even though nonunion open shop workers are not represented in national-level collective bargaining, there are organizations that provide services such as retirement benefits and health insurance to nonunion printers. The advantage of open shop work is that the wage level is not necessarily linked to union pay scales. Open shops emphasize previous skills combined with knowledge gained on the job. There is a national nonunion certification called the Master Craftsman Program, which is coordinated through the Printing Industries of America. Many open shops also provide on-the-job training.

Career Advancement

Advancement in the printing industry is based on performance. The most skillful managers and workers gradually assume more responsibility through practice and additional training. Technical skills and a thorough understanding of digital workflow technologies are critical in today's industry, with many quality organizations providing continuous updating and training to the printing professions. Three examples are the Graphic Arts Technical Foundation (GATF), the Printing Industries of America (PIA), and the National Association of Printers and Lithographers (NAPL). All of these nonprofit organizations are designed to meet the research, technical, and educational needs of their members. They are supported by printers, suppliers, manufacturers, graphic-arts educators, and students. They are each involved in solving industrial problems, conducting applied research, publishing the results of their work in the form of books and audio visual aids, and conducting workshops.

Many other types of printing organizations serve both professional and social needs (See Appendix B.) There are several management organizations, a number of fellowship groups, and even student clubs. The printing industry is made up of a vast group of people all devoted to the goal of fulfilling the print communication needs of a technical world.

Key Terms

ideographs
printing
relief printing
intaglio printing
gravure
screen printing
lithography
electrostatic printing

image design
image conversion
image carrier preparation
image transfer
finishing
commercial printing
trade shops
special purpose printing

quick printing
in-plant printing
publishing
package printing
related industries
closed shop
open shop

Review Questions

1. What is a pictograph?
2. What is an ideograph?
3. What is a phonetic symbol?
4. What are the five main printing processes?
5. What is the sequence of steps that all printers follow regardless of the printing process they are using?
6. What is the purpose of the board of directors of a printing company?
7. What is the task of the production manager in a printing company?
8. What is one job of the production-planning department in a printing company?
9. What kind of printing services do trade shops provide for the printing industry?
10. What is the difference between a closed shop and an open shop in the printing industry?
11. List the different ways to enter, train, and advance in the different levels of the graphic-arts industry.

2

The Tradition of Foundry Type

Historical Background

The inventor of printing in the Western world is generally considered to be Johannes Gutenberg, who was born in the city of Mainz, Germany, in 1397. The wealth of the Gutenberg family freed Johann for a life of leisure and pleasure during which he developed an interest in technology, primarily seal making and goldsmithing. In 1438 Gutenberg started a business that produced religious mirrors in Strasbourg. By that time he was considered a master craftsman in metalworking.

There is evidence that by 1444 Gutenberg had returned to Mainz to set up a printing shop. As a goldsmith he had cut letters and symbols into precious metals and into wax to form molds to cast jewelry. It is unknown exactly how he conceived a casting letters for printing. However, the concept of mirror images was common knowledge.

Gutenberg's casting process involved first cutting a letter by hand in reverse on a piece of hard metal, then punching the letter shape into a soft copper mold to form a die called a matrix. He next needed a suitable metal to cast in the matrix. He experimented with pewter hardened with large quantities of antimony, but the mixture shrank when it cooled and pulled away from the matrix. The letters formed were imperfect.

Gutenberg's experience with lead in mirror manufacturing encouraged him to try a combination of lead, tin, and antimony. His original formula (5 percent tin, 12 percent antimony, and 83 percent lead) is used nearly unchanged in casting today. Characters can be perfectly cast with this alloy because it expands when it cools and forms a duplicate of the matrix cavity. Using Gutenberg's system, two workers could cast and dress (trim away excess material) twenty-five pieces of type an hour.

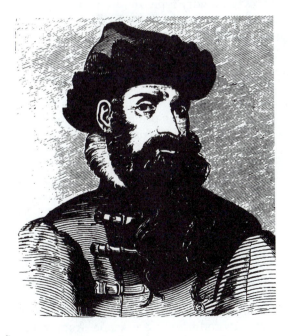

Johannes Gutenberg—the father of printing

Gutenberg's most notable work, a forty-two-line-a-page Bible, was begun in 1452 and completed by 1455. Each page contained around 2800 characters. Two pages were printed at the same time, so 5600 pieces of type were needed to make each two-page printing. It was the practice for the next two pages to be composed during the press run of the current two, so at least 11,200 letters were needed to even begin printing. Working a normal workday (12 hours), it took two craftsmen more than 37 workdays just to prepare the initial type. At this rate, more than three years were needed to complete just 200 copies of Gutenberg's Bible.

Much of the language of modern printing comes from the craft of foundry type composition developed by Gutenberg and his workers more than 500 years ago. Terms such as form, leading, uppercase, lowercase, type size, impression, and make-ready originated with Gutenberg. All printers today owe the hundreds of early craftsmen who followed Gutenberg in the tradition of hand-set foundry type and gave us both a language and an art.

Objectives

After completing this chapter you will be able to:

■ Identify the major parts of a piece of foundry type.

■ Describe the procedure for composing a line of foundry type.

■ Name the advantages that line-casting and character-casting composing machines have over foundry type composition.

Introduction

Until recently relief printing (printing from a raised surface) was the most important reproduction process. Photographic and computer technology has drastically reduced use of the relief process, however. The influence of relief printing continues despite its decline because nearly all contemporary concepts and vocabulary are based on the relief technique. In addition, the goal of this chapter is to provide a historical context for understanding and appreciating the revolutionary changes that have occurred in the last 50 years.

All relief printing involves printing from lead-based metal type, called **foundry type** or **hot type**. Printing from lead-based hot type is often referred to as **letterpress** printing. For more than 400 years after Gutenberg invented casting, letterpress printing accounted for almost all of the industrial printing done in the world. With the introduction of other printing processes, particularly lithography, letterpress's share of the printing market declined. Today letterpress printing accounts for only a small share of the printing industry and is primarily used in finishing operations for applications such as perforating, scoring, and embossing. These applications will be discussed in chapter 17. Most relief printing done today is done with flexography, a process that prints from a raised rubber surface in much the same way reproductions are made from rubber stamps. Although flexography is now more common, it is important to understand the letterpress process. Much of the terminology printers use comes from the tradition of foundry type and the letterpress process.

Foundry Type Composition

Composition is the process of assembling type for printing. The methods used for hot type composition of foundry type for letterpress have changed little since the days of Gutenberg. Individual characters are cast on separate bodies by type founders. The printer composes words and sentences by placing the appropriate cast characters, symbols, and spaces next to each other in a composing stick. (See "Composing a Line of Type," page 23.)

Identifying Foundry Type

To work with foundry type, you must be able to identify the significant parts of each cast character (figure 2.1). The actual printing surface is called the *face*. The sides of the character are cast at an angle (called the *beard*) for

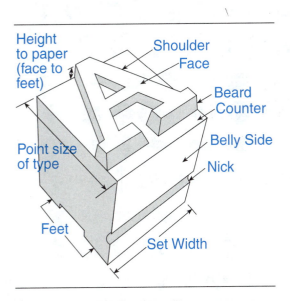

Figure 2.1 **Example of a foundry type character.** Foundry type characters are cast on individual bodies.

greater strength. The beard slopes down to the nonprinting shoulder and counter. The *feet* are parallel to the face. The distance from the face to the feet is the height to paper or **type-high**. For most English-speaking countries, type-high is 0.918 inch.

All characters in a **font** (a collection of type of the same style and size) have a nick cut in the same position on the type body. When setting a line of foundry type, it is easy to glance at the row of nicks. If one nick does not line up with all the rest, the printer knows it is probably a wrong font character. The nick side is often called the belly side. The distance from the belly to the back side is the **point size** of the piece of type. Note that the type body in figure 2.1 is larger than the character *A*. Type point size is defined by the point size of the body, not by the size of the character.

The distance across the nick or belly side of the type is an important measure called the **set width**. The letter *m*, for example, is wider than the letter *i*. Therefore, the set width of *m* is greater than that of *i*, or, stated another way, the set width is proportional to the size of the letter on the type body. Most typewriters form nonproportional letters. This makes it possible to type the letter *m*, backspace, and type the letter *i* in the same visual space.

Special Characters

By using variations of the 26 letters of our Latin alphabet, many characters can be cast as foundry type to meet a special purpose. Gutenberg cast nearly 250 different characters and symbols to print his Bible. He cast that many characters because he was attempting to duplicate the variations inherent in scribe hand-lettering.

A **ligature** is two or more connected letters on the same type body (figure 2.2). The most common are *fi* and *fl* combinations. When any portion of the printing face extends over the body of the type, the character is said to

fl fi ff

Figure 2.2   Examples of ligatures

be **kerned**. *Kerns* are very common in italic faces.

Another classification of special characters is called **dingbats**. Dingbats are commonly used symbols such as bullets, asterisks, outline boxes, and pointing fingers (figure 2.3).

Type Storage Systems
The earliest relief printers stored identical characters in small compartments or bins. As the number of type styles grew, each font was stored in what was termed a *case*.

A once-popular type storage system was the **news case**. An entire font of letters was stored in two cases: capitals were in one case and small letters were in another. The case with capitals was traditionally stored on a shell directly over the case with small letters. Our terms *uppercase* and *lowercase* to indicate CAPITAL or small letters, respectively, come from the use of the news case.

The most popular type case is the **California job case** (figure 2.4). It is designed to hold one font of characters made up of upper- and lowercase letters, numerals, punctuation marks, ligatures, special symbols (such as $), and spacing material in a total of eighty-nine small boxes. Lowercase letters and symbols are assigned positions and spaces in the case according to how frequently they are used.

The Printer's Measurement System
Printers use a special system to measure almost all printed images. This system was developed from the measurement of foundry type and continues to be used today. In this system 6 **picas** equal 1 inch, and 12 **points** equal 1 pica.

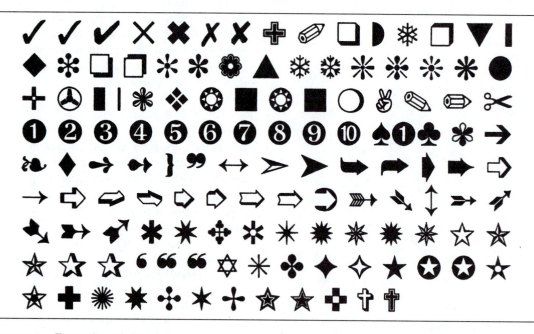

Figure 2.3   Examples of dingbats

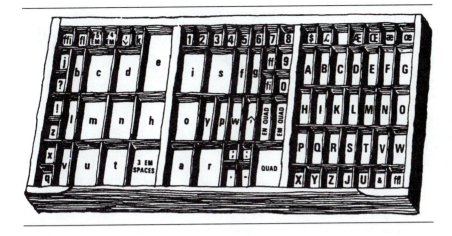

Figure 2.4 **Example of a California job case.** Courtesy of Mackenzie and Harris Inc., San Francisco, CA.

Type size is almost always described in points. Common type sizes are 6, 7, 8, 9, 10, 11, 12, 14, 16, 18, 24, 36, 42, 60, and 72 points (figure 2.5). Traditionally, anything over 72 points was measured in inches (because 72 points/12 points = 6 picas = 1 inch). However, with contemporary digital typography, you can create any point size in three-decimal increments from 5 to 500 point.

Space between lines of type is also measured in points. When a customer requests a type page to be set "10 on 12" (10/12), the printer understands that the letters will be 10 points high, with 2 points of space between each line (12 points − 10 points = 2 points).

The length and depth lines of type are specified in picas. Most newspaper columns are 13 picas wide. A 36-pica line is 6 inches long (because 1 inch equals 6 picas). Column depth is measured in picas from the top of the first line on a page to the bottom of the last line of type.

Word-Spacing Material

All hot type spacing material in a given font is the same point size. Each space must match the point size of the type it is being used with and must be less than the height of the type (usually 0.800 inch or less) (figure 2.6).

Within any font size, then, is a collection of different pieces of spacing material. The basic unit of spacing material in each font is an **em quad**, sometimes called the mutton quad. The em quad is a square piece of spacing material. Each side of the em quad is the point size of the font the em quad is from. For example, an em quad from a 12-point font of type would measure 12 points × 12 points on the face and would be less than type-high; an

6 7 8 9 10 11 12 14 16 18 24 36 42 60 72

Figure 2.5 **Point sizes.** Common foundry type point sizes.

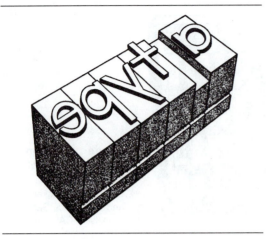

Figure 2.6   Example showing spacing material between words. Spacing material used between words must match the point size of the type and be less than the height of the type.

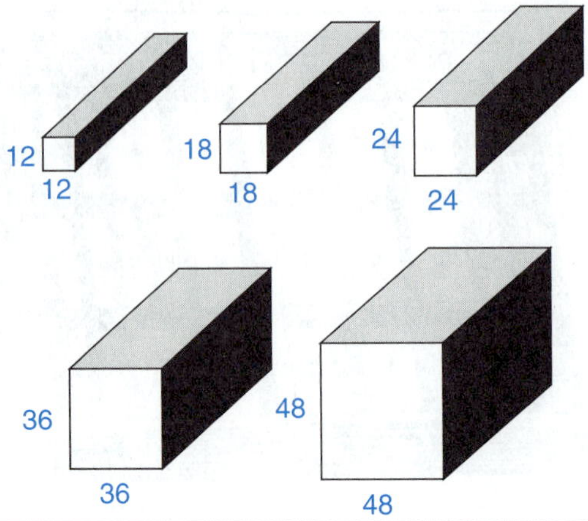

Figure 2.7   Examples of em quads. The em, or mutton, quad is the basic word-spacing unit in each font.

18-point font would contain em quads that are 18 points in each dimension on the face (figure 2.7).

All other spacing material in a font is based on the size of the em quad. Two **en quads**, or nut quads, placed together equal the dimension of one em quad. For example, if the font size is 12 points, the en quad will measure 6 points × 12 points on the face. A 3-em space (abbreviated from "three to the em") is one-third of an em quad. The smallest space typically found in a job case is the 5-em space, which is one-fifth of an em quad. Some spaces, such as the 2-em quad or the 3-em quad, are larger than the em quad.

For most composition, the em quad is used to indent the first line of a paragraph, the en quad is used to separate sentences, and the 3-em space is placed between words. Combinations of all spacing material are used to achieve equal line lengths of type composition.

There is one more class of spacing material called thin spaces. The most common mea-sure of thin spaces is 1/2 point (generally made of copper) and 1 point (usually made of brass). Thin spaces are generally only used for spacing between letters (called *letter spacing*).

Line-Spacing Material

The space between lines, called **leading**, must be controlled with line-spacing material. Line-spacing material is less than type-high and is generally cut from long strips to the length of line being set. All line-spacing material is classified according to thickness. **Leads** are generally 2 points thick, but anything from 1 to 4 points thick is considered a lead. **Slugs** are typically 6 points thick, but any piece up to 24 points (2 picas) is labeled a slug. Both leads and slugs are made from type metal. Any line-spacing material that is 24 points thick or thicker is called **furniture**. Furniture is made from type metal, wood (generally oak), or an aluminum alloy.

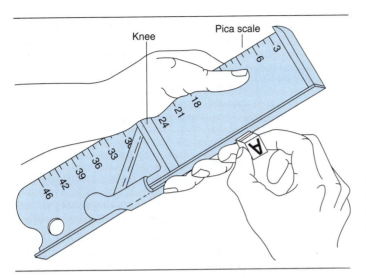

Figure 2.8 Example of a composing stick. When using a composing stick, hold the stick in your left hand and place the first character, nick up, against the knee. Always compose from left to right.

Composing a Line of Type

Foundry type characters are placed in a **composing stick** to form words and sentences. The most common composing sticks have slots which seat an adjustable knee to an exact pica or half-pica position. Type is always set with the right hand. The composing stick is held in the left (figure 2.8).

To set type in the composing stick, begin by adjusting the knee to the desired line length. Then place a piece of line-spacing material in the stick. The first character of the first word is always seated against the knee of the composing stick, nick up. All other characters and spaces are set in order after this first character. The thumb of your left hand applies pressure against the last character set to keep the line from falling out of the stick.

When all characters have been set, it is necessary to fill the gap remaining at the end of the line. The line must be held snugly in place within the preset line length. This is accomplished by filling the gap with spacing material. If the gap is large, begin with em quads or 2-ems until only a small space is left. Then select combinations of spacing to fill the line

perfectly. Ideally, the last space will slide into place with only slight resistance, and the entire composing stick can be turned upside down without the line falling out. This process of making the line tight in the stick is called **quadding out**. To set another line of type, insert a piece of line-spacing material and repeat the techniques used to set the first line. The amount of line-spacing material added between two lines of type determines the leading of the two lines.

Because cast characters are smaller than the type body, it is possible to set type with no leading and keep the letters on one line from touching the letters on the line below. Type that has been set with no leading between lines is referred to as *set solid*.

Centering a Line of Type

A printer frequently wants to reproduce a series of centered lines, one over the other. To do this, set the entire first line in the stick against the knee. Quad out the line by placing equal amounts of spacing material on each end of the line.

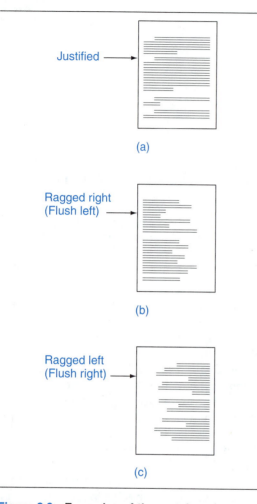

Justified (a)

Ragged right (Flush left) (b)

Ragged left (Flush right) (c)

Figure 2.9   Examples of three styles of composition. (a) Justified composition is set flush left and flush right. (b) Copy can also be set **ragged right** (flush left) or (c) **ragged left** (flush right).

Straight Composition

Straight composition or **justification** is the process of setting type so that both the left and right margins form straight lines (figure 2.9). Hand-set straight composition involves setting each line of type against the knee of the composing stick, determining the amount of space left at the end of the line, then dividing the space equally between the words in the line. Spacing material from the case is inserted between words in the line so that the words are separated from each other by nearly equal amounts and the line is tight in the composing stick.

Storing the Form

The composition process creates what printers call a form. A **form** is the grouping of cast characters, symbols, and spaces that makes up a job or complete segment of a job (such as one page to be printed in a book). Composed forms are stored in shallow metal trays called **galleys**.

Proofing Techniques

Once set, hot type composition is difficult to read because the characters are cast in reverse. A sample print of type composition is called a **proof**. Printers check for typesetting errors by proofing, which means comparing composed copy to the rough or manuscript copy provided by the customer. Most companies employ proofreaders to proof copy for errors. Over the past century a collection of special proofreader's marks or notes have been developed to communicate to the printer what corrections need to be made on the proof (figure 2.10). These same symbols are used when proofing foundry, photographic, or computer composition.

If the printer sets the **copy** (the original words or information supplied by the customer) exactly as provided, but the customer makes changes to the copy, the customer pays for author's alterations, or "AA's." However, if the printer makes mistakes setting the copy they are called **typos**, and corrections must be made without charge.

⊗ Defective letter		⊙ Colon	
⊕ Push down space		ℓ𝑓 Boldface	
⌗ Make paragraph		𝟫 Turn over	
⤵ Take out (delete)		Two-em dash	
∧ Insert at this point		One-em dash	
□ Em-quad space		// Space evenly	
⊏ Move over		# Insert space	
◡ Close up entirely		‖ Straighten lines	
⸗ Hyphen		⊙ Period	
⩊ Quotation		⋏ Comma	
⩔ Apostrophe		*no* ⌗ No paragraph	
⸝ Semicolon		*lig* Ligature	
wf Wrong-font letter		⌣ Less space	
stet Let it stand		*out-see copy* Out—see copy	
tr Transpose		*spell out* Spell out	
ⓥ Verify		*caps* Capitals	
lc Lowercase letter		*sc* Small capitals	
ital Italic		*rom* Roman letter	

Figure 2.10 Examples of commonly used proofreader's marks. Proofreader's marks are used to indicate type corrections that must be made on proof sheets.

Galley Proofs

A **galley proof** is pulled on a device called a galley proof press. It is called a galley proof because foundry type jobs are usually transferred from composing sticks to galleys. Galleys match the bottom thickness of composing sticks (0.050 inch).

The galley press is designed so that during composition the printer places the composing stick or a galley filled with forms on the bed; inks the type with a brayer, or ink roller; sets the paper on the form; and pulls the roller over the paper. Galley proofs are delivered to the printing customer before the job goes to press.

Reproduction Proofs

Reproduction proofs are high-quality proofs made on a reproduction proof press (figure 2.11). There are three primary considerations when pulling a reproduction proof: precision, quality type forms, and a good ink-and-paper combination.

Because reproduction proofs are designed to be photographed, they must be puffed from perfect pieces of type. Many companies reserve special fonts of foundry type to be used exclusively for "repro" proofs.

Machine Composition of Hot Type

It probably was not long after the pages of Gutenberg's first Bible were dry that printers began thinking of ways to improve the speed of hand-set composition. Many ideas were tried—even suspending a composing stick around the printer's neck by a rope so type could be set with both hands.

Machine hot type composition is a refinement of the hand-set foundry type concept. Instead of individual pieces of raised type, matrices are placed together to generate words and sentences. Molten type metal is then forced into the matrices to form the raised printing surface. When the metal cools to form a solid cast character, each matrix is returned to a storage system to be used again. Most machines use a keyboard (like a typewriter) to control the position of each matrix. After the type has been used, it can be melted and returned to the machine to be reused.

Line-Casting Machines

On July 3, 1886, the first truly automatic typesetting machine was demonstrated in the com-

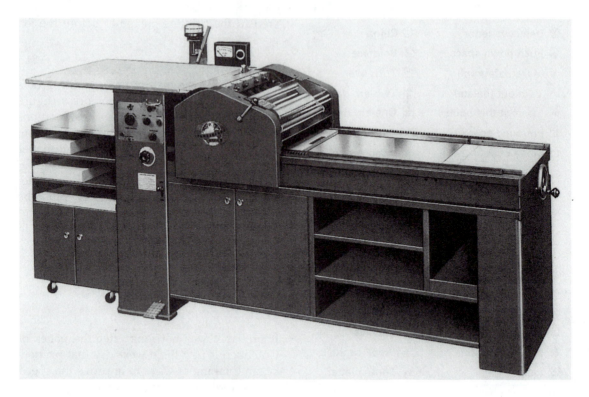

Figure 2.11   **A reproduction proof press.**
Courtesy of Vandersons Corporation, Chicago.

posing room of the *New York Tribune*. The device was designed by Ottmar Mergenthaler. His invention, the **Linotype machine**, has been called one of the ten greatest in the history of the human race (figure 2.12).

The Linotype machine is based on the concept of a recirculating matrix which is continually reused in the machine. The Linotype performs the following four basic operations with the matrices:

1. Matrices and spacebands are activated by keyboard control;
2. The line is justified;
3. The slug is cast; and
4. Each matrix and spaceband is returned to its storage position.

The Linotype can be, and probably has been, set up to do nearly every typesetting function in almost every language.

A second line-casting machine (although not completely automatic) was the **Ludlow**, named after its inventor, Washington I. Ludlow. The device was designed around 1888 and could cast type from 8- through 144-point characters from hand-set matrices.

Character-Casting Machines

The **Monotype system** was designed by Tolbert Lanston in 1889 to cast and assemble individual pieces of hot type in a line. The system was made up of two machines: a keyboard device which punched holes into a long paper

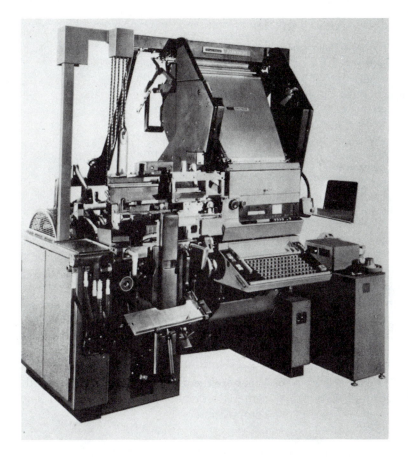

Figure 2.12 **A Linotype machine.**
Courtesy of Mergenthaler Linotype Company

tape and a casting mechanism which cast type automatically from the information on the tape.

Character sizes up to 36 points and line lengths up to 60 picas (90 picas with a special attachment) could be cast on the same Monotype machine. For small faces, up to 150 characters per minute could be cast. Because of the machine's speed and versatility, several key-boards could be constantly functioning to feed a single caster.

After forms were composed, they were assembled to make plates. Although the making of relief plates is no longer pertinent to the study of contemporary printing, the use of traditional letterpress devices does continue for certain specialty applications. These will be discussed in chapter 17.

Key Terms

foundry type	California job case	ragged right
hot type	pica	ragged left
letterpress	point	form
composition	em quad	galley
type-high	en quad	proof
font	leading	copy
point size	lead	typos
set width	slug	galley proof
ligature	furniture	reproduction proof
kerned	composing stick	Linotype machine
dingbats	quadding out	Ludlow
news case	justification	Monotype system

Review Questions

1. Identify the major parts of a piece of foundry type.

2. What dimensions of a piece of foundry type determine set width and point size?

3. What is the point size of an en quad in a 12-point font of foundry type?

4. How thick are leads and slugs, and what are they used for?

5. What is meant by "quadding out"?

6. What are the differences between justified, centered, ragged right, and ragged left composition?

3

Basic Design and Traditional Preparation

On March 9, 1972, an unmanned United States rocket, *Pioneer 10*, began a one-half-billion-mile journey to the plant Jupiter and beyond. It was our country's first effort to leave this solar system. On the ship were a robot and a 6- × 9-inch, goldplated aluminum plaque attached to the rocket's antenna supports. The plaque carried a message for any extraterrestrial creatures who might encounter it. The message explained the robot's purpose and who built it.

Once the decision had been made to send a message with the rocket, the problem was deciding what to say and how to say it. If there were other creatures like us in the universe, what language would they speak—English, Russian, French? What experiences could we share with creatures who were not from Earth?

The solution was to use lines to draw the basic shapes of a man and a woman standing in front of a scale outline of *Pioneer 10*. That image could communicate our animal type and our size. A code was then devised that used the wavelength of radiation given off by a hydrogen atom (the most common element in the universe). The code described the origin of the rocket and the distance of our sun from the center of the galaxy.

Traveling at a speed of seven miles a second, it should take *Pioneer 10* more than 80 thousand years to reach the nearest star. The chances that the message will collide with an inhabited planet are slim. But that small grouping of lines and symbols stands as our first attempt to communicate with and confirm the existence of humanity to the rest of the universe.

Objectives

After completing this chapter you will be able to:

- Recognize and explain the design considerations of balance, dominance, proportion, and unity.
- Identify the common elements of alphabet design.
- Discuss the six basic typestyles.

- Identify tools and materials for traditional layout and pasteup
- Acquire a basic understanding of traditional pasteup and layout procedures
- Explain the three basic types of color printing, and identify tints, surprints, reverses, and bleeds.
- List and explain the design steps used to produce a printed product.

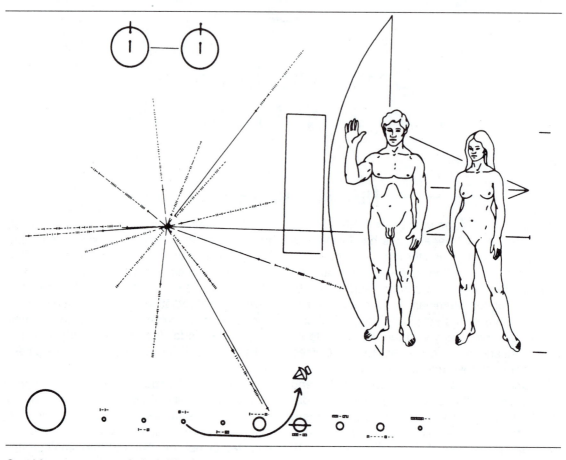

Graphic message carried on Pioneer 10.
Courtesy of NASA.

Introduction

Printing is a manufacturing process. Printing produces multiple, identical copies of graphic images. Image design is the first step in a typical printing job. The purpose of image design is to create an image which meets the customer's need—to influence, inform, sell, or persuade. If the customer's need is not met then the printing job is useless. The purpose of printing is to reproduce an image.

An image may be created by the customer or by a professional graphic designer. It may be a simple page of text, or it may be a complex color printing job requiring several colors, scoring, embossing, and folding. Whether the job is simple or complex, the printer must provide reproductions that meet the customer's expectations and are at a price the customer can afford. Thus, the printer must be efficient and provide quality work to compete.

Efficiency and quality cannot be achieved by the printer alone, however. The printer and the graphic designer must work together. In a traditional workflow, the designer gave the printer the specifications regarding completion of the job and typically did not participate in the prepress process. The printer had to understand and satisfy the designer's specifications during printing (and still must today). This chapter introduces some of the design considerations that need to be considered in both analog and digital workflow, along with an overview of the traditional pasteup and layout process. Digital job preparation will be discussed in detail in chapters 8 and 9. Even though pasteup and traditional layout methods have been replaced by the computer, an understanding of the techniques gives context to modern digital workflow and an appreciation of the magnitude of the changes of the past decade.

Section 1: Design Considerations

It is impossible in a book of this nature and scope to provide more than a brief introduction to the graphic design process. Graphic design is an art and a skill; it is mastered only after years of study and practice.

A graphic designer's art is in imagining and creating a graphic image that meets a specific need. Artistic decisions about balance, dominance, proportion, and unity must be made. The purpose of the printed piece influences design decisions about the type of illustrations, paper, and binding. All of these decisions are further influenced by the budget for the piece.

A graphic designer's skill is in presenting the image design to the printer properly and with clear specifications and directions so the printer can reproduce it accurately. More printing jobs are sent back to the printer for rework due to misunderstandings between the designer and the printer than because of printing errors. Type measurement and specification and the ability to prepare both type and illustrations for printing are among the many skills a graphic designer needs.

Balance

Balance is a term that describes the equilibrium and visual weight of a graphic page. The visual weight of an image on the printed sheet depends on the image's size, color, and density in relation to other images on the sheet. Solid areas have more visual weight than outlines. Circular forms generally appear heavier than rectangles. Visual equilibrium is achieved when a page is perfectly balanced. Color can be used to make an image visually heavier or lighter.

There are three kinds of visual balance:

- Formal
- Informal
- Subjective

Formal balance (figure 3.1a) places identical visual weight on the top, bottom, and sides of a visual center. Designers often use formal balance in situations that demand dignity. Wedding and other formal invitations often have formal balance. Designs in which im-

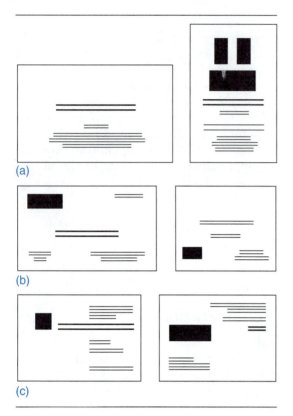

(a)

(b)

(c)

Figure 3.1   Examples of visual balance.
Examples of balance shown here are (a) formal,
(b) informal, and (c) subjective.

ages create a sense of visual balance around a visual center because of their sizes, weights, and positions have **informal balance** (figure 3.1b). With **subjective balance** (figure 3.1c), designers have complete freedom with image positions as the name implies, but they still seek to achieve visual balance.

Not all designs require visual balance, however. Sometimes designers purposely create images that are unbalanced to direct a reader's eyes to one spot or to communicate chaos.

Dominance

Dominance refers to the main purpose of a printed piece—to communicate a message. If a message does not dominate a piece, the reader has to search for the piece's meaning.

Dominance can be achieved by contrasting the most important parts of the message with the rest of the sheet. Some lines of type can be set larger than others. Boldface, italic, or underlining can help create dominance. Words can be printed in special colors or tints, reversed, or dropped (figure 3.2).

Good control of contrast can also direct the eye to the most important part of the message, even though it might not be the largest part. A prime example of contrast is the use of white space around densely set copy.

Proportion

Proportion is concerned with size relationships. Both the size of the sheet and the size and placement of the images on the sheet are important to proportion. A sheet that measures 1 inch × 11 inches is probably not a good page proportion (depending upon use). However, 8 1/2 inches × 11 inches is considered a good page proportion.

The idea of acceptable proportion is closely related to culture. When we see and use a particular proportion frequently it becomes appealing. For example, in most Western culture page designs the two side margins are equal, the top margin is larger than the side margins, and the bottom margin is larger than the other three (figure 3.3).

The final use of a piece must also be considered when setting margin proportions. In book design a certain portion of the page must be reserved for binding. In addition, the visual proportion of each book page is smaller than the actual page size. In practice the designer specifies the visual page size and the printer calculates the necessary or actual page size.

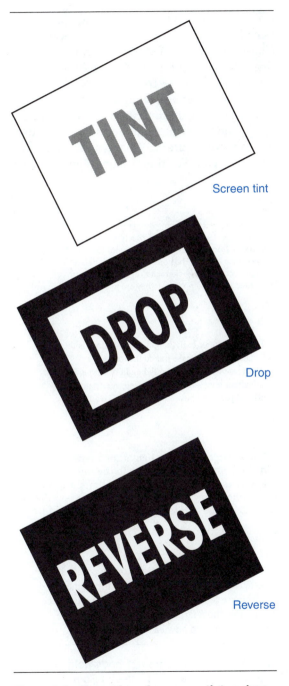

Figure 3.2 **Examples of a screen tint, a drop, and a reverse**

Screen tint

Drop

Reverse

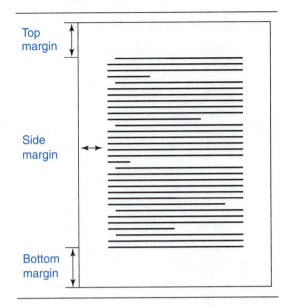

Top margin

Side margin

Bottom margin

Figure 3.3 **Margin proportions.** Margins must appear proportionally correct on the page. The top margin is usually larger than the side margins, and the bottom margin is usually larger than the top margin.

Unity

The idea of **unity** connects all of the design functions. It is concerned with how an entire piece flows together into a complete message. The best designs deliver one message; the worst have competing, and often confusing, messages. The classic example of poor unity design is a nineteenth-century circus poster—every act is featured and no single act attracts the eye.

This idea of unit is enhanced with the selection of appropriate typefaces and art for the message being printed. The characteristics of letterforms create feelings and moods. Mixing type designs typically creates disunity. A fundamental rule for young designers is to work with only one family or type for any given job.

Alphabet Design

Graphic designers work with the placement of images and the manipulation of white or open space. The most basic images used in graphic design are the 26 symbols of our Roman alphabet. Just as each individual writes in a different and distinctive style, printers reproduce the alphabet in many different **typefaces**.

Symbol Characteristics

Different letterforms are created using only five variables:

- x-height
- Ascenders and descenders
- Stroke
- Stress
- Serifs

These variables can deliver an unlimited number of typeface designs.

x-Height and Ascenders and Descenders

Typefaces are described using a very specific vocabulary (figure 3.4). Our alphabet is made

up of uppercase (capital) and lowercase (small) characters. Both upper- and lowercase characters are formed along a common base line. The **x-height**, or **body height**, of a typeface is the distance from the base line to the top of the lowercase letter *x*. The body height of a typeface can affect how large characters appear on the printed page and how easy they are to read (figure 3.5). Larger characters are easier to read. For this reason, typefaces with

The x-height, or body height, of a typeface is the distance from the base line to the top of the lowercase letter *x*. The body height of a typeface can affect how large characters appear on the printed page and how easy they are to read.

The x-height, or body height, of a typeface is the distance from the base line to the top of the lowercase letter *x*. The body height of a typeface can affect how large characters appear on the printed page and how easy they are to read.

The x-height, or body height, of a typeface is the distance from the base line to the top of the lowercase letter *x*. The body height of a typeface can affect how large characters appear on the printed page and how easy they are to read.

The x-height, or body height, of a typeface is the distance from the base line to the top of the lowercase letter *x*. The body height of a typeface can affect how large characters appear on the printed page and how easy they are to read.

Figure 3.5 **Comparison of body heights.** These examples are all printed in Roman typefaces with the same point size and line spacing. The primary variable is x-height.

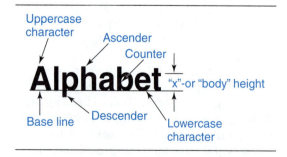

Figure 3.4 **Elements of typeface design**

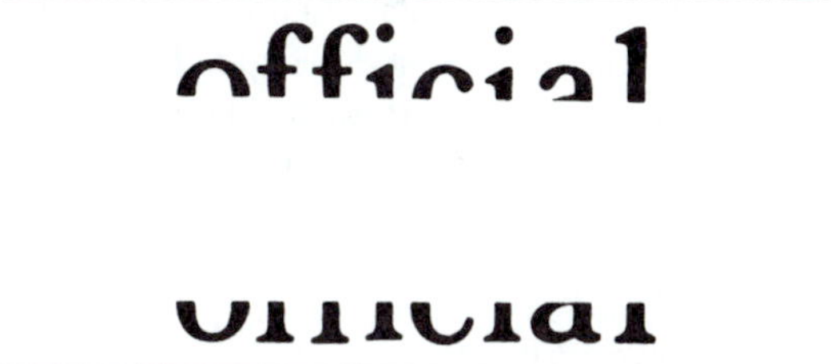

official

official

Figure 3.6 Recognizing words by their forms. Cover the top line and ask someone to read the bottom. Then reverse the procedure. Which was easier?

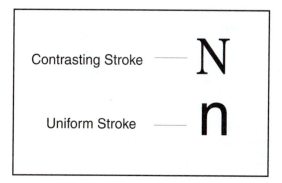

Figure 3.7   Stroke. The stroke or thickness of typeface varies from design to design.

large body heights are often used in children's books.

Any part of a letter that drops below the x-height is called a **descender**; any letter part that extends above the x-height is called an **ascender**. Accurate recognition of words depends on the visual impact of ascenders and descenders (figure 3.6). We tend to read word-forms or word shapes rather than individual letters. As an experiment try the exercise shown in figure 3.6. Be sure to do it with someone who has not yet seen the full illustration.

Stroke

There are three major variables in letterforms: stroke, stress, and serifs. **Stroke** refers to the thickness or weight of the lines that form a character (figure 3.7). The stroke might be uniform, as with the Helvetica typeface, or contrasting, as with the Bodoni typeface.

A scribe hand lettering manuscripts with a quill pen originated stroke variation. Today stroke can be varied with a thick felt-tip pen. Hold the pen firmly in your hand and draw a vertical line. Without changing your hand position and without lifting the tip of the pen from the paper, slowly move the pen to the right to make an arc. You will see that the line thickness varies.

Stress

Stress refers to a slant of a character. Mathematically, stress is defined as the angle of a line that passes through the center of a character (figure 3.8). This can be visualized as if the *o*'s were large tires or inner tubes. If you pushed on an upright inner tube it would depress, but its base would remain in place.

Italic typefaces generally have slight negative stress. In other words, they slant a bit to the right rather than to the left. However, stress is not the only element that defines an italic typeface. Type designers actually modify each letter to create an italic image. For ex-

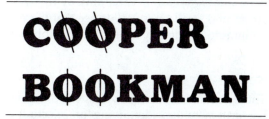

Figure 3.8   Comparison of stress. The Bookman typeface has vertical stress. The *o*'s in the Cooper typeface are stressed (slanted) from the upper left to the lower right.

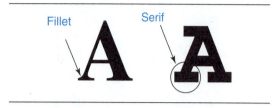
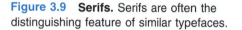

Fillet   Serif

Figure 3.9   Serifs. Serifs are often the distinguishing feature of similar typefaces.

ample, examine the italic letter *e* in figure 3.17. Notice that more than just stress affects its appearance.

Serifs

Serifs are small strokes that project out from the top or bottom of main letter strokes (figure 3.9). Serifs can be vertical or horizontal strokes. Horizontal serifs are parallel to the base line. Vertical letter strokes or serifs are at right angles to the base line, or slightly off 90 degrees.

A fillet is added to some letterforms. A **fillet** is an internal curve between the serif stroke and the main stroke. Fillets are generally considered to add a sense of elegance to the basic alphabet design.

Serifs can vary in thickness and stress. Serifs can also be square or rounded. In fact, there are endless serif variations. With serifs, stress, and stroke, it is easy to see that there is no limit to the design of our Roman alphabet.

Typeface Classification

The unlimited number of variations in alphabet design makes identifying or selecting a typeface difficult for young designers. There are numerous choices, and there is no universally accepted classification system for type

design. The most popular method is to organize typefaces by type style. **Type style** is defined by variations in stress, stroke, and serif. There are six basic styles in this system:

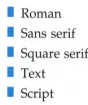

- Roman
- Sans serif
- Square serif
- Text
- Script
- Occasional

Roman

The text in this book is set in **Roman** typeface. Body composition is set in Palatino, while figure notes use Helvetica. Ms. Rachel Baker, the art and design coordinator for *Printing Technology*, 5e, selected these faces because "they are classic and easily read."

The Roman style is based on the characteristics of letterforms cut into granite by early Roman stonemasons. Iron chisels were used to cut horizontal and vertical lines. Where strokes did not intersect, the tool left a ragged appearance at the end of a line. A cut made with the tool straightened the unevenness. The cut was called a "serif."

The Roman typeface style is defined by two main characteristics: serifs and stroke variation.

There are three subcategories of the Roman design: oldstyle, transitional, and modern (figure 3.10). Oldstyle Roman has little stroke variation. There is usually a slight rounding of the serif base, and fillets occupy the area between main and serif strokes. A modern Roman character is formed from thick strokes contrasted with almost hairline strokes. There is generally no rounding or filleting of the serif. Between the two stylistically is transitional Roman with greater stroke vari-

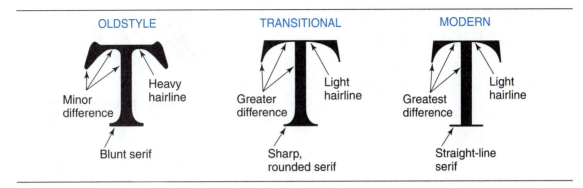

Figure 3.10   **Roman designs.** Roman designs can be oldstyle, transitional, or modern.

ation than oldstyle but less variation than modern Roman.

Most alphabets with a Roman design are considered easy to read. Many books, magazines, and newspapers are set in Roman typefaces.

Sans Serif

Sans serif means "without serifs" (figure 3.11). Sans serif characters are typically formed with uniform strokes and with perfectly vertical letter stress. These type designs generally communicate a modern, clean visual appearance.

Triumvirate

Avant Garde Gothic

ALDOUS VERTICAL

Figure 3.11   **Examples of sans serif typefaces**

Square Serif

Square serif typefaces are sometimes referred to as Egyptian typefaces. The serifs on square serif typefaces are not rounded but rather appear as blocks or slabs connected to the main character strokes (figure 3.12). Square serif faces are often used in larger point sizes for display type. When set in smaller sizes, they tend to make the printed page appear dense and black.

Square serif faces generally communicate a feeling of strength or power.

Text

Text typefaces, also referred to as *black letter*, attempt to recreate the feeling of the era of medieval scribes (figure 3.13). They are generally used in very formal pieces, such as wedding invitations. Text characters are difficult to read

Lubalin Graph Book

Figure 3.12   **An example of a square serif typeface**

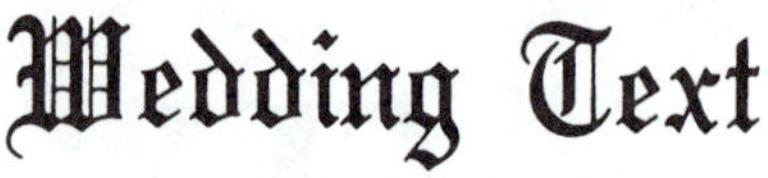

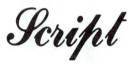

Figure 3.13   An example of a text typeface

and become almost illegible when set all uppercase (figure 3.14).

Script

Script (or cursive) designs attempt to duplicate the easy, free-flowing feeling of hand lettering (figure 3.15). As with text, script is not easy to read when set all uppercase.

Occasional

The last typeface, **occasional**, is really an "other grouping" or catchall category. Anything that cannot be placed in one of the other five categories is labeled occasional (figure 3.16). Some **typographers** (type designers) use the labels *novelty* or *decorative* for an occasional typeface, but whatever it is called, it has no design limits. Occasional typefaces are usually created to meet a specific design need. Companies often design and copyright a particular letterform so that consumers will associate it with their product or service.

Typeface Families

Each unique combination of stress, stroke, and serif is a type style. Within each style further

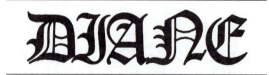

Figure 3.14   An example of all uppercase text.
Words in a text typeface that are set in all capital letters are almost unreadable. This word is *Diane*.

Figure 3.15   An example of a script typeface

variations are possible. These variations define a **type family**. Just as human families are made up of various members—sisters, brothers, cousins, aunts, and so on—who have a family resemblance, type families are made up of letterform variations that have a resemblance. These variations are all based on the main type family characteristics of stroke, stress, and serif (figure 3.17).

There are thousands of different type families; each is identified by a specific name. Examples include Lubalin, Bodini, or Zapf. Others get their names from their intended use. In 1887 *The London Times* newspaper commissioned a new design. The type family used was called New Times Roman, or simply Times.

A type family variation may be created by making the characters in the basic family

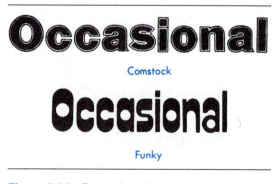

Comstock

Funky

Figure 3.16   Examples of occasional typefaces

Century Light

Century Light Italic

Century Bold

Century Bold Italic

Century Bold Condensed

Century Bold Extended

Century Textbook

Century Textbook Italic

Century Textbook Bold

Figure 3.17 **An example of a type family.** The family name of this type is Century. Its variations are combinations of different weights—light, bold, regular—and different stress.

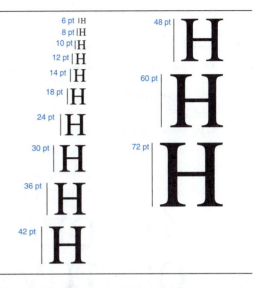

Figure 3.18 **Type size.** Type size is measured in points, shown here from a small letter of 6 points to a display letter of 72 points.
Courtesy of Mackenzie and Harris, Inc., San Francisco.

design bold, light, condensed, expanded, extra bold, extra light, italic, or combinations of several variations, such as extra bold condensed. Nine different members of the Century typeface are shown in figure 3.17. The word that describes the variations, for example, bold or italic, is added to the type family name to distinguish between each member in the type family such as Lubalin bold or Lubalin italic.

Type Fonts

Alphabet point size is measured with the printer's measurement system explained in chapter 2. Every member (variation) of a type family can be reproduced in a range of **point sizes** (figure 3.18). A **font** is a collection of all of the characters, including punctuation marks and special symbols, of one type family variation that are the same point size. All of the characters and symbols in a font of 10-point

Century Bold, for example, make up a *font* of type Century Bold variation of the Century *type family*, which is one of many type families in the *Roman* style (figure 3.19).

Graphic designers use type specimen books as their primary reference (figure 3.20). Such books typically show families of type set in sizes from 6 to 72 points. They also often display paragraph composition to show how text will appear in a job.

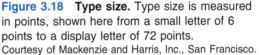

Figure 3.19 **A font of type.** A font is a collection of all characters—alphabet, punctuation marks, and special symbols—for one member of a type family in one size.

Times

6 pt.   ABCDEFGHIJKLMNOPQRSTUVWXYZabcdefghijklmnopqrstuvwxyz0123456789!?,"$&%{}*

7 pt.   ABCDEFGHIJKLMNOPQRSTUVWXYZabcdefghijklmnopqrstuvwxyz0123456789!?,"$&%{}*

8 pt.   ABCDEFGHIJKLMNOPQRSTUVWXYZabcdefghijklmnopqrstuvwxyz0123456789!?,"$&%{}*

9 pt.   ABCDEFGHIJKLMNOPQRSTUVWXYZabcdefghijklmnopqrstuvwxyz0123456789!?,"$&%{}*

10 pt.   ABCDEFGHIJKLMNOPQRSTUVWXYZabcdefghijklmnopqrstuvwxyz0123456789!?,"$&%{}*

12 pt.   ABCDEFGHIJKLMNOPQRSTUVWXYZabcdefghijklmnopqrstuvwxyz0123456789!?,"$&%

14 pt.   ABCDEFGHIJKLMNOPQRSTUVWXYZabcdefghijklmnopqrstuvwxyz0123456

18 pt.   ABCDEFGHIJKLMNOPQRSTUVWXYZabcdefghijklmnopqr

48 pt.   ABCDEFGHIJKLMNOP QRSTUVWXYZabcdefg hijklmnopqrstuvwxyz012 3456789!?,"$&%{}*

10/10

Lorem ipsum dolor sit amet, consectetuer adipiscing elit, sed diam nonummy nibh euismod tincidunt ut laoreet dolore magna aliquam erat volutpat. Ut wisi enim ad minim veniam, quis nostrud exerci tation ullamcorper suscipit lobortis nisl ut aliquip ex ea commodo consequat. Duis autem vel eum iriure dolor in hendrerit in vulputate velit esse molestie consequat, vel illum dolore eu feugiat nulla facilisis at vero eros et accumsan et iusto odio dignissim qui blandit praesent luptatum zzril delenit augue duis dolore te feugait nulla facilisi. Lorem ipsum dolor sit amet, consectetuer adipiscing elit, sed diam nonummy nibh euismod

10/12

Lorem ipsum dolor sit amet, consectetuer adipiscing elit, sed diam nonummy nibh euismod tincidunt ut laoreet dolore magna aliquam erat volutpat. Ut wisi enim ad minim veniam, quis nostrud exerci tation ullamcorper suscipit lobortis nisl ut aliquip ex ea commodo consequat. Duis autem vel eum iriure dolor in hendrerit in vulputate velit esse molestie consequat, vel illum dolore eu feugiat nulla facilisis at vero eros et accumsan et iusto odio dignissim qui blandit praesent luptatum zzril delenit augue duis dolore te feugait nulla facilisi. Lorem ipsum dolor sit

10/14

Lorem ipsum dolor sit amet, consectetuer adipiscing elit, sed diam nonummy nibh euismod tincidunt ut laoreet dolore magna aliquam erat volutpat. Ut wisi enim ad minim veniam, quis nostrud exerci tation ullamcorper suscipit lobortis nisl ut aliquip ex ea commodo consequat. Duis autem vel eum iriure dolor in hendrerit in vulputate velit esse molestie consequat, vel illum dolore eu feugiat nulla facilisis at vero eros et accumsan et iusto odio dignissim qui blandit praesent lupta-

Point size:	6	7	8	9	10	11	12	13	18	20	24	36
Chars/Pica:	5	4.29	3.75	3.33	3	2.73	2.5	2.31	1.67	1.5	1.25	0.83

Cap height::	0.25"	0.5"	0.75"	1"	1.25"	1.5"	2"	2.25"	2.25"	2.5"	2.75"	3"
Approx. pt. size:	26.32	52.64	78.97	105.29	131.61	157.93	184.25	210.58	236.9	263.22	289.54	315.86

Figure 3.20   **An example of a type specimen book page**

Type Copy

The term *copy* is used widely in both printing and graphic design. In the most general sense, **copy** is any image or information that is part of a design or printing job. It is a noun, not a verb. The following guidelines apply:

- An author's written words that are set into type is copy.
- A photograph inserted in an ad is copy.
- Typeset words ready to become part of a book are copy.
- A copy editor is someone who works with an author's words before final typesetting.

Type copy is all copy that will appear as type in the printed piece. Designers use their knowledge of type design to select and specify the typefaces and sizes for use on the printed piece. All type in a job is either display copy or body copy, depending on its size and function.

Display Type

Display type is typeset in a large point size, typically 14 points or larger. Uses for display type include newspaper headlines, book chapter headings, and book covers. Most printed advertisements include some display type.

Most books use display type to help organize information and make it easy to understand how ideas relate. These words are often called A-heads, B-heads and C-heads. *Printing Technology*, 5th edition, uses distinct display type to help the reader:

Type Copy	A-head
Type Mesurement	B-head
Measuring Type Point Size	C-head

Body Copy

Body copy is typeset in smaller point sizes than display copy, usually 14 points or less. Body composition is sometimes called *text copy*. The words you are reading right now are an example of body copy. Graphic designers pick body type that is easy to read and does not detract from the author's message.

Type that is too small strains the eye and can cause headaches. Lines that are too long (line measure) and too close together (line leading) make it difficult for the eye to move easily from the end of one line to the beginning of the next. An old typesetting rule of thumb is to never set a line of type longer than the length of the line of a font's capital and lowercase letters set together (example: ABCDEFGHIJKLMNOPQRSTUVWXYZ abcdefghijklmnopqrstuvwxyz). However, contemporary designers often ignore this rule if there is sufficient line spacing. The column width for newspaper body composition is selected so you can read the entire line without moving your eyes.

𝔖𝔬𝔪𝔢 𝔱𝔶𝔭𝔢 𝔰𝔱𝔶𝔩𝔢𝔰 𝔞𝔯𝔢 𝔦𝔫𝔞𝔭𝔭𝔯𝔬𝔭𝔯𝔦𝔞𝔱𝔢 𝔱𝔬𝔡𝔞𝔶 𝔣𝔬𝔯 𝔟𝔬𝔡𝔶 𝔠𝔬𝔪𝔭𝔬𝔰𝔦𝔱𝔦𝔬𝔫 𝔟𝔢𝔠𝔞𝔲𝔰𝔢 𝔱𝔥𝔢𝔶 𝔡𝔦𝔰𝔱𝔯𝔞𝔠𝔱 𝔣𝔯𝔬𝔪 𝔱𝔥𝔢 𝔦𝔫𝔣𝔬𝔯𝔪𝔞𝔱𝔦𝔬𝔫. 𝔉𝔬𝔯 𝔢𝔵𝔞𝔪𝔭𝔩𝔢, 𝔞 𝔱𝔢𝔵𝔱 𝔱𝔶𝔭𝔢𝔣𝔞𝔠𝔢 𝔦𝔰 𝔥𝔞𝔯𝔡 𝔣𝔬𝔯 𝔪𝔬𝔰𝔱 𝔦𝔫𝔡𝔦𝔳𝔦𝔡𝔲𝔞𝔩𝔰 𝔱𝔬 𝔯𝔢𝔞𝔡, 𝔢𝔵𝔠𝔢𝔭𝔱 𝔦𝔣 𝔱𝔥𝔢𝔶 𝔯𝔢𝔞𝔡 𝔬𝔫𝔩𝔶 𝔞 𝔣𝔢𝔴 𝔩𝔦𝔫𝔢𝔰 𝔞𝔱 𝔞 𝔱𝔦𝔪𝔢. 𝔍𝔱 𝔰𝔦𝔪𝔭𝔩𝔶 𝔯𝔢𝔮𝔲𝔦𝔯𝔢𝔰 𝔱𝔬𝔬 𝔪𝔲𝔠𝔥 𝔠𝔬𝔫𝔠𝔢𝔫𝔱𝔯𝔞𝔱𝔦𝔬𝔫. 𝔅𝔬𝔡𝔶 𝔱𝔶𝔭𝔢 𝔰𝔥𝔬𝔲𝔩𝔡 𝔟𝔢 𝔦𝔫𝔳𝔦𝔰𝔦𝔟𝔩𝔢 𝔣𝔯𝔬𝔪 𝔱𝔥𝔢 𝔦𝔫𝔣𝔬𝔯𝔪𝔞𝔱𝔦𝔬𝔫.

Specifying Copy Measurement

A designer must specify the sizes for display copy and body copy. Selection of type size is a design decision, but it is based in part on the amount of space available for type matter on the printed piece. Display type for a business card, for example, probably would be too large if it were set in 72-point type; for this application 24-point type might be more appropriate. If this textbook were set in 14-point type instead of 10-point type, many more pages

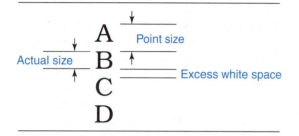

Figure 3.21   Comparison of actual size and point size. The characters above are all set in 24-point type with no leading. Their actual size is about 16 points, which leaves about 6 points of excess white space between them.

would be required to set the same amount of copy because fewer characters would fit on each text page.

Specifying Type Point Size

There is a difference between the actual height of a typeset character and the point size of the character. Recall from our discussion of foundry type in chapter 2 that type point size is the size of the foundry type body from the belly to the back side (figure 2.1). Thus the height of a typeset foundry type character is actually less than the point size of the lead body on which it is cast. A small amount of white space remains above and below the character when the character is typeset (figure 3.21).

This extra space above and below type-set characters exists whether the characters are generated from foundry type, a computer, or phototypesetting. Thus, even if lines of type are set solid (with no extra leading between them), there will always be some space between each line of type (figure 3.22). The amount of space above and below the typeset character depends on the point size in which the character is set. A 48-point character will have more extra space above and below it than will a 24-point character.

Measurement is the only way to precisely determine the actual height of a 48-point

(a)

A small amount of white space remains above and below the character when the character is typeset. Thus, even if lines of type are set solid (with no extra leading between them) there will always be some space between the lines of type.

Copy set 9/9, Century Book

(b)

A small amount of white space remains above and below the character when the character is typeset. Thus, even if lines of type are set solid (with no extra leading between them) there will always be some space between the lines of type.

Copy set 12/12, Century Book

Figure 3.22   Type set solid. The first paragraph above (a) is set solid in 9-point type; the second paragraph (b) is set solid in 12-point type. The amount of extra white space between the lines depends on the point size of the type.

character from a specific typeface when it is typeset. Transparent type rulers, like to the one in figure 3.23, aid in type measurement and specification. A display of the uppercase *E*, typeset in point sizes from 6 to 84, is printed across the face of the rule. To use a type ruler the character size display is moved over the typeset composition. A designer can compare the *E* in this rule to a typeset uppercase character in print. The number on the rule face printed next to the *E* that most closely matches the height of the typeset character gives an approximation of the typeset character's point size.

The relationship of the typeset height of a character to its specified point size can also be approximated by applying the *two-thirds*

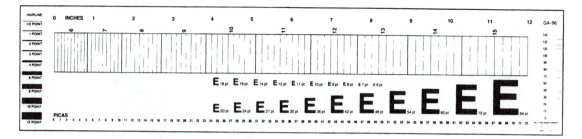

Figure 3.23 **A type rule.** *Note*: rule has been photographically reduced and is not shown in accurate scale.
Courtesy of C-Thru Ruler Company.

rule. On average, the height of a typeset character is approximately two-thirds its specified point size. Applying this rule, an uppercase character specified at 48 points will be approximately 32 points high when typeset (48 points × 2/3 = 32 points).

Type specimen books also help the designer to determine and specify to the printer desired sizes.

Specifying Line Spacing

Line spacing is defined as the vertical distance between one base line and the next, measured in points (figure 3.24). The term **leading** is sometimes used as well.

Graphic designers typically specify type size and line space together. For example, a 9 point type set with 3 extra points of space would be specified as 9/12, read "nine on twelve."

It is sometimes necessary to measure the line spacing on existing typeset copy. The ruler shown in figure 3.23 provides a means of gauging leading. Notice the set of vertical lines above the character size display. The lines in the set of vertical lines to the far right are 15 points apart. By turning the ruler so that these lines are horizontal and by moving this portion of the transparent rule over the existing type it is possible to position each group along the type base line. When any two ruler lines fall exactly on two adjacent base lines line spacing has been determined.

Specifying Line Length and Depth

The length of a typeset line, called the line measure or line length, and the vertical distance that type occupies on the typeset page, called the depth, are both specified in picas. **Picas** can be converted to points by multiplying the total number by 12.

It is important to keep in mind the following basic printing measurement units:

- 72 points = 1 inch
- 6 picas = 1 inch
- 12 points = 1 pica

Conversion charts can be used to make pica-to-point conversions.

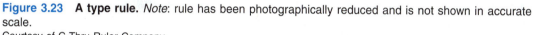

"Line spacing" is defined as the vertical distance between one baseline and the next, measured in points. The term "leading" is sometimes also used.

Line spacing

Figure 3.24 **Measuring line spacing**

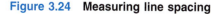

Copyfitting

Traditionally, **copyfitting** has been used to determine the space that one or more lines will occupy after typesetting. Designers needed to predict how much space the original copy would occupy when typeset. They needed to know how much type would fit in any area of their design. Today most designers deliver digital page layouts complete with graphics and text and are no longer concerned with manually calculating the number of characters to be typeset. Most software applications have the ability to do word counts, and adjustments can be made quickly.

Traditional Art Copy

There are two basic types of traditional art copy: **line copy** and **continuous-tone copy**. Line copy (figure 3.25a) is composed entirely of lines and/or dots. An illustration drawn with technical pens is a good example of line copy. The lines can be drawn with a variety of thicknesses, but all the lines are the same tone. As a result, each line is just as dense and black as all the others.

Continuous-tone copy (figure 3.25b) consists of images in a variety of tones. One common type of continuous-tone copy is a black-and-white photograph. A black-and-white photograph has tones ranging from white and gray through black.

No printing press can print more than one tone in one ink color from a single printing plate. Thus it is not possible to print all of the tones in a continuous-tone photograph as a range of tones from white to black. To print a black-and-white, continuous-tone photograph, the photo must be converted to a **halftone**. In **halftone conversion**, all the different tones on the original black-and-white photograph are converted to dots. The different sizes of these dots gives the illusion of various tones. Many large dots together appear as a darker, black area in print; small dots

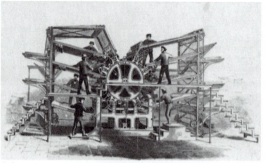

(a)

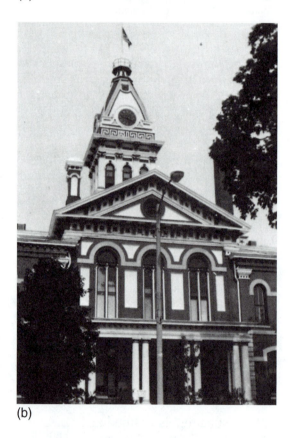

(b)

Figure 3.25   Two types of art copy. Line copy (a) consists entirely of lines and/or dots. Continuous-tone copy (b) consists of shades from white to black and must be converted to a halftone for printing.

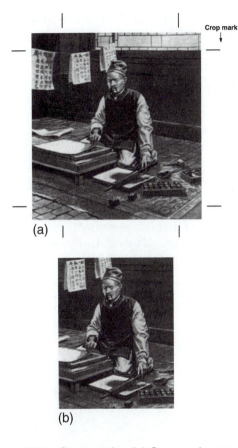

Crop mark

(a)

(b)

Figure 3.26 **Crop marks.** (a) Crop marks are used to indicate which part of the photograph should be printed. The cropped photograph is shown in (b).

appear as a lighter, gray area (figure 3.25b). Halftone conversion is explained in detail in chapter 7.

Cropping

Originally, **crop marks** (figure 3.26) had to be dense black and made with a grease pencil in order to reproduce clearly on a film negative so that they would provide a reference when stripping for positioning of the cropped image. Today most cropping of images occurs after being scanned and brought in to an image editing program.

Scaling Art

When reproducing hard copy in the traditional manner, it is often necessary to enlarge illustrations or photographs to fit specific spaces in the design. These adjustments can be produced photographically either as negatives, which are assembled with the type image during stripping, or as paper positives, which can be pasted up on a mechanical. The industry refers to these paper positives as **photostats**, or simply stats. Utilizing this method, designers and printers use a **proportion scale** (figure 3.27) to determine and specify the percentage that the image should be enlarged or reduced.

In **scaling**, 100 percent is considered the original size. A 5-inch image copied at 100 percent would result in a stat image 5 inches long. A 50 percent reduction would give an image $2\frac{1}{2}$ inches long. In contrast, a 200 percent enlargement would be 10 inches long.

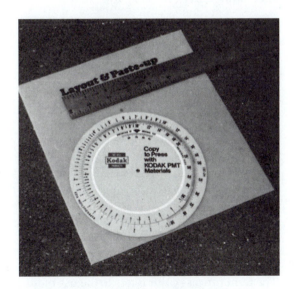

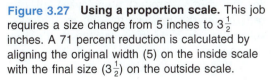

Figure 3.27 **Using a proportion scale.** This job requires a size change from 5 inches to $3\frac{1}{2}$ inches. A 71 percent reduction is calculated by aligning the original width (5) on the inside scale with the final size ($3\frac{1}{2}$) on the outside scale.

Use of Color

Most printing processes (except embossing and digital printers) create an image using ink to create the colors needed. The term *color printing* generally refers to multiple colors on the same sheet. Printing with more than one color is expensive because each color requires an additional printing plate and an additional impression on the printing press. Ink and paper considerations also affect the cost of color printing (see chapter 16).

Printers classify color printing in the following three groups:

- Fake
- Spot
- Process

Fake Color

A one-color reproduction printed on a colored sheet is known as **fake color**. Any ink color and sheet combination could be used, but the sheet must carry only one layer of ink.

Spot Color

The inks the printer purchases or mixes for a specific job are called **spot colors**. Spot colors can be specified from a color-matching system or hand mixed to match a color submitted by the designer. A color-matching system generally employs a swatchbook with samples of ink colors printed on both coated and uncoated papers (see chapter 16). All colors are numbered, and mixing formulas are included. If the designer specifies a swatchbook number, the printer can easily mix the required color. Hand mixing of colors to match a color sample is a more difficult trial-and-error process.

Process Color

The term **process color** refers to the use of four specific colors—process blue (cyan), process red (magenta), process yellow, and black—suspended in a translucent vehicle. Because the ink is translucent the pigment colors act as

filters and blend to form other colors. **Four-color process printing** is used to reproduce continuous-tone color images, such as color photographs. Chapter 5 discusses the use of four-color process printing to create the illusion of nearly any color on the printed sheet.

Tints, Surprints, Reverses, and Bleeds

An interesting technique for creating the illusion of different tones or color hues with a single color is the use of a **screen tint**. Tints break solid areas into uniform series of dots. The size of the dot is specified as a percentage of the paper area that is covered with ink. A 60 percent screen tint places dots over 60 percent of the image area (figure 3.28).

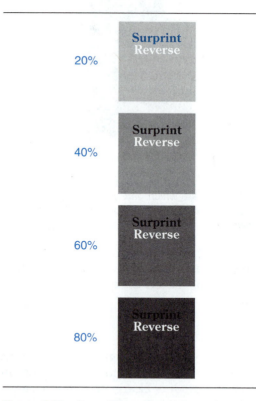

Figure 3.28   Surprints and reverses shown on selected screen tints. Note the effect of a dark background, such as an 80 percent tint, on a surprint.

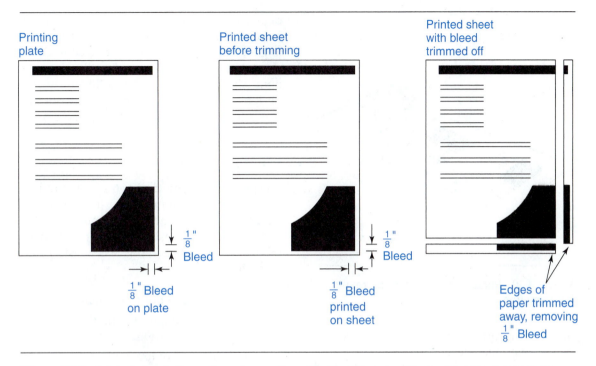

Figure 3.29 **Printed sheet dimensions larger than the bleed image.** When a bleed is required, the image is printed beyond the trim size and then trimmed.

Both **surprints** (often called *overprints*) and **reverses** are images positioned over another design. Surprints are reproduced as solids; reverses are reproduced as open areas. Both techniques are often used to set words over a picture or an illustration. It is important to consider the density of the background area when deciding whether to use a reverse or a surprint (figure 3.28). A surprint will not show up well in a dark background, and a reverse will not show up well in a light background.

A common printing design technique is to *bleed* an image off the edge of the page. A **bleed** is a design that extends an image to the edge of the printed sheet. The technique is not difficult, but it is often confusing to novice designers. During printing, the bleed edge of an image is actually printed beyond the dimensions of the trim size for the printed sheet.

When the printed sheets are trimmed to final size, the part of the bleed that was printed beyond the trim sheet size is cut away, leaving the image printed to the edge of the trimmed sheet (figure 3.29).

Image Positions on the Printing Plate

Most presses ink printing plates with ink rollers. The rollers pick up ink from a reservoir system, pass over the plate to ink the image areas, then return to the reservoir to re-ink. Halftone images require more ink during printing than does most other type copy. If several halftone images are placed so that they fall in a line at right angles to the ink rollers, it is difficult to obtain uniform ink coverage across the printed sheet.

One common result of improper image placement, particularly on small presses, is ink

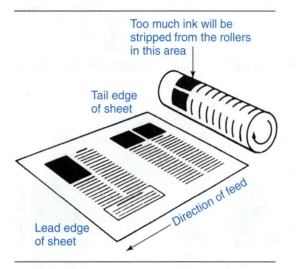

Too much ink will be stripped from the rollers in this area

Tail edge of sheet

Direction of feed

Lead edge of sheet

Figure 3.30   Image position that can result in ink depletion

depletion (figure 3.30). As the ink roller revolves over the sheet, it has enough ink to properly print the first halftone on the lead edge of the sheet, but not enough ink to print the remaining images in line with the halftone on the tail edge of the sheet. The ink becomes

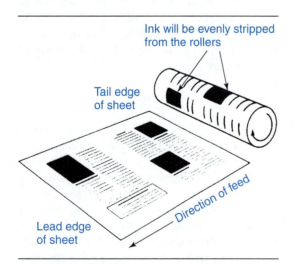

Ink will be evenly stripped from the rollers

Tail edge of sheet

Direction of feed

Lead edge of sheet

Figure 3.31   Image position that will help avoid ink depletion

depleted from the ink rollers faster than it can be replaced from the ink reservoir. The result is good ink coverage on the lead edge of the sheet, but poor ink coverage on the tail edge of the sheet. Correct image position during the design stage can balance ink distribution needs to avoid ink depletion (figure 3.31).

Design Steps

The primary graphic design task is to produce an image that communicates the customer's desired message to the intended audience. The **design steps** that designers have traditionally followed to accomplish this task consist of the following:

1. Prepare a set of thumbnail sketches.
2. Prepare rough layouts based on the preliminary thumbnail sketches.
3. Prepare a comprehensive layout.
4. Prepare a final layout or mechanical.

Thumbnail Sketches

The process begins with a series of **thumbnail sketches** (small, quick pencil renderings that show the arrangement of type, line drawings, and white space). They are proportional to, but always smaller than, reproduction size (see figure 3.32). Thumbnails do not indicate the text that will ultimately appear, but serve to give a general idea of the design. They are still an important part of the design process today.

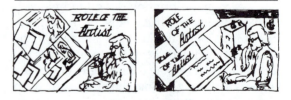

Figure 3.32   Thumbnail sketches

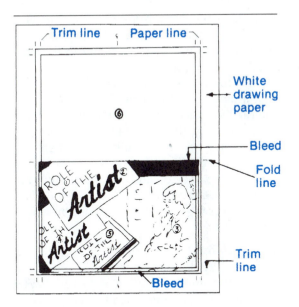

TYPE AND ILLUSTRATION SPECIFICATIONS for "Role of the Artist" mailer

1. Role of the *36 pt. Spartan Book*
2. Artist *60 pt. Brush*
3. Two-tone posterization of artist
4. Lettering to represent rough layout
5. Lettering to represent thumbnail layout
6. Space for the address

Figure 3.33 The rough layout

Rough Layouts

Before the advent of page layout software, a **rough layout** would provide all the necessary printing information. In essence, it is a detailed expansion of the thumbnail. Any printer should be able to produce the final reproduction from the directions on the rough layout. The rough layout is generally the same size as the final product and contains the actual wording of the piece, margin specifications, image placement for any line drawings or halftone photographs, and type specifications (type-

faces and sizes to be used). (If there is a great deal of body copy, typewritten copy is sometimes attached and the rough indicates where it is to be placed after typesetting.) In addition, any special operations, such as folding, trimming, or perforating, to be performed, are indicated on the rough layout. The drawing is done in pencil and may be sketched, but it must be an accurate representation of the final printed sheet (figure 3.33).

All image positions, whether type or illustrations, should be indicated accurately. Photographs are generally sketched in place and the originals are placed in a work envelope with the rough.

In addition to the rough layout, the graphic designer prepares a detailed work sheet for each job (figure 3.34). A work sheet should contain any information that is necessary to print the job.

Comprehensives

In traditional design and preparation, the customer approves the rough and the design immediately goes into production. In some cases, however, such as for expensive multicolor jobs, the customer expects to see a compre-

WORK SHEET FOR "Role of the Artist" mailer

1. Type of stock: Warren, Cameo Dull Cover
2. Weight of stock: Cover 80
3. Color of stock: White
4. Finish of stock: C2S (coated two sides)
5. Basic sheet size: 20 × 26
6. Number of basic size sheets needed: 500
7. Process of production: Offset
8. Finish trim size: 5 5/8 × 7 1/2
9. Ink color: Black
10. Length of run: 4,500
11. Imposition: 1-up
12. Finishing techniques: Score for fold
13. Special processing: Trim

Figure 3.34 Job work sheet. The work sheet contains all printing and materials specifications.

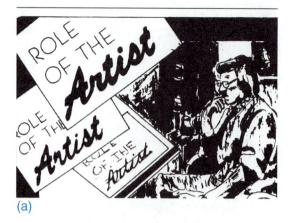

(a)

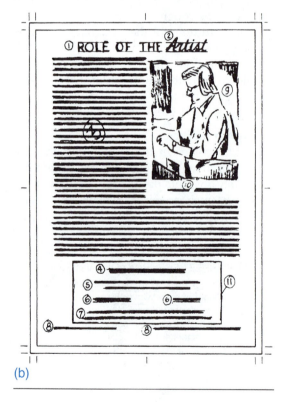

(b)

Figure 3.35   Comprehensive layout. The cover layout is illustrated in (a). The text copy comprehensive is illustrated in (b).

hensive layout. Most printing customers have had little experience interpreting roughs and are unable to use them to visualize the final product.

A **comprehensive** is an artist's rendering that attempts to duplicate the appearance of the final product. It is drawn to final size and carries no guidelines or printing instructions. In it display type is skillfully hand lettered or shown in a manner that resembles the actual type styles and sizes, and any illustrations are drawn in place. Figure 3.35 shows the comprehensives for a cover and text of a brochure.

Final Layout

Traditionally, the designer would produce a mechanical after completion of the rough. The **mechanical** is a camera-ready layout, made from detailed information on the rough. A negative made from the mechanical is used to make the actual printing image. Figure 3.36 shows the camera-ready layout for the sample job.

Today the vast majority of designers work digitally after the initial thumbnails are created. The job is then delivered to the printer through storage media, accompanied by a black-and-white or color laser proof. Output information still must be specified (that is,

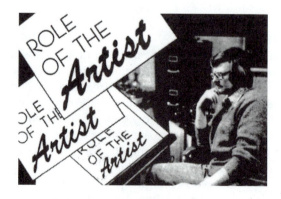

Figure 3.36   Camera-ready copy

color and weight of stock, type of printing, finishing techniques, and the like), but this can be indicated on a separate job ticket.

Dummy

Jobs that are made up of *signatures* formed by folding one or several press sheets can be very confusing in the final layout stage. To simplify the process, a **dummy** is usually prepared. A blank press sheet that is identical in size to the paper that will be used for the job is folded in the order that it will be folded after the press run. The sequence of folds is important and will influence page placement.

Without trimming the folded sheet, the printer numbers each page and cuts a notch through the top of the folds. When the dummy is unfolded, the notch indicates the head of each page and the pages appear in their proper order for the final layout. Figure 3.37 illustrates the dummy preparation process.

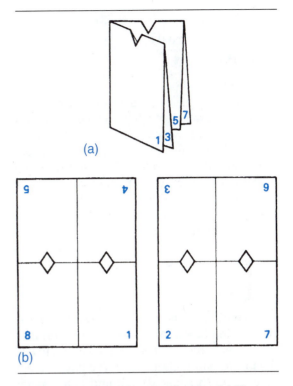

Figure 3.37 Preparing the dummy. (a) The press sheet is folded, numbered, and notched at the top. (b) The opened sheet, which is numbered on the front and on the back, is a guide to correct positioning of the pages.

Section 2: Traditional Layout and Pasteup

The goal of traditional layout and pasteup was to bring all the different pieces of composition together into a final form that met job specifications and was of sufficient quality to be reproduced photographically. As discussed in Section 1, designers and printers have traditionally referred to this camera-ready copy as a **pasteup** or a mechanical.

Traditional cold-type assembly techniques were the industry standard from the 1960s to the early 1990s. Since then, the pace of change has accelerated in the printing world, and for most of the industry traditional layout and pasteup have been eliminated. **Prepress** is the term that describes the method of digitally preparing copy for reproduction, which has literally transformed the copy preparation steps traditionally taken prior to reaching the printing press. Although rarely practiced now, much of the terminology used in today's graphic software stems from the traditional cold-type assembly techniques.

Surfaces, Materials, and Tools for Traditional Layout and Pasteup

Surfaces

Two types of pasteup surfaces generally are used to assemble cold type images. One is a **drafting board**, which has a surface set at an angle to eliminate light reflection from the paper or board and to reduce back strain for the pasteup artist (figure 3.38). The second type of surface is a **light table** (figure 3.39), which is used during stripping to bring pieces of transparent film together. It makes it possible to see through most layout papers and accurately line up images with preprinted guidelines.

Materials

The most stable and expensive board is called **illustration board**. Also used is 110-pound index paper, although it is not uncommon to use 60- to 70-pound offset paper. The pound measure refers to paper weight and is a general description of paper thickness (see chapter 16). **Polyester** or **acetate sheets** are stable-based

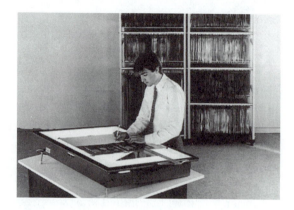

Figure 3.39   **Light table.** A light table is also used for pasteup.
Courtesy of Foster Manufacturing Co.

sheets mainly used as overlays to carry images for a second color. A stable-based sheet does not change size with moderate changes in temperature and humidity and allows for dimensional stability, which is important when two or more colors need to be registered accurately.

Tools

The three basic tools are a **T-square**, a **triangle**, and a **ruler** (figure 3.40). Both plastic and steel tools are used, and layout rulers come with both English units (inch) and printer's units (pica). **X-ACTO®** **knives** and **single-edge razor blades** are the two most common handheld cutting tools (figure 3.41). Masking tape is used to secure the board to the working surface with cellophane tape used to tape clear plastic sheets in place.

Burnishers are used in the layout room to adhere dry-transfer images or small pieces of pressure-sensitive materials to the pasteup board (figure 3.42). Part of the layout artist's job is to add layout and image lines to the pasteup. All guidelines not intended to print are drawn with a light blue (nonreproducing) pencil or pen. These light blue lines on the lay-

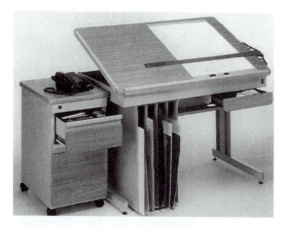

Figure 3.38   **Drafting board.** A drafting board is an inexpensive pasteup surface.
Courtesy of Foster Manufacturing Co.

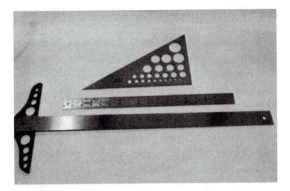

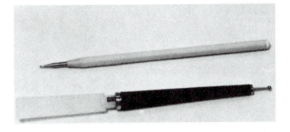

Figure 3.42 **Two types of burnishers**

Figure 3.40 **Three basic layout and pasteup tools.** T-squares, triangles, and rulers are available in various lengths in both plastic and steel.
Courtesy of Bill Hurlburt/Maple Glenn, PA.

out are not recorded on the film used to make the negative for the printing plate.

Pasteup Adhesives

The main goal in traditional cold-type pasteup is to adhere different pieces of copy to the pasteup board in the proper printing positions for a specific job. Several different **adhesives** can be used to hold the images in place. One is a **wax coater** (figure 3.43), a device designed to place a uniform layer of wax material on one side of a sheet of paper. The adhesive used remains tacky and can be moved and repositioned many times. Rubber cement is also used, but copy must be positioned correctly quickly, because this adhesive is quick drying.

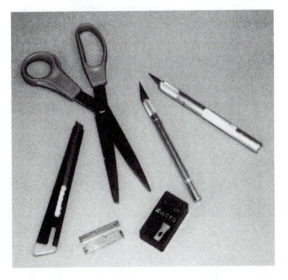

Figure 3.41 **Cutting tools.** X-ACTO® knives (or other stick-type cutters) and single-edge razor blades are commonly used to cut pieces of art. The blades should be replaced often to ensure clean, smooth edges.
Courtesy of Bill Hurlburt/Maple Glenn, PA.

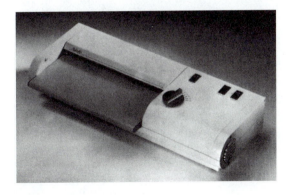

Figure 3.43 **A wax coater.** The drive roller pulls the paper through the wax in the wax coater.
Courtesy of Schaefer Machine Company, Inc.

Types of Art

Jobs with images for pasteup come to the traditional layout room in several forms. *Line work* (such as type, ink drawings, and clip art) and *continuous-tone photographs* are the two most common sorts of images (figure 3.44). Most pasteup jobs have black images on an opaque paper base. **Clip art** traditionally has been camera-ready material, usually line art, that is purchased by printers and designers in forms ready for pasteup. Today, clip art is available on disk, CD-ROM, and the Internet and can be inserted digitally into a variety of programs.

Working with Photographs

Many jobs include photographs. Because most printing processes cannot directly reproduce continuous-tone images, it is necessary to adapt the mechanical. The main methods that a traditional layout artist utilizes to handle photographs are using prescreened halftones or forming a window on the negative.

Basically, halftones are continuous-tone images that have been converted to dots (halftones are discussed in chapter 4). Dense, black areas of the halftone have large dots; light areas have small dots. The resulting image tricks the human eye into thinking it sees continuous tones.

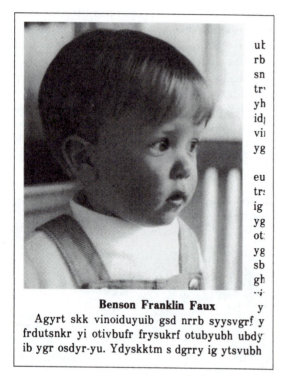

ut
rb
sn
tr
yh
id
vi
yg

eu
tr
ig
yg
ot
yg
sb
gh

Benson Franklin Faux   y
Agyrt skk vinoiduyuib gsd nrrb syysvgrf y
frdutsnkr yi otivbufr frysukrf otubyubh ubdy
ib ygr osdyr-yu. Ydyskktm s dgrry ig ytsvubh

Figure 3.44   A prescreened print pasted on a mechanical. Random letters are used here to visualize copy applied to a typical job.

E
ub
rbg
snr
trv
yhr
idg
vin
ygr

Y
euy
trs
ig
ygr
otr
ygr
sbf
ghi
vin
ygr

Benson Franklin Faux
Agyrt skk vinoiduyuib gsd nrrb syysvgrf yi
frdutsnkr yi otivbufr frysukrf otubyubh ubdyty
ib ygr osdyr-yu. Ydyskktm s dgrry ig ytsvubh o

Figure 3.45   A blockout on a mechanical. When this layout is photographed, the black area will appear on the negative as a clear rectangle window into which the halftone negative will be positioned.

Prescreened Halftone

An opaque **prescreened halftone** can be pasted into a mechanical and rephotographed with the rest of the job as line copy. These are sometimes referred to as *stats* or *photostats*.

Windows on the Negative

A **window** can be created on the negative by adhering a layer of red or black material, sometimes called a *blockout*, to the area on the pasteup where the photograph is to appear in the final reproduction (figure 3.45). When the layout is photographed, the black or red blockout forms a clear area (a window) on the negative. A **halftone negative** can then be attached under the window during stripping prior to making a printing plate.

Working from the Rough Layout

The **rough layout** is a detailed guide used to identify and position every piece of art on the pasteup. It is a "floor plan" that predicts and describes the final product and should contain all the information necessary to produce the job. Incorrect roughs lead to redoes and lost profits.

Reviewing Instructions

The first step in beginning a traditional pasteup job, or even a modern job being prepped on the computer, is to examine the work order, special instructions, and rough layout. The goal of this step is to clearly understand the customer's expectations.

The job jacket should contain certain information, the most common of which is the following:

- Type content and specifications (such as size and style)
- Final product dimensions

- Image positions for all elements
- Finishing operations (such as folding, trimming, scoring, or perforating)
- Press specifications (including paper, length of run, imposition, and ink color)

The traditional layout artist, as well as the modern graphic designer working digitally, must consider every part of the rough (or project), including finishing operations such as **folding** and **trimming**, in addition to considering image positions.

Checking for Completeness

After reviewing the job instructions, it is important to ensure that all necessary pieces are in the **job jacket**. It is frustrating and costly to begin pasteup and discover when nearing completion that one piece of copy is missing. This same issue exists in modern prepress workflow, and the term **preflighting** is now used to describe the process of reviewing all parts of a job digitally before it enters production (see chapter 9).

Single-Color and Multicolor Pasteup

In preparing for a traditional pasteup, the following steps are taken:

- Select and mount the pasteup board on the layout table
- Add layout lines to the pasteup board. These include center lines, fold lines, trim lines, and image guidelines.
- Attach the copy and check alignments
- Cut masks for halftone windows, screen tints and special overlay images.
- For multicolor pasteups, it is necessary to add register marks (figure 3.46).

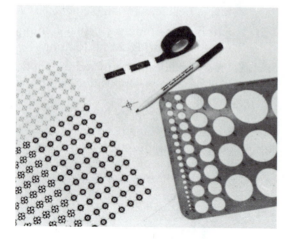

Figure 3.46 **Register marks.** Register marks can be purchased in pressure-sensitive or preprinted form, or they can be created by hand with a black ruling pen.

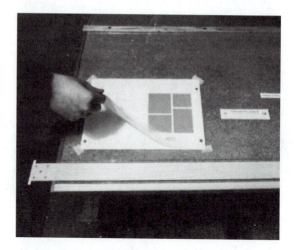

Figure 3.47 **Adding the color overlay.** Hinge a piece of plastic over the board to receive the second set of images. Be sure to cut away the areas over the register marks.

As with single-color work, every multi-color job begins by setting up the pasteup board. Draw the paper lines, fold lines, and image guidelines in nonreproducing blue. Place all image guidelines for each color on the same pasteup sheet. Add trim or fold marks for the finishing room in black India ink or in repro felt-tip pen.

The production process now follows the designer's directions. There are several methods of stripping the job. With one method, the photographer shoots two film negatives of the pasteup. The stripper then prepares two separate flats and unwanted images are simply masked out. Another method is to make only one negative. During stripping, masks are cut that flip back and forth to cover or uncover images. The platemaker then follows the stripper's directions to prepare two separate printing plates.

Adding Register Marks

For multicolor work it is necessary to add **register marks**. Register marks help the press operator to align one color over another in per-

fect register. A minimum of three register marks should be placed on the board to ensure good registration. In today's digital workflow, register marks are added within the page layout application.

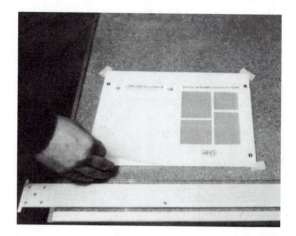

Figure 3.48 **Mounting the second-color copy.** Following the image guidelines on the first sheet, affix the second set of images to the overlay sheet.

Working with an Overlay

An **overlay sheet** is used in pasteup to carry images for a second color. A clear or frosted plastic overlay sheet is hinged over the first color (figure 3.47) and carries artwork and composition for the second. For each additional color, another overlay is hinged from an edge of the board (figure 3.48).

Although many of the procedures discussed in this chapter are rarely done anymore, they still provide a framework for understanding modern digital workflow. They also help us to appreciate the incredible speed and efficiency that computers have brought to the page preparation process.

Key Terms

balance	display type	pasteup
formal balance	body copy	prepress
informal balance	line spacing	drafting board
subjective balance	leading	light table
dominance	pica	illustration board
proportion	copyfitting	polyester sheet
unity	line copy	acetate sheet
typeface	continuous-tone copy	T-square
x-height	halftone	triangle
body height	halftone conversion	ruler
descender	crop marks	X-ACTO® knife
ascender	photostats	single-edge razor blade
stroke	proportion scale	burnisher
stress	scaling	adhesive
serif	fake color	wax coater
fillet	spot color	clip art
type style	process color	prescreened halftone
Roman	four-color process printing	window
sans serif	screen tint	halftone negative
square serif	surprints	rough layout
text typeface	reverses	folding
script	bleed	trimming
occasional	design steps	job jacket
typographers	thumbnail sketch	preflighting
type family	rough layout	register marks
point size	comprehensive	overlay sheet
font	mechanical	
copy	dummy	

Review Questions

Section 1

1. Define x-height, ascenders, and descenders.
2. What are the six typeface categories?
3. Define the term *font*.
4. What is the difference between display copy and body copy?
5. What are the differences between fake, spot, and process colors?
6. Thumbnails, roughs, comprehensives, mechanicals, and dummys are all used during the traditional design process. Discuss the purpose of each.

Section 2

7. What are the two most common types of images in traditional pasteup?
8. What are the main methods used in traditional layout to include photographs?
9. When are register marks used?

4

Traditional Line and Halftone Photography

Historical Background

The first commercial halftone illustration reproduced in a mass circulation publication appeared in the March 4, 1880, issue of the New York *Daily Graphic*. It was a picture of a scene in Shantytown, New York. As the picture's cutline advertised, it was a "reproduction direct from nature." Even before it ran the first halftone illustration, however, the *Daily Graphic* was a startling venture in both design and manufacture. An editorial in the *Daily Graphic* from the same period observed that "the boldness of the experiment, when it was proposed to start and maintain in the city of New York a daily illustrated newspaper, was well fitted to take away the breath."

Before halftones, the only way to add illustrations to a printed piece was to include the drawings by artists. It was the day of the "sketch artist," or the "artist on the spot," as many newspapers advertised. The task of providing enough

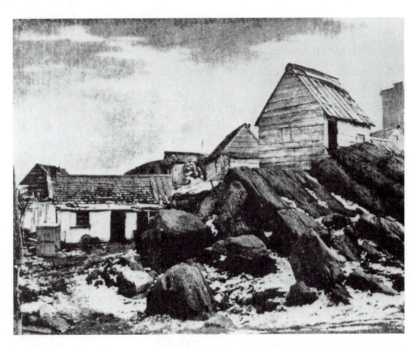

The first commercial halftone illustration. Courtesy of Smithsonian Institution, Photo No. 73–5138.

artists' illustrations to fill twelve pages of newspaper was a mammoth undertaking.

The person responsible for the *Daily Graphic's* success was a young man named Stephen H. Horgan, then 26 years old. As early as 1875 Horgan conceived of a method to make the density gradations of a photographic negative into lines, and the halftone illustration was born.

Horgan's first commercial halftone was made with a negative screen formed from a series of fine rulings, all slightly out of focus. A print was made by projecting the original photographic negative through the negative screen. The result was then treated exactly like a line drawing by the production workers.

Horgan's early work was with single-line screens. In other words, the gradation lines from opaque to transparent on the screens ran parallel. The resulting reproductions looked, to many printers, somewhat like the artists' drawings that they had been working with for many years. The single-line screens were coarse and well suited to reproduction on fast letterpress equipment using inexpensive paper.

The single-line illustrations were all right, but there was room for improvement. The next challenge was to print cross-line halftones. Every press operator, however, said only a fool would suggest that a cross-line halftone could be printed without looking like a "puddle of mud."

The "foolish" ideas of people like Stephen Horgan contributed to the growth and refinement of halftone photography, the subject of the second section of this chapter.

Objectives

After completing this chapter you will be able to:

- Classify photographic films.
- Understand traditional basic camera concepts.
- Understand the basics of film development.
- Differentiate between density, tone, and contrast.
- Discuss the purposes of reflection, transmission, and dot area densitometers.
- Discuss the significance of a gray scale in the photomechanical process.
- Explain the difference between a halftone screen and a screen tint.
- Explain how a halftone screen produces dots of varying sizes.
- Explain how to determine appropriate highlight and shadow dot sizes.
- Identify highlight, midtone, and shadow areas of continuous-tone copy.
- Understand the importance of dot size and dot gain.

Introduction

This chapter deals with the basics of line photography and halftone photography. It is rare for pages to be prepared using photographic processes now, but what has become commonplace in digital prepress today is rooted in the traditional printing processes. The basic concepts need to be understood even though it is not necessary to re-create the actual processes anymore.

All of the major printing processes place one consistent layer of ink on some receiver, such as paper. This idea cannot be overemphasized. *Printers only reproduce lines.* These lines can be so big that we see them as huge ink areas or so small that we need a magnifying glass to see them, but they all have the same ink density (figure 4.1). The primary concern of this chapter is the production of line images that can be used with the printing processes. This process is called **line photography.**

A line negative either passes light in the image area, or blocks the passage of light in the nonimage area, to a printing plate. If all images that needed to be reproduced were made only of lines, then simple line exposures would meet all printing needs. There is, however, a large group of images that do not have line characteristics—continuous-tone images. Except by using special techniques, it is not possible to print a continuous-tone photograph. **Continuous-tone photographs** have varying shades of gray called **tones.** A picture reproduced in a book or a magazine is not a continuous-tone image. Such a picture is reproduced through **halftone photography.**

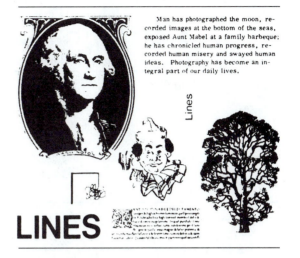

Figure 4.1 **Examples of line reproduction.** This illustration shows some different images that are reproduced by lines.

This process breaks the tones of a picture into small, dense dots that trick the eye into seeing what appear to be various tones. Chapter 7 deals with halftone photography.

Section 1: Line Photography

The Nature of Light

It is generally agreed that light is electromagnetic radiation measured in wavelengths emitted from either a natural source (the sun) or an artificial source (such as a camera light) (figure 4.2). All electromagnetic radiation, whether gamma rays, visible light, heat, or radio and television signals, travels in waves. The effect of radiation is determined by wavelength, which is measured as the distance from one wave crest to the next (figure 4.3). The top scale in figure 4.2 shows that X-ray radiation has a very short wavelength while radio waves have a long wavelength. Figure 4.2 also illustrates the relationship of visible light to the spectrum of known electromagnetic radiation.

Light has wavelengths in the spectrum that stimulate our optic nerves. These wavelengths comprise the **visible spectrum**.

Because light waves are short, they are generally measured in millimicrons (mμ) (1 mμ = 1 billionth of 1 meter or 25 millionths of 1 inch), or in nanometers (1 nm = 1 billionth of 1 meter). Each color of the visible spectrum has a unique wavelength. White light is the balanced presence of radiation from the visible spectrum.

The human eye can perceive wavelengths from about 400 mμ to about 700 mμ. In other words, if we can see it we call it *light*. The shorter wavelengths (closer to 400 mμ) produce the colors on the blue end of the spectrum; the longer wavelengths (closer to 700

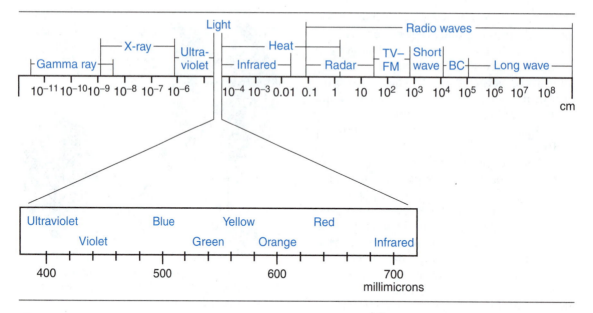

Figure 4.2   Wavelengths of different colors of the visible light spectrum

mμ) produce the colors at the red end of the spectrum. The human eye is most sensitive to the green portion, or center portion, of the visible spectrum, between 500 and 580 mμ.

The basis of photography is a chemical change caused when radiation in the visible spectrum contacts a light-sensitive material called an **emulsion**. Graphic arts photographic processes use artificial light sources that vary in the range of wavelengths of visible light they produce. Some light sources produce wavelengths high in the blue end of the spectrum; others produce wavelengths high in the red end. As will be seen in what follows, light-

sensitive emulsions are formulated to record select wavelengths of light. That is, emulsions are produced that are sensitive to some colors in the spectrum but not to others.

Light-Sensitive Materials

All light-sensitive materials, whether films or plates, can be classified according to three main variables:

■ Color sensitivity

■ Contrast

■ Film speed

Color Sensitivity

Color sensitivity describes the area of the visible electromagnetic spectrum that causes a chemical change in a particular emulsion. A **wedge spectrogram** is often used to show a film's reaction to light across the visible spectrum (figure 4.4a). Notice, for example, that blue-sensitive film (figure 4.4b) is only ex-

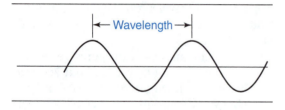

Figure 4.3   Diagram of wavelength

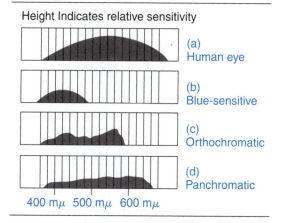

Height Indicates relative sensitivity

(a)
Human eye

(b)
Blue-sensitive

(c)
Orthochromatic

(d)
Panchromatic

400 mμ 500 mμ 600 mμ

Figure 4.4   Examples of wedge spectrograms.
A wedge spectrogram shows a film's reaction to
light across the visible spectrum.

posed by wavelengths of light from the left
end of the visible spectrum, from about 400 to
550 mμ. The height of the graph indicates sensitivity. Wavelengths near the center of the
sensitivity range, around 475 mμ, produce the
fastest chemical reactions. A greater amount
of light is needed from the 400-mμ or 550-mμ
ends to obtain the same film exposure.

There are three basic types of light-
sensitive emulsions: blue-sensitive, orthochromatic, and panchromatic materials.

Blue-sensitive materials are often called *color
blind* because they react to only the blue end
of the spectrum (figure 4.4b). On a negative
they record high densities from blue light, but
they record very little from the green or red
end of the spectrum. Roomlight film, which
can be used outside the darkroom, is blue-light
sensitive.

Orthochromatic material is not red sensitive, but it is sensitive to all other portions
of the visible spectrum (figure 4.4c). Because
they are not sensitive to red light, "ortho films"
can be safely handled under a red darkroom
safelight.

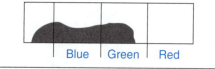

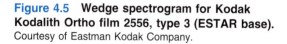

Blue | Green | Red

**Figure 4.5   Wedge spectrogram for Kodak
Kodalith Ortho film 2556, type 3 (ESTAR base).**
Courtesy of Eastman Kodak Company.

Most film manufacturers provide a
wedge spectrograph for each of their films.
Figure 4.5 illustrates the sensitivity of one type
of ortho film. The most efficient and accurate
photographs are obtained when the peak sensitivity of a film's spectrograph corresponds to
the peak output of a light source.

Panchromatic material is sensitive to all
visible colors and is approximately as sensitive as the human eye (figure 4.4d). Because
they are sensitive to all of the colors that humans see, "pan films" can be used to record
variations in tone and are ideally suited for
continuous-tone photography. Being sensitive
to all wavelengths of light also means that a
panchromatic emulsion is exposed by any visible light that strikes it. Therefore, pan films
must be processed in total darkness.

Contrast

Contrast, the second variable that can be used
to classify light-sensitive materials, is a term
that describes the compression or expansion of
the shades or tones of original copy on the film
or plate. (Refer to figure 4.17 for a comparison
of normal- and high-contrast pictures.)

Contrast is described by a film's **characteristic curve**, also called a log E curve, H &
D curve, Density-log E curve, D-log E curve,
or sensitometric curve (figure 4.6).

Film manufacturers provide characteristic curves for each of their films. Figure 4.7 illustrates the curves for Kodak's Ortho 3, an extremely high-contrast film. These curves reveal
that a very slight change in exposure provides

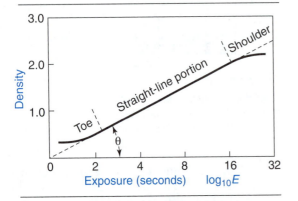

Figure 4.6 Example of a film's characteristic curve. The toe of the curve is a gradual incline because a light-sensitive material does not produce a predictable density when exposed by a small amount of light. In other words, a predictable amount of density is not developed until a specific exposure time is reached. The straight-line portion represents an expected density development for each exposure. Eventually, the curve shoulders off even as exposure is increased; that is, the film fails to produce an expected amount of density as the exposure increases. The film fails to reciprocate.

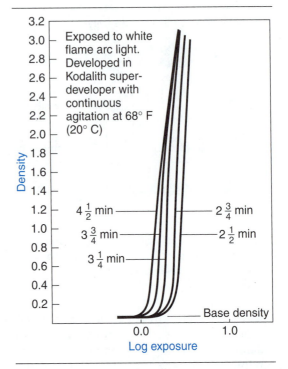

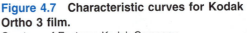

Figure 4.7 Characteristic curves for Kodak Ortho 3 film.
Courtesy of Eastman Kodak Company.

a rapid jump in film density. This quality is ideal for printing production because the film records sharp, clean lines between image and nonimage areas of the original copy.

Film Speed
Film speed is the third main variable that can be used to classify light-sensitive materials. Each film or plate material requires a different amount of light to cause a chemical change in the emulsion. Emulsions that require little light are called *fast*, while those that require a lot of light are called *slow*. Because there are so many different emulsions requiring different amounts of light, the concept of fast versus slow is meaningless, however. For that reason, an **exposure index** is assigned to each film by the manufacturer. The ISO system (developed by the International Standards Board)

applies a number scale to relative film speed—the higher the number, the faster the film. For example, a film with an ISO rating of 25 requires twice as much light to create the same image density as does a film rated at ISO 50. Exposure index is assigned as a function of the type of light source used to expose the film.

It is important to understand that color sensitivity, contrast, and film speed are unrelated variables that cannot be compared directly. It is possible to produce films that exhibit any combination of these three characteristics.

Film Emulsions
All photographic films use some type of light-sensitive material called an emulsion to record an image. The characteristics of the light-

sensitive emulsion, as well as the quantity and type of light reaching that emulsion, determine the sort of image recorded on the film. Most film emulsions are formed from silver halide suspended in a gelatin compound (picture fruit suspended in a bowel of gelatin). The most common film emulsion component is silver bromide (AgBr), which reacts rapidly and predictably. Silver iodide (AgI) and silver chloride (AgCl) are less common emulsion components and are almost always used with silver bromide to produce different film characteristics.

Despite their chemical differences, all films are structured in the same general manner (figure 4.8). The emulsion is bonded to a base material by an adhesive lower layer. Glass was long used as base material because it is transparent and extremely stable. Most materials change size or shape when the temperature changes. It is very important in graphic arts photography that the base supporting the emulsion not change size. If it does, an image may distort or fail to fit exactly in the desired location on the printed page.

Glass is still used in some topographic mapping and electronic circuitry—fields in which perfect registration (image location) is critical and in which the size of the film must not change with humidity, temperature, or age. In contrast, graphic arts films are usually made from a cellulose-ester- or polystyrene-based material. The advantage these materials have over glass is that they are flexible and much less expensive.

In addition to the stability problems of base materials, there are stability problems caused when the emulsion and the base are laminated because each part is affected differently by the environment and by age. For many years film was formed from only the base and the emulsion material. This type of film had several problems, however. During exposure the light would pass through the camera lens, strike and expose the emulsion, and then pass through the base material. It would reflect from the back of the base material and again pass through the emulsion, re-exposing it (figure 4.9a). To prevent this effect, an **antihalation dye** is now placed over the back of the film base. Instead of being reflected, the light is absorbed by the dye and

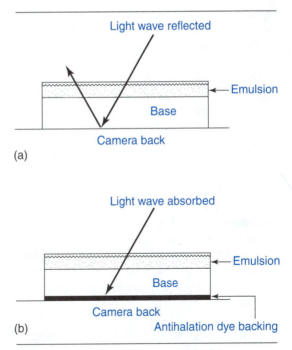

(a)

(b)

Figure 4.9 Comparison of light rays through two types of film structure. Without the antihalation dye layer (a) light reflected from the back of the film base reexposes the emulsion. The antihalation dye (b) absorbs the light rays and prevents reexposure.

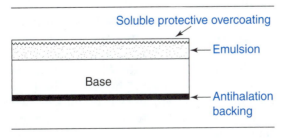

Figure 4.8 A typical film structure

exposes the film only once (figure 4.9b). The antihalation dye also serves as an anticurl agent with flexible base films. The antihalation dye dissolves during chemical processing.

Another problem a film made of only a base and an emulsion had was the gelatin material in the emulsion was frail. To overcome this weakness, the emulsion is blanketed with a transparent protective layer called overcoating (figure 4.8). This **overcoating** protects the gelatin material from fingerprints and adds an antistress factor during handling. Like the antihalation dye, the overcoating dissolves during chemical processing.

Camera Fundamentals

Line photography is also called *process photography*, *reproduction photography*, or *high-contrast photography*. Whatever label is applied, the goals are the same: to make precision enlargements and reductions, and to critically control line dimensions with a process camera. Although process cameras have been rendered obsolete due to modern prepress operations, an understanding of basic camera concepts is still relevant today. Modern analog photography is still concerned with the amount of light entering through the lens and the duration of the shutter opening. Digital photography also uses aperture settings as one of the measures determining the quantity of light striking the scanning array.

Process cameras vary in type, size, complexity, and cost. Regardless of their differences, all process cameras provide four basic services:

- A place to mount the light-sensitive film and the original image
- A means of focusing an image on the film
- A system to enlarge or reduce the original image on the film
- A system to control the amount of light that reaches the film emulsion

Process Camera Concepts

To understand how a process camera works first build a general understanding of how any photographic system operates. Then move on to how line photography uses the same approach. All that is required for process photography is a light source, a light-tight box to hold the film, a way to focus an image on the film, a way to control the amount of light that reaches the film, and, of course, something to photograph.

Whatever the light source, it should be directed at the object to be photographed because film records reflected light. It is easy to position an artificial light source so that all areas of the object receive the proper amount of light. If we use natural light (the sun), we have to position the object to get the proper illumination. In line photography, artificial light is always used to illuminate the image because uniform illumination across the image is required.

Process Camera Controls

Process cameras all have the same controls. There must be some sort of opening through which to pass and aim light. This is called the **lens**. It is necessary to be able to move the lens so the light reflected from the object is sharp and clear on the film. This movement is called **focusing**. If the image is not in focus, a blurred picture results.

After the image is focused, there must be a way to control the amount of light that passes through the lens. This is important. If too little light reaches the film, no image is recorded. If too much light strikes the film, then the film is completely exposed. The two ways to control this passage of light are by controlling:

- The size of the lens opening
- The amount of time the lens is open

A simple way to understand how light is controlled is to think of a camera lens as a water faucet and of light as the water that passes through the pipe. First, consider the size of the pipe. It seems logical that a 2-inch pipe will pass nearly twice the amount of water as a 1-inch pipe in the same amount of time. If we run water through the 1-inch pipe for twice as much time as through the 2-inch pipe, the same amount of water should pass through each pipe. This example is not mathematically accurate in terms of the amount of water passed, but it does show the importance of the relationship between time and area. Actually, the amount of water—or light—that passes through an opening is a function of the area of the pipe, not the diameter.

The light controls for a camera operate like the water faucet. We can accurately control the amount of time the lens or "pipe" stays open with the **shutter**. This amount of time is called **shutter speed**. It is also possible to vary the size of the lens opening. This opening is called the **aperture**. The aperture is controlled by the **diaphragm**. The size of the aperture is based on the f/stop system (figure 4.10).

The **f/stop system** is based on the ratio of the aperture diameter to the focal length of the camera lens. **Focal length** is the distance from the node, or center, of the lens to the film board when the lens is focused at infinity (maximum reduction for graphic arts cameras). The formula to determine an f/stop number is

f/stop number = focal length/diameter of
the aperture

For example, if the lens has an 8-inch focal length, a 1-inch aperture is assigned the f/stop value of f/8 (8÷1 = 8). A 1/2-inch

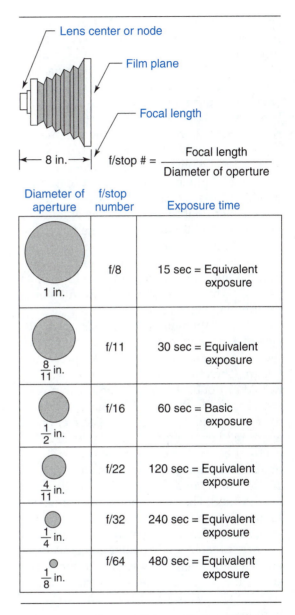

$$f/stop \ \# = \frac{Focal \ length}{Diameter \ of \ operture}$$

Diameter of aperture	f/stop number	Exposure time
1 in.	f/8	15 sec = Equivalent exposure
$\frac{8}{11}$ in.	f/11	30 sec = Equivalent exposure
$\frac{1}{2}$ in.	f/16	60 sec = Basic exposure
$\frac{4}{11}$ in.	f/22	120 sec = Equivalent exposure
$\frac{1}{4}$ in.	f/32	240 sec = Equivalent exposure
$\frac{1}{8}$ in.	f/64	480 sec = Equivalent exposure

Figure 4.10   Camera f/stops. Camera f/stops are the relationships between focal lengths and lens opening sizes. In this figure, the focal length is always 8 inches but the lens opening sizes vary from 1 inch to 1/8 inch. The basic exposure time is 60 seconds (f/16). Equivalent exposure times are given for the remaining f/stops.

aperture is f/16 (8÷1/2 = 16). In theory it is possible to create any f/stop number. An aperture diameter of 3/8 inches produces f/21.33 (8÷3/8 = 21.33). However, lens manufacturers have agreed upon a sequence of the most efficient f/stop numbers or ratios. The numbers are f/1.4, f/2, f/2.8, f/4, f/5.6, f/8, f/11, f/16, f/22, f/32, and f/64. Graphic arts process cameras generally use ratios from f/8 to f/64.

All these numbers—or ratios—differ by a factor of 2 in the amount of light they pass. In other words, moving from one f/stop to another either doubles or halves the amount of light. Notice in figure 4.10 that the larger the f/stop number, the smaller the aperture. Changing the f/stop from f/32 to f/22 doubles the aperture. Moving from f/16 to f/22 halves it. This is an especially powerful tool in determining equivalent exposures.

The diaphragm and shutter work together. Each f/stop either doubles or halves the cross-sectional area of the preceding f/stop. Therefore, the shutter speed can be halved or doubled to correspond with a one-step diaphragm change. (Remember, changing the f/stop actually changes the diameter of the aperture.) For example, if the film were being exposed correctly at f/16 for 40 seconds, an **equivalent exposure** could be made at f/8 for 10 seconds (f/16 at 40 sec = f/11 at 20 sec = f/8 at 10 sec). The same amount of light would hit the film, and the film record would be the same. An understanding of this relationship is a powerful tool for any photographer. A camera operator often seeks to reduce the exposure time to save time and camera lights which, like any artificial light source, wear out with use.

Because f/stop numbers result from mathematical formulas that are based on focal length and aperture diameter, information can be accurately compared between different cameras. In other words, f/16 on a 35-mm camera and f/16 on a large process camera pass the same amount of light.

Process Camera Classifications

The process camera is large, as large as a printing plate, because it must be able to hold large sheets of film, but it is really nothing more than a sophisticated light-tight box. The film end of the camera opens to show a **filmboard** (figure 4.11), which holds the film in place during the exposure. A vacuum-back filmboard is generally used to hold the film flat on the filmboard and ensure that it does not shift during exposure. The filmboard hinges closed and is parallel to the copyboard at the opposite end of the camera. The **copyboard** is simply a glass-covered frame that holds the copy to be photographed. There are general guidelines on both the film and the copyboard that, if followed, ensure that the image records in the center of the film.

Process cameras have an artificial light source that directs light at the copyboard. Most light systems are controlled by the camera shutter. When a timer opens the shutter, the lights go on. They automatically shut off when the timer closes the shutter.

One great advantage of the process camera was that it could enlarge and reduce original copy. Size changes are referred to by the percentage of the original that is to be recorded on the film. A 100 percent or 1:1 reproduction exposes an image on the film that is the same size as the original copy. A 25 percent reduction exposes an image that is one-quarter the original size. A 200 percent enlargement exposes an image that is twice the size of the original copy. The percentage of enlargement or reduction is controlled by changing the positions of the camera lens and the copyboard. Today's digital workflow can create whatever size is required through software and choice of output device.

Process cameras can be classified in terms of their design. A **horizontal process camera** (figure 4.11) has a long stationary bed. The film end is usually in the darkroom and the lights and lens protrude through a wall

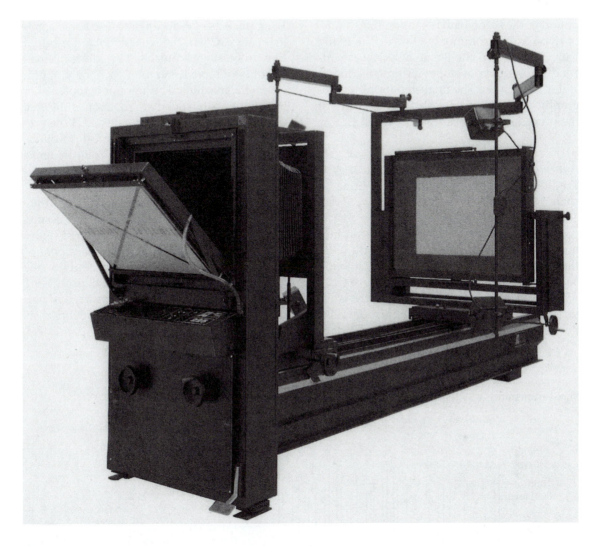

Figure 4.11 A horizontal process camera.
Courtesy of ACTI Cameras Inc.

into a normally lighted room. A **vertical process camera** is a self-contained unit that takes up little space in the darkroom.

Film Processing

For litho or orthochromatic films, at least three chemical solutions and a water bath are used during film processing. First is the developer, which is a complex solution designed to make the latent image visible. The next step is to stop the development, which is done by plunging the film in an acid solution, referred to as a *stop-bath*. After the development is stopped, the image on the piece of film is visible, but not permanent. A fixing bath is used to remove any remaining unexposed silver crystals and make the image permanent. The main compound in the fixing bath is sodium thiosulfate, or hypo as it is commonly known. The fixing bath also hardens the image, which was softened during the development process due to water absorption. The final step for all photographic processes is to wash away all traces of the processing chemicals.

Automatic Film Processing

Traditionally, film processing was done in shallow trays and controlled manually. Today automatic processors are used.

In automatic film processing a continuous belt or roller system passes the film through a developer, a stop-fixer combination bath, a washing tank, and a dryer (figure 4.12). With deep-tank chemical storage, there is little problem with oxidation because there is little surface area of the liquid exposed to air.

Long periods of disuse will cause some activity change. Chemical exhaustion as a result of film processing is controlled by adding a small quantity of replenisher after each piece of film enters the machine. The amount of replenisher that is generally added is a function of the area of the sheet of film being processed. When replenishers are used, the chemical solutions generally need to be removed from the tanks only several times a year for machine maintenance.

Automatic film processing is an attractive alternative to shallow-tray processing. Most automatic film processing units (figure 4.13) are designed for dry-to-dry (operator touches no liquids) delivery in four to five minutes. In addition, automatic processing provides accurate time, temperature, and agitation control and reduces production costs through faster processing.

Film Processing

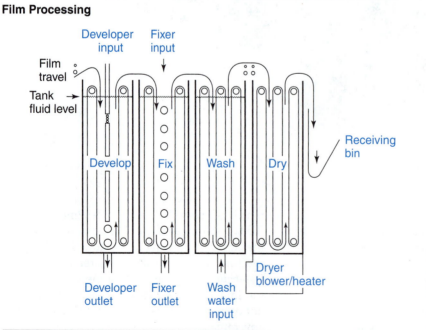

Figure 4.12 Side view diagram of a typical automatic film processor. Rollers move the film from tank to tank.

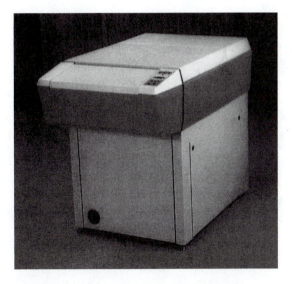

Figure 4.13 An automatic film-processing unit. A unit like this machine provides greater accuracy and control of agitation, time, and temperature than is possible with manual processing methods.
Courtesy of Log E/LogEtronics, Inc.

Rapid Access Processing

Traditional graphic films are commonly called **lith films**, and the developers used with them are called **lith developers**. The primary disadvantage of lith processing is the lack of latitude during development. Development time, temperature, and agitation have to be critically controlled. If all of these conditions are not in control, then it is impossible to predict results exactly. For large-line images, there is generally not a problem. However, much production time can be lost trying to obtain an acceptable film image with any other type of original copy.

Rapid access processing nearly eliminates dependence upon time, temperature, and agitation controls. Rapid access processing offers much wider latitude than lith, which

gives it several advantages. Development requires only one solution and the fixer is simpler in chemical composition than that used for lith. Thus, whether shallow-tray or automatic processing is used, no replenisher is needed. The processor operator need only keep the developer and fixer topped off to the appropriate levels. In addition, because of the differences in developer chemistry, the developer is not easily exhausted through oxidation. Although rapid access developer eventually becomes exhausted from processing film, it can be left in the development tray and exposed to air for a day or more without becoming exhausted through oxidation.

The latitude for rapid access processing is also increased because the three major development variables (time, temperature, and agitation) are far less crucial than they are for lith development. If properly exposed, film developed in rapid access chemistry almost completely stops developing at the proper point. As a result, there is almost no chance of over- or underdevelopment. The exposed emulsion moves rapidly to maximum density and then slows to almost no chemical activity.

Most rapid access chemistry requires a minimum development time of 90 seconds. However, the film will not overdevelop if it is left in the developer for far longer. Because the film stops developing at the proper point, development time does not need to be controlled for copy variations. A piece of film used to record fine-line detail can be developed for the same length of time as a piece of film used to record normal detail. Another advantage of rapid access is that it can be used to process a range of film materials, including process camera films, contacting films, duplicating films, and even some typesetting papers.

All of these advantages add up to processing simplicity and productivity in the camera room, particularly with automatic processing. Critical chemical replenishment and monitoring through control strips is not needed with a rapid access film processor, and the processor can be used to process a wide range of film materials without changing chemistry. The speed of development time also increases productivity. Automatic processors can process rapid access materials from dry-to-dry in two minutes or less. Many automatic processors designed for lith processing can be converted easily for rapid access processing.

When they were first introduced, rapid access materials and chemistry proved excellent for line work but not for halftone reproduction. Within a few years manufacturers introduced halftone screens specially designed for use with their rapid access materials. Halftones produced with these screens and developed in rapid access chemistry are acceptable for a variety of applications where reproduction quality need not be the highest possible.

To meet the need for high-quality halftones, manufacturers have introduced a new producer called **high-speed lith** that is a cross between traditional lith and rapid access. High-speed lith is said to offer the same high-quality development available with traditional lith, but at much faster speeds and with simpler processing procedures.

Section 2: Halftone Photography

Density, Tone, and Contrast

Before proceeding to a discussion of halftone photography, it is necessary to establish a basic understanding of the terms *density*, *tone*, and *contrast* and to determine what they mean to the graphic arts photographer.

Density

In the most general terms, **density** describes the ability of a material to absorb or transmit light. It is well known in the construction industry that a house with a white roof is much cooler in the summer than one with a black roof. The white shingles reflect a great deal of light and, consequently, heat. The black shingles absorb the light and store the sun's heat in the house. In the tropics, light-colored clothing is much cooler and more comfortable than clothing that is dark because it reflects light and heat.

In printing production, the density of the copy, film emulsion, and printing plate emulsion are all important (figure 4.14). In printing, a film negative is used to either pass or absorb light. If properly exposed and processed, the film negative passes light in the image areas and blocks light in the nonimage areas to expose a light-sensitive printing plate. In other words, the film emulsion must be more dense in the nonimage areas than in the image areas. Thus, the density of the film emulsion in the nonimage areas directly influences the quality of the printed piece (figure 4.15).

Reflectance and Transmittance

The printer is concerned with both the density of the image on the original copy and with the density of the emulsion on the piece of film. The density of the image on the copy is defined by the term **reflectance**. The density of the film emulsion is defined by the term **transmittance**.

Reflectance is a measure of the percentage of direct light, or **incident light,** that is reflected from an area of the copy. Transmittance

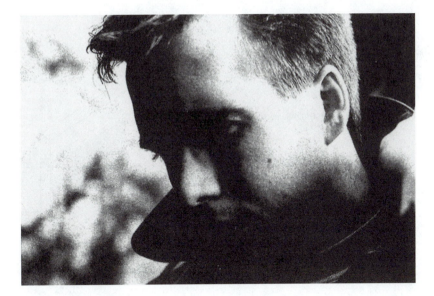

Figure 4.14 **A high-contrast reproduction of a continuous-tone image.** There are only black-and-white areas in this type of print. There are no gray tones.

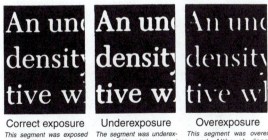

Correct exposure	Underexposure	Overexposure
This segment was exposed correctly. The negative areas are either clearly transparent or densely opaque. Edges are sharp and detail proportions are true to the original.	The segment was underexposed. Although transparent areas are clear, the dark areas have low density. A positive made from a negative of this type shows thickening of all detail.	This segment was overexposed. Although dense areas are opaque, density appears in some areas which should be clear. A positive made from a negative of this type shows loss of fine detail.

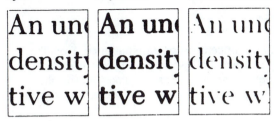

Figure 4.15 **Examples of correct exposure, underexposure, and overexposure.** It is possible to judge underexposure or overexposure by comparing the reproduction with the original copy.

is a measure of the percentage of directed light that passes through an area on a piece of film. For example, if 100 units of light are directed from the camera lights to the copy and only 50 units of light are reflected back from an area on the copy to the camera lens, reflectance for that area of the copy is 50 percent. If 100 units of light are directed at an area on a piece of film and only 50 units of light pass through that area of the film, transmittance in that area of the film emulsion is 50 percent. See figure 4.16.

Tone and Contrast

Up to this point in the discussion of line photography, we have been concerned only with copy that is either all black in the image areas or all white in the nonimage areas. Our object has been to reproduce every area with no density (every nonimage area) on the copy as an area of density on the film emulsion, and every area with density (every image area) on the copy as an area with no density on the film emulsion.

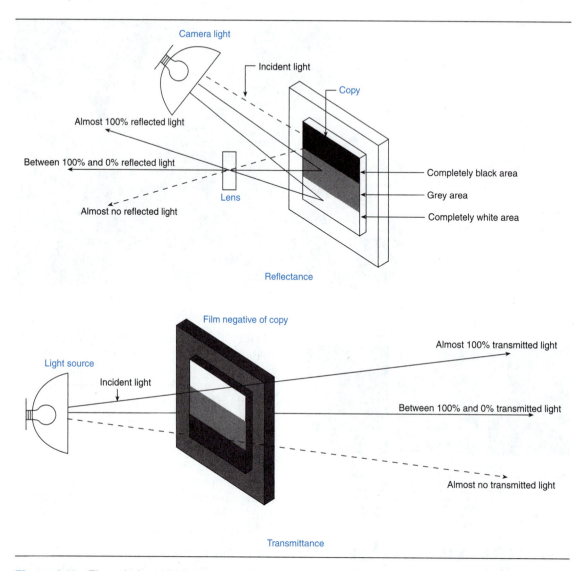

Figure 4.16 **The relationship between incident light and reflectance or transmittance.** From the diagram we can see that there is an inverse relationship between the light that is reflected from the original image area and the light that is transmitted through the negative. That is, almost no light is reflected from the black area of the image. However, in the corresponding area of the negative, almost 100 percent of the light is transmitted.

Halftone copy such as a snapshot is not composed of only black-and-white areas. Halftone copy is made up of white, black, and grey areas. These differing shades from white through gray to black are called tones. Different tones have different densities.

Line copy that is either all black or all white is called **high-contrast copy** because the two tones of the copy (black and white) are very different in appearance. **Contrast** is simply a measure of how different the tones on a piece of copy are in appearance. Two tones on line copy can be called discontinuous if they are very different.

Halftone copy is called **continuous-tone copy** because all (or most) of its tones are on a continuum from white to black. Each of these tones has a different density on the copy. In fact, the differing densities in these tones give the copy contrast and detail (figure 4.17).

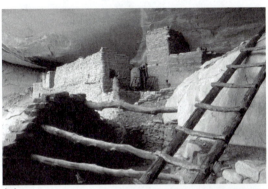

(a)

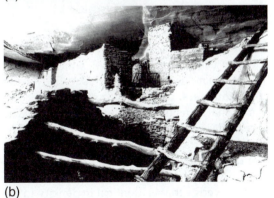

(b)

Figure 4.17 Comparison of a normal-contrast picture and a high-contrast picture. (a) A normal-contrast picture shows shades or tones from white through gray to black. (b) A high-contrast picture shows only two colors, white (no ink) and black. Picture (a) contains more information than picture (b).

Remember that high-contrast film is used in graphic arts photography. When exposed and processed, high-contrast film emulsion has only two tones or areas of density. The emulsion is either clear and transmits light or it is black and transmits no light.

Graphic arts film has to be high contrast because printing presses cannot print varying tones. A printing press puts ink density in the image areas and no ink density in the nonimage areas. The printer's problem when dealing with a continuous-tone photograph is how to record a continuous-tone image on a high-contrast film. In fact, it cannot be done. What can be done, however, is break a high-contrast image into a series of dots of varying shapes and sizes (but all of the same density) to give the illusion of tone variations. The dot patterns are produced by using a special screen. The resulting dot formation is called a **halftone**. The screen used to produce halftone dot patterns is discussed later in this chapter.

Densitometry

Measurements of density belong to an area called **densitometry**. Reflectance and transmittance can be expressed algebraically as follows:

$$\text{Reflectance} = R = \frac{I_r}{I_{rw}}$$

where R = reflectance

I_r = intensity of light reflected from copy

I_{rw} = intensity of light reflected from white paper

$$\text{Transmittance} = T = \frac{I_t}{I_i}$$

where T = transmittance

I_t = intensity of transmitted light

I_i = intensity of incident light

As discussed earlier, transmittance is a measure of the light that passes through film; reflectance is a measure of the light that reflects from copy.

These formulas describe the examples in the reflectance and transmittance section of this chapter: A light source is directed at a piece of copy. One hundred units of light are reflected back from the white or nonimage area of the paper (I_{rw}) and 50 units are reflected back from an image or tone (I_r); reflectance is 50 percent ($50 \div 100 = 0.5$ or 50%). We could use percentages for I_{rw} and I_r, but nothing in life functions as perfectly as mathematical examples in textbooks. In reality, I_{rw} might be measured at 112.76 units and I_r as 48.89. Doing the arithmetic ($48.89 \div 112.76$), we find that reflectance equals 43.357573608%. Such a long number has little meaning. Is 43.400000000% significantly denser than 43.357573608%? Can we really perceive the difference—probably not—but is it denser than another material? The problem is that the numbers simply become too large for us to understand and interpret. The solution is logarithms.

Logarithms are a way to express large quantities by using small numbers. Logarithmic information is readily available from tables in any mathematics book. Table 4.1 shows some common transmittance and density relationships. Although in theory there is no maximum density reading, realistically, for printing, there is no need to measure an optical density much greater than 3.0.

A density reading is nothing more than a logarithmic scale ranging from 0.0 to around 3.0 that equates a numeric value to the relative ability of a material to absorb or transmit light. The higher the density reading, the denser the material. Remember that dark areas on a piece of copy are denser than light areas.

So now you understand the mathematics of densitometry. You can use densitometry to gain information about a photograph or a film negative without using mathematical for-

Table 4.1. Some common transmittance and density relationships

Transmittance	Density
100%	0.0
10%	1.0
1%	2.0
0.1%	3.0
0.01%	4.0
0.001%	5.0
.	
.	
.	
0.0000001%	9.0
.	
.	
. and so forth	

mulas, however. Printers do not have to be able to manipulate logarithms in order to work with optical density. Densitometric tools read transmittance and provide readings that are already translated to logarithmic numbers. A variety of tools measure transmittance and reflectance using logarithmic scales.

Densitometers

Density is measured by a tool called a **densitometer**. The first densitometers, called **visual densitometers**, use human judgment to compare tonal densities visually (figure 4.18). The device has a set of known density wedges. The printer inserts the material to be measured in the densitometer and visually compares it to the previously known densities. After identifying a wedge that is identical in density to the test material, the printer records the logarithmic value printed on the wedge. To determine the density of another image, the printed standards are compared to the area by eye. When a known area is judged to match the unknown area, the printed value is assumed to be the density.

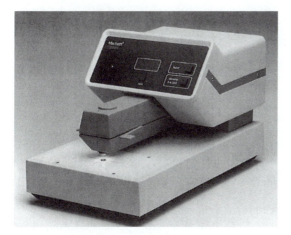

Figure 4.18 **A visual densitometer.** Visual densitometers allow the operator to compare copy, which is placed under the probe, to labeled densities that are seen through the viewing element.

designed to measure: opaque or transparent. Any ink or emulsion on a solid base (such as paper) that is not designed to pass light is called opaque copy. Examples of opaque materials are drawings, pasteups, continuous-tone paper photographic prints, or sheets of paper from a printing press. The density of opaque materials is measured using reflected light with a device called a **reflection densitometer** (figure 4.19). Before any reading is taken, the device is always calibrated to the same reading (usually 0.0, but some devices calibrate to 0.10) using a standard white opaque wedge to ensure accurate measurements. This calibration process is called **zeroing**. After zeroing, the reflection densitometer directs a narrow, controlled beam of light at a 45-degree angle onto an area of the opaque material. The amount of light that is reflected

A **photoelectric densitometer** operates on the logarithmic measure of incident light. A controlled beam is projected onto the material to be tested, and the machine measures the transmittance or reflectance. Most photoelectric densitometers have readout devices that immediately report the logarithmic density.

Visual densitometers are less expensive and more rugged than photoelectric densitometers, but they depend too much on the operator's judgment. Most individuals become tired after 20 to 30 single-tone visual measurements. Color densities are even more difficult to perceive than densities on visual densitometers. For these reasons, visual densitometers are almost never used today in the printing industry. In contrast, photoelectric densitometers are independent of the operator's judgment, provide extremely consistent results, and usually have color heads that accurately read primary color densities.

Photoelectric densitometers are classified according to the type of materials they are

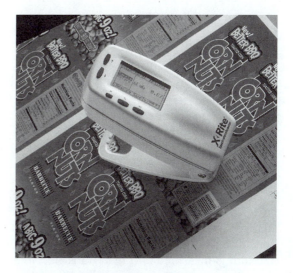

Figure 4.19 **Reflection densitometer.** The reflection densitometer is placed over a specific area of copy. Light is projected from the densitometer and reflects back to the densitometer probe. This reflected light is measured and displays digitally as density units. Courtesy of X-Rite, Inc.

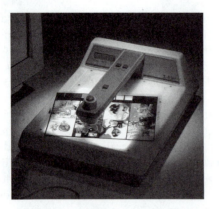

Figure 4.20 **Transmission densitometer.** A negative or positive film image can be placed between the densitometer probe and the densitometer table. Light is passed (transmitted) through the film to the densitometer probe. The amount of light transmitted through the film is read and recorded on the densitometer display. Courtesy of X-Rite, Inc.

is measured photoelectrically and is then translated to a logarithmic number.

Any ink of emulsion that is on a clear base (such as glass) and is designed to pass light is called transparent material. Graphic arts film is one example of transparent material. Another example is a color photographic slide. The density of transparent material is measured by light passing through the base with a device called a **transmission densitometer** (figure 4.20). A transmission densitometer passes a narrow beam of light at a 90-degree angle to an area on the transparent film. The amount of light that passes through the film is measured and then translated to a logarithmic number. Care must be taken when zeroing a transmission densitometer. The base material of all transparent film has some small amount of density, sometimes called fog. The device should be zeroed on a clear area of the piece of film being measured. This subtracts density that is unrelated to the image density.

Gray Scale and Density

It is important to understand that the graphic arts gray scale discussed earlier is simply a visual illustration of the logarithmic density scale. Each step on the gray scale is an area of specific, measurable density. The number of steps is arbitrary, however. Most printers use 10-, 12-, or 21-step gray scales. Gray scales are available commercially in opaque or transparent forms. The opaque scale can be used as a crude sort of visual densitometer, but it is best used to indicate film density during and after chemical processing.

Examine the gray scale in figure 4.21. It only approximates a 12-step gray scale (an opaque scale could not be reproduced here because it is made up of different tones),

Figure 4.21 **A 12-step gray scale.** This scale is divided into 12 steps representing densities from 0.00 to 1.65. Courtesy of Stouffer Graphic Arts Equipment Co.

but it illustrates the usefulness of the tool. Each of the evenly divided 12 steps of the scale represents an increase in density from around 0.00 (no density) to 1.65. Printed next to each step are the manufacturer's density values in increments of 0.15. Figure 4.21 shows an uncalibrated gray scale. Uncalibrated gray scales can be measured with a reflection densitometer.

From the scale it can be seen that step 4 represents a density of 0.45. If this small scale were placed on a copyboard and photographed, the light reflected by step 4 would be the same as the light reflected by any part of the copy having a density of 0.45. *This is the key to this tool.*

The white nonimage areas for high-contrast copy such as line copy all have about the same density. This density is 0.45 or less. When determining the basic exposure for line shots on the process camera (see appendix A), we select an exposure time and aperture that cause step 4 on the gray scale to fill (go solid) with controlled development conditions. In doing so, we ensure that all white nonimage areas on the copy record as solid black areas on the film negative when a solid step 4 is reached during film development. Any images on the copy (lines, dots, or even fingerprints and smudges) with density greater than 0.45 (darker than a step 4 on the opaque gray scale) record as clear areas on the film negative when the film is developed to a solid step 4.

Understanding the gray scale steps as specific blocks of density is a powerful tool for the graphic arts photographer. With it the photographer can predict how different camera apertures or shutter speeds will affect the density of the film emulsion.

Graphic arts photographers have learned that a change of one f/stop number on the camera produces a 0.30 density shift on a sheet of film. For example, assume that after processing a line negative, a solid step 2 with a density of 0.15 was produced from an exposure of f/16 for 20 seconds. If a solid step 4 (density of 0.45) was desired for normal copy, changing the exposure one f/stop to f/11 for 20 seconds (or f/16 for 40 seconds) would add 0.30 density to the film (0.15 + 0.30 = 0.45). This one f/stop change in exposure will produce a solid step 4 which is appropriate for normal copy.

This concept of a predictable density shift as a result of exposure was discovered last century and can be used in all phases of photography, whether continuous-tone, line, halftone, special effects, or color separation.

Traditional Halftone Screens

Halftone screens are the traditional tools used by the graphic arts photographer to convert continuous-tone images to halftone images that can be reproduced on a press. This section reviews the terminology and classifications of these basic tools.

Halftone Screen Rulings

The most common method of printing a continuous-tone photograph is to convert the image to line copy by a process called halftone photography. With this method, the continuous-tone image is broken into a series of dots of varying size but equal density. The dots combine in such a way as to trick the eye into believing that the picture is still continuous tone (figure 4.22). This illusion is accomplished by placing a ruled halftone screen between the copy and the film in a process camera (figure 4.23). On the camera, light is reflected from the white highlight areas of the copy and is absorbed by the black shadow areas. (See the Areas of Continuous-Tone Print section, page 89, for more about highlights and shadows.) The middle tones (gray areas) absorb light to varying degrees, depending on their densities. The reflected light then passes through the openings in the halftone screen

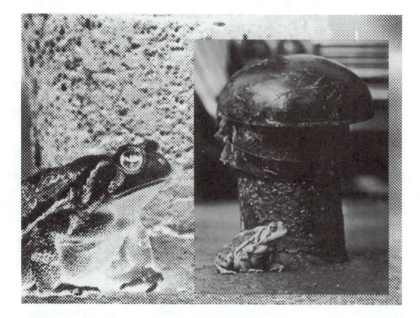

Figure 4.22 Halftone reproduction. A halftone photograph is a series of lines or dots so small that they trick the eye into seeing a continuous-line image. Note that the dot pattern is visible in the detail enlargement on the left of the halftone.
Courtesy of Chris Savas.

and forms dots on the halftone negative. The size of each dot is controlled by the amount of light that passes through the screen, which is in turn controlled by the amount of light reflected from the different areas on the copy.

It is perhaps easiest to understand a halftone screen by picturing crossed solid lines, like the texture of a window screen used to keep insects out of your home. The openings between the lines pass light; the lines

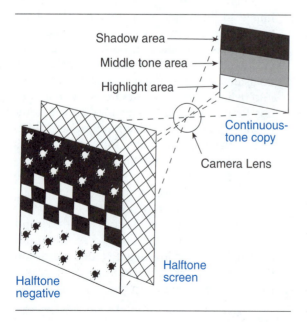

Figure 4.23 Diagram of halftone screen use. A halftone screen is placed between the continuous-tone copy and the film when exposing the film to break the continuous-tone copy into dots of varying sizes and shapes. White or highlight areas of the copy produce big, black dots on film. Middle tone areas produce intermediate-size dots, and black or shadow areas produce small dots.

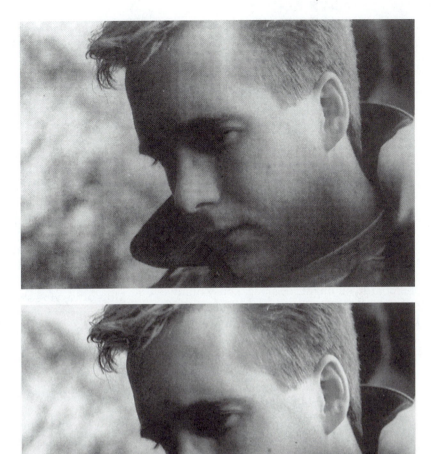

Figure 4.24 **Examples of 65-line and 133-line screen halftones.** Notice that you can actually see 65 line dots with the naked eye, but 133 lines per inch require magnification to detect.

themselves do not. If we were to count the number of parallel lines in 1 inch of the screen, we would have a rough idea of the size of dot that would be produced with that screen.

The more lines per inch of screen, the smaller the average dot produced. This measure is referred to as **screen ruling**. Figure 4.24 shows the same image produced using a 65-line screen (there were 65 parallel lines in any given inch in the screen that produced the halftone negative) and a 133-line screen (there were 133 parallel lines in any given inch of the screen). It is apparent from this figure that the finer screen ruling (133-line screen) produces a more natural appearing picture.

Three variables help decide what screen ruling to use for a halftone photograph:

- Normal viewing distance
- Process of reproduction
- Type of base material

Normal Viewing Distance

A halftone photograph appears to have continuous tone because the eye cannot detect minute line detail at normal viewing distance. Normal viewing distance varies with the function of the printed piece. This book is intended to be read at about 14 inches (or 36 centimeters) from your eyes. Therefore, the normal viewing distance for this book is 14 inches. A billboard you might see along a busy highway is designed to be read from approximately 300 yards (or 275 meters). Three-hundred yards, then, is the normal viewing distance for the billboard. The best halftone screen ruling for a billboard might be as coarse as 10 lines per inch. As viewing distance gets smaller so too must the screen ruling. Screen rulings range from the huge dot size of a billboard to the fine dots produced from a 300-line screen.

Process of Reproduction

The method and material of reproduction also influence the selection of screen ruling. For example, with current technology, a 300-line halftone is much too fine to be used with screen printing; stencils cannot be made that will adhere to any support fabric. For some printing methods, a 300-line screen ruling is possible, but it becomes a test of sophisticated reproduction control.

Type of Base Material

The ink-absorbing characteristics of base materials in printing vary widely. Newsprint rapidly absorbs ink and tends to spread or increase dot size. A 300-line screen printed in your newspaper would probably look like a puddle of black ink as a result. Clay-based or coated papers, such as those used for most popular magazines, do not absorb or spread ink and can hold fine detail with little trouble.

For most processes and paper characteristics, screen rulings of 65, 85, 100, 120, 133, and 150 lines per inch are the simplest to manipulate and are the most widely used.

Halftone Screen Structure

Although the crossed-solid-line pattern of a halftone screen is easy to visualize, it is not an accurate image of how the most commonly used screens are made. The dots formed by the clear openings between solid line rulings in screens would all have the same shape and size. To produce a halftone, however, we need dots of varying shapes and sizes and therefore openings of varying sizes in the screens.

There are solid-line screens, called **screen tints**, but they are not used to produce halftone photographs. The typical halftone screen is constructed using a photographic emulsion to form a **vignetted screen pattern**. Figure 4.25 is an artist's rendering of what the intersection of two crossed lines in solid-line screen and vignetted screen areas might look like greatly magnified.

Screen tints are used for many purposes. The most common is to create the illusion of two colors when really only printing one color. If a 30 percent screen tint is used with a solid red, the tint appears pink. The job can then have areas of solid red and other areas of pink, but only one color is printed on press. Notice that screen tints have rigidly controlled openings (figure 4.25a). Screen tints are classified according to the amount of light they pass to the piece of film. A 40 percent screen tint passes 40 percent of light through its openings and blocks 60 percent by its solid lines. Figure 4.26 shows the range of typical screen tints. The lines in some solid-line screens do not cross. These screen patterns are generally referred to as *special-effect screen tints* (figure 4.27). Screen tints and solid-line special effect screen tints

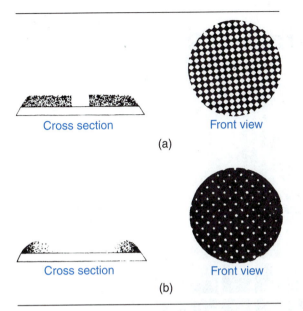

Cross section   Front view

(a)

Cross section   Front view

(b)

Figure 4.25 Comparing a solid-line screen to a vignetted screen. (a) A solid-line screen with evenly shaped and sized openings is used to produce an even tone tint. (b) A vignetted screen produces variations in the sizes and shapes of the dots which result in the continuous-tone appearance of halftones.

are not used to produce halftones (although special effect halftone screens do exist). Solid-line screen tints produce dots of uniform size. Halftone dots must be of different sizes.

As mentioned earlier, to appear continuous, a halftone must be formed from dots of varying shapes and sizes. Figure 4.25b illustrates the structure of the vignetted screen that produces these variations. The center portion of the screen opening (the area between the intersection of two dots) is clear, but the density of the screen's photographic emulsion increases as the diameter of the opening grows larger. Visualize this as a pile of sand, high and deep at the center, but gradually decreasing in depth until there are no grains of sand.

When light reflected from the copy passes through the vignetted screen opening, a dot the size of the clear part of the opening

forms on the film immediately. As the quantity of light reaching the screen increases, more light penetrates the denser portion near the outer edge of the opening and the dot recorded on the film becomes larger. Within any halftone photograph, there is a wide range of individual dot size. These variations are related directly to the amount of light reflected from the copy and focused through the camera lens onto the halftone screen. The more light that is reflected from the copy, the more light that penetrates the denser portions of the vignetted dots and the larger the dots recorded on the film.

All of this makes sense if you remember that more light is reflected from the white highlight areas of the copy and less light is reflected from the dark shadow areas. You would want larger dots in the highlight areas on the film negative to block more light from reaching the printing plate. If more light were blocked, small dots would be produced on the plate. These small dots would print as small dots on the final page, thereby providing white highlight areas that have little density because little ink is printed in them.

Dot Size and Shape

To control individual dot size variation, it is necessary to identify and measure dot size (the area the dot covers on the printed sheet). Dot size is measured in terms of percentage of ink coverage. Thus, a printer speaks of a printed halftone as having a 5 or 10 percent dot in the highlight area, and a 90 or 95 percent dot in the shadow area. What is meant is that 5 percent of the highlight area is covered by dots and 95 percent of the shadow area is covered by dots.

Dot size varies according to screen ruling. A 20 percent dot produced from a 65-line screen is larger than a 20 percent dot produced from a 133-line screen. This presents no problems for the printer, however, because a 20 percent dot produced from a 65-line screen

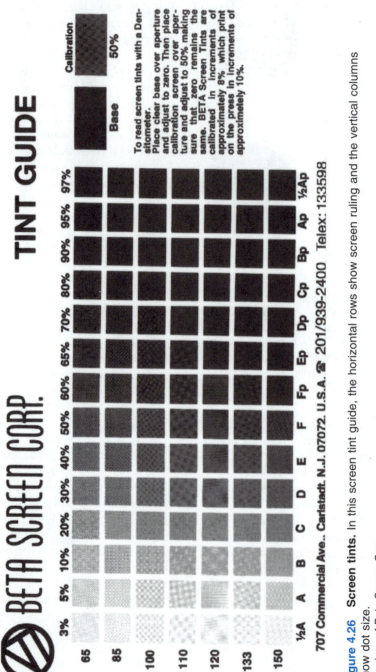

Figure 4.26 **Screen tints.** In this screen tint guide, the horizontal rows show screen ruling and the vertical columns show dot size.
Courtesy of Beta Screen Corp.

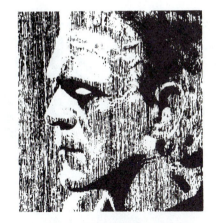

Mahogany

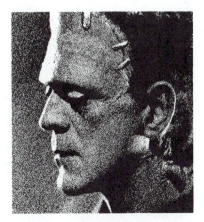

Mezzotint

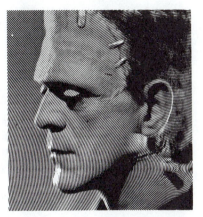

Circleline

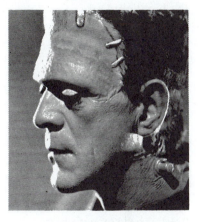

100 Straightline

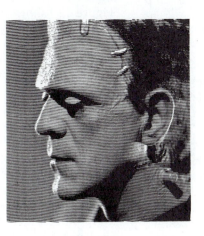

Wavyline

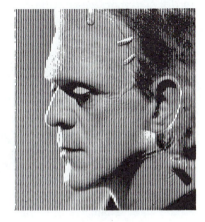

50 Straightline

Figure 4.27
Examples of special-effect tints. Special-effect screen tints can be used to create different impressions with the same image.
Courtesy of James Craig, Production Planning.

covers 20 percent of the printed area with ink. Likewise, a 20 percent dot from a 133-line screen covers 20 percent of the printed area with ink. One dot would be smaller than the other, but the percentage of ink coverage produced in each area would be the same. Comparing dot size between different lined screens is done only when printers select a screen for a job. Comparing dot percentage sizes produced by the same screen, however, is done whenever printers attempt to assess the results of a halftone they have made, decide whether they have put the correct-sized dot in the highlight and shadow areas of the negative, or determine if they printed the correct-sized dot in the highlight and shadow areas of a halftone reproduction.

Traditional halftone screens are designed to produce one of two different types of dot structure:

■ Square
■ Elliptical

Square Dot Structure

Figure 4.28 illustrates the typical range of dot sizes for a conventional *square dot structure*. Although the square dot screen is commonly used, it has some problems, In the area of the 50 percent dot there is a sudden visual jump in dot size that does not reproduce the original photograph accurately (figure 4.29).

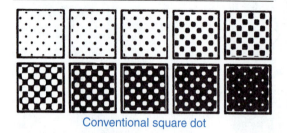
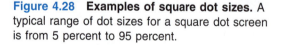
Conventional square dot

Figure 4.28 **Examples of square dot sizes.** A typical range of dot sizes for a square dot screen is from 5 percent to 95 percent.

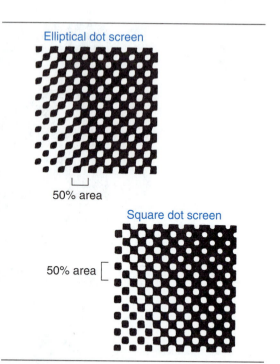

Elliptical dot screen

50% area

Square dot screen

50% area

Figure 4.29 **Comparing a square dot screen to an elliptical dot screen.** The 50 percent area of the square dot screen jumps suddenly. The elliptical dot screen has a slower visual shift in the same area.
Courtesy of Eastman Kodak Company.

Elliptical Dot Structure

Figure 4.30 shows the elliptical dot size range that was developed to overcome the square dot's limitations. Notice that in the 50 percent area the elliptical dot structure provides a smooth transition to where one dot finally touches another on all four sides.

Measuring Dot Area

Both square and elliptical dots are produced using a halftone screen in exactly the same manner. Whatever dot structure is used to produce the halftone, there are two techniques printers use to measure dot area:

■ Visual inspection
■ Dot area meter

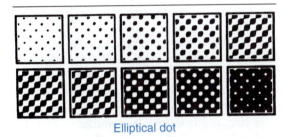

Elliptical dot

Figure 4.30 **Examples of elliptical dot sizes.** Shown is a typical rnage of dot sizes (5 to 95 percent) for an elliptical dot screen.

Visual Inspection. It is possible to use a **linen tester** or magnifying glass to view dots of any size (figure 4.31). Using this tool to compare figure 4.28 or 4.30 with a halftone negative, we can approximate dot size. This is done less by comparing the actual size of the dot to the illustration than by comparing the configuration of an area of dots. As was mentioned previously, the 50 percent dot is easy to recognize. If a square dot screen was used to re-

produce the negative, a 50 percent dot is found on the negative in an area where the dots just start to touch on all four corners. If an elliptical dot screen was used to produce the negative, the 50 percent dot is found in an area on the negative just before the dots start to touch on two corners. By viewing the amount of white space around a printed 10 percent dot, it becomes easy to identify an area on a negative that will produce a 10 percent dot.

Visual dot size identification is not as complicated as it may seem. When graphic arts photographers make halftones, they are mainly concerned with the dots that will reproduce the highlight areas of the copy (typically around 5 to 10 percent dots, depending upon the printing method) and the dots that will reproduce the shadow areas of the copy (typically around 90 to 95 percent dots). Some practice is required, but an experienced printer

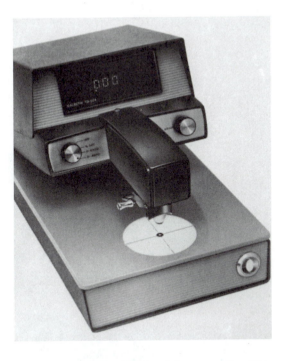

Figure 4.32 **Example of a dot area meter.** This transmission dot area meter measures dot sizes on transparent materials.

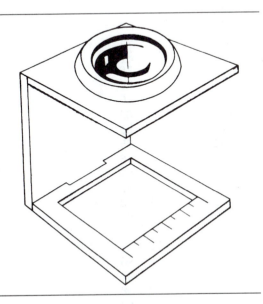

Figure 4.31 **A linen tester.** A linen tester is used to view dot structure.

can at least estimate highlight and shadow dot size visually. However, this becomes somewhat of a subjective problem. Is a dot 9, or 11, or 13 percent? As much as a 7 percent variation in visual judgment, even among experienced camera operators, is possible.

Dot Area Meter. Although printers can work with this inaccuracy, one solution is to use a **dot area meter** (figure 4.32). This device *integrates* or averages the amount of light passing through a selected area on a halftone neg-

ative and equates that measure to a dot area reading.

It is also possible to adapt the information from a transmission densitometer to measure dot area, although there is some slight loss in accuracy. With this technique, density reading of the target area on a halftone negative is made using the transmission densitometer. The density number is then located on a density-dot area conversion table (table 4.2). However, it is preferable and more accurate to use a dot area meter.

Table 4.2.   Conversion from density readings to percent dot area

Integrated Halftone Density	Percent Dot Areas	Integrated Halftone Density	Percent Dot Areas
0.00	0	0.36	56
0.01	2	0.38	58
0.02	5	0.40	60
0.03	7	0.42	62
0.04	9	0.44	64
0.05	11	0.46	65
0.06	13	0.48	67
0.07	15	0.50	68
0.08	17	0.54	71
0.09	19	0.58	74
0.10	21	0.62	76
0.11	22	0.66	78
0.12	24	0.70	80
0.13	26	0.74	82
0.14	28	0.78	83
0.15	29	0.82	85
0.16	31	0.86	86
0.17	32	0.90	87
0.18	34	0.95	89
0.19	35	1.00	90
0.20	37	1.10	92
0.22	40	1.20	94
0.24	42	1.30	95
0.26	45	1.40	96
0.28	48	1.50	97
0.30	50	1.70	98
0.32	52	2.00	99
0.34	54		

Areas of a Continuous-Tone Print

There are three areas that both printers and photographers identify as the most significant measures of the quality of a continuous-tone print (figure 4.33):

- Highlight area
- Shadow area
- Middle tone area

The **highlight area** is that portion of a picture that contains detail but has the least amount of density. The darkest areas of the print are called the **shadow areas**. All the shades of gray between the highlights and the shadows are called the **middle-tone areas**. Middle tones contain the most pictorial detail or information.

A special kind of highlight, called a **spectral highlight**, has no detail or density. Examples include the gleam of the chrome on an automobile or the pinpoint iris of a model's eye. Spectral highlights contain no detail and should not carry a halftone dot.

It is possible to compare the density of these three areas of a print with the density of the steps on any graphic arts gray scale. We can also equate these densities to the size of halftone dots on the film negative and on the final printed sheet. For example, in figure 4.33:

1. The highlight detail begins in step 1, or with a density near 0.05. The highlight dots begin with the smallest reproducible dot (generally about 5 percent) and extend to about a 20 or 25 percent dot.

2. The shadow detail ends in step 10, or with a density of about 1.45. The shadow dots extend from about 75 or 80 percent to the largest reproducible dot (generally about 95 percent) before solid black is reached.

3. The middle-tone area for this photo is roughly from step 3 to step 7, but it is not a definite range. Middle-tone dots typically range from about a 25 to 75 percent dot.

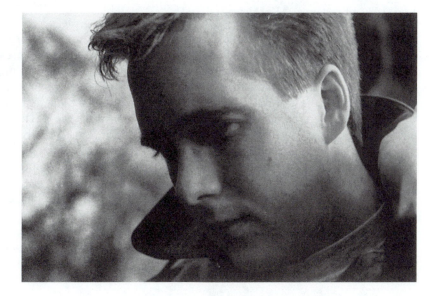

Figure 4.33 Areas of a continuous-tone print. In this continuous-tone print, the highlight areas correspond to steps 1 and 2 on the gray scale. From the gray scale, we see that the middle range is from 3 to 7. The shadow area ranges from 8 to 11 on the gray scale.

Several things need to be emphasized with respect to this comparison. Printers do not typically measure a particular highlight, middle tone, or shadow density. They are primarily concerned with density extremes (the density difference from the lightest highlight to the darkest shadow). This measure is called the **copy density range (CDR)** of the photograph. The CDR is the shadow density minus the highlight density. This is an important relationship to remember. The CDR of figure 4.33 is 1.40 (1.4 − 0.05). The typical continuous-tone photograph has a CDR of approximately 1.70.

Comparing the dot size and the gray scale tonal area should not be taken to mean that a certain dot size should be formed in any particular part of the gray scale for every halftone negative. Printers are concerned that the smallest dot appear in the highlight step and that the largest dot appear in the last shadow step. The placement of any dot sizes between these two extremes controls the contrast of the halftone and depends on the photograph being reproduced. There is no rule that states in which step any dot should be placed.

Understanding Halftone Dots

The density variations in a continuous-tone original are represented in a halftone reproduction as dots of various sizes. The size of these dots in any area of the halftone negative is determined by the amount of light reflected from the original to that area during the main and bump exposures, as well as by the amount of exposure produced by the flash. Halftone dots communicate information or detail from the original. Where there are no dots on a printed halftone, there are either completely open, inkless areas or completely filled in, inked areas.

The object of making a halftone is to produce a printed piece that reflects the tonal range of the original through variations in dot size and placement. The more closely the halftone approximates the tonal range of the original, the more closely it shows the detail of the original.

Printable Dots

It is impossible to observe all of the dot sizes on a halftone negative during film development to check for accurate dot size. Instead, printers use *aim points* that are typically at either extreme of the original's density range. They try to place the smallest dots or aim points that can be printed in the detail highlight areas of the original to show highlight detail in the print; the largest dots that can be printed are placed in the detail shadow areas. Thus, the positions of the smallest and largest printable dots on both the negative and the printed piece are important.

Remember that on the negative, the *smallest* printable dots appear as small, clear openings surrounded by black, exposed emulsion (density). During platemaking, these small openings expose only small dots on the printing plate. These small dots transfer small dots (highlight dots) to the printing paper and reproduce detail in the highlight area of the printed piece.

The *largest* printable dots appear on the negative as small areas of density surrounded by large, clear openings. During platemaking, these large openings expose large dots on the printing plate, which transfer large dots to the printing paper. These large dots (shadow dots) reproduce detail in the shadow area of the printed piece.

A press operator refers to a dot that is printable as a dot that the press can *hold*, or as a dot that can be *held* on press. A 5 to 10 percent highlight dot can be held with most offset presses (see chapter 12). Dots that are smaller are too small to print accurately and consistently; some may not print at all. The largest printable shadow dot that can be held with most offset processes is a 95 percent shadow dot. On press, these dots appear as tiny, unprinted areas surrounded by ink. Shadow dots larger than 95 percent tend to fill in on press and go solid.

The smallest and largest printable dots are of concern to the camera operator. If the highlight dots on the negative (small, open areas surrounded by density) are too small, they will not pass enough light during platemaking to expose printable dots on the printing plate, and detail will be lost in the highlight areas. If the large, open areas on the negative that produce shadow dots in the print are too large, they may fill in during platemaking and become plugged with ink on press.

To make an acceptable halftone, the camera operator must know something about printable dot size. The correct size of a printable dot (such as 5, 10, or 95 percent) is determined through knowing about the printing process to be used, the working conditions in the printing plant, and the ink and paper (or other substrate) to be used for printing. This information is given to the camera operator before the halftone is made.

Dot Gain

One very important consideration when determining printable dot size is **dot gain**. Halftone dots tend to grow in size during platemaking and when on press. Critical exposure and development control is needed during platemaking to reproduce the dot structure on the negative accurately. Improper plate exposure or processing produces dot sizes on the plate that differ in size from those on the negative. If the dots recorded on the printing plate are larger than those on the negative, larger dots will be printed and detail will be lost.

Even if the dots' sizes are recorded on the plate accurately, dot gain can still occur on press. In the offset printing process, improper ink and water balance can cause dot gain or loss. The type and condition of the press can also affect dot gain, as can the paper-and-ink combination being printed. Uncoated papers, such as bond or newsprint, absorb ink (see chapter 16). A dot printed on uncoated paper tends to spread and grow larger—ink is absorbed and spreads into the paper like water into a sponge. Small highlight dots get bigger; large shadow dots fill in. Coated paper has better *ink holdout*. It does not absorb as much ink, and dots do not spread as much as they do on uncoated paper.

Dot size is inspected visually with a magnifying glass or a dot area meter. The sizes of the smallest and largest dots that can be reproduced (plated and printed) are determined by comparing dot size on the negative to the actual printed dot size. Through this comparison, a historical record of expected dot gain for a variety of processing and printing conditions on a variety of paper-and-ink combinations can be developed. Equipped with this knowledge, camera operators can recognize the smallest and largest printable dots for particular processes and working conditions, and they can place them in the correct density areas on the negative.

If no information is known about dot gain, shop tests must be run. One common test is to plate the negative made during the main test, print it on a number of paper types commonly used in the plant, and measure for dot gain. In practice, a variety of control devices are available to the camera operator, plate department, and press operator to monitor and control dot gain.

The move toward computer-to-plate prepress eliminates one source of dot gain, because there is no intermediary material between the digital image and the plate. The digital data are written directly to the plate by laser. This will be examined further in chapter 10.

Key Terms

line photography
continuous-tone photograph
tones
halftone photography
visible spectrum
emulsion
color sensitivity
wedge spectrogram
blue-sensitive material
orthochromatic material
panchromatic material
contrast
characteristic curve
film speed
exposure index
antihalation dye
overcoating
process camera
lens
focusing
shutter

shutter speed
aperture
diaphragm
f/stop system
focal length
equivalent exposure
filmboard
copyboard
horizontal process camera
vertical process camera
lith film
lith developer
rapid access
high-speed lith
density
reflectance
transmittance
incident light
high-contrast copy
contrast
continuous-tone copy

halftone
densitometry
densitometer
visual densitometer
photoelectric densitometer
reflection densitometer
zeroing
transmission densitometer
screen ruling
screen tints
vignetted screen pattern
linen tester
dot area meter
highlight area
shadow area
middle-tone area
spectral highlight
copy density range (CDR)
dot gain

Review Questions

Section 1

1. What common characteristic of all printing processes forms the primary concern of line photography?
2. What is the basis of photography?
3. What determines the effect of electromagnetic radiation such as light?
4. What does film speed tell about a film emulsion?
6. What is the purpose of the antihalation backing (or dye) on a piece of film?
7. What is the change in quantity of light passed through the lens when the aperture is changed from f/16 to f/22?
8. Why are process cameras so large?
9. How does rapid access processing differ from lith processing?
10. What was high-speed lith designed to do?

Section 2

1. In general terms, what does the term *density* mean?
2. What does the term *contrast* describe about tones on a piece of photographic film?
3. What is the difference between a transmission densitometer and a reflection densitometer?
4. What does the term *screen ruling* mean?
5. What is the difference between a vignetted screen structure and a solid-line screen structure?
6. Which will produce a larger dot on the printed page, a 40 percent or a 60 percent screen tint?
7. What is the purpose of a dot area meter?
8. What three areas of a continuous-tone photograph are considered the most significant measures of print quality?

5

Color

Historical Background

In 1862, Louis Ducos du Hauron sent a letter to M. Lelut of the Academie de Medecine et Sciences in Paris describing his ideas for a "Physical Solution of the Problem of Reproducing Colors by Photography." Du Hauron said:

> The method which I propose is based on the principle that the simple colors are reduced to three—red, yellow, and blue—the combinations of which in different proportions give us the infinite variety of shades we see in nature. One may now say that analysis of the solar spectrum by means of a glass which passes only one color has proved that red exists in all parts of the spectrum, and the like for yellow and blue, and that one is forced to admit that the solar spectrum is formed of three superimposed spectra having their maxima of intensity at different points. Thus one might consider a picture which represents nature as composed of three pictures superimposed, the one red, the second yellow, and the third blue. The result of this would be that if one could obtain separately these three images by photography and then reunite them in one, one would obtain an image of nature with all the tints that it contains.[1]

Du Hauron's ideas were responsible, in part, for the later development of successful additive color plates and film.

A man named Frederick E. Ives was a journeyman printer who became interested in photography. He was familiar with du Hauron's ideas about color reproduction and worked to refine them. In 1880 Ives moved from Ithaca, New York, to Philadelphia. From that time on he only did research in color photography and photomechanical printing.

By the end of 1881, Ives had received two United States patents for a specialized halftone printing process and was beginning to spend most of his energy on color. In 1885, at the Philadelphia "Novelties Exhibition," he exhibited a process of photographing colors and a photomechanical method for reproducing them.

In May 1892, Ives was invited to present a paper outlining his ideas before the Society of Arts in London. At that time he displayed the Photochromoscope camera he had invented. Using a single exposure, the device recorded a three-color image on three separate plates. The transparent separations could then be viewed through red, green, and blue color filters.

Ives produced the illustration on page in 1893 with his tricolor process. It is perhaps the first photomechanically printed color image. It is uncertain whether it was reproduced by using a relief plate or a gravure cylinder, but the halftones were certainly made from cross-line screens.

By the turn of the century, almost all printers and photographers understood the color separation process, and national publications such as the *National Geographic* had begun to use full-color picture printing.

[1]Louis W. Sipley, *A Half Century of Color* (New York: Macmillan, 1951), p. 22.

Objectives

After completing this chapter you will be able to:

- Define hue, value, and saturation.
- Describe what is meant by color space.
- Define process inks.
- Explain additive color theory.

- Discuss how subtractive colors relate to additive colors.
- Explain how a color filter works.
- Discuss how four black-and-white halftones can produce a full-color reproduction.
- Briefly describe the purpose of a mask.
- Differentiate between UCR and GCR.

Introduction

Around 1454 Johann Gutenberg printed his famous 42-line Bible. He printed almost all of the lines of type with black ink. The initial letter on opening pages, however, was hand painted in multiple colors by special artists called illuminators. By painting the opening letters, Gutenberg was attempting to duplicate the work of scribes who illustrated their finest work in decorative colors.

For nearly three centuries after Gutenberg, most printing was done in one color—black. Although by the nineteenth century color plates and inserts in books had become more common, they were only done in flat color. Flat color refers to a solid ink purchased or mixed for a specific use.

By the beginning of this century, printers and photographers clearly understood the color separation process, and they were printing "color photographs" in a wide number of publications. However, these color images were not the process color common today at every newsstand, book store, or grocery store. Process color is the use of ink with a translucent base that allows for creation of many colors by overprinting only four (cyan, magenta, yellow, and black).

Since the end of World War II, there has been an accelerated increase in the use and sophistication of printed color images. Color printing has now become an expectation rather than the exception. There are literally thousands of weekly or monthly magazines with color illustrations on every page. Every major metropolitan newspaper features process color in its Sunday edition, and there is even a national daily newspaper printed in four colors.

As people become accustomed to color illustrations, their demands for more and higher-quality color reproductions increase. It no longer suffices that a page merely carries several colors. Now the goal is to eliminate printing defects such as poor fit, inaccurate color balance, or insufficient ink density, and to produce a perfect color reproduction that matches or enhances the quality of the color original.

Within the last decade there have been major advances in color separation, color correction, and color reproduction technology. The purpose of this chapter is to introduce the basic concepts of color theory, color separation, and color correction.

Basic Color Theory

It is important to establish a firm foundation of basic color theory understanding. This section introduces key concepts and terms.

Light and Color

Isaac Newton demonstrated the hues of the visible spectrum by passing a beam of light through a glass prism (plate A). He not only produced a rainbow of color, he passed the rainbow through a second prism and reconstructed the original beam of light. Newton therefore proved that color is in light and that what we see as white light is really a mixture of all colors.

The idea of wavelength was introduced in chapter 4. Recall that the visible spectrum is that portion of electromagnetic radiation from approximately 400 mμ (millimicrons) to around 750 mμ (figure 5.1). Every distinct color in the spectrum, from blue at one end to red at the other, has a unique wavelength. However, we rarely see just one wavelength color; we more commonly perceive the effect of combinations of different wavelengths. For example, sunlight is natural white light made up of relatively uniform amounts of each wavelength in the spectrum.

Recall also the difference between reflected light and transmitted light. If you look up at the sun, you see transmitted light—light that is directed at you from a light source. If you hold a color slide between you and the sun, you see the image on the slide by transmitted light. Light passes in a straight line from the sun, through the slide, and to your eye.

If you were to look down from the sun at any object, you would see by reflected light. White light travels from the sun to an object; that light would bounce back or reflect to your eye. Every object absorbs or reflects different wavelengths of light and in different quantities.

For example, an apple might appear a strikingly bright red or a dun red. When white light strikes an apple, the apple absorbs most

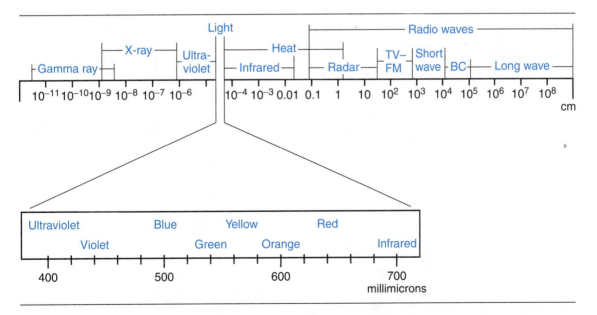

Figure 5.1 **Plot of the visible spectrum (lower bar) compared to the electromagnetic spectrum (upper bar)**

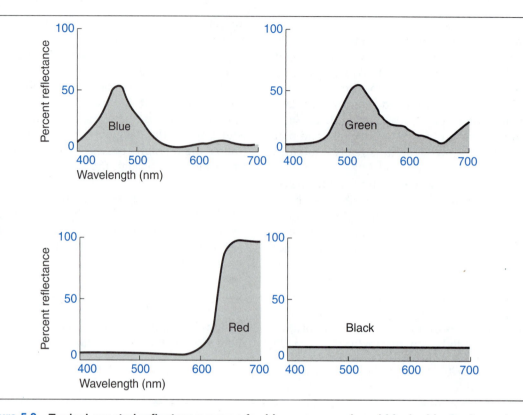

Figure 5.2   Typical spectral reflectance curves for blue, green, red, and black objects. An apple appears red because it reflects wavelengths of light in the 600- to 700-nm range and absorbs wavelengths in the 400- to 600-nm range. Black objects absorb all wavelengths of light; white objects reflect approximately equal amounts of all wavelengths.

of the wavelengths below around 600 mμ on the visible spectrum and reflects most wavelengths above 600 mμ (figure 5.2). This combination of reflected wavelengths creates the color impression humans see as red. The **hue, saturation,** and **value** of a color describe their colorimetric properties. The hue of a color is the actual name of a color created by the wavelengths that define that color.

A saturated color describes a color at its maximum hue. It also describes the extent of the purity property of the color. The less gray or contaminants of another color present, the more saturated the color is. A completely desaturated color achieves a neutral gray. **Chroma** is a quality of a color combining hue and saturation, with *chromatic* referring to something having hue or color. *Achromatic* means having no hue, *polychromatic* having many hues, and *monochromatic* having one hue only.

A color's value is a measurement of its relative lightness or darkness. This is also referred to as its brightness, and this characteristic depends on the quantity of wavelengths that are reflected.

Color Systems

To be consistent and accurate color needs to be defined precisely and classified according to a specific **color space**. The term *space* defines the limits of the particular color model being used. The full range of colors that can be defined within a given color space are referred to as its **gamut**. Absolute and relative systems are used to facilitate these kinds of specifications. An **absolute system** is one composed of permanent color chips, but is expandable up to a theoretical color limit as new permanent colors are discovered. An example of this kind of system is the Munsell system, based on human perception. This is the most frequently used of all the color order systems. It uses hue, value, and chroma (its reference to saturation) to describe color attributes and is composed of five basic hues: yellow, green, red, blue, and purple. **Relative systems** are utilized by the printing industry for halftone color composed of varying percentages of cyan, yellow, magenta, and black, as represented on various substrates and ink-mixing colors specific to recording ink-mixing formulas for a given color.

CIE

The Commission Internationale de L'Eclairage, or the **International Commission on Illumination (CIE),** was formed in 1931 to address the unique challenges of color specifications. The printing industry has adopted this system of color definition as the most workable in relationship to reproduction issues. The CIE approach is to measure the responses of the human eye to different light waves, which results in a less perceptually uniform color representation than the Munsell system (refer to plate K). Improvements to the system have been made over time, notably the CIELAB and the CIELUV systems, but a true, *perfect* color space does not exist. This is important to understand, because color reproduction is not an exact science and depends not only on the color system that one is working with, but on the characteristics of the substrate or viewing medium and the ambient conditions under which an individual is viewing the image, whether reflective or transmissive.

Additive Primary Colors

The visible spectrum is often described as being made up of three colors: blue, green, and red. Actually, these colors are combinations of wavelengths in each third of the spectrum. Red, green, and blue are called the **additive primary colors** because they can be combined to form every other color of light in the spectrum. Figure 5.3 shows the plot of reflected light for each of these primary colors. It is very important to understand this fundamental idea: Objects display color by absorbing and reflecting different wavelengths of light in the visible spectrum. In the case of transmitted light, looking through the color slide, the idea is the same. We perceive color because portions of the slide absorb certain wavelengths of light and pass (transmit) others.

Subtractive Primary Colors

The three **subtractive primary colors** are cyan, magenta, and yellow. They form when two of the additive primary colors combine. For example, a banana appears yellow because it absorbs wavelengths at the blue end of the visible spectrum and reflects light at the middle (green) and red ends (figure 5.3). Yellow light is therefore a combination of green and red light.

In a similar manner, when an object absorbs red light but reflects green and blue, the color cyan forms (figure 5.3, plate F). When green light is absorbed but blue and red light are reflected, the color magenta forms.

Where all three of the additive colors overlap, white light forms. Where any two of

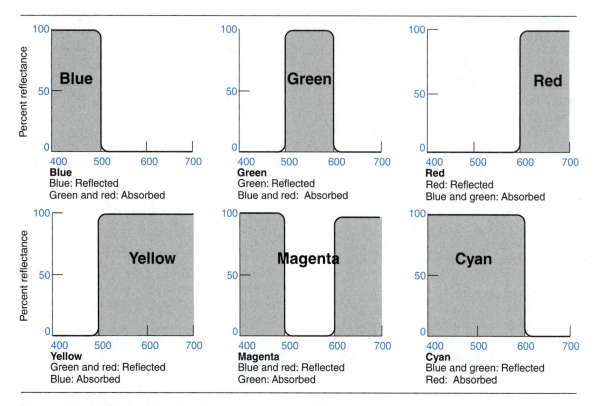

Figure 5.3   Additive and subtractive primary colors. The additive primary colors (top row) each reflect about one-third of the wavelengths of light in the visible spectrum and absorb the other two-thirds. The subtractive primary colors (bottom row) each reflect about two-thirds of the wavelengths of light in the visible spectrum and absorb the other one-third.

the colors overlap, one of the subtractive primaries forms. Printers use magenta, cyan, and yellow inks to create the reflected colors of the spectrum. These are called **process inks**. Process inks are specially formulated to be somewhat translucent. *Translucent* means that they both transmit and reflect light.

When white light hits cyan ink, the ink reflects blue and green light (blue and green light create cyan) but absorbs red. Similar relationships exist for magenta and yellow inks, respectively. Process inks are translucent, which means that there is an additive effect if two process colors are printed one over the

other. If equal amounts of magenta and cyan process ink overlap, the visual effect is blue. Only blue light is reflected by both magenta and cyan. Therefore, blue is the only color you see. If less magenta ink is printed than cyan, then the result will be a greener blue. By controlling the amounts of cyan, magenta, yellow, and black, printers can create the illusion of any color of the visible spectrum.

Basic Separation Theory

The task, then, of color separation is to separate the hues of a continuous-tone color orig-

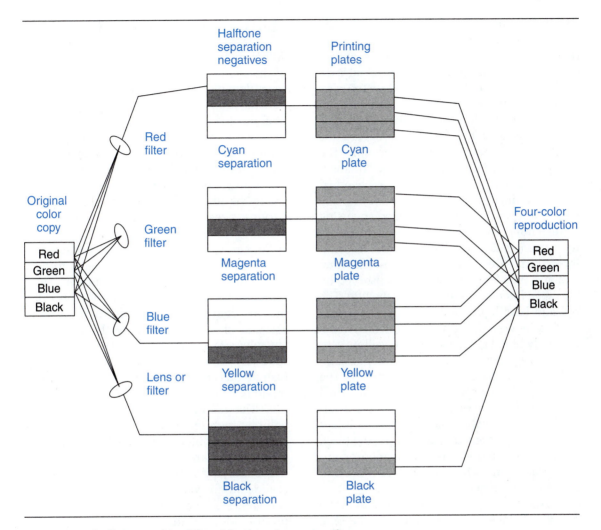

Figure 5.4   A diagram of traditional basic color separation

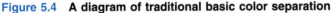

inal into four negatives or files to prepare cyan, magenta, yellow, and black printing plates. Figure 5.4 illustrates the basic concept of color separation as was done in traditional prepress before the advent of the computer.

When viewing this figure, it is important to keep two ideas firmly in mind:

■ A color filter transmits only its own color and absorbs all other colors.

■ Light that reaches the film exposes the emulsion and becomes nonimage area; the reproducible image is that area of the film that has not been exposed to light. This unexposed area of film is a record of the two additive primary colors that were absorbed by the filter.

In the traditional color separation process, the additive primary colors—red, blue, and green—are used as filters to prepare the cyan, magenta, and yellow separation negatives. The separation process begins with a color original. The light from the original is directed through a red filter to produce the cyan separation negative (figure 5.4). Because a red filter transmits only red color, the red patch is the only area of the original to expose the emulsion and form density on the film. The unexposed areas then represent the combination of blue and green light that was absorbed by the red filter. We see this color as cyan. The magenta separation negative is made by using a green filter. The wavelengths reflecting from the green patch of the original transmit through the green filter and expose the film. Red and blue light, however, are absorbed by the green filter and do not expose the film. The red and blue light combine to form the magenta color we see. The blue filter, which transmits only blue light, produces the yellow separation negative by exposing the negative in all but the red and green areas (figure 5.4). The black separation negative is exposed in such a way that shadows or dark areas of the original do not record on the film. The primary hues, however, record as density on the black negative. In other words, information or image detail from each primary color is used to create the black negative.

After the negatives are exposed to printing plates, the clear areas on the film become areas of density on the plate. When the four plates are printed together in their proper combinations on one sheet, the results should duplicate the range of colors of the original copy.

In today's digital world, the process of color separation has been immensely simplified and the time frame drastically reduced. It is now a matter of settings within software that determine the output of specific plates. Determining correct setup for your digital files will be explored in detail in chapter 9.

Halftone Dots and Color

Although figure 5.4 is a good conceptual view of the color separation process, it only represents flat color and does not accurately show how the full range of colors is produced on the final printed sheet.

Most color separation is done from continuous-tone color originals that must be screened during the reproduction process. Recall from chapter 4 that halftone photographs create the illusion of tones by using dots of varying sizes. For example, 15 percent dots surrounded by 85 percent white space appears as light gray; correspondingly, 35 percent dots with 65 percent white space appears to be a darker gray. That same dot structure produces a range of values within a given subtractive primary color for process color reproduction. The dots of varying sizes from the four different color separations overlap to accurately reproduce the color original. It is possible to illustrate this concept with a set of color proofs (plate J).

The yellow proof in plate J is actually a halftone represented in one color (yellow); it consists of a limited range of values. These values of yellow are produced by many halftone dots of varying sizes. When the magenta proof is added to the yellow proof, additional colors and values become noticeable. When the cyan proof is added to these two proofs, the image appears to be complete. All of the colors and values of colors seem to be visible. Adding a black proof, however, increases density in the shadow areas and strengthens the values of each color.

Because the various values of each color are produced by overlapping dots, it is important that each halftone separation be prepared with dots at differing screen angles. If these angles are not controlled properly, an objectionable moiré (pronounced *more-ray*) pattern can be formed (figure 5.5). The problem

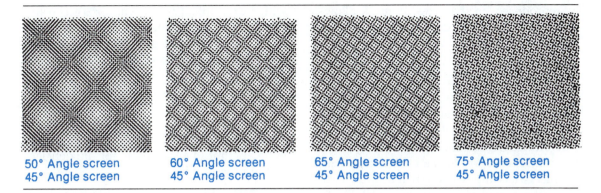

| 50° Angle screen | 60° Angle screen | 65° Angle screen | 75° Angle screen |
| 45° Angle screen | 45° Angle screen | 45° Angle screen | 45° Angle screen |

Figure 5.5 Moiré patterns. The moiré patterns were formed by a 33-line screen at approximately 20 percent tone value.

is caused by individual dots overlapping at an inappropriate angle. The typical contact screen, whether solid line or vignetted halftone, has a built-in 45° angle. When overprinting two screen patterns, you must angle the second screen 30° from the first.

Halftone screens used to make color separations anticipate the problem and build in special angles. For example, the cyan separation is typically made at a 45° angle, the magenta at 75°, the yellow at 90°, and the black at 105°. Angle control is discussed in greater detail in chapter 9.

Color Masking

Color masking has three distinct goals in color reproduction:

- To compress the density range of the color original (called **tone correction**)
- To compensate for color deficiencies in process inks (called **color correction**)
- To enhance the detail of the final reproduction (called **sharpness enhancement**)

While electronic color separation has a built-in masking function, the term *masking* is still widely used and describes what continues to be an important photographic process. Traditionally, a color mask was made by exposing a color original to **pan masking film** (a continuous-tone film) through a special filter. The mask was then physically placed over unexposed film during the separation process. However, electronic color scanning is doing the masking step electronically today. A computer can be programmed to adjust the final separated digital images before they are output onto film or printing plates. Whether a physical film mask is used or electronic adjustments are made, the three goals of masking remain the same.

Tone Correction

Color transparencies typically have a maximum density of around 2.60, and color prints may reach a density of 2.00 (refer to chapter 4 for a discussion of density measurement). Although four layers of ink on a printed sheet of paper can match a 2.00 reflection density, the 2.60 density of a transparent image cannot be reproduced on the press. A mask allows the tonal range of the image to be compressed to a usable range without causing color imbalance.

Color Correction

A second goal in color masking is to compensate for the inherent limitations of printing inks. Although color theory says that cyan ink is a combination of blue and green pigments, in practice it is impossible to manufacture cyan ink without some red pigment as well. Figure 5.6 shows plots of each process ink color. Each segment of the figure compares the ideal ink

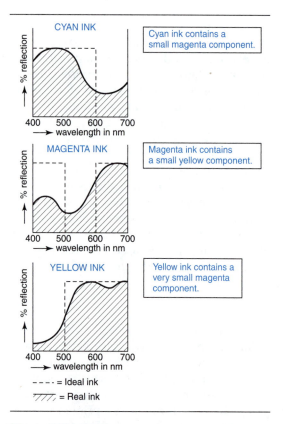

Figure 5.6 caption region:

Cyan ink contains a small magenta component.

Magenta ink contains a small yellow component.

Yellow ink contains a very small magenta component.

- - - - = Ideal ink

///// = Real ink

Figure 5.6 Comparison of real inks with theoretically ideal inks.
Courtesy of D.S. America.

with the real ink. If cyan ink absorbs green and blue pigments, as expected, but also a bit of red pigment, then it is necessary to reduce both the magenta and yellow separation negatives in areas where cyan is printed on the final reproduction. These types of interactions occur between all colors. The process of masking (whether photographic or electronic) reduces select areas of the separation negatives in an attempt to compensate for the deficiencies of process inks.

Sharpness Enhancement

The third purpose of color masking is to enhance the detail of the individual separation. A blurry or unsharp photographic mask produces a sharp separation. Such a photographic mask is produced by placing a diffuser sheet (generally frosted acetate) between the original and the pan masking film during the mask exposure. The diffused mask then slightly increases the contrast of the edges of the images, which in turn gives more detail to the reproduction. In the electronic version of the process, the computer exaggerates the density difference (contrast) of the image edges.

UCR and GCR

One purpose of masking, as discussed in the previous section, is to adjust for the differences between ideal and real printing inks. For example, ideal cyan ink absorbs red light and reflects blue and green light. In reality, while cyan ink does reflect most blue and green light, it also absorbs some blue and green light. This makes the ink appear contaminated with magenta and yellow inks. The solution is to reduce magenta and yellow ink wherever cyan is also printed. The computer is ideally suited to automatically make such adjustments for all color interactions. Once the operator has set the machine for the actual press conditions, ink, paper, and press printing characteristics, the computer can take information from the color transparency and modify the data to produce the best possible set of separations.

Another reason for color correction is intended use. A printed sheet looks different depending upon its viewing situation. For example, supermarkets always place warm (slightly red) lights over their meat counters. Customers tend to buy more meat when it appears rich red at the point of purchase. If a package with a process color image is to be placed in or near the meat counter (such as a box of frozen shrimp), then the color separations should be adjusted to reduce the magenta printer. However, an adjustment in the magenta printer affects every other color separation. Therefore, the cyan and yellow printers must also be corrected where the two overlap with magenta. The scanner's computer can be set up to make such corrections and, with the operator's direction, can produce a set of four appropriate printers.

The operator may also make adjustments to improve the color balance of an inferior color original. The system may be used to adjust for the type of paper to receive the image. The separations used to print a color image on newsprint should be different from those used for a high-quality, coated offset paper (see chapter 16).

Undercolor removal (UCR) is the process of diminishing the amount of cyan, magenta, and yellow ink printed in the shadows, while increasing the amount of black ink in the areas of the original where the three primary subtractive colors have been removed. Equal amounts of cyan, magenta, and yellow create a neutral gray. The basic idea is to remove equal amounts of the three colors to the extent that each individual color's clarity is retained, but to diminish neutral gray, which adds nothing to the image (figure 5.7).

The results of UCR are the prevention of ink buildup, which tends to cause picking (see chapter 12), and increased detail in the shadow

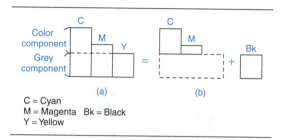

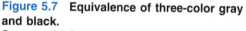

Figure 5.7 **Equivalence of three-color gray and black.**
Courtesy of D.S. America.

areas because of added density in the black printer. The goal of UCR is increased image quality, but one important side result is the savings gained by reducing use of expensive color inks and replacing them with relatively inexpensive black ink.

A color separation technique that is unique to the modern electronic color scanner is **achromatic color**. The technique is also known as **gray component replacement (GCR)**. The GCR process is an extension of UCR (undercolor removal). While UCR only removes cyan, yellow, and magenta in the darker neutral gray areas of the separation, GCR replaces cyan, yellow, and magenta wherever they overprint to produce a neutral gray, even in the highlights. Traditional electronic separations produce a black (ghost) separation that prints from the midtones into the shadows. The GCR process produces a more full-range black. With GCR, the black printer is responsible for producing a full range of neutral gray tones from highlight to shadow. The result is that the process inks—cyan, yellow, and magenta—only print where necessary to produce the color portion of the image. Where black is required, black prints, rather than building the color black with equal parts of each process color as is done with traditional separations. The press is now able to lay

Undercolor removal of the gray component
works on neutral colors only.

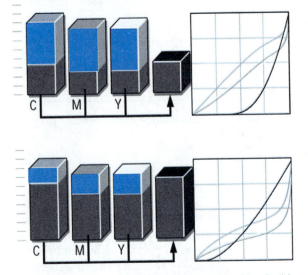

The gray component of CMY is indicated as blue in this
diagram. The part of this gray component that is converted
to black, is indicated as a dark gray.
Courtesy of AGFA

**Figure 5.8   UCR uses black ink to
replace other process colors in the
shadow areas of an image and in
neutral shades**

down a heavier film of the process inks without the possibility of upsetting the gray balance of the separation. In addition, much of he
more expensive process ink is replaced by the
less expensive black ink. Color adjustments

can now be corrected from within the software
program used for output of the files. Color is
a critical part of publishing and will be discussed in chapter 9 as it relates to the digital
workflow.

Key Terms

hue
saturation
value
chroma
color space
gamut
absolute system
relative system

International Commission on
    Illumination (CIE)
additive primary colors
subtractive primary colors
process ink
color masking
tone correction
color correction

sharpness enhancement
pan masking film
undercolor removal (UCR)
achromatic color
gray component replacement
    (GCR)

Review Questions

1. Describe the difference between hue, saturation, and value.
2. Define the term *color space*.
3. Discuss the CIE approach to color.
4. What are the additive primary colors?
5. What are the subtractive primary colors?
6. When using subtractive primary inks, what color results from a combination of yellow and magenta?
7. What is the purpose of adding black ink if a combination of three subtractive inks approximates all colors?
8. What are the three main goals of masking in color separation?
9. What several advantages does color separation by electronic scanning have over other techniques?
10. The GCR process is an extension of what masking function of the electronic color scanner?

6

Traditional Image Assembly and Platemaking

Historical Background

Stripping refers to the process of preparing and positioning a piece of film for exposure to a printing plate. The term originally described a process, used commonly as recently as the 1950s, in which a wet emulsion was removed from a special *stripping film*. Stripping film was cumbersome to work with when compared to today's flexible, stable-base photographic materials, but at the time it was considered an efficient, simple material.

The stripper could use a variety of techniques when stripping. One of the most common was to manufacture the film from existing materials in the darkroom. The process started with the careful cleaning of a sheet of glass. The glass was then polished with a soft rag and a powder called *French chalk*. Next, a substratum

of rubber solution or egg albumen solution was poured on the glass, followed by a layer of rubber and naphtha. The final layer to be applied was a light-sensitive stripping emulsion.

While the emulsion was still wet, the plate was rushed to the camera and an exposure was made of the image to be reproduced. The plate was then taken to the developing area and processed. The wet plate then went back to the stripper, who immersed it in an acetic acid–water bath.

When the emulsion began to lift from the plate, the stripper started at one corner and actually stripped the membrane from the plate. While this was going on, another worker prepared a new glass plate by covering it with a small pool of gum Arabic solution. The wet emulsion was positioned on the second plate and finally squeegeed into place. Depending on the printing process used, the emulsion could be placed on the plate either right reading or wrong reading. If a halftone or new piece of line art needed to be added, the stripper used a sharp knife to cut away the unwanted area and put a new wet piece in its place. With computers changing the way prepress is handled, stripping, when used today, mainly consists of stripping flats together for imposition purposes. Although it is now rare to strip individual pages and images, assembly on a computer requires the same criteria, language, and attention to detail that was required when wet sheets of emulsion were stripped from a glass sheet.

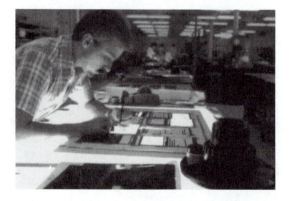

Stripping film on a light table.
Courtesy of Kingsport Press, an Arcata National Company.

Objectives

After completing this chapter you will be able to:

- Understand the purpose of stripping and proofing in the printing process.
- Recognize the equipment and supplies used in mechanical stripping and proofing.
- Recall and explain the basic mechanical stripping steps.
- Recall and explain the basic methods of preparing single-color proofs.
- Describe the basic concepts of opaque and transparent color proofs.
- Describe the basic components of a platemaker.
- Explain what is meant by actinic light and tell why platemakers produce this type of light.
- Explain why offset plates are grained.
- Explain the basic components of light-sensitive coating for offset plates.
- Differentiate between negative-working and positive-working plates.
- List the steps involved in processing a subtractive lithographic plate and an additive lithographic plate.
- Describe the basic characteristics of presensitized photopolymer surface plates.

Introduction

This chapter is divided into two main sections. The first section describes the basics of film stripping prior to platemaking and the analog proofing methods used to check the accuracy and quality of the position of the stripped film images. The second section reviews conventional platemaking techniques. Familiarity with traditional approaches to page assembly and platemaking helps us to better understand both the scope of the digital workflow that has replaced it and much of the terminology that has been carried forward as new techniques have been developed.

Section 1: Traditional Image Assembly

Stripping Transparent Materials

After the final layout has been completed and converted to transparent film, the film image must be transferred photographically to the printing plate. Although the type of plate used will differ according to the method or process of reproduction (relief, lithography, screen, or gravure), mechanical stripping and proofing steps from the darkroom to the plate room are basically the same.

The Purpose of Stripping

Mechanical **stripping** is the process of assembling all pieces of film containing images that will be carried on the same printing plate and securing them on a masking sheet that will hold them in their appropriate printing positions during the platemaking process. (For more about masking sheets, see the next section.) The assembled masking sheet with pieces of film attached is called a **flat**. After the flat is stripped, it is generally tested on some inexpensive photosensitive material to check image positions and to ensure that no undesired light reaches the plate. This process is called **proofing**. If the proof is approved by the customer, the flat is placed in contact with a printing plate, light is passed through the film, and the plate is exposed.

Most printers view the stripping process as the most important step in the printing cycle. The stripper can often correct or alter defects in the film image by etching away undesired detail. The stripper also directly controls the position of the image on the final page. If the film is not stripped square in the masking sheet, the image will appear crooked on the printed page. However, the stripping process cannot correct poor work that started on the mechanical or in the darkroom, no matter how skillful the stripper.

Stripping Equipment and Supplies

The stripper uses a variety of tools that center around a quality T-square and triangle. Tools made of plastic or other easily nicked materials are not used because the tools must serve as cutting edges for razor blades or X-ACTO® knives when trimming pieces of film or masking sheets. Most printers use one quality steel T-square and one steel 30-degrees by 60-degrees by 90-degrees triangle.

Measurements can be made with an architect's scale and an engineer's scale. Stainless steel straightedges with fractional gradations to one one-hundredth of an inch are also commonly used. For greater accuracy, an ordinary needle or a special purpose etching needle is used to mark the masking sheet when laying out a flat. The etching needle can also be used to remove unwanted emulsion from a film negative or a film positive.

Detail is added to a piece of film with a brush. Most strippers have an assortment of red sable watercolor brushes on hand. Start your collection of brushes with #0, #2, #4, and #6 brushes. In addition, your stripping area should have such things as a pair of scissors, a supply of single-edge razor blades, a low-power magnifying glass (10X), pencils (#2H and #4H), erasers, and several felt-tip marking pens for labeling flats.

Almost all stripping is done on a glass-topped light table (figure 6.1). One side of the glass is frosted, and a light source (generally fluorescent) is located under the glass so that

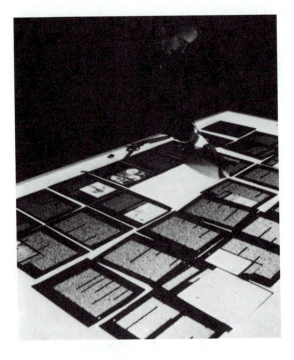

Figure 6.1   A glass-topped light table. On this light table, negatives for a 32-page signature or section are being assembled and stripped.
Courtesy of Pre-Press Co., Inc.

the surface is illuminated evenly. When a film negative or positive is placed on the lighted glass, it is easy to view the image and to detect any film defects. A variety of light tables are available. Most are equipped with accurately ground straightedges on each side so that if a T-square is placed on any side, lines will always be at right angles to each other.

Several types of supplies are needed for the stripping operation. For negative stripping, **masking sheets** that do not pass light to the printing plate must be used. The most common material is "goldenrod paper," which blocks **actinic light** (any light that exposes blue light- and ultraviolet light-sensitive emulsions) because of its color. For jobs that require greater dimensional stability, orange colored (sometimes red) vinyl masking sheets are typically used.

Special "red" translucent tape can be used to secure film negatives during stripping. This tape blocks actinic light. **Opaque** is a liquid material used to cover pinholes and other unwanted detail on film negatives. Red opaque is easier to apply than black opaque, but black colloidal-graphic opaque is thinner and thus more efficient for extremely small areas, such as when retouching halftones. Both water- and alcohol-based opaques are available.

Imposition

Imposition refers to placing images in the correct positions on the printing plate so they print in the desired locations on the final printed sheet. Several types of imposition are commonly used. The type of imposition used depends on several factors:

- The design of the printed piece (whether it is multicolor, process color, or single color; whether one or both sides of the sheet are to be printed; whether one or several duplicate images are to be reproduced on the same sheet; and the type of finishing operations that are required, such as folding, trimming, and binding)
- The type and size of the press to be used (whether the press is sheet fed or web fed, and if the job is ganged, the size of the press sheet, and whether to use a large sheet or a single unit)
- The type of paper to be used during printing (whether image position in relation to grain direction will affect folding operations)

Types of Imposition

In general, the best imposition is the one that produces a quality job with maximum efficiency, minimum press time, minimum amount of paper, and minimum time in the finishing operations that follow. Without careful planning in the stripping operation, a job could be stripped, plated, and run on the press only to discover that it cannot be folded correctly.

One-Side Imposition

The simplest form of imposition is one-side imposition. In one-side imposition, one printing plate is used to print on one side of the shet as it passes through the printing press. This type of imposition is common in small, offset press operations.

Sheetwise Imposition

Two printing plates are used in sheetwise imposition. One printing plate is used to print on one side of a press sheet. A second plate containing different information is then made, the sheets are turned over, and the sheets are printed on the other side from the second plate.

Ganged Imposition

Often the job to be printed is smaller than the press can handle, or it is so much smaller than

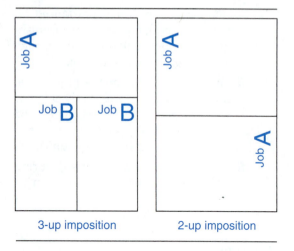

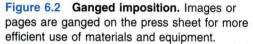

3-up imposition   2-up imposition

Figure 6.2 Ganged imposition. Images or pages are ganged on the press sheet for more efficient use of materials and equipment.

the standard press sheet size that printing only that one job on each press sheet would be a very inefficient use of equipment. For example, it would be impossible to print $2 \times 3^{1}/_{2}$ inch business cards on an 11×17 inch press. To overcome this problem, several jobs are often *ganged* together, reproduced on a large sheet, and then cut to their final trim sizes with a paper cutter figure 6.2). When a press sheet carries only one job, it is called one-up imposition. When more than one job is run on the same sheet, it is called two-up, three-up, four-up, and so on, depending on the number of final jobs run on each press sheet. It makes no difference if the same or different images are printed; the same terms are used.

Signature Imposition

A large single sheet is frequently passed through a printing press and then folded and trimmed to form a portion of a book or magazine. This process is called **signature imposition**. Four-, eight-, twelve-, sixteen-, twenty-four-, and even forty-eight-page signatures are common press runs (figure 6.3). The printer

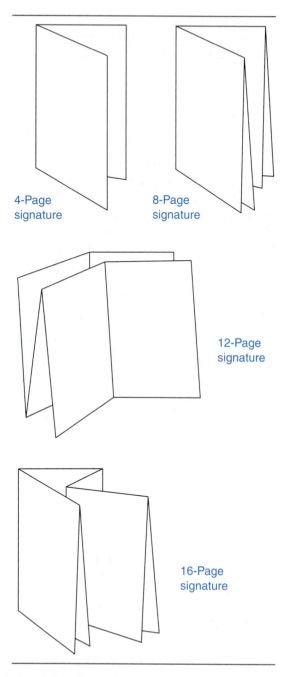

4-Page signature   8-Page signature

12-Page signature

16-Page signature

Figure 6.3 Folded signatures. A folded signature of several pages is the result of signature imposition. The number of pages that are folded is predetermined.

must impose the pages in the proper positions so they will be in the correct sequence when folded in the final publication.

Work-and-Turn Imposition

Another common form of imposition is the work-and-turn. **Work-and-turn imposition** employs one printing plate to print on both sides of a single piece of paper (figure 6.4). The sheet is first printed on one side, the pile is turned over, and the sheet is fed through the press again with the same **lead edge** (first edge that enters the press).

Work-and-Tumble Imposition

Work-and-tumble imposition also uses one plate to print on both sides of one piece of paper. On the second pass through the press, however, the pile is tumbled (or flopped) so that the opposite edge enters the press first figure 6.5). Both work-and-turn and work-and-

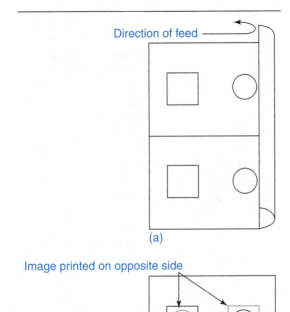

Figure 6.4 **Work-and-turn imposition.** (a) On the first run through the press, the first side of the sheet is printed. (b) The back of the sheet is printed on the second run through the press.

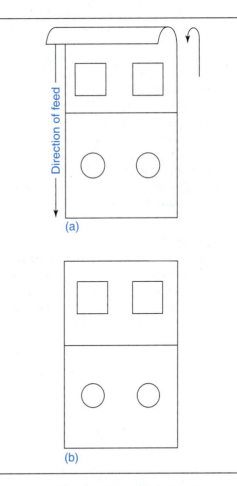

Figure 6.5 **Work-and-tumble imposition showing first run (a) and second run (b)**

tumble techniques are more efficient than sheetwise imposition because only one printing plate is prepared. Work-and-tumble imposition is generally not used where fit (critical image position) is desired, such as in multicolor jobs, because using two different lead edges requires additional press adjustments.

Elementary Stripping Techniques

Traditional stripping requires careful placement of numerous pieces of film. Today image editing programs that place digital images directly into page layout programs prior to film output are used. Stripping now more commonly refers to placing individual sheets of film on a flat in the proper order for imposition based on the size of the press and the job's specifications. The trend is also moving toward imposetters, which output complete signatures. The techniques in this section are intended to introduce the basic concepts of traditional stripping, thus providing historical context for today's digital prepress.

Masking Sheets

The position of the images on the printing plate is determined by the film positions on the masking sheet. Thus the masking sheet *represents* the printing plate and must be at least the same size as the printing plate. Care must be used in placing the film images on the masking sheet to ensure that they are in the correct printing positions and are parallel to the lead edge of the masking sheet. Identifying the following four areas on the masking sheet helps to position the film images accurately in their correct printing positions:

■ The cylinder line
■ The gripper margin
■ The point where the image begins on the printed piece (Figure 6.6a)
■ The plate center line

The **cylinder line** represents the masking sheet area used to clamp the lithographic plate to the press cylinder. Most offset lithographic plates are flexible and wrap around a press cylinder, which is called the **plate cylinder**. The lead edge and tail portions of the plate are covered by the clamps that hold the plate in place, so no image can be printed from these areas (figure 6.6b). The **gripper margin** is the area of the press sheet held by the mechanical fingers that pull the press sheet through the printing unit (figure 6.6b). Because these fingers cover part of the paper, it is also not possible to print an image in the gripper margin.

The top of the uppermost image on the printed piece dictates how far down from the bottom of the gripper edge the film image is stripped onto the masking sheet. Information on this dimension should be included on the rough. The center line of the masking sheet is used to line up the center of the film image area so that it is exposed squarely in the center of the lithographic plate and consequently prints in the center of the press sheet. (There are instances when an image is to be printed off center on the final press sheet; for these images, too, however, the center line of the masking sheet must be identified in order to position the film correctly.) Once these four areas are marked on the masking sheet, film can be stripped onto the sheet with confidence that the images will appear in the correct locations on the printing plate and the final press sheet.

The stripper's job is to create a flat by positioning the film on the masking sheet so that the plate transfers images in the required locations on the final press sheet. Press adjustments to change image location are possible, but they are time consuming and costly. Press

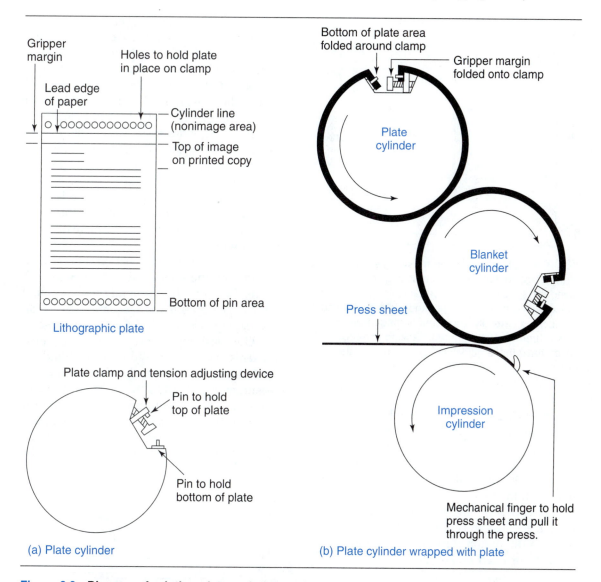

Figure 6.6 **Diagram of printing plate and plate cylinder.** The printing plate is wrapped around the plate cylinder and held in place on the top and bottom with clamps.

adjustments for image location are also limited. For example, it is difficult, if not impossible, for a press operator to salvage a plate that has an image above the cylinder line. Often an incorrectly stripped flat must be com-pletely restripped, and a new plate must be made. This wastes both time and money. The situation becomes even more critical when several flats are used to expose images on the same plate.

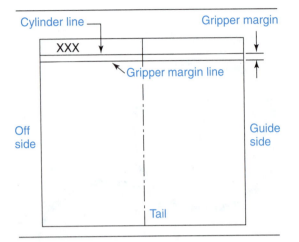

Figure 6.7   **Marking blank masking sheets.**
Many strippers lay out blank masking sheets using the specifications for a particular press. The cylinder line, gripper margin, and plate center line are located carefully. All layout is made from these three lines. Preprinted masking sheets, which have these guidelines provided, are also used.

Masking sheets can be purchased with or without preprinted guidelines. In either case, the stripper's tasks remain the same: identify the cylinder line, plate center line, gripper margin, and top image distance, and strip the images into their correct printing positions (figure 6.7). Stripping for both lined and unlined masking sheets is discussed in this chapter. The discussion starts with stripping procedures for lined masking sheets.

Laying Out a Preprinted Masking Sheet
To begin the discussion, let us pick a simple one-color, single-flat stripping job: one image must be printed on $8\frac{1}{2}$ inch × 11 inch paper using an 11 inch × 17 inch duplicator. For this example, we will strip a negative film image.

The stripper's first job is to select the correct masking sheet. There is no problem if there is only one size of press sheet in the shop.

However, if the shop has several different size presses, careful masking sheet selection becomes necessary. Our job requires a preprinted masking sheet for an 11 inch × 17 inch duplicator. Often the masking sheet carries the name of the press manufacturer and a symbol or size marking to identify for which press the masking sheet is designed. If your shop does not have masking sheets with this information, a simple measurement will help locate the correct sheet; or you can compare the sheet to a plate from the press on which the job is to be run. The masking sheet should be the same size as or slightly larger than the plate that will be used with it.

Place the masking sheet on a light table and line up one edge of the sheet with a T-square. Tape the sheet securely in two places on the edge opposite the T-square (figure 6.8). Masking tape can be used for this purpose.

Our masking sheet is prelined in a $\frac{1}{4}$-inch grid. This grid can be used as a rough indicator of measurements on the sheet, but exact measurements should always be made carefully with a ruler. Not only is the $\frac{1}{4}$-inch grid not perfectly accurate, but we taped the masking sheet in place based on the location of the edge of the sheet against our T-square, not the

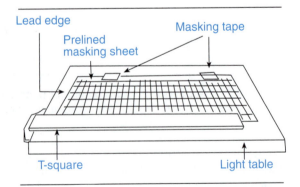

Figure 6.8   **Placing the masking sheet on the light table.** Line the masking sheet up against the edge of a T-square and tape it on one side.

printed grid. There is no reason to assume that the grid printed on the masking sheet is parallel to the edge of the masking sheet. It may be close, but it is probably not perfectly parallel. Using the T-square and ruler for all image location ensures that the images end up positioned correctly and perfectly straight on the sheet.

After the masking sheet is taped in place, look it over carefully. As shown in figure 6.7, the cylinder lines, gripper margin, and center line should be clearly identified. It is often a good idea to draw a line over the bottom of the gripper margin line and down the center line on the masking sheet. This helps you refer back to these locations as you lay out the sheet.

Now check the rough layout to determine top margin: the distance from the top of the paper to the top of the image on the printed piece (figure 6.9). A line representing the top of the image should be drawn across the masking sheet, below the bottom of the gripper

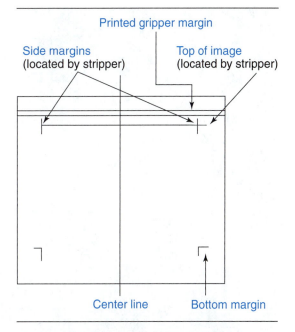

Figure 6.10 **Diagram of a masking sheet.** Lines representing the top, side, and bottom margins are drawn first on the masking sheet. The top image margin should always be below the gripper margin.

margin; lines representing side and bottom margins should also be drawn (figure 6.10).

For this example, there is only one film negative. Lay it emulsion side down near the masking sheet on the light table. Examine the negative carefully. Corner marks that indicate image extremes or center lines (or both) should be recorded on the negative (figure 6.11). These marks help you position the film negative in the proper location under the masking sheet.

Attaching Film Negatives

With rare exception, all printing plates are exposed with the emulsion side of the plate against the emulsion side of the film. Recall from chapter 4 that negatives are right read-

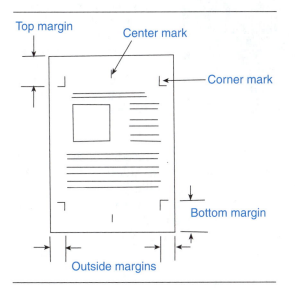

Figure 6.9 **Rough layout with margins identified**

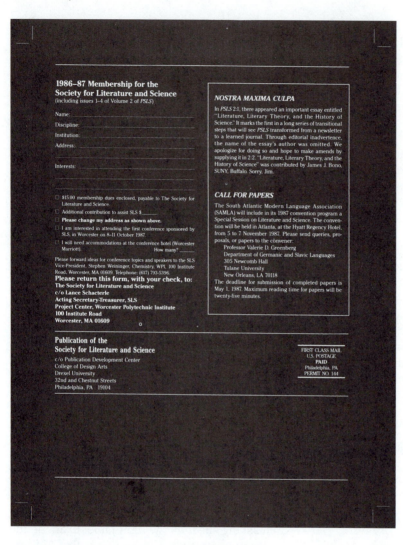

Figure 6.11 Example of a negative with corner marks. If corner marks are placed on the paste-up board, they appear as images on the film negative. These negative corner marks can then be lined up with the top, side, and bottom margins on the masking sheet.

ing through the base. In other words, if the piece of film is placed on the light table so that the image can be read from left to right, the base side is up and the emulsion side is against the glass. If there is any question about which is the emulsion side of the film negative, the emulsion side can be identified in one of two ways: by comparing the finish of the two sides of the film or by scratching the film edge. If the film is folded over on itself, the emulsion side is the duller of the two sides. Also, the emulsion side of the film can be scratched. A

small pin scratch on the edge of the film outside the image area quickly identifies the emulsion side of the film.

Begin by placing the negative emulsion side down on the masking sheet in its appropriate position, with the images roughly falling in place with the image margins. If there is more than one negative in a job, never allow the pieces of film to overlap on the flat. If the overlap is near an image area, there may be some distortion when the plate exposure is made. With the negative in place, mark where any pieces overlap. If possible, cut any over-lapping sheets to within $\frac{1}{2}$ inch of any film image. If, because of imposition (image location on the final press sheet), the cut must be less than $\frac{1}{2}$ inch from an image area, delay trimming the film until both pieces have been attached. This procedure is discussed in this section. After trimming, all negatives should be removed and set aside until they are needed again.

Because the masking sheet is translucent, it is possible to see through the material to the glass surface below. With right-reading stripping, untape the masking sheet and set it aside or flip it back out of the way. Place the negative, emulsion side down, on the light table. Accurately align the image margins or *tick marks* with a T-square and triangle, and tape the film in place on the light table (figure 6.12).

Next, replace the masking sheet over the film and move it until its image lines are positioned with the image margins on the negative. It should be easy to see both sets of marks line up as you look down through the flat. Use

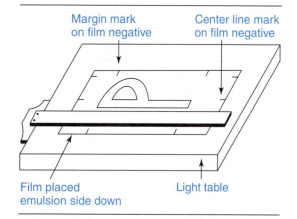

Figure 6.12 **Positioning the negative on the light table**

a T-square to ensure that the margins and type lines run parallel to the edge of the masking sheet.

After the negative is in place, smooth the masking sheet and cut two small, triangular openings in the masking sheet over the negative in the nonimage areas (figure 6.13). It is

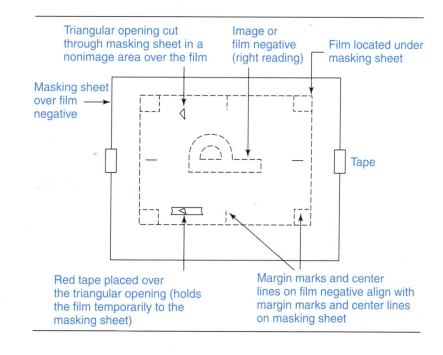

Figure 6.13 **Cuffing triangular openings.** Looking down through the masking sheet to the film negative below, cut two small triangular openings in the masking sheet covering a nonimage area in the film. Tape over these openings with red tape to temporarily hold the film to the masking sheet.

important that you cut only through the masking sheet and not into the film. Practice several times on a scrap sheet. Still holding the film in position under the masking sheet, place a small piece of red tape over each triangular opening and apply pressure. This temporarily attaches the negative to the masking sheet and forms the flat.

Before untaping the flat from the light table, again check all film images for position and squareness. Improper image placement at this stage reflects throughout the rest of the job.

After the negative has been attached temporarily and checked for accuracy, release the flat from the light table by removing the tape, and carefully turn it over. Now secure the negative to the masking sheet at each corner with a small piece of cellophane tape (figure 6.14). Be sure to smooth the negative as the tape is applied to ensure that there are no buckles in

the film. Once the film is taped securely to the masking sheet, turn the masking sheet over again (lined side up) and recheck the image placement.

If two pieces of film overlap, it is necessary to cut the negatives so they butt against each other. To do this without cutting into the masking sheet, insert a piece of scrap film or acetate beneath the overlapping portions of film and use a steel straightedge and a single-edge razor blade or frisket knife to cut through both pieces of film (figure 6.15). Do not remove the straightedge until you are certain that you have cut completely through both sheets of film. Remove the loose pieces and the scrap film, and tape the negatives to the masking sheet on the nonimage edges only. Do not put tape over the image areas on a negative.

After all the negatives have been located and taped in place on the masking sheet, turn the masking sheet over again so that the film emulsion is against the light table. Now cut away the masking sheet in the image areas. The masking material should be removed to

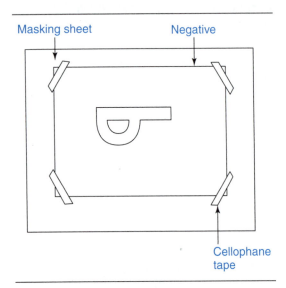

Figure 6.14 Taping the negative to the masking sheet. Turn the masking sheet over and tape each corner of the film negative with cellophane tape. For larger films, tape the long edges at their centers.

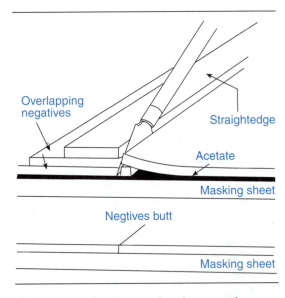

Figure 6.15 Cutting overlapping negatives

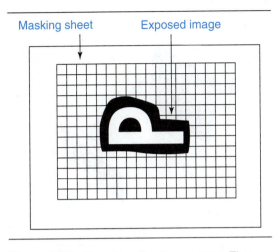

Masking sheet   Exposed image

Figure 6.16 **Exposing the image area.** The masking sheet is cut away to expose the image area of the film negative.

within $\frac{3}{8}$ inch of the image areas. The less non-printing area that is exposed, the better (figure 6.16).

Opaquing and Etching the Flat

Although theoretically the flat is now ready to be sent to the plating room, in actuality there are usually small defects that must be corrected. The most common defects are **pinholes**. These are small openings in the emulsion that pass light. They may be caused by dust on the copyboard when the camera exposure was made or by dirty original copy. Pinholes ultimately appear as ink on the final press sheet. Pinholes are undesired images and, therefore, must be blocked with opaque. Most opaques are water based. Alcohol-turpentine- or petroleum-based materials are also available. Opaque should be applied in as thin a coat as possible yet still block light through the negative.

The final step, after all opaquing and etching are complete and checked, is to label the flat. The platemaker typically handles many flats in a single day, so each must be identified. Place all information in the trailing edge of the masking sheet, out of the paper limits. The notations depend on the individual shop, but such things as the name of the account, job title or production number, sequence of the flat, ink color, or any special instructions such as the inclusion of a screen tint are all commonly included.

Stripping Halftones

Several techniques for adding halftone images to printed materials were discussed in chapter 3. One method suggested including a red or black pressure-sensitive material on the paste-up that would reproduce on the film negative as a clear open window. A halftone negative could then be added to the window later in production. It is the stripper's responsibility to combine the halftone negative with the negative holding the window on the flat. This must be done in such a way that the halftone appears in the proper position on the final printed sheet and the added piece of film carrying the halftone image does not interfere with the existing images on the negative that has the window.

To add a halftone negative to a window in a main negative, first prepare the masking sheet; add the main negative(s); and complete all cutting, opaquing, and etching. Then turn the flat over on the light table so that the film is emulsion side up. Trim the halftone to be stripped into the window so that it is larger than the window opening and yet does not overlap any image detail near the window. Position the trimmed negative over the window emulsion side up, in line with the rest of the image detail on the flat, and tape it in place with clear cellophane tape. The halftone must be mounted in this position because the emulsions of both the main negative and the halftone negative must contact the printing plate when the plate exposure is made (figure 6.17).

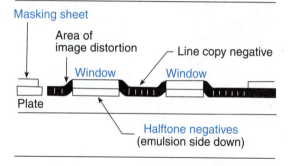

Figure 6.17 Positioning the halftone negatives. The emulsions of both the line copy and the halftone negatives must contact the emulsion of the printing plate.

Check to be sure that the halftone image completely fills the window. Any open area around the edges of the window prints as a solid line on the final reproduction.

When you are stripping positive flats, treat a halftone exactly as you would treat all other pieces of film. Cut it to size and secure it in place with clear tape or a thin layer of rubber cement.

It is often not possible to add a halftone negative to an existing flat without overlapping image detail and creating an area of image distortion. This happens when two halftones butt together on the final printed sheet or the halftone window is too close to other image detail. In such cases, the stripper cannot work with the halftone on a single flat. The solution is to use two **complementary flats**. One flat carries the main printing detail; the second holds the halftone image (figure 6.18). If properly stripped, each flat can be exposed successively in the platemaker to combine the two images in their proper positions on one printing plate (figure 6.19). The Multiflat Registration section that follows is concerned with the problem of controlling the positions of film images that are mounted on more than one flat.

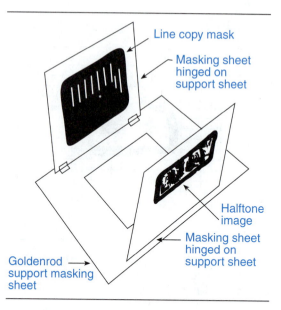

Figure 6.18 Complementary flats. In this example of complementary flats, the two masking sheets hinge on a larger support sheet.

Multiflat Registration

It is important to realize that almost all printing plates can be exposed from five or six different flats before the sum effect of light leading through the goldenrod or yellow vinyl masking sheets begins to expose the plate emulsion in nonimage areas.

The problem of multiflat exposures is registration. The stripper must place the separate film images on each flat and then control the placement of the images from each flat on one plate. When the plate is processed, all images must appear in their proper printing positions relative to each other and to the limits of the printing press. Some form of mechanical punch or guide is generally used to aid in the multiflat registration process.

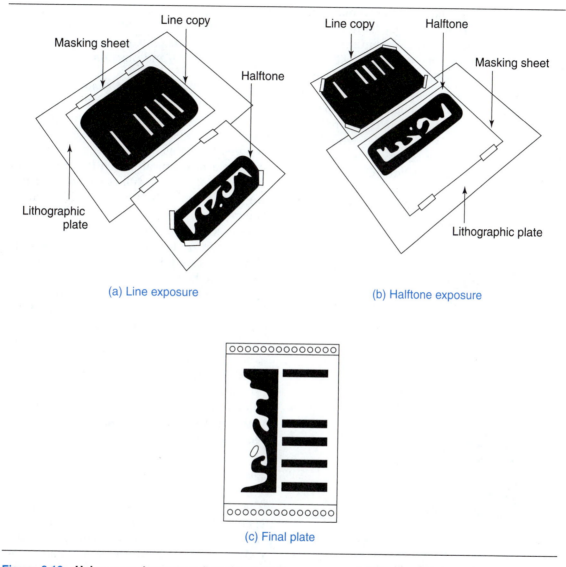

(a) Line exposure

(b) Halftone exposure

(c) Final plate

Figure 6.19 **Using complementary flats for double exposures.** (a) The complementary flat uses one exposure to record the line copy and (b) one exposure to record the halftone. (c) The final plate carries both images.

The Purpose of Registration Systems

Registration determines the accurate placement of successively printed colors with respect to each other. Proper registration aims to eliminate gaps between colors and overlap of images. In contemporary workflows, register marks are applied within the page layout application.

In mechanical image assembly, many situations besides complementary halftone flats require the stripper to use the multiple flat process. Commonly, the stripper must print two separate screen tint values in the same color using the same plate. It is possible to place both images on one negative and to use folding masks to make the plate exposure (figure 6.20). Two separate exposures would be made with a screen tint between the flat and the plate during each exposure. Only the desired areas would be opened for each exposure, and the proper screen would be placed between the flat and the plate each time the plate was exposed. If images are extremely close together, however, or if many different areas are spread over the entire flat, this technique is not usable. It is then necessary to place all images of common screen tint values or sizes on separate flats. With proper multiflat registration techniques, these images can be assembled on one plate in the proper tint values, screen angle, and position (figure 6.21).

Punch and Register Pin Method

In traditional stripping, the most efficient way of controlling registration is to apply the punch and register pin method from camera to press. With this method the camera operator uses a mechanical punch (figure 6.22) on each piece of film, as well as register pins (figure 6.23) to hold the film in position on the camera back. This is especially effective for process color separation work where the copy does not move between exposures. Once the film is processed, the stripper works opaques and etches the film, and then mounts the film on a punched masking sheet if necessary. When the total system approach is used, the printing plate is also punched to line up with the film or masking sheet holes before plate exposure, and register pins are placed on the printing press to receive a punched plate. If used throughout the process, the technique results in printed images that line up perfectly with few press adjustments. This significantly reduces costs in all areas.

Multiflat Stripping for Process Color Work

This section is concerned primarily with the specific techniques involved in stripping for four-color process printing. The general procedures apply to all other multiflat stripping, whether it is flat color, more than four colors (such as topographic mapping where five are used), or single color (where several flats are used to generate one plate).

The most accurate method of positioning multiple flats is to use some type of master image stripped into a master flat as a guide for all subsequent images and flats. There are two basic approaches: blueline flat and single master flat.

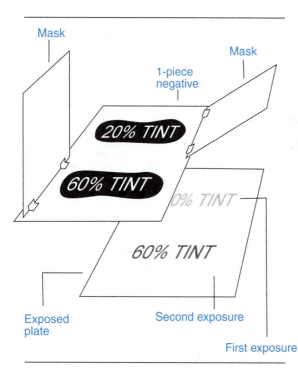

Figure 6.20 **Using folding masks to control multiple plate exposures**

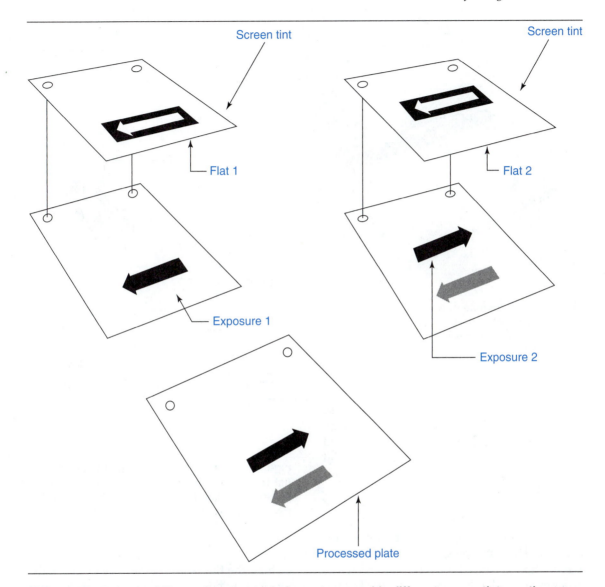

Figure 6.21   Using multiflat registration techniques to assemble different screen tints on the same plate

Blueline Flat Method

With the **blueline flat method** a special flat is prepared. This flat is generally assembled using negatives and holds any detail needed to position all film images for the job, as well as all necessary registration marks. After it is as-

sembled, the blueline master flat is exposed to a special light-sensitive solution that has been coated on a piece of clear plate glass or plastic. The processed emulsion produces a blue image that does not expose a printing plate if the clear base is used for positive stripping. If

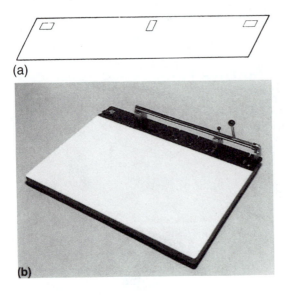

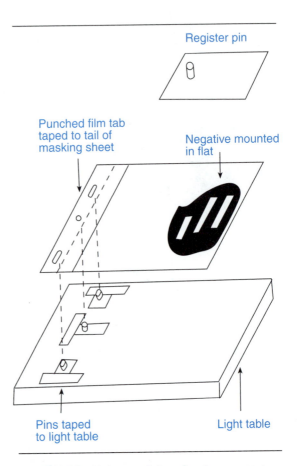

Figure 6.22   **Example of a punched tab (a) and a mechanical tab (b).**
Courtesy of Dainippon Screen Mfg. Co., Ltd., distributed by DS America, Inc.

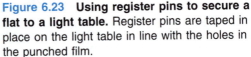

Figure 6.23   **Using register pins to secure a flat to a light table.** Register pins are taped in place on the light table in line with the holes in the punched film.

negatives are used for stripping, you can use the blueline image as a guide to register all flats. For positives, prepare a laterally reversed blueline for each flat. Then take the master flat apart and strip all pieces of film with their appropriate color.

Single Master Flat Method

The most common registration technique for color negative stripping is the **single-master flat method** in which the single master flat acts as a guide for all other flats in the job. For flat color, the master flat is generally the flat that carries the greatest amount of detail. For four-color process work, the cyan, magenta, or black separation negative can be used, depending on which color carries the greatest detail. Four-color stripping with a master flat is covered here.

Prepare the master flat using common stripping techniques. After opaquing and etching the flat, apply some type of pin register device and turn the flat over on the light table with the emulsion side of the film facing you. Apply the pin system to a second masking sheet and position it over the first flat. Then place the second set of negatives, emulsion side up, in register with the first image.

Each piece of film carries duplicate halftone and register mark images for each of the four color separations. The register marks are your first guides. As you impose the sec-

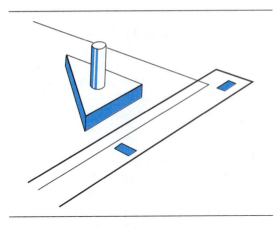

Figure 6.24 **Example of a sighting tube**

ond negative over the first, the register marks on the negatives line up. With four-color reproductions made up of halftone images, the alignment is critical. If you view register marks on any but a 90 degree angle, the thickness of the film might cause a distortion that will put the two images out of register. To eliminate the possibility of this type of error, some strippers use a **sighting tube** to view the register marks (figure 6.24).

After all register marks are in line, hold the negative in place with some weighted material (a leather bag filled with lead pellets is often used) and examine the detail registration in the halftones themselves.

If the job is made up of only four flats to print as four different colors, all flats are registered individually to the master flat. If there are more than four flats to be reproduced with only four colors (such as when using two different screen tint percentages in the same color, or when line copy falls too close to a halftone image to include it on one flat), the sequence of flat registration is important. Examine each color grouping. For each color, the flat that contains the greatest amount of image detail becomes the key flat for that color. Register each key color flat to the master flat and register all other flats in the color group to the key.

Proofing Transparent Materials

After the job has been stripped and checked, it is ready to be converted to some form of plate or image carrier after another step—proofing each flat or job—occurs.

The Purpose of Proofing

It is difficult to interpret the image on the flat. Both printers and printing customers are distracted by such things as the masking sheet, tape, opaque, notations, or instruction marks. Moreover, the image on the flat is often a negative. It is also not possible to fold a flat to check for accuracy of image position for a work-and-turn or a signature job. The function of proofing is to check for image location and quality, and to obtain the customer's final approval to run the job. There are two basic ways to proof transparent materials: by using press proofs and by using photomechanical proofs.

Press Proofs

Press proofs are made using the same types of ink and paper that are used on the final job. Press proofing has the disadvantage of high cost. The customer must assume the costs of press time (set up, make-ready, actual running time, and clean up) and materials in press proofing. Therefore, press proofing is reserved for extremely high-quality, long-run jobs.

A *press check* occurs when a customer comes to the plant to give final approval while the job is being run. With press proofing the customer can see how the final job will look (including the final colors). However, if changes must be made, the cost is very high. Press checks are usually conducted not to check accuracy of words or image position, but rather to approve colors on the final printed sheet. The customer rarely stays for the entire press run—only to approve the first images.

With some reproduction methods, the job is actually mounted on a press and a few hundred images are produced as a proof. This is common with gravure printing (see chapter 14). Where the plate cylinder is exceptionally time consuming and costly to prepare in gravure printing, a press proof is safe insurance for both the printer and customer.

Photomechanical Proofs

Unlike press proofs, **photomechanical proofs** require no large investment in special proofing equipment and generally use existing platemaking equipment. Most photomechanical proofing systems use a light-sensitive emulsion coated on some inexpensive carder, such as paper or plastic, which is then exposed through the flat in the same way the plates are exposed. The emulsion is next processed chemically to produce an image that represents the final press sheet. Contrary to what many proofing manufacturers claim, no photomechanical proof matches the quality and color of a press proof. However, the low cost of photomechanical proofs vastly outweighs this disadvantage. Photomechanical proofs are generally classified as either single color or multiple color.

Single-Color Photomechanical Proofing

Single-color photomechanical proofing is the least expensive of the proofing systems. Most methods use a vacuum frame to hold the flat in contact with a light-sensitive coating on a sheet of paper and a light source to expose the emulsion. This equipment is discussed in detail in the following section of this chapter. Single-color proofs do not show the actual ink color of the final press run. They are used only to check such things as imposition, image position, and proper masking and opaquing. Two common types of materials used for single-color proofs are diazo and instant image proof papers.

Diazo Paper

Diazo paper produces a positive image when exposed to transparent film positives. Its exposed emulsion develops when placed in contact with a special liquid or gas (generally ammonia fumes). This paper has the advantage of relative dimensional stability because it is not moistened with water during development.

Instant Image Proof Paper

Instant image proof paper produces dry image proofs without processing equipment and chemicals. One example is Du Pont's Dylux papers, which are exposed with ultraviolet (UV) light and produce a visible image without chemical processing. The resulting proof can be fixed, or deactivated, by bright white light exposure. Typical exposure light sources are Sylvania BLB lamps, pulsed xenon with an ultraviolet filter, mercury vapor with a UV filter, or carbon arc with a UV filter. Dylux papers are coated on one or two sides, with either a blue or near-black image. The paper can be handled under normal room light for several minutes. Different colors can be proofed for fit by using different screen tint values to represent each color.

Diazo and instant image proofs can all be used to check imposition for jobs that involve image alignment on both sides of a press sheet. Most papers can be purchased from the manufacturer with both sides sensitized. The first flat to be proofed is positioned on the paper, small notches that line up with the center lines of the flat are cut—or the proofing material is punched with the same punch system used for flats—and an exposure is made. The proofing paper is then turned over, the center lines of the second flat are placed in line with the small notches, and the second exposure is made. Once processed, the proof can be folded or cut to approximate the final job. If paper that is sensitized on both sides is not available, two separate sheets can be glued together for the same effect.

Multiple-Color Photomechanical Proofing

It is possible to proof some types of multicolor jobs, such as jobs requiring spot color (see chapter 3), on a single-color photomechanical proofing material by varying the exposure time for each color. The intensity of the image recorded varies with exposure time. Thus, if each color is exposed with a different exposure time, each color records as a different shade. Similar effects can be achieved by using various screen tint values to expose each color on a single-color proofing material. Both of these techniques for showing color are acceptable for checking registration and the fit of one image with another. They are not widely used, however, because the customer usually prefers seeing proofs in color.

While registration and fit are important to the printer, the designer or customer is interested primarily in what the job will look like after printing. Thus, multicolor proofing is typically used to proof the job in color so the printer and the customer can predict how the colors, whether flat or process, will appear on the final press sheet. Therefore, the proofing system's ability to produce an image that is as close as possible to the image that will print on the final press sheet is important. A press proof can provide a nearly exact reproduction of the image that will print during the press run. But as this is time consuming and expensive, high-quality photomechanical proofs are most often used to represent the final image that will run on press. Photomechanical color proofing materials can be classified as either transparent or opaque based.

Transparent Color Proofs

Transparent color proofs are generally formed from separate sheets of clear-based plastic (each one carrying one color image). One product used for photomechanical color proofing is Colorkey,™ manufactured by Imation. The Imation Colorkey™ Negative Proof-

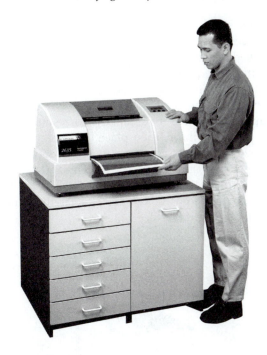

Figure 6.25 Example of a processing and laminating unit. This unit can do Matchprint™ single-sheet color proofs and Colorkey™ overlay proofs.

ing Films are factory coated with process ink pigment colors. For each color, the film must be exposed, processed, and mounted. During the exposure process, the color separation film is placed emulsion side down on the coated side of the Colorkey™ color sheet and exposed according to the exposure value determined for the magenta color layer. The film is then processed in a proofing processor using proofing developer (figure 6.25). The mounting sequence for the four-color process proof is yellow, magenta, cyan, and black. They are mounted in register, coated side up on a paper base with each sheet secured to the base with tape.

Opaque Color Proofs

Opaque color proofs are generally prepared by adhering, exposing, and developing each color emulsion on a special solid-based sheet successively. Imation produces a product called Matchprint™ Negative Color Proofing Films. The production steps involve laminating, exposing, and processing. The first color sheet is laminated, coated side down, to the appropriate base material. The corresponding separation film is then placed emulsion side down and exposed according to a predetermined exposure value. The Matchprint™ negative proof is then processed. Each color is laminated, exposed, and processed in the same manner (figure 6.26).

It is important that all color proofs be viewed under a common light source. Any variation in color temperature, light intensity, amount of reflected room light, evenness of illumination, or surrounding color environment changes human judgment concerning color values. Many problems result when the printer and the customer use two different light sources or viewing situations to view color proofs. In the industry, 5,000 K color temperature emitted from an artificial source is generally accepted as the standard for color viewing. Several companies have developed color viewing systems that meet the industry's specifications (figure 6.27).

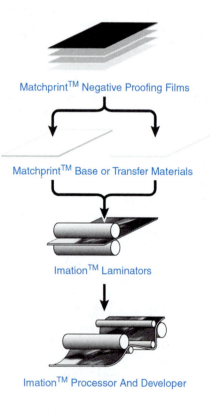

Matchprint™ Negative Proofing Films

Matchprint™ Base or Transfer Materials

Imation™ Laminators

Imation™ Processor And Developer

Figure 6.26 **Opaque proofing sequence.**
Courtesy of Imation.

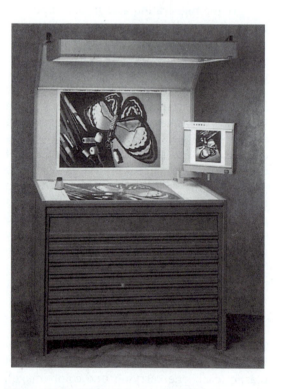

Figure 6.27 **Example of a color viewer.**
Courtesy of GTI Graphic Technology, Inc.

Section 2: Offset Platemaking

The preparation and printing of most modern metal plates used in lithographic printing is based on the original concepts of stone printing developed by Senefelder nearly two hundred years ago. Senefelder's invention was intended and used as an industrial process. Printers used this technique to reproduce images such as advertisements, business forms, maps, and many other printed products.

Lithography developed a reputation as a fine arts process in America through the products of the Currier and Ives Company that operated from 1835 to 1895. Today, stone lithography remains an art process. Historically it has formed the foundation for a major portion of the commercial printing industry. A brief review of the steps taken by a stone lithographer will help you better understand contemporary industrial techniques.

A slab of lithographic stone (generally limestone) is first cleaned and ground to a perfectly flat surface using a smaller stone and water mixed with carborundum. This process is called **graining**.

Once the stone is grained and dry, the artist-printer begins to draw on its surface with a lithographic grease crayon (a refinement of Senefelder's original correction fluid). This process forms the printing image. Graining creates a slight tooth, or texture, which makes it easier to draw on the stone with the grease crayon. The grease absorbs slightly into the pores of the stone.

A gum arabic solution (generally mixed with a small quantity of nitric acid), called an **etch**, is then worked into the entire stone surface. The gum absorbs into the nonimage areas of the stone and solidifies the grease, or image, areas in a process called etching. **Etching** seals the open parts (nonimage areas) of the stone against grease but keeps these open parts receptive to water. After the crayon residue is removed with turpentine, the stone is ready to print.

A roller of ink is prepared, and a layer of water is wiped on the stone with a damp cloth. The water is repelled by the grease crayon image areas, but it remains in the nonimage or open areas. As the ink roller moves over the stone, the film of water acts as a buffer that repels ink. Wherever there is no water (as on the crayon image), the ink remains.

If a prepared piece of paper is positioned carefully over the stone and pressure is applied, the image on the stone will be transferred to the sheet. A skillfull stone lithographer can prepare a stone and pull one print every ten minutes.

Contemporary printers do not print from lithographic stones. Rather than a litho stone, printers use thin aluminium plates. The basic concepts are the same, however, whether using a stone or plate. One important difference is that early lithographers had to create reversed images on the stone, since the paper came directly into contact with the stone surface. Reversing the image on the stone made it right reading on the paper. Modern lithography creates a right-reading image on the plate. On the press, the plate image is transferred to a blanket (which reverses or offsets it), which then transfers the image to the paper (reversing it again)—hence the term *offset lithography* (see chapter 12).

Equipment for Proofing and Plating

This section introduces the basic equipment used to prepare proofs and offset lithographic plates.

Exposure Systems

Most proofing materials and most offset plates contain photoemulsion surfaces that form images when exposed to light. During platemaking, light passing through a transparent image carrier, such as a film negative or a film positive, strikes the plate or proofing material emulsion. The areas of emulsion that are affected by the light become the image or the nonimage areas, depending upon the type of photoemulsion used on the proofing or plate material. Most proofing materials and offset plates can be exposed in the same type of exposure unit.

Whether exposure systems are used for platemaking, proofing, or daylight-handling film exposures, they are usually referred to as **platemakers**. The simplest exposure system is made up of a vacuum frame and some high-intensity light source. The vacuum frame holds the film or flat in contact with the proofing material, film, or plate; the light source provides the light needed for exposure. Some platemakers have the vacuum frame and light source set within a cabinet (figure 6.28). In other systems the frame and lights are on rolling stands that can be moved closer together or farther apart, or they can be used as an overhead light source.

Most proofing and plate photoemulsions have peak sensitivity in the blue and ultraviolet end of the visible spectrum and little sensitivity in the remaining areas of the spectrum. Light in the blue and ultraviolet end of the visible spectrum is referred to as *actinic light*. Because most proofing, daylight film, and plate photoemulsions are primarily sensitive to actinic light, they must be handled in a special environment. Most facilities use a yellow filter to block actinic light from normal illumination sources.

The most efficient light sources for exposing proofing materials and offset plates produce light that is high in the acitinic end of

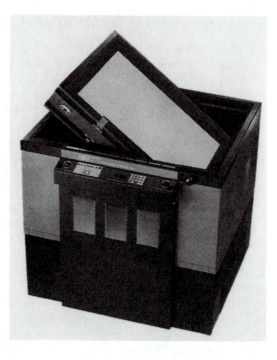

Figure 6.28 **A flip-top platemaker.**
Courtesy of nuArc Company, Inc.

the spectrum. The two most commonly used light sources for platemaking are metal halide and pulsed xenon. Carbon arc lamps are also sometimes used. However, carbon arc lamps emit fumes and dirt that must be removed from the plateroom with a ventilation system; this is a major disadvantage of carbon arc lamps.

Processing Systems

The equipment for processing printing plates varies. The simplest type of equipment is a smooth, slanted, hard surface set in a sink with a water source (figure 6.29). This type of equipment, called a **platemaking sink**, is generally used for hand processing lithographic plates, but it can also be used for developing several types of photomechanical proofs.

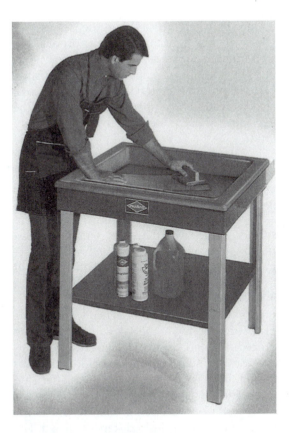

Figure 6.29   A platemaking sink.
Courtesy of nuArc Company, Inc.

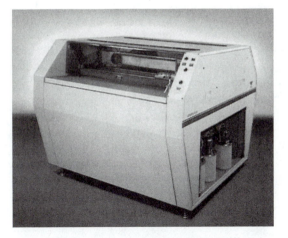

Figure 6.30   An automatic plate processing unit.
Courtesy of Western Litho Plate and Supply Company.

Most companies use automatic processing units that produce plates ready for press without any hand finishing (figure 6.30). Although the specific configuration varies from unit to unit, all automatic systems accept the exposed plate for insertion at one end; use automatic drive rollers for uniform feeding; and deliver a finished, gummed, and dried plate at the other end.

A variety of special purpose platemakers and processing units are designed for use with specific processes (such as an electrostatic platemaker for the electrostatic platemaking process).

Light Source Calibration

Exposure is the most important variable in the plating and proofing processes. The simplest form of platemaker control has a toggle switch that can be plugged into an automatic timer or controlled manually by an operator with a watch. The problem (as with line photography) is that accurate exposure is not necessarily related to time. Variables such as line voltage, light source position, and the age of the lamp can influence exposure. The most accurate tool for controlling exposure is a **light integrator** (figure 6.31). With a phototube sensing unit mounted on the platemaker vacuum frame, the integrator automatically controls the units of light reaching the plate or proof and alters exposure time with any line or light source variation. Such a system ensures that there is no more than a 0.5 percent difference in the amount of light that strikes the plate from any two exposures made at the same time setting.

Whether you use a simple toggle switch system or an integrated system, the initial

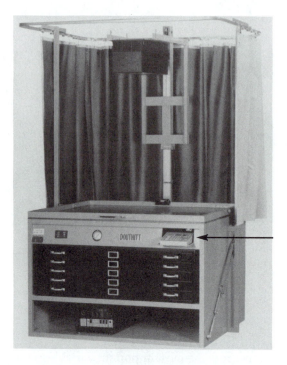

Figure 6.31 **Light integrator.** A light integrator mounted on the front of a console overhead platemaker.
Courtesy of Douthitt.

problem is to determine the quantity of exposure needed to produce a quality plate or proof image. Most plate or proofing material manufacturers provide recommended exposures for general lighting situations. However, the actual exposure differs for each working situation. To calibrate or to determine this actual exposure, you must use a transparent gray scale or sensitivity guide.

The Sensitivity Guide

The **sensitivity guide** is a continuous-tone density scale. (Remember it is a transparent gray scale.) The density of each step on the guide increases from around 0.0 density at step 1 to generally around 3.0 density at the last step. There is generally a 0.15 density dif-

ference between steps. The guide passes progressively less light to the plate or proof as the step numbers increase.

In addition to suggesting an exposure, plate or proofing material manufacturers will also indicate which specific step reading the exposure should record on the sensitivity guide.

To determine the actual exposure for a specific working situation, place a test sheet of the plate or proofing material in the platemaker, with the emulsion positioned as specified by the manufacturer. Place a sensitivity guide over the sheet with the right-reading side of the transparent gray scale facing the exposure lamp. Mask all other areas of the emulsion with a masking sheet. Make an initial exposure according to the manufacturer's recommendations. Then process the plate or proofing material with appropriate procedures and controls. If the resulting image shows a step reading that is less than required, increase the exposure. If a higher step is recorded, decrease the exposure and run another test. Continue using this trial-and-error technique until the desired step is reached. The exposure that produces the desired step density becomes the actual exposure for that specific material.

For greatest consistency of results, a sensitivity guide should be stripped into the flat in a nonimage area for every plate. Another alternative is to test the exposure with the guide daily. If variation occurs, either each processing step should be reexamined for any variation, or the entire system should be recalibrated. Of course, the test should be rerun every time a new type of plate material is used.

Lithographic Printing Plates

The basis of all industrial lithography today is a combination of photographic principles and Senefelder's original observation that oil and water do not mix. Almost all modern lithographic presses employ the offset principle and use a thin paper, plastic, or metal sheet as an image carrier, called a **plate**, which can be wrapped around the plate cylinder. When prepared for printing, the plate surface consists of two areas: image areas, which repel water (and thus remain dry and accept ink), and nonimage areas, which accept water. Therefore, the basic requirement of almost all lithographic printing plates is the ability to produce a plate surface that has *hydrophobic* image areas; that is, they repel water. The nonimage areas of the plate must be *hydrophilic*; that is, they must accept water. Offset plates differ largely in the methods they use to separate the image from the nonimage areas.

Base Plate Materials

The great majority of plates used in offset lithography are made of thin metal sheets. Metal plate thicknesses range from 0.005 inch to around 0.030 inch, depending on the size of the plate and the type of press. The entire plate must be of uniform thickness, however. It is generally held to a gauge tolerance of 0.0005 inch. Most metals for plates are cold rolled to the final plate gauge or thickness to produce a hard printing surface.

Zinc was the standard plate material of the industry for years, but it has been replaced almost totally by aluminum for all but special purpose plates. Some types of plates are made from materials such as steel, stainless steel, chromium, copper, and even paper, but aluminum enjoys the most widespread use.

Just as Senefelder had to prepare, or grain, the stone surface before an image could be added to it, modern lithographic plates must also be grained. The term *graining* is actually misleading because relatively little roughness is imparted to the surface. On metal surface printing plates, graining is a roughening process that must be performed so that a

uniform layer of photoemulsion will adhere to the plate. All graining processes can be classified as either mechanical or chemical.

Mechanical Graining

The simplest form of **mechanical graining** of the plate surface is accomplished by placing the plate in a rotating tub filled with steel ball bearings, water, and some form of abrasive material. Assembly-line techniques have been applied to the process so that a continuous row of plates passes under a series of nylon brushes with a spray of water and pumice. Sandblasting has also been used, but this procedure presents some problems because small pieces of abrasive become embedded in the metal plate surface.

Chemical Graining

Chemical graining of lithographic plates is similar to Senefelder's first trial acid etch of a piece of stone. The plate is submerged in an acid bath that creates surface roughness. One chemical graining technique uses an electrolytic reaction in a solution of hydrofluoric acid to create surface roughness on the plate. Almost all presensitized surface plates (see following sections) are formed from anodized aluminum. The surface is treated chemically and then sealed. The anodized surface is unaffected by almost all acids but remains water receptive.

Coating Materials

All photosensitive lithographic metal plates have a photoemulsion surface consisting of some form of light-sensitive material combined with a collodion coated on a grained metal surface. A **collodion** is an organic compound that forms a strong, continuous layer. When mixed with the light-sensitive solution and then exposed to light, the **colloid** or emulsion becomes insoluble and forms a strong, continuous coating on the printing plate. Gum arabic is a collodion commonly used in many emulsions. It is also used for a variety of other purposes in the lithographic process, such as in press fountain solution (see chapter 12) and as a protective coating over finished plates.

Ammonium bichromate combined with egg albumin was used previously as the photoemulsion in the photolithography process. Albumin has been replaced gradually by other solutions, however, until now it is very nearly obsolete. Popular industrial coatings today are polyvinyl alcohol (PVA), diazo, and photopolymers.

Classifying Lithographic Plates

Lithographic plates can be classified in several ways. The most common method is to group them according to structure and action.

Lithographic plate structure can be described as surface or deep etch. **Surface plates** can be visualized as being formed from a colloid sitting on the surface of the metal (figure 6.32). **Deep-etch plates** are formed when the colloid material bonds into the plate surface (figure 6.33). There are, of course, special purpose plates that defy classification.

A second way to classify lithographic plates is by action. Almost all industrial lithography uses the photographic process to produce the image area on the plate. Plate emulsions can be formulated for use with either film negatives or film positives. When the

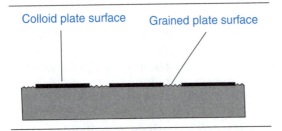

Figure 6.32   **Cross section of a lithographic surface plate**

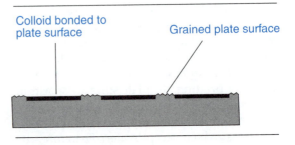

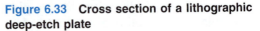

Figure 6.33   **Cross section of a lithographic deep-etch plate**

plate image is formed by passing light through the clear or image areas of a negative, the plate is called **negative working**. When a positive is used to expose the plate, the plate is called **positive working**. Plate action is not necessarily associated with plate structure, however. Surface plates can be designed for use with either film negatives or film positives, but only film positives can be used with deep-etch plates. For the purposes of our discussion, we will examine surface plates.

Surface Plates

Wipe-On Surface Plates

The **wipe-on metal surface plate** is a refinement of the early attempts to sensitize a lithographic stone with a photographic emulsion. To make this type of plate, an emulsion is hand or machine coated onto a pregrained plate immediately prior to plate exposure.

The base material in this process usually is either aluminum or zinc. All wipe-on surface plates are supplied to the printer with a fine-grain surface and are treated with a protective coating that acts as a link between the future emulsion coating and the base metal. The emulsion is generally mixed in small quantities shortly before it is applied to the pregrained plate. All current emulsions are formed by mixing a dry diazo powder and a liquid base.

There are two techniques for coating the light-sensitive emulsion onto a wipe-on surface plate: by hand or with a mechanical roller. With the hand process, the emulsion is applied with a damp sponge (or cheesecloth). The goal is to place a fairly uniform layer of emulsion over every portion of the plate surface.

The mechanical roller approach for wipe-on plates employs a dual roller device (figure 6.34). As the plate passes between the two rollers, a perfectly uniform layer of emulsion is distributed over one side of the plate. The gap between the rollers can be adjusted to ap-

ply the desired thickness of emulsion on the plates. There is no problem with coating consistency or streaking with this process, two major difficulties with the hand process.

Almost all lithographic plates now used for production are negative working (some positive working plates are currently used as image carriers for press proofing). Most wipe-on surface plates are exposed through a film negative, using a vacuum frame and a high-intensity light source. Specific exposure times vary according to the individual plate and emulsion combination and the working environment. Manufacturers' specifications should always be followed.

Wipe-on plates are processed by one of two methods. The first technique involves two steps. A pool of desensitizer gum is first poured onto the wipe-on plate and is rubbed into the entire plate surface with a damp sponge. The gum solution serves the dual function of removing any unexposed emulsion and making the nonprinting area water receptive. Any excess gum solution is removed. A second solution, made primarily of lacquer, is then rubbed over the entire plate. Finally, the plate is washed with water.

The image area of the wipe-on plate, which hardened during exposure, would theoretically accept ink and could be used on the printing press. However, adhering a layer of lacquer to the exposed areas of the wipe-on plate greatly increases the number of copies that can be made from the plate. The lacquer strengthens the image bond to the plate. With the two-step process, a final layer of desensitizer gum is generally buffed into the entire surface of the plate until it is dry. This last step serves to protect the plate until the job is run on the press and also ensures that all unexposed emulsion is removed.

The second alternative wipe-on processing technique involves one step in which a lacquer developer removes the unexposed emulsion while the lacquer adheres to the image

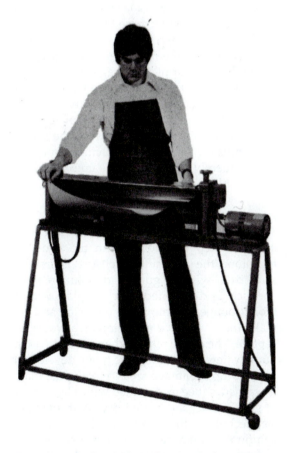

Figure 6.34 Coating a wipe-on surface plate with a mechanical roller.
Courtesy of Western Litho Plate and Supply Company

areas. After the plate is washed with water, it is buffed with a coating of gum arabic until its entire surface is dry.

Presensitized Surface Plates

Presensitized surface plates are by far the plates most widely used for commercial offset lithography. These plates are called presensitized because they are supplied from the manufacturer with the emulsion surface already coated on the metal base. The first presensitized metal plates were introduced by the 3M Company in 1950. Since that time, many other manufacturers have developed similar plates.

Presensitized plates offer several advantages. Because they are precoated with a photoemulsion, the platemaker need not be concerned with mixing and wiping on the emulsion, or using and maintaining emulsion-coating equipment. Presensitized plates are used by the platemaker directly from the manufacturer's wrapper with no surface preparation. In addition, the plates are processed with ease, have reasonably long shelf lives (generally up to six months), and can be produced for high-quality, long-run press situations.

The base material for presensitized plates can be paper, aluminum foil laminated to paper, or a sheet of aluminum. Paper and foil plates are generally used only for very shortrun jobs. As discussed previously, the presensitized metal plates are typically grained and then anodized. Aluminum plates can be sensitized on one or both sides.

Almost all presensitized emulsion-coating materials used today contain diazo. The specific makeup of the solution varies from manufacturer to manufacturer, but the primary ingredient of all solution types is nitrogen. When the plate emulsion is exposed to a sufficient quantity of light, the nitrogen is released from the solution and the material becomes insensitive to additional light. The insensitive emulsion then can readily accept dyes that become the printing, ink-receptive surfaces.

Presensitized plates are available in a wide range of capabilities, from plates that handle short runs of less than 1000 copies to emulsions that can easily produce as many as 300,000 impressions. With their anodized metal surfaces, diazo emulsions, and mass production techniques, presensitized plates compete easily in quality and cost with other types of surface plates.

In addition to being either negative or positive working, presensitized plates can also be classified as additive or subtractive. Recall that for wipe-on plates a lacquer is adhered to the image areas to increase the plate's potential life. The lacquer, then, is the surface that actually accepts the ink. The same concept is used when preparing the image areas for presensitized plates. When the printer applies a lacquerlike material to the image areas during plate processing, the presensitized plate is **additive**. When the printing surface is built into the emulsion by the manufacturer and the printer merely desensitizes the unexposed areas, the plate is **subtractive**.

Processing Additive Plates

Additive plates can be processed with a two- or a one-step technique. With the two-step technique, the plate, after exposure, is first desensitized with a gum–acid solution. The chemical is distributed over the plate with a moist sponge to remove the emulsion and/or make the unexposed emulsion area water receptive. The entire plate is then rubbed with a gum–water–lacquer mixture (plate developer) to build up the image areas. Finally, the plate is washed, squeegeed, coated with a light layer of gum arabic, and buffed dry. With the one-step technique, the desensitizer (the gum–acid solution) and lacquer–developer functions are combined. The plate is developed with that single solution and is then washed, squeegeed, gummed, and buffed dry.

Processing Subtractive Plates

Negative-working presensitized emulsions are exposed by light passing through the open or image areas of a film negative. With negative-working subtractive plates, only one developing step is taken. After exposure, a special developer that is supplied by the plate manufacturer is used to remove the unexposed lacquer emulsion that was added during the presensitizing process. Again, the plate is washed and squeegeed. Often, a special subtractive gum must be used to coat and protect the plate for storage.

Positive-working presensitized plates are exposed by light passing through the open or nonimage areas of a film positive. As mentioned earlier, positive-working presensitized plates can be classified as either additive or subtractive. In general, after exposure, the exposed emulsion of a positive-working additive plate is removed by wiping it with a special developer supplied by the manufacturer. The unexposed or image area remains in place. The developing action is then halted by a fixing agent. As with negative-working additive plates, lacquer is rubbed into the positive-working plate. The lacquer adheres to the image areas and increases the potential length of the press run. After the plate is washed and squeegeed, it is coated with gum arabic and buffed dry. Positive-working subtractive plates are processed in a similar manner, but without the lacquer step.

Presensitized Photopolymer Surface Plates

One disadvantage of presensitized surface plates that have diazo emulsions is that they cannot be used for extremely long press runs. Until the development of presensitized **pho-** **topolymer plates**, only deep-etch or bimetal plates (bimetal plates are no longer popular and are not discussed in this chapter) could be used for offset press runs of a million or more copies. When exposed and processed properly, photopolymer emulsions on presensitized plates produce image areas that are extremely hard and wear resistant, which means that they can be used for press runs that are much longer than plates with diazo emulsions. At the same time, the exposure and development process for photopolymer emulsions is far less involved and less time consuming than that for deep-etch or bimetal plates.

Negative-working photopolymer emulsions consist of molecules called **monomers**. When exposed to actinic light, these monomers link and cross-link with each other chemically to form polymers. **Polymers** can be thought of as complex chains of monomers that are linked so strongly that they behave as one hard, wear-resistant molecule. Photopolymer plates are developed in a manner similar to presensitized diazo emulsion plates. The developer removes the unexposed plate coating but leaves the exposed coating (image area) on the plate.

Positive-working photopolymer plates can be baked in large ovens for a specific time, at a specific temperature. The baking firmly adheres the image to the plate surface, as well as adheres a special baking gum to the nonimage portions of the plate. Plate life of more than one million impressions is possible. Newer, negative-working photopolymer plates are now available that reach this plate life without the need for baking.

In chapters 10 and 15, we will examine other types of platemaking systems, along with computer-to-plate technology.

Key Terms

stripping
flat
proofing
masking sheets
actinic light
opaque
imposition
signature imposition
work-and-turn imposition
lead edge
work-and-tumble imposition
cylinder line
plate cylinder
gripper margin
pinholes
complementary flats
blueline flat method

single-master flat method
sighting tube
press proof
photomechanical proofs
diazo paper
instant image proof paper
transparent color proofs
opaque color proofs
lithography
graining
etch
etching
platemaker
platemaking sink
light integrator
sensitivity guide
plate

mechanical graining
chemical graining
collodion
colloid
surface plate
deep-etch plate
negative working
positive working
wipe-on metal surface plate
presensitized surface plate
additive
subtractive
photopolymer plate
monomer
polymer

Review Questions

1. What is the purpose of the masking sheet when preparing a negative flat?

2. What does the term *imposition* mean?

3. What is a signature?

4. Why should no image be printed in the gripper margin?

5. What is the purpose of opaquing a film negative?

6. What are complementary flats?

7. Explain the total system approach of the punch and register pin method.

8. What are the two basic approaches of multiflat stripping for process color work?

9. What is the purpose of proofing?

10. What are the two common types of single-color photomechanical proofing?

11. What are the two basic types of multicolor photomechanical proofs?

12. What is meant by actinic light?

13. What is the purpose of lithographic plate graining?

14. What is the difference between a negative-working plate and a positive-working plate?

15. How do presensitized surface plates differ from wipe-on plates? What are the advantages of presensitized plates?

16. Discuss the main advantages of a presensitized photopolymer surface plate.

7

Working with Digital Data

Historical Background

In 1943, World War II raged across Europe, and United States troops, tanks, and artillery were deployed overseas. Back home, a civilian army of female mathematicians (called "computers") at the Aberdeen Proving Ground in Maryland and the University of Pennsylvania worked furiously to prepare firing tables for the artillery.

The enormity of the task was quickly apparent. The tables were critical, but extremely time consuming because it took a month to prepare the trajectories for firing different artillery according to variables such as wind speed, elevation, humidity, temperature, and shell size. Factories built artillery faster than the tables could be computed, but without the tables the weapons were useless. The military needed a machine that was faster than the people who actually did the computing.

In April 1943, the Army turned to two scholars at the University of Pennsylvania's Moore School of Electrical Engineering: John Mauchly and Presper Eckert. The pair had been working on an idea for an electronic adding machine. Their device was called the Electronic Numerical Integrator and Computer, ENIAC, the world's first electronic digital computer. Presper, Mauchly, and their entire team invested 200,000 worker-hours on the $486,804.22 project, working around the clock seven days a week. Presper, a graduate student, was the chief engineer

for the project, while Mauchly, a faculty member, served as a project consultant. The two men assembled a team of 12 engineers, including Lieutenant Herman H. Goldstine, a Reserve officer of the Ordnance Department and an accomplished mathematician, who was assigned the duty of supervisor of the computational and training activities at the University of Pennsylvania. Six women were chosen from the "computers" to program the machine, a daunting task given its complexity and the lack of instructions.

By the fall of 1945, ENIAC was finally ready for service, but by then the war had ended. The final product was massive. ENIAC weighed 30 tons, occupied 1,800 square feet, and required 174 kilowatts of power to operate. It contained 17,468 vacuum tubes, 70,000 resistors, and 10,000 capacitors. When ENIAC was finally presented to the public in a news conference on February 14, 1946, the press was amazed. ENIAC could perform 5,000 additions, 357 multiplications, or 38 divisions in one second. Trajectory calculations that took humans 20 hours to compute by hand could be done in 30 seconds by ENIAC.

The machine was disassembled and moved from the University of Pennsylvania to the Aberdeen Proving Grounds, where it spent eight years calculating firing tables, assisting

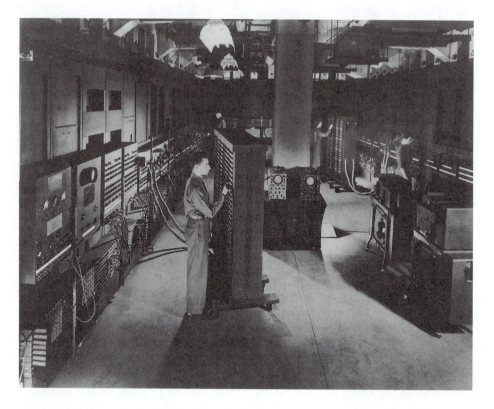

ENIAC, 1946.
Courtesy of University of Pennsylvania.

scientists developing the hydrogen bomb, and solving equations used in wind tunnel design and atomic energy problems. Eventually, the ENIAC became too costly to operate as newer, faster, and less expensive computers were developed. Its operations were shifted to the other machines, and at 11:45 P.M. on October 2, 1955, the power to ENIAC was removed.

Objectives

After completing this chapter you will be able to:

- Define digital data.
- List the basic unit sizes of digital data.
- Define hardware and software.
- Identify the different components of a computer.

- Discuss factors that determine a computer's capability.
- Define the two types of processors in use today.
- Define LAN and WAN networks.
- Discuss the way in which data are transmitted over a network.

■ Define basic network topologies and connective media.

■ Define network technology and discuss its most widely used implementation, Ethernet.

■ Discuss analog and digital telecommunication methods.

■ Differentiate between primary, removable, and backup storage solutions.

Introduction

The digital revolution has become the digital standard. Traditional hand methods of preparing images—whether type, line drawings, or continuous-tone images—have been almost completely replaced by digital technology. Understanding the digital infrastructure as it relates to printing and publishing is a fundamental necessity.

The computer used as a prepress tool has moved far beyond basic typesetting. It can generate, manipulate, edit, and output nearly any form of monochrome or color image; be used to assemble full pages of type and graphic images; separate complex images into primary colors; scan and digitize type and images prepared by hand; and receive information from telephone lines, cable, and satellite. Content can be sent to equipment in the same facility or across the world and be published as reflective copy on the Internet or on multimedia CD-ROMs. The computer can track work in progress, compile work standards, and deliver data that were impossible to gather and monitor even a decade ago.

This book is not intended to provide details on the operation of any specific system or device. Manufacturers can supply detailed operating procedures for their equipment. The goal of this chapter is to provide a basic understanding of the digital components that comprise the digital infrastructure of a modern printing facility. Understanding these components will allow a full appreciation of the critical concept of digital workflow, which will be discussed in greater depth in chapters 8, 9, and 10.

The Concept of Digital Information

A computer accepts data and stores them, and software allows the data to be manipulated into a message or information that is understandable to humans. To understand the process of converting information into digital data (covered in chapter 8), we first need a basic understanding of what **digital data** are (figure 7.1).

All data entered into a computer by the operator and each instruction entered by the software are converted to **alphanumeric code** and stored as numbers. In a computer, all data are based on the current state of electrical switches. The switch is either on or off, represented by 0 or 1. Using only these two symbols, computers are said to be operating in base 2, or in **the binary system** (figure 7.2).

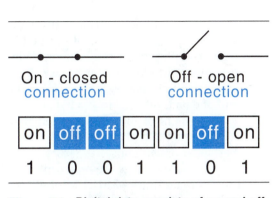

Figure 7.1 **Digital data consists of on and off bits**

Binary Code

	64	32	16	8	4	2	1
1							1
2						1	0
3						1	1
4					1	0	0
5					1	0	1
6					1	1	0
7					1	1	1
8				1	0	0	0
9				1	0	0	1
10				1	0	1	0
20			1	0	1	0	0
50		1	1	0	0	1	0
100	1	1	0	0	1	0	0
127	1	1	1	1	1	1	1
	64	32	16	8	4	2	1
Read From Right							

Figure 7.2   Binary code

Everything you see represented on the monitor is comprised of a series of 1's and 0's, with a switch either on or off. Each on or off switch is referred to as a bit, or **binary digit.** This is the smallest possible unit of data. The next unit of data is referred to as a **byte** (8 bits) and is the amount of information needed to make up a single **alphanumeric character** (number, letter or symbol).

Memory and storage are represented by multiples of bytes (figure 7.3). A **kilobyte** (K) is 1024 bytes, a **megabyte** (MB) is 1024 K (or over a million bytes), and a **gigabyte** is 1024

bit	smallest unit
byte	8 bits
kilobyte	1024 bytes
megabyte	1,048,576 bytes
gigabyte	1,073,741,824 bytes
terabyte	1,000 gigabytes
petabyte	1,000 terabytes

Figure 7.3   File sizes

MB (or over a billion bytes). Typical computer storage drives today can range from 2 GB to over 20 GB, with special storage systems running into the **terabyte** range (1024 GB, or over a trillion bytes) (figure 7.4).

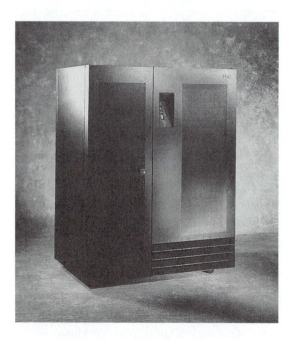

Figure 7.4   Terabyte storage system.
Courtesy of IBM.

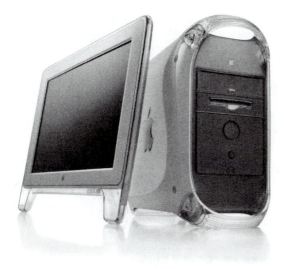

Figure 7.5 **CPU and monitor.**
Courtesy of Mark Laita Photography & Apple Computer, Inc.

Computer Basics

A computer is an electronic device whose function is to process data. To understand how computers operate requires an understanding of hardware and software. **Hardware** (figure 7.5) refers to the physical apparatus, such as the wires, computer, mouse, and hard drive. **Software** is the set of instructions that enables a computer to perform its tasks.

Hardware Terminology
Logic Board

The heart of the computer is the **logic board** (figure 7.6), sometimes referred to as the *motherboard.* The logic board contains the central processing unit (CPU), a system clock, input and output connections, memory, and a feed line from the power supply. It can also have accelerator cards, video, and network cards connected to it.

The Central Processing Unit

The **central processing unit,** or CPU, is essentially the brain of the computer. It is contained in the microprocessor (figure 7.7) and consists of two basic parts: the **control unit,** which manages the computers resources, and the **arithmetic logic unit,** which carries out mathematical operations. The rate at which the CPU processes data plays a significant part in determining the cost of the computer and the computer's ability to process the large graphic files used in the printing and publishing industry.

Power Macintosh G4 (PCI Graphics) Logic Board Diagram

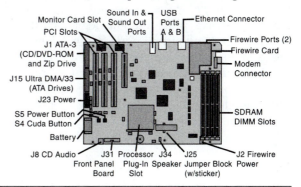

Figure 7.6 **Computer logic board diagram.**
Courtesy of Apple Computer, Inc.

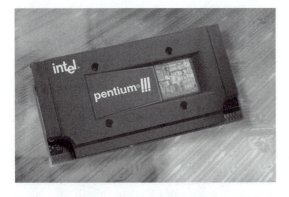

Figure 7.7 Computer microprocessor
Courtesy of Intel Corporation.

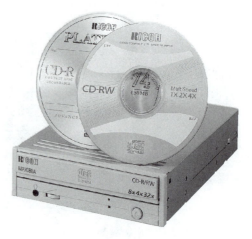

Figure 7.8 CD-RW Burner. This unit allows you, with the correct media, to make rewritable CDs.
Courtesy of Ricoh Company, Ltd.

System Clock

Every computer has a **system clock** driven by a quartz crystal. Electricity causes the crystal to vibrate at several million beats per second, with the vibrations determining the speed at which the computer can process information. This speed is measured in **hertz** (Hz), which is a measure of cycles per second; cycles are the time it takes to turn a transistor off and back on again. Megahertz (MHz) means millions of cycles, and today speeds of 600 to 800 MHz are common. Every action of the computer, such as booting up, reading memory, loading programs, and checking input and output ports, is coordinated by the speed of the quartz clock.

Input and Output Ports

External devices plug into the logic board through input and output ports (I/O). A keyboard, mouse, and digital camera are examples of **input devices.** A monitor, printer, and CD-ROM burner are **output devices** (figure 7.8). A modem, an external disk drive or a removable media drive, can also input data to and receive data from the logic board.

Memory

Memory chips are placed in the logic board to store instructions and data. There are two ba-

sic kinds of memory: **read-only memory (ROM)** and **random-access memory (RAM).**

Read-only memory chips hold permanently written instructions. These instructions are accessed by the microprocessor upon start-up and prepare the computer for use. ROM chips retain their contents even when the power is turned off. Random-access memory stores data as you use the computer system. RAM is the computer's main memory; it stores data as long as the microprocessor needs them. As new data enter RAM memory locations, old data are eliminated. This exchange of data slows the computer's processing, however. Processing speed can be increased by installing large amounts of RAM, which allows more application and project data to reside in active memory, and by increasing the amount of cache memory. **Cache memory,** in the form of additional chips connected to the logic board, works by storing a copy of data read from RAM, thereby making these data more readily available the next time the memory is accessed. Instead of having to load program

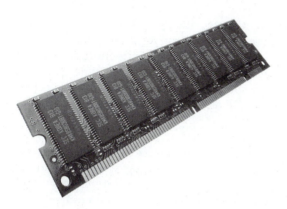

Figure 7.9 **Dual in-line memory module.**
Courtesy of NewerRam.

instructions for data into RAM every time they are needed, the CPU first checks to see if the data are already in cache memory. This allows more application and project data to reside in active memory. To add memory (figure 7.9) to the logic board, you need to install **single in-line memory modules (SIMMs)** or **dual in-line memory modules (DIMMs).** The size and speed of the chips needed depend on the complexity of the work to be done, but in general a production workstation has at least 250 MB of RAM. A single DIMM can range from 16 MB to 256 MB, with a high-end workstation capable of addressing 1 gigabyte or more of memory.

Computers with limited RAM can use a technique called **virtual memory** (Apple) or **swap file** (PC). Virtual memory divides programs and data into segments, which are stored on disk and loaded into memory when needed. This technique requires that the start-up or default (scratch) drive have adequate open space. Using virtual memory is not as productive as using RAM. On a PC, the swap files function lets you use a disk file as an extension of the main memory, but the process is managed by the system software, not by the user as on an Apple computer.

The Power Supply

The **power supply** is not on the logic board, but it is very important because it converts alternating current from the plug in the wall to the direct-current voltages needed to run a computer's system board. Because the current coming from the plug in the wall can fluctuate and damage the logic board, it is important to connect the logic board to a voltage stabilizer.

Classifying Computers

Several types of computers are available for prepress applications. Traditionally, they have been categorized as mainframe computers, minicomputers, and microcomputers, or PCs. Although these classifications still exist, the definition of each type of computer is constantly changing. A **supercomputer** is considered the most powerful computer made; it is mainly utilized in mission-critical applications and operations that need a vast amount of computational power (figure 7.10). A **main-**

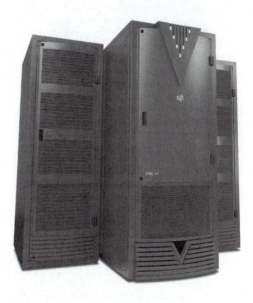

Figure 7.10 **Supercomputer.**
Courtesy of Cray, Inc.

frame computer has traditionally been the largest commonly used computer that is capable of handling large amounts of software and data. It can accommodate large numbers of users simultaneously and consists of the mainframe itself, with users being connected by terminals. It is not a common configuration in prepress and printing production and is more likely to be found in the administrative part of a large company. A **minicomputer** is slower than a mainframe, but faster and able to handle a heavier load than a microcomputer or PC. It can be designed for a single user or can handle hundreds of terminals. The **microcomputer** has evolved rapidly from a simple desktop computer to a more powerful machine capable of doing very high end tasks when compared to minicomputers of a few years ago. **Workstations** (figure 7.11), one type of microprocessor being used today in the

graphic arts industry, have extremely fast processors (and can have more than one), are networked, and are able to **multitask,** or handle more than one task at a time. They can function as individual stations or as a server. (We will discuss client–server networks later.)

Computer Capability

A computer's processing speed depends on the power of its microprocessors and the orchestration of its electronic components. Microprocessors are being produced with more power than ever imagined. They are rated by three factors: the amount of memory (RAM) that their chips can control, work length or bits of information that they can handle, and how fast they can process data (clock speed), expressed as millions of cycles per second (megahertz or MHz).

The two types of microprocessors used in the graphic production environments are the **complex instruction set computing (CISC)** processors and the **reduced instruction set computing (RISC)** processors. The CISC processors found in the older Motorola 680×0 and Intel 80×86 families can handle instruction sets typically containing 200 to 300 instructions at a time. The move to RISC processors was based on the design theory that a smaller and simpler CPU can process more instructions during a given time period. RISC technology is found in many midsized computers, such as the IBM RS/6000 and high-end UNIX machines like those built by Sun Microsystems (figure 7.12). Apple computer also utilizes this technology in its PowerPc's and G series processors.

As the quest for speed continues, microprocessors will continue to improve and become faster. In the mid-1990s, a processor running at 80 MHz was considered powerful and fast. As of this writing, systems of 400 and 500 MHz are commonly used, even in the home. Systems running at 1 GHz have been an-

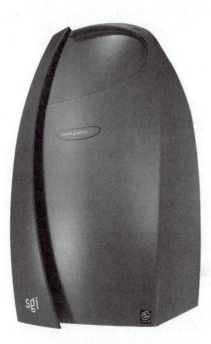

Figure 7.11 **High-end workstation.**
Courtesy of Silicon Graphics, Inc.

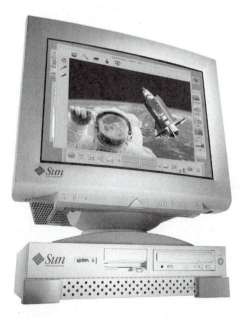

Figure 7.12 **UNIX computer utilizing RISC technology.**
Courtesy of Sun Microsystems.

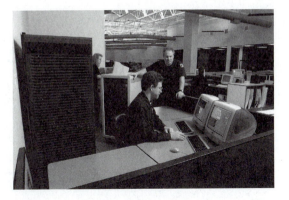

Figure 7.13 **Digital prepress environment.**
Courtesy of Quad/Graphics.

nounced by the major chip manufacturers and are available for commercial use. This is extremely important to the graphics arts industry, because processing speed is critical to digital imaging technology and a profitable workflow.

Moving and Storing Data

As digital prepress becomes more sophisticated and images become more complex, file sizes continue to grow. The cover of a magazine can run up to 150 MB, with the entire job topping 20 GB. Moving these files from computer to computer, storing them, transmitting them to various output devices, and sending them to distant locations by numerous transmission technologies are key concerns in today's world of printing and publishing (figure 7.13).

Networking

A network is a system of interconnected devices that can communicate with each other and share hardware and software resources. There are two types of networks: **local area networks (LAN)** and **wide area networks (WAN).** A LAN (figure 7.14) typically is made up of connected devices in relatively close proximity, such as a prepress production room. When two or more LANs connect across a wide geographical area, they are referred to as a WAN (figure 7.15).

The **network** is the backbone of a successful digital workflow. It is the infrastructure that allows for transmission of data for databasing, archiving, editing, outputting, and transmitting to other locations. An understanding of how a network is configured and how data are transmitted allows for more informed choices when designing the most effective workflow configuration for a prepress or printing facility.

Transmitting Data

Networks transmit data in the form of packets governed by a specific network protocol. **Packets** (figure 7.16) are an assemblage of bits consisting of a **header** (information about the

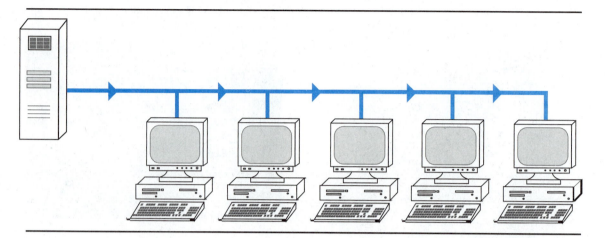

Figure 7.14 Local area network

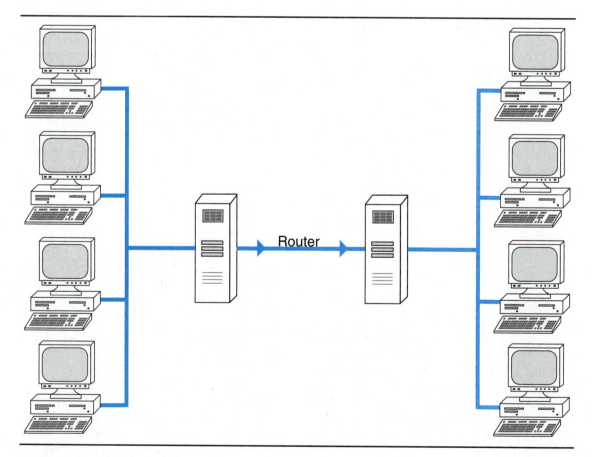

Router

Figure 7.15 Wide area network

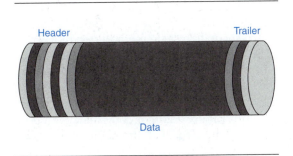

Header   Trailer

Data

Figure 7.16 Components of a packet

source address and destination address), **data** (the actual data being transmitted), and **control elements** or **trailer** (the error-checking component to ensure integrity of the data when they reach their destination). This process of breaking a message into packets for transmission on a network and then reassembling the data at their destination is referred to as **packet switching.**

Each LAN is governed by a specific **protocol,** the rules and formats that detail the method by which data are sent and received. The most common protocol in use today is **TCP/IP** (Transmission Control Protocol/Internet Protocol). This protocol is used to define packet switching on the Internet and is also the most common protocol used in the graphic arts industry.

Topology

There are three basic **topologies,** or the physical layouts of cables, that connect the components of a network: bus, ring, and star. Each computer on the network is referred to as a **node,** and output and input devices are considered **peripherals.** There are advantages and disadvantages to each topology depending on the purpose of your network and on the issues of cabling, distance, and efficiency of transmission to be considered.

The **bus topology** (figure 7.17) connects all terminals and peripherals to a single back-

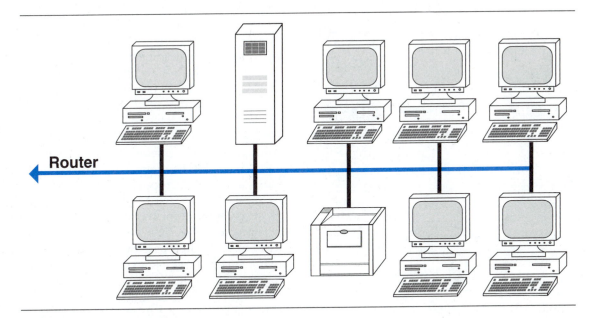

Router

Figure 7.17 Bus topology

bone. Data transmitted are sent along this backbone, with each node checking to see if the destination and node address match. If the address does not match, the data continue along the bus until the destination and node address match. Although this a common configuration, one weakness is the potential for **data collision** if two nodes transmit simultaneously. This can be corrected with extra software and circuitry, but transmission speeds can slow down appreciably on a bus network if each node has to continue retransmitting data to achieve successful delivery. Another weakness is that all or part of the network can crash if there is a broken connection.

The **ring topology** (figure 7.18) connects the nodes in a circular fashion. Data pass from one node to the next, with each computer acting as a repeater to boost the signal and send

it on. There are no collisions on this type of network, but the failure of one node can bring down the whole system if additional override features are not installed.

The **star topology** (figure 7.19) is perhaps the most common in a prepress and printing production environment. It consists of a central **hub** (figure 7.20), or central switching location, connected to all the nodes and peripherals on the network. All data are routed through the hub on the way to their destination. This configuration offers the advantages of centralized resources and management. If one connection is broken, the network remains operational (unless the hub itself goes down). It is a common topology for a client–server network, which describes a **hierarchical network** strategy in which the server provides services to the node, or end user, such as storage, processing, and printing.

Network Operating System

The **network operating system (NOS)** provides management for resources on a network. It allows for protection of information by maintaining passwords and authentication procedures, managing the network users, and tracking and monitoring statistical data to improve the production facility's workflow. The most common NOSs used in the graphic arts industry are Windows NT, Novell, and UNIX.

Network Media and Technology

All networks need media to link their nodes and servers. Media refer to the actual cabling, wires, and other methods by which data travel from one piece of hardware to the next. The most common types of media today are twisted-pair cable, fiber-optic cable, and wireless links. **Twisted-pair cable** is made up of two insulated strands of copper wire twisted together. To shield it from outside electromagnetic interference, it is incased in a metal shield and is referred to as **shielded twisted-**

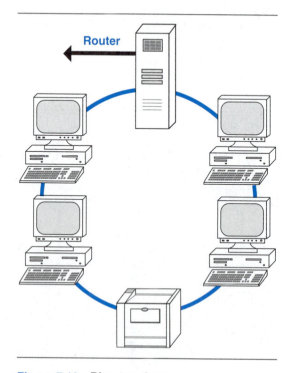

Figure 7.18   **Ring topology**

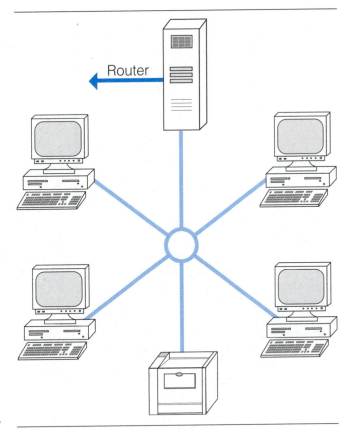

Router

Figure 7.19 **Star topology**

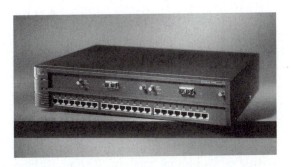

Figure 7.20 **Example of an Ethernet hub.** This is a 24-port 10/100 BaseT hub.
Courtesy of Cisco Systems, Inc.

pair cable (STP). It is the most common form of cabling within a LAN. **Fiber-optic cable** is made of pure glass and is resistant to electromagnetic interference. It transmits light, rather than electrical frequencies, and can carry data as fast as 1,300 Mbps (millions of bits per second). It is more expensive and difficult to install than twisted-pair and is most often used to connect WANs, whether across the street or the country. It is frequently used in the communications industry where large amounts of information such as digital video and voice data must be transmitted at high speeds. **Wireless networks** (figure 7.21) offer obvious advantages as far as flexibility of network layout, but they are not that widely used in prepress

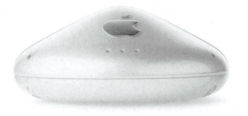

Figure 7.21   A wireless hub for networking.
Courtesy of Mark Laita Photography & Apple Computer, Inc.

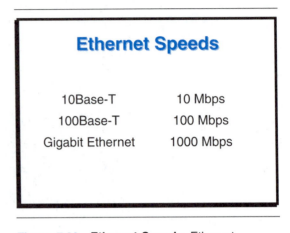

Figure 7.22   Ethernet Speeds. Ethernet technology can achieve speeds up to 1,000 Mbps (megabits per second).

and printing production due to distance limitations, interference issues (from ambient light and structures intersecting the line of sight), and relatively low transmission speeds.

Network technology refers to the transmission method being utilized. The most popular one is **Ethernet,** originally developed by Xerox and standardized in 1980. It is widely used in the star topology with twisted-pair cabling. To avoid the problems of data collision inherent in the Ethernet standard, **CSMA/CD** (carrier sense multiple access/collision detection) is employed. This allows for two nodes on a network to detect if they are both transmitting simultaneously and to retransmit their data one at a time. This can often result in delays or the slowing down of a very busy network.

The most widely used implementation of Ethernet is called **10Base-T.** The number 10 stands for a transmission rate of 10 megabits per second. Base indicates baseband transmission, which carries one signal per cable, as opposed to **broadband transmission,** which carries multiple signals per cable. The T refers to twisted-pair telephone wiring, which is limited to a distance of about 100 meters. With additional network cards installed in a workstation, **Fast Ethernet,** or **100Base-T** can be employed. This allows for speeds up to 100 Mbps and is becoming the standard in pro-

duction environments. With the development of **Gigabit Ethernet** in 1998, Ethernet network technology can now scale to transmit as fast as 1000Mbps, or 1 gigabit per second (figure 7.22).

As production environments upgrade existing equipment and connections, most will be compelled to upgrade their transmission technology in the pursuit of faster turnaround and efficient workflow.

Telecommunications
Analog
A computer's digital signal must be converted to an analog signal before it can be transmitted over a traditional phone line. This requires the use of a **modem,** which **modulates** a signal (converts to analog) and **demodulates** a signal (converts to digital) (figure 7.23). Speeds of 56 Kbps (kilobits per second) are attainable with a conventional modem. Although these types of modems are still used in the home and were once prevalent in the graphic arts industry as the initial way that files were trans-

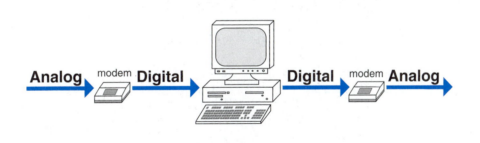

Figure 7.23 **Modulation and demodulation.** Information traveling from a modem (analog) to a computer (digital) and back.

mitted from one location to another, the average size of graphic files today precludes the use of modems in commercial settings.

Digital

Many different types of digital transmission are available today. The most widely used services are ISDN, DSL, T-1, and T-3 (figure 7.24). These services, all offered by the phone company, provide varying speeds of transmission and are chosen according to data transfer needs and budget.

Integrated Services Digital Network (ISDN) is a set of standards for digital transmission of data over analog phone lines. There are two standards: Basic Rate Interface (BRI) and Primary Rate Interface (PRI), which can transmit from 128 Kbps to 1.544 Mbps, respectively. Data are transmitted over regular phone lines, and each end of the connection must have an ISDN adapter installed.

Digital Subscriber Line (DSL) uses advanced technology to transmit a higher number of bytes than ISDN over standard twisted-pair cable (figure 7.25). One version, **Asymmetric Digital Subscriber Line (ADSL),** supports faster transmission rates when downloading than uploading. This is more applicable to personal use than industry, where fast rates are needed in both directions.

T-carrier lines (commonly known as T-1 or T-3) carry multiple signals over a single digital communication line utilizing a technique called multiplexing. A **T-1 line** can carry 24 separate signals at a speed of 1.544 Mbps. A **T-3 line** is the equivalent of 28 T-1 lines and can transmit data as fast at 44.736 Mbps. T-1 lines are most frequently used in medium and large organizations. The Internet **backbone,** or high-speed network that connects **Internet Service Providers (ISPs)** and regional and local networks to the Internet, utilizes T-3 lines.

Broadband packet-switching services are also used by businesses to move files at transmission rates above 1.544 Mbps. This method of transmission sends information over separate inbound and outbound channels that can transmit television, data, voice, and other services simultaneously. These services include Frame Relay and ATM (Asynchronous Transfer Mode) and are offered by most major telecommunications carriers.

Carrier Technology	Rate	Description
OC-1	51.8 Mbps	Optical Fiber carrier
T-3	44.7 Mbps	Twisted pair copper wire - Typically used to connect an ISP or large companies to the Internet backbone.
Cable	512 Kbps to 52 Mbps	Coaxial Cable for downstream transfers with phone lines for upstream data transfers
T-1	1.54 Mbps	Twisted pair copper wire - Typically used to connect an ISP or large companies to the Internet backbone.
DSL	512 Kbps to 8 Mbps	Digital Subscriber Line (digital twisted pair)
Satellite	400 Kbps	Radio frequency in space (wireless)
ISDN	64 Kbps to 128 Kbps	BRI (twisted pair for home and small business use) PRI (T-1 line for medium to large companies)

Figure 7.24   Digital telecommunication methods

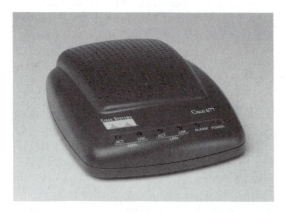

Figure 7.25   DSL modem.
Courtesy of Cisco Systems, Inc.

Storage

Storing data is a major concern of printers and publishers and those who create content. For the content creator, issues of spooling space become paramount when working with large image files (this will be discussed in more detail in Chapter 9). For the production facility, data handling and storage are important issues in terms of workflow and even profitability because these relate to fast retrieval of customer files. A complete digital file for a 64-page four-color publication can be as large as 15 or 20 GB.

In addition to being concerned about proper and adequate storage, printers and publishers are concerned about the possibility of losing or damaging files and realize that they need to back up all work. They also realize it is important to be able to move or transport large amounts of data from site to site or from workstation to workstation when networking or telecommunication is not practical or possible.

To simplify the discussion of storing digital information, we will assume that there are three basic types of storage devices: primary, removable, and backup.

Primary Storage Device

A **primary storage device** is the hard drive traditionally purchased with the CPU; it contains the system folder, applications, and all other resources necessary for daily production. It also houses online production work during assembly, so it is best to purchase the largest you can afford, since there never seems to be enough storage space for project work. A hard disk drive is referred to as **magnetic storage** because it records data in magnetic fields. It consists of a series of same-sized metal **platters** that spin on one spindle. They are sealed in a vacuum chamber and made from a rigid metal (usually aluminum) that allows for very fast spin speeds. The most common platter size for production PCs is 5.25 inches, with capacities typically from 6 GB up to 40 GB. Laptop drives can run as small as 2.5 inches; the MicroDrive by IBM, which is the size of a matchbook, has the capacity to hold 1 GB of data (figure 7.26).

Removable Storage Devices

The media used in **removable storage devices** (figure 7.27) allow for transportation of files when there are no connecting physical networks. These devices are an easy and economical way for customers to deliver files to a prepress or printing facility and allow for transportation of data in production when it is not economical to add an additional transmission burden to the existing network. Some

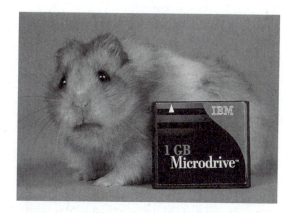

Figure 7.26 Micro drive. Small media with a very large capacity.
Courtesy of IBM.

types of removable media also play a part in backup strategies, which we will discuss in the next section.

The main types of removable media used in removable drives are magnetic, magneto-optical, and optical. The most common **magnetic** and **magneto-optical drives** have capacities from 100 MB to 2 GB. Magnetic storage media record data in magnetic fields, as does an internal drive, but they have only one plat-

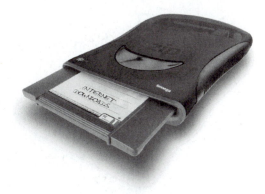

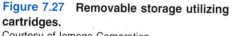

Figure 7.27 Removable storage utilizing cartridges.
Courtesy of Iomega Corporation.

ter within the cartridge. Magneto-optical media use a hybrid of magnetic and optical technologies by employing a laser beam that briefly focuses on the surface of the disk and melts the coating long enough to allow a magnet to affect the orientation of the surface crystals. Both technologies are rewritable and provide an easy way to transport data from content producers to production facilities, with magneto-optical being more stable and archival; it can maintain integrity for up to 30 years. The most common optical storage device is the **CD-ROM drive,** which can hold up to 650 MB of data. Information is written to the disk surface by a laser that creates microscopic pits (indentations) and leaves lands (flat areas) (figure 7.28). Light reflects from these pits and lands and is converted into bits that the computer can process. CD-recordable has great advantages in the stability of the media

and the ubiquity of drives, but can only be written to once (either to the complete 650 MB or in contiguous series of writes). Rewritable CD is available, but requires special hardware and software and currently has slow write speeds. The **DVD (digital video disk)** will most likely eclipse this development, because DVD technology is capable of storing from 4.7 to 17 GB, and rewritable versions are becoming available (figure 7.29). Due to the proliferation of optical drives already installed and the inherent stability of the materials used, it is also thought that the future of removable storage in production will move toward DVD.

Backup Storage

Saving work in a safe place requires a reliable backup device and established procedures. Removable cartridges and optical disks are often used, but when storing or backing up large

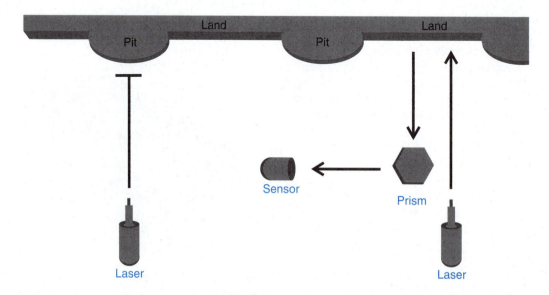

Figure 7.28 **Pits and lands.** Information written by laser to a CD surface creating pit and lands that represent data.

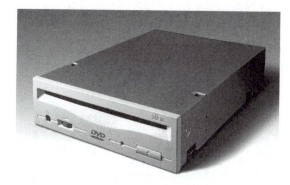

Figure 7.29 **DVD drive.**
Courtesy of Aopen.

amounts of in-progress projects or archiving older data that may not be accessed in the near future, a **tape backup** device is most appropriate. **Digital audiotape (DAT)** has been one of the most common choices until recently. The cartridge is a cross between audio technology and helical-scan video technology (the recording tracks are diagonal rather than longitudinal). Each DAT tape can hold up to 24 GB of data, thus offering high-capacity storage at a relatively low cost per megabyte. But due to the rapidly expanding amounts of data moving through prepress and printing facilities, there is a need for larger capacity backup options. **Digital linear tape (DLT)** offers storage capacities up to 70 GB and can store files in excess of 100 MB per minute. Tape data are expected to last from 10 to 20 years based on the quality of storage conditions. Tape backup is not the most appropriate choice if one needs frequent access to the data because it is stored sequentially and can result in long search times if the needed data are stored near the end of the tape.

There are many strategies and procedures for backup. The best strategy is to save and back up frequently. This pertains to the operators working on specific jobs and the production supervisor who should manage the complete production backup strategy. Numerous software solutions provide cataloging,

indexing, and data management paths that can be tailored to the equipment used and the type of work passing through a given facility.

Online Storage Solutions

The most typical set-up for a mid- to large-sized prepress or publishing facility is to have perhaps 50 to 100 MB of online storage available for immediate use connected to high-capacity near-line storage, such as a tape system for less frequently accessed data. One common approach to online storage is to use a method referred to as a RAID disk. **RAID (redundant arrays of inexpensive disks)** is a solution that allows a large amount of storage to appear as one single logical storage unit or drive, but actually consists of two or more disks (figure 7.30).

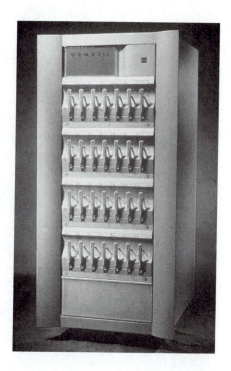

Figure 7.30 **Large RAID storage solution.** This RAID system is scalable up to 1 terabyte of online storage.
Courtesy of MicroNet Technology, Inc.

The basic idea of RAID is to combine multiple small, inexpensive disk drives into an array of disk drives that yields performance exceeding that of a single large-capacity disk. A RAID disk can reach capacities of 1 terabyte (1,000 GB) of storage, but most commonly runs less than 100 GB for online graphic production access. Besides speed, its primary benefit is security of data. There are five levels of RAID that allow for different combinations of redundancy and methods of writing data. Through **mirroring** of data (writing to two disks at a time) and **parity** (an error-checking procedure in which one drive provides mirroring for the rest of the primary drives), greater security of data is afforded in the event of drive failures (figure 7.31).

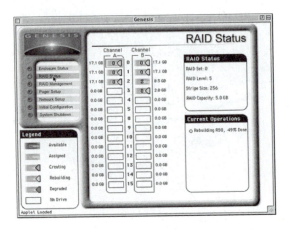

Figure 7.31 **RAID software control panel.**
Courtesy of MicroNet Technology, Inc.

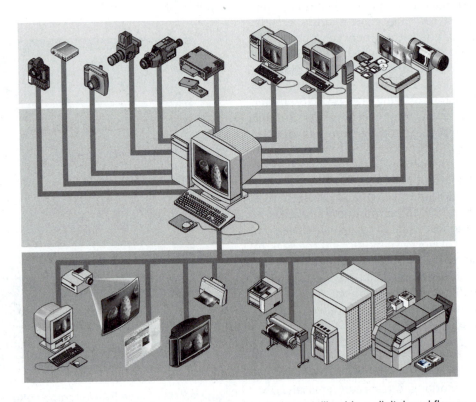

Figure 7.32 **Digital workflow.** Various forms of input and output utilized in a digital workflow.
Courtesy of Agfa Corporation.

Digital Workflow

All manufacturing processes require an efficient **workflow,** or method in which their products are produced (figure 7.32). The graphic arts industry has an added challenge in that each product (job) is unique. In addition, with the advent of digital design, control has moved from the hands of the printing facility to being shared in part with the content creator. There are so many variables to be considered now in the printing process that a well-designed workflow process is absolutely necessary. And today's workflow is digital.

The analog preparation methods discussed in earlier chapters have been replaced by digital counterparts. The advantage is the ability to create a fully automated workflow that streamlines the printing or publishing process, shortens turnaround, and reduces cost to the customer. The challenge is implementing it properly and cost effectively. The issue of digital workflow will be looked at numerous times in the following chapters as we explore the components that contribute to an effective and profitable digital workflow in the graphic arts industry today.

Key Terms

digital data
alphanumeric code
binary system
binary digit
byte
alphanumeric character
kilobyte
megabyte
gigabyte
terabyte
hardware
software
logic board
central processing unit (CPU)
control unit
arithmetic logic unit
system clock
hertz
input devices
output devices
read-only memory (ROM)
random-access memory (RAM)
cache memory
single in-line memory module (SIMM)
double in-line memory module (DIMM)
virtual memory
swap file
power supply
supercomputer
mainframe
minicomputer
microcomputer

workstation
multitask
complex instruction set computing (CISC)
reduced instruction set computing (RISC)
local area network (LAN)
wide area network (WAN)
network
packets
header
data
control elements
trailer
packet switching
protocol
TCP/IP
topology
node
peripherals
bus topology
data collision
ring topology
star topology
hub
hierarchical network
network operating system (NOS)
twisted-pair cable
shielded twisted-pair cable
fiber-optic cable
wireless network
network technology
Ethernet

CSMA/CD
10Base-T
broadband transmission
Fast Ethernet
100Base-T
Gigabit Ethernet
modem
modulate
demodulate
Integrated Services Digital Network (ISDN)
Digital Subscriber Line (DSL)
Asymmetric Digital Subscriber Line (ADSL)
T-1 line
T-3 line
backbone
Internet Service Provider (ISP)
primary storage device
magnetic storage
platters
removable storage device
magnetic drive
magneto-optical drive
CD-ROM drive
digital video disk (DVD)
tape backup
digital audiotape (DAT)
digital linear tape (DLT)
RAID (redundant arrays of inexpensive disks)
mirroring
parity
workflow

Review Questions

1. Explain how data are represented by a computer.
2. Discuss the parts of a CPU and the functions that they carry out.
3. In addition to RAM, what other kind of memory can you add to the logic board, and how does it improve the processing speed of the computer?
4. What is the most common type of computer found in a production facility and what are some features that they should have?

5. Discuss what packet switching is and how packets are assembled.

6. Define the three basic network topologies. Which one is most often used in graphic arts production environments?

7. What are the transmission rates of the various forms of Ethernet and how many signals per cable can each carry?

8. Which digital transmission method would be best for a mid-sized to large company and why?

9. Discuss the differences between magnetic, magneto-optical, and optical storage technology.

10. What are the primary advantages of a RAID?

11. Discuss the basics of what is meant by digital workflow.

8

Digital Prepress
Creation and Input

Historical Background

In 1983, with the release of Lisa, Apple Computers introduced the first **graphical user interface** (GUI), which revolutionized the computer user's experience. Two decades later we take for granted the ease with which we navigate the intricacies of computer applications. Colorful icons, layered windows, and the point and click technology that the GUI interface offers make our experience intuitive and hierarchical. The GUI takes the multitude of applications operating on our CPU and provides them all with a similar set of graphical representations and principles.

The GUI technology released with Lisa was first explored at the Xerox Palo Alto Research Center (PARC). In the late 1970s, along with GUI technology, PARC was also researching cutting-edge areas, such as object-oriented programming (OOP) and Ethernet networking. PARC released two computers with a basic GUI interface, the Alto and the Star. Although these machines received limited commercial distribution, Apple furthered the interface ideas and technology with the development of the Lisa, and the later Mac 128 in 1984. Lisa incorporated preemptive multitasking, a hierarchical file system, cut and paste options between programs, and black and white graphics resembling those of modern GUIs. Lisa was designed with seven applications that included word processing, spreadsheet, drawing, scheduling, and modem communication capabilities. Many of the features of this early GUI, including rulers, toolbars, and discerning icons, are now familiar features of our application and system software.

Objectives

After completing this chapter you will be able to:

- Discuss the two types of image file formats that are created or brought into graphics software.
- Define dpi, ppi, and lpi.

- List and describe the various printing file formats.

- List and describe the various Internet file formats.

- Understand and discuss the two main types of digital capture: scanning and digital photography.

■ List and describe the three important characteristics that determine the quality of an electronic scanner.

■ Define XY scanning.

■ Understand and describe the differences between single-pass and triple-pass digital photography.

Introduction

As we have seen, the original methods for producing artwork and type for reproduction were photomechanical. The conversion process involved taking original art or photographs and, through photographic processes, translating the information onto film, which would then be used to burn plates. The desktop computer has brought about an amazing revolution in the way that information is prepared for publication. And now information must also be ready to be disseminated to not only reflective copy, but also to the World Wide Web and distributed media such as CD-ROM and DVD disks. Issues such as size, color, space, and file formats must be taken into account.

This chapter will examine three main areas of creating digital content: actual content creation on the computer, scanning, and digital photography. To understand these methods of creation and acquisition, an understanding of file types and formats must first be acquired.

Digital Image Types

Two types of images are created in or brought into graphics software: bitmapped (raster) or object-oriented (vector) (figure 8.1).

Raster Images

Bitmapped or **raster images** are created in paint-type applications or by scanning (scan-

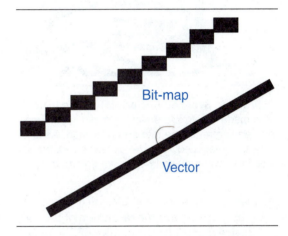

Figure 8.1 Example of a bitmap and vector line

ning is discussed later). Bitmapped, line art images are represented by picture elements **(pixels)** that are assigned a value by the computer (figure 8.2). Scanned line art images are assigned one bit (0 or 1) per pixel, either black or white. The quality of these images depends on input and output resolution.

Resolution refers to the number of samples that a scanner or capture device makes per inch and is measured in dots per inch **(dpi)** or pixels per inch **(ppi).** The number of bits used to record the information for one pixel is called the bit depth of the file. When an image is output to a laser printer or an imagesetter, its resolution is described by the number of dots that the output device can generate in 1

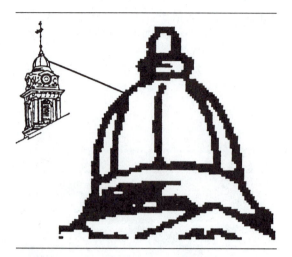

Figure 8.2   Scanned line art. Bit-mapped line art is made up of picture elements and is produced by scanning an image into an application. As is shown, the jagggedy or pixel appearance is very noticeable when these images are enlarged.

inch (dpi). The resolution at which a line image is bitmapped and the resolution of the output device determine the quality of the image.

Assume that a 300-dpi laser printer is used. In an attempt to improve image quality, a scan is made at 600 dpi. When the image is sent to the laser printer, it adopts the resolution of the output device, or 300 dpi. Scanning at a dpi higher than that of the output device does not improve image quality; it just increases the file size.

Gray-scale or continuous-tone images pose a slightly different bitmapping problem. A gray-scale image is made up of black, white, and intermediate tones. A one bit per pixel cannot represent a shade of gray, however. It can only represent black or white. Most gray-scale images are eight bits, which is enough to distinguish 256 levels of gray through various combinations (figure 8.3). When scanning continuous-tone images, the output device must therefore be set to make an 8-bit sample for black and white or gray-scale images and a 24-bit sample when doing a color scan (the sample actually contains three eight-bit values for red, green and blue) (figure 8.4).

Images are imageset as halftones, and the minimum input resolution is 1 ppi for each

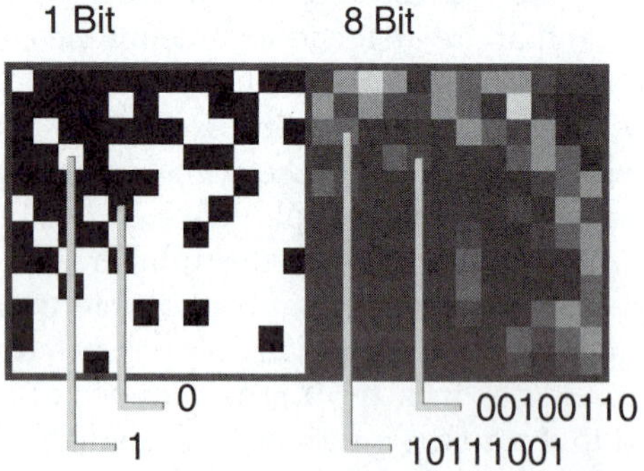

Figure 8.3   Bit depth. The greater the number of bits used, the greater the number of different colors that can be stored by the computer. Courtesy of Agfa Corporation.

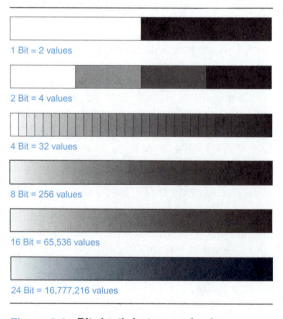

1 Bit = 2 values

2 Bit = 4 values

4 Bit = 32 values

8 Bit = 256 values

16 Bit = 65,536 values

24 Bit = 16,777,216 values

Figure 8.4   Bit depth in terms of values represented

line per inch **(lpi)** of the halftone. The best halftone reproduction occurs if the input resolution is 1.5 to 2 times the lpi of the halftone. Therefore, if a halftone is to be printed at 133 lpi, it should be scanned at 200 ppi (133 × 1.5 = 199.5 or 200 lpi) to produce the correct file size.

Enlarging bitmapped images requires planning. If the image is not going to be enlarged, the optimum image can be obtained if the input resolution is 1.5 to 2 times the lpi of the halftone. When a bitmapped image is enlarged, its resolution reduces. Basically, printing a bitmapped image gives you the resolution the image was created at. If a 200-dpi image is printed on a 2,400-dpi printer, a 200-dpi image will still result. A bitmap file is referred to as **resolution dependent.** This can result in a very large file if a high-resolution bitmapped image is created, because every pixel on the page must be defined. If the halftone lpi and the size of the final image are known in advance, the proper input resolution can be determined in an effort to avoid creating a larger file than is needed. The advantage of a bitmapped image is evident in image-editing programs such as Adobe Photoshop, with which images can be manipulated and edited at the pixel level (figure 8.5).

Vector Images

If line art is scanned into an application, it is a bitmapped, resolution-dependent image. If it is created in a paint program, it is also a bitmapped image. When it is created in an illustration or a draw program, however, it is an object-oriented or a **vector image.** Vector images are made up of mathematically described paths called **vectors** (figure 8.6).

Vector software does not store the lines of an image as a string of picture elements, but rather as drawing instructions or formulas that describe the directions of lines. The addresses of two different points define a line. Additional equations can define attributes such as thickness and color. The outline of an alpha-

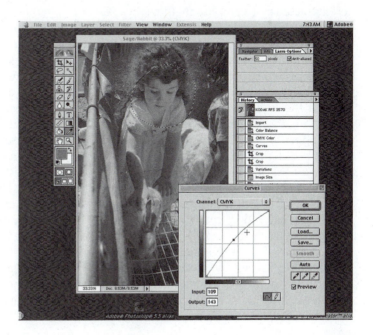

Figure 8.5 Image editing at the pixel level.
Courtesy of Adobe Systems, Inc.

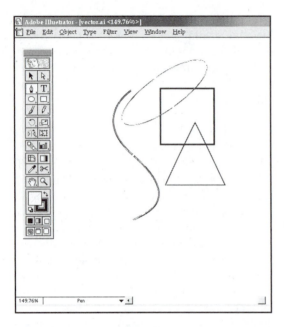

Figure 8.6 Vector illustration composed of mathematically described paths.
Courtesy of Adobe Systems, Inc.

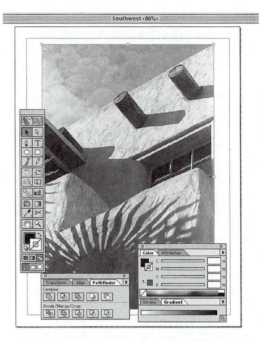

Figure 8.7 A raster image brought into an object-oriented program.
Courtesy of Adobe Systems, Inc.

bet character is a complex mathematical expression in a vector image.

Vector art has many advantages over raster or bitmapped art. It can be reshaped, rotated, enlarged, reduced, and manipulated in many other ways without sacrificing quality. Because the image is described as a mathematical equation, it requires far less computational effort to alter it than a bitmapped image, for which the program has to calculate the movement of numerous individual pixels. Vector formats are usually smaller than raster formats and sometimes print faster. Raster images can be brought into an object-oriented application such as Adobe Illustrator or Macromedia's Freehand either through drag-and-drop or directly by opening it from the application (figure 8.7). Using the raster file as a template, the image can be redrawn or au-

tomatically traced with tools such as Adobe Illustrator's Auto Trace tool. (Conversely, a vector image can be brought into a bitmapped program and turned into raster data.)

In addition to resizing and shaping capabilities, vector art has an advantage over raster art during output. The drawing application used to create vector art mathematically determines the shape of the object and allows output at a printer or imagesetter's highest resolution. This is why vector images are said to be **resolution independent:** they are not governed by the resolution of the input. Vector images are excellent for line illustrations or any artwork that requires changing, resizing, or manipulating.

Once raster and vector files are created, they must be saved and stored on disk. Refer

The following procedure can be used to estimate file size. Here is a formula that allows you to estimate file size using your own file variables:

(tonal resolution/8) × (spatial resolution)^2 × (dimensions) = file size

Divide the **tonal resolution** by 8 bits to determine bytes per sample. Squaring the **spatial resolution** gives the number of **samples per square inch.** Multiply that number by the number of bytes per sample to get the number of bytes per square inch. Multiply that number by the **size of the job in square inches** to get the tonal **number of bytes in a job.** Divide that number by 1,024 to get kilobytes or by 1,048,576 to get megabytes.

Tonal resolution: Depth of gray-scale or color. A line art scan is only 1 bit deep because 1 bit is all that is needed to distinguish black from white. Most gray-scale images are 8 bits deep in order to distinguish 256 levels of gray. Color images are commonly 24 bits deep in order to distinguish 16.7 million different colors.

Spatial resolution: Laser printer and imagesetter resolution is only two dimensional. It is dependent on the number of dots in the horizontal and vertical directions. Scanners have horizontal and vertical directions—and also depth. Both scanners and imagesetters describe horizontal and vertical resolution in terms of dots per inch (dpi) and sometimes in pixels per inch (ppi) or samples per inch.

1. Assume that a 4-inch × 5-inch line illustration will be scanned at 300 dpi. What is the file size?
   (tonal resolution/8) × (spatial resolution)^2 × (dimensions) = file size
   (1/8) × (300)^2 × (4 × 5) = file size
   .125 × 90,000 × 20 = file size
   225,000 bytes = file size
   225,000/1,024 = file size of 219 kilobytes

2. Assume that a 4-inch × 5-inch black and white photograph will be scanned at 300 dpi. What is the file size?
   (tonal resolution/8) × (spatial resolution)^2 × (dimensions) = file size
   (8/8) × (300)^2 × (4 × 5) = file size
   1 × 90,000 × 20 = file size
   1,800,000 bytes = file size
   1,800,000/1,048,576 = file size of 1.7 megabytes

3. Assume that a 4-inch × 5-inch black and white photograph will be scanned at 300 dpi. What is the file size?
   (tonal resolution/8) × (spatial resolution)^2 × (dimensions) = file size
   (24/8) × (300)^2 × (4 × 5) = file size
   3 × 90,000 × 20 = file size
   5,400,000 bytes = file size
   5,400,000/1,048,576 = file size of 5.14 megabytes

Figure 8.8 **Determining file size**

to figure 8.8 for an outline of a procedure to determine file size, which is important to know for storage and for predicting amounts of production time needed. There are many different file formats for structuring data as they are recorded to disk. The following section addresses the characteristics of some of the most commonly used file formats.

File Formats

After an image is created or captured (scanning and digital photography), it must be saved in an appropriate format. These file formats must be able to be imported into page layout programs and subsequently be able to retain integrity through the whole digital production process. The entire industry has moved away from proprietary formats that only work in specific systems based on a vendor's equipment and software. Images need to be saved in a format that has wide acceptance and known parameters.

Printing File Formats

The two most commonly used formats in printing are **TIFF** (Tagged Image File Format) and **EPS** (Encapsulated PostScript). TIFF files are bitmapped files and are used for picture images, both gray scale and color. Gray-scale TIFF can hold 256 grays and color TIFF can handle 16.7 million colors. A refinement of this standard called **TIFF/IT** (Tagged Image File Format for Image Technology) improves on the format by incorporating more high-end requirements and allowing for easier exchange between high-end and desktop environments.

An EPS file is basically a **PostScript** file with a preview. PostScript was developed by Adobe in the early 1980s and is a page description computer language that was developed to convert a document into an instruction set that any output device could interpret. PostScript and formats such as PDF are discussed in more detail in chapters 9 and 10.

The advantage of an EPS file is that it can be created from an object-oriented or bitmapped editing application and can also include function information such as screen rulings and separation information. It also provides a low-resolution bitmapped PICT preview that can be displayed without Post-Script interpretation. Most color images enter the prepress process as EPS files.

A third type of file, **DCS** (Desktop Color Separation) is also used to allow for file information to be saved as a set of EPS files containing preseparated color data (figure 8.9). This format was developed by the software company QuarkXpress; it creates a composite CMYK (cyan, magenta, yellow, and black) file and a PICT view file for screen display. One of its advantages is that it allows an image-editing program to fully prepare separations before sending them on to a page layout program. This format is also referred to as a five-file EPS.

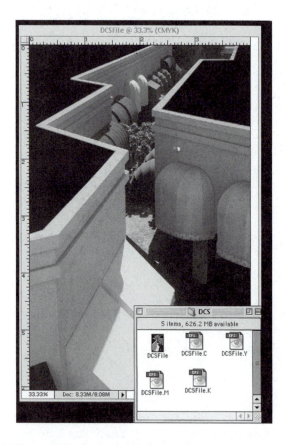

Figure 8.9   **Desktop Color Separation file**

Internet File Formats

In today's printing industry almost all business customers maintain an Internet Web site in addition to the printed material that they produce (figure 8.10). This creates the need for images that are suitable for viewing in a transmissive space as well as on a substrate. They must meet a specific resolution of 72 dpi for display on a monitor and be compressed enough to load in an acceptable amount of time. The two most commonly recognized image file formats used in web creation are JPEG (Joint Photographic Experts Group) and GIF (Graphic Interchange Format).

The **JPEG** standard is able to store 24 bits of information (16 million colors) (figure 8.11). Combined with the ability to handle subtle gradations of color, JPEG is the best choice for photographs or complex illustrations. Al-

though this format is also used in printing production when storage and transmission speeds are an issue, it has been embraced as a standard on the World Wide Web (WWW). Images displayed on the WWW need to load fast, especially if they want to reach a wide audience that may include individuals with slow online connections. The JPEG file format utilizes a compression scheme referred to as **lossy** (figure 8.12). This method achieves compression through the elimination of data and can result in files with a compression ratio of 10 : 1. Image-editing programs such as Adobe Photoshop provide several levels of compression when saving a file as a JPEG, with each level resulting in different amounts of information being removed.

The **GIF** format was designed specifically for online delivery by CompuServe in the

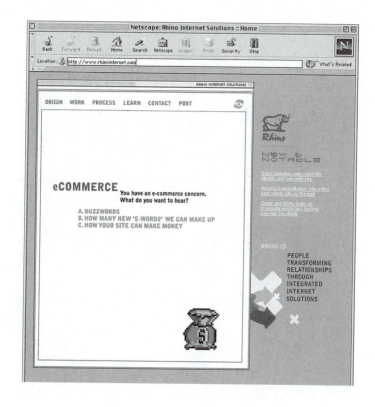

Figure 8.10 Many companies specialize in offering web-related services to the business community.
Courtesy of Rhino Productions.

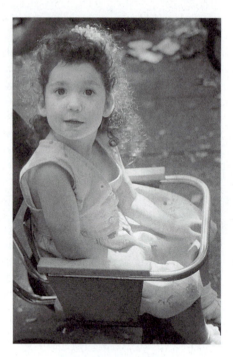 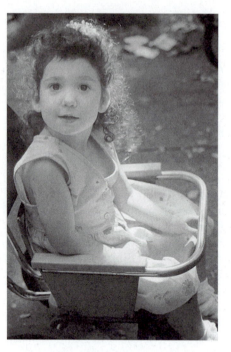

Full resolution = 5.9 MB   JPEG Medium Quality = 325 K

Figure 8.11 **Example of a full-resolution image and a JPEG file of the same image.** When opened, there is little difference in quality.

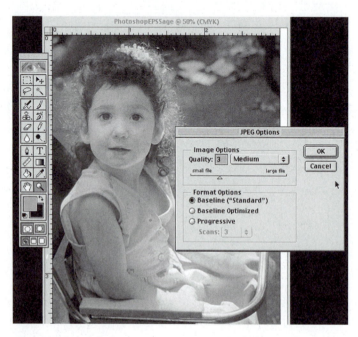

Figure 8.12 **JPEG compression window**

late 1980s. It uses a compression scheme referred to as a **lossless** algorithm, which means that no image degradation should occur during compression. But because it is an eight-bit file format (256 colors or less), it is best used for illustrations without complex gradations and for solid blocks of color. It exists in a color space referred to as indexed color, as opposed to RGB (red, green, blue) for JPEG and CMYK (cyan, magenta, yellow, black) for EPS and TIFF. The GIF palette can be adjusted to meet the lowest common denominator color palette used on all platforms in an effort to avoid unwanted color shifts when viewing on different platforms.

Digital Image Input

The two main methods of digital image input are scanning and digital photography. The late 1990s saw a tremendous increase in the capabilities of these technologies concurrent with price reductions that have changed the face of digital capture.

Scanners and Scanning

Scanners are input devices that convert analog information to digital information and digitize various types of copy for editing with software. There are many different types of scanners at various levels of quality. Scanner selection is determined by the kind of input used and the quality of output desired. An inexpensive desktop scanner would be very appropriate for an office environment for which the output printer is between 300- and 1,200-dpi resolution. A small- to medium-sized printing organization reproducing quality halftones and detailed line art would require a more expensive scanner with higher resolution. A company capturing color transparencies, negatives, and color prints would require an even higher quality scanner and possibly more than one type.

Flatbed Scanners

One of the most popular scanners for both the consumer market and prepress facilities is the flatbed scanner (figure 8.13). This scanner is capable of scanning or digitizing both monochrome (black and white) and color prints and transparent film. A scanner's price depends on its size, its ability to scan both opaque and transparent copy, its maximum scanning resolution, and its maximum color sample per pixel. Professional-level flatbed scanners are now available at a low enough cost and high enough quality that they are becoming the norm in prepress and printing facilities of all sizes. There are also less expensive film scanners for 35-mm format film that are popular with designers and consumers.

Flatbed scanners use **CCD** (charge-coupled device) technology, which is characterized by the use of an array of light-sensitive elements that translate analog signals into digital information (figure 8.14). Light reflected from the original is detected by the CCD array and converted into digital data or pixels. The number of CCD elements determines the actual optical resolution possible, rather than a software-interpolated resolution.

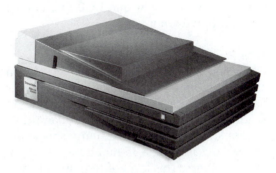

Figure 8.13 **Prepress flatbed scanner.** This scanner is capable of a maximum optical resolution of 5080 dpi.
Courtesy of Purup-Eskofot.

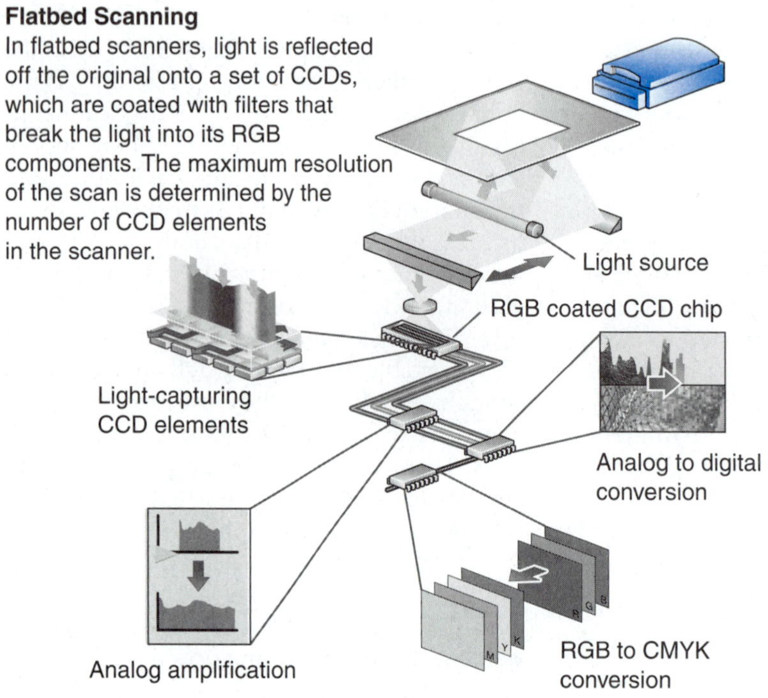

Flatbed Scanning

In flatbed scanners, light is reflected off the original onto a set of CCDs, which are coated with filters that break the light into its RGB components. The maximum resolution of the scan is determined by the number of CCD elements in the scanner.

Light source

RGB coated CCD chip

Light-capturing CCD elements

Analog to digital conversion

RGB to CMYK conversion

Analog amplification

Figure 8.14 Flatbed scanner illustration.
Courtesy of Agfa Corporation.

The scanner can utilize either a three-filter method, in which the scanning element makes three passes through RGB filters or projects RGB light at each pass, or the more sophisticated single-pass methods in which the scanning head is equipped with a **dichroic filter** that splits the light into RGB that is then directed to the array.

Film Scanners

Film scanners must be capable of high-resolution capture, because 35-mm slides and negatives have more gradations from highlight to shadow and are normally smaller than prints (figure 8.15). Some desktop film scanners are capable of sampling a 35-mm transparency at over 5,000 ppi. This level of resolution is necessary when working with small images.

Take, for example, a 35-mm slide that is only 1 inch on its short side. Assume that a

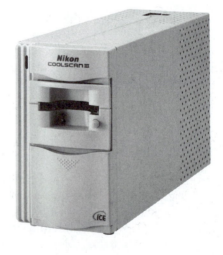

Figure 8.15 Film scanner.
Courtesy of Nikon, Inc.

scan of this slide is made at 1,200 dpi at 100 percent and that the resulting image will be printed in a magazine at a dimension of 8 inches on the short side. As the image is enlarged in the page layout software, resolution decreases proportionately. At 1 inch the image has a resolution of 1,200 dpi. At 2 inches the resolution reduces to 600 dpi, then to 300 dpi at 4 inches, and finally to 150 dpi at 8 inches. Normally, the digital halftone requires 1.5 to 2 times as many pixels as the halftone screen frequency that will be used in the final printing. Therefore, the 8-inch image at 150 dpi is adequate only to produce a quality 75- to 100-lpi halftone (75 lpi × 2 = 150). The magazine may require that all pictures be reproduced at 120 or 133 lpi (133 lpi × 2 = 266). A 75-to 100-lpi halftone may be adequate for newspaper work, but it is not adequate for a quality magazine.

Determining Scanning Quality

Three characteristics are important when determining the quality of an electronic scanner: dynamic range, bit depth, and resolution.

Dynamic range refers to a scanner's ability to capture a range of densities representing both the highlights and shadow detail found in the original copy. The higher the dynamic range, the greater the amount of detail that can be captured at both ends of the image spectrum. Desktop scanners can have a dynamic range of up to 3.6, while high-end CCD scanners can reach 4.0. The actual number is arrived at by a logarithmic measurement that measures the how much brighter the highlight is than the shadow.

Bit depth relates to the amount of information that a scanner can capture and has an effect on color, size of file, and the smoothness of image gradation. Bit depth determines the amount of colors that can be defined with 8-bit color only capable of 256 levels. To produce millions of colors, a bit depth of at least 24 is

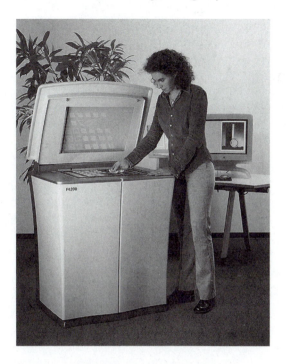

Figure 8.16 **High-end production scanner.** Courtesy of Heidelberg USA, Inc.

needed (24 to the second = 16,777,216 colors). A typical desktop scanner now captures at least 36-bit color. High-end CCD scanners are capable of 36-bit color enhanced to 48 (over 281 trillion colors) (figure 8.16).

Resolution in a scanner refers to the number of pixels per linear inch. The greater the number, the finer the detail that can be captured and the higher the image quality. A scanner's optical resolution refers to the actual pixel sample captured at a particular frequency. For example, a scanner with a resolution of 1,000 ppi can take a sample every 1/1,000 inch. This resolution is achieved by the scanner's actual optical capability. Another way that resolution is measured is through **interpolation,** by which software is used to artificially enhance the number of pixels in the sample. There is a point of diminishing return where too much software interpolation does not result in any more improvement in a scanned image, but increases the file size enough to require much more processing capability than is necessary to produce a quality image.

XY Scanning

There are two approaches to flatbed scanning technology: traditional and **XY technology.** In a traditional flatbed scanner, the optical assembly moves in only one direction—down the length of the flatbed (referred to as the x-direction). To achieve different optical resolutions, multiple lenses covering different widths must be used. Depending on the resolution chosen, the optimal scanning area could be significantly reduced to just a strip running down the center of the bed. Thus, if the material being scanned is not placed precisely on what is called the "sweet spot," the overall quality of the scan will be compromised (figure 8.17). This was once one of the biggest disadvantages of a flatbed technology when compared to drum scanners (discussed in the next section).

XY technology makes it possible to place images anywhere on the scanning bed and get high resolution over the entire scanning area, maximum uniform quality and sharpness, and almost unlimited resolution for enlargements of any original size. This is achieved through movement of components on both the x (horizontal) and the y (vertical) directions. In essence, this allows the sweet spot to be moved anywhere needed on the bed of the scanner. The image is actually scanned in several pieces, which are then stitched together using

In non-XY scanners the optimum or highest scanning area on the bed is often called the "sweet spot". Located in the center of the scanning bed, this is where the highest quality image data can be captured. It limits the size of an original that can be scanned, even for scanners with large scanning beds.

XY scanning technology allows an image to be scanned up to the maximum resolution of the sensor on any one area of the scanning bed.

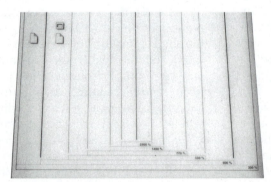

This photo of a non-XY scanner bed shows that in order to obtain the maximum enlargement of 2,500%, the original must be placed within the two center lines of the bed. Maximum achievable enlargement goes down to 300% at the edge of the bed. XY scanners with stitching are designed to capture the entire bed area at maximum enlargement.

Figure 8.17 XY sweet spot.
Courtesy of Graphic Arts Technical Foundation.

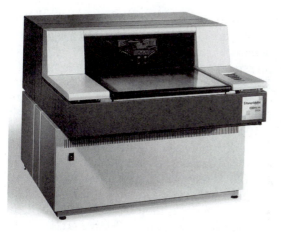

Figure 8.18 **High-resolution scanner.** This scanner is capable of scanning resolutions up to 2,540 dpi and incorporates CopyDot technology for digitizing color separations.
Courtesy of Purup-Eskofot.

software. This stitching allows originals of any size to be scanned at any resolution anywhere on the flatbed. It also allows for batch scanning to occur, which is valuable in a busy production house.

XY technology has enabled the development of **copy-dot scanning,** which allows black and white line and halftone separations to be digitized into a high-resolution bit-mapped image (figure 8.18). This allows pre-screened films to be brought into a digital workflow, which is a profitable and necessary service as long as customers still have film output that they would like digitized. The pre-screened material is converted into continuous-tone data by digitally eliminating the original screen through scanning at extremely high resolutions.

Drum Scanners

Drum scanners are input devices for high-end reproduction applications (figure 8.19). At one

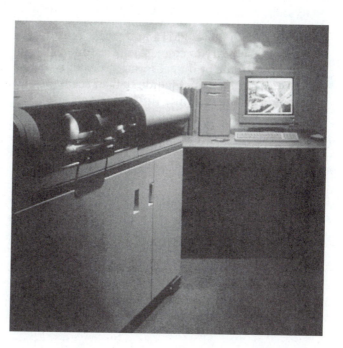

Figure 8.19 **Drum scanner**

time it was the only choice for high-quality professional scans; but flatbed technology has evolved to such a degree and become so much more affordable that some predict the inevitable end of production of high-end drum scanners. This remains to be seen, because the wide-format printing market has a need for enlargements as much as 3,000 percent of their original size. Even though it may become more of a niche-market technology eventually, drum scanning is still in use today because many companies feel that it is still the best choice for extremely high quality scanning.

An illustration, a photograph, or a transparency is fastened to the scanner's rotating drum, and efficiency is achieved because the drum has three photomultipliers (red, green, and blue) scanning the original at once with a very accurate beam. Drum scanners perform functions such as sharpening the focus and converting RGB (red, green, and blue) to CMYK (cyan, magenta, yellow, and black) during the input process. Images scanned using flatbed and film scanners normally capture only a RGB scan. Adjusting, sharpening, and converting the image to CMYK when using a flatbed or film scanner is done using image manipulation software, such as Adobe Photoshop.

Basic Drum Scanner Operation

When scanning a color transparency, it is first mounted on the transparent revolving drum. Some devices have a vacuum system for this purpose or secure the film with clear cellophane tape or mounting oil. Although the position of the transparency is not crucial, it is important that the transparency not move or shift as the drum rotates. Drum scanners can be either stand-alone or desktop units.

Next, a narrow beam of light passes through a condenser lens and is deflected by a mirror, which is set at a 90-degree angle to the drum surface. The lamphouse of the scanner contains the light source and lenses. The two most common light sources are high-pressure xenon and tungsten–halogen lamps. The light from the mirror passes through the color transparency and is split into four light paths by microscopic optics. Each light path enters a **photomultiplier tube** (PMT). The PMT is the most important element of the scanner because it has the ability to change light to an electrical signal. The PMT can send a signal that varies in strength according to variations in the intensity of light that it receives. When scanning reflective art, the light source reflects back from the original to the PMT.

Three of the PMTs in the scanner are covered with red, green, and blue filters, respectively. The amount of light passing into any single PMT is proportional to the density of a primary color from a spot on the color transparency. Photomultiplier tubes are able to sense this light and amplify it into strong electronic signals, which can then be converted into digital information ready to enter the digital production workflow (figure 8.20).

This entire operation occurs as the transparency drum rotates at a high speed of up to 1,600 rpm. The number of samples per revolution and the speed at which the sensor moves along the drum determine the resolution that can be achieved. A high-quality drum scanner can scan at resolutions up to 11,000 dpi without interpolation.

The operator may also make adjustments to improve the color balance of an inferior color original (figure 8.21). The system may be used to adjust for the type of paper to receive the image. The separations used to print a color image on newsprint should be different from those used for a high-quality, coated offset paper. Originally, color correction was done at the scanner and film was output at that time. Today, color correction and

Drum Scanning

In drum scanners, a light source is moved in tiny increments across the original. The reflected or transmitted light is then sent through a photo-multiplier tube, which breaks the light into its RGB components. Other circuitry converts the analog (light) information to digital, CMYK separations.

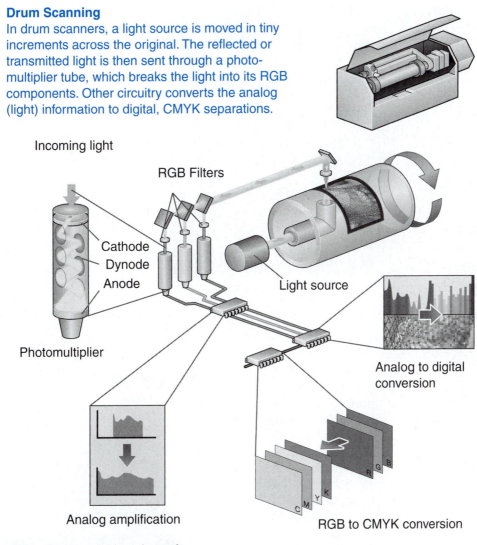

Incoming light

RGB Filters

Cathode
Dynode
Anode

Light source

Photomultiplier

Analog to digital conversion

Analog amplification

RGB to CMYK conversion

Figure 8.20 **Drum scanner schematic.**
Courtesy of Agfa Corporation.

management are done at image-editing stations and managed through software and profiles (discussed in chapter 9) with film output by an imagesetter, if film is used at all. But even though the method by which color correction occurs has changed, certain basics still apply, such as UCR and GCR (discussed in chapter 5).

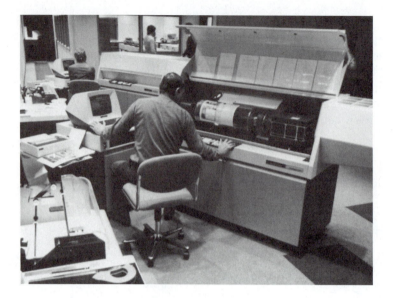

Figure 8.21 **Scanner operator**

Digital Photography

Digital photography uses CCD technology and is in essence a scanner. Its value is in photographing three-dimensional objects and capturing movement. Digital photography has grown so successful as a capture device in prepress that it has replaced film-based photography in all but a few areas of photography. Images are captured as RGB data typically in the TIFF format and then converted to various color spaces and file formats as needed. Two types of digital photography are used in commercial photography today: single-pass and three-pass systems.

Single-Pass Camera

A **single-pass digital camera** system is a camera built specifically for digital capture. It may be mounted on a modified body derived from a traditional analog body, but it can only capture digital information (figure 8.22). At the consumer level, single-pass cameras come with a fixed lens or offer one or two changeable lenses, but they are not as sophisticated as traditional optical lenses. High-end single-pass cameras often use existing optical lenses from manufacturers such as Nikon, Canon, or Hasselblad. (refer to plate M).

The CCD in a single-pass digital camera is assembled as an **area array** that captures an

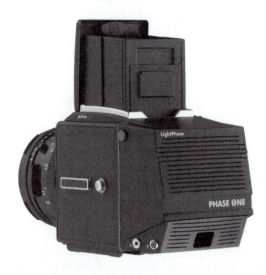

Figure 8.22 **Single-pass digital camera.**
Courtesy of Phase One, Inc.

ity of information gathered, it may encroach on the dominance that three-pass systems have had in high-end studio work.

Three-Pass Camera

Three-pass cameras basically use three separate exposures to obtain complete RGB data using a linear array. They are most often characterized by scanning backs that are mounted to the back of medium- and large-format traditional cameras (figure 8.24). The CCDs are arranged in a single row, and the image is captured one row of pixels at a time with an RGB filter wheel in front of the sensor. A variation on this is a **trilinear sensor.** Three linear arrays coated with a color in lieu of a filter are mounted side by side. Even though the image

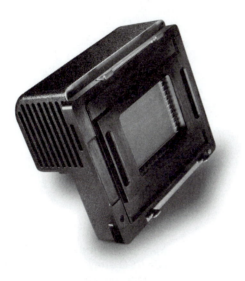

Figure 8.23 **Scanning back.**
Courtesy of MegaVision, Inc.

entire scene in one exposure (figure 8.23). The CCD itself is overlaid with color filters positioned over each pixel. Through adjacent color pixel interpolation, the three color channels are computed. The disadvantage of this method is the potential for the creation of artifacts, that is, areas of incorrect color that are obvious in the image.

An advance in chip technology has been the development by Phillips, the Dutch electronic company, of CCDs made up of modular one-megapixel (1 million pixel capture) blocks stitched together. Six blocks make up a 24- by 36-mm six-megapixel sensor that equates to the size of a 35-mm frame. Megapixel sensors capture RGB files as large as 36 MB with 48-bit color (16 bits per color). The exposure is then refined through processing down to typically an 18-MB or 24-bit image. Images can be taken as fast as 4.5 frames per second, although this will speed up as the technology advances. In fact, as single-pass technology improves in the amount and qual-

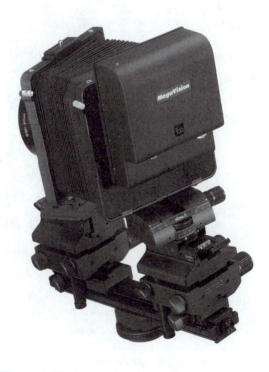

Figure 8.24 **Three-pass camera.**
Courtesy of MegaVision, Inc.

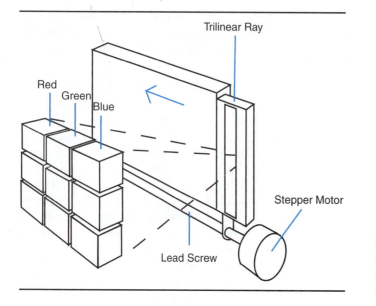

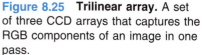

Figure 8.25 **Trilinear array.** A set of three CCD arrays that captures the RGB components of an image in one pass.

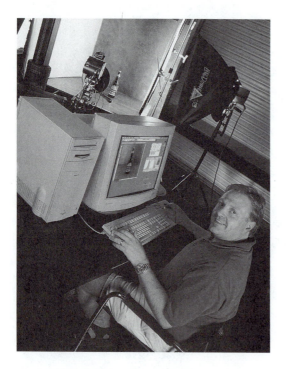

Figure 8.26 **Digital photo shoot.**
Courtesy of R & R Images.

information is captured in one pass, time is needed to actually complete the image process, so no movement can be photographed with this method (figure 8.25).

Both single- and three-pass systems are used extensively in publishing. Single-pass systems are most often used for portraiture and fashion, with high-end three-pass systems used for product photography (figure 8.26). A typical catalog shoot might incorporate both types of systems. For example, if a digital studio is photographing (shooting) a fashion catalog, they may have people and products to shoot. The advantages of shooting digitally as opposed to conventional are numerous. With a film-based camera, Polaroids are needed to check lighting conditions and the framing of the shot. The film must then be processed and digitized to be brought into image-editing and page-layout software. When shooting digitally, the photographer and customer can immediately see on the computer monitor if they are capturing what they need. The images can then be transferred right into production, edited, and placed in the page. Today, most catalogs and newspaper inserts incorporate some if not all digitally captured images. This ability to immediately see and correct an image, in addition to having it be digital data ready to insert into the workflow, has ensured digital photography's place in production.

Key Terms

graphical user interface (GUI)
raster image
pixel
resolution
dpi
ppi
gray scale
lpi
resolution dependent
vector image
vector
resolution independent
TIFF

EPS
TIFF/IT
PostScript
DCS
JPEG
lossy
GIF
lossless
scanner
CCD
dichroic filter
dynamic range
bit depth

resolution
interpolation
XY technology
copy-dot scanning
drum scanner
photomultiplier tube
digital photography
single-pass digital camera
area array
three-pass digital camera
trilinear sensor

Review Questions

1. Discuss the difference between raster images and vector images.

2. Describe the differences regarding resolution in raster and vector images,

3. Define resolution independent and resolution dependent.

4. What is the difference between the TIFF file format and the EPS file format?

5. Discuss the approach to compression in GIF and JPEG file formats.

6. Define CCD technology and how it is utilized by a flatbed scanner.

7. List and describe the three characteristics that are important in determining the quality of an electronic scanner.

8. What is the main difference between traditional and XY scanning technology?

9. What is a PMT and why is it the most important element of a drum scanner?

10. Discuss the differences between a single-pass digital camera and a three-pass digital camera.

9

Digital Prepress
Assembly

Historical Background

Before World War II, almost all printing was done with the letterpress process using cast metal type. The growth of offset lithography after World War II forced printers to develop alternative methods of setting type. No longer were all images printed directly from raised metal type. Instead, most images were arranged on a flat paper surface and photographed to produce a film negative. The negative was then used to produce a printing plate. The term *hot-type composition* had been used to describe cast type images, so it seemed natural to give the name *cold-type composition* to this new photographic method of producing images.

Cold-type composition had several advantages over hot-type composition. One major advantage was that artists had far more flexibility and ease in producing images for printing. Almost any two-dimensional image could be photographed and printed. In addition, cold-type images could be enlarged, reduced, or cropped without being recast. A second advantage of cold-type composition was the speed with which images could be produced. Cold type allowed printers to expand their type libraries and eliminated the time-consuming step of casting the image onto a type-high lead body. It allowed

heavy type cases and banks of type cabinets to be replaced with computers that could reproduce hundreds of different typefaces at speeds impossible to achieve with cast metal type.

With the development of cold-type composition came a new occupation in the printing industry—pasteup artist. The pasteup artist was responsible for arranging cold-type images into proper printing position and pasting them up on a flat surface so that they could be photographed. Pasteup artists worked with stiff paperboard or plastic sheets that were specially formulated for dimensional stability.

The computer has changed printing so dramatically that the job of pasteup artist no longer exists. Along with the craft of stripping images into film flats, the tasks of page assembly have all moved to the computer and been absorbed in the new digital workflow. Now those involved with page assembly are referred to as *prepress operators* and more often are checking incoming files for correctness, rather than building them from an artist's sketch. It will be interesting to see what the next transformation will be as technology continues to change the processes that we use to produce and disseminate information.

Objectives

After completing this chapter you will be able to:

- Describe the elements of digital page layout.
- Identify methods of creating and using low-resolution images during the assembly process.
- Describe the differences between vector and raster images.
- List processes that can be accomplished with image-editing software.
- Discuss the benefits of accurate preflighting.
- Define digital halftone technology.
- Define frequency, angle, and dot shape.
- Describe the difference between process and spot color.
- Discuss the variables encountered with color on the Internet.
- Define the three main components of the ICC color management system.
- Define trapping and imposition.

Introduction

Traditionally, designers provided their mechanicals to the prepress facility to be assembled for output. Today, the designer or content creator is a full participant in the digital production process and is responsible for a level of knowledge beyond the creative side of the project. This has presented challenges to the production process that are ultimately resolved by a collaborative effort between the designer and the production facility. Issues such as correct page layout, font usage, image editing, and color correction must be addressed to enable a successful digital workflow.

This chapter will examine different facets of the modern digital assembly process and job preparation prior to output. Because the designer is now an integral part of this process, we will begin with the page-layout processes utilized in creating a printed piece.

Page Layout

Page-layout software allows for digital assembly of all page elements prior to being sent to the specified output device (figure 9.1). These elements include text, line art, and photographs in one file. Because files generated from a page-layout program need to be integrated seamlessly with the rest of the digital workflow, prepress production facilities generally use a solution from one vendor to simplify the process. This also allows third parties to justify research and development of plugins and extensions, because a large market will be readily available.

Page-layout software programs such as Adobe InDesign and QuarkXpress allow designers, typesetters, layout artists, advertisers, editors, and anyone who communicates using print products the opportunity to assemble an attractive product (figure 9.2). Aldus helped to spark the desktop publishing revolution in 1985 when it introduced its page-layout program called PageMaker. Using a page-layout program on a 1-megabyte Macintosh Plus limited the operator to mainly typographic layouts. It was not until the early 1990s that hardware and software allowed text and graphics, which included high-resolution line art, gray

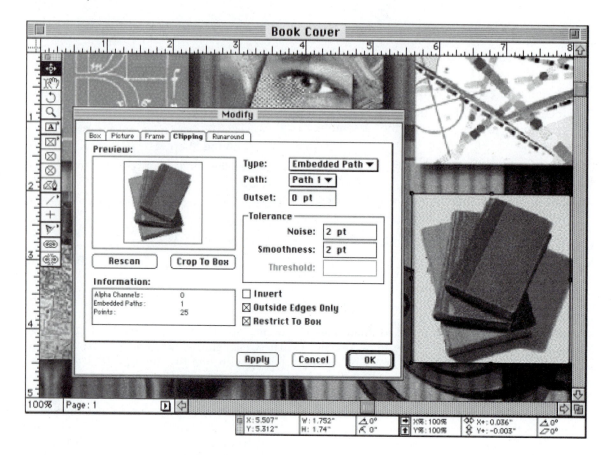

Figure 9.1 **Assembling page elements.**
Courtesy of Quark, Inc.

scale images, and 24-bit color images with special effects, to be integrated. Today, inexpensive high-speed workstations, quality scanners, and fast imagesetters have allowed all members of the graphic communication community to access personal prepress technology.

Traditionally, prepress operators used thumbnail sketches, rough layouts, and comprehensives to achieve customer approval. Using thumbnails and roughs to develop an idea before going to a page-layout program is still not a bad idea. Establishing the size and for-

mat of a piece is very helpful to get off to a quick start. Also, knowing approximate picture sizes, image-resolution requirements, type sizes, and column lengths allows operators to work smart by keeping file sizes as small as possible.

Establishing the product format on the computer as soon as possible has many advantages. While a prepress person develops the design or layout, the comprehensive is actually being developed. In a sense, the final mechanicals, films, or plates are also being created at the same time. Job progress can be

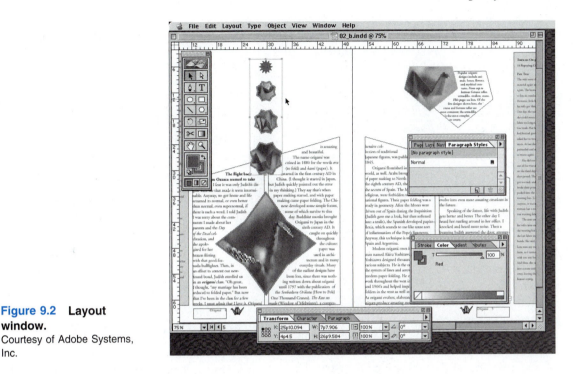

Figure 9.2 Layout window.
Courtesy of Adobe Systems, Inc.

shown easily to fellow workers and clients at any time, and changes can be made on demand.

Integrating photographs with text can be a problem during the early stages of product development, however. When scanned at appropriate resolutions for production, continuous-tone images create large files. When high-resolution images are placed in a layout during the early stages of development, screen redraw and overall operating speeds are adversely affected. It is recommended that, after scanning continuous-tone images at the proper resolution, they be stored temporarily, and low-resolution **FPO (for position only)** files be created for use during the design stages. The primary way this is handled is through the use of **OPI (open prepress interface)** software and with the high-resolution images generally maintained at the prepress facility (figure 9.3). OPI software addresses the

bottlenecks that can occur when dealing with large color image files. Initially developed by the Aldus Corporation, it describes a procedure by which high-resolution images are stored on a central server, with the corresponding low-resolution files being distributed to the designer or individual production computers working on the layout. A limited number of operations can be performed on the FPO images, with these operations being applied to the high-resolution images when the complete file is ultimately output to the imagesetter, platesetter, or digital printer. This procedure increases production and eliminates storage problems.

Understanding all the ramifications of an efficient digital workflow can be very demanding. Knowing the entire prepress process, knowing all printing concerns, understanding computer operation and maintenance, having design and layout abilities,

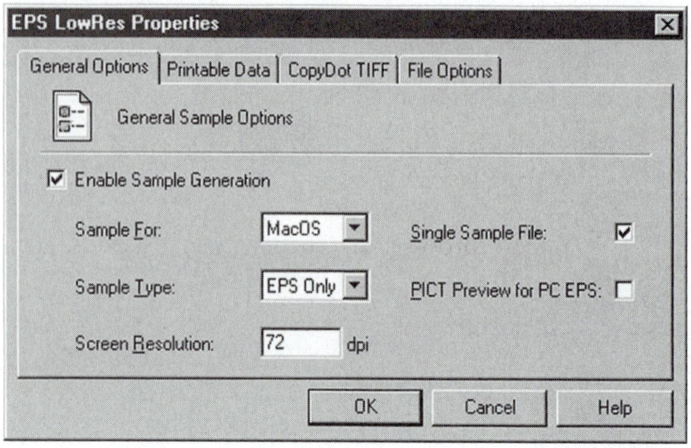

Figure 9.3 **Setting low-resolution choices in OPI software.**
Courtesy of IPTech.

knowing telecommunications, and using a prepress facility require a capable, well-prepared individual. This may be the case in the thousands of small establishments typical of the printing and publishing industry. In larger organizations an appropriate division of labor can be established, and **prepress specialists** with clearly identified job descriptions can be identified.

Digital prepress page layout has become the standard for the graphic communicator for the following reasons:

- Ability to produce design variations
- Ability to make changes to the final layout
- Local control of image input and manipulation
- Inexpensive, low-resolution proofing
- Film and/or plate output directly from the computer
- Quick turnaround on customer alterations, proofs, films, and overall production
- Ability to keep the entire production cycle in-house

Illustration and Image-Editing Software

Two types of artwork must be considered, line work and continuous-tone images (refer to chapter 8). In software this is handled by vector or illustration programs for line work and bitmap or image-editing programs for continuous-tone images. Bitmap, or image-editing software, is quickly becoming comprehensive enough to handle the creation of type and some line work previously only handled in vector or illustration programs.

Drawing or Illustrating Software

Drawing or illustration software produces vector or object-oriented art and type. Object-oriented software programs use the graphic capabilities of the **PostScript** language to manipulate this art and type (discussed further in chapter 10). PostScript handles these images well because they are mathematically based. PostScript objects are created by establishing and manipulating vector or control points with a variety of drawing tools (figure 9.4). When an image is created, each line or curve is assigned its own mathematical definition. In

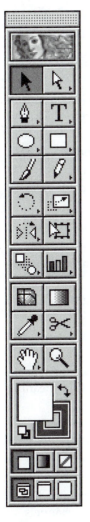

become **encapsulated PostScript (EPS)** files. When a file is saved in EPS format, it is written in the PostScript language that contains the code necessary for printing. PostScript images, whether separate or integrated with text in a page-layout program, must be converted to bitmaps before they are printed. The conversion process for interpreting PostScript to bitmaps is called *rasterizing*. This is accomplished with a **raster image processor (RIP).** A RIP converts the object-oriented and bitmapped images from any graphics software to pixels or bitmaps that the output device understands (figure 9.5). RIPs can be stand-alone devices or they can be incorporated into all PostScript printers. They will be discussed in more detail in chapter 10.

Figure 9.4 Object-oriented software tools palette.
Courtesy of Adobe Systems, Inc.

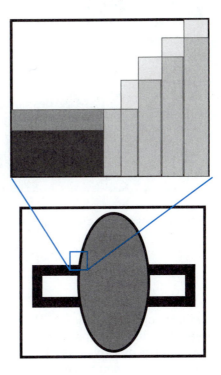

Figure 9.5 RIP. A RIP converts graphic information to bitmaps that an output device can understand.

other words, as the operator draws lines the direction is mathematically computed by the software, and vector points are established by the software. The lines are called **Bézier curves.** These curves are defined by the control points placed by the operator. This also means that these images can be enlarged, reduced, or manipulated without losing detail or quality.

When saved or exported for use in a page-layout program, object-oriented images

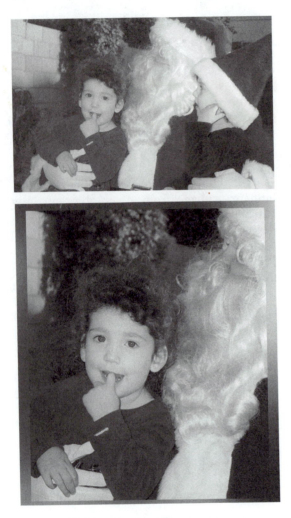

Figure 9.6   An example of cropping

sulting bitmapped image is ready for some of the following manipulations or processes:

- Cropping, sizing, and establishing appropriate resolution
- Adjusting highlight, shadow, and intermediate tones between black and white
- Adjusting hue, saturation, brightness, and contrast
- Adjusting or correcting color balance
- Sharpening images
- Removing scratches, blemishes, or unwanted images
- Restoring damaged or incomplete image sections
- Creating composite images from more than one original
- Creating special effects or altering images to better communicate ideas
- Removing and/or creating backgrounds to improve picture meaning or quality
- Controlling undercolor removal, gray component replacement, and dot gain
- Encapsulating or embedding screen ruling and tone value adjustments
- Color separating an image into yellow, magenta, cyan, and black channels
- Compressing data
- Saving an image as separations in the appropriate format

Image-Editing Software

Image-editing software such as Adobe Photoshop offers the digital prepress operator the ability to complete quickly tasks that were traditionally very time consuming (figure 9.6). Once photographs are either scanned or digitally captured through photography, the re-

An example of image editing done within Adobe Photoshop is illustrated by the *sharpening* process. All sharpening tools are meant to visually emphasize differences in an image to increase the impression of detail. In particular, the unsharp masking tool is considered the most efficient at creating the illusion of sharpness. It works by increasing the contrast that already exists between contrasting pixels. The unsharp mask filter allows you to pick the radius of pixels surrounding high-contrast edges that are to be sharpened. It also lets you determine the threshold value that indicates the minimum amount of contrast that an area must have to be modified.

When the manipulated and processed images are saved in the proper format on the hard drive or removable storage, they are ready in most cases to be placed in a page-layout software program such as Adobe In-Design or QuarkXPress.

Fonts

A typeface family is made up of all the possible variations of a typeface. In digital prepress this is referred to as a **font,** which is often interchangeable with the term *typeface.* Fonts are an extremely important design element, and corrupt or improperly made fonts can result in numerous output problems, including reflow problems and missing text.

In digital typography one still needs to be concerned with traditional typography issues. The advantage is the ease with which character attributes can be applied. Some typical font adjustments might be the following:

- *Kerning:* selectively adding or subtracting space between letters and words
- *Tracking:* subtracting space between a group of letters, applied to all the letters using the same value
- *Formatting:* changing fonts, size, color (tint), scale, type style (bold, italic, outline, subscript, etc.)
- *Leading:* the measurement of space from baseline to baseline, generally

larger than the font point size (for example, 10/14 indicates 10-point type with 14 points of leading)

When a designer creates a file with specific font choices, the specified fonts need to be collected for output and delivered to the prepress facility along with the file. This is important even if the prepress facility has the exact same file. Different font companies can create their own versions of a popular file, and even a universally used font such as Helvetica can go through revisions. If the font at the production facility is not identical to yours, output problems can occur.

In addition, due to copyright considerations, the prepress provider must own a licensed copy of the exact same font. Licenses typically are based on the number of a specific device on premise, such as five PostScript output devices per license, or that it can be used on five computers. These licenses are adjustable and subject to different pricing.

Types of Fonts

Two basic types of fonts are in common use today: **PostScript Type 1 fonts** and **TrueType fonts.** The major difference between them is that PostScript fonts have two components, a screen font and a printer font, whereas True-Type fonts include the display and output information in a single file. When using Post-Script Type 1 fonts, you must send both the screen and printer font to the prepress provider for accurate output. Although True-Type sounds more convenient due to having one file, it can often cause problems on high-end PostScript output devices. New font formats are being considered, including a format called **OpenType font,** that strive to combine the attributes of PostScript and TrueType fonts, but they are not widely available or used at present.

Preflight

Preflight is a procedure by which a file is checked for omissions and set-up errors to ensure a smooth passage through to output (figure 9.7). Failure to accurately preflight a job can cause costly errors and production delays, which can affect the profitability of a printing facility negatively. Although the final and most critical preflighting will occur at the prepress facility, the designer needs a basic understanding of its principles to weed out the most egregious errors.

Some of the most common things that good preflighting prevents are the following problems:

- Corrupt or missing fonts
- Missing images
- Improper trapping
- Wrong page sizes
- Incorrect color designations
- Inadequate bleeds
- Unusable media

Preflighting typically occurs when a job enters a prepress or printing facility, and often a workstation is devoted to that task. A variety of preflight software packages is available, such as FlightCheck by Markzware, that scan documents electronically and reports on

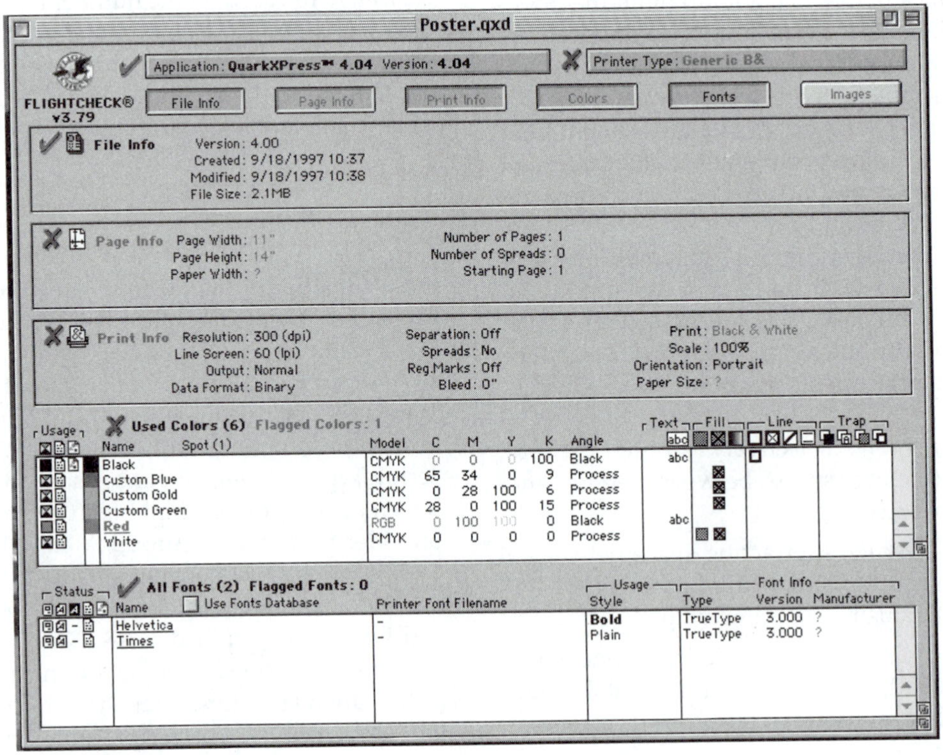

Figure 9.7 **Preflight window.**
Courtesy of Markzware, Inc.

errors or missing items in a variety of categories. They are comprehensive enough to not only list errors found, but to suggest solutions and indicate from where in the document the error reports are being generated.

A certain amount of error correction may be undertaken by a prepress provider, but there will usually be additional charges for any major rework or cleanup done to a file. Efficient preflighting can ensure smooth passage through production, whereas errors caught late in the workflow can cost time and money.

Digital Halftones

Digital halftones are generated for output to imagesetters, computer-to-plate, and laser printers. These output devices print spots, representing either on or off bits as communicated from the computer, on the material or substrate. But if all the spots are the same size and are either on (black) or off (white), a method is needed to create variations in tone. By creating a **halftone cell** made up of a number of spots, a corresponding halftone dot is made that can appear as varying degrees of light or dark when printed. The number of spots either on or off within the halftone cell will determine the level of gray represented (figure

9.8). The greater the amount of spots contained within a cell, the greater the levels of gray that can be achieved.

Screening

There are three things to consider when it comes to understanding digital screening: frequency, angle, and dot shape. Although there are many similarities to traditional screening, in that both are used to create the illusion of a continuous-tone image, digital halftoning allows a more sophisticated and complex approach.

Frequency

The **frequency** of a halftone tells you the number of dots per inch in the halftone. This frequency is referred to as lines per inch (lpi). A lower-frequency screen makes the image appear coarser and, conversely, a higher-frequency screen allows for a finer-looking image (figure 9.9). This is because the higher-frequency screen actually has more halftone dots or spots per inch. In producing digital screens directly from your software application, the computer performs screen algorithms that convert the stored image information into the correct pattern of spots to create the desired dot upon output.

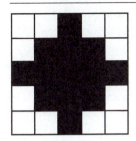 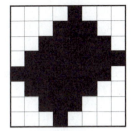

The halftone cell on the left has 25 spots, while the one on the right has 64 spots that compose printer spots. The one on the right contains a greater number of gray levels.

Figure 9.8   Digital halftone cell

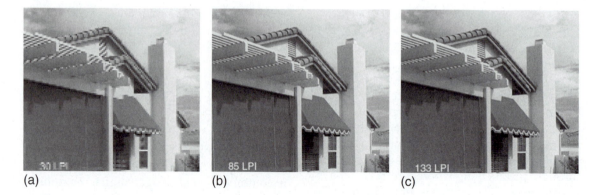

(a)   (b)   (c)

Figure 9.9   Frequency screens. (a) An image screened at 30 lpi. (b) The same image screened at 85 lpi. (c) The image screened at 133 lpi. The difference that the screening makes in image reproduction is obvious.

Screen Angle

The method by which you align your four-color halftone screens is referred to as the **screen angle.** This refers specifically to the angle at which the row of halftone dots runs in relation to the horizontal. Using the correct screen angles is important to avoid problems such as *moiré.* Moirés are created when overlapping screens create the appearance of lines and patterns, and one goal of screening is to reduce this visual result (see chapter 5). The printing industry most often utilizes the following angles to minimize the creation of moiré: the yellow separation at 0°, the magenta separation at 15°, the black separation at 45°, and the cyan separation at 75°. The farther from the horizontal or vertical axis that a separation is, the less likely that a moiré will be created. This is referred to as **rational tangent (RT)** screening because it defines the angle of rotation in terms of discrete numbers on a reference grid of horizontal and vertical image spots (figure 9.10). Because the tangents of 15° and 75° are not rational (whole) numbers, this is not always a perfect solution, and manufacturers tend to suggest screen rulings and angles advisable for their output devices. An example of this are the Adobe recommended

RT angles, which changes the cyan screen angle to 71.5° and the magenta screen angle to 18.5°.

To more accurately describe screen angles, **supercell** screening algorithms were developed that defined a screen angle using a larger reference grid of image spots than the original screening methods. The resulting larger halftone cell allows more precise spot rotation, permitting the spot to get closer to the desired angles. It requires more computational power, which was an issue when originally introduced, but with today's powerful systems this is less of a concern.

Stochastic or frequency-modulated (FM) screening takes a different approach. In conventional halftones, dots are of variable size with fixed spacing (or screen ruling). This is also referred to as amplitude-modulated (AM) screening. Stochastic screening instead varies the frequency of the spacing and keeps the dot size fixed (figure 9.11). This more random appearing placement of the dots eliminates the problem of interference from screen lines that causes moiré. In addition, there is a reduction in dot gain (discussed in chapter 4) and file size. The main challenge with this type of screening is tiny dot size, which can make

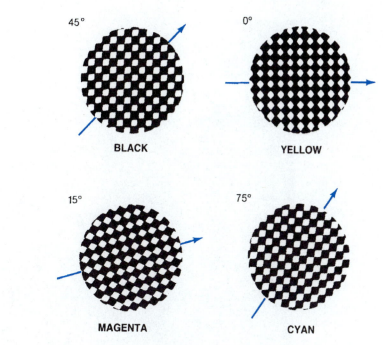

45°   0°

BLACK   **YELLOW**

15°   75°

MAGENTA   **CYAN**

Figure 9.10 **The typical screen angles used in process color printing**

proofing and platemaking difficult, but the technology is rapidly improving to minimize this concern.

Dot Shape

Traditional halftone screens are designed to produce square and elliptical dot structures.

In digital halftones you have more options regarding the shape of the halftone dot, and this can greatly affect your printed piece.

    Due to dot gain, which can be caused by pressure between the blanket cylinder and impression cylinder on a press and/or the porousness of the substrate, spots can dra-

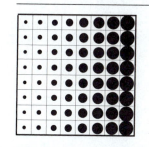

In traditional halftone screening dots are of variable size with fixed spacing

Stochastic screening varies the frequency spacing of the dot while keeping the size of the dots constant

Figure 9.11 **Traditional halftone screening versus stochastic screening**

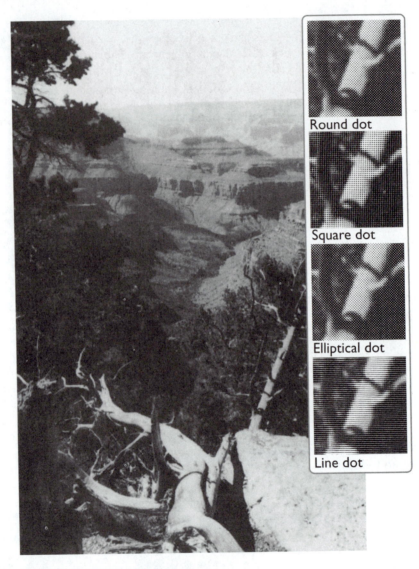

Round dot

Square dot

Elliptical dot

Line dot

Figure 9.12 **The most commonly used dot shapes**

matically spread, especially in the mid-tones. This can create blocked up shadows and muddy mid-tones. Dot gain is measured in percentages and can be compensated for in your image-editing software by decreasing or increasing the percentage of gain expected for the highlight, mid-tone, and shadow areas. Not only do we have the physical dot gain just described, but there is also a perceived phenomenon called optical dot gain. This is due to the decrease of reflected light from the substrate surface because of the increased density of inks in the area.

The shape of the dot can have an effect on dot gain and image appearance (figure 9.12). The basic halftone spot is round, starting small and getting bigger until it fills the halftone cell. Due to its shape, it is very prone to optical dot gain in the dark areas. PostScript devices create a variation on the round dot, which allows for changes in the actual dot shape as the size increases. It begins as a round black dot, transforms into a square shape at the midtones, and then inverts to a small white spot on a black background.

The **elliptical dot** is also used in digital halftones and is in fact more diamond-shaped than truly elliptical. This shape can help to reduce optical dot gain by having two distinct merging points, where the sides meet and where the ends meet, creating a smoother transition than would occur with a round dot. There is also a halftone dot called the **transforming elliptical dot** that changes shape as it moves from the highlight to shadow tones, much the way the PostScript dot does.

The **square dot** is used most often for very high quality color work because it gives the best illusion of sharpness. It also results in more optical dot gain in the mid-tones, which produces contrast and enhances the sense of sharpness.

Color

Basic color theory, as discussed in chapter 5, does not change when we move into the digital realm. But there are different issues to be aware of and different ways to specify color that need to be handled through your page-layout and image-editing software.

Digital color is concerned with conversions of color from one color space to another. If publishing to the Internet, RGB and Index color are color models that need to be understood; if going to print, CMYK (process) and spot colors comprise your color space. Although there are more color spaces than the ones just specified, we will explore the models involved with output to substrate (printing) and output to a transmissive environment (the Internet).

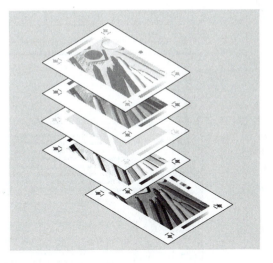

Figure 9.13 Process color.
Courtesy of Agfa Corporation.

Process and Spot Color for Printing

Cyan, magenta, yellow, and black are called **process colors.** In conventional prepress, the method or process of creating four distinct color separations is referred to as *process color* (figure 9.13). The process involves overlaying of the inks that, when combined, can create the illusion of millions of colors. Spot color is used when you need the color exactly as defined by the ink (not a overlay of any of the process colors). A separate plate is produced for spot color, with the actual hue being designated within a color matching system, such as Pantone Matching System (PMS). This ink color is premixed and matches a swatch booklet that the designer and prepress operator can refer to.

In page-layout software, such as QuarkXpress, you can specify your colors from your Colors dialogue box (in addition to the six default colors: cyan, magenta, yellow, black, white, and registration). It is important to be familiar with this type of box in any page-layout program, and it is one of the areas always checked during the preflight process (figure 9.14).

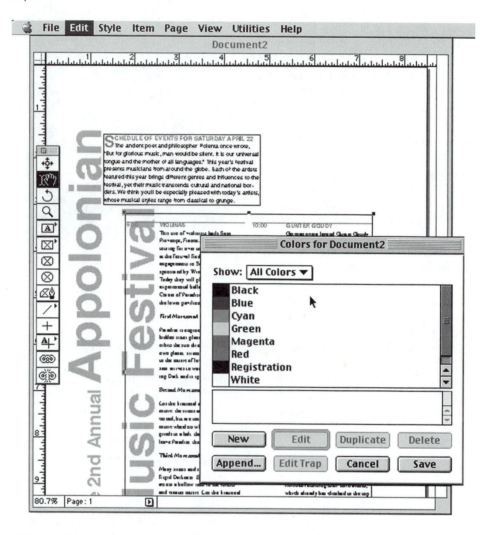

Figure 9.14 **Colors dialogue box.**
Courtesy Quark, Inc.

If you are printing a CMYK job and inaccurately list a process color as printing as a spot color or plan on a spot color and do not specify it, your job will output incorrectly. For example, if you have a spot color that you want in your job, but fail to choose that attribute for the color, it will default to process and separate into four colors.

Tints and blends are other areas that have become easy to apply with the advent of digital prepress (figure 9.15). A **tint** is another way of describing the saturation of a color, or how light a particular hue is. For example, you could print a spot color (or process color) at 25 or 65 percent of its value, depending on the saturation that you want. In page-layout soft-

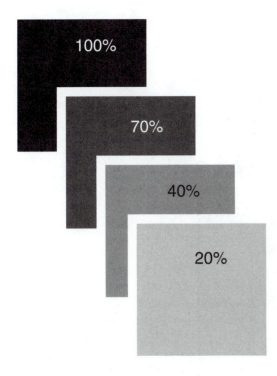

Figure 9.15 **Tints**

transition from one color or shape to another with varying degrees of smoothness. A pitfall to be avoided is **banding,** which is often a challenge in digital halftone technology (figure 9.16). Banding, that is, the separate steps of a blend becoming visible in what is meant to be a smooth blend, occurs when you create a blend with more levels of gray than can be described due to the screen frequency and ability of the output device.

Color and the Internet

Print is a reflective medium dealing with the CMYK color space. Move to the Internet and you enter a transmissive world that operates in RGB. And unique to this environment is the fact that the viewer can affect the look of your output. When you print a magazine, aside from the quality of light that it is viewed in, the viewer cannot really alter the final piece. When something is published on the Internet, you have issues such as color depth, luminescence of the display, the currency of the browser, and the skill level of the viewer to contend with. We will look at the color variables faced in an RGB world and how to plan for them in your workflow.

Many companies today produce Web sites in tandem with printed pieces or as adjuncts to them. Others sell over the Web, but often have a printed piece available on request. The challenge is not to have color vary too widely and to keep a complementary sense of design.

ware, you cannot only accurately specify the percentage tint that you want, but you can also adjust the halftone screen angle and frequency of the tints. This is important if the tint of your spot color is going to overprint another tint of some other color.

Computer-generated **blends,** also referred to as **gradations,** describe the gradual

Figure 9.16 **Banding.** Separate tones of a blend become visible.

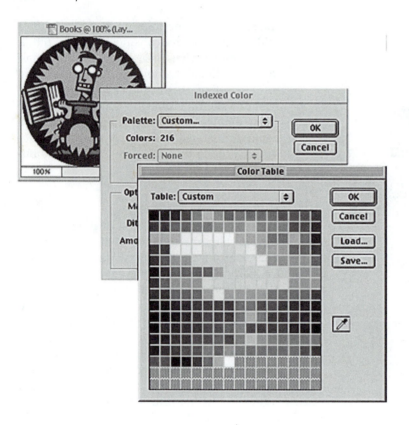

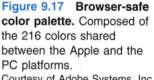

Figure 9.17 Browser-safe color palette. Composed of the 216 colors shared between the Apple and the PC platforms.
Courtesy of Adobe Systems, Inc.

The ability of a monitor to produce numerous colors depends on the video RAM installed. An eight-bit video card can only create 256 colors, whereas as a 24-bit video card can display up to 16.7 million colors. The display capability affects how the user will experience your Web site. To plan for this and to have a published site vary as little as possible due to viewer variables, a **browser-safe color palette** is often used (figure 9.17). This palette is composed of 216 mathematical color combinations based on the shared colors utilized by all current browsers, on both the Mac and PC platforms. This assures the least color variation from display to display. In chapter 10, we will explore more issues regarding output to the World Wide Web.

Color Management

Color management has traditional been the responsibility of the prepress and printing professional who relied on analog film and proofing methods to ensure an exact match to the printing press. Digital prepress changed everything, with color decisions and choices being made far earlier in the process and less highly trained individuals being able to output proofs on relatively inexpensive proofers. With the multitude of proofing options (including soft proofs) and designers working in an RGB space with colors far exceeding the gamut of a printing press, some kind of standardized management of color has been essential. Different vendors, such as Kodak,

EFIColor, and Agfa, have developed their own color management systems, but these are application-level approaches, rather than system-level approaches. The ICC (International Color Consortium) was formed to address this issue and the goal of consistent color output independent of the output device or application being used. The result is the ICC color management system which involves three main components: profiles, Color Management Modules (CMMs), and the Color Management System (CMS).

The main goal of a **profile** is to describe specific characteristics of a particular output device. Different output devices can create different ranges of color, or **gamuts.** These characteristics are determined by measuring the output of a specific device against a standard target. Print output is measured by printing a software-generated target and measuring the target values with a spectrophotometer, a device that measures and analyzes the wavelengths reflected off a surface (figure 9.18).

This profile can also be referred to as the *footprint* of the device. A monitor's color value is measured by evaluating a software-generated target that would be read with a colorimeter, a device that measures color in terms of different color temperature light sources. A scanner's output is measured against the known values of the target scanned. The resulting profile itself is embedded into the image file as additional data that travel with it through the production cycle.

Once the profile is determined, a **Color Management Module,** or CMM, actually performs the color conversions based on the profile information. A CMM converts the data from the specific characteristics of one device to another. The **Color Management Solution,** or CMS, is the operating-system-level software that facilitates the whole color management process. The CMS utilizes the CMM to do the color transformation. Apple ColorSync and Microsoft ICM2 are examples of a CMS that utilizes profiles for consistent color from image creation to output.

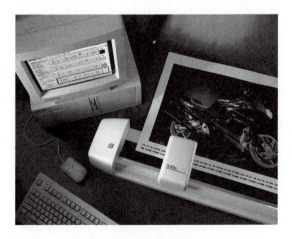

Figure 9.18 **Spectrophotometer.** A spectrophotometer is used to measure press sheet color bars at various intervals throughout the press run. The measurement data are displayed on the computer.
Courtesy of X-Rite, Inc.

Digital Trapping and Imposition

Trapping and imposition (the latter is discussed in chapter 6) have always been a part of the printing process. What has changed in the last decade is where these operations can occur.

Trapping, the allowance for an overlap of two colors so as to compensate for misregister and the resultant gaps between colors, has traditionally occurred during stripping (refer to plate N). With the demise of traditional stripping, the process has been incorporated into either the design or the output phase of production. In software such as Adobe Illustrator and QuarkXpress, there are choices to adjust your colors to *choke* (making the background area smaller) or *spread* (making the foreground area larger, figure 9.19). The problem is that the designer does not always know

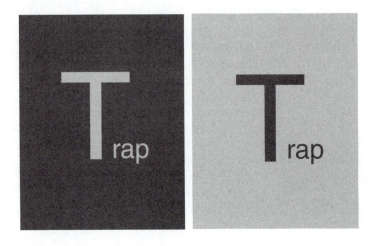

Figure 9.19 **Trapping.** The trap filter creates spread with a light object on a dark background. The trap filter creates choke with a dark object on a light background.

what device the work will be output on or what substrate will be used. More often than not, the prepress or printing facility will ask to handle the trapping choices within production.

Imposition is the correct positioning of pages on a press sheet so that, when folded into a signature and cut, the sequence of pages will be correct (refer to chapter 6). Traditionally, this was not a concern of the designer, but, once again, digital prepress has allowed for the movement of processes to earlier points in the workflow. Although available as a plug-in for many popular page-layout programs, it is not advisable to let this decision be made too early and by an individual not familiar with all the finishing processes that may occur. Imposition and trapping at the late stages of output will be discussed in more detail in chapter 10.

Key Terms

page–layout software
FPO (for position only)
OPI (open prepress interface)
prepress specialists
PostScript
Bézier curves
encapsulated PostScript (EPS)
raster image processor (RIP)
font
PostScript Type 1 fonts
TrueType fonts

OpenType font
preflight
digital halftone
halftone cell
frequency
screen angle
rational tangent (RT)
supercell
stochastic
elliptical dot
transforming elliptical dot

square dot
process colors
tint
blends
gradations
banding
browser-safe color palette
profile
gamut
Color Management Module (MM)
Color Management Solution (MS)

Review Questions

1. What are some advantages of developing a layout on a computer?
2. What is the primary method of creating low-resolution files for use in production?
3. Define bitmap and vector images.
4. What is the function of a raster image processor?
5. List at least five different operations that image-editing software does in far less time than it would take with traditional prepress.
6. What are some problems that can be encountered with fonts?
7. Why is preflighting so important?
8. Define digital halftone and how different levels of gray are represented.
9. Describe frequency, angle, and dot shape as they relate to digital screening.
10. What is the difference between supercell screening and stochastic screening?
11. Define process color and spot color.
12. Describe the difference between a tint and a blend.
13. What is meant by a browser-safe color palette?
14. What is the main goal of a color profile?
15. Define trapping and imposition.

10

Digital Prepress
Output

Historical Background

In 1978, Charles Geschke, a talented research scientist at Xerox's Palo Alto Research Center, hired an engineer named John Warnock. Together the two men began working on a piece of software that would revolutionize the publishing industry. Geschke and Warnock spent years as part of a PARC team developing Interpress, a page description language that en-abled printers to reproduce content exactly as it appeared on a computer screen. Prior to Interpress, the differences in resolution between the computer and the printer meant that documents appeared one way on screen, but would frequently print as a scrambled mess. Xerox liked the technology, but refused to release it commercially until it could reengineer all of its printers to the new standard, a process that would take years.

Frustrated, Geschke and Warnock left the company in 1982 and formed Adobe Systems, Inc. A year later, Apple CEO Steve Jobs showed Adobe executives an early Macintosh and, impressed with their technology, invested $1.5 million in the company to develop PostScript for the Apple LaserWriter printer, which debuted in 1985.

Buoyed by its success with PostScript, Adobe went on to develop market-leading design and document products, such as Photoshop, Illustrator, Acrobat, and InDesign. These and other products such as the Adobe Type Library, have combined to make Adobe the fourth-largest software producer in the world, with recent sales topping $1 billion.

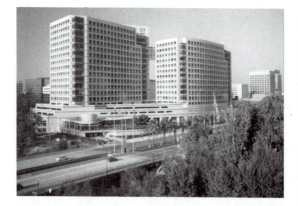

Adobe headquarters in California.
Courtesy of Adobe Systems, Inc.

Objectives

After completing this chapter you will be able to:

- Discuss and define PostScript.
- Explain the three main functions of raster image processing.
- List the advantages of a PDF workflow.
- Define digital imposition and trapping.
- Discuss outputting to film from a digital workflow.
- Differentiate between preliminary and contract proofs and soft proofs.
- List the options that digital halftone proofing provides.
- Discuss the differences between computer-to-plate substrates and imaging systems.
- List the three types of plate exposing systems.
- Discuss options when publishing to the World Wide Web.
- Explain the importance of databasing and archiving.

Introduction

Output in today's publishing world encompasses a much broader arena than it did in the past. Until the 1990s, output meant creating film, burning plates, and running a printing press, which generally operated by placing ink on a given substrate. Now we can output directly to plate or to a toner-based digital press or multimedia or the Internet. This chapter will explore the technologies and methods used to output content in a variety of ways. We will discuss specific press technologies in later chapters. To begin, we must understand the language of digital workflow, which primarily revolves around PostScript.

PostScript

PostScript is a page description language invented by Adobe Systems that is device independent. This allows any document created with it to be understood by any PostScript-compatible output device. The other powerful feature of PostScript is that it translates the fonts and most images into mathematical vec-

tor equations, allowing the file to be output at the highest quality on the output device being used (figure 10.1). PostScript itself is actually a computer programming language. When a designer finishes a file in a page-layout program and chooses the print command, a **Post-**

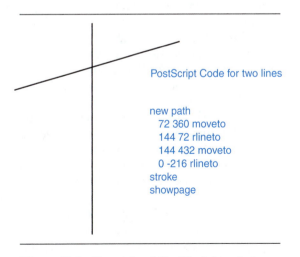

Figure 10.1 Example of PostScript code to create two lines

Script driver begins the process of converting the file into PostScript code. After the code is created, it is sent from the computer to the designated output device. The designated devices are usually characterized as raster output devices. They are typically imagesetters, laser and inkjet printers, or digital presses and computer-to-plate (CTP) devices, which will be covered later.

The **RIP** (raster image processor) is where the PostScript information gets converted into the actual on and off commands that will allow the device to create the image. It can be a software RIP (a program running on a computer that also has other functions) or a hardware RIP (residing on a dedicated computer whose only purpose is RIPping). The RIP has three main functions: interpretation, rasterization, and screening.

Interpretation or rendering is the beginning of the process. Here the commands contained within the PostScript code are redrawn as a series of objects. In **rasterization,** the resolution-independent objects are converted into squares of variable density data, also known as *pixels* (figure 10.2). The resultant file is referred to as the raster image. **Screening** is the point at which the raster image is converted into a bilevel bitmap consisting of on and off commands that can be understood by the marking engine of the output device. For example, if the output device is capable of 1,200 dpi, the bilevel bitmap will be made up of a grid consisting of 1,200 on and off commands per linear inch. Also during screening, scanned images, digital photographs, and other pixel-based data are incorporated. High-resolution images stored on OPI servers join the file at this time.

Some of the limitations of working with a pure PostScript file are that, once the file is converted to PostScript, it is for all practicable purposes uneditable. It is also a very complex page description language and creates a large file.

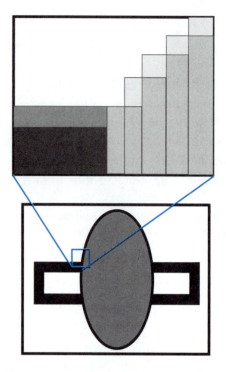

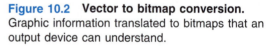

Figure 10.2   Vector to bitmap conversion. Graphic information translated to bitmaps that an output device can understand.

Portable Document Format

The **Portable Document Format (PDF),** was developed by Adobe in 1993. The original concept focused on bypassing paper and creating a digital document viewable and annotatable by many and independent of specific application software, font, or operating system. It was not originally designed to handle high-end printing needs involving color separations. But the publishing industry saw the potential for this type of file format in the early stages of digital workflow development, and Adobe pursued a path that has resulted in robust and comprehensive file formatting that addresses numerous publishing needs.

The basic components of a PDF file are a view file that displays the file as created, embedded type, graphic objects, and links to other types of data, including job ticket information. Information from the original file is processed through the Distiller, which is an included function in Adobe Acrobat 4.0. This **distillation** process actually creates the PDF and includes various assignable settings, depending on the eventual output device (figure 10.3). The main areas of output can be categorized as follows:

- *Screen:* Internet or viewing on a display and local laser or ink-jet printing
- *Print:* high-speed laser printer reproduction or CD-ROM/disk distribution
- *Press:* high-end printing

Although the page descriptions in a PDF file still must be converted into PostScript before printing, the distillation process in essence handles the file interpretation and, as a result, assures less variability during final output.

One of the main benefits of PDF in digital workflow is that it produces a more manageable file that maintains integrity and yet can be edited, is **page independent** (individual pages can be accessed, which cannot be done in PostScript, and can be output at a variety of different settings. For many of the following reasons, PDF is becoming an integral part of the printing and publishing workflow.

- Ability to incorporate numerous data formats such as bitmap or raster images, vector-based artwork, and text, while remaining platform independent (not dependent on any one operating system).
- Compactness of file. There is approximately a 10 : 1 compression factor between the original file and the PDF file.
- Eliminates the variability of PostScript. The interpretation and display list functions normally handled in the RIP are executed during distillation. This creates a file with only the essen-

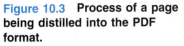

Figure 10.3 Process of a page being distilled into the PDF format.
Courtesy of Adobe Systems, Inc.

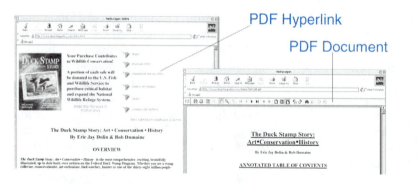

PDF Hyperlink

PDF Document

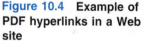

Figure 10.4 Example of PDF hyperlinks in a Web site

tial information needed and therefore a much cleaner PostScript output to the imaging device.

■ Full text search available within the Acrobat software. Hypertext features allow linking of various parts of a document, and comprehensive navigation features allow for quick retrieval of information (figure 10.4).

■ Repurposing of data is easy because PDF files can be published to the Internet as viewable and/or downloadable documents accessible through any popular browser by a browser plug-in. This allows for concurrent publishing streams to print and the Internet.

■ The ability to embed fonts in the document that preserves cross-platform font fidelity and allows printing at any resolution.

■ The ability to do last minute editing on files through an extensive offering of third party software.

Imposition and Trapping

The traditional methods of handling imposition and trapping have been altered by the advent of digital technology. In particular, there

are now more choices as to when these actions can occur. Imposition in today's digital workflow can be classified as either (1) PostScript imposition or (2) RIP-based imposition.

Imposition

Originally, as detailed in chapter 6, imposition occurred after film was made. A stripper would gather the film output and strip the pages into flats based on press and finishing considerations. Now, with workflow automation a major trend in printing, imposition software is being used at the design stage or at the RIP to produce a more efficient and faster production workflow.

PostScript-Based Imposition

PostScript-based imposition can include plug-ins designed for page-layout programs that create imposed PostScript files during output (figure 10.5). Or it can consist of a stand-alone program designed solely to arrange the pages of the job into the correct signature, consisting of both the front and back forms based on the sheet size to be used. There are also programs designed to impose PDF files directly, eliminating the need to first translate the files to PostScript. What distinguishes the top PostScript imposition software programs is the ability to save configuration

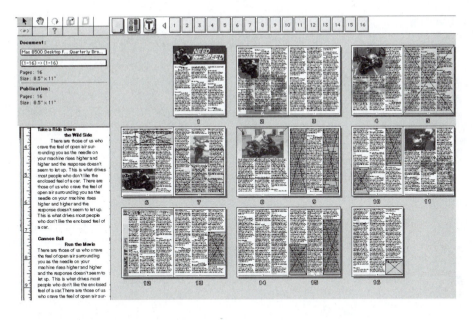

Figure 10.5 **Reader's mode imposition.** An imposition plug-in that operates within layout software. Courtesy of DK&A, Inc.

information on variables such as page layout and page order as custom templates.

RIP-Based Imposition

RIP-based imposition is done through software that is actually incorporated into the RIP. There are a variety of approaches, including proprietary ones that are based on vendor-specific equipment and workflow. Incoming files (TIFF, Postscript, EPS, or PDF) can either be converted to an intermediary multipage file format, which is then imposed into a single file prior to screening, or rasterized as individual pages, imposed, and then screened. The advantage of RIPing the file as independent pages rather than as one large multipage file is the ability to make last-minute imposition changes without having to re-RIP the entire file. This ability to effect changes to individual pages late in the output process is often re-

ferred to as **late binding.** RIP-based imposition is the more frequent choice because it is incorporated into the production workflow, rather than being chosen at the design stage.

Trapping

In printing there is the possibility of gaps or incorrect overlaps of color due to misregistration while the job is being run on the press (figure 10.6). There can be misregister due to stretching and the inherent flexibility of the substrate as it moves through the press. The technique of **trapping** seeks to reduce this possibility by either enlarging the background or foreground color slightly to compensate for the possibility of gaps between adjacent colors. Traditionally, this has been handled by either a photographic overexposure of film to make the foreground image slightly larger than the original (known as a *spread*) or to

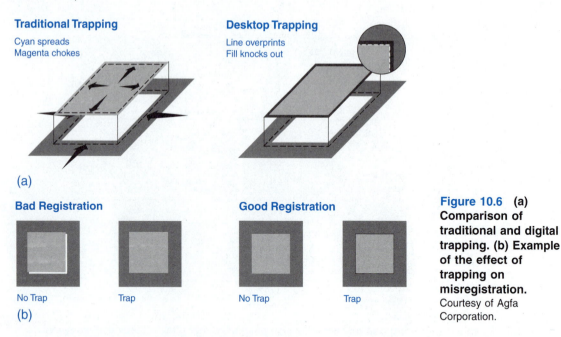

Traditional Trapping

Cyan spreads
Magenta chokes

Desktop Trapping

Line overprints
Fill knocks out

(a)

Bad Registration

No Trap   Trap

Good Registration

No Trap   Trap

(b)

Figure 10.6 **(a)
Comparison of
traditional and digital
trapping. (b) Example
of the effect of
trapping on
misregistration.**
Courtesy of Agfa
Corporation.

make a photographic enlargement of the background image which then overlaps the foreground image slightly (known as a *choke*).

Trapping was once exclusively handled by the prepress or printing facility because they were solely responsible for shooting film and producing color separations. With digital prepress, the ability to do trapping can now occur at the program level on the desktop, within dedicated trapping software or at the RIP.

Vector and Raster-Based Trapping

There are two basic approaches to digital trapping: vector trapping and raster trapping. **Vector trapping** involves vector-based graphics being analyzed for trapping problems. If one is encountered, the software analyzing the file mathematically changes the width and depth of the object based on what needs to be done to effect the best trap. This method is somewhat less effective with scanned or raster data, because the program must determine the trap on a pixel by pixel basis. **Raster trapping** is designed to analyze rasterized or bitmap images and add pixels as needed. This can take a sizable amount of RAM and disk space, but it is the most convenient form of trapping when done at the point that all data have been converted to screened bitmaps. The majority of high-end prepress systems analyze raster data when trapping. A third approach is called **hybrid trapping** and involves both vector and raster data analysis.

Trapping occurring within an application such as Illustrator, Freehand, or Quark-Xpress works with vector data and can be done by the designer or the prepress facility during assembly (figure 10.7). But there are limitations, such as the ability to trap adjacent gradients and complex raster data. The ideal approach is to always ask the prepress or printing facility where in the workflow they want to handle trapping; most often the response will be at the production facility and most likely it will be integrated with the RIP software.

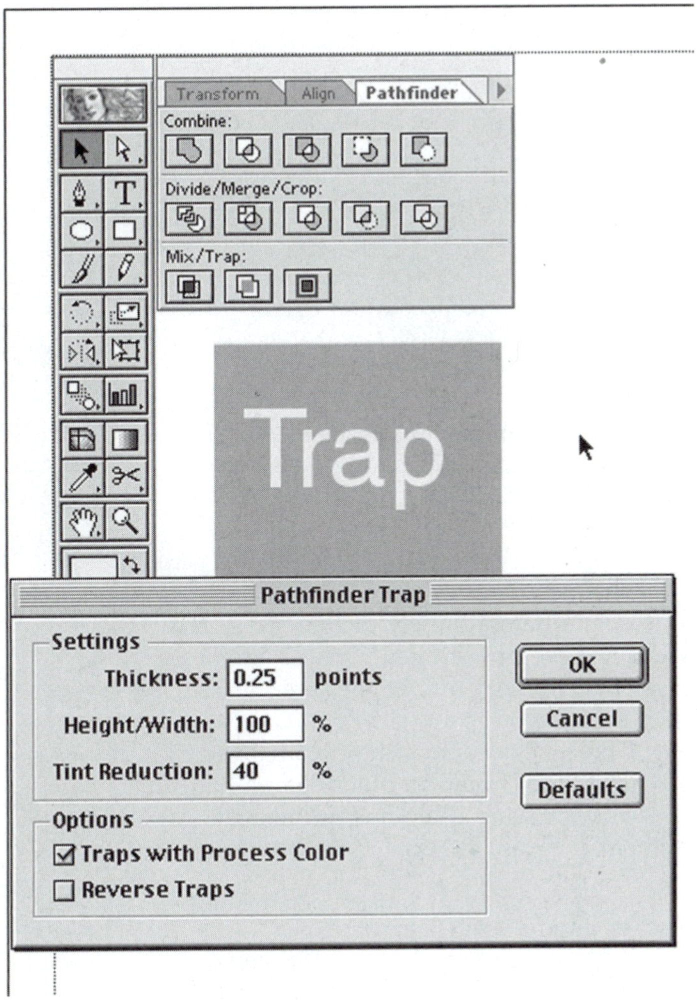

Figure 10.7 **Trapping window within illustration software.** Courtesy of Adobe Systems, Inc.

Output to Film

Although a purely digital workflow would not incorporate film, the ability to send to an imagesetter requires a digital front end in your job production. The advances in imagesetting technology and the competitively low cost when compared to investing in computer-to-plate (CTP) equipment have ensured that imagesetters will continue to play an important role in digital prepress until CTP technology has dropped in price sufficiently to allow companies of all size to adopt its many benefits. Imagesetters also allow for outputting of certain types of plate material, such as polyester, further preparing for the transition to full digital workflow.

The term **imagesetter** is used to describe an output device that records processed data to photographic paper, film, or plate material (figure 10.8). Many companies produce imagesetting devices that record at various reso-

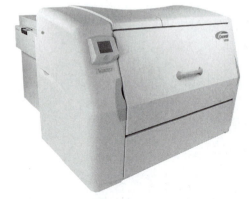

Figure 10.8 **Multilaser imagesetter.** This two-laser system can produce up to 29 plate-ready flats per hour at 2,438 dpi.
Courtesy of Fuji Photo Film, U.S.A., Inc.

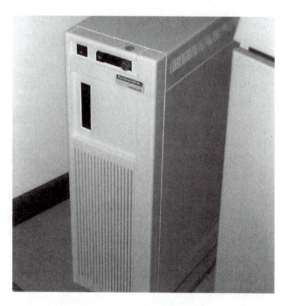

Figure 10.9 **Raster image processor.** A raster image processor converts various types of digital data to machine bitmaps understood by the recorder to which it is attached.

lutions and onto a variety of film sizes. The smaller, less sophisticated devices are less costly than the high-resolution, large-film size, color-separation-capable systems.

Three major components are involved in producing film from computer data: a hardware or software RIP, a film imager or recorder (imagesetter), and a film processor.

Raster Image Processor

The raster image processor, or RIP converts PostScript and raster data to the **machine bitmap** that the recorder can process (figure 10.9). This conversion process requires a highly productive RIP one characterized by a fast microprocessor, quality screening hardware, sufficient storage and spooling capability, and a network connection.

Film Imager or Recorder

The **film image recorder** exposes the single-color, spot-color, or process-color separations on a light-sensitive substrate. Imagesetters can offer a range of resolutions up to ±3,000 dpi. This ensures quality output with a full range

of tones at commonly used halftone ruling screens of 133 to 150 lpi and higher. Imagesetters are designed for prepress facilities, printers, magazine publishers, or any manufacturer processing and recording computer-generated graphics or color separations.

Film Processor

The **film processor** develops, fixes, washes, and dries exposed light-sensitive output from the imagesetter (refer to chapter 4 for more information on film processing). A processor with adequate developer storage and control is necessary to produce film negatives or positives with appropriate maximum densities. It is recommended that you discuss these requirements with the imagesetter and film manufacturer before purchasing a processor.

A calibration procedure is needed to orchestrate all these devices into one productive test system. Calibration exposure tests are produced and measured with a densitometer. If the calibrated films do not meet specifications, software and hardware adjustments must be made until quality output is achieved.

Digital Proofing

Digital proofing involves sending files electronically from a scanner or workstation directly to a proofing mechanism that makes a color proof from the digitized information (figure 10.10). A variety of proofing solutions is available, from high-end contract proofers to desktop models used in the initial design stages. The many categories of digital proofing encompass design comps, revision approvals, imposition dummies, and final contract proofs. One dividing line that can be drawn is between those that produce a continuous-tone image and the digital proofing systems that simulate the actual halftone dot of the images to be printed on press.

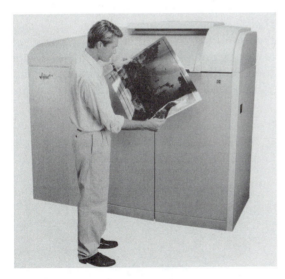

Figure 10.10 **A contract quality digital proofer.**
Courtesy of Kodak Polychrome Graphics, Inc.

Preliminary Proofs

The basic purpose of a **proof** is to check type, graphics, page construction, and color. The level of quality required to evaluate these characteristics changes depending on where you are in the production cycle. Color is less critical, as is dot gain, in the early design comp stages, revision processes, and certainly for imposition set-up. These **preliminary proofs** are critical for an efficient digital workflow, but are not necessarily accurate predictors of final press results.

The main proofing technologies employed in preliminary proofing are laser, thermal wax, ink jet, and dye sublimation.

Laser Printers

Laser printing marries the technologies of electrostatic or electrophotographic printing and the computer. The word **laser** is an acronym for the phrase "light amplification by stimulated emission of radiation." Simply stated, a laser beam is a concentrated beam of light that is capable of microscopic precision. Information sent by a computer causes the printer laser to expose an internal electrically charged drum or cylinder to the light that reflects from the nonimage areas, causing the charge to dissipate. The charged areas remaining represent the image areas, which attract oppositely charged particles of toner. The toner that corresponds to the image areas is transferred to the substrate passing beneath the drum. Color laser printers are increasingly being used for preliminary proofs and can produce resolutions of up to 1,200 dpi. They are capable of high page per minute counts and a low per copy cost (figure 10.11).

Solid-Ink Printers

The thermal-wax printer was at one time one of the more popular preliminary proofers. This technology created 300-dpi images by transferring wax from a yellow, magenta, cyan, and black ink cartridge onto a special substrate us-

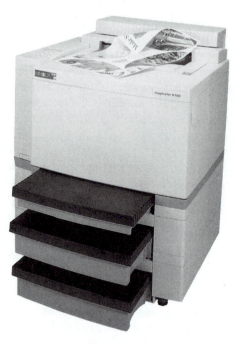

Figure 10.11 **Color laser printer.**
Courtesy of Minolta-QMS

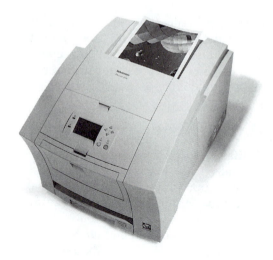

Figure 10.12 **Solid-ink printer.**
Courtesy of Tektronix (Xerox), Inc.

ing a thermal printing head. The thermal head contained heating elements that caused the wax to melt and adhere to the substrate. This basic concept has not changed, but now, in addition to wax-based inks, resin-based **solid inks** are used and resolutions up to 1,200 dpi are possible. The new formulation and improved printer design permit up to ten color pages per minute with accurate dot registration due to a single-pass architecture and the ability to print on a variety of substrates (figure 10.12).

Ink-Jet Printers
Ink-jet printers offer liquid and solid-ink imaging technology. Dyes mixed in a fluid vehicle or carrier are propelled through tiny nozzles in the form of droplets to the substrate surface (figure 10.13). Ink-jet printers are relatively inexpensive, but the ink-jet cartridges

can be costly. Although ink-jet printers are very popular for preliminary proofing, there are also ink-jet solutions for high-end proofing requirements. Ink-jet printing will be discussed in greater detail in chapter 16.

Dye-Sublimation Printers
Dye-sublimation printers are capable of achieving photographlike quality. They do not use the **dithering** process used by ink-jet and wax-thermal printers, which is the technique

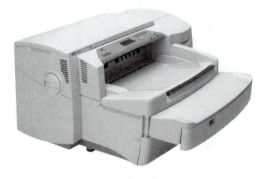

Figure 10.13 **Ink-jet printer.**
Courtesy of Imation, Inc.

of using a noncontinuous pattern of yellow, magenta, cyan, and black dots to create the illusion of tone. A dye-sublimation printer is instead a continuous-tone imaging system that transfers colored dyes from a plastic ribbon to a special plastic sheet. Continuous tones are created when the dyes from the ribbon are vaporized by heat and then absorbed into the special sheet. Instead of producing a specific number of dots per inch, the dye-sublimation printer transfers vaporized dyes to *areas per inch,* blending them seamlessly.

Although considered an intermediate proof, high-quality dye-sublimation proofers are occasionally being used as final proofs in well-controlled and color managed workflows that repeatedly output the same type of publication to the same press.

Contract Proofs

A **contract proof** supplies what its name implies: a visual tangible product that serves as the contract between the prepress facility or printer and the customer. Both parties accept the proof as an accurate predictor of what the final on-press product will look like. Traditionally, this proof was done with the same film that would burn the plates; but with a true digital workflow there is no film and therefore no original physical output to approve prior to running on press. The digital proof that comes closest to simulating the actual press output is one that can produce halftone dots.

Digital Halftone Proofing

A halftone consists of a collection of dots of varying sizes that serve to simulate the appearance of a continuous-tone image. A **digital halftone proofer** seeks to create dots as they would appear on the final sheet on press and to simulate all the controls one would have in a conventional proofing operation (figure 10.14). Proofers such as the Kodak

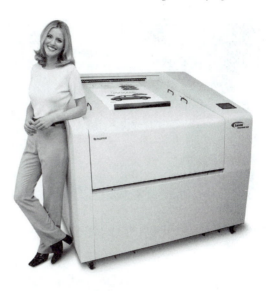

Figure 10.14 Digital halftone proofer.
Courtesy of Fuji Photo Film, U.S.A., Inc.

Approval allow an operator to choose the following:

- Exact screening algorithms
- Resolutions up to 2,500 dpi
- Dot shape
- Screen angles
- Specifications and settings of densities of CMYK individually
- Halftone dot gain adjustment

Often a quality digital halftone proofer will use a common RIP and imaging technology as the platesetter to achieve the proof that is the most accurate representative of the final product.

Soft Proofing

A **soft proof** is presented on a display and attempts to predict the color and content of the image to be printed (refer to Plate 0). Correct color is difficult to achieve on a display, be-

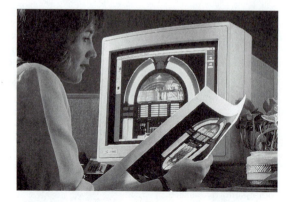

Figure 10.15 **Example of soft proofing.**
Courtesy of Imation, Inc.

cause variables such as video card resolution, ambient light, and monitor calibration are hard to control. Add to this the facts that a display works in a transmissive RGB mode and print is based on CMYK and reflective light and you have many factors that may alter the color markedly from the final output. The best use for soft proofing is as an intermediary or preliminary proof for checking overall appearance, text, and image placement. It is especially useful for remote proofing prior to producing a contract proof (figure 10.15).

Computer to Plate

Computer-to-plate (CTP) technology eliminates one of the most enduring symbols of the printing process, the film. It allows digital data direct from the computer to guide lasers in the direct imaging of a plate without any intermediate material. It greatly reduces mechanical concerns such as registration problems and dot gain because there is no generational loss between media. The imaging technology involved allows for extremely accurate dot placement and high-quality plates. It is a critical component of a completely digital workflow (figure 10.16).

CTP Plate Substrate

Plate imaging is achieved through the use of light-sensitive coatings. Different surfaces in combination with different imaging systems have varied results. As with conventional plates, they can be described as either positive or negative acting. A negative-acting plate creates the image areas through exposure, and a positive-acting plate creates the nonimage areas though exposure.

Metal plates used in CTP are made from aluminum alloys that are grained to improve coating adhesion and water control. They are then anodized (to create an aluminum oxide layer) to increase durability and to help resist scratching. Four basic categories of lithographic plates can be imaged directly from digital data: silver halide, thermal conversion, thermal ablation, and photopolymer.

Silver halide plates are positive-working plates with silver halide suspended in a gelatin layer (figure 10.17). They are extremely light sensitive and relatively inexpensive, but can

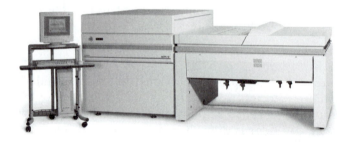

Figure 10.16 **Digital platesetting system.**
Courtesy of Agfa Corporation.

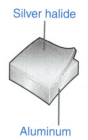

Silver halide

Aluminum

Figure 10.17 Plate layers. In a silver halide plate, a laser exposes nonimage areas of the plate, which are removed during development. The plate is rinsed in water, with minimal finishing required.
Courtesy of Agfa Corporation.

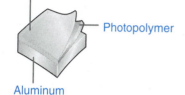

Thermo-sensitive Layer

Photopolymer

Aluminum

Figure 10.18 Plate layers. In thermal conversion plates, an infrared laser exposes the image areas. The plate is then developed in potassium hydroxide to dissolve the nonimage areas and the plate is rinsed, gummed (refer to chapter 6), and baked.
Courtesy of Agfa Corporation.

develop inconsistencies at high-press-run lengths. After exposure, they require processing to remove the unexposed silver halide and then stabilization. Silver halide plates can also be on a polyester base. **Polyester plates,** once considered appropriate for only short-run and single- or spot-color work, are now able to handle jobs once reserved exclusively for metal plates. Polyester plates rated up to 20,000 impressions and for full four-color work are now used on a variety of hybrid presses, such as the Heidelberg QuickMaster 46/4 DI Press.

Thermal conversion plates are coated with a reactive material that undergoes a conversion process when exposed to heat from an infrared laser (figure 10.18). After exposure, the plate is sent through an alkaline bath to dissolve the nonimage area. The plate is then rinsed and gummed, or desensitized, and baked twice. Thermal plates are considered true digital plates; they hold a very fine dot structure and can be handled in both yellow-safe light and certain daylight situations. They require higher laser energy to create image areas than do conventional plates, but can support resolutions greater than 300 lpi and are appropriate for very long press runs.

Thermal ablation plates use laser technology that selectively heats the nonimage area until the reactive material vaporizes; they do not require postexposure chemical treatment (figure 10.19). If dry plate technology is used, the waste can be vacuumed off, making this plate ideal for imaging on press. Wet plate technology using thermal ablation is capable of long press runs, but requires curing after imaging.

Photopolymer plates are negative-working plates that represent the earliest development in digital plate technology and are

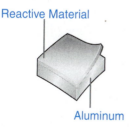

Reactive Material

Aluminum

Figure 10.19 Plate layers. In the thermal ablation plates, a YAG or laser diode vaporizes nonimage areas. The plate is then vacuumed to remove debris. Minimal finishing may be required.
Courtesy of Agfa Corporation.

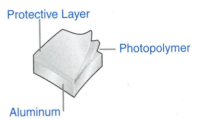

Protective Layer

Photopolymer

Aluminum

Figure 10.20 **Plate layers.** Photopolymer plates have the image areas exposed with frequency doubled YAG lasers and developed in an alkaline solution. They are then finished with gum.
Courtesy of Agfa Corporation.

derived from conventional presensitized plate technology (figure 10.20). The photopolymers used are mainly sensitive to ultraviolet radiation, with exposure initiating a polymerization process that creates long chains of higher-molecular-weight molecules, resulting in an extremely durable plate. The plate is then heated and developed. It can be baked for greater strength, with certain curing processes creating a strong enough plate for a press run of a million impressions.

Imaging Systems

In a CTP system, plates can be imaged using visible light or thermal lasers. A laser beam is an extremely focused beam of coherent light that provides a great deal of energy. In CTP technology, lasers are usually used either as a single beam reflecting off a high-speed rotating mirror to the substrate, or in an array that effectively increases the coverage area.

Visible Light Lasers

Visible light lasers in CTP systems work the same as in an imagesetter with the laser exposing the plate line by line. The size of the spots created is determined by the intensity and duration of the laser beam. The plate's substrate determines the amount of light energy needed to image the spot. Lasers in this

category range in frequency from 410 to 532 nanometers (nm) and include argon ion and frequency doubled YAG. Argon ion lasers were once the standard lasers used in early platesetters, but have been eclipsed by newer technologies. Frequency-doubled YAG lasers operate at a frequency of 530 nm in the visible green and are often used on slower or less sensitive substrates due to this laser's high power (see Plate P).

Thermal Imaging

Thermal imaging systems use an infrared laser to create two types of responses depending on the substrate used. **Thermal conversion** heats reactive material on the substrate, causing a spot to appear. **Thermal ablation** has the laser actually removing material from the substrate, which decreases the amount of finishing steps required for processing the plate after exposure (figure 10.21). Thermal lasers range from 650 to 1,064 nm in the infrared part of the spectrum.

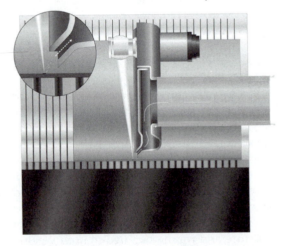

Figure 10.21 **Ablation process.** The image or nonimage area is removed by heating it to the point where the bonds to the substrate break. The debris is then vacuumed off the plate.
Courtesy of Agfa Corporation.

Platesetter Architecture

Platesetters are generally categorized by the size of plate that they accommodate. They can range in size from a very large format (VLF) platesetter of up to 80 by 58 inches to platesetters as small as 22 by 28 inches. There are three types of plate-exposing systems: flatbed, internal drum, and external drum (figure 10.22).

Flatbed platesetters are similar in design to capstan imagesetters with a stationary imaging head and the plate moving beneath. Plate handling in a flatbed system is easy, and the platesetters are usually configured with a visible-light imaging source. This contributes to fast throughput and is appropriate for newspaper printers, for whom speed is critical.

Internal drum platesetters incorporate a moving imaging head with a stationary plate. The plate is held within the drum by vacuum pressure. This architecture can support both high-speed visible-light and thermal imaging heads and utilizes a single-beam laser.

External drum platesetters have the plate wrapped around the circumference of the drum and held by clamps and vacuum pressure. This architecture uses multiple laser beams to expose multiple spots and is the most practical design for imaging very large format plates. It rotates slower than an internal drum system to prevent dislodging the plate during exposure.

Output to the Internet

Publishing no longer means information only sent to a physical substrate. The same customer that comes to a printing facility to have his annual report published may also require publication to the graphical portion of the Internet, the World Wide Web (referred to hereafter as the Web). A large part of the challenge involved in repurposing data is dealt with at the design stage. Illustrations for print and the Web are handled differently, as discussed in chapter 8. Publications created using page-layout programs cannot just be uploaded as is into a Web site. There are layout constraints due to templating and the use of tables in Web page design. Correct computer languages must be used and formats developed to accommodate publications that need regular additions. Taking digital content and sending it to a variety of output solutions is now referred to as a **cross-media** approach and involves print, Web, and multimedia. Some approaches being used are page-layout programs that have an HTML plug-in allowing document conversion to Web format, XML-based publishing, and PDF technology. And there are always proprietary third-party solutions that a print customer can access on its own and self-publish.

HTML Conversion Tools

A common approach is for a program to have a feature that allows the user to save the document as an **HTML** (hypertext mark-up language) document. One challenge of this kind

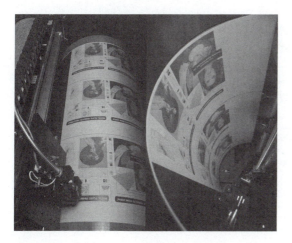

Figure 10.22 **External and internal drum architecture.**
Courtesy of Kodak Polychrome Graphics, Inc.

of straight conversion is that most formatting is lost. HTML is not a very sophisticated mark-up language and does not provide mechanisms for precise placement and the nuances that can be achieved with page-layout programs.

XML

XML (extensible mark-up language) is a more robust Web language than HTML. The advantages it brings to publishing on the Internet are the ability to structure the pages more precisely and to automate content exchange in an effort to repurpose existing digital data. Data become portable, or media independent, because they carry the data description. XML is built on the concept of **tags,** which allow you to specify attributes such as formatting or even data relationships. Several page-layout programs, such as QuarkXpress, have incorporated mechanisms to translate publications formatted for print output into XML content, which are then easily published to the Web (figure 10.23). They essentially take existing style sheets that apply to the document destined for print and correlate these with ele-

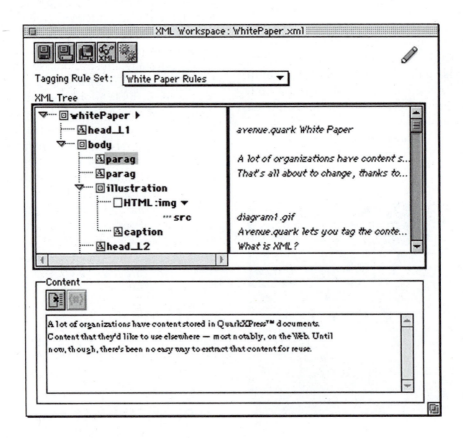

Figure 10.23   XML conversion. Dialogue window in avenue.quark, which tags the content of a QuarkXpress document and then extracts the content in XML format.
Courtesy of Quark, Inc.

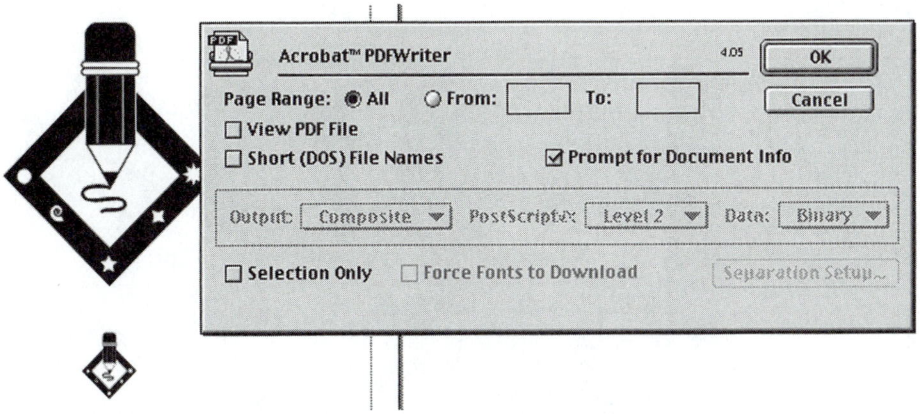

Figure 10.24 The Acrobat PDFWriter plug-in.
Courtesy of Adobe Systems, Inc.

ments as expressed in XML. Other software manufacturers have designed programs that can further repurpose XML documents into a variety of other web formats.

PDF Publishing

PDF publishing allows faithful re-creation of a document for use on the Web without altering the original look. It utilizes a plug-in loaded in the Internet browser that launches as needed. This approach is often used to repurpose advertising and brochures that need to retain the impact of their original design (figure 10.24). It then appears as a choice embedded in an existing Web site as hyperlink.

Databasing and Archiving

In today's printing and publishing world, digital data comprise a printer's most valuable asset. **Asset management** involves databasing and archiving data for easy retrieval and reuse as needed. Prior to the digital age, print jobs remained in physical job jackets with films

stored for three to five years or longer. This information was placed in storerooms and accessed according to company name and date. With prepress facilities almost exclusively handling digital layouts and film gradually being replaced by computer-to-plate workflows, methods must be developed to catalog and retrieve information for future revenue streams. To effectively compete and publish in the current cross-media environment, a digital infrastructure is essential to manage the content that travels through the digital production process.

A **database** is a computer system designed for the storage and retrieval of specified data. In printing and publishing, a database needs to handle the unique elements that can make up a document. Digital assets in publishing can be made up of text, images and graphics, logos, video, and audio files. A database can be as simple as one listing the files as records or one that utilizes thumbnails that detail production data and customer information (figure 10.25).

Archiving digital assets requires a company to decide what is important to archive

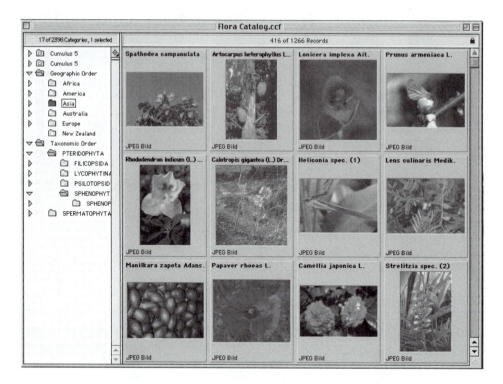

Figure 10.25 **An image database that displays thumbnails.**
Courtesy of Canto Software, Inc

and how the files will be cataloged. Original graphics and final output would be appropriate to archive, whereas intermediate revisions may not be worth retaining. Decisions must be made as to what media to archive to and what software will be used for retrieval. If a company archives to CD-ROM, it has to work within the constraints of the capacity of each disk, 650 MB. Or tape can be used with far more storage per piece of media and a lower per megabyte cost, but data are stored sequentially with no random access and therefore are more time consuming to retrieve.

A new option that is becoming available is **online archiving.** This is a centralized storage and archiving service that can be accessed from anywhere at anywhere through the Web, but it comes with ongoing costs, contractual obligations to an outside service provider, and higher per megabyte costs than writing to in-house media.

Some general rules to follow when planning your backup and archiving procedures are the following:

- Develop a backup plan that includes how often you backup and to what media.
- Backup frequently.
- Automate your backups to ensure that it gets done.

- Do **incremental backups,** which only add new or changed files to your original backup.
- Make several copies of your backup.

- Verify backups and restore a few files to check integrity.
- Use compression to further extend your storage space.

Key Terms

PostScript
PostScript driver
RIP
interpretation
rasterization
screening
Portable Document Format (PDF)
distillation
page independent
PostScript-based imposition
RIP-based imposition
late binding
trapping
vector trapping
raster trapping
hybrid trapping
imagesetter
machine bitmap

film image recorder
film processor
digital proofing
proof
preliminary proof
laser printing
laser
solid inks
ink-jet printer
dye-sublimation printer
dithering
contract proof
digital halftone proofer
soft proof
computer-to-plate (CTP)
silver halide plates
polyester plates
thermal conversion plates
thermal ablation plates

photopolymer plates
visible light lasers
thermal imaging system
thermal conversion
thermal ablation
flatbed platesetter
internal drum platesetter
external drum platesetter
cross-media
HTML
XML
tags
PDF publishing
asset management
database
online archiving
incremental backup

Review Questions

1. Define PostScript and its most important features.

2. Discuss the three main functions of the raster image processor.

3. What are the basic components of a PDF document?

4. Discuss the difference between PostScript-based imposition and RIP-based imposition.

5. Discuss the difference between vector trapping and raster trapping.

6. Discuss the three major components involved in producing film from computer data.

7. When would you use a preliminary proof and when would you use a contract proof?

8. What functions can a quality digital halftone proofer provide?

9. What are the four basic categories of lithographic plates used in CTP technology?

10. Define and discuss the two types of imaging systems utilized in CTP technology.

11. List and define the three types of platesetter architecture available.

12. Discuss the characteristics of HTML, XML, and PDF publishing to the Web.

13. Why is asset management so important to a company?

11

Printing Presses: An Overview

The first high-speed printing press was designed around 1450 by Johann Gutenberg in Germany. Gutenberg tried several different designs, but he settled on the basic form of a wine press. He placed the bed of the press so that it could be rolled out from under the plate, activated the screw by a lever, and added a frame, or tympan, to hold the paper. With this device Gutenberg printed his famous forty-two-line Bible (called the Gutenberg Bible). It took him just over three years to print two hundred copies.

Gutenberg's press worked so well that three hundred years later Benjamin Franklin used a similar design (see illustration). Two men were needed to operate Franklin's press. The type was locked in place on the bed of the press, the raised portions of the type were inked, and the paper was positioned on the tympan frame and swung into place over the type. The bed was then rolled under the platen and the lever (a pressure plate) was activated to press the sheet against the type. The press was then opened, the printed sheet was hung on a line to dry, and the entire process was repeated. Using this method, two press operators could make about three hundred impressions in a single twelve-hour work-day. The basic steps of feeding the paper, registering the paper to the form, printing, and finally delivering the sheet remain in printing today. Modern processes, however, are more accurate and more rapid than the modified wine press.

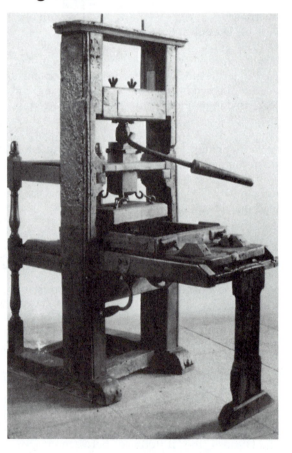

A replica of Benjamin Franklin's press.
Courtesy of Smithsonian Institution, Photo No. 17539-B.

Objectives

After completing this chapter you will be able to:

- Recall the four units that make up any printing press.
- Discuss the development of press designs from platen presses to rotary presses.
- Explain the principle of offset printing.

- Diagram the cylinder configuration of an offset perfecting press.
- Explain how the feeder unit, registration unit, printing unit, inking unit, dampening unit, and delivery unit operate on an offset lithographic press.
- Give a general description of the operation of a web offset press.

Introduction

A **printing press** is a machine that transfers an image from a plate or an image carrier to a substrate, such as paper. It is certainly possible to transfer images from a plate without using a machine—consider a rubber stamp or a stencil—but printing presses are much faster and print more accurately than hand methods.

Gutenberg's version of the wine press could be operated at the then fantastic rate of one copy every three minutes. Contemporary high-performance automatic presses can operate at extremely high speeds, with some configurations producing up to 60,000 copies per hour. When the paper is fed from a continuous roll (called *web feeding*), the paper can pass under a printing plate as rapidly as 3,000 feet per minute, depending on the type of press.

The design of Gutenberg's original press has been refined a bit, but modern presses still perform the same basic operations of feeding, registering, printing, and delivering that Gutenberg's press performed more than five centuries ago. It is important to understand that every printing press—relief, gravure, screen, lithographic, and electrostatic—is built from four basic units (figure 11.1):

- Feeding unit

- Registration unit
- Printing unit
- Delivery unit

The actual buttons and switches that cause a press to run differ from machine to machine. However, every press has these four fundamental elements regardless of size, manufacturer, complexity, or cost. If you first learn the basic tasks of each unit and then how the units function together you will always have the skills to advance and adapt in the printing industry. It is easy to learn buttons and switches—the individual who understands systems will be able to operate any press.

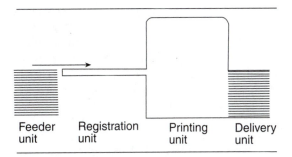

Figure 11.1 **The four units common to all presses**

The goal of the **feeding unit** is to feed stock into the press rapidly and uniformly. The feeding unit can be as simple as a human hand picking up a sheet of paper or as complex as an air-vacuum device that automatically fans the top sheets of a paper pile and lifts a sheet with mechanical fingers.

The **registration unit** is designed to ensure that the press sheet is held in the same position for each impression. It is important that the printed image appear in the same spot on every sheet. Registration is especially important for color printing, which requires two or more impressions on each press sheet. The different colored images made during each impression would not line up if the position of the paper were not controlled during printing.

Once the sheet is held firmly in the proper position, the image is transferred from the plate to the press sheet in the **printing unit**. The placement of the plate or image carrier might vary with the type of printing (relief, screen, gravure, or lithography), but there are general similarities between all presses.

After printing, the completed sheet must be removed from the press by the **delivery unit**. Five centuries ago, Gutenberg picked up each printed sheet and hung it on a wire line to dry. Modern presses generally deliver a uniform stack of sheets that can be easily folded, collated, packaged, or cut.

This chapter discusses the development of printing presses and the operation of the four press systems. Much of this discussion centers around the systems used on offset lithographic presses because offset lithographic printing is the printing method used most commonly in industry. Gravure, screen, and flexographic presses are discussed in more detail later in the text.

Press Development

Since Gutenberg developed his first printing press, major improvements have been made in press design. These improvements have in-creased both the speed and the quality with which work can be printed. Modern press designs are the result of changes in the method used to move paper through the press and in the method used to transfer an image. A brief look at press development will help you understand the operation of a modern offset press.

Platen Press

If it were in operation today, Gutenberg's converted wine press would be labeled a **platen press**. On this type of press, the paper is placed between the type form and a flat surface called a **platen** (figure 11.2a). The type form and the platen are then brought together, and an image is transferred to the press sheet (figure 11.2b). Although the feeding, registration, and delivery units have now been automated, the basic problems inherent in the platen press design remain. The paper must be inserted, held in place, and printed, and it must remain in place until the platen opens sufficiently for the sheet to be removed. The process is slow.

In addition to being slow, the platen press process is limited to the page size that can be printed. The platen press requires 175

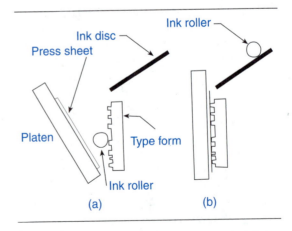

Figure 11.2 **Diagram of a platen press.** (a) A press sheet is positioned on a platen when the platen press is open. (b) The image is transferred when the press is closed.

pounds of pressure per square inch (psi) to transfer ink from the type form to the press sheet. A press capable of printing an 11 inch × 14 inch image must be able to produce 26,950 pounds of pressure. (This is why early wooden printing presses were built in the basement or first floor of a two-story building. The press was the main support for the floor above.) Speed and size were the two factors that led to the development of the flat bed cylinder press.

Flatbed Cylinder Press

An improvement over the platen press, the **flatbed cylinder press** is constructed so that the press sheet rolls into contact with the type form as a cylinder moves across the press (figure 11.3). Mechanical fingers, or **grippers**, hold the press sheet in place during the cylinder's movement and automatically open at the end of one rotation. Ink rollers are usually attached to the cylinder assembly so that as an image is being printed, the form is also being reinked. After each impression, the cylinder raises automatically and rolls back to the starting point to receive another sheet. On some models the cylinder is stationary and the type form moves.

One advantage of the flatbed cylinder design is that, because only a very narrow portion of the sheet is being printed at any given instant, much less pressure is required to transfer the image than is required for the

platen design. A slight modification is to place the type form in a vertical position so that the bed and the cylinder rotate in opposite directions. This cuts the printing time in half because the cylinder makes only a 180-degree turn for each impression. However, motion is still wasted when the cylinder and/or the type form return to their original positions and no image is being transferred.

Rotary Press

The **rotary press** is formed from two cylinders. One cylinder, called the **plate cylinder**, holds the type form while the other cylinder acts as the **impression cylinder** to push the press sheet against the type form (figure 11.4). As the cylinders rotate, a press sheet is inserted between them so that an image is placed in the same position on every sheet. Ink rollers continually replace ink that has been transferred to the press sheets. The impression cylinder can usually be moved up or down to adjust impression pressure for the weight or thickness of the material being printed.

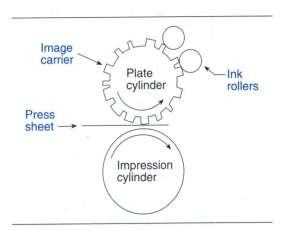

Figure 11.4   Diagram of a rotary press. A rotary press moves the press sheet between two cylinders: the plate cylinder, which holds the image carrier, and the impression cylinder, which pushes the press sheet against the type form or image carrier.

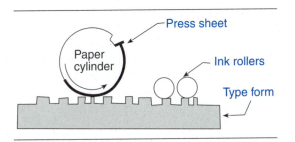

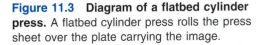

Figure 11.3   Diagram of a flatbed cylinder press. A flatbed cylinder press rolls the press sheet over the plate carrying the image.

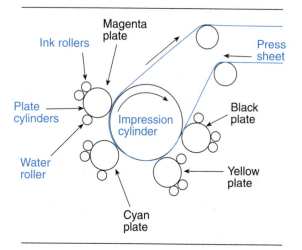

Figure 11.5   **Diagram of a multicylinder rotary press.** A rotary, web-fed press can be adapted to place several plate cylinders around a single impression cylinder for multicolor work.

The rotary press is efficient. Because one impression is made with each cylinder rotation, there is no wasted motion. The rotary press is the only press design that can transfer an image to a continuous roll of paper. This process is called **web printing**. The rotary configuration can also be easily adapted to multicolor presswork. One common rotary press of this design places several plate cylinders around a single impression cylinder (figure 11.5). All modern offset lithographic presses are rotary presses.

Offset Press

The term *offset* is generally associated with the lithographic process, but the offset principle can be applied to a variety of printing processes. An **offset press** transfers (or offsets) an image from an inked printing plate cylinder to a rubber **blanket cylinder**. The blanket cylinder reverses the image. The blanket cylinder then transfers the reversed image to the press sheet (figure 11.6).

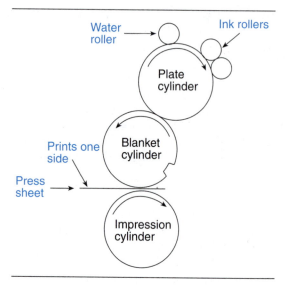

Figure 11.6   **Diagram of an offset rotary press.** Using the offset principle, the offset press transfers an image (or offset) from the plate cylinder to the blanket cylinder, which reverses the image. The reversed image is then passed to the press sheet as it moves between the blanket and impression cylinders.

Transferring an image from a blanket cylinder to the press sheet, rather than transferring the image directly from the plate cylinder to the press sheet, has several advantages. Paper has an abrasive effect on printing plates. If the paper were allowed to contact the printing plate throughout the press run, the plate would soon become too worn to print properly. Having the plate contact the rubber blanket cylinder instead of the printing press sheet, lengthens the life of the plate cylinder. In addition, whenever an image is transferred from one carrier to another, the symbols are reversed (recall that foundry type is cast in reverse). When a blanket cylinder is used on an offset press, the characters on the printing plate must be right reading. The characters will print in reverse on the blanket cylinder, then be reversed again (back to right reading) on the press sheet. Right-reading characters are more convenient for people to work with and assemble during the composition and stripping processes. A rubber blanket cylinder also tends to diminish unwanted background detail or "scum" that might accumulate on the printing plate.

A **perfecting press** can print simultaneously on both sides of the press sheet as it passes through the printing unit (figure 11.7). The most common perfecting presses use the rotary configuration and can be designed for either sheet-fed or web-fed reproduction. (See the Feeding Unit section of this chapter for more about sheet-fed and web-fed reproduction.)

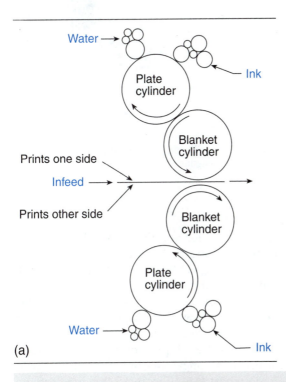

(a)

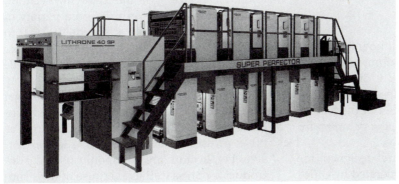

(b)

Figure 11.7 **(a) Diagram of a blanket-to-blanket perfecting press configuration. (b) Perfecting press.**
Courtesy of Komori Corporation.

Understanding Offset Press Operation

Offset lithographic presses, which are presses that can feed sheets larger than 11 inches × 17 inches, can be classified and described in many different ways. For example, one press might be labeled a "five-unit, perfecting in-line web." Another might be called a "single-color, sheet-fed" press. The terms are meaningful to experienced printers, but they are foreign to new students in the field. Whenever people move to learn something in a new field, they have to learn the field-specific language.

The purpose of this section is to describe in some detail the process and vocabulary of basic press operation. Of course, it would be possible to write volumes about each category of operation. However, you must understand the main controls and variables within each press unit before you begin the process of printing. This description provides that understanding. Once you are proficient in this content, you can move to the volumes of advanced technical manuals on printing presses and their operation.

Classifying Offset Lithographic Presses

Offset lithographic presses are classified most simply as either duplicators or presses. These types are based on the maximum size of press sheet the press can print.

Offset Duplicators

Duplicators are any offset lithographic machines that can feed a maximum press sheet size of 11 inches × 17 inches. A duplicator is assumed not to have the degree of control found on a larger offset press, but the feeder, registration, printing, and delivery units are always present in a duplicator.

Tabletop duplicators are designed for short-run work and can be operated by office personnel. Most models have friction paper

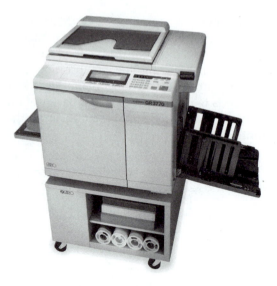

Figure 11.8   **600 dpi digital duplicator.**
Courtesy of Riso, Inc.

feed, control registration by positioning of the paper pile, and use a simple gravity delivery system. Figure 11.8 shows a common pedestal-type duplicator. Pedestal duplicators are usually more rugged than tabletop duplicators and have a few more sophisticated controls than the tabletop devices.

An offset duplicator can do any job a larger press can handle, but each handles a different sheet size. (See the following section.) Modern duplicators can print on a variety of paper stock thicknesses at speeds of 5,000 to 10,000 impressions per hour. They are also available with a web-fed design and multiple printing units for efficient multicolor printing.

Duplicators are versatile machines that meet the short-run demands of the printing industry. They have the same basic controls as offset presses yet are significantly less expensive. Duplicators are commonly used for introductory press training because of their similarity to larger offset presses.

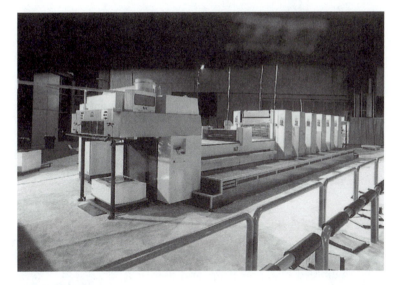

Figure 11.9 **A lithographic offset press.**
Courtesy of Miller Printing Equipment Corp.

Offset Presses

A true offset press can feed a sheet size greater than 11 inches × 17 inches. Sheet-fed offset presses (see the Feeder Unit of this chapter) can print press sheets from $12\frac{5}{8}$ inches × 18 inches to 54 inches × 77 inches. Figure 11.9 shows a common lithographic offset press.

Although presses and duplicators are technically different, the word *duplicator* is rarely used. Rather, both duplicators and larger presses are referred to as *presses* in everyday use.

The Systems Approach to Learning about Presses

It is critical to keep firmly in mind that all presses are designed and built using four basic units: feeding, registration, printing, and delivery. The following material describes the printing process as a sheet of press paper goes from one end of the press to the other. It is also critical to always remember the simple visualization presented in figure 11.1. If you think of the overall system while learning the specifics, you will ultimately become a more skillful press operator.

Finally, remember that while this discussion focuses on offset lithographic presses, these concepts apply to every other printing method. If you understand how the four units of an offset press function, then you could walk up to a flatbed relief press, and with brief instruction on buttons and switches, probably run it. This approach of classifying units, looking at specifics, and transferring learning to other applications is called the systems approach. It will serve you well throughout your life.

Feeding Unit

One method of categorizing presses is by the form of the material sent through the feeding system. When a roll of paper is placed in the feeding unit, the press is classified as **web fed** or, simply, web (figure 11.10). When the feeding unit picks up individual press sheets from a pile, the press is classified as **sheet fed**. Our primary concern in this discussion is sheet-fed presses. Web presses are discussed later in this chapter.

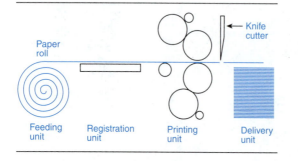

Figure 11.10   **Diagram of a web-fed press**

The feeding unit for a sheet-fed offset press must separate the top sheet of paper from the infeed pile, pick it up, and deliver it to the registration unit. This process must be done consistently for each sheet in the pile. Only one sheet can be fed at a time, and each sheet must reach the registration unit at a precise moment to be registered and sent to the printing unit.

Loading Systems

The simplest and most common sheet-feeding system is **pilefeeding** (figure 11.11). With this system a pile of paper is placed on a feed table while the press is turned off. The table is then raised to a predetermined feeding height and the press run begins. As each sheet is removed from the pile, the press moves the table up so that the top of the pile remains at a constant height.

Pilefeeding presents no difficulties when all the sheets for a single job can be placed in one pile. However, when the press must be stopped and started several times during an extremely long run to add more paper, problems are often encountered. When a job is first set up on a press, a certain amount of paper is spoiled during **make-ready** (preparation work) to obtain a quality printed image. During a steady press run, it is relatively easy to maintain consistent quality. Whenever the press is stopped, however, not only is pro-

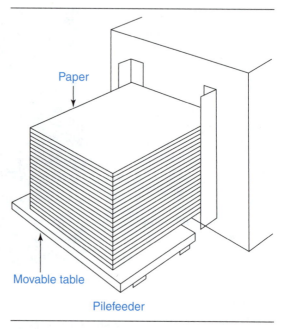

Figure 11.11   **Diagram of a press with a pile feeder**

duction time lost, but more paper wastage could occur before a quality impression is obtained again.

Continuous sheet feeding provides a means of adding sheets to a feeding system without stopping the press in the middle of a run. There are two common continuous-feed designs. The older of the two designs generally has a feed table located over the registration unit (figure 11.12). The printer fans the paper, and the pile is spread on the infeed table. A continuous belt then moves the pile around and under the feed table to the registration unit. Additional paper is fanned and added to the moving pile as needed.

The second continuous sheet-feeding system provides continuous feeding by loading new paper under an existing pile while the press is running (figure 11.13). Before the pile has run out, temporary rods are inserted between open channels in the table, and the fresh

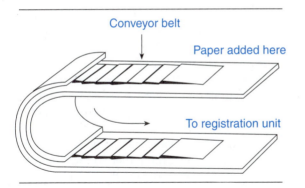

Figure 11.12 **Diagram of a continuous sheet-feeding system**

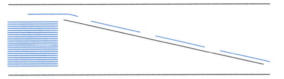

Figure 11.14 **Diagram of a successive sheet-feeding system**

pile is elevated into feeding position. The rods are then removed, and a single stack of paper is again in the feeding unit.

Types of Feeders
The most common type of mechanical feeder is the **successive sheet-feeding system** (figure

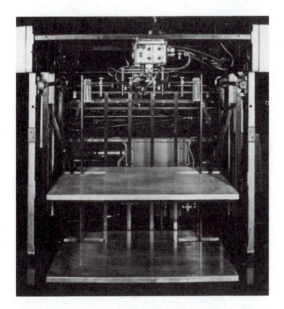

Figure 11.13 **Example of a continuous sheet-feeding system that uses dual tables.**
Courtesy of Miller Printing Equipment Corp.

11.14). Mechanical fingers pick up one sheet from the top of the paper pile and direct it into the registration unit.

Usually, an air blast is used to separate the top press sheet from the rest of the pile. This blast can be adjusted for papers of different weight and for different atmospheric conditions. On dry days, when press sheets tend to cling together because of static electricity, the air blast can be increased. Heavy papers require a stronger air blast than light papers. Coated papers, too, generally require a stronger air blast than uncoated papers. The air blast must be strong enough to float the top piece of paper above the pile at a specified height below the sucker feet.

The **sucker feet** are small vacuum tubes that grab the floating top sheet and send it down the registration board where the registration unit takes over. (The registration board consists of conveyor belts and a registration system.) The amount of vacuum in the sucker feet can be adjusted for the weight of paper being printed. Heavy papers generally require more vacuum than light papers. The object is to adjust the vacuum so that only one piece of paper is picked up by the sucker feet and delivered to the registration unit.

In actual operation, the sucker feet grab the top press sheet from the pile and move it forward a short distance to where it is picked up by pull-in wheels (or some other device) that put it squarely on a conveyer belt system on the registration board. The press automatically controls the precise moment when the sucker feet grab the top sheet, as well as movement of the sheet toward the registration board and the precise moment when the vacuum is cut off and the sheet enters the registration unit.

As the press removes paper from the infeed table, the height of the paper pile decreases. However, the paper pile must be maintained at a constant distance from the sucker feet. This requirement is accomplished automatically by the press. As the press removes paper from the infeed pile, the infeed table automatically moves up, which moves the infeed pile closer to the sucker feet.

The feeding system must be adjusted for air blast, vacuum, paper pile height, and upward movement of infeed table as the paper is used.

The paper feed must be synchronized with the printing unit: each time an impression is made, the feeder must be ready to insert a fresh press sheet. In high-speed presses with successive sheet-feeding systems, the paper literally flies through the registration unit to keep up with the printing unit. It is not easy to hold accurate registration when high-speed printing with a single sheet feeder. The paper may misalign as it enters the registration board due to the high rate of speed.

In contrast to a successive sheet feeder, a **stream feeder** overlaps sheets on the registration board and slows the rate of sheet movement significantly (figure 11.15). With a stream feeder, sheets move through the registration unit at a fraction of the speed of the printing unit. This makes accurate registration control less difficult.

Automatic Feeder Controls

Whatever the method of paper loading or feeding, there are common feeder system controls on all sheet-fed presses. When the paper pile is loaded into the feeding system, it is centered on the press. A scale is usually provided somewhere on the feeder to ensure accurate paper position. Once the pile has been centered, movable side and back guides are positioned to just touch the paper so that the pile will not shift position during the press run (figure 11.16).

The height of the pile can usually be adjusted and maintained automatically by the press. Usually some type of sensing bar touches the top of the pile immediately after a sheet has been fed and directs a gear-and-

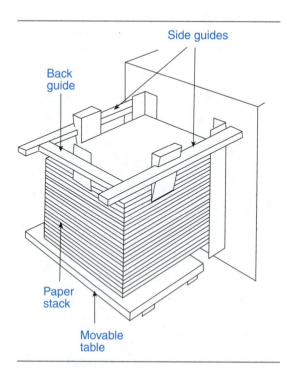

Figure 11.16 Diagram showing movable guides. The movable side and back guides hold the pile in position.

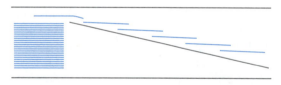

Figure 11.15 Diagram of a stream-feeding system

chain pile height control. The pile height that is required depends on such factors as the paper weight, environmental conditions, and feeding method. The top of the pile must be as level as possible for consistent feeding. This is usually a problem only with large press sheets. Wedges or blocks are often placed under a pile of large press sheets to keep the sheets level.

To ensure that only one sheet feeds into the registration unit at a time, the top sheet must be separated from the rest of the pile. Various mechanisms are used on different machines, but they are all called **sheet separators**. The most common is a blast of directed air, which was just discussed. Blower tubes, which can be directed at the front, side, or rear of a pile, place a blanket of air under the first few press sheets (figure 11.17). Another common approach is to combine a blast of air with a mechanical **combing wheel**, which curls one edge of the paper above the rest of the stack (figure 11.18). With either technique, a sucker foot moves to the top sheet, applies suction,

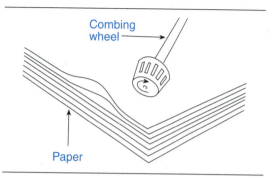

Figure 11.18   A mechanical combing wheel

and forwards it into the registration unit. (Sucker feet were discussed in more detail in the previous section.) Most sheet separators have at least two sucker feet. Both the volume of air to separate the top sheet and the amount of vacuum pull in the sucker feet can be adjusted for different paper characteristics.

The final consideration is to ensure that only one sheet feeds into the press from the feeder to the registration unit at a time. Multiple sheets can jam the press, give poor image impression, fail to be held in register, and even damage the printing unit. Most presses have **double-sheet detectors** (figure 11.19) to check for multiple sheets. These devices either eject double sheets from the registration system or stop the press when double sheets are detected. Usually a double-sheet detector merely gauges the thickness of the passing paper using a sensing switch. The gap from the switch to the paper can be set to any thickness. When the allowable gap is exceeded (there are double sheets and the paper is too thick), the switch is tripped and the double sheets are ejected. On some presses, the paper feeder shuts down when a double sheet is detected. If all paper-feed adjustments have been made properly, the feeder should rarely feed multiple sheets.

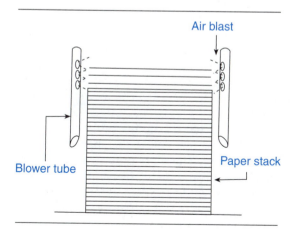

Figure 11.17   Diagram showing blower tubes. Blower tubes force a blanket of air under the first few sheets of paper and float them above the rest of the pile.

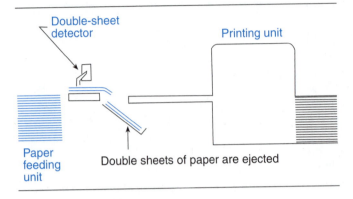

Double-sheet detector

Printing unit

Paper feeding unit

Double sheets of paper are ejected

Figure 11.19 **Diagram showing a double-sheet detector**

The Registration Unit
Importance of Registration

Registration is the process of controlling and directing a press sheet as it enters the printing unit. The goal of registration is to ensure consistent image position on every sheet printed. When one color is to be printed over another on a single sheet, the image will not fit on the sheet unless all sheets are held in register throughout the press run. The ideas of registration and fit are often confused. **Fit** refers to the image position on the press sheet. This term is often used when discussing flat color work. Two colors that are printed adjacent to each other in the proper positions are said to have proper fit. Fit can be affected by a variety of factors, including the original mechanical, the camera operations used to reproduce that mechanical, and the stripping of the job. Registration refers to the consistency of the position of the printed image during printing. An image that has the proper fit in stripping can be made to register properly. However, if the fit was wrong in stripping, no amount of adjustments on press will bring the image into correct register.

Typical Registration Designs

After leaving the infeed pile, the press sheet is moved along the registration board toward the registration unit. As mentioned earlier, the registration board consists of a conveyer belt system and some type of registration system. The paper is carried along the conveyer belts until it reaches the registration unit, where it is stopped momentarily and squared to the plate cylinder along its top edge by a headstop. A **headstop** is a mechanical gate that stops the paper on the registration unit. At the same time the paper is being aligned by the headstop, it is either being pushed or pulled slightly sideways and placed in the proper printing position. It is important to understand that before each press sheet is printed, the registration unit places it in exactly the same position as the preceding sheet. This position determines where the image will print on the press sheet. The registration unit must be adjusted for paper width as well as image location.

The actual registering of the press sheet is performed just before the sheet enters the printing unit. There are only two basic types of sheet-fed automatic registration systems: three-point guide and two-point pull rotary.

In a three-point guide system, the press sheet advances along the registration board and halts against the headstops (figure 11.20). Next, side guides push the sheet into the proper printing position, the front guides move out of the way, and the sheet moves into

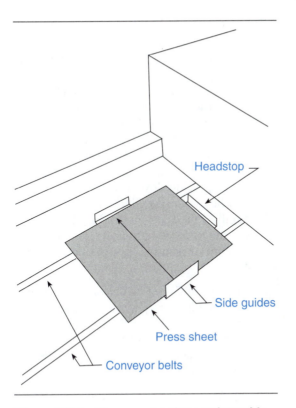

Figure 11.20 **Diagram of a three-point guide system**

The Printing Unit

In offset lithography the printing unit places ink and a water solution on the printing plate, transfers the image to the press sheet, and forwards the press sheet to the delivery unit. The printing unit must be adjusted so that the proper amount of ink and water solution deposits on the printing plate. It must also be adjusted so that the image transfers to the printing paper accurately, evenly, and consistently. Every offset printing unit is made up of the following three systems:

- ■ Cylinder system
- ■ Inking system
- ■ Dampening system

the printing unit. There is a tendency for heavy paper stock to bounce back as it contacts the headstop. In contrast, extremely lightweight materials buckle easily with this push system. Either condition can lead to misregistration.

The two-point pull rotary system reduces the possibility of the press sheet misregistering (figure 11.21). With this system the headstop still swings into position at the head of the registration board, but one side guide is locked into position and does not move. As the press sheet meets the headstop and comes to rest, a finger or roller lowers against the sheet. The sheet is then pulled by a rolling, or rotary, motion against the stationary side guide or pull guide. Once the sheet is in register, it moves into the printing unit.

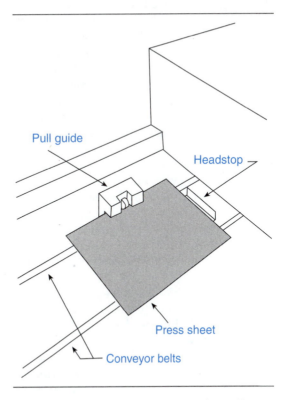

Figure 11.21 **Diagram of a two-point pull rotary system**

Each system serves an important function in the total image transfer process and thus each is examined in detail.

Cylinder System

The cylinder system for any offset press has three functioning parts: a plate cylinder, a blanket cylinder, and an impression cylinder. The function of the plate cylinder is to hold the plate and revolve it into contact with the blanket cylinder during the printing process. The plate cylinder generally has some form of clamping system that holds the plate squarely and firmly in place. Ink and water **form rollers** contact the plate while it is attached to the plate cylinder, thereby causing the image areas on the plate to be inked. The plate image is then transferred to the blanket cylinder, and the image is reversed. Next the press sheet passes between the blanket cylinder and impression cylinder, and the image is offset back to right-reading form on the press sheet. The impression cylinder applies the pressure that is needed to transfer the image from the blanket cylinder to the press sheet.

Figure 11.22 shows one common plate, blanket, and impression cylinder configuration called the **three-cylinder principle**. Notice that because the blanket cylinder is above the impression cylinder, the press sheet travels in a straight line from the feeder to the delivery unit. Note also the direction of rotation of each cylinder and the logical placement of the dampening and inking systems. Remember that the plate must be moist before it is inked.

Figure 11.23 illustrates an alternative cylinder configuration called the **two-cylinder principle**. With this design the functions of the plate and impression cylinders are combined on one main cylinder that has twice the circumference of the blanket cylinder. During the first half of the main plate/impression cylinder rotation, the image is offset from the plate section of the main cylinder to the blanket cylinder. During the next half of the revolution, the press sheet passes between the impression section of the main cylinder and the blanket cylinder. Because the blanket cylinder is beneath the impression cylinder, the delivery system must flop the press sheet to have the printed image face upward on the outfeed table. This also means that the press sheets being fed into the press must be placed on the infeed table facing downward.

While the three-cylinder configuration is commonly found on both duplicators and presses, the two-cylinder design is never used on contemporary offset presses because it is too slow.

Impression Cylinder Adjustments. The gap between the blanket cylinder and the impression cylinder affects the final image quality. The pressure must be sufficient to transfer a dense ink image but not so great that it smashes the blanket cylinder or the press

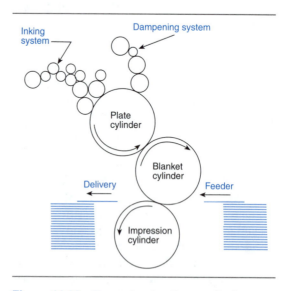

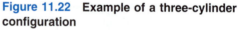

Figure 11.22   Example of a three-cylinder configuration

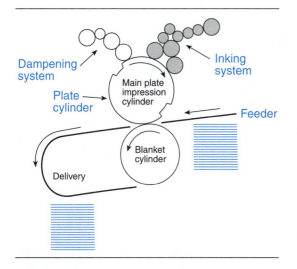

Figure 11.23 Example of a two-cylinder configuration

sheet. Controlling this gap is referred to as adjusting **impression**. Each time the thickness of the paper being printed changes, the impression must be readjusted. Heavier papers need a wider gap than lighter papers.

On most duplicators, the impression cylinder can be raised or lowered by a simple set-screw arrangement. On most presses, impression is controlled by adding or removing packing from behind the blanket cylinder or by a cam adjustment which moves the impression cylinder closer or nearer to the blanket. On some presses, both the impression cylinder and the blanket cylinder require packing.

Blanket Cylinder Concerns. An offset press blanket cylinder is consumable. Blankets wear out and must be replaced. Remember that one of the advantages of the offset technique is that paper never touches the plate cylinder. Paper is abrasive and greatly reduces plate life if allowed to contact the plate cylin-

der during priming. Moreover, paper often carries lint, which can be carried back into the ink and dampening systems.

Most blankets are made from a vulcanized rubber, which is bonded to a fiber support base. Blankets can stretch around cylinders and they can also deform, just like automobile tires wear unevenly, develop cracks, from bubbles, and grow brittle with age. With proper care, however, a blanket can be used for many hundreds of thousands of impressions.

When it is time to replace the blanket, clamps on the cylinder are loosened and the old blanket is removed. A new blanket is inserted under the clamps and stretched around the cylinder. Blankets are purchased according to press specifications and are sized to exactly match a specific cylinder circumference.

The Inking System

The goal of any inking unit is to place a uniform layer of ink across every dimension of the printing plate. The lithographic process is unique in that it requires the ink form rollers to contact the nonimage areas of the plate without transferring ink to them.

Inking System Configurations. All lithographic inking units are made up of four main sections:

- Ink fountain and fountain roller
- Ductor roller
- Ink distribution rollers
- Ink form rollers (figure 11.24)

The ink fountain stores a quantity of ink in a reservoir and feeds small quantities of ink to the rest of the inking system from the fountain roller. The ink distribution rollers receive ink by movement of the ductor roller, and work it into a semiliquid state that is uniformly delivered to the ink form rollers. The ink form

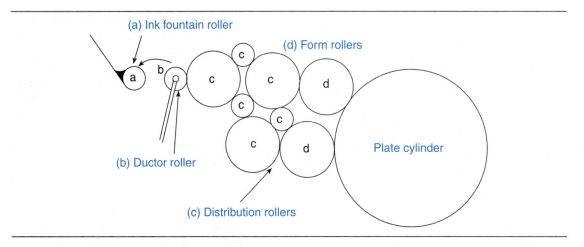

Figure 11.24 **Example of a typical inking unit.** A lithographic inking system consists of the ink fountain (a), the ductor rollers (b), the distribution rollers (c), and the ink form rollers (d).

rollers then transfer a thin layer of ink to the image portions of the lithographic plate.

Inking System Operation. The ink **fountain** (figure 11.24a) holds a pool of ink and controls the amount of ink that enters the inking system by feeding small amounts of ink from the **fountain rollers**. The most common type of ink fountain consists of a metal blade that is held in place near the fountain roller. The gap between the blade and the fountain roller can be controlled by adjusting screw keys to vary the amount of ink on the fountain roller. The printer adjusts the screw keys in or out as the fountain roller turns to obtain the desired quantity of ink. If the image to be printed covers only half of the plate, half of the screw keys are closed. If the plate image covers the whole plate evenly, all of the screw keys are moved to place a uniform layer of ink on the fountain roller.

The ink is transferred from the fountain to the ink distribution rollers by a **ductor roller** (figure 11.24b). The ductor roller is a movable roller that flops back and forth between the fountain roller and the distribution rollers. As the ductor roller swings backward and contacts the fountain roller, both rollers turn and the ductor roller is inked. The ductor roller then swings forward to contact a distribution roller and transfers ink to it. The rate of rotation of the fountain roller and the gap between the fountain blade and the fountain roller control the amount of ink added to the ink distribution system.

The ink **distribution rollers** spread the ink out to a uniform layer before it is placed on the plate (figure 11.24c). There are two general types of distribution rollers: rotating distribution rollers and oscillating distribution rollers. **Rotating distribution rollers** rotate in one direction. **Oscillating distribution rollers** rotate and also move from side to side.

The rollers that actually ink the plate are called form rollers (figure 11.24d).

A simple indication of the quality of a printing press is its number of distribution and form rollers. The greater the number of distribution rollers, the more accurate the control of ink uniformity. It is difficult to ink large, solid areas on a plate with only one form roller. With three form rollers (generally the maximum) it is relatively easy to maintain consistent ink coverage of almost any image area on the plate.

The Dampening System

Recall that most lithographic plates function on the principle of water- and ink-receptive areas. In order for ink to adhere only to the image areas on a plate, a layer of moisture must be placed over the nonimage areas before the plate is inked. The dampening unit accomplishes this by moistening the plate consistently throughout the press run.

Dampening System Configurations. There are no radical differences between the basic designs of most conventional, direct dampening units (figure 11.25). Like inking units, dampening units all contain some form of fountain, a fountain roller, a ductor roller, distribution rollers, and one or more form rollers.

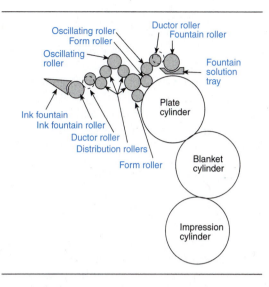

Figure 11.26 Diagram of an indirect dampening unit

Not all manufacturers use direct dampening systems where the ink and dampening rollers are separate, however. An indirect dampening system, such as the aquamatic system found on A.B. Dick duplicators, combines the ink and dampening rollers and carries the water solution to the plate on the ink-covered form rollers (figure 11.26).

Dampening System Operation. In a direct dampening system, the dampening fountain roller sits in a pool of fountain solution stored in the dampening fountain. As the press runs, the dampening fountain roller turns, picking up fountain solution from the fountain and holding it on its surface. A ductor roller jogs back and forth from the fountain roller, where it picks up fountain solution, to a dampening distribution roller. The distribution roller takes the fountain solution from the ductor roller to the dampening form rollers, where the fountain solution is transferred to the plate.

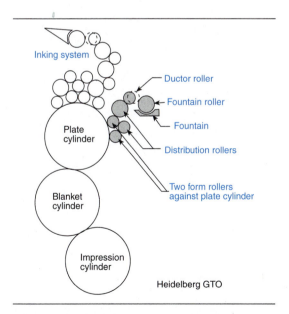

Figure 11.25 Diagram of a direct dampening unit

In an indirect dampening system, the dampening distribution and form rollers are also the inking distribution and form rollers. In this type of system, all the rollers in the ink and water train are first inked. Then fountain solution is added to the fountain. Because the dampening fountain roller and every other roller in the roller train is inked, the fountain solution literally rides on the surface of the inked rollers and is carried to the plate.

In both systems, the rate at which the dampening fountain roller rotates in the fountain can be varied. The faster the fountain roller turns, the more fountain solution it delivers to the dampening system. By changing the rotation speed of the fountain roller, the quantity of moisture reaching the plate can be adjusted.

Waterless Printing

Waterless printing breaks with the tradition of using water or a dampening system in the normal operation of printing press. Instead, it utilizes a special silicone-rubber-coated printing plate and special inks (figure 11.27). Waterless printing requires that a specific temperature be maintained for accurate transferring of ink to the substrate, rather than the maintenance of a correct water-to-ink balance. A waterless plate is an intaglio plate with image areas recessed from the surface of the plate. Waterless plates eliminate the chemically tainted waste produced from traditional printing processes. They also allow for very clean and sharp images because, with the removal of the water dampening chemistry, the printing ink cannot become emulsified. These

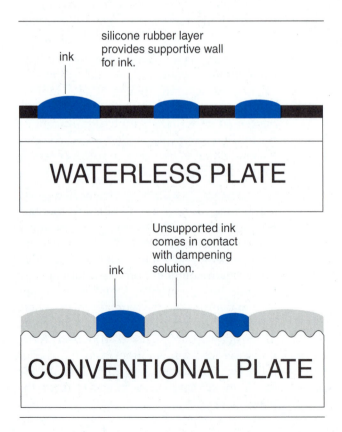

Figure 11.27 Waterless plate versus conventional plate.
Courtesy of Waterless Printing Association.

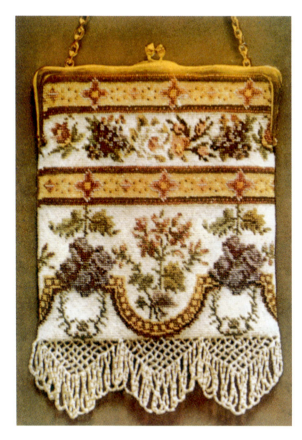

Colorplate A

Ives early tricolor experiment. Original proof of tricolor halftone reproducton made by Frederic E. Ives about 1893. Perhaps the first three-color illustration ever produced with a crossline halftone screen.

Courtesy of 3M Company, from the Joseph S. Merle Collection.

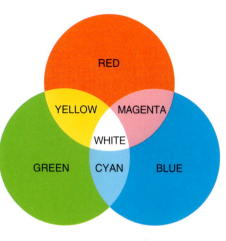

Colorplate B

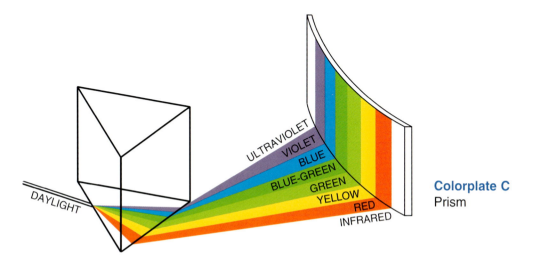

Colorplate C
Prism

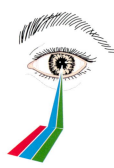

Colorplate D
Cyan Ink
absorbs red
reflects blue
reflects green

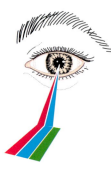

Colorplate E
Magenta Ink
reflects red
reflects blue
absorbs green

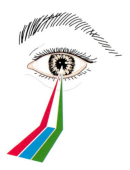

Colorplate F
Yellow Ink
reflects red
absorbs blue
reflects green

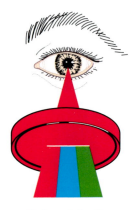

Colorplate G
Red Filter
transmits red
absorbs blue
absorbs green

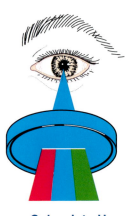

Colorplate H
Blue Filter
absorbs red
transmits blue
absorbs green

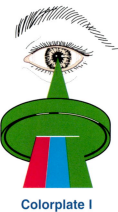

Colorplate I
Green Filter
absorbs red
absorbs blue
transmits green

FIRST control target for job start up/job run

Ink Trap Patches, CM, MY, CY. If less than 100% coverage produces the highest density, these scales must contain that screen value in each overprint target.

Process Color Patches, C, M, Y. Should remain 100%.

Exposure guide. Micro-fine rules assess proper photopolymer face exposures and are approximately the width of a 3% dot. Values are given below, width of microline is in thousandths.

lpi	width
55	.003
65-85	.0025
100-120	.002
133-175	.0015
200	.0013

Solid Density patch. The 100% area of this element must represent the maximum screen values of the areas intended to print with the highest density.

Slur patch. Coarser patch for 55-85 lpi, finer patch for 100-200 lpi.

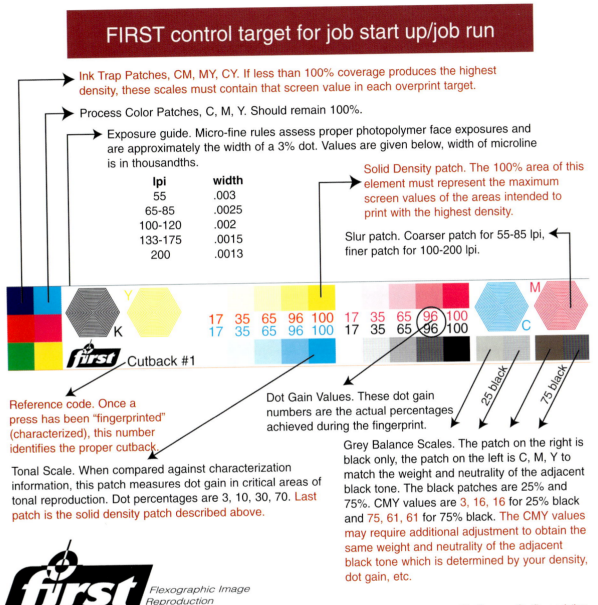

Reference code. Once a press has been "fingerprinted" (characterized), this number identifies the proper cutback.

Tonal Scale. When compared against characterization information, this patch measures dot gain in critical areas of tonal reproduction. Dot percentages are 3, 10, 30, 70. Last patch is the solid density patch described above.

Dot Gain Values. These dot gain numbers are the actual percentages achieved during the fingerprint.

Grey Balance Scales. The patch on the right is black only, the patch on the left is C, M, Y to match the weight and neutrality of the adjacent black tone. The black patches are 25% and 75%. CMY values are 3, 16, 16 for 25% black and 75, 61, 61 for 75% black. The CMY values may require additional adjustment to obtain the same weight and neutrality of the adjacent black tone which is determined by your density, dot gain, etc.

Flexographic Image Reproduction Specifications & Tolerances

NOTE: Fields described in red are entered by the user after fingerprinting

Colorplate R

A FIRST Color Control Target: FIRST is a set of specifications and tolerances for flexographic image reproduction.

Courtesy of Flexographic Technical Association

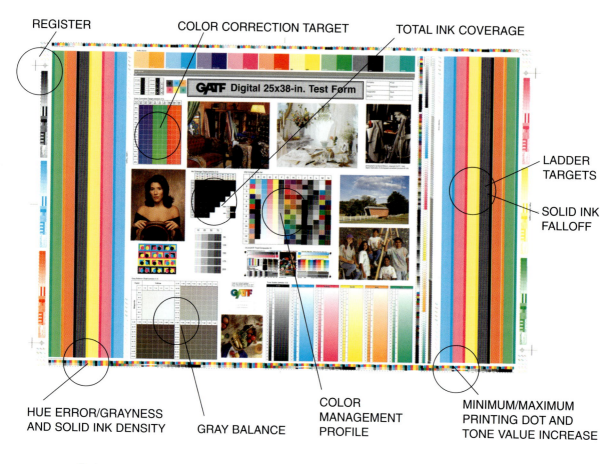

REGISTER

COLOR CORRECTION TARGET

TOTAL INK COVERAGE

LADDER TARGETS

SOLID INK FALLOFF

HUE ERROR/GRAYNESS AND SOLID INK DENSITY

GRAY BALANCE

COLOR MANAGEMENT PROFILE

MINIMUM/MAXIMUM PRINTING DOT AND TONE VALUE INCREASE

Colorplate Q

The GATF 25x38-inch Digital Sheetfed Test Form. This is a digital version of GATF's film-based 25x38-inch Sheetfed Test Form. It provides a digital file to generate a press form that is used to diagnose and calibrate a 25x38-inch printing press with up to six units. It can also be used to calibrate a filmsetter or platesetter.

Courtesy of The Graphic Arts Technical Foundation

Colorplate O

A soft proof strives to match the display and reflective piece as closely as possible.

Courtesy of Imation, Inc.

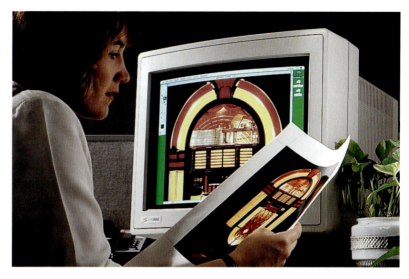

Colorplate P

Characteristics of lasers used in computer-to-plate technology.

Courtesy of Agfa Corporation

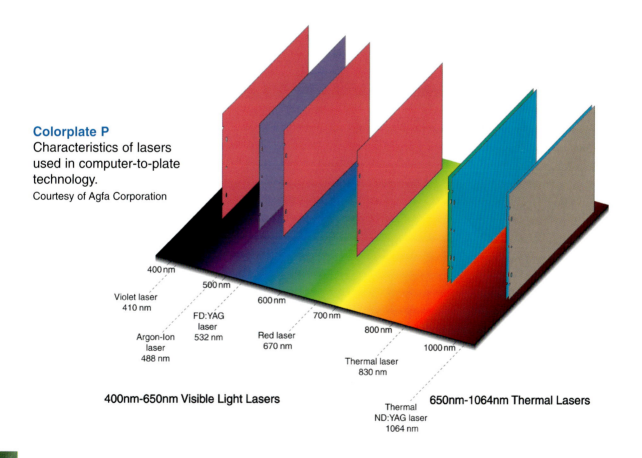

400 nm

500 nm

Violet laser
410 nm

600 nm

FD:YAG
laser
532 nm

700 nm

Argon-Ion
laser
488 nm

Red laser
670 nm

800 nm

Thermal laser
830 nm

1000 nm

400nm-650nm Visible Light Lasers

Thermal
ND:YAG laser
1064 nm

650nm-1064nm Thermal Lasers

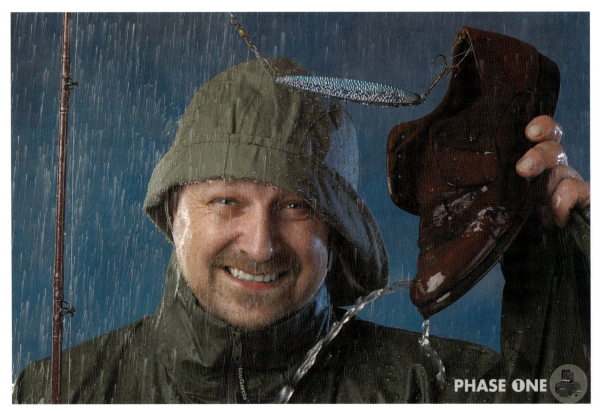

Colorplate M
Image taken with a professional high resolution single pass digital camera.
Courtesy of Phase One, Inc.

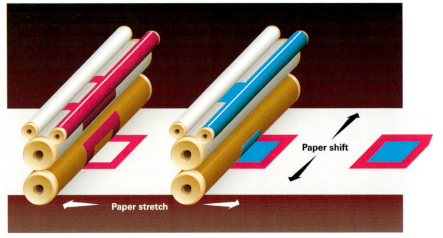

Paper shift

Paper stretch

Colorplate N
Trapping corrects for misregistration problems due to paper stretch and shift on the press.
Courtesy of Agfa Corporation

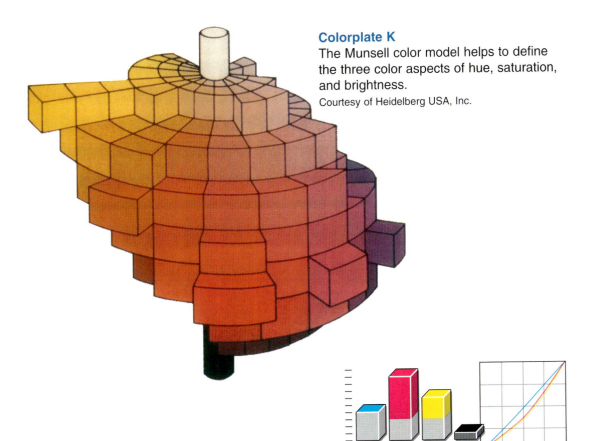

Colorplate L
Gray Component Replacement

The Gray component of CMY is indicated as a light gray in this diagram. In different settings of GCR, different portions of this Gray component (indicated as dark gray) are converted to black.

The effect of reducing ink costs is visualized when looking at the CMY curves in the diagram on the right. The lower the CMY curves drop, the less ink you are printing on press.

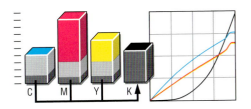

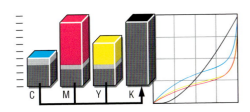

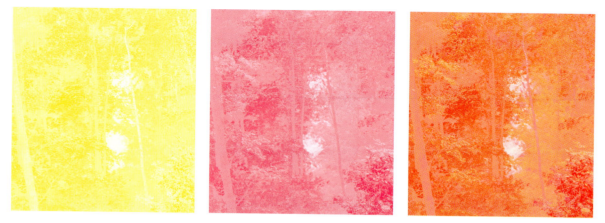

Yellow

Magenta

Yellow plus Magenta

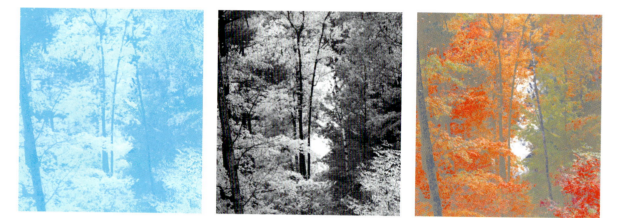

Cyan

Black

Yellow, Magenta, plus Cyan

Colorplate J
Separations (left and center)
Progressive Proof (right)
Yellow, Magenta, Cyan, plus Black (bottom right)

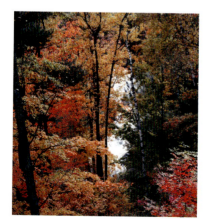

plates are becoming standard on the new digital imaging presses that will be discussed in chapter 16.

The Delivery Unit

The delivery unit takes the paper from the printing unit and places it on an outfeed table. There are two common designs for sheet-fed press delivery units: gravity delivery and chain gripper delivery. **Gravity delivery** is the simpler and less dependable of the two designs. As the press sheet leaves the printing unit, it drops into a delivery pile. The basic limitation of this system is that paper cannot be delivered faster to the pile than gravity can pull it into place. With lightweight papers, air resistance reduces the possible press speed even more. For these reasons, gravity delivery is usually found on only the smallest, least expensive duplicators.

The most popular design for delivery units is **chain gripper delivery** (figure 11.28). With chain gripper delivery, the press sheet can be either pulled through the printing and delivery units by the same chain system or it can be transferred from the mechanical fingers or **grippers** on the impression cylinder in the printing unit to a different set of grippers on the chain of the delivery unit.

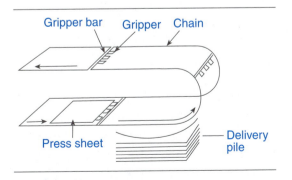

Figure 11.28 Diagram of a chain gripper delivery system

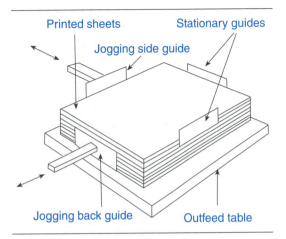

Figure 11.29 Diagram showing jogging side and back guides

As the press sheet leaves the printing unit, a set of grippers grabs the leading edge of the sheet and pulls it out of the printing unit. The gripper bar is attached to a continuous chain that moves the printed sheet to a paper pile, releases it, and moves the grippers back to receive another sheet. The chain moves at the same rate and in synchronization with the feeding, registration, and printing units. As one sheet is being delivered to the paper pile, another sheet is being placed on the registration board. Presses with chain gripper delivery systems can print at high speeds because the gripper chain moves the press sheet and does not depend on gravity to remove the sheet from the printing unit.

Delivery Pile Controls

Ideally, the delivery unit forms a perfectly neat stack of paper on the outfeed table. If a perfect pile forms, the printer can easily move it back to the feeding unit to print another color; can stack it in a paper cutter to trim it to a finished size; can collate it with other sheets; or can punch, drill, fold, or package it.

Jogging side and back guides are usually used to control the outfeed pile (figure 11.29).

As a sheet drops onto the stack, the guides are open. As the sheet drops into position on the stack, the guides begin to close until they gently push the sheet into place. Most pile control systems are designed so that the two stationary guides can be adjusted to the paper extremes. The jogging guides are adjusted to touch the remaining two paper sides on their innermost motion. As the press operates, the delivery pile is continually touched by all four guides. This keeps the stack straight. The entire outfeed table typically lowers automatically as the height of the delivery pile increases.

A static electric charge frequently builds on a press sheet as it passes through the printing unit. Charged sheets tend to cling to each other and often do not stack properly in the delivery unit. The most common **static eliminator** is a piece of copper tinsel attached to a thin copper wire. The tinsel is stretched across the delivery unit so that each press sheet must brush against it. The wire is grounded through the press and removes the static electricity from the sheet.

Multicolor Sheet-Fed Presses

Multicolor presses are becoming the standard choice for presses. **Multicolor sheet-fed presses** operate in the same manner and with the same functional units as single-color sheet-fed presses, but they are equipped with two or more printing units arranged in a line following each other. Each color printing unit is capable of delivering one color of ink to the press web sheet. In today's fast changing printing landscape, 12-color sheet-fed presses are being introduced, but they are most often used by high-end, large-volume printing companies. To understand the basics of multicolor sheet-fed press operation, we will focus on presses with between two and six units.

Multicolor Press Design

Most multicolor presses are designed with two, four, five, or six printing units. Two-color presses are ideal for jobs that require spot color, such as a page of text in which the words are printed in one color and the display type or graphic elements (rules, boxes, decorative borders, or illustrations) are printed in another color. Four-color presses are designed especially for four-color process printing. At five- or six-color press (figure 11.30) increases printing possibilities even further by allowing a press sheet to be printed with four process colors followed by a flat color, a match color, or a varnish. Varnish is a clear, inklike substance that changes the reflectance characteristics of the printed piece where it is applied. A var-

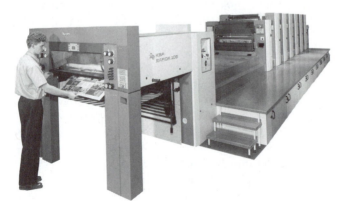

Figure 11.30   Medium-format flexible unit sheet-fed offset press. Depending on the number of units (up to 12 possible), this press can achieve speeds of up to 12,000 sheets per hour.
Courtesy of Koenig & Bauer AG.

nished area stands out visually and has a different texture than the rest of the press sheet.

The primary advantage of a multicolor press is that more than one color can be printed in a single pass through the press. Without a multicolor press, the press sheet would have to be printed with one color, then replaced on the infeed table and run through the press again for each additional color. Not only is this a time-consuming operation, but it can lead to registration problems. As has been mentioned, paper is not dimensionally stable. When press paper passes through the press, each piece is subjected to both ink and water. Moisture from the dampening system tends to make the press sheet stretch; the sheet then shrinks as it dries. Absorption and drying of ink on the printed sheet can have a similar effect. Also, when a single-color press is used for a multicolor job, some time elapses before the press sheet is put through the press for the next color. During this time, the press sheet may shrink, stretch, or warp slightly due to humidity and other environmental conditions in the printing plant. The overall result of all these effects is that on the second pass through the press, the press sheet is not exactly the same size as it was on the first pass through the press. This makes critical registration, such as is required for process color work, difficult and sometimes impossible. A multicolor press can reduce this problem.

One additional advantage of a multicolor press is that press operators can judge the quality of the printed sheet immediately when it comes off the press, and they can make press adjustments based on their evaluations. When printing process color, all four colors must be printed with the correct press settings if the colors on the final job are to be correct. When a single-color press is used to print process color, improper press adjustments during the printing of the first color may only be discovered as the fourth color is being printed. By this time, all of the sheets have been printed with three colors, and it is too late to make any corrections. The whole job would have to be scrapped and reprinted.

Perfecting Transfer

To increase press flexibility, the multicolor press shown in figure 11.30 is equipped with a perfecting transfer system. The perfecting transfer system on this press is designed and patented by the Miller Printing Equipment Corporation, but other press manufacturers offer perfecting presses that operate on a similar principle. A schematic of a two-color press equipped with a perfecting transfer system is shown in figure 11.31. With this system it is possible for a two-color press to print two colors on one side of the press sheet, or one color on each side of the press sheet, in one pass through the press. A four-color press equipped with the perfecting transfer system has even greater printing flexibility. It can print four colors on one side, or three colors on one side and one color on the other side, or two colors on each side. Five- or six-color presses can also be equipped with a perfecting transfer system, which again increases printing flexibility.

The **perfecting transfer system** introduces several additional cylinders to the press which work in conjunction with the impression and blanket cylinders commonly found on an offset press. As shown in figure 11.32, the Miller perfecting transfer system uses two transfer cylinders and one perfecting cylinder. Together these cylinders can pass a press sheet from one printing unit to another so that the press sheet reaches the second printing unit with either its printed side facing the second blanket cylinder (multicolor mode) or with its unprinted side facing the second blanket cylinder (perfecting mode). The cylinders are especially designed so that freshly printed ink does not smear when the printed side of the sheet presses against them.

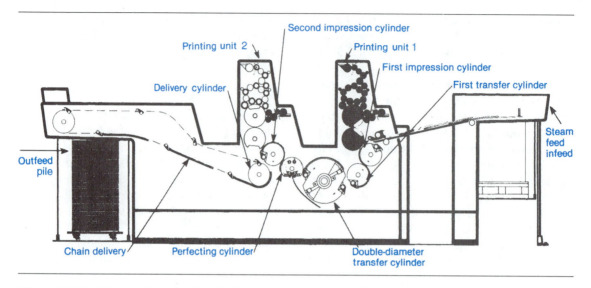

Figure 11.31   A two-color, sheet-fed offset press equipped with a perfecting transfer system. The two transfer cylinders and the perfecting cylinder in this press allow for printing one color on each side of the press sheet or two colors on one side of the press sheet.
Courtesy of Miller Printing Equipment Corp.

In perfecting mode, the printed sheet passes from the first impression cylinder to the first transfer cylinder. At this point the printed side of the sheet is against the face of the first transfer cylinder. The first transfer cylinder then passes the sheet to the second transfer cylinder, printed side away from the face of the second transfer cylinder. The perfecting cylinder is equipped with two sets of grippers. In the perfecting mode, the perfecting cylinder grips the *tail* edge of the sheet using one set of grippers, and passes the sheet to the second impression cylinder, printed side against the face of the second impression cylinder face, using the second set of grippers, to be printed on its unprinted side. Thus, the sheet leaves the press printed on both sides. In the multicolor (nonperfecting) mode all of the cylinders still handle the press sheet, but only one set of grippers is activated on the perfecting cylinder. In this mode the perfecting cylinder grips the printed sheet on its *lead* edge and passes it to

the second impression cylinder printed side away from the face of the second impression cylinder. Thus, the sheet is printed with two colors on the same side.

Multicolor Press Monitoring and Control Systems

It is relatively easy for one operator to control infeed, registration, ink and water balance, and outfeed on a single-color press. However, as the number of color units in the press increases and registration becomes more critical, press control becomes a bigger problem. Until recently, the answer to this problem has been to provide each press with enough operators to monitor all press functions. Thus, a six-color press might require four to six operators. Even with the required number of operators, press control still presented problems, not the least of which was the inability of the press operators to react quickly enough to

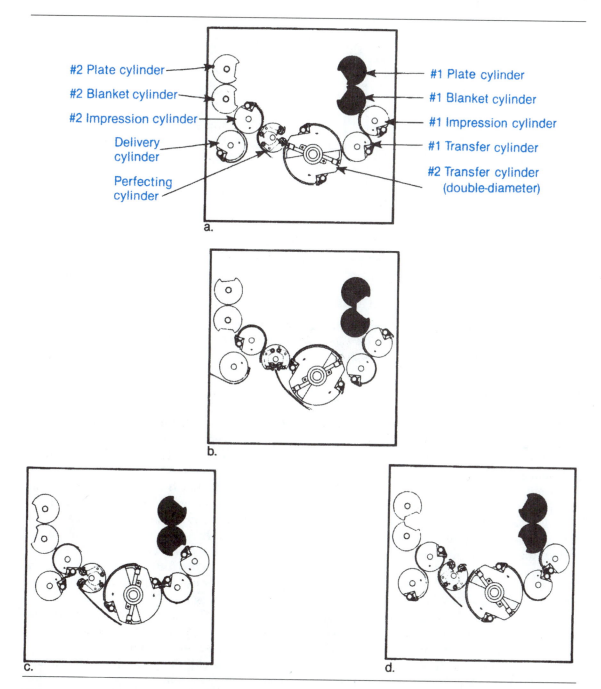

Figure 11.32 **Schematic of the Miller perfecting transfer system, perfecting mode.** Note the two-gripper system on the perfecting cylinder which grips the sheet by its tail edge with one gripper (a), then passes the sheet to the second gripper (b and c), and on to the second impression cylinder (d). Courtesy of Miller Printing Equipment Corp.

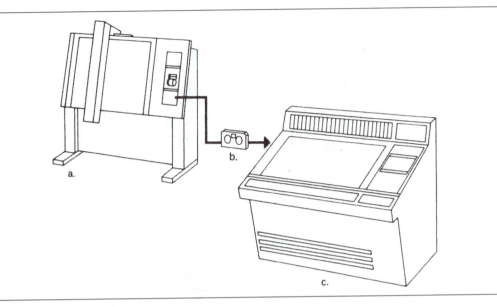

Figure 11.33 **Schematic of an automated, multicolor press control system with plate scanner.** The plate scanner (a) scans the plate and prints information needed to set the press ink system on cassette tape (b) for automatic system setting through the press console (c).
Courtesy of Miller Printing Equipment Corp.

make needed press adjustments without a great deal of paper spoilage.

The use of computers has reduced this problem and has greatly improved the quality of printed products while at the same time has reduced make-ready time and spoilage. An automated, multicolor press control system is shown in figure 11.33. This system involves the use of a plate scanner and a press console.

The Plate Scanner

The **plate scanner** (figure 11.34) is typically installed in the platemaking room. After a plate is made, it is scanned by the plate scanner. The scanner moves across the plate, optically measuring the image area of the plate, and calculates the settings needed on the press ink keys and the amount of **roller stroke** needed (the stroke length required on the ink fountain roller). This information can be stored on cassette tape, digital computer disk, and/or on a printout. The data is then passed with the plate to the press room. On fully automated systems, information from the storage medium can be fed directly to the press from the press console. Adjusting the ink system is done automatically when the press reads the information on the tape. When the press is not equipped with this fully automatic feature, the press operator can use the information on the printout to preset the ink system. A plate scanner significantly reduces both make-ready and spoilage because presetting produces almost the final ink settings required for the job with the first sheet off the press. The plate scanner has experienced some decline in recent years as automated workflows, including computer-to-plate, and increasingly sophisticated press consoles have become more prevalent.

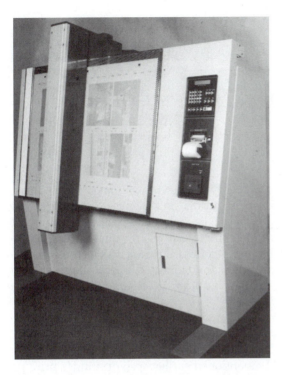

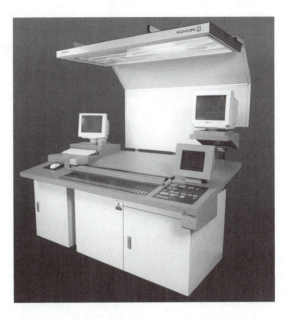

Figure 11.35 **Press console.** This console incorporates a scanning densitometer, a print-quality monitor, and a complete digital management system.
Courtesy of Komori, Inc.

Figure 11.34 **A plate scanner.** Note the printout tape in the center of the control panel and the slot for cassette tape at the top of the panel. The plate scanner is built into the vertical bar positioned over the plate.
Courtesy of Miller Printing Equipment Corp.

The Press Console

The **press console** is the heart of the automated press system (figure 11.35). As prepress has become digitally driven, press operations have become more and more automated. Operations that were once labor intensive and required many operators now are directed from a console that can read information and job parameters directly from digital files. Although a press operator is still critical to maintaining proper operation of the press and determining that the sheets meet the goal of the customer contract proof, more and more jobs are being handled as part of an automated system, thus requiring fewer press operators.

Automated presses offer many advantages. Some areas being automated in today's printing presses are the following:

- Plate changing
- Ink delivery and distribution
- Registration
- Color control (in-line densitometers and spectrophotometers) (Fig. 11.36)
- Blanket and press cylinder cleaning
- Error checking (streaks, scratches, misprints)
- Feeder adjustments

Because the press console is programmed with the parameters for each job, printing problems can be recognized instantly and jobs returned quickly to the quality standards established on

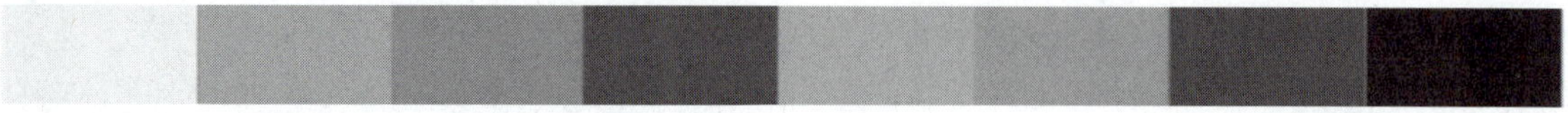

Figure 11.36   One type of color bar. Colors printed on this test strip can be read by a scanning densitometer and used to monitor press operation.

the *OK sheet* (the sheet approved by the printer or press operator). As a result, the printer can deliver better quality faster and at a lower cost. This makes the printer more competitive in a highly competitive printing market.

Although the introduction of automated press operations means that fewer press operators are required to run a press, computer systems have not reduced the number of press operators required in the industry overall. Instead, computers have increased the amount of quality color printing being done, and therefore the number of printers needed, and they have greatly increased the knowledge needed and the type of skills required by press operators.

Most educational institutions are equipped with manual presses because the knowledge gained from manual press operations is still valuable. No matter how automated press systems become, there will always be a need for skilled press operators who understand the basics of press operation and the concepts of print quality. This type of knowledge is gained during manual press operation, and it provides a firm foundation on which to build the skills needed to operate an automated press.

Web Offset Presses

An in-depth description of web offset press operation is beyond the scope of this text. However, the growth of web offset printing, particularly for printing books, newspapers, business forms, magazines, directories, and packaging, has made the process a major part of the commercial printing industry. The following is a brief introduction to the web offset process and to the types of web presses and auxiliary equipment commonly used in the industry.

Sections of the Web Offset Press

As mentioned earlier, web printing is printing on a continuous roll of paper (or some other substrate) rather than printing on individual sheets. The method of image transfer in web offset is not the same as the offset printing method used for sheetfed work. In both methods the image is transferred from a printing plate to a blanket cylinder, and from a blanket cylinder to a printing substrate. However, because the substrate is wound on a roll in web printing and travels continuously through the press, the feeding, registration, and delivery units on web presses differ from those on sheet-fed presses. The major sections of a typical web press are the infeed unit, the printing unit, and the delivery unit (figure 11.37).

Infeed Unit

The infeed unit delivers paper to the web press. The infeed unit typically contains a **roll stand**, which holds the paper rolls; a **splicer**, which automatically splices the end of one web to the beginning of another web; a **web-**

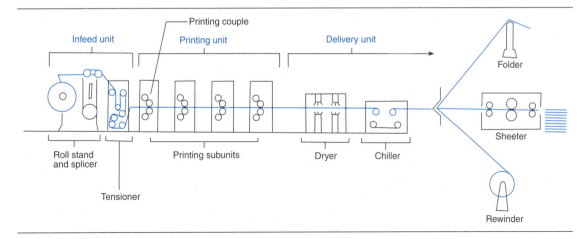

Figure 11.37 **Major units of a web offset press**

steering device, which controls the **sidelay** (side-to-side position) of the infeeding web; and a **tensioner**, which maintains the proper tension on the web as it enters the press.

Printing Unit
The printing unit of the web press is made up of one or more printing subunits. Each printing subunit contains one or more printing couples. A **printing couple** contains an inking system, a dampening system, a plate cylinder, a blanket cylinder, and an impression cylinder. Each printing couple prints one color of ink.

Delivery Unit
The first major component of every delivery unit is an ink drying device. After the ink dryer, the delivery unit can consist of a variety of devices ranging from a simple **sheeter**, which cuts the moving web into sheets of the required size, to a combination sheeter and folder, which both folds the web into final signatures and trims the signatures to size. Where no folding or cutting is required, the delivery unit can contain only a rewinder, which winds the web into a roll for later processing.

Types of Web Presses
The most popular web presses for commercial printing are the blanket-to-blanket and the common impression cylinder (CIC) presses. In-line presses are also common.

Blanket-to-Blanket Web Press
A **blanket-to-blanket web press** uses two printing couples to print on both sides of the web simultaneously. Thus, it is a perfecting press. However, as you will note from figure 11.38, each blanket cylinder serves a dual function; it serves as the blanket for one printing couple and as the impression cylinder for the other printing couple. As a result, impression pressure develops between two blanket cylinder surfaces, rather than between a blanket cylinder and an impression cylinder.

Common Impression Cylinder (CIC) Web Press
Common impression cylinder (CIC) web presses use one large, central impression cylinder in conjunction with a number of printing couples (figure 11.38). The web travels around the common impression cylinder

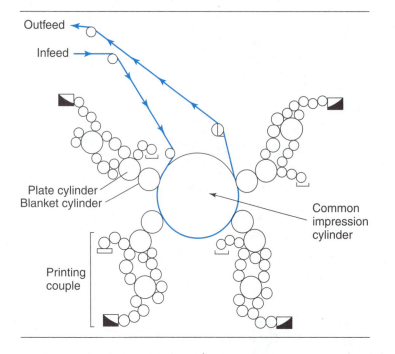

Outfeed

Infeed

Plate cylinder
Blanket cylinder

Common
impression
cylinder

Printing
couple

Figure 11.38   **Schematic of a
common impression cylinder
web press**

and passes under one or more of the blanket cylinders, which are each part of a printing couple. The advantage of a CIC press is that the paper or other substrate has uniform stretch around the large impression cylinder. This uniformity makes obtaining proper register, and keeping register consistent, much easier than it is on a blanket-to-blanket press.

In-Line Web Press

In addition to blanket-to-blanket and CIC web presses, in-line web presses are also common, particularly for printing forms (figure 11.39a). The major feature of an **in-line web press** is that each printing unit consists of only one blanket cylinder and one impression cylinder combined with an inking and dampening system (figure 11.39b). Thus, in-line presses are not perfecting presses and are used mostly for work that needs to be printed on one side only, such as business forms and labels. However, some in-line presses can print on both sides of

the web by inserting a **turn bar** between printing units (number 6 in figure 11.39b). The turn bar turns the web over so that the remaining units can print on the back side of the web. Typical in-line presses can print two to four colors on one side of the web or one to two colors on both sides of the web.

Components of a Web Press

The major components of the printing couple for offset printing (the plate cylinder and blanket cylinder, and associated ink and water systems) have already been discussed. The Web Offset Presses section touched upon the components unique to a web press. The following discussion focuses in more detail on those components of a web press that are not typically found on a sheet-fed offset press.

Roll Stand

The roll stand holds one or two webs of paper, and it meters or measures the paper feed

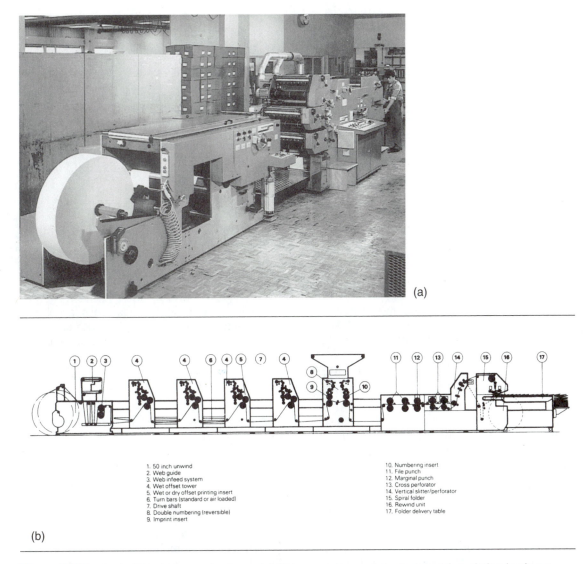

(a)

1. 50 inch unwind
2. Web guide
3. Web infeed system
4. Wet offset tower
5. Wet or dry offset printing insert
6. Turn bars (standard or air loaded)
7. Drive shaft
8. Double numbering (reversible)
9. Imprint insert

10. Numbering insert
11. File punch
12. Marginal punch
13. Cross perforator
14. Vertical slitter/perforator
15. Spiral folder
16. Rewind unit
17. Folder delivery table

(b)

Figure 11.39 **An in-line forms web press.** (a) This press is specially designed for printing business forms, checks, lottery tickets, envelopes, data mailers, and other direct mail applications. (b) Equipped with four printing couples and a rewinder, this press can print from one to eight colors.
Courtesy of Müller-Martini Corporation.

into the press. On most web presses, the roll stand is placed in line with the printing couples. However, it is possible to place the roll stand to one side of the press or beneath the press to conserve space or to keep paper roll-handling operations out of the press room (figure 11.40). Many presses are equipped with auxiliary roll stands so that more than one web can feed to the press at once (figure 11.41a). This provides great flexibility on a multiprint-

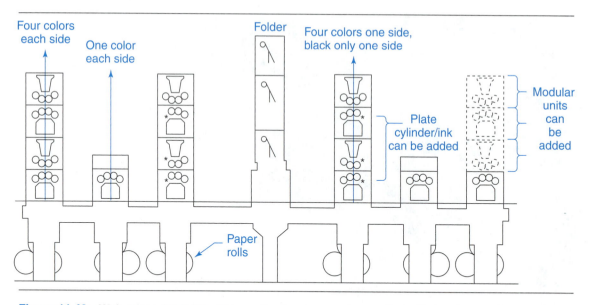

Figure 11.40 **Web press flexibility.** This multiunit web press is supplied with four base units to which other vertical printing couples can be added. With a modular unit design such as this, the press can be configured for the type of job to be printed, and press flexibility is greatly increased. Note that the paper is fed from rolls beneath the press room floor.
Courtesy of Graphic Systems Division, Rockwell International Corporation.

ing unit web press because one paper web can be printed by up to four or more printing couples (figure 11.41b). Thus, on a six-color web press, a two-color job can be printed by two printing units while a four-color job is being printed on the remaining four printing units.

A **dancer roller**, operating in conjunction with a brake on the roll stand, controls the web as it unwinds from the roll stand and enters the printing unit. The infeeding web wraps around the dancer roller, which actually rides on the moving web and presses its weight against the moving web paper. The dancer roller is free to move up and down; this up-and-down movement controls the brake on the roll stand (figure 11.42). As shown in figure 11.42, if the web feeds too rapidly, the paper under the dancer roller becomes slack and the dancer roller drops, which automatically applies the brake to the roll stand and slows

paper feed. If the web feeds too slowly, just the opposite occurs. The paper under the dancer roller becomes taut and lifts the dancer roller, which releases the brake on the roll stand and allows the web to feed more rapidly.

Splicer
In addition to the dancer roller, it is common for a roll stand to include a splicer, sometimes called a *paster*. The splicer automatically positions a new web for infeed and splices the lead end of the new web to the tail end of the web being printed. There are two types of splicers: flying splicers and zero-speed splicers. Both operate automatically, and both use adhesives to connect the two webs. The difference between them is that a **flying splicer** connects the two webs while each web rotates at press speed. It does so by pressing both the adhesive lead edge of the new web and the tail edge

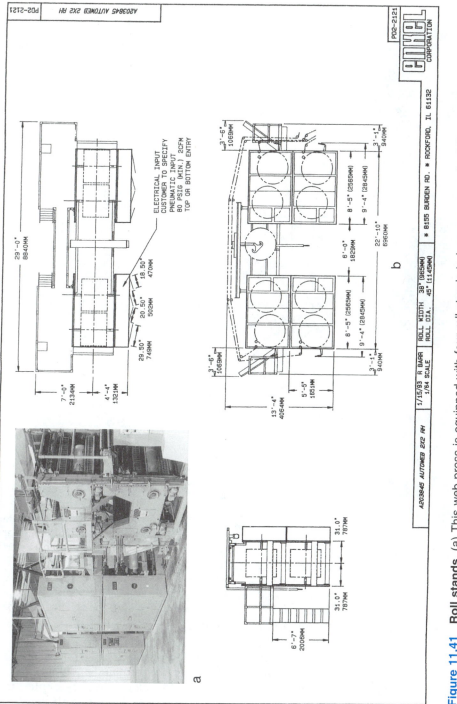

29'-0"
8840MM

ELECTRICAL INPUT
CUSTOMER TO SPECIFY
PNEUMATIC INPUT
80 PSIG (MIN.) 2CFM
TOP OR BOTTOM ENTRY

18.50
470MM

20.50"
502MM

29.50"
749MM

7'-0"
2134MM

4'-4"
1321MM

3'-6"
1069MM

3'-1"
940MM

8'-5" (2565MM)

9'-4" (2845MM)

22'-10"
6960MM

6'-0"
1829MM

8'-5" (2565MM)

9'-4" (2845MM)

3'-6"
1069MM

3'-1"
940MM

13'-4"
406MM

5'-5"
1651MM

b

31.0"
787MM

31.0"
787MM

b

6'-7"
2006MM

a

| A203845 AUTOWEB 2X2 RH | 1/15/93 | R BARR | ROLL WIDTH | 38" (965MM) | * 8455 BURDEN RD. * ROCKFORD, IL 61132 |
| | 1/64 SCALE | | ROLL DIA. | 45" (1145MM) | |

Figure 11.41 Roll stands. (a) This web press is equipped with four roll stands to increase press flexibility. (b) This schematic shows roll-stand configuration. Courtesy of Enkel Corporation.

253

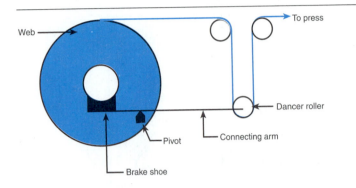

Web

To press

Dancer roller

Pivot

Connecting arm

Brake shoe

(a) Normal position of dancer roller

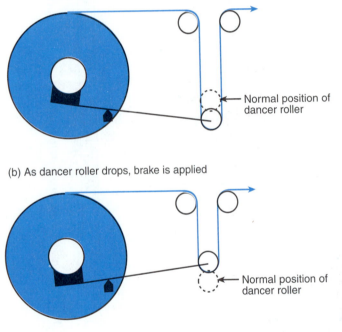

Normal position of dancer roller

(b) As dancer roller drops, brake is applied

Normal position of dancer roller

(c) As dancer roller rises, brake is released

Figure 11.42 Schematic showing operation of dancer roller and roll stand brake. Up or down movement of dancer roller controls the brake on the roll stand.

of the printing web against a splicing arm figure 11.43). The **zero-speed splicer** uses a **festoon**, which consists of several rollers. A festoon is a mechanism built for multiple-web rollers; the unit raises or falls. As shown in figure 11.44, the festoon holds enough paper to feed the press during the splice. As a result, the splice can be made while both the old and

new web are stationary and the press is running.

Web Tensioner

Although the roll stand and dancer roller work together to meter the web as it enters the printing units, they cannot control web tension completely. Several factors, such as the tension

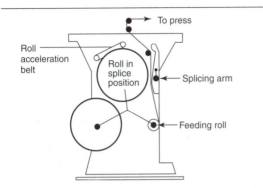

a) Splice in preparation, new roll accelerated, and splicer arm in position

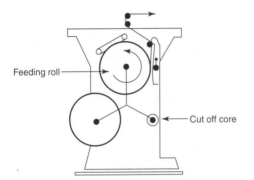

b) Splice is made, new roll feeding and old roll cut, leaving core

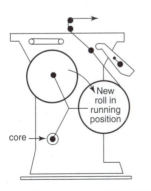

c) New roll moved into running position; splicer arm and acceleration belt moved aside

Figure 11.43 **A flying splicer.** After the splice is made, the core is removed and a new web is mounted.

with which the web was rolled at the mill, the type of paper or other substrate on the web, and the configuration of the press itself, affect web tension during printing. The dancer roller and brake mechanism cannot compensate for all of these factors to maintain adequate and proper web tension. Web tension is critical. Improper tension can lead to improper image registration. In the worst case, improper tension can break the web, forcing the operator to shut down the press.

Most presses employ a tensioner to maintain consistent web tension (figure 11.45). The tensioner consists of a series of rollers over which the infeeding web passes. As the infeeding roll passes over the tensioner rollers, it recovers from the tension with which it was wound at the mill and is regulated to the proper, even tension for the press run. Many tensioners consist of a series of variable speed rollers, followed by a second dancer roller. This configuration ensures proper web tension and minimum variation.

Dryer and Chill Rolls

The **dryer** and the **chill rolls** work together to ensure that the ink on the printed sheet is dry and set when it comes off the web. If the web were allowed to leave the press with wet ink, ink setoff would be a problem, and the wet ink would almost certainly smear as the web passed through the folder, cutter, or rewinder. Most web printing inks are heat-set inks. A web printed with a heat-set ink passes from the last printing unit through a dryer, which brings the moving web up to a temperature of about 300°F in a few seconds. This temperature is high enough to evaporate most of the ink solvent. It also softens the resin that binds the ink pigments together during chilling. Chilling immediately follows drying. Chilling is accomplished by passing the web over a series of water-cooled chill rolls. During chilling, web temperature is reduced to about 90°F, which is cool enough to set the binder and pigment and produce a dry print.

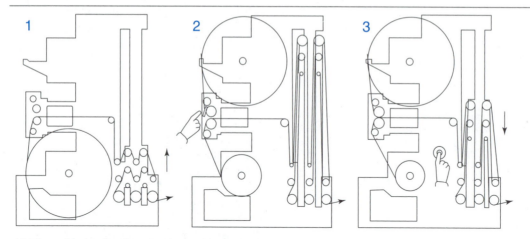

(1) The roll is feeding into the press, and the festoon has begun rising. (2) The festoon has expanded to store a full 80 feet of paper; a new roll has been mounted, and its lead edge has been prepared for the splice. (3) The expired roll has been stopped, and paper feeds into the running press from the collapsing festoon. The lead edge of the splice roll has been placed close to the surface of the expiring web.

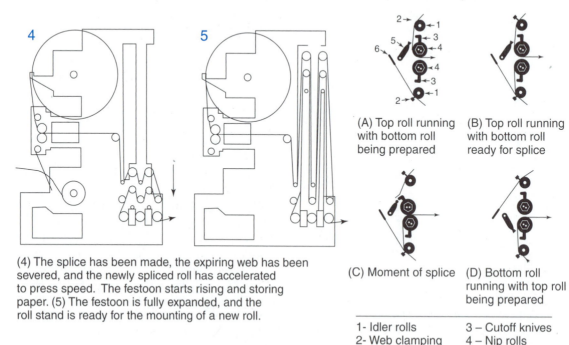

Detail view of splice

(4) The splice has been made, the expiring web has been severed, and the newly spliced roll has accelerated to press speed. The festoon starts rising and storing paper. (5) The festoon is fully expanded, and the roll stand is ready for the mounting of a new roll.

(A) Top roll running with bottom roll being prepared

(B) Top roll running with bottom roll ready for splice

(C) Moment of splice

(D) Bottom roll running with top roll being prepared

1- Idler rolls	3 – Cutoff knives
2- Web clamping brushes to hold severed web	4 – Nip rolls
	5 – Cutoff brush
	6 – Vacuum blade

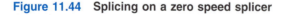

Figure 11.44   Splicing on a zero speed splicer

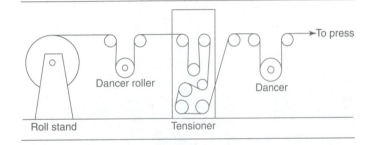

Figure 11.45 **A web tensioner.**
Dancer rollers placed before and
after the tensioner help maintain
proper web tension.

Folding and Cutting

Because of the nature of web press work, most
web presses are equipped with one or more
folders that fold the webs into signatures as
they leave the press. The type of folder required depends largely on the type of work
being printed on the web press. There are three
basic types of folders: former folders, jaw folders, and chopper or quarter folders. Often, all
three folding devices are incorporated into a
combination folder, as shown in figure 11.46.

A **former folder** folds the web by pulling
it over a triangular-shaped former board. This
action makes one "with-the-grain" fold by
folding the web along its length. Folds made
after the former fold are made with jaw and
chopper folders. A **jaw folder** folds the web
across its width (across its grain) by allowing
it to travel around a cylinder equipped with a
tucker blade. The tucker blade forces the paper into a jaw (opening) on an opposing cylinder. After passing through the folding jaw, the
web is automatically cut into individual signatures and, if necessary, passes to a chopper
folder. In the **chopper folder** each signature is
forced between two rotating fold rollers that
make the final with-the-grain fold.

Press Console

Modern presses run at median speeds of
25,000 impressions per hour. Much paper
would be wasted if the press operator had to
examine printed signatures while the press
was running in order to determine if press ad-

justments were needed, and then had to go to
the appropriate printing unit and make the required adjustments. High-speed web presses
are equipped with press consoles similar to
those used on automated sheet-fed presses.

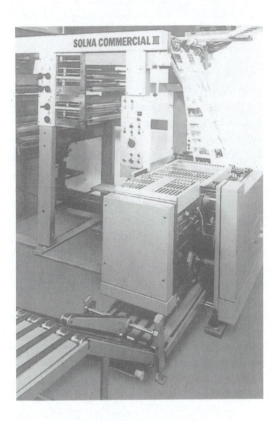

Figure 11.46 **A combination folder.**
Courtesy of Solna, Incorporated

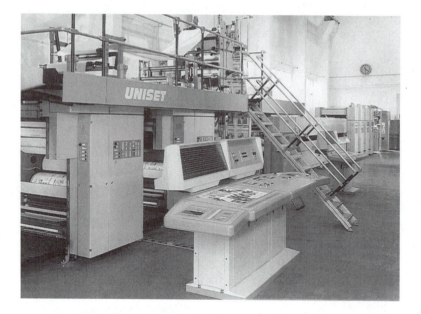

Figure 11.47   A web press console. This web press console is designed for complete press control in a single location. Courtesy of M. A. N.-Roland, ISA, Inc.

Press consoles provide electronic control for register and image quality on the moving web (figure 11.47). Information such as web side-lay, register, color consistency, and backup (the position of the image being printed relative to the top and bottom of the web) is computer controlled. Press adjustments can be made *on the fly* (as the press is running at printing speed). Settings for each printing unit or couple, such as ink and dampening settings and horizontal and vertical register, can be made directly from the console. Once the press operator has the press set properly, computers continually monitor press performance and make adjustments to maintain those initial settings. The press operator monitors the console and, if necessary, makes press adjustments by adjusting switches on the console, which in turn causes the appropriate adjustments to be made on the press itself. The console greatly reduces wastage by reducing the amount of misprinted material and by reducing the amount of press downtime. Many presses have automatic blanket washing units

that are controlled from the press console. Consoles also reduce the number of people required to operate the press.

Toward Total Automation

We have discussed the basic components and operation of sheet-fed and web presses. The same digital revolution that transformed the prepress processes has now begun to change the printing press workflow. Digital files can now arrive at the press console directly from prepress with more than just press settings indicated. All information pertinent to the successful completion of the print job can now remain integrated with the file. The driving force behind the creation of this new file format is the **CIP3** group, which stands for *International Cooperation for Integration of Prepress, Press, and Postpress*. Since its introduction in 1995, the goal has been to create a vendor-independent interface called the **Print Production Format (PPF)**. This file format contains instructions for machines involved in a CIP3 automated workflow. The file format is PostScript based and can contain all necessary data for printing and processing the job (excluding screened high-resolution data). For example, rather than visually examining plates or using a plate scanner to determine ink coverage, the CIP3 data are used to preset the ink key fountains. The following data can be stored in the CIP3 PPF file.

- Administrative data (job name)
- Preview images for color separations that enable automatic ink key presets
- Transfer curves (needed to calculate real-area ink coverage)

- Color and density measurements
- Register marks
- Cut data
- Folding data
- Private data, such as application- or vendor-specific data
- Information about collection, binding, stitching, or trimming

Automation can lead to faster production cycles that, in turn, can satisfy the customer's demand for faster turnaround. But automation alone will not produce a satisfactory product. A well-trained press operator is still a critical component.

Key Terms

printing press
feeding unit
registration unit
printing unit
delivery unit
platen press
platen
flatbed cylinder press
grippers
rotary press
plate cylinder
impression cylinder
web printing
offset press
blanket cylinder
perfecting press
offset lithographic press
duplicator
web-fed press
sheet-fed press
pilefeeding
make-ready
continuous sheet-feeding system
successive sheet-feeding system
sucker feet

stream feeder
sheet separators
combing wheel
double-sheet detector
registration
fit
headstop
form rollers
three-cylinder principle
two-cylinder principle
impression
fountain
fountain roller
ductor roller
distribution roller
rotating distribution rollers
oscillating distribution rollers
waterless printing
gravity delivery
chain gripper delivery
grippers
static eliminator
multicolor sheet-fed press
perfecting transfer system
plate scanner

roller stroke
press console
roll stand
splicer
web-steering device
sidelay
tensioner
printing couple
sheeter
blanket-to-blanket web press
common impression cylinder
  (CIC) web press
in-line web press
turn bar
dancer roller
flying splicer
zero-speed splicer
dryer
chill rolls
combination folder
former folder
jaw folder
chopper folder
CIP3
Print Production Format (PPF)

Review Questions

1. What four units are common to all presses?

2. How does a platen press differ from a flat-bed cylinder press?

3. Why is the rotary press design efficient for printing?

4. Explain the offset principle.

5. Draw the cylinder configuration for a blanket-to-blanket perfecting press.

6. Differentiate between an offset duplicator and a true offset press.

7. How does a successive sheet-feeder feed paper to a press? What controls are available on this type of feeder?

8. What is the difference between registration and fit?

9. How is registration controlled on a sheet-fed offset press?

10. Describe the three- and two-cylinder configurations used on offset presses.

11. Why must control impression be adjusted?

12. Describe the roller train for the inking and dampening systems on a press equipped with a conventional direct dampening system.

13. Explain the operation of a chain delivery system.

14. What makes waterless printing different from conventional printing?

15. What are the major units of a web offset press?

16. How does a common impression cylinder press differ from a blanket-to-blanket press?

17. How do the roll stand and dancer roller control web travel?

18. Why are a dryer and chill rolls needed on a high-speed web offset press?

19. Describe the three types of folders commonly found on a web offset press.

20. What is the purpose of a press console?

21. Who created the Print Production Format interface and what is its function?

12

Offset Press

Historical Background

Alois Senefelder, the inventor of lithography, designed the first lithographic press sometime between 1798 and 1800 by borrowing the basic idea of a press that was used to reproduce copperplate engravings using a relief process. Senefelder took what was basically a flat bed cylinder design and added a tympan frame

and frisket to hold the paper, a flexible blade instead of a roller to apply the pressure, and a lever–counterweight system to control the blade tension.

During production, two workers operated Senefelder's device. The workers first drew a design by hand on a slab of limestone with a

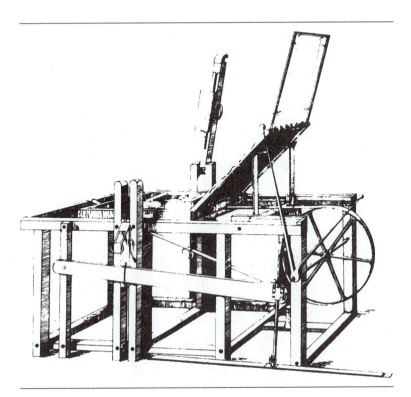

Original drawing of Senefelder's lithographic press design

grease crayon-like material and placed the "plate" on the movable bed of the press. They next covered the stone with a water and gum arabic solution. The liquid flowed off of the greasy image but covered the nongreasy stone surface. Then the workers vigorously rolled an ink-covered leather roller back and forth over the stone. The ink was repelled by the water film but attached to the grease image. The stone was ready to print after the workers carefully wiped it with a clean cloth to remove any excess moisture.

The workers then moved to the press where they mounted a sheet of previously dampened paper on the tympan, closed the frisket to hold the sheet in place, and lowered the frame into contact with the processed stone. Then they lowered the blade against the back of the tympan. One worker stood on the pressure lever while the others slowly turned a wheel to slide the bed under the blade. This scraping pressure caused the ink to transfer from the stone to the sheet of paper. There was always danger that the blade would apply too much pressure and the stone would break or that the sheet would slip under the scraping action. After one pass, the workers released the blade, hinged the tympan frame out of the way, and hung the sheet on a line to dry. Then they repeated the whole process.

Senefelder's press was considered a marvel of its time. In an average twelve-hour day, two craftspeople could produce perhaps fifty acceptable copies using this press. Senefelder's later designs included an automatic dampening and inking system and a lever scraper blade that moved across the stone instead of the stone moving under the blade.

Although steam power was applied to a lithographic press around 1866, Senefelder's basic design was not changed until the offset press was introduced in 1907.

Objectives

After completing this chapter, you will be able to:

■ Recall the most common inking unit configuration and describe its setup operations.

■ Recall the most common dampening unit configuration and describe its setup operations.

■ Describe the basic steps in setting up and operating an offset lithographic press.

■ Recall press concerns when printing process color on sheet-fed offset lithographic presses.

■ Describe several quality control devices commonly used in offset printing.

■ Recall common roller and blanket problems and solutions, and describe mechanical adjustments that are possible on most presses.

■ Recall common press concerns.

■ Recognize a troubleshooting checklist and be able to use it to suggest solutions to press problems.

■ List common press maintenance steps.

Introduction

There are so many different offset presses on the market today with so many minute operational differences that it is easy to become bogged down trying to learn press operation by the "which-switch-does-what" method. The problem with this method is that the operator is lost if moved to another type of machine.

An operation manual prepared by the press manufacturer is unparalleled for teaching "switches." Such a manual can provide more detailed on-the-job information for a production situation than any textbook could provide. The purpose of this chapter is not to serve as a general operation manual, but rather to deal with fundamental understandings that will enable you to run any offset duplicator or sheet-fed press after reviewing the manufacturer's operation manual.

This chapter is divided into two sections. Section 1 covers the information necessary to run an offset press. Section 2 gives important information on troubleshooting press concerns.

Section 1

As just mentioned, the purpose of this section is to examine the general operation of any sheet-fed offset press or duplicator. Refer to a machine's operation manual for details on operating that specific machine.

Offset Press Operation

In an industrial situation each press is usually assigned one operator or group of operators. The operator assigned to a press knows the press's characteristics and typically runs only a few standard sheet sizes. Experienced press operators typically set up the ink and water sections of the printing unit before adjusting the paper feed. Novice printers, however, do not have the advantages of being familiar with the press, knowing the sheet size run previously, or being confident around a machine as complicated as an offset press. For these reasons, it is recommended that students adjust the paper feed before adding ink or fountain solution to the printing unit when learning press operation. When the press sheets pass through the press consistently and without jamming or misfeeding, students can direct their attention to obtaining proper ink-water balance.

Feeding the Press Sheet

It is important that the press sheets are cut accurately to the same size, are the same thickness (paper weight), and are not wrinkled or stuck together. To feed the paper, begin by fanning the pile of press sheets to remove any static electricity that might be holding the individual sheets together (figure 12.1). Place the pile slightly off center in the feeder unit of the press. When the press sheet is momentarily held in place in the registration unit—just before it enters the printing unit—the paper is generally jogged or pulled $\frac{1}{8}$ inch to $\frac{3}{16}$ inches into final position. It is this action that causes *registration*. For this reason it is important to load the pile in the feeder unit just a bit off center.

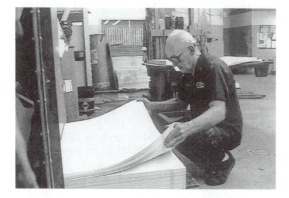

Figure 12.1 **Fanning the press sheets.** The press sheets are fanned to remove any static electricity.

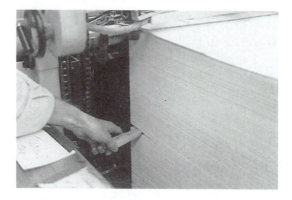

Figure 12.3 **Using wedges to level the paper.** Push wedges into the pile of paper to level the surface of curled stock.

Push the pile forward so that it is seated squarely against the front plate of the feeder when held by the side and back guides (figure 12.2). The top of the paper pile must be perfectly level and parallel to the registration board. If the pile sags, place a heavy board (such as a binder board cut slightly smaller than the paper size) under the pile. If the pile curls, insert wedges at several points in the pile to make the surface level (figure 12.3).

Next, adjust the pile height below the feeder mechanism (figure 12.4). Pile height is generally measured from the sucker feet. Heavy paper must be closer to the sucker feet than light paper. To set the pile height, turn the press on and allow the automatic pile height control to raise the pile to its previously set position. When the pile is in position, turn

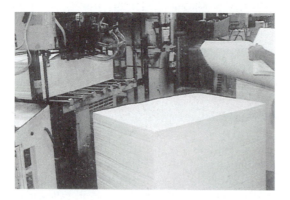

Figure 12.2 **Adding paper to the feeder unit.** Seat the pile of press sheets squarely against the front plate of the feeder.

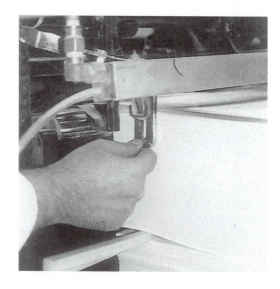

Figure 12.4 **Adjusting the pile height**

the press off and check the distance between the pile and the sucker feet when the feet are in their lowest position. If the distance is not between $\frac{1}{8}$ inch and $\frac{1}{4}$ inch, lower the pile manually, readjust the pile height control, and allow the press to rerun and lift the paper pile to the new setting. Feeding problems will result if the pile height is not set properly. If the paper pile is too high, the sucker feet will pick up double sheets, or jamming will result because the air and vacuum system is not allowed to do its job. If the pile is too low, no sheets will be picked up or misfeeds will occur.

As mentioned in chapter 11, the purpose of the air blast in the feeder unit is to float the top few sheets of the pile above the rest of the pile on a blanket of air. The amount of air blast needed varies depending on the weight and size of the paper being printed. In general, the air blast should be adjusted so that the press sheets do not vibrate and the topmost sheet nearly contacts the sucker feet (figure 12.5). Too much air causes the top sheets to press together rather than separate. The vacuum should be sufficient to draw the top sheet the short distance into contact with the sucker feet but not enough to pick up more than one sheet.

Before allowing the feeder mechanism to send a press sheet to the registration unit, the pull-in wheels (not on all machines) and the double-sheet detector must be set. Adjust the pull-in wheels to a uniform pressure so that they pull each sheet squarely from the feeder onto the registration board. Double-sheet detectors either open a trap door and eject multiple sheets to a tray below the registration board or they mechanically (or electronically) cause the press to stop when a double sheet is detected. Set the detector to allow the thickness of one sheet to pass but to trip the press if more than one sheet is fed.

Registering the Press Sheet

Next, allow the press to feed a press sheet into the registration unit until the press sheet contacts the headstop (figure 12.6). The paper is moved along the registration board by moveable conveyer tapes, straps, or skid rollers that move the tape to align with the sheet size. Then adjust the sheet jogger or pull guide to push or pull the sheet about $\frac{1}{8}$ inch. The press sheet should lie flat in the registration unit without binding or curling. Inch the sheet into the grippers that pull it between the impression cylinder and the blanket cylinder and al-

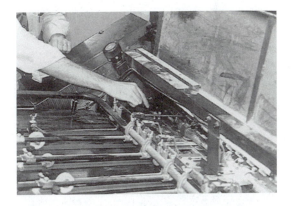

Figure 12.6   Adjusting the registration unit.
Adjust the registration unit by allowing a sheet of paper to contact the headstop. Then position the sheet jogger or pull guide.

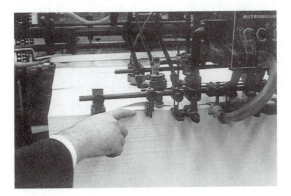

Figure 12.5   Adjusting the air blast

low it to be transferred to the delivery unit. Heavier paper is more difficult for the sheet jogger to move and should be closer than $\frac{1}{8}$ inch.

Delivering the Press Sheet

Before the sheet is released from the chain grippers, adjust the delivery table side guides (figure 12.7). Allow the press sheet to drop onto the delivery table and position the table end jogger.

In order to check the entire printing system, start the press and allow paper to pass from the feeder to the delivery unit. The sheets should feed smoothly and consistently to the registration board. Each sheet should be registered and transferred uniformly to the printing unit. The delivery unit should remove each sheet and stack a perfect pile on the outfeed table. Final adjustments for image registration are made after the printing unit has been inked and the first few printed sheets have been checked.

It is wise to place some make-ready or scrap sheets on top of the press sheet pile. Make-ready sheets can be used for initial press

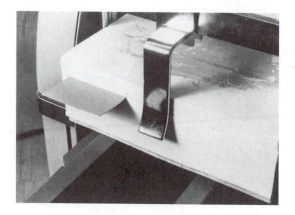

Figure 12.8 **Using make-ready sheets.** Notice that a marker is placed between the make-ready or scrap sheets and the clean press sheets on the infeed table.
Courtesy of SUCO Learning Resources and R. Kampas.

setup. Be certain, however, that the make-ready sheets are of the same weight and surface finish as the final sheets (figure 12.8).

Preparing the Printing Unit

Recall from chapter 11 that two basic systems are used to put water solution and ink on the printing plate: the direct system and the indirect system. In the direct system, moisture is transferred to the plate directly from a dampening form roller. In the indirect system, the water is transferred to the plate from the ink form rollers. The major difference in preparing the printing unit for these two systems is that with the indirect system, the fountain solution cannot be added to the water fountain until the press is inked completely. In the direct system, however, the ink and fountain solution can be put into the ink and water fountain during the same step. It is important to keep in mind with which system you are working as you read the following.

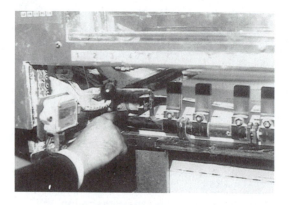

Figure 12.7 **Adjusting the delivery unit side guides**

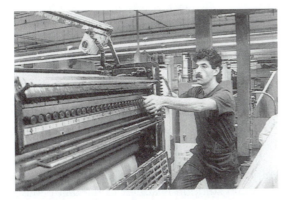

Figure 12.9 **The ink fountain.** The ink fountain holds a pool of ink that is passed to the inking system. The amount of ink that is passed is controlled by ink fountain keys.

Adjusting the Ink System

Ink is transferred from the ink fountain reservoir by a ductor roller that contacts the fountain roller. The consistency of the ink layer over the fountain roller directly influences the amount of ink fed to the distribution unit.

Many ink fountains are set up with ink fountain keys that allow the press operator to adjust the ink feed to allow for variation in ink coverage needed on the plate (figure 12.9). If large solids or halftones cover one section of the plate, it is necessary to feed additional ink to that section of the plate (figure 12.10).

When setting up an ink fountain, assume that the ink feed needs adjustment. Begin by loosening all of the ink fountain keys. This brings the ink fountain doctor blade out of

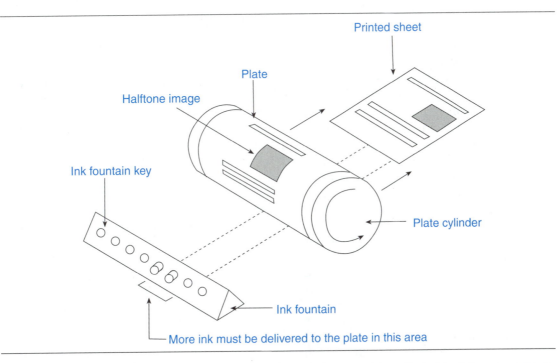

Figure 12.10 **Adjusting the ink fountain.** The ink fountain keys must be adjusted to deliver more ink to areas where large halftones or other kinds of dense copy will print from the plate.

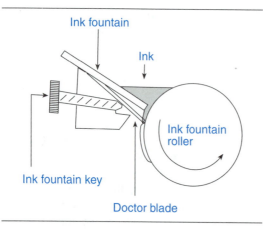

Figure 12.11 Diagram of an ink fountain key. As the ink fountain key is adjusted, it moves the doctor blade either toward or away from the ink fountain roller, and thereby decreases or increases the amount of ink that is deposited on the roller.

contact with the fountain roller (figure 12.11). Reverse the process by gently tightening each fountain key until you feel blade pressure against the fountain roller. Then move the fountain keys out slightly to allow a small gap between the doctor blade and the fountain roller.

When the doctor blade is straight and parallel to the fountain roller, you can add ink to the ink fountain. To check for uniform ink distribution, manually rotate the press until the ink ductor roller touches the ink fountain roller. Then turn the ink fountain roller and observe the ink coverage on the ductor roller. If the surface of the ductor roller is covered evenly, the fountain keys are set properly. If heavy or light areas are noticeable across the ductor roller, adjust the fountain keys until the ink layer is consistent. If some areas of the plate require more ink than others, open the fountain keys that are in line with those sections.

Once the first rough ink adjustments have been made, and without bringing the water or ink form rollers into contact with the plate cylinder, turn the press on and allow the systems to ink up. As the distribution rollers work the ink to a fine layer, make small adjustments to ensure ink train uniformity. Do not overink the system. It is easier to add ink to the system than it is to remove it.

Adjusting the Dampening System

Fountain solution is added to the dampening fountain of most presses and duplicators from a storage bottle that works by gravity feed. This bottle should be placed into position at this time. Remember, if you are operating an indirect dampening system, the fountain solution should not be added until the whole roller train is inked. In contrast, the fountain solution can be added to a direct dampening system before, after, or during ink adjustments.

None of the ink and dampening rollers in indirect dampening systems have covers or sleeves. The dampening ductor and form rollers in direct dampening systems generally have cloth or fiber covers. If the dampening covers in the direct system are extremely dry (this may occur after a long period of press shutdown), turn on the press, bring the dampening ductor roller into contact with the fountain roller, and turn the fountain roller by hand to add extra fountain solution to the dampening ductor roller. This action speeds the dampening process. Be careful not to soak the ductor roller, however, as soaking over-dampens the press.

Another way to speed the dampening process is to soak a cotton wipe in the fountain tray and squeegee the dampening solution onto the ductor roller. The form roller cover should be damp to the touch, but it should not be dripping wet. Once the dampening unit is inked and moistened adequately, stop the press and insert the plate.

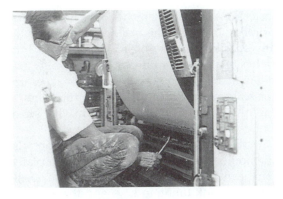

Figure 12.12   **Mounting the plate on the press**

Attaching the Plate

Mount the plate on the press by inserting the front edge of the plate in the lead clamp of the plate cylinder, and tighten the plate into position (figure 12.12). If packing is required to help control impression, select and cut the appropriate packing material, and position the packing material between the plate and the cylinder. Then rotate the cylinder forward so that the plate curves into contact with the plate cylinder. When the rear plate clamps become exposed, insert the tail edge of the plate and tighten the clamp. The plate should be tight around the cylinder, but it should not distort or stretch.

Starting Up and Proofing

Most lithographic plates have some form of gum preservative coating to protect the plate surface between development and press placement. Moisten a sponge with plain water or fountain solution and wipe the entire plate to dissolve this coating. If a direct image plate is being used, a special etch or starter solution must be used at this point.

Inking the Plate

If you are operating an indirect system, start the press and allow it to operate for a moment.

Then move the form rollers into contact with the plate. The plate should pick up ink in its image areas and no ink in its nonimage areas. If no ink is picked up anywhere on the plate after several press revolutions, check to make sure that the form rollers are contacting the plate. If there is contact, you must either cut back on the moisture or add ink until the image appears on the plate. To determine which adjustment is necessary, stop the press and observe the plate. If the plate is moist with only a thin film of fountain solution (not dripping), more ink is probably needed. If the plate is overdampened, adjust the water fountain to deliver less moisture.

If you are operating a direct dampening system, start the press, let it operate for a moment, and lower the dampening form rollers into contact with the plate. Release the form rollers, stop the press, and check the plate. The surface of the plate should be moist, but dampening solution should not drip from it. If the plate is not moist, adjust the fountain system to deliver more moisture and repeat the processes of dampening and checking. Once the dampening form rollers are delivering enough moisture to the plate surface, lower the ink form rollers into contact with the plate. Ink should transfer only the image areas of the plate. If ink deposits in nonimage areas, there is probably a lack of moisture. If ink appears in nonimage areas, called scumming, place additional fountain solution onto the dampener form roller in that area.

Press Proofing

Once the plate is properly inked, place the press *on impression* (lower the plate cylinder into contact with the blanket cylinder) and allow several make-ready sheets to pass through the printing unit.

The only initial concern is image position, not image quality. Examine the first few printed sheets for consistent image placement, and compare the image placement with the proofs or layout specifications for the job. All offset presses allow the image to be raised or lowered on the sheet by moving the position of the plate image on the blanket cylinder. On most presses you can skew the plate on the plate cylinder or the paper on the registration board to square the image on the press sheet. Before final side-to-side and up-and-down adjustments of the image are made, the image must first be square to the lead edge of the press sheet. The side-to-side image position can then be adjusted by moving the registration system.

After obtaining the desired image position, start the press, lower the dampening and ink form rollers into plate contact, and begin the run with the make-ready sheets. As the sheets pass through the press, assess the image quality and make appropriate adjustments to the ink or dampening system and the impression cylinder. As the first clean sheets begin to feed, set the press sheet counter to zero and begin the press run. A counter automatically counts each sheet as it passes through the press.

Achieving Proper Ink–Water Balance

The ink–water balance is crucial in offset printing. If not enough moisture is on the plate, the image scums on the press sheet. If too much moisture reaches the plate, the image appears light and washed out (not dense enough) on the press sheet. Adding ink to an overdampened plate does not correct the ink–water balance problem. In fact, it makes matters worse because when the correct amount of moisture is finally delivered to the plate, the press will be overinked.

It is important to remember that small changes made at the fountain rollers take time to work through the distribution and form rollers and to the plate. Most fountain rollers are adjusted by a ratchet. A lever along the ratchet is moved forward or backward so many clicks to make the fountain roller turn

faster or slower. Often the lever has a scale printed next to it. This scale does not refer to any specific quantity of ink or moisture, but rather relates to the rate of fountain roller rotation at any given time. Moving the lever up the scale makes the fountain roller rotate more rapidly. Moving the lever down the scale causes the roller to rotate more slowly.

The water fountain roller alone controls the amount of moisture placed on the plate. On the inking system, however, both the opening of the ink fountain keys and the rotation rate of the ink fountain roller control the quantity of ink reaching the plate. To achieve proper ink–water balance, the ink fountain keys, the ink fountain roller rotation rate, and the water fountain roller rotation rate must all be adjusted properly. When these elements are adjusted properly, and the press can run through several thousand impressions without the press operator touching the ink or water adjustments, the ink and water systems are said to be *in balance*.

Ink–water balance can be achieved only while the press is actually printing. An inexperienced press operator may have to print many make-ready sheets to achieve this balance. Even experienced press operators allow up to six percent spoilage for a run of 1,000 sheets. In other words, the experienced operator expects to print up to 60 press sheets to get the press to feed properly and to reach the correct ink–water balance. These spoiled sheets, called the *spoilage allowance*, are added to the 1,000 sheets needed for the final run and are paid for by the customer as part of the job.

The ink and water settings necessary to achieve proper ink–water balance differ with each printed job. One job may have large, dense image areas and require more water and ink than another job. When colors are printed, whether process color or flat color, proper ink–water balance must be achieved for each color. As a result, the spoilage allowance increases for color work.

The mark of an experienced press operator is the ability to get the press feeding and reaching ink–water balance with the least amount of spoilage. This takes practice and familiarity with a particular press. Novice printers do not have this experience. However, the following considerations may make achieving ink–water balance a bit easier for the novice.

1. Remember that the gauge of any printing job is the press sheet. Experienced press operators watch the outfeed table and pull every twenty-fifth, fiftieth, or one hundredth press sheet to compare with the first acceptable press proof. A quick check of the press sheet shows density inconsistencies across the image area, scumming or ink in the nonimage areas, and **set-off** (an image printed on the back of the press sheet). Checking the ink rollers and registration board will not help determine whether the printed image is acceptable, however.

2. On direct system presses, the ink and water form rollers can be lifted from the plate separately. It is always a good idea to raise the form rollers from the plate when the ink or dampening system is being adjusted. This will help keep the plate from becoming overdampened or overinked.

3. Most ink and water fountain rollers can be stopped without stopping the ductor roller or the distribution rollers. If the press appears too dry, but the ink quantity seems right, stop the paper feeder, lift the form rollers, and turn off the ink fountain roller before adjusting the water fountain roller. It may take 50 to 100 press revolutions for a small change in the ink fountain roller adjustment to work its way to the plate. If the press is inking all this time and no paper is being printed, the ink will build up on the ink rollers. Once the water system is properly adjusted, the press will be overinked.

4. Feed jam-ups are frequent problems for inexperienced press operators. Generally, a jam-up can be corrected in a short time simply by shutting off the press and removing the jammed paper. Occasionally, however, jam-ups take longer to clear. If the press is shut down for much more than two minutes during a run, the ink–water balance has to be reachieved before final sheets are printed again. Unless new make-ready sheets are placed on the infeed table after the jam-up is cleared, spoilage increases.

Remember that all the time the press is shut down, the dampening rollers are drying. If the shutdown is lengthy, it may take several press revolutions before the dampening system is back to proper moisture level. After a long press shutdown, it is best to run the press for a few minutes with the inking system off, the form rollers off of the plate, and the dampening system on. Once the dampening system is back to proper moisture level, the dampening form roller(s) can again be engaged to moisten the plate, the press can be stopped briefly, and the plate can be examined for moisture content.

Cleanup Procedures

With the availability of rubber-based inks, many small job shops clean their ink and water systems only once a week. Some operators only cover their presses with a cloth to keep dust out; others spray the ink fountain and rollers with a commercial antiscum material that coats the ink with a thin layer of lacquer and, in effect, forms a seal that prevents the ink from drying. The disadvantage of all these approaches is that paper lint and other impurities in the ink and water systems eventually build up and affect production quality. Therefore, the most effective cleanup procedure is to clean the entire printing unit thoroughly at the end of each workday.

First, however, before the inking system is cleaned, the water fountain is generally drained. A tube leading from the water fountain is used for this purpose.

The ink cleanup systems on all but the smallest offset duplicators are almost totally automatic. One common system moves a doctor blade or squeegee against an ink roller (figure 12.13). If the wash-up solution is applied to the press while it is running, the ink dissolves and passes across the squeegee into a sludge tray.

There are specific procedures to follow when cleaning the inking system. First, remove as much ink as possible from the ink fountain. Next, remove the ink fountain itself and clean it by hand with ink solvent. On most presses, the rest of the inking system is cleaned almost automatically. While the press is off, attach or engage the squeegee or other transfer roller cleanup device. Then start the press and

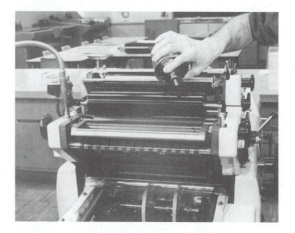

Figure 12.14   Applying wash-up solution

apply press wash-up solution to one side of the distribution rollers (figure 12.14). Most of the ink rollers are driven by friction against two or three geared rollers. If solvent were applied across the entire system, friction would be reduced and not all the rollers would turn. Apply wash-up solution until half of the system becomes clean and dry. Then apply the solvent to the remaining inked portion. Continue the procedure of applying solvent to one side of the system at a time until the entire system is clean.

The cleanup attachment of the press functions more efficiently if the leading edge of the squeegee blade is wiped clean after each use. If ink dries and hardens on the blade, the blade will not contact the roller properly. Some cleanup attachments are removed completely from the press after cleanup. Others merely hinge out of contact with the press rollers.

An alternative to the mechanical cleanup system is a blotter pad. Blotter pads are absorbent paper sheets that are cut and punched to the exact plate size for the press being used. To clean the inking system using a blotter pad,

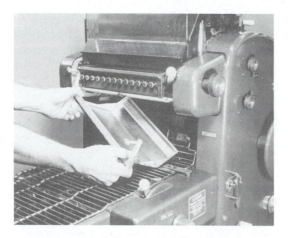

Figure 12.13   A doctor blade

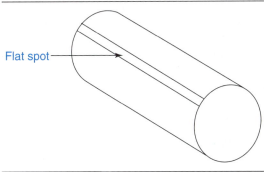

Figure 12.15   **A roller with a flat spot**

mount a blotter pad on the plate cylinder, turn on the machine, and lower the ink form rollers into contact with the pad (take special care to raise the water form roller out of contact with the plate cylinder). Apply solvent much the same as you would when using a mechanical cleaning device. With this approach, however, the dissolved ink transfers to the blotter pad.

Many presses and duplicators have systems (often called *night latches*) that separate the distribution rollers when the press is shut down. If the rollers are left in contact during lengthy shutdown periods, they develop *flat spots* where they rest together (figure 12.15). Flat spots can cause uneven ink distribution throughout the roller train. Consult the operating manual for the press that you are running to determine whether there are night latches that should be set after the press is cleaned.

Printing Process Color on Sheet-Fed Offset Presses

Most offset lithographic presses can be used to reproduce quality process color work as long as good separations, plates, paper, ink, and, most important, a skilled operator are available.

Press Concerns

The concerns when working with four-color, process printing are the same as for any quality single-color job: the sheets must be fed, registered, printed, and delivered. However, it is important when printing process color to hold accurate and consistent registration throughout the entire press run.

There is a simple method to check registration controls prior to printing a four-color job. First, set up the press for the most consistent feeding and registration and print a different job that includes both line and halftone copy. Without changing the press settings, remove the printed sheets from the delivery system and move them to the feeding system to be fed through the press a second time. The goal is to print a second layer of ink—both halftone dots and line copy—over the first image with **dot-for-dot registration**. If, after two printings, only one sharp image is observed, quality registration is being held. If the image is blurred or if there is a double image, however, either the system is not properly adjusted or the press is incapable of quality color reproduction.

When a single press is used to reproduce four-color work, color contamination between runs is always possible. Even though an ink unit is cleaned thoroughly, residual ink may interfere with the purity of the next color. This is more of a problem when a dark color, such as black, is followed by a light color, such as yellow, because impurities are more evident in a light color.

One solution is to ink the press first with a small quantity of the new ink and, after a uniform ink layer is obtained on all rollers, wash the press. The press is then reinked with the same new color in proper quantities for the production run. With this procedure the press actually gets cleaned twice, and there is little chance for color contamination. This technique, called a *color wash-up*, is unnecessary when a light color is followed by black.

Sequence of Colors

Recall that process color involves overprinting four separate images in a combination that approximates the appearance of nearly any color in the visible spectrum. During printing, the sequence of colors can vary depending on the type of ink, paper, or press or on the preference of the operator. There are, however, several common sequences.

The sequence of cyan, then yellow, magenta, and finally black is used often. Yellow, magenta, cyan, and black is another frequent color order. The cyan image generally resembles a normal halftone reproduction. In other words, if process cyan is the first color placed on the sheet, detail is usually carried across the sheet wherever the final image appears. Using progressive color proofs, it is possible to compare press sheets with each color to match density and detail positions, and it is relatively easy to fit all colors into their proper positions after cyan is printed. One disadvantage with printing cyan first is a large quantity of ink is laid down on the press sheet the first pass through the press. With so much ink detail on the press sheet, all colors following cyan tend to dry rather slowly because the paper has already absorbed ink over much of its area. There is also the possibility that as the paper becomes more ink saturated with each added color, adhesion can build up between the sheet and blanket cylinder.

Many printed jobs have process color on the same page as line copy such as headlines or paragraph composition, which must appear in black. Often the color position on the page is defined by the location of this black copy. In these situations, it is necessary to print the black copy first and then fit all of the other colors in their correct positions on the sheet. The typical color sequence is black, yellow, magenta, and cyan. This approach has the added advantage of reducing the adhesion between the press sheet and the blanket cylinder because the colors that typically carry the least amount of ink detail are printed first. In instances where progressive proofs are not available, this sequence also enables the press operator to correct any color deviations on the first three colors by adjusting the cyan printer.

Quality Control Devices

Although visual inspection of the press sheet can be used effectively to determine print quality of single-color line images, the quality of halftone images, or images which require critical registration, is best determined with quality control devices. Many companies have developed quality control devices that can be stripped, plated, and printed in nonimage areas of the press sheet. Under magnification, these devices can aid the press operator in determining overall press sheet image quality and in making press adjustments. In the following section, we discuss only a few of the many quality control devices available. All the devices discussed here have been developed by the Graphic Arts Technical Foundation (GATF), which for years has been at the forefront of research and development in the graphic arts. Readers who desire further information about these and other quality control devices can write to GATF directly at 200 Deer Run Road, Sewickley, PA 15143-2600. Note that the following reproductions of GATF quality control devices are for illustration only. When supplied by GATF, these devices are of extremely high quality and fine line detail. The reproductions here in no way reflect the original film images provided by GATF.

The GATF T-Mark

The GATF **T-Mark** consists of a configuration of thin, accurately ruled lines that are used to identify image centers, folds, trims, and bleeds during printing production (figure 12.16). The T-shaped center lines signify final trims, folds,

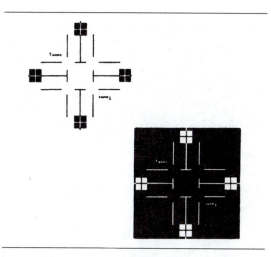

Figure 12.16 **GATF T-mark for trims, centers, and bleeds.**
Courtesy of GATF.

or the center-of-image points. During stripping, the cross stroke of the T is positioned $\frac{1}{8}$ inch (3 mm) outside of the final image area so that is trimmed off after printing. The set of outer marks indicate standard bleed or trim allowances. In negative form, these marks provide accurate references for film assemblers when cutting masks for bleeds. When printed on the press sheet, these marks guide the press operator in image fit and aid bindery operators when trimming press sheet signatures before folding. The reverse image cross marks that appear in the small squares at the end of the T-marks indicate vertical and horizontal center-of-image points on film sheets. These cross marks are especially useful for aligning images during step-and-repeat operations.

In addition to the previous aids, film negative T-mark images can be positioned on master flats during four-color stripping so that they reproduce in identical locations on each of the plates used to print the job. During printing, the press operator checks to see that these marks line up for each press sheet color.

These checks are an aid in achieving initial color register and in monitoring register during the press run.

The GATF Star Target

The GATF **Star Target** is a small, circular pattern of solid and clear pie-shaped wedges (figure 12.17). When printed on a press sheet, the Star Target gives the press operator a quick and effective measure of the following:

- **Ink spread:** Spreading in all directions of the edges of ink dots and lines on the press sheet beyond their corresponding areas on the plate

- **Slur:** Smearing of the trailing edges of dots, resulting in ink film tapering into the white areas

- **Doubling:** Printing of a double image, which consists of a full solid and a weak second image, slightly out of register with the full solid

In practice, the Star Target is stripped into the flat so that it plates in the trim areas at each corner of the trailing edge of the press sheet. These corner areas are usually the most sensitive in showing any ink slur or doubling. The image of the Star Target on the press sheet shows the amount of ink spread and its direction by the way the center wedges of the target fill in with ink. Figure 12.18a shows a press sheet image with very little ink spread. Note that the wedge-shaped images are open

Figure 12.17 **Image of the GATF Star Target shown in same size it appears on a press sheet.**
Courtesy of GATF.

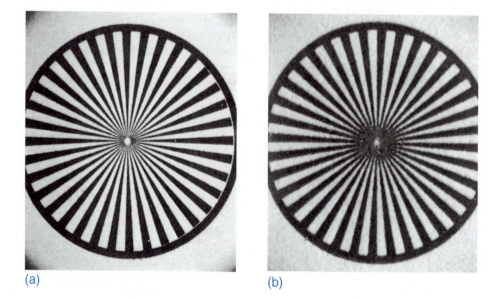

(a) (b)

Figure 12.18 **Photomicrographs of Star Target images on press sheets (6x).** Target (a) shows very little ink spread. Target (b) shows considerable ink spread. Courtesy of GATF.

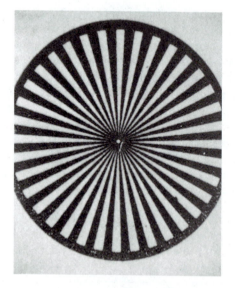

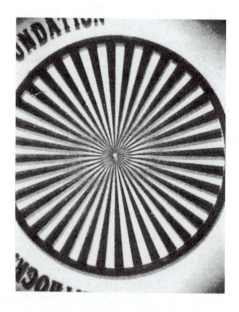

Figure 12.19 **Photomicrographs of Star Target image showing slur (6x).** Press slur in vertical direction has caused the center of the target to spread to an oval shape. Courtesy of GATF.

Figure 12.20 **Photomicrographs of Star Target image showing doubling (6x).** Note weak double image adjacent to full printed image in target. Courtesy of GATF.

almost to the white center. Compare this figure to figure 12.18b, in which ink spread has caused the wedges to fill in and create a central disk of considerable darkness and size.

Slur is recognized in a Star Target when image spread is not uniform in all directions. In figure 12.19 note that the ink spread in the center of the target is greater in one direction, producing an oval-shaped center. Doubling of an image is clearly shown in figure 12.20 where each wedge shows a double, and the center of the target forms an oval or a figure eight.

The GATF Quality Control Strip

The GATF **Quality Control (QC) Strip** is a patterned device that helps the press operator

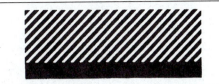

Figure 12.21 **10x enlargement of a segment of a GATF QC strip.**
Courtesy of GATF.

control print quality throughout the press run (figure 12.21). The QC strip is stripped and plated to print parallel to the gripper edge (figure 12.22a). The press operator follows standard procedures to produce a properly printed sheet, which is called the *OK sheet*. During the press run, the operator pulls in-

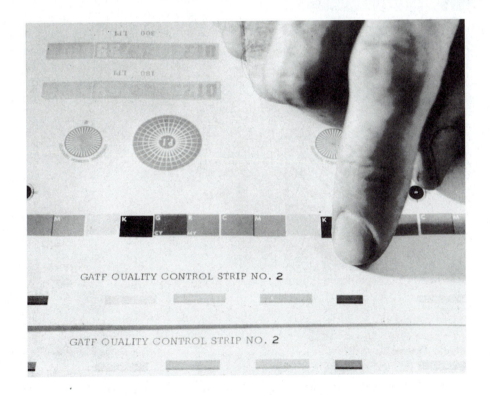

(a)

Figure 12.22a **Closeup of QC Strips on OK and inspection press sheets.**
Courtesy of GATF.

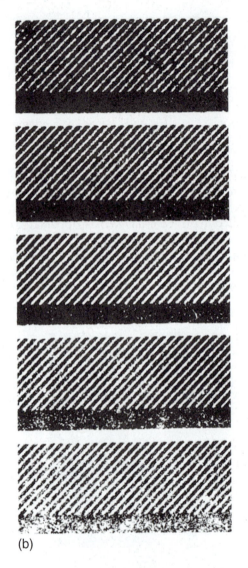

(b)

Figure 12.22b   10x enlargements of a QC Strip segment used to compare five different press sheets.
Courtesy of GATF.

vides a quick and effective method of comparing image quality on the inspection press sheet to image quality on the OK sheet. If the images on the two sheets do not match, press adjustments are made until an inspection sheet is produced with a QC image that matches the OK press sheet image.

The GATF Dot Gain Scale and Slur Gauge

The GATF **Dot Gain Scale** is used to determine if the dot areas of printed halftones match the dot areas on the halftone negatives or positives used to produce them. Fine screen tints are more sensitive to dot gain than coarse screens. The GATF Dot Gain Scale is designed to give numerical values to any dot sharpening (uniform loss in dot size) or dot gain (uniform gain in dot size). The scale is made up of ten 200-line screen tint steps which are graduated in density. These steps form numbers from 0 to 9 on a uniform background of 65-line tint density. When reproduced with halftone copy, some of the numbers appear

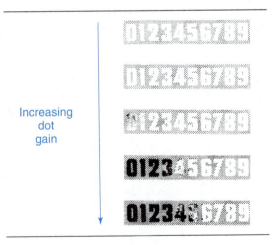

Increasing dot gain

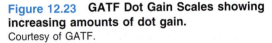

Figure 12.23   GATF Dot Gain Scales showing increasing amounts of dot gain.
Courtesy of GATF.

spection sheets from the outfeed pile, compares the QC strip printed on the OK sheet to the QC strip printed on the inspection sheet, and looks for a perfect matchup. As shown in figure 12.22b, when enlarged the QC strip pro-

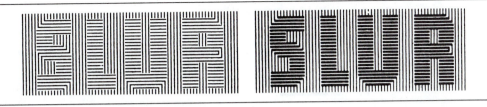

Figure 12.24 Enlarged GATF Slur Gauge. Image on left shows no slur; image on right shows slur. Courtesy of GATF.

darker than the background, and some appear lighter. Because the density differences from one number to the next are small, there is usually one number that is about as dense as the background. This number, therefore, is visible to the naked eye on the OK press sheet. The press operator uses the Dot Gain Scale to compare the numbers on the inspection sheet to those on the OK sheet to make sure that the same number remains invisible throughout the press run. If, for example, the number 3 were invisible on the OK sheet, but it began to appear during the press run, the press operator would be alerted to a dot gain condition and could make adjustments accordingly (figure 12.23).

Dot gain causes a dot to grow in all directions. It can result from improper exposure or development in platemaking, excessive cylinder pressures on press, too much ink, or a variety of other press factors. However, slur or doubling, which are directional, can also appear as dot gain. GATF has developed a **Slur Gauge** to help the press operator determine whether slur is occurring (figure 12.24). The Slur Gauge consists of fine horizontal lines that form the word SLUR on a vertical line background. Because the horizontal and vertical lines have the same density value, the word SLUR is invisible when all lines are printed with equal thickness. When slur occurs, however, the horizontal or vertical lines thicken, and the word SLUR appears darker than the background, alerting the operator to the slur and the slur direction. Because slur can often be confused with uniform dot gain, GATF has combined its Dot Gain Scale with its Slur Gauge (figure 12.25). This combined scale allows the press operator to determine the cause of apparent dot gain quickly so that the problem can be corrected with minimum paper waste.

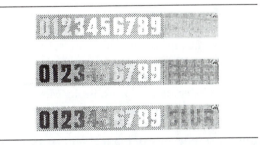

Figure 12.25 Combined Dot Gain Scale and Slur Gauge. The top scale is sharp, the second scale shows dot gain without slur, and the bottom scale shows dot gain caused by slur. Courtesy of GATF.

Section 2

This section covers some common press problems and concerns. Like all machines, presses need occasional adjustments to operate correctly. It is impossible to achieve proper ink-water balance or to print a quality image on a press that is not adjusted correctly.

Roller and Blanket Problems and Adjustments

Press operators often encounter several roller and blanket problems. Many of these problems can be corrected by relatively simple adjustments. Others require roller or blanket replacement. A press operator should be familiar with the adjustment procedures for most of the rollers in the roller train and be able to recognize solutions for many of the more common roller and blanket problems.

Blanket Considerations

As discussed in chapter 11, most offset blankets are formed from vulcanized rubber bonded to a fiber support base. A wide range of blanket quality is available within these basic materials, however. There are special purpose formulations designed to be used with specific materials, such as ultraviolet drying inks or coated stock, for example. Most printers do not change blankets every time a different ink or paper is fed through the press, but the importance of blanket and special materials compatibility must be stressed. Lithographic suppliers are prepared to identify the appropriate blanket for any press situation.

Blanket Problems

There are two common problems that occur with offset blankets that the press operator must be able to recognize and correct: glazing and smashes.

Glazing

Blankets become glazed because of long periods of improper cleaning or age. A very smooth, hard, glossy surface is created when the pores of the blanket fill with ink, ink solvent, and gum known as **glaze**. A glazed blanket loses its ability to transfer enough ink to produce an acceptable ink density on the press sheet. Commercial deglazing compounds are available to clear blanket pores, but the best measure to take to prevent glazing is to wash the blanket properly after each press run.

A good technique for keeping the blanket clean is to dampen the blanket with water and to use a good blanket wash while the blanket is still wet. The water loosens any dried gum that is not dissolved by the blanket wash, and the blanket wash removes dried ink. A properly washed blanket should look like smooth velvet.

Smashes

Blankets become smashed when more material passes between the impression and blanket cylinders than the gap between the two permits. Each time the press sheet wrinkles or folds as it travels through the printing unit, the blanket becomes smashed or creased. If enough pressure is applied to the blanket, the smashed areas of the blanket push in too far to receive ink from the plate cylinder and are unable to transfer images to the press sheets. If a smash is small, a commercial *blanket fix* is available to fix it. When this fix is painted over a smashed area, it causes the surface of the blanket to swell. Do not apply fix to a blanket in a halftone or tint area, however. The swelling caused by blanket fix is not uniform and will not print a uniform halftone or tint pattern. In these situations, the blanket should be replaced. The blanket should also be replaced if there are tears in the surface of the blanket. If a large blanket area has been smashed but there are no visible breaks, it might be possible to return the blanket to usable condition by removing it from the press and soaking it in a water bath for several days.

New blankets should not be stored near excessive heat. If a blanket is exposed to high temperatures, the rubber may lose its give, or elasticity. Blankets should be stored in flat positions with cover sheets to protect their surfaces from damage.

Plate-to-Blanket Packing and Adjustments

When the paper being printed passes between the impression cylinder and the blanket cylinder, the amount of pressure among these three elements must be uniform and sufficient to transfer ink. At the same time, this pressure cannot be so great that it is abrasive to the plate when the image is offset from the plate to the blanket.

The uniformity of the plate-to-blanket pressure can be checked easily by the operator. Turn off the dampening system and ink the entire surface of a used plate that is mounted on the press. Stop the press and lower the plate cylinder into contact with the blanket cylinder ("on impression"). Separate the two cylinders and inspect the ink band that was transferred to the blanket. If the band is approximately $\frac{1}{8}$ inch wide across the entire width of the blanket, the system is aligned properly. If the image is light, heavy, or irregular, consult the press manual for specific recommendations.

On most offset duplicators, plate and blanket cylinder pressure is either controlled automatically by spring pressure or it can be changed by a manual screw adjustment.

On presses, plate-to-blanket pressure is usually adjusted by placing packing under the blanket and/or the plate. Packing press cylinders improperly could cause serious registration problems. Press manufacturers specify appropriate packing for their equipment. Refer to the press manual for detailed plate-to-blanket packing procedures.

Glazed Ink Rollers

Even with the most efficient cleanup procedures, ink rollers can eventually become glazed with dried ink. As mentioned earlier, glaze is a buildup on the rubber rollers that prevents the proper adhesion and distribution of ink. Commercially prepared deglazing compounds are available that can be used easily to remove any dried ink from the rollers. One common technique is to apply a pumice compound to the rollers in the same manner as ink is applied. Allow the pumice to work into the rollers by running the press for 5 to 10 minutes. Then wash the system with a liquid deglazing solution. Both the compound and the solution can then be removed by using wash-up solution and standard cleanup procedures. Many press operators deglaze their rollers regularly as part of a preventive maintenance system.

Dampening Rollers

Water does not adhere readily to smooth roller surfaces. Therefore, several dampening rollers are covered with some material that carries usable quantities of the water fountain solution to the plate easily. The ductor roller and form rollers are covered typically with two types of dampening covers: molleton covers and dampening sleeves.

Molleton Covers

Molleton covers are thin cloth tubes that slip over the rollers and are tied or sewn at each end. It is important that the molleton covers cover the entire roller uniformly. If the ends are tied so tightly that a taper forms in the roller, insufficient moisture is delivered to the plate and the outside edges of the plate scum with ink. A new molleton cover placed on a roller should be broken in. Soak the cover with water and squeeze out any excess water by rolling the covered roller over a sheet of uncoated paper. The breaking-in process removes any lint or loose threads from the cover.

Thin cloth sleeves can be used to cover badly inked molleton covers. Thin cloth and fiber sleeves react more readily to operator adjustments and make maintaining consistent moisture control easier than with the traditional molleton cover.

Dampening Sleeves

Dampening sleeves are thin fiber tubes that, when dry, are slightly larger in diameter than the roller. To apply the dampening sleeve, slide the dry sleeve over the clean roller and soak both with warm water. Within minutes the fibers in the sleeve shrink into position on the roller and the roller is ready to be installed on the press. Dampening sleeves are generally used only on form rollers. Because the sleeves are exceptionally thin compared to molleton covers, the rollers must be oversize compared to those usually supplied with the press. Despite this inconvenience, dampening sleeves are lintless and are easy to install and easy to keep adjusted to the plate cylinder.

Cleaning Dampening Rollers

At the end of each workday, remove the dampening solution from the water fountain tray. If the metal fountain roller becomes coated with ink, it can be cleaned with pumice powder and water. Coating the fountain roller with any commercial desensitizing etch occasionally ensures continued water transfer during the production day.

Cloth and fiber dampening covers and sleeves can be cleaned with a commercial dampening roller cleaner. To clean the covers and sleeves, first saturate them with water so the cleaner soaks into the fabric and not the fibers. Then scrub the surface of the covers and sleeves with a stiff brush and roller cleaner. Rinse the covers and sleeves with water and allow them to dry.

It is best to have two sets of dampening rollers for each press so a clean, dry roller is always available for use. If the press has only one set of rollers and a roller is needed immediately after cleaning, roll the needed roller against a blotter pad or cleaning sheets until all water is removed. Covers should not be cleaned daily; they should only be cleaned as necessary. They should, however, be changed when the cover material no longer accepts water.

Distribution Roller Adjustment

All distribution rollers in the ink and dampening systems must contact each other uniformly to achieve proper ink and water distribution. Most rollers are adjustable in at least one direction and are relatively simple to move.

A common method for adjusting distribution rollers involves using strips of 20-pound paper. Cut six pieces of paper, 8 inches or 9 inches long. Four of the pieces should be approximately 2 inches wide and two should be 1 inch wide. To check for uniform pressure between the two rollers, roll a set of three strips (two that are 2 inches wide and one that is 1 inch wide) between a set of rollers at each end of the rollers and then gently pull the middle pieces out (figure 12.26). The strips should slide with slight uniform resistance, but they should not tear.

Form Roller Adjustment

The ink and water form rollers must all be adjusted so that they touch the plate with the correct amount of pressure and have uniform pressure across the width of the plate. Form rollers all have some type of easy adjustment for skew and pressure.

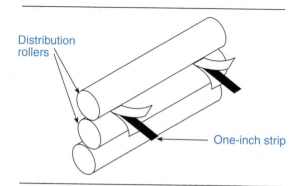

Figure 12.26 **Adjusting the distribution rollers.** Distribution roller adjustment can be checked by placing a set of three pieces of paper between rollers and then gently pulling the middle strips. The strips should slide with slight, uniform resistance.

Dampening Form Roller Adjustment

If the dampening roller is not parallel to the plate cylinder, moisture will not be distributed evenly across the plate. If all portions of the plate surface are not moistened uniformly, ink

scumming occurs on the plate. The need to adjust and align the dampening form roller and plate is often indicated when one side of the plate scums and the other side does not. This adjustment must be made with the dampening form roller in place on the press.

Cut two 1-inch-wide strips of 20-pound bond paper and place one under each end of the dampening form roller (figure 12.27). Lower the dampening form roller into position against the plate cylinder. Slowly pull each paper strip to check for uniform resistance. If unequal resistance is observed, the dampening form roller is not parallel to the plate cylinder and must be reset. Both duplicators and presses have adjustments to control this form roller-to-plate alignment.

Ink Form Roller Adjustment

Ink form roller-to-plate pressure is critical. Too much pressure results in a blurred or enlarged image. Too little pressure transfers no ink. Proper adjustment requires not only that you have the proper amount of pressure, but that

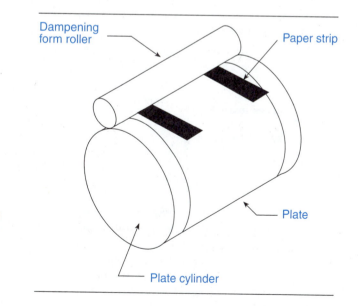

Figure 12.27 **Checking the dampening form roller adjustment.** Dampening form roller adjustment can be checked by placing two strips of paper under each end of the dampening form roller and comparing resistance.

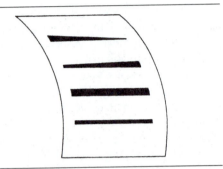

Figure 12.28   Examples of test strips to check for ink form roller-to-plate pressure. The top two test strips show rollers that contacted the plate with uneven pressure. The third strip indicates too much pressure. The last strip is uniform and not too wide, which indicates correct pressure.

the pressure be even across the width of the plate. Ink form roller pressure is checked by first inking the press and then turning the press off in such a way that the plate cylinder is beneath the form rollers. With the plate

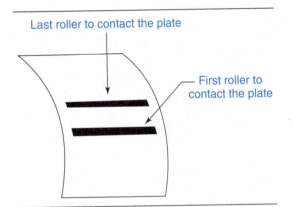

Figure 12.29   Examples of different tracks left by the first and last roller. The ink track left on the plate by both rollers should be even across the width of the plate. The track of the first roller, however, should be slightly wider than the track of the last roller.

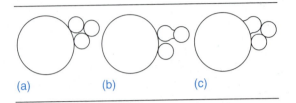

Figure 12.30   Diagram of ink form roller adjustment. The proper adjustment of form rollers is shown in (a). Misalignment of form rollers is shown in (b) and (c).

cylinder in this position, bring the form rollers into contact with the plate by moving the press to the *print* mode. Immediately bring the press off ink and rotate the plate to where you can examine the ink tracks left on it by the form rollers (figure 12.28). As shown in figure 12.29, the first roller to contact the plate should have the heaviest ink line ($\frac{1}{8}$ inch to $\frac{3}{16}$ inch) while the last roller should have the lightest ink line ($\frac{3}{32}$ inch to $\frac{1}{8}$ inch). All rollers, however, should transfer a uniform width of ink across the plate. Figure 12.30a shows proper form roller positions against a plate cylinder. Figures 12.30b and 12.30c illustrate two possible adjustments that diminish image quality on the final sheet.

Common Press Concerns

Many concerns are common to all press designs or models. This section does not contain an exhaustive list, but it should help you understand some basic press problems.

The Dampening Solution and pH

The moisture applied to the surface of a lithographic plate actually serves two functions. First, moisture in the nonimage areas repels ink. If only pure water were used as the dampening solution, however, the action of the ink would rapidly cause the nonimage areas to become ink receptive. The second purpose of the moisture, then, is to ensure that the nonimage areas of the plate remain water receptive. Alois Senefelder recognized the dual role of the moisture layer on the stone and used a solution made from a combination of water, acid, and gum arabic.

Ready-mixed dampening solutions are available from a commercial supplier or they can be purchased as separate components and mixed. Most dampening solutions are now made from an acid concentrate, gum arabic, and a gum preservative.

For lithographers, the most meaningful measure of dampening solution usability is its level of acidity. The numeric scale that measures acidity in a range from 0 (very acid) to 14 (very alkaline or basic) is called the **pH scale** (figure 12.31). The midpoint of the scale, 7, is considered neutral. Plate manufacturers recommend a pH level to be used with their plates. A reading between 5.5 and 4.5 is acceptable for most plates.

The printer can measure pH in several ways. Litmus paper pH indicators are available from printing suppliers and give acceptable readings of the acidity levels of most production situations (figure 12.32). To perform a test, remove a small piece of litmus paper from the roll and dip it into the fountain solution. The wet paper changes color and can be matched to color patches supplied with the roll of litmus paper. A pH number identifies each color patch. If the pH of the fountain solution is not in the recommended range, remix it.

Some presses have built-in sensors that monitor the pH level of the dampening solution continually. With these sensors, the required pH is dialed into the unit, and the device automatically compensates for any variation in pH by adding water or acid concentrate.

A variety of problems can occur when a fountain solution is too acidic (pH reading from 1 to 3). A strongly acidic fountain solution can greatly shorten plate life. The acid tends to deteriorate the image area of all surface plates and can eventually remove the plate emulsion. When this happens, printers say the image "walked off the plate." When humidity in the press room is high, the action of the acid on the ink causes drying problems on the press sheets (especially high-acid content press sheets). A high-acid bath also breaks down the ink. In this case, the high-acid content of the fountain solution attacks the ink, and the ink becomes paste like, or **emulsified**. The rollers appear glazed, and no quantity of ink that is added to the system will correct the problem. The rollers must be cleaned and the unit must be reinked.

If the acid level of the dampening solution is too low (pH reading from 7 to 14), the action of the moisture layer on the nonimage areas decreases water receptivity, and the plate scums with ink.

Ink and Paper Considerations for Lithographic Printing

Ink and paper are probably the two most common ingredients of any printing job. The customer does not want to be concerned with the details of production problems, but the printer must live with ink and paper problems on a day-to-day basis. Some characteristics of these two important ingredients of offset litho press operation are worth examining.

Working with Lithographic Ink

Ink is affected by the paper on which it is put. Many printers add materials, such as a drier or an extender, to their ink indiscriminately at the beginning of each workday and believe that they are improving the ink in so doing. There is a trend in ink manufacturing to supply inks that require no special mixing and that match each different type of press sheet and job characteristic. Under no circumstances

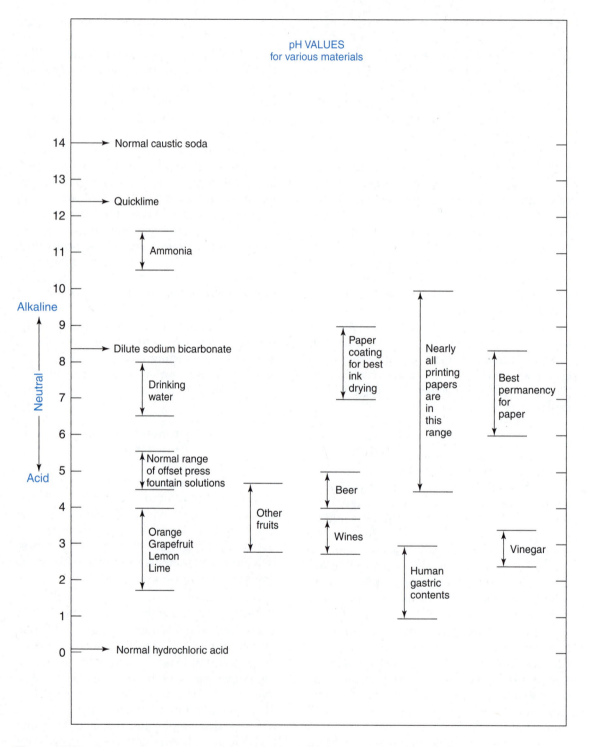

Figure 12.31 **The pH values for various substances.**
Courtesy of Mead Paper.

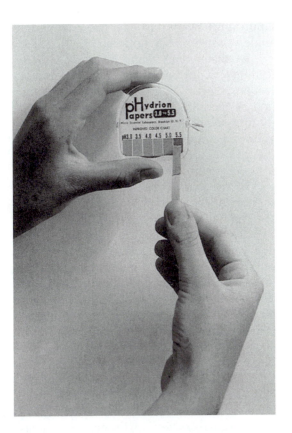

Figure 12.32 **Example of a litmus paper pH indicator.** Litmus paper pH indicators are used to check the water fountain solution in most working situations.
Courtesy of Micro Essential Lab., Inc.

should additives be mixed with any ink without consulting an ink supplier.

Troubleshooting Ink Difficulties

Beyond mechanical problems caused by inexact press adjustments, there are often difficulties resulting from ink characteristics that can be corrected easily with appropriate additives. Three common problems are tinting, picking, and slow drying.

Tinting is identified by a slight discoloration over the entire nonimage area, almost like a sprayed mist or the pattern created by a

five or ten percent screen tint. Generally, the situation is caused by a reaction between the ink and the water fountain solution. If the ink is too water soluble, it bleeds back into the water fountain through the dampening system. If tinting occurs, both the ink and the dampening systems should be cleaned. A different ink formulation should also be used.

Picking is similar in appearance to small hickies over the entire image area of the press sheet (figure 12.33). A **hickey** can result from linty or poorly coated paper, but it more commonly results from ink that is too tacky. Small particles of paper tear from the surface of each press sheet and feed back into the inking system to cause the hickies. If picking is observed, the inking system should be cleaned and the ink should be mixed with a small quantity of reducer or nonpick compound.

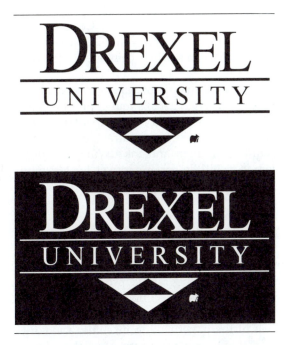

Figure 12.33 **Example of a printer's hickey.** Hickies are defects in a printed image caused by small particles of ink or paper attached to the plate or blanket.

Solving the problem of slow ink drying can be elusive unless all possible causes are recognized. Simple drying problems can generally be eliminated by adding a drier compound to the ink, but too much drier compound can actually increase drying time. Overinking a coated (nonabsorbent) stock can significantly increase drying time. On humid days, too high an acid content in the dampening solution (low pH) can cause difficulties. This combination of problems is almost impossible to solve without moving the press sheets to a humidity-controlled environment. Delayed drying can be a special problem when the press sheet must be flopped or turned to receive an image on the second side.

Paper Acid Content

In general, uncoated papers will not dry properly in a humid atmosphere if the pH of the paper is below 5 (see figure 12.31). Most coated papers have a pH of above 7.5. Coatings with a pH between 6 and 7 would also cause ink-drying problems when combined with high humidity.

Testing the pH of papers can be a cumbersome and time-consuming process. Acid content information for any paper lot is available from the manufacturer. If the room humidity is high and ink drying is a problem, consult the paper supplier for testing or information.

Paper Grain

Paper grain direction is an important characteristic that is related most closely to the ability of the individual sheets to be run through a sheet-fed lithographic press. Most paper forms when cellulose fibers combine and interlock. As paper forms on the moving wire belt of the papermaking machine, a majority of the cellulose fibers turn parallel to the direction of travel. Press sheets are defined as **grain long** when most of the paper fibers are parallel to the longest dimension of the sheet.

Grain short means the paper fibers are at right angles to the longest dimension of the sheet.

A distinction should be made between feeding and printing as they relate to grain direction. In grain-long feeding, the grain direction is parallel to the direction of travel through the press. In grain-short feeding, the grain direction is at a right angle to the direction of press travel (figure 12.34). Grain-long printing occurs when the paper grain is parallel to the axis of the plate cylinder. Grain-short printing occurs when the paper grain is at a right angle to the plate cylinder axis.

The Mead Paper Corporation suggests that cellulose fibers expand as they absorb moisture. This expansion can be up to five times as great across the width of a fiber as along its length. This fact should suggest to lithographers that the direction of grain feed could present significant registration problems when multicolor runs are printed on a single sheet-fed offset press. In other words, on a lithographic press, press sheets contact moisture from the fountain solution. The individual cellulose fibers in the paper sheets can then change size, with the greatest increase being in the dimension across the grain. If the sheet has to be run through the press several times to receive different ink colors, each pass can add more moisture to the fibers and can cause different changes in sheet size. These changes can make it extremely difficult to fit one color image to another.

Almost all offset paper is supplied grain long. It is to the printer's advantage, when involved with multicolor runs, to print with the paper grain parallel to the axis of the plate cylinder. For most presses, the printing plate is longer across the cylinder dimension than it is around. If the greatest paper expansion is going to take place across the grain, it is wise to feed the sheet so that the greatest change takes place across the smallest plate or image dimension. Also, on most presses, it is far simpler to make registration adjustments by ro-

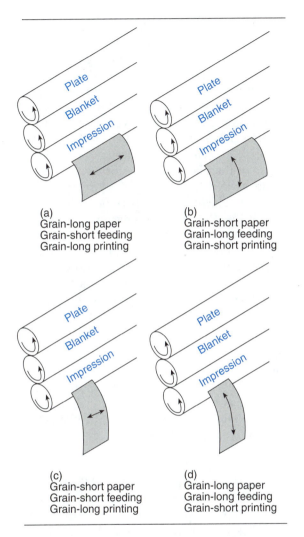

Figure 12.34 **Grain direction in printing**

(a) Grain-long paper / Grain-short feeding / Grain-long printing

(b) Grain-short paper / Grain-long feeding / Grain-short printing

(c) Grain-short paper / Grain-short feeding / Grain-long printing

(d) Grain-long paper / Grain-long feeding / Grain-short printing

tating the printing cylinders than it is by moving the infeed pile.

It is important to understand that not all lithographic press work is done with grain-long printing. Grain is of little importance for simple, single-color runs or for multicolor images that do not have critical registration requirements. There are also instances when a multicolor job *must* be printed short grain. For example, when printed sheets are to be folded, grain direction is very important. Such jobs must generally be printed so that the fold is parallel to the paper grain.

Surface Texture

A wide variety of textures can be formed on the surface of all papers. This texture is generally referred to as **finish**. Because lithography transfers an image from a flat printing plate, it is difficult to print a detailed design on a very rough paper surface. Ink would never reach the valleys of rough textures. For this reason, almost all offset materials are relatively smooth. Lithographers are concerned with two main classifications of papers: coated and uncoated.

Almost all papers form by the interweaving of cellulose fibers. The surface of **uncoated paper** is made up of nothing more than these raw, interlocking fibers. Although the fibers can be polished by **calendering** (pressing the fibers between rollers or plates to smooth or glaze them), the ink image sits on, and is often absorbed into, the fibers. A **coated paper** surface has an added layer of pigment bonded to the original cellulose fibers to smooth the rough texture of this natural material. Coated papers generally carry more printed detail and produce a better finished image, but they are more difficult to print than uncoated papers. Coated papers are available coated on one side (C1S) or coated on both sides (C2S). Both types of paper are made in at least two grades, and the surface appearance can vary from a dull to a high gloss.

There are several areas that lithographers have learned to watch when printing coated stocks. Most jam-ups occur because of static electricity between the coated sheets on the infeed table. The pile of paper should be fanned *carefully*, and the feeding should be adjusted with start-up sheets before the actual run begins. The blanket should be checked carefully for quality, specifically for glaze buildup. Glaze has a tendency to pick and split or tear coated paper. Ink quantity is more critical with coated materials than with uncoated ones. Too much ink causes set-off (the transfer of an image from the printed face of one sheet in the pile to the bottom face of the next sheet in the pile) of the image in the delivery pile. Overinking could also cause the paper to stick to the blanket cylinder and generally increases drying time. Roller and cylinder alignment is also more critical with coated stock and should be checked carefully.

A Troubleshooting Checklist

In theory, press setup and operation are simple. Unfortunately, difficulties may develop in every situation and prevent a quality image from printing on the final press sheets. The true craft of printing is identifying and correcting these problems. This process is called troubleshooting. The following sections identify common press and duplicator difficulties and outline probable causes and solutions.

Scumming

Scumming is a condition in which nonimage areas accept ink.

Too Much Ink

If the press is overinked, the ink system rollers appear highly textured and a hissing sound is often heard from the rollers as the press idles. To remove excess ink without a wash-up, turn the machine off and manually roll scrap sheets of paper between two of the upper ink distributing rollers. Repeat the procedure until the required amount of ink is removed.

Dampening System Difficulties

Scumming can also be caused by insufficient moisture, dirty dampening covers, dampening covers tied too tightly, light dampening form roller pressure to the plate, or low acid level of the fountain solution.

First, study the pattern of the scum carefully and trace its position back to the dampening form roller. If the scumming covers the entire plate, it could be the result of overall lack of moisture (increase the fountain feed), poor form roller pressure (readjust), or a dirty dampening form roller cover (clean with a commercial dampening roller cleaner or replace). If the scumming pattern is on the outer edges of the plate only, the form roller cover could be tied too tightly or the ductor roller cover may have slipped (retie or replace covers). If the plate is scumming in a band that extends around the circumference of the cylinder, that area of the dampening form roller might be inked and may not be allowing the moisture to pass to the plate (clean the form roller). Scum on the plate can also be caused by improper platemaking or gumming.

Blurred Copy (Double Image)
Loose Blanket

As blankets are broken in, and during press runs, they press against the plate cylinder and tend to flatten or stretch out. If the blanket is new, immediately check for tightness.

Excessive Impression

Too much impression tends to roll the blanket ahead of the impression cylinder and causes a set-off from the press sheet back to the blanket. This in turn results in a blurred image (back off or reduce impression).

Too Much Ink

Refer to the solution under the previous Scumming section.

Gray, Washed-out Reproduction
Too Much Moisture

If moisture is dripping off the plate or spraying onto the press sheets, water is flooding into the image areas and the plate cannot accept sufficient quantities of ink. Turn off the fountain ductor roller, lower the dampening form roller into contact with the plate, and allow the press to run. This process allows the excess fountain solution to coat the plate and evaporate. If an extra set of dampening form rollers is available, it could replace the overmoistened set. The rollers could also be removed from the press and rolled against clean, absorbent paper.

Not Enough Ink

If the inking system is carrying too little ink, a dense image cannot be transferred to the press sheet. Check the appearance of the ink coating and increase the ink feed if necessary. However, always check for too much moisture before increasing ink feed.

Incorrect Plate-to-Blanket Pressure

If the blanket image is light but the plate is inking well, the plate-to-blanket pressure is insufficient and should be readjusted, or the packing should be increased.

Incorrect Impression-to-Blanket Pressure

If the ink and dampening systems are set correctly and the blanket is receiving a good image, the impression cylinder position should be checked. Increase impression until a dense, sharp press sheet image is obtained.

Gray, Washed-out Reproduction and Scumming
Glazed Ink Rollers

If the inking system rollers appear shiny and hard, glazed ink rollers are interacting with the moisture system and passing inconsistent or inadequate amounts of ink to the plate. Use a commercial deglazing compound to clean the inking system.

Glazed Blanket

If the blanket surface appears shiny and hard, clean it with a commercial deglazing compound.

Too Much Form Roller Pressure

If the ink and/or dampening form rollers are set too close to the plate cylinder, then sufficient ink or water solution transfer will not take place. Readjust the form roller pressure.

No Reproduction on Press Sheet

Check for insufficient ink form roller pressure (readjust), not enough plate-to-blanket pressure (reset), not enough impression (increase impression), or too much moisture and glazed blanket and ink rollers (decrease moisture and deglaze blanket and rollers).

Printer's Hickey

Hickeys are caused by small particles of ink or paper attached to the plate or blanket (figure 12.33). Stop the press and clean the plate and blanket.

Press Maintenance

Unfortunately, maintenance is often viewed as an activity that takes place after a problem occurs. Manufacturers always provide recommended maintenance programs for their machines. However, several general areas of concern should be considered for every press.

The motor that provides motion for the press is often concealed in a position that would seem to challenge a professional contortionist's skills. Because the motor is out of sight does not mean it is unimportant. Check for lubrication points and examine the belt and pulley systems often.

Chains on infeed and outfeed tables need to be kept greased and free of paper pieces or dirt. Infeed rollers become smooth from use. A piece of fine-grit, abrasive paper can be used to roughen and remove any dirt from the roller surface. Vacuum pumps usually have an oil reservoir that should be kept filled. The pump itself should be flushed several times a year.

All roller and cylinder bearings must be lubricated, usually daily. Some presses have a single oil reservoir that delivers lubrication to bearing surfaces continually.

The importance of a consistent maintenance schedule cannot be overstated. It is far cheaper to spend time each day doing preventive maintenance than to wait until a major malfunction takes place and the press is *down* for several days awaiting new parts.

A printing press is a machine that is controlled by humans. Some printers claim that each press has a distinctive personality and assign human names and characteristics accordingly: "It's Monday and Harold is kind of sluggish" or "Jane is mad at me today—she's throwing paper all over the place." However, a mechanism cannot perform tricks beyond what a human programs it to do. Every press problem has a cause and a solution. The printer works with a press, but it is the printer, not the machine, who controls each situation.

Key Terms

set-off
dot-for-dot registration
T-Mark
Star Target
ink spread
slur
doubling
Quality Control (QC) Strip
Dot Gain Scale

Slur Gauge
glaze
molleton cover
dampening sleeve
pH scale
emulsified
tinting
picking
hickey

grain long
grain short
finish
uncoated paper
calendering
coated paper
scumming

Review Questions

1. Discuss the steps and procedures for setting up the paper feed on an offset press.
2. Explain how the printing unit is prepared for printing, including adjustments for ink and water for both direct and indirect dampening systems.
3. Describe the method for achieving proper ink and water balance.
4. How is press cleanup accomplished?
5. What is one way to solve possible color contamination when running process colors on a lithographic press?
6. Describe the T-Mark, Star Target, QC Strip, Dot Gain Scale, and Slur Gauge produced by GATF, and tell what quality control checks can be made with each.
7. What causes a lithographic blanket to glaze?
8. What is the purpose of dampening covers in the dampening system of a lithographic press?
9. Why is accurate alignment of form rollers against the image carrier (printing plate) so important?
10. How are printing inks formed?
11. What does the term *pH* mean?
12. What generally causes tinting on a lithographic press sheet?
13. What is the difference between grain-short and grain-long press sheets?
14. What are two possible causes of scumming on a lithographic press?

13

Screen Printing

Historical Background

This illustration is a famous playing card called the Knave of Bells that dates from about A.D. 1500. There is some debate as to how the card was actually printed, but it was probably printed from a stencil. The Knave was part of a set of forty-eight playing cards found in the inner lining of a book cover that was printed and bound sometime around the turn of the sixteenth century. Paper was such a precious commodity then that discarded or inferior sheets were often used to stiffen book bindings. Many valuable early pieces of printing have been found in such hiding places.

As we understand the process today, the stenciled Knave card was made using a perforated metal plate. To create the stencil, many small holes were punched through the thin metal plate in the shape of the desired image. The illuminator, as the stencil maker was called, positioned the plate over the paper and applied ink to the plate with a brush. The brush forced the ink through the small openings in the plate and onto the page. Several different colors were often used; a separate plate was used for each.

No one knows exactly when playing cards were invented, but evidence of their existence is documented in a 1392 account book kept by the treasurer of King Charles VI of France, in which a notation was made on the purchase of three packs of cards for the king. Several scholars, however, have found references to games of hazard, as card games were called, in French poetry as early as 1328.

The exact evolution of the printed card design is also difficult to trace. By 1550 printers had nearly universally adopted the four card suits we know today as symbols of the four classes of society. Hearts symbolized the clergy. Spades were a refinement of the Italian *spada*, a sword, and represented the nobility. Clubs meant the peasantry. Diamonds symbolized the citizens or burghers.

There are some experts who suggest that playing cards were the first printed product ever produced in Europe. Some even believe that the widespread use of games of hazard started an interest in learning for many uneducated peasants. There is little doubt that a demand was created for a printed product.

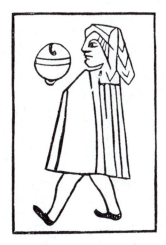

The Knave of Bells. A printed playing card from about A.D. 1500.

Objectives

After completing this chapter, you will be able to:

- Explain the basic concepts of screen printing.
- Classify types of screen stencils.
- Classify types of screen fabrics.
- Describe methods of stretching screens.
- Describe the steps in preparing and mounting indirect photographic stencils.
- Describe the steps in preparing and mounting direct photographic stencils.
- Describe the different techniques of masking stencils.

- Select the appropriate type of stencil, screen, and ink for different screen printing jobs.
- Identify important considerations when selecting a squeegee and ink.
- Explain basic screen printing techniques, including registration, on- and off-contact printing, printing, and cleanup.
- Recall multicolor printing techniques.
- List methods of ink drying.
- Recall methods of screen printing halftones.
- Classify high-speed production screen printing presses.
- Recognize special screen printing machine configurations.

Introduction

The basic process of screen printing has changed little in the last several hundred years. The standard printing device remains a stencil attached to a piece of fabric stretched over a wooden or metal frame. A flexible squeegee is used to force ink through the stencil opening. Even though the basic printing device has changed little, the printer's understanding of the variables that affect image quality has increased substantially.

Screen printing is one of the five basic printing processes. The concept is to transfer an image by allowing ink to pass through openings in a stencil that has been applied to a screen mesh (refer to figure 1.4c). Although such terms as silk screen, mitography, seriography, and selectine might be classified within this framework, screen printing is the label the industry recognizes and uses.

This chapter is divided into two sections. Section 1 examines the basics of stencil, screen, and fabric preparation. Section 2 examines the basics of both hand operated and automatic screen printing presses.

Section 1

Basic Concept and Classification of Stencils

The Stencil

The basic concept of screen printing is simple and is based on the idea of a stencil. By taking a piece of paper, drawing some outline or sketch of an object, and then cutting out the sketch, we can make a **stencil** (figure 13.1). By placing the stencil over another sheet of paper, it is possible to paint, spray, or otherwise force ink through the stencil opening (figure 13.2). When the stencil is removed from the paper,

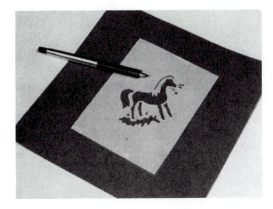

Figure 13.1 **Paper stencil cut with Ulano swivel knife**

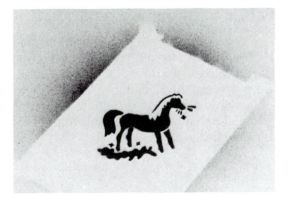

Figure 13.3 **A stenciled image**

all that remains on the printed sheet is a reproduction of the opening on the stencil (figure 13.3). This process can be repeated as long as the original stencil holds its shape.

Today the advantages of screen printing are impressive. It is ideally suited for low-cost production of high-quality, short-run printed materials. Screen printing is extremely versatile. It is possible to print on nearly any surface, texture, or shape. The process is limited only by the size of the screen frame. Fine line detail and even halftones may be reproduced

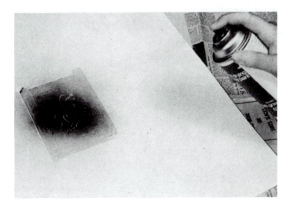

Figure 13.2 **Spraying ink through a paper stencil**

by screen printing. Many types of ink, from acid etches to abrasive glues, are available with this process. Ink densities on the printed page are such that any color may be overprinted (printed over another color) without the first color showing through.

Types of Stencils

Stencils can be classified into three groups:

- Hand-cut
- Tusche-and-glue
- Photographic

As the name implies, **hand-cut stencils** are prepared by removing the printing image areas manually from some form of base or support material. **Tusche-and-glue**, an art process, involves drawing directly on the screen fabric with lithographic tusche (an oil-based pigment) and then blocking out nonimage areas with a water-based glue material. **Photographic stencils** are generally produced by using a thick, light-sensitive, gelatin-based emulsion that is exposed and developed either on supporting film or directly on the screen itself. Only hand-cut and photographic stencils are used in commercial printing.

Fabric and Frame Preparation

Screen printing preparation involves selecting and controlling screen fabrics, screen frames, fabric stretch on the frame, fabric treatment to accept a stencil, stencil preparation, and stencil masking. As with all printing processes, it is critical to control every variable to produce a quality image on the final sheet.

Screen Fabrics

There is no one fabric that can be used for all screen printing applications. The type of ink to be screened, the fineness of image line detail, the quality of the paper or base material that is to receive the image, the number of impressions, and the type of stencil must all be considered when selecting the screen fabric.

Screen fabrics are made from either natural fibers, such as silk, or man-made fibers, such as polyester, rayon, or nylon. They are also classified as either multifilament or monofilament materials. **Multifilament screens** are made up of strands of fibers twisted together into threads (figure 13.4). Silk is a multifilament fabric. **Monofilament screens** are woven

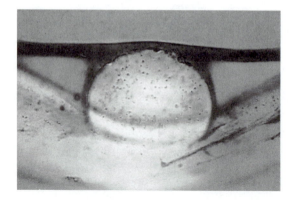

Figure 13.5 **Magnified view of cross section of man-made monofilament strands.**
Courtesy of J. Ulano Company, Inc.

from single round strands (figure 13.5). Nylon is a monofilament fabric.

As was mentioned in the Historical Background, silk was the first fabric used to carry screen printing stencils. Multifilament silk strands provide greater cross-sectional area than monofilament strands and allow for the strong adhesion of nearly any hand-cut or photographic stencil (figure 13.6). However, silk is not dimensionally stable, which means it changes shape and size with changes in tem-

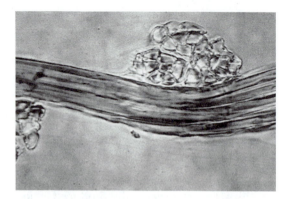

Figure 13.4 **Magnified view of cross section of multifilament strand.** Notice that the multifilament strand is made up of individual fibers.
Courtesy of J. Ulano Company, Inc.

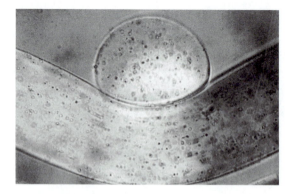

Figure 13.6 **Magnified view of stencil applied to silk fibers.**
Courtesy of J. Ulano Company, Inc.

perature and humidity. This makes it unsuitable for work requiring critical control of registration and color fit. Moreover, many special purpose inks, such as abrasives or chemical resists, can quickly destroy silk fibers.

Although man-made multifilament fibers, such as multistrand polyester, do not have the natural coarseness of silk, they are stronger and can be woven more uniformly. Polyester is useful for critical registration work because it is dimensionally stable, can withstand many abrasive materials, and can pass a uniform layer of ink.

Monofilament fabrics, such as single-strand polyester, nylon, or wire cloth (copper or stainless steel), have uniform weaves and pass pigments freely through mesh openings. However, because monofilament fabric is so smooth, it can be difficult to adhere a stencil. For this reason, it is generally necessary to treat or roughen the monofilament surface to obtain good stencil adhesion (figure 13.7).

Each fabric type has its own characteristics. Nylon tends to absorb moisture and reacts to changes in room humidity. Metal screens absorb no moisture but react to temperature changes and pass nearly any abrasive pigment with little difficulty. Monofilament polyesters have low moisture absorption rates,

stabilities, and strengths. Because they are also less expensive than most other screen materials, they are rapidly becoming the main material for commercial screen printing work.

Screen fabric is purchased by the yard. Two systems are used to classify screen fabric. Silk and multifilament polyesters are classified according to the ratio of open or link-passing area to thread area per inch. Numbers ranging from 0000 to about 25 are assigned to fabrics accordingly. The smaller the number, the larger the percentage of open area per inch. These fabrics are also assigned a strength indicator. A 12XX fabric is stronger than a 12X fabric. Most other fabrics, such as nylon and metal cloth, are classified according to the number of threads per inch. These fabrics are available in a range from about 60 threads per inch to a maximum of around 500 threads per inch. The two classification systems can be compared to identify equivalent opening sizes (table 13.1).

Specific recommendations cannot be made here about the type of fabric and mesh count to use in a given situation. Many variables can influence that decision. To decide which fabric type and mesh count to use, identify the type of ink to be used and consult the manufacturer's data for the screen material the manufacturer suggests is used with that ink. Manufacturers specify minimum screen mesh sizes based on the maximum pigment particle sizes in the ink (the particles, which are suspended in the liquid *vehicle*, must be able to pass freely through the screen openings). Manufacturers also indicate whether the ink vehicle will interact with any commercial screen fabrics. If the vehicle is a liquid that dissolves polyesters, for example, then the printer must avoid polyester fabrics.

The next step in deciding which fabric type and mesh count to use is to consider the fineness of the line detail of the image to be screen printed. A coarse screen mesh passes a heavy layer of ink, but it does not hold a fine

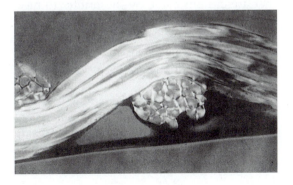

Figure 13.7 **Magnified view of stencil applied to monofilament fibers.**
Courtesy of J. Ulano Company, Inc.

Table 13.1   A Comparison of Mesh Classification Systems

XX system used for silk and multi- or monofilament polyesters	Silk	Multifilament polyesters	Nylon	Monofilament polyesters	Stainless steel	Silk	Multifilament polyesters	Nylon	Monofilament polyesters	Stainless steel
6XX	74	74	70	74	70	47	43	45	34	55
8XX	86	86	90	92	88	45	32	42	42	48
10XX	109	109	108	110	105	40	20	43	39	47
12XX	125	125	120	125	120	32	28	45	30	47
14XX	139	139	138	139	135	30	26	47	35	47
16XX	157	157	157	157	145	31	25	41	24	46
18XX	166	170	166	175	165	31	31	38	34	47
20XX	173	178	185	—	180	28	29	43	—	47
25XX	200	198	196	200	200	23	26	44	32	46
			230	225	230			42	42	46
			240	245	250			39	38	36
			260	260	270			36	35	32
			283	280	—			37	34	—
			306	300	—			34	29	—
			330	330	325			30	27	30
			380	390	400			22	18	36

line stencil. In general, use a 12XX (or equivalent number) fabric for hand-cut and indirect photographic stencils with normal images and a 14XX (or equivalent number) or finer fabric for photographic stencils containing images with fine line detail. Multifilament fibers are generally not suitable for halftone or extremely fine line reproduction.

Organdy is often used for short-run situations where bold line detail is required, but organdy is not an industrial fabric and is not recommended for fine detail.

Screen Frames

One of the great advantages of screen printing is that there is no standard size or shape for a screen printing frame. The screen frame must hold the screen fabric without warping, be deep enough to hold the quantity of ink being printed without spilling, and be at least 4 inches wider and 4 inches longer than the largest stencil to be reproduced.

Commercially constructed frames are available, but they are not required. Frames that are custom made by the printer to meet individual needs are often just as acceptable as their commercial counterparts. Most custom-made frames are made from wood because wood is inexpensive, fairly stable, and easily cut to any dimension. The high tension that develops when modern synthetic fabrics stretch on a frame warps wooden frames constructed with common butt joints. As a result, the joints must be constructed such that the frame cannot spring in any direction (figure 13.8).

Wooden frames are not recommended for close registration work because wood has a tendency to swell and shift when damp.

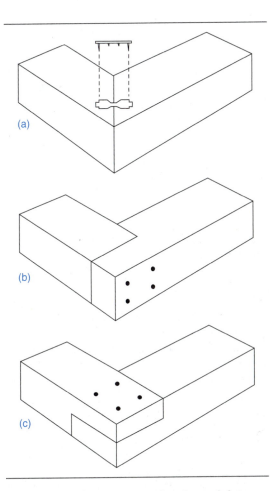

Figure 13.8 **Common wooden frame joints.**
Common joints used for custom-made wooden
screen frames are a reinforced miter joint (a), a
rabbet joint (b), and an end-lap joint (c).

When exact registration is required, as in
printed circuits or color process reproductions, steel or aluminum is a preferable frame
material.

Fabric Stretching Techniques

Fabric manufacturers recommend the amount
of tension that should be placed on their fabrics. Generally, silk should be stretched 3 to 4

percent of its original dimensions in two directions. Nylon should be stretched from 4 to
7 percent, and polyesters should be stretched
from 1 to 4 percent. Most suppliers recommend using a mechanical stretching system.
With this system it is easy to control the exact
amount of tension for any frame.

Mechanical Stretching

The basic process of **mechanical stretching** is
straightforward and relatively simple. The
fabric is cut to the size of the screen, but with
an additional amount in each dimension that
is sufficient to clamp the fabric into the stretching device. The empty screen frame is then
centered in the stretching system, and the fabric is clamped into place.

The fabric is then stretched to the desired
percentage. Next, the material is stapled to the
frame, the pressure is released, and the excess
fabric is cut away. An optional last step is to
seal the staples and fabric to the frame with
glue or epoxy, which provides a stronger
bond.

This same basic technique is used when
stretching fabric over commercial metal frames
except that a cord and clamp are used instead
of staples.

Hand Stretching

The easiest method of attaching screen fabric
is by tacking or stapling the material to the underside of a wooden frame. It is not possible
to control for tension percentage with this approach. However, for small-run jobs with
coarse line detail, many printers find it acceptable.

Use number 4 carpet tacks or $\frac{1}{4}$-inch staples in a general purpose industrial staple gun.
Space the tack or staples approximately $\frac{1}{2}$ inch
(1.27 cm) apart in two rows. Start by placing
the loose fabric over the frame so that the
strands are parallel to the frame edges. The
rough-cut fabric should be at least 2 inches
(5.08 cm) larger in each dimension of the

frame. Next, place three fasteners in the upper right-hand corner of the fabric. Pull the fabric diagonally and fasten a second corner in place. Then stretch and fasten the upper left-hand corner and, next, the lower right. Now begin at the center of any long frame edge and begin spacing a row of fasteners completely around the frame. As you fasten, pull the material with fabric pliers to remove all warps from the screen surface. Go back to the starting point and alternate a second row of fasteners around the frame just inside the first. Finally, cut the surplus fabric from the frame with a sharp razor blade and mask the staples with gummed tape (figure 13.9).

An alternative method for hand stretching fabric on a wooden frame is a starched cord and groove technique. Cut a single notch partially through each frame side with a saw (figure 13.10). An inexpensive piece of $\frac{3}{16}$-inch woven clothesline will nearly perfectly fill the groove left by a standard table saw blade. The inside groove may have to be rounded to prevent cutting the fabric, however. By carefully working from one corner, you can stretch the fabric by forcing both the clothesline and the fabric into the groove (figure 13.11). Special

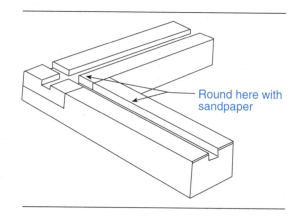

Figure 13.10   Wooden frame with sawed notch

tools have been developed to insert the clothesline in the groove (figure 13.12), but any device that will not tear the cloth is acceptable. Whatever method is used, the fabric should be drumhead tight, without warps or tears.

Fabric Treatment

As mentioned earlier in the chapter, monofilament fabric, such as nylon or polyester, must be treated before a stencil can be adhered. A

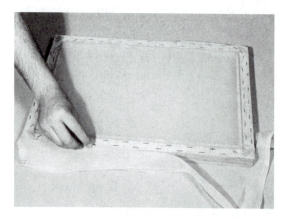

Figure 13.9   Cutting away surplus fabric

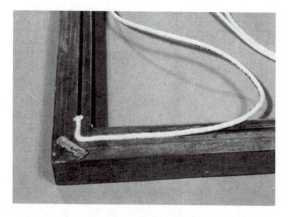

Figure 13.11   Clothesline forced into the notch to secure the screen

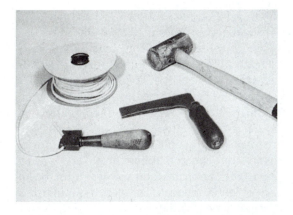

Figure 13.12 **Tools used to insert clothesline into notch**

tooth must be produced on the smooth monofilament fibers so the stencil can be held in place.

To produce a tooth, slightly dampen the monofilament fabric with water and pour half a teaspoon of 500-grit silicon carbide for each 16 inch × 20 inch (40.64 cm × 50.8 cm) area on the back, or stencil, side of the screen. Carefully scour the fabric with a wet rag for two to three minutes. Make sure to scrub the entire screen surface. Then thoroughly rinse both sides of the screen with a strong water spray. The 500-grit silicon carbide will not clog even the smallest mesh screen opening. This operation must be repeated each time the screen receives a new stencil.

Some printers use a very fine waterproof silicon carbide paper (sandpaper) to produce a tooth on monofilament fabrics. When using this paper, wet the screen and lightly rub the entire surface of the stencil side for four to five minutes. Then thoroughly rinse both sides of the screen with a strong water spray. This technique is recommended only if no alternative method is available because the sandpaper could destroy the screen if applied too roughly.

All fabrics, whether new or used, must be cleaned and degreased to ensure proper film or emulsion adhesion. If the screen is old, be sure that all ink has been removed and no foreign particles are clogging the mesh openings (figure 13.13). Ink manufacturers recommend the proper degreaser for their products. To clean and degrease a screen, first wet the screen with cold water and sprinkle both sides with powdered trisodium phosphate. If trisodium phosphate is not available, use a commercial nonsudsing automatic dishwashing detergent. Then thoroughly scrub both sides with a soft bristle brush. Next, rinse the screen with a powerful water spray. Allow the screen to drain and dry, but do not touch the fabric—skin oils on the fibers might prevent stencil adhesion. Do *not* use commercial abrasive cleansers like Ajax because the cleanser particles can clog the screen on fine mesh fabrics and cannot be removed with the water spray.

After the fabric has been cleaned, it is ready to accept the stencil. It is important not to store the clean screen for a long period before attempting to adhere the stencil. Air carries impurities and dirt that could clog a clean screen.

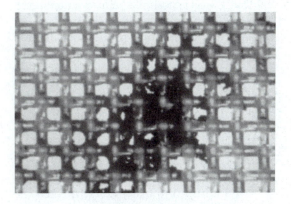

Figure 13.13 **Magnified view of a clogged screen.**
Courtesy of J. Ulano Company, Inc.

Photographic Stencil Methods

The primary reason for the explosive growth of the screen printing industry has been development of the photographic stencil. The idea of photographic stencils is not new, however. The basic process was developed in Great Britain in 1850 by William Henry Fox Talbot. Actually, Talbot was concerned with developing a continuous-tone negative/positive process. He found that certain materials, such as gelatin, egg albumin, and glue, when mixed or coated with a potassium bichromate solution, hardened when exposed to light. The unexposed areas remained soft and could be washed away readily. It was not until 1914 that someone applied Talbot's work to the screen printing industry. Today, photographic emulsions far more sophisticated than egg albumin are available through commercial suppliers.

In photographic screen printing, printers expose light-sensitive material through a positive transparent image. After processing, unhardened areas on the stencil are washed away. The stencil is fixed, or made permanent, masked, and then printed.

The primary advantage of photographic stencils is the possibility for intricate and high-quality line detail. Step-and-repeat images, halftones, exact facsimile reproductions, and high-quality process color stencil prints are all possible and commonplace. The introduction of photographic screen printing allowed the screen printer to enter the field of packaged product illustration. A color image can be screen printed with nearly any ink on nearly any surface shape (flat, cylindrical, or irregular) with this process.

All photographic stencil processes are divided into three types:

- Indirect or transfer image method
- Direct image method
- Film emulsion or direct/indirect image method

Indirect Process

The **indirect process** uses a dry emulsion on a plastic support sheet. The stencil emulsion is sensitized by the manufacturer and is purchased by the printer in rolls or sheets. The stencil film is exposed through a transparent, right-reading positive and is then treated with a developer solution. The areas that light reaches (the nonimage areas) harden during exposure. The remaining areas are washed away with a warm-water spray to form the image or printing areas. The stencil is adhered to a clean screen while it is wet from the spray, and the support sheet is removed after the stencil dries (figure 13.14).

Direct Process

The **direct process** uses a wet emulsion that is coated directly on a clean screen. The emulsion is exposed through a transparent positive to harden the nonimage areas. The image areas are washed away with a warm-water spray. When the emulsion is dry, the stencil is ready to print (figure 13.15). Direct emulsions have a limited shelf life when compared to indirect materials which are basically unlimited because they are stored in an inactive form.

Direct/Indirect Process

The **direct/indirect process** combines the indirect and the direct photographic processes. An unsensitized film material is placed under the stencil side of the screen on a flat table. The stencil emulsion is stored in two parts, a liquid emulsion and a sensitizer. When the two are mixed and coated on the screen, they become light sensitive and coat through the screen to the film support. When the emulsion is dry, the backing sheet of the stencil is removed and normal direct exposure techniques are carried out (figure 13.16). The main advantage of the direct/indirect process is the uniform emulsion thickness. Because the direct/indirect process uses the procedures of both the direct

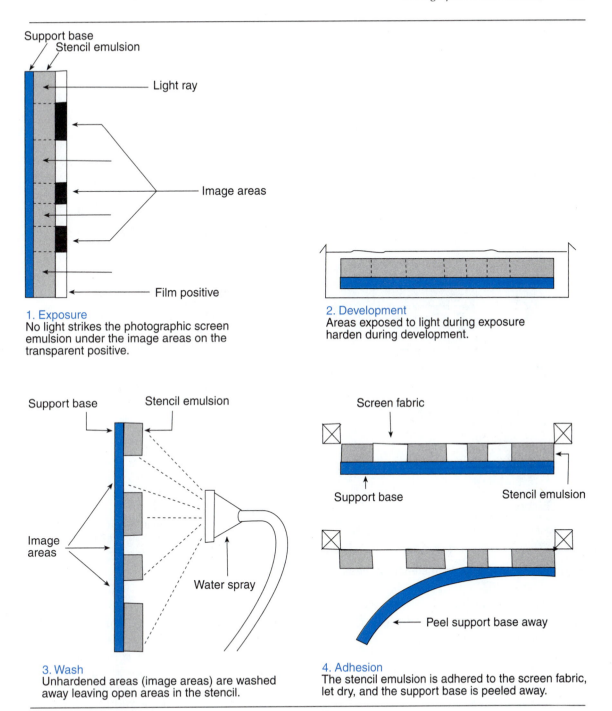

1. Exposure
No light strikes the photographic screen emulsion under the image areas on the transparent positive.

2. Development
Areas exposed to light during exposure harden during development.

3. Wash
Unhardened areas (image areas) are washed away leaving open areas in the stencil.

4. Adhesion
The stencil emulsion is adhered to the screen fabric, let dry, and the support base is peeled away.

Figure 13.14   Indirect screen stencil process

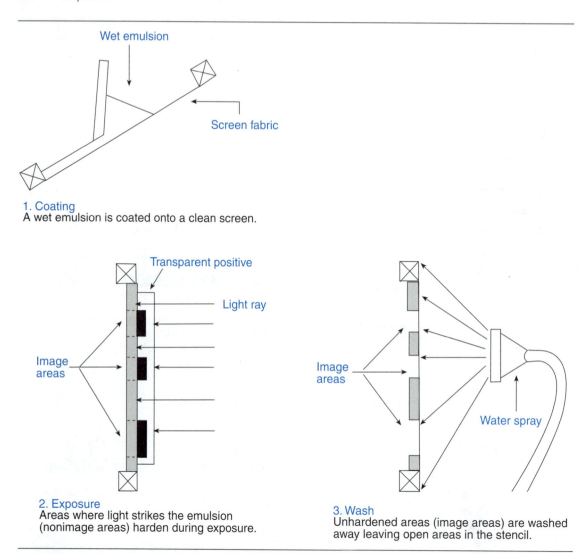

1. Coating
A wet emulsion is coated onto a clean screen.

2. Exposure
Areas where light strikes the emulsion (nonimage areas) harden during exposure.

3. Wash
Unhardened areas (image areas) are washed away leaving open areas in the stencil.

Figure 13.15   Direct screen stencil process

and the indirect stencil methods, it is not discussed in detail in this chapter.

Determining Photographic Stencil Exposures

Most photographic stencil emulsions have a spectral sensitivity that peaks in the ultraviolet to blue region of the visible spectrum (see Light Sources in appendix A). Because the stencil emulsion must be exposed through a transparent positive, good contact is important to ensure accurate line detail. Vacuum frames are generally used to hold the stencil and film in place during exposure.

Proper exposure is also important for photographic screen stencils. An underexposed stencil produces an emulsion that is too

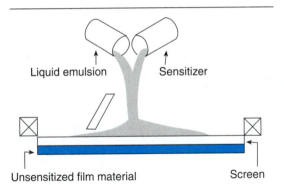

Liquid emulsion   Sensitizer

Unsensitized film material   Screen

1. Coating
The two parts of the stencil emulsion are mixed and coated on the screen material. Note the piece of insensitized film material under the screen.

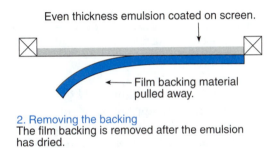

Even thickness emulsion coated on screen.

← Film backing material pulled away.

2. Removing the backing
The film backing is removed after the emulsion has dried.

Figure 13.16 **Direct/indirect screen stencil process**

thin. A thin emulsion is difficult to adhere to the screen material and can possibly pass ink in a nonimage area. In contrast, an overexposed stencil results in an emulsion that is too thick. A thick emulsion closes the fine line detail of an image and, if on an indirect photographic stencil, might not adhere to the fabric properly.

A commercial **step wedge** manufactured by the J. Ulano Company, Inc. (figure 13.17) can be used to calibrate correct stencil exposure. An alternative calibration device is a transparent positive made up of normal and hard-to-produce copy. The step wedge is

preferable because it contains identified line weights.

In practice, a series of exposures is made through the step wedge to the photographic stencil. If an indirect stencil is used, the emulsion must be exposed through the base material (figure 13.18). If a direct stencil is used, the transparent positive is exposed through the bottom side of the screen (figure 13.19).

Most stencil manufacturers recommend exposure times, but it is best to calibrate the exposure to the specific working conditions. Begin with the manufacturer's recommended exposure time for the specific light source and distance. If no time is recommended, start with 60 seconds. From the recommended time, determine exposures that are 50, 75, 100, 125, and 150 percent. For example, if 60 seconds is the recommended exposure time, then five separate exposures would be made through the step wedge: 30 seconds (50 percent of 60 seconds), 45 seconds (75 percent of 60 seconds), 60 seconds (100 percent of 60 seconds), 75 seconds (125 percent of 60 seconds), and 90 seconds (150 percent of 60 seconds).

A test exposure is easy to make if these time percentages are used. Place the transparent positive in contact with the stencil. First, expose through the positive for the shortest exposure time. For this example, the shortest exposure would be 30 seconds. Then mask one-fifth of the step wedge with opaque paper or masking film and expose the remaining uncovered portion for 15 seconds. (See the Masking the Stencil section later in this chapter for more on masking.) Move the masking sheet to cover two-fifths of the wedge and again expose the uncovered area for 15 seconds. Continue masking an additional one-fifth of the wedge and exposing the uncovered area until the entire step wedge has been masked and exposed. Develop and wash the stencil. (See the following sections outlining the specific procedures for each type of stencil.)

Mount the stencil on the screen that will be used in the shop, allow it to dry, and make

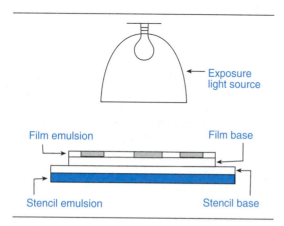

Figure 13.17 **Ulano step wedge.** The Ulano step wedge is a precision tool that can be used to determine the correct exposure time for any type of photographic stencil. The illustration shown is only an approximation and in no way attempts to duplicate the quality of the original instrument.
Courtesy of J. Ulano Company, Inc.

a print with the desired ink. Examine the image in detail. First identify the step that has reproduced the original line detail most faithfully. Consider the narrowest line that was reproduced, then select the exposure that has

the thickest emulsion but has held that line dimension. If no step appears ideal, expose another stencil with smaller percentage difference (such as 80, 90, 110, or 120 percent of the recommended time).

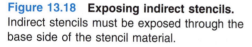

Figure 13.18 **Exposing indirect stencils.**
Indirect stencils must be exposed through the base side of the stencil material.

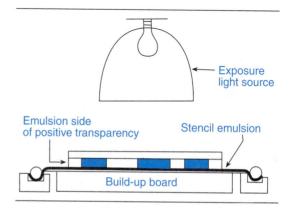

Figure 13.19 **Exposing direct stencils.** A direct stencil is set up to be exposed through the bottom of the screen.

Indirect Photographic Stencil Process

The indirect photographic stencil process is known by several different names in the industry: transfer, carbon tissue, and pigment paper are a few. The process is also identified by several trade names representing indirect stencil material that is supplied by individual dealers.

The **indirect photographic stencil** is exposed through a transparent film positive. Where light strikes the stencil (nonimage areas), the emulsion hardens. Where light does not strike the stencil (image areas), the emulsion remains soft and can be washed away. Logically, the better the film positive, the better the reproduction. Chapter 4 provides detailed information on the production of positive film images.

An indirect photographic stencil is the easiest screen stencil to produce. It involves the following six steps:

1. Exposure
2. Development
3. Washing
4. Application of the stencil to the screen
5. Drying
6. Removal of the base material

Exposure

All indirect emulsions are coated onto a transparent support sheet by the stencil manufacturer. It is always necessary to expose the stencil through the support material. Some sort of contact frame is generally used to bring the positive into contact with the presensitized stencil. It is important that the right-reading side of the positive be against the base side of the stencil. Place the positive on a tabletop so that the image reads exactly as it would on the final print. Place a sheet of stencil material over the positive so that its emulsion side is up. Be sure that the stencil extends at least 1

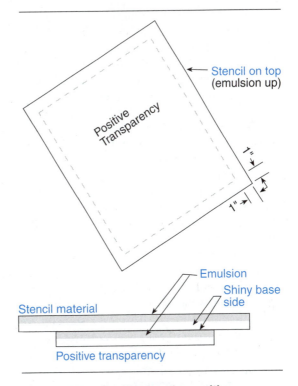

Stencil on top (emulsion up)

Positive Transparency

Emulsion
Shiny base side

Stencil material

Positive transparency

Figure 13.20 Positioning the positive transparency. The right-reading side of the positive must be placed against the base side of the stencil.

inch (2.54 cm) beyond all image extremes (figure 13.20). Then pick up both pieces and turn them over. To expose the stencil, the light must pass through the clear areas of the positive. Place the two sheets in the contact frame and expose the stencil for the time that was determined from the test exposure.

Development and Washing

The developing process removes all areas not hardened by exposure to light (all image areas). Any area covered by the positive image is washed away. Depending on the type of emulsion, indirect stencils are developed by one of two techniques: a hydrogen peroxide bath or plain water.

Some emulsions require a hydrogen peroxide bath to harden their exposed areas. These stencils are placed in the bath emulsion side up and are agitated constantly for one to three minutes, depending on the manufacturer's recommendations. The stencils are then removed and sprayed with warm water (95°F to 105°F). The spray washes away the unhardened stencil areas, leaving a stencil outline of the image areas.

Other emulsions are developed in plain water immediately after being removed from the contact frame. A cool-water (70°F) spray is directed over the entire emulsion surface until the image areas wash away.

With both developing methods the concern is with stopping development as soon as the image areas are clear. Excess warm-water spray removes the hardened emulsion and can create a thin stencil. All indirect stencils are fixed by a stream of cold water (gradually decreasing the temperature).

Application of the Stencil

Indirect stencils adhere very easily to the screen fabric. Place the chilled stencil emulsion side up on a hard, flat buildup board (figure 13.21). Position the clean screen over the sten-

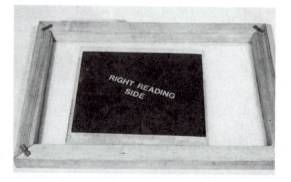

Figure 13.22 Positioning the screen over the stencil

cil so that the clear printing area of the stencil is in the center of the screen frame (figure 13.22). Do not move the screen once it has contacted the stencil and do not use excessive pressure—merely allow the weight of the frame to hold the screen in position. Excess moisture is removed from the stencil by blotting it through the screen with clean newsprint or inexpensive paper towels (figure 13.23). The function of blotting is to remove excess moisture and to blot up through the fibers the soft top of the emulsion. Lay the newsprint flat and gently wipe the newsprint with a soft, clean

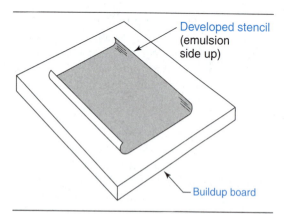

Developed stencil (emulsion side up)

Buildup board

Figure 13.21 Placing the indirect stencil on a buildup board

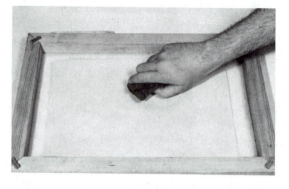

Figure 13.23 Removing excess moisture

rag; *do not use pressure.* Keep changing the newsprint until it does not pick up moisture from the stencil. Excessive pressure during blotting pushes the fabric threads of the screen into the emulsion, which can cause pinholes or a ragged sawtooth edge during printing.

Drying

Indirect stencils should not be forced dry with hot or warm air. Rapid drying could result in poor adhesion or a warped stencil. To dry the emulsion properly, place the frame in a position so that air is allowed to flow over both of its sides—a gentle room air fan may be used. Spotty light and dark areas indicate that the stencil is drying. The emulsion is completely dry when the entire stencil area is a uniform color.

Removal of the Base Material

When the emulsion is dry, its clear support base can be peeled off (figure 13.24). After printing, all indirect photographic stencils can be removed from the screen fabric with a high-pressure, hot-water spray. For difficult materials, enzymes are available that will help to dissolve the old material. On metal or synthetic screens, bleach is commonly used for this purpose.

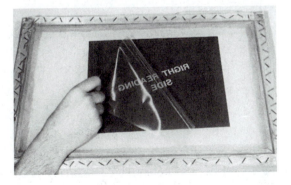

Figure 13.24 **Peeling off the support material**

Direct Photographic Stencil Process

With the direct method of stencil preparation, a wet photographic emulsion is applied directly to the screen fabric by the printer. The entire screen is then exposed to a positive image, developed, and printed.

The main requirement of the direct process is some form of liquid, light-sensitive emulsion. All emulsions currently used fall into the following types of chemical formulations:

- A synthetic-based material, such as polyvinyl alcohol
- A gelatin-based chemical material
- A combination of synthetic and gelatin materials

Most printers use commercially prepared emulsions rather than prepare their own. Commercial emulsions are more economical, higher in quality, and can be formulated by the supplier to meet any printing requirements. Commercial emulsions are available in two forms: presensitized and unsensitized liquids.

The five steps in preparing a **direct photographic stencil** are relatively simple:

1. Preparation of the sensitized emulsion
2. Application of the emulsion to the screen
3. Drying the emulsion
4. Exposure
5. Development

Preparation

Unsensitized, direct screen emulsions are provided by the manufacturer in two parts: a liquid unsensitized emulsion and a dry powder sensitizer. First, the dry powder sensitizer is dissolved in warm water according to the

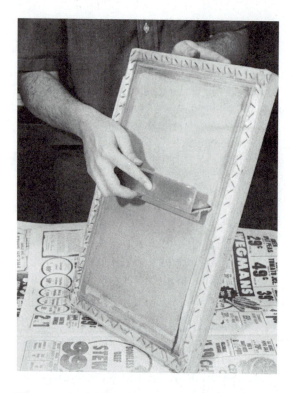

Figure 13.25 **Using a scoop coater on the emulsion**

the corner to the other end of the screen using smooth, continuous strokes (figure 13.25). Turn the frame over and immediately squeegee the inside of the screen until it is smooth. The quantity of liquid applied for the first coat depends on the length of the screen, but it is better to apply too much liquid and squeegee off the excess than it is to use too little liquid and not cover the screen totally.

Drying
Store the frame flat in a dark place. A circulating air fan can be used to hasten drying. When the first coat is dry, apply a second coat to the inside of the screen and allow it to dry. The thickness of the ink deposit can be controlled somewhat by the number of emulsion layers. If a thick ink deposit is desired, a third emulsion coating should be placed on the bottom side of the frame.

Exposure
Special contact frames must be used to hold the screen frame and film positive during exposure. Place the right-reading side of the

manufacturer's recommendations. The liquid sensitizer is then added to the dry powder sensitizer dissolved in water to create an active, sensitized emulsion. The emulsion may be stored in a closed amber or light-tight bottle, but it usually must be applied to the screen as soon as possible.

Application
The screen should be coated with the liquid emulsion in yellow or subdued light. One application technique is to pour a quantity of the emulsion on one edge of the bottom side of the frame rather than on the screen itself. With this technique the liquid does not seep rapidly through the screen mesh. With a round-edge scoop coater, squeegee the emulsion from

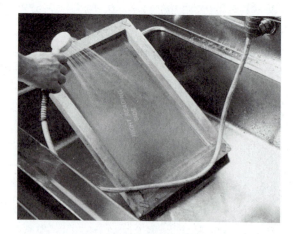

Figure 13.26 **Developing the image.** Gently spray both sides of the screen with warm water.

transparent positive against the underside sur-face of the screen. The light must pass through the positive to expose the screen emulsion. Ex-pose the screen stencil material through the positive for the time determined from the test exposures.

Development

The stencil image is developed by first wetting both sides of the screen in warm (95° to 105°F) water, then gently spraying both sides with warm water until the image areas are com-pletely clear (figure 13.26). Allow the frame to drain and blot the emulsion dry with newsprint.

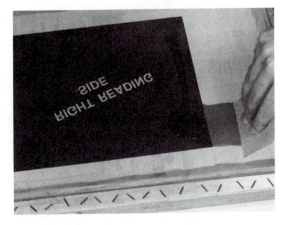

Figure 13.27 **Using a liquid mask**

Masking the Stencil

The idea of a stencil is that ink passes through any open areas on the screen. It is necessary to block or mask the areas of the screen that are not covered by the stencil material and are not intended to print. There is generally a gap between the edge of the stencil and the screen frame that must be covered to prevent ink pas-sage.

Preparing a Paper Mask

A paper **mask** works well for blocking nonimage areas in short runs. Cut a piece of kraft paper (brown wrapping paper) slightly smaller than the inside dimensions of the frame. Lay the masking paper on the screen and trace the rough outline of the image area on the paper with a pencil. Remove the mask-ing paper and cut out an area that is about 1 inch (2.54 cm) larger than the image extremes. Replace the masking paper on the screen and apply gummed tape around the edges of the frame. Then tape the edges of the masking pa-per to the stencil material. It is important that the tape be at least $\frac{3}{4}$ inch (1.91 cm) from the

nearest image and in perfect contact with the solid stencil.

Preparing a Liquid Block-out Mask

A second method of masking employs a liq-uid block-out mask which is a fluid (figure 13.27). These types of fluids are usually water based and are easy to use. Materials such as LePage's glue will work in this capacity, but specially formulated commercial products are inexpensive and work much better. Brush or scrape one coat of the fluid on the underside of the screen wherever the fabric is exposed but an image is not desired. Allow the fluid to dry and then apply a second coat on the in-side area of the screen.

It is often necessary to touch up any im-perfections, such as pinholes, in the stencil. The liquid block-out is ideal for small correc-tions and should always be applied to the un-derside of the screen.

The processes of printing and cleaning the screen and stencil are discussed in detail in Section 2.

Section 2

The term **printing press** might sound strange when associated with the most basic screen printing frame, but the screen printing frame is a press in every sense; it has the four basic press units: feeding, registration, printing, and delivery. The receiver in screen printing (whether paper, metal plastic, or even wood) must be fed and registered under the stencil. The ink must be transferred to the receiver. The printed product must be removed and stored for later distribution. Screen printing presses can range in complexity from an elementary homemade, hand-operated wooden frame (figure 13.28) to a sophisticated system that automatically inserts, registers, prints, and removes any receiving material, including cylindrical surfaces.

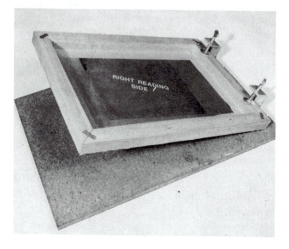

Figure 13.28 Basic screen printing unit. The wooden frame hinges on a particle baseboard. Courtesy of SUCO Learning Resources and R. Kampas.

Squeegee and Ink Considerations

Selecting the Proper Squeegee

The **squeegee** (figure 13.29) causes the image transfer to take place because it forces the ink through the stencil and the fabric openings onto the receiver. All squeegees have two parts: a handle and a blade. The handle can be any design that is comfortable for printers and meets their needs, but great care must be taken when selecting the squeegee blade. Four primary blade considerations must be examined prior to printing:

- Shape
- Chemical makeup
- Flexibility
- Length

Shape

The first blade consideration is blade shape. The blade shape generally determines the sharpness and thickness of ink deposit. There

are six basic blade shapes (figure 13.30). A square blade (figure 13.30a) is the most common blade shape and is a good general purpose design that can be used to print on flat surfaces with standard poster inks. A double-bevel, flat-point blade (figure 13.30b) is good for working with ceramic materials such as

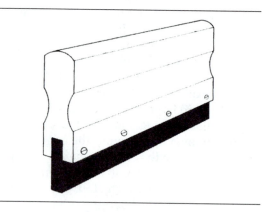

Figure 13.29 Printer's squeegee

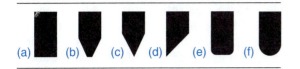

Figure 13.30 **Basic shapes of squeegee blades.** The six basic shapes are (a) square, (b) double bevel, flat point, (c) double bevel, (d) single bevel, (e) square edge with rounded corners, and (f) round edge.

glazes or slip. The double-bevel form (figure 13.30c) is used for printing on uneven surfaces or for placing a fine layer of ink on a surface when stenciling extremely fine line detail. The single-bevel blade (figure 13.30d) is generally used when printing on glass. The square-edge with rounded corners shape (figure 13.30e) is generally used when screening light colors over dark backgrounds, and the round-edge design (figure 13.30f) works well when printing on fabrics. The round-edge design also has the advantage of forcing an extra-heavy amount of ink through the screen. Everyone but the special purpose printer will find the square form acceptable for almost every job.

Chemical Makeup
The chemical makeup of the squeegee blade is the second blade consideration. The base for some inks could actually dissolve the blade if the wrong type of blade were used. Most squeegee blades are cast from rubber or plastic. Blades that are designed for vinyl or acetate printing are water soluble and therefore cannot be used with a water-based pigment. Synthetic blades, such as polyurethane, retain their edges longer and resist abrasion better than do blades of any other material. They are significantly more expensive, however. A good general purpose squeegee blade is neoprene rubber. It can be used for vinyl, lacquer, oil, poster enamel, and ethocel inks. When selecting the chemical makeup of a blade, decide

what type of ink will be used, identify the ink base, and determine which blade formulation is acceptable.

Flexibility
The third consideration for squeegee blade selection is flexibility. Flexibility is measured on a scale called Shore A ratings. As the number increases, so does hardness. Rubber hardness is measured in terms of **Shore durometer** readings. An average blade for general use has a 60 Shore A rating. Most squeegee manufacturers translate the value into the terms hard, medium, and soft. Soft blades (around 50 Shore A) deposit a fairly thick layer of ink. Hard blades (around 70 Shore A) deposit a sharp, thin ink layer. A medium squeegee blade (60 Shore A) meets most shop needs.

Length
The length of the squeegee is the fourth and final important consideration. As a rule, the blade should extend at least $\frac{1}{2}$ inch (1.27 cm) beyond the limits of the stencil image, but it should be able to pass freely between the edges of the screen frame.

Squeegee Preparation
Whatever the shape, makeup, or hardness of the blade selected, the major factor controlling image quality is blade sharpness. Several types of commercial squeegee sharpeners are available that can be used to prepare any shape of blade edge (figure 13.31). Most sharpeners operate with a moving abrasive belt or drum. The blade is mounted in the sharpener with a series of clamps, and it passes against the cutting surface.

If a sharpening machine cannot be obtained, 6- and 8-inch (15- and 20-cm) widths of garnet cloth are suitable for sharpening square-edge blades. The cloth is mounted (generally with staples) on a hard, flat surface. The blade is held in a perfectly vertical posi-

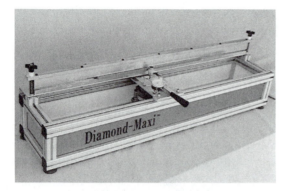

Figure 13.31 Commercial squeegee sharpener.
Courtesy of Naz-Dar Company.

tion and is dragged back and forth over the abrasive cloth until a sharp edge forms.

It is important that the squeegee be absolutely clean prior to printing. Any dry ink left on a blade from previous printing runs will contaminate the ink used with other printing jobs. This is especially important when a dark color is followed by a light color because the light color reveals impurities more readily.

Selecting the Proper Ink

The ink pigment and ink vehicle in screen printing must freely pass through screen fabric and create an image of acceptable density on the receiving surface. Screen inks are thinner than letterpress or lithographic inks, but thicker than inks used in gravure. (See chapter 14 for more about gravure.) Early screen inks were very similar to ordinary paint. The creation of new fabrics and stencil materials, the growth of printing on nontraditional materials (any material but paper), and the application of screen printing to specialized industrial needs (such as printed circuits) have resulted in the development of a wide variety of screen inks.

There are so many different materials intended for so many different applications in screen printing that both novice and experienced printers become confused easily. Choosing the appropriate ink becomes easier to understand if all elements of a particular job are examined in detail and several specific questions are answered.

Product Characteristics

The first area of concern should be the characteristics of the printed piece. What is the function of the final product? Will it be exposed to harsh weather conditions (as is a billboard)? Will it contact harsh chemicals (as does printing on a detergent bottle or even a cola container)? Should the image have a gloss finish or a flat finish? What is the surface of the image receiver? Will the ink have to dry by absorbing into the material? Will it need to be heat set? Will it have to air dry?

Production Limitations

After considering the characteristics of the printed piece, the printer must address the limitations of the production situation. Ink manufacturers recommend a minimum **screen mesh count**, or screen opening, that can be used with each of their inks. If the screen mesh count of a screen is smaller than the recommended minimum, no ink will pass through the screen.

Any material that can be ground to a fine powder can be mixed with a liquid vehicle and used as a screen ink. The solvents for the stencil and for the ink must not be the same. For example, if a water-based ink is used with a water-based stencil, the ink and stencil rapidly become a puddle on the screen.

By making a list of both product and production limitations, it is possible to eliminate all but a narrow category of possible ink choices. More information about screen inks for specific applications is given in chapter 16.

Ink Preparation

Many manufacturers advertise that their inks are "ready to use directly from the can," but the printer usually has to prepare the ink before printing. **Ink viscosity** (resistance to flow) is very important in ink preparation. The goal is to keep the ink as dense as possible to form an acceptable printed image. At the same time, however, the ink must be thin enough to pass freely through the screen openings without clogging. The difficulty is that the required viscosity can be different for every job. The higher the screen mesh count, the thinner the ink must be. In very general terms, the ink should "flow like honey" from the ink knife. It should move slowly and smoothly and should flow immediately when the knife is tipped.

Many different additives can be mixed with screen inks to yield certain ink characteristics. Ink viscosity can be decreased by adding a compatible thinner and/or reducer, for example. Adding a transparent base makes ink somewhat translucent. An extender base increases the quantity of usable ink without affecting density. A drier functions to hasten the drying of the ink on the receiver, but it can also increase the possibility of the ink drying in the screen fabric. A binder can be added to increase the adhesion of the ink to the paper or receiver. Individuals inexperienced with additives should always consult a screen ink supplier for information.

Basic Screen Printing Process

The basic techniques for screen printing are discussed here in terms of a hand-operated, hinged-frame system. For this section it is assumed that the printing frame is held to a wooden or particleboard base with a pair of heavy-duty hinge clamps. The hinges can be either common butt hinges or special hinges purchased from a screen printing supplier.

The sequence of screen printing steps, as with any press system, is to feed, register, print, and deliver the paper. Because the simple screen system is hand fed and delivered, this section considers only registering the paper and printing the image. The processes of drying the image, cleaning the screen, and removing the stencil are also discussed.

Basic Registration Techniques

As with all printing systems, registration is placing the image in the same position on every press sheet. Recall from chapter 2 that three metal gauge pins are used on the tympan of a platen press to hold the press sheet in place. It is also possible to form *gauge pins* from a narrow strip of paper. These gauge pins hold the press sheet in register during screen printing. To create these gauge pins, cut three pieces of 20- to 40-pound paper $\frac{1}{2}$ inch $\times$ 2 inches (1.3 cm $\times$ 5 cm) and make a simple Z-fold tab (figure 13.32). Tape the Z tabs to the baseboard under the screen frame.

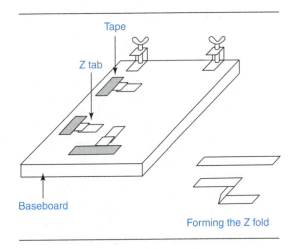

Tape

Z tab

Baseboard

Forming the Z fold

Figure 13.32 Making gauge pins. Three Z tabs taped in place on the baseboard serve as gauge pins used to register the press sheet.

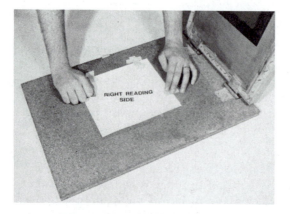

Figure 13.33 Setting the image position. The Z tabs are placed against the positioned stock and carefully taped in place.

Commercial printers use several methods to locate the image in the appropriate screen printing position. One simple method is to first place the original drawing or film positive used to produce the screen stencil so that it is right reading on a piece of the press sheet. Tape the original to the sheet so that the image is in the desired printing position. Place the sheet with the taped image on the baseboard and lower the screen frame into printing position over the sheet. Move the sheet until its taped image aligns with the stencil opening on the screen, then carefully hinge the screen up and out of the way. Without moving the press sheet, carefully insert the gauge pins and tape each one to the baseboard (figure 13.33). The pins should be positioned so that there are two pins on a long side of the press sheet and one pin on a short side. It is also important that the pins be placed as far from the image areas as possible. Remove the press sheet and tape the inside portion of the pins to the base. If every press sheet is seated against the inside of the three pins, the image will print in the same position on each sheet.

On-Contact and Off-Contact Printing

Two common printing methods are used for hinged-frame printing: on-contact and off-contact printing. With **on-contact printing**, the screen and stencil contact the press sheet throughout the image transfer process. With this method, the press sheet generally sticks to the screen. After the image is transferred, the frame must be hinged up and out of the way and the stock must be peeled away carefully. One method of preventing the press sheet from sticking is to place several pieces of thin, double-backed adhesive in nonimage areas on the baseboard. On-contact printing is the most common technique for small job shops or for short-run jobs that do not require extremely sharp impressions. However, off-contact printing should always be done if possible to prevent the press sheet from sticking.

In **off-contact printing**, the screen and stencil are raised slightly (generally no more than $\frac{1}{8}$ inch or 3.2 mm) from the press sheet by small shims, or spacing material, under the hinge and frame. With this technique the stencil touches the press sheet only when the squeegee passes over the screen. Once the image transfers across the squeegee line, the screen snaps back away from the receiver (figure 13.34). Off-contact printing helps keep the

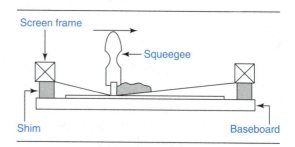

Figure 13.34 Diagram of off-contact printing. In off-contact printing, the screen touches the press sheet only when the image is transferred by the squeegee.

press sheet from sticking to the screen and usually prevents image smearing. It is often used to produce sharp impressions on smooth surfaces.

A vacuum frame base can be used with either on-contact or off-contact printing to help keep the press sheet from sticking to the screen. Vacuum bases are available as single units or as tables and are found on most semi-automatic sheet printing machines.

Printing the Stencil

Section 1 outlined several procedures for masking the nonimage portions of the screen. Before printing the stencil, however, two tasks remain. First, check to ensure that there are no pinholes or other unwanted openings in the stencil. Block any areas with the recommended block-out solution for the type of stencil being used. Second, seal off the inside edge of the stencil, between the fabric and the frame. Sealing can be done with any wide commercial tape (2-inch or 5-cm width tape is recommended). If the press run is exceptionally long or if special inks (such as water-based) or abrasive materials (such as ceramic glaze) are used, a plastic solvent-resistant, pressure-sensitive tape should be used. Otherwise, a water-moistened gummed tape will suffice.

Begin printing by positioning a press sheet on the baseboard in the registration system and lowering the screen frame into position. Pour a puddle of prepared ink away from the image at one end of the screen and in a line slightly longer than the width of the image (figure 13.35). Hold the squeegee at about a 60-degree angle to the screen surface and, pressing firmly, draw the puddle of ink across the stencil opening with one smooth motion (figure 13.36). It is important that the movement is uniform and does not stop until the squeegee is out of the image area. Make only

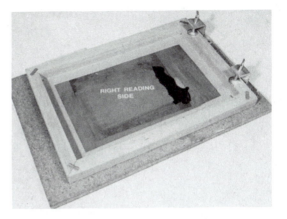

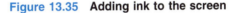

Figure 13.35 **Adding ink to the screen**

one pass. Then remove the squeegee, raise the frame, prop the screen away from the image surface, and remove the press sheet (figure 13.37).

Examine the printed image for correct position, ink uniformity, and clarity of detail. If necessary, readjust the registration pins for proper registration. If ink clogs or dries in the screen fabric it can cause the layers of ink on the image to be nonuniform or of a lower qual-

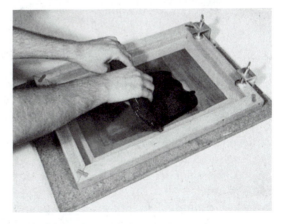

Figure 13.36 **Distributing the ink**

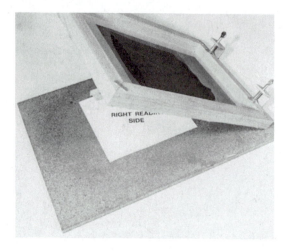

Figure 13.37 **Removing the press sheet**

ity line detail. To correct clogging or drying, remove as much ink from the screen as possible and add thinner to the ink. Clean the clogged portions of the screen by gently wiping the underside of the stencil with a rag moistened with thinner. Then reink the screen and pull a second impression. Once an acceptable image is obtained, continue inserting a press sheet, passing the squeegee across the stencil, and removing the printed sheet until the job is completed.

Multicolor Printing

The primary concern of multicolor screen printing is the method of registration. It is important that the first color be placed accurately. If placement of the first printed image varies on the page, it will be impossible to register the second image to it.

A two-color screen printing job requires two separate stencils. Multicolor runs require careful planning of printing sequence and color overlaps to eliminate gaps. When opaque colors are used, the images must overlap by at least 1/16 inch (1.6 mm). It is not necessary to overlap transparent colors except where a third color is desired.

Several techniques can be used to control accurate color fit. One technique is to register the first color using standard positioning methods, but to mark the first sheet as a proof. While the proof sheet is still held by the Z tabs, mark the position of the tabs with a pencil. Most press sheets are cut with some slight variation on the edges. If, for the second color, the Z tabs are placed in the same position as for the first color, the possibility of misregistration is lowered.

To position the second color over the first, mount a sheet of clear acetate over the baseboard and tape it from one edge so it can be hinged out of the way when necessary. With the acetate in place, swing the second stencil down into printing position and pull an impression. When the frame is removed, the second image position is defined on the acetate. Slip the proof sheet from the first color under the acetate and line up both colors. Then carefully hinge the acetate out of the way and mount the register tabs on the baseboard in line with the edges of the proofsheet of the tab positions. The two colors should now fit for the second printing. Any number of additional colors may be registered with this technique.

Problems with registration are not always the operator's fault. Fabrics that are loosely stretched on the frame tend to cause problems with multicolor registration. Frame hinges can also become loose. If not taped securely, register tabs move out of position. Whatever the reason, when colors do not fit, all possible variables should be carefully examined.

Drying the Image

Most screen printing inks dry by absorption, aerial oxidation (air drying), a combination of both absorption and aerial oxidation, or by heat-setting action. Screen prints cannot be delivered from the press and stacked because all types of screen inks require some drying time. To reduce work and conserve production space, a drying rack is often used to receive press sheets (figure 13.38). Racks are available in a wide variety of sizes, and commercial models come equipped with spring systems

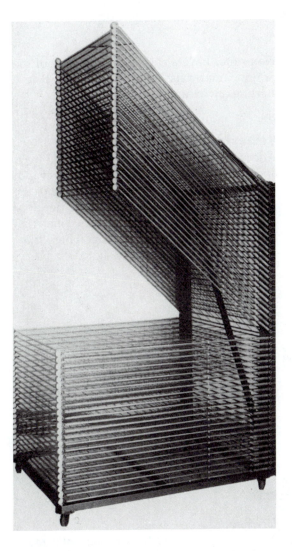

Figure 13.38 **Floating bar print drying rack.**
Courtesy of Naz-Dar Company.

attached to floating bars that swing each shelf down into position as needed.

Inks that dry by absorption into the press sheet or by aerial oxidation can generally be stacked and shipped within 30 minutes. It is possible to hasten drying time by passing the press sheet through a heat oven.

Heat-setting inks require an intense direct heat source. Some form of commercial curing or baking oven is generally used (figure 13.39). Most ovens heat to about 320°F, have forced air circulation and a temperature control device, and are equipped with a variable-speed, conveyer-belt feeding system.

Cleaning the Screen

To clean the screen, first remove any large deposits of ink remaining on the screen and squeegee with an ink knife. It is generally wise to discard the ink from the screen surface and thereby avoid contaminating any fresh ink remaining in the can. Next, place 10 to 15 open sheets of newspaper on the baseboard and lower the screen into printing position. Place a quantity of compatible solvent on the squeegee side of the screen. It is important to dissolve all ink before any solvent is removed. If a rag were applied to the screen immediately, the solvent would be absorbed but no dissolving action would take place. Now, using your hand, rub the solvent into the entire surface of the screen. (Plastic gloves are practical during this process.) After all ink is dissolved, remove both the ink and the solvent from the screen with a dry cloth rag. Lift the screen and remove the several layers of newspaper. Repeat this operation until all ink has been removed. As a final step, moisten a clean rag with solvent and rub the underside of the screen to remove any remaining ink.

Commercial screen cleaning units (figure 13.40) also dissolve all ink and leave the screen perfectly clean. With these devices, the frame is placed on a washing stand, and a solvent

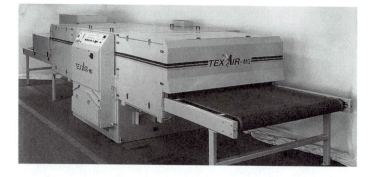

Figure 13.39 **High-volume modular drying system.** This gas dryer system is used for water-, plastisol-, and solvent-based inks. Courtesy of American M&M.

spray is directed over it. The solvent drains back into a container where the ink and dirt settle or are filtered out, and the clear solvent is recirculated through the machine.

There is a tendency for novice printers to mix dissimilar solvents during the cleanup operation. Stencil material and printing inks are chosen so that their bases will not dissolve one another. If the stencil is water based, the ink is lacquer based, and water accidentally mixes with the ink, problems occur. The stencil may not wash away, but the ink will emulsify and hopelessly clog the screen. It is important that

the printer have a clear understanding of the printing materials and their solvents before starting any cleanup.

Removing the Stencil

After all ink has been cleaned from the screen and any remaining ink solvent has evaporated, the stencil can be removed. One of the great advances in recent years is the development of a quality water-based stencil material. Whether hand-cut or photographic, most water-based stencils are designed to be re-

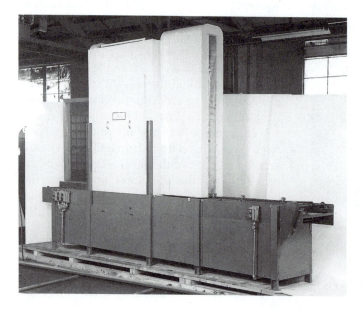

Figure 13.40 **Commercial screen washing system.** Courtesy of American M&M

moved with a hot-water spray. With some stencils, a commercial enzyme is recommended to achieve removal.

To remove a stencil that requires an enzyme, wet both sides of the stencil and sprinkle on the enzyme. After letting the stencil and enzyme stand for five minutes (or whatever time is recommended by the manufacturer), spray the screen with hot water. It is necessary to neutralize the enzyme remaining on the wet screen by wiping the screen with a five percent acetic acid or white vinegar solution. After neutralizing, thoroughly rinse the screen with cold water and allow it to air dry.

If nylon, polyester, or stainless steel screens are used with water-based stencils, you can use a household chlorine bleach presoak in place of the commercial enzyme. One method is to wet both sides of the stencil with a sodium hypochlorite solution (bleach) and allow it to stand for five minutes. Then carefully rinse the bleach solution from the stencil (avoid splashing or contacting the eyes) and spray with hot water. This technique should *not* be used if a natural fiber, such as silk, is used.

Lacquer stencils must be removed with lacquer thinner. Lay several layers of newsprint on a flat surface and pour lacquer thinner on both sides of the stencil. Allow the thinner to sit on the stencil for several minutes before rubbing with a cloth. Lacquer thinner has a tendency to dry very rapidly, so several applications of the solution might be necessary before the screen is clean.

Troubleshooting Clogged Screens

A clean screen is the first requirement when preparing to print. A clogged screen should not be used because a stencil will not adhere to it well. If the stencil does adhere, the quality of the printed image will be very poor. In a learning situation where many different individuals use the same equipment, it is not always possible to identify what material is clog-

ging a screen. It could be stencil emulsion, block-out material, ink, or even some foreign substance.

There are several steps to follow to clean a clogged screen when you do not know what is causing the problem. First, try using the household chlorine bleach mentioned in the preceding section (as long as the fabric is not silk) or a commercial enzyme (this should remove any water-based substance). Next, try the solvent for the ink that was used for the last printing. If the screen is still clogged, try scrubbing the area with lacquer thinner. Finally, try alcohol. It is important that the screen is dried thoroughly after each step. If the screen remains clogged after all of these attempts, discard the screen and restretch the frame.

Halftone Reproduction in Screen Printing

Screen printing halftone images have several advantages over relief or lithographic processes. First, it is ideal for short-run posters or illustrations and is less costly than any other method in terms of both time and materials. It can print extremely large image sizes as well. Finally, a wide range of inks can be used that have a brilliance, opacity, and texture unmatched by any other method.

There are, however, special considerations when screen printing halftones. Although 85- and 110-line halftones are screened commonly in the printing industry, a small job shop without critical stencil preparation and printing controls should stay with rather coarse halftone screen rulings (85 lines per inch or coarser) because the highlight and shadow dot structure must be carefully controlled in this process, and a film positive must be produced.

The reproducible halftone dot sizes of the final film positive in screen print should be 10 to 15 percent for highlights and 85 to 90 percent for shadows. Any dot size not within these ranges will probably not reproduce on the final printed sheet.

Methods of Halftone Preparation for Screen Printing

The basic challenge when preparing halftone images for screen printing is to work within the limits of the production facilities. Although a 65-line contact screen is readily available from printing suppliers, it is common only in those shops that prepare illustrations for newspaper production or in screen companies that specialize in halftone printing.

Basically four methods can be used to prepare film halftone positives in any printing company.

1. If a 65-line halftone screen is available, first make a film halftone negative to the reproduction size. Then make a contact film positive of the halftone negative.

2. Using an available halftone screen (such as 133-line screen), make a reduced halftone negative that can fit into a film enlarger (like that used to make continuous-tone prints). Then project through the negative in the enlarger onto a fresh piece of high-contrast film to make a film positive at the reproduction size.

3. Using the available halftone screen, make a same-size film halftone negative from the original. Then place the negative on a black-lighted process camera copyboard and enlarge it to the required reproduction size on a fresh piece of high-contrast film.

4. Using an available diffusion transfer halftone screen (usually 100-line type), make a diffusion transfer opaque halftone positive the same size as the

original. Then enlarge the positive on a process camera to the required reproduction size by using either a second set of diffusion transfer materials with a transparent receiver sheet or high-contrast film to make a film negative. Then contact print a film positive.

If the last three methods are used, it is necessary to be able to calculate percentage changes to make halftones that are the required screen rulings using available in-plant materials.

Assume, for example, that a 5 inch × 7 inch continuous-tone photograph must be printed as a 9 inch × 12 inch halftone reproduction with a 50-line ruling. The available screen is a 133-line negative gray contact screen. The printer decides to produce the final film positive by projection using an enlarger (method 2).

First, use the following equation to determine the percent enlargement (PE) of a 133-line ruling that is needed to obtain 50 lines per inch:

$$PE = \frac{\text{Available screen ruling}}{\text{desired screen ruling}} \times 100$$
$$= 133/50 \times 100$$
$$= 133 \times 2$$
$$= 266 \text{ percent}$$

In other words, it is necessary to enlarge a halftone with a ruling of 133 lines per inch 266 percent to obtain a 50-line ruling.

An enlarger is being used for this example, so it is necessary to determine the size of the first halftone negative. The easiest method of doing so is to refer to a proportion scale. Set the wheel at 266 percent enlargement. Then read from the required size (9 inches × 12 inches) across the wheel to obtain the negative size to be placed in the enlarger. For this example, the first halftone negative must be reduced to $3\frac{3}{8}$ inches × $4\frac{1}{2}$ inches from a 5 inch ×

7 inch original. Calculations for all four methods can be made in a similar manner.

Fabric Selection

When selecting fabric for screen printing halftone images, the screen mesh count is the major concern. In general, monofilament fabrics should be used with halftones. The specific mesh count depends on the halftone ruling of the film positive. The Ulano Company recommends multiplying the halftone ruling by 3.5 to 4.0 to obtain a usable screen mesh range. For example, if the halftone ruling is 60 lines per inch, any mesh count between 210 and 240 can be used ($60 \times 3.5 = 210$, $60 \times 4.0 = 240$).

Whatever screen mesh count is used, the smallest halftone dot must attach to at least four fiber intersections (figure 13.41). For example, if a 133-line halftone stencil is attached to a number 12 fabric, which has approximately 125 threads to the inch, many individual dots would drop through the screen during the printing operation because there would be insufficient fabric support.

Moiré Patterns

A **moiré pattern** (an objectionable optical pattern discussed in chapter 5) may form when two screen patterns overlap (such as when a halftone image is placed on the fabric screen pattern). This is a problem particularly when the screen mesh count is too coarse for the halftone screen ruling. One way to avoid the moiré pattern is to place the clean, stretched screen over the film halftone positive on a light table before making the stencil. Rotate the positive under the screen until the moiré pattern disappears. Then mark the location or angle of the positive so that the stencil can be adhered in the same position.

Printing Considerations

Special inks designed for halftone reproduction are available from screen printing suppliers. Halftone ink is made from fine-ground pigment and can be purchased in either transparent or opaque versions. As with normal ink preparation, halftone ink should form a dense image on the receiving surface but it should not be so thick that it clogs the screen. If the ink is too thin, the halftone dots may bleed together on the press sheet, resulting in a loss of image detail in the shadow areas.

A double-bevel squeegee blade is recommended for halftone work. A sharp, square blade can also be used, but the amount of pressure should be less than is applied typically for normal production runs.

When screen printing halftones, a vacuum base or off-contact printing will help prevent the press sheet from sticking to the screen and thereby diminish the possibility of a blurred image.

High-Speed Production Presses

The basic problem with any hand-operated, hinged-frame screen printing press is the small number of impressions that can be made per hour. Production is limited by how rapidly the printer can feed the press sheets, close the frame, position the squeegee, pull the

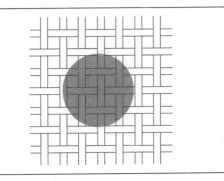

Figure 13.41 **Halftone dot on screen printing fabric**

impression, remove the squeegee, and deliver the printed sheets. Even the most skilled press operator has difficulty screen printing more than 50 impressions an hour with only a small stencil.

Low print output was no problem with the early, slow-drying inks because most printers could not store an output of several thousand wet prints an hour that required overnight drying. With the introduction of fast-drying inks, however, greater production speeds have become more important. High-speed screen printing presses can be classified as hand operated, hand fed, or hand delivered; semiautomatic; or automatic units.

Lever-Action, Hand-Operated Presses

Figure 13.42 illustrates one type of lever-action screen printing press. The advantage of this press is that one operator can screen print images of nearly any size. The screen frame is counterbalanced over a vacuum frame that holds the press paper. With light pressure the frame swings down into position. The squeegee is attached to a lever that automati-

cally springs up and out of contact with the screen. The operator grasps the lever handle, lowers both the screen and the squeegee, and, with a simple motion, drags the blade across the stencil.

Although this press is still hand operated, the action of lowering the screen, positioning the squeegee, and pulling the impression is shortened significantly. Large images are also easy to handle with this device because the lever action ensures uniform pressure across the stencil.

Semiautomatic Presses

Semiautomatic screen printing presses (figure 13.43) are generally hand fed and delivered by the operator, but the actual image transfer is automatic. The operator first inserts and positions (registers) the press sheet. The machine then lowers the frame, draws the squeegee across the stencil, and raises the frame. Some semiautomatic devices have a 5- to 30-second built-in time delay for the press sheets to feed. Others have a foot switch to activate the squeegee that is controlled by the operator. As

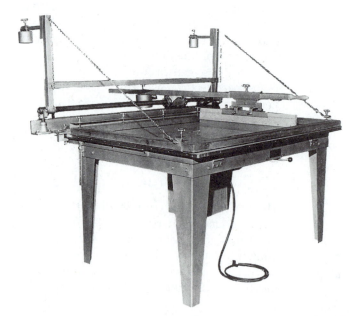

Figure 13.42 Lever-action screen printing unit.
Courtesy of American M&M.

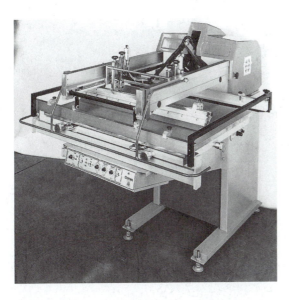

Figure 13.43 **Semiautomatic screen printing press.**
Courtesy of American M&M.

with lever-action presses, the speed of a semiautomatic press is limited by the speed of the operator.

Fully Automatic Presses

True high-speed screen printing is not achieved until the responsibility for feeding and removing each individual press sheet is taken from the operator and given to the press. The techniques for the automatic screen printing press are the same as for any automatic press, except that the screen printing press uses no rollers or cylinders. The image transfer concerns are the same as for the hand-operated hinged system discussed earlier in this chapter, however.

One area of special importance in an automatic press is the delivery system. Because wet press sheets are removed from the press at a relatively high rate of speed, their handling becomes problematic. Devices are available that can be synchronized with any pro-

duction press speed to deliver dry press sheets for stacking or packaging.

Special Machine Configurations

As touched upon earlier, screen printing has been applied to a wide variety of nontraditional materials and uses. One example is the production of printed circuits for the electronics industry (figure 13.44). Major machine de-

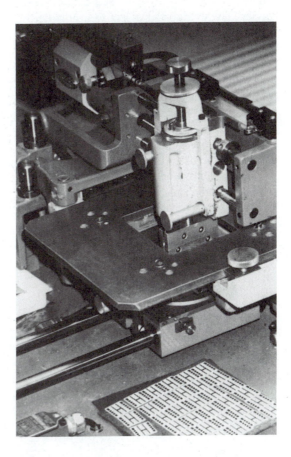

Figure 13.44 **Automatic screen printing press.** This press is used to produce screen printed electronic circuits.
Courtesy of Electronic Products Division, E.I. Du Pont de Nemours and Company, Inc.

signs have been developed since World War II to meet the special demands of the screen printing industry and its customers.

Screening Cylindrical Surfaces

One major area of growth has been the printing of labels directly on cylindrical or conical containers such as bottles, cans, and drinking cups.

Whether automatic or hand operated (figure 13.45), all of these devices function according to the same basic principle. The familiar flat screen is always used as the stencil carrier. The cylindrical object to be printed is positioned beneath the screen and rests on ball bearings or some other system that allows the object to rotate. A squeegee is then lowered into contact with the screen and the cylindrical object and is locked into position. To transfer the image, the screen frame is moved along a track. The weight of the squeegee (which is stationary) pressing the screen against the cylindrical object rotates the object.

Figure 13.46 shows a fully automatic screen printing press that can feed, print, and

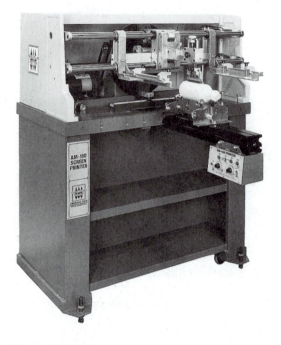

Figure 13.46 **Automatic container and bottle printer.** This system is able to print on cylindrical, elliptical, conical, spherical, and flat surfaces. Courtesy of American M&M.

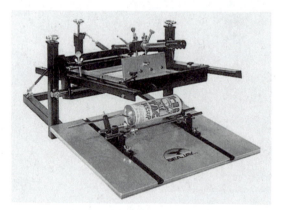

Figure 13.45 **Hand-operated cylindrical screen printing press.** Courtesy of Naz-Dar Company.

deliver 6,000 cone-shaped containers per hour. It operates with the same stationary squeegee and moving-screen idea.

Cylindrical Screens

There is a vast consumer market for continuously repeating images on long rolls of materials such as wallpaper or bolt fabrics. A single flat screen stencil was traditionally used to meet this need. The stencil was prepared carefully so that the printer could step the image down the sheet. This method is still used with specially designed equipment, but it is slow and costly. Figure 13.47 shows a multicolor rotary screen printing press that is designed for this type of continuous web printing. In this press the stencil is carried by rigid screen mesh

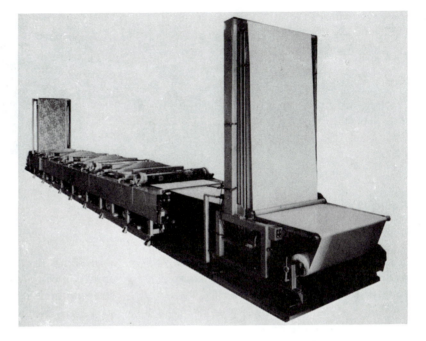

Figure 13.47 Multicolor rotary screen printing press.
Courtesy of Naz-Dar Company.

cylinders. Both the ink and squeegee ride inside the cylinders, which rotate as the line of material passes beneath them. With this approach a continuous multicolor image (up to sixteen colors with this model) can be placed on a roll of paper, plastic, or fabric at a rate of 240 feet a minute.

Carousel Units

A popular method of screening multicolor images on materials such as T-shirts is **wet-on-wet printing** (figure 13.48). With this technique the individual pieces of material are mounted on **carousel carriers** that rotate under each different stencil color sequentially. The wet ink from the first color contacts the bottom of the second stencil, but because it touches in the same place each time, no blurring or loss of image detail occurs.

Registration is generally controlled with a pin system that positions each screen stencil

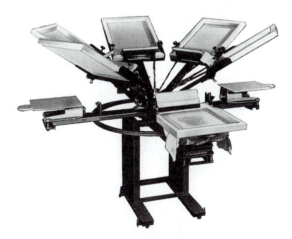

Figure 13.48 Multicolor wet-on-wet screen printing press.
Courtesy of American M&M.

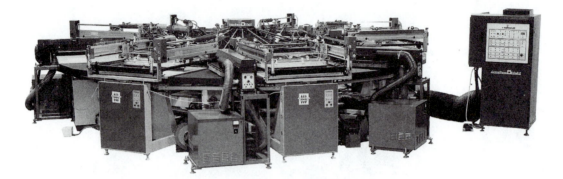

Figure 13.49 **Automatic multicolor carousel printing system.**
Courtesy of American M&M

accurately. Because the material is not moved until the entire printing cycle is complete, color fit should be perfect.

Some printers use automatic printing units that can be configured with the carousel design (figure 13.49).

Key Terms

screen printing
stencil
hand-cut stencil
tusche-and-glue
photographic stencils
multifilament screens
monofilament screens
mechanical stretching
tooth

indirect process
direct process
direct/indirect process
step wedge
indirect photographic stencil
direct photographic stencil
mask
printing press
squeegee

Shore durometer
screen mesh count
ink viscosity
on-contact printing
off-contact printing
moiré pattern
wet-on-wet printing
carousel carriers

Review Questions

1. What is the basic concept of screen printing?
2. What are the three groups of stencil preparation methods?
3. How are screen fabrics classified?
4. Will a 6XX or a 14XX mesh count pass a coarser ink pigment?
5. Why must a tooth be produced on a monofilament fabric and not on a multifilament one?
6. Why should commercial household abrasive cleaners not be used to clean or degrease a screen?
7. What is the primary advantage of photographic stencils?
8. What are the three types of photographic stencils?
9. Briefly outline the six steps necessary to prepare an indirect photographic stencil.
10. Briefly outline the five steps necessary to prepare a direct photographic stencil.
11. What is the purpose of masking?
12. Why is the chemical makeup of the squeegee blade important?
13. Why must the solvent for the ink differ from the solvent for the stencil base?
14. What is the difference between on-contact and off-contact screen printing?
15. Briefly describe the techniques that can be used to control accurate color fit when doing multicolor screening.
16. How do most screen printing inks dry?
17. What are the highlight and shadow reproducible dot sizes when screening halftone images?
18. How can a moiré pattern be prevented when mounting a stencil with a halftone image?
19. What is the advantage of a lever-action, hand-operated screen printing press?
20. Briefly describe the operation of a semiautomatic screen press.
21. What is the advantage of a cylindrical screen?
22. What does the term *wet-on-wet printing* mean?

14

Gravure Printing

Historical Background

The history of gravure printing begins with the work of creative artists during the Italian Renaissance in the 1300s. Fine engravings and etchings were cut by hand into soft copper. The designs were cut away, leaving a channel, or sunken area, to hold the ink during printing. The term *intaglio*, which we use today to describe a class of printing, is an Italian word meaning to print with a sunken pattern or design. Gravure is a type of industrial intaglio printing that is used for extremely long press runs.

Intaglio quickly gained widespread recognition as a rapid, high-quality printing process that could be put to many different uses. The French artist Jacques Callot developed his reputation by sketching the fighting on battlefields and then rushing back to his studio to print etchings of the scenes. He would sell the etchings only a few days after the battle. Callot is sometimes called the first photojournalist because of the speed with which he distributed copies of his sketches.

The first photographic intaglio prints were made by Joseph Nicephore Niépce in about 1814. Niépce, who called his process *heliography*, printed his products on a copperplate

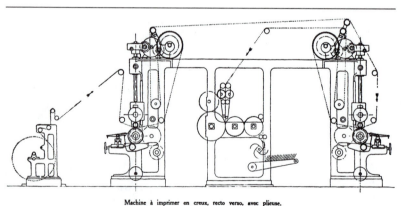

Machine à imprimer en creux, recto verso, avec plieuse.
(Société alsacienne de Constructions Mécaniques.)

An early patent design for a French rotogravure press

press. Fox Talbot refined Niépce's work and developed the first film negative in addition to working on heliography.

The person who is recognized as the inventor of modern gravure printing, however, is Karl Klif (born Klitsch). Klif began experimenting with photographic copper etching in 1875. By about 1879 he had refined the process and formally announced his "heliogravure" process to the Vienna Photographic Society. Klif produced very high-quality reproduction for art collectors but gained little recognition outside Vienna because he wanted to keep his techniques secret. Klif eventually sold his "secret," but continued to refine the process until his death in 1926. He made the revolutionary move from flat printing plates to printing from cylinders. He developed the first doctor blade, or squeegee, and even designed a method of printing color on a web press. Klif originated the term *rotogravure* for printing from a cylinder.

After Klif shared his secrets, others became interested in rotogravure and began designing and building equipment for the process. By the beginning of this century, rotogravure had developed a relatively widespread reputation for fine reproductions. By 1920 huge presses with four or five color units were being used for gravure. Postcards, calendars, book illustrations, and even magazines were being printed in full color.

One of the major uses of gravure that began in the 1920s was the printing of the supplement section of the Sunday newspaper. The section carried human-interest stories, many advertisements, and lots of color photographs. The supplement section was, and continues to be, a favorite item that readers look forward to each week.

The supplement section and rotogravure printing gained such widespread public recognition that Irving Berlin wrote a Broadway play that used the two as a theme. Although Berlin was one of America's most famous songwriters, few remember that 1934 play called *As Thousands Cheer*. However, almost everyone remembers the play's opening song, called "Easter Parade." The most famous lines of the song mention both rotogravure printing and the Sunday supplement because the two terms had come to mean the same in the public's eye.

> On the Avenue, Fifth Avenue, the photographers will snap us, and you'll find that you're in the rotogravure.

Objectives

After completing this chapter, you will be able to:

- Understand the organization of the gravure industry and the importance of professional associations in its growth.
- Recall the major methods of cylinder preparation, including diffusion etch, direct transfer, electromechanical, and laser cutting.
- Recognize the variables in gravure printing, including well formation, film positive quality, etching and plating techniques, cylinder balance, cylinder and doctor blade considerations, and impression rollers.
- Recall the major steps in cylinder construction and preparation.
- Recognize the parts of a gravure press and recall cylinder, doctor blade, and impression roller functions.

Introduction

Recall from chapter 1 that intaglio is one of the five major printing processes (figure 14.1):

- ■ Relief forms an image from a raised surface.
- ■ Screen passes ink through openings in a stencil.
- ■ Lithography prints photochemically from a flat surface.
- ■ Electrostatic prints electromagnetically.
- ■ Intaglio transfers ink from a sunken surface.

Students new to the printing industry sometimes have difficulty visualizing how it is possible to print from a sunken or negative surface. As you will see in this chapter, preparing industrial intaglio plates is perhaps the most sophisticated and technically demanding of all current methods, yet they are the simplest to print on a high-speed press. The intaglio process also delivers the most significantly consistent, high-quality results.

Terms associated with intaglio include *etching*, *engraving*, *drypoint*, and *collagraphy*. Artists use these terms to describe images printed from lines cut into the surface of metal or plastic.

Industrial intaglio is called **gravure** printing, or **rotogravure**. *Roto* means "round." Therefore, rotogravure is printing from a cylinder. All industrial intaglio transfers an image from sunken areas cut into the surface of a cylinder (figure 14.2). Except for small proof presses, most industrial gravure presses are web fed (figure 14.3). As the plate cylinder turns, a continuous roll of paper, foil, or plastic passes through the press to receive the image. After printing, the roll is either re-

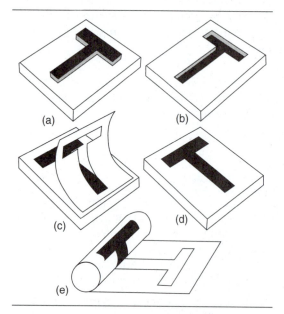

Figure 14.1 Five of the major printing processes. Relief printing (a), intaglio printing (b), screen printing (c), lithographic printing (d), and electrostatic printing (e).

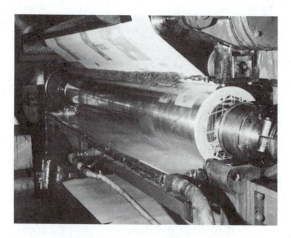

Figure 14.2 A gravure press cylinder. Rotogravure means printing from a cylinder.

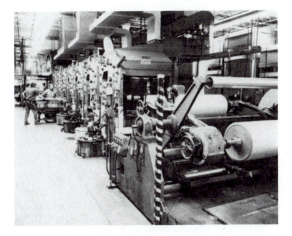

Figure 14.3 **A web-fed gravure press.** Almost all production gravure presses are web fed. Courtesy of the Morrill Press.

wound for shipment to the customer or cut into sheets at the end of the press by a device called a slitter.

The Gravure Industry

Gravure is a major printing process. Over 18 percent of all printing in this country is done by gravure. The gravure industry has enjoyed a relatively steady growth rate and, with recent technical advances, will continue to gain a larger share of the printing market. Several important characteristics make gravure an ideal process for jobs requiring high quality and extremely long press runs.

■ Gravure is the simplest of all printing systems, with the fastest press start-up and the most direct press controls.

■ Gravure's easy press control results in very little paper waste. Gravure has less than half the paper spoilage rate of lithography.

■ Gravure press speeds are extremely high. The largest gravure presses can operate as rapidly as 45,000 impressions an hour.

■ Gravure cylinders are especially hardy. Several million impressions from the same cylinder are common. Some printers report press runs as long as 20 million copies without the cylinder wearing out.

■ Gravure gives the highest-quality image of the five major printing processes. It has a reputation for delivering excellent color and ink density, even on low-quality printing papers.

Traditionally, the most significant disadvantage of gravure was the length of time required to prepare the cylinder. New technology has automated much of the process, but this has not changed the fact that gravure cylinders are enormously heavy and require special equipment to maneuver them and significant plant space to store them. Gravure presses are also massive, expensive, and out of the reach of smaller shops. Traditionally, gravure has only been used for jobs of 60,000 or more, but this is changing as automation improves and turnaround time decreases.

Industry Organization

Gravure printing is divided into three broad product areas, each with its own special problems and solutions. The first area is **packaging printing**. This includes producing folding cartons, bags, boxes, gift wrappers, labels, and flexible materials that eventually form containers.

The second area is **publication printing**. Publication printing includes producing newspaper supplements, magazines, catalogs, and mass mailing advertisements. Gravure is ideally suited for the long press runs required for the Sunday newspaper supplement sections that are distributed on a national basis.

The third area of gravure printing is **specialty printing**. In this area, gravure is used to print such materials as wallpaper, vinyl, floor coverings, and even textiles for both decoration and clothing fabrication.

Companies have found that they become more efficient and cost effective by limiting the jobs they accept to a specific product area.

The Gravure Association of America

One reason for the steady growth of gravure printing in the United States has been the cooperative efforts of gravure printers, suppliers, and manufacturers who focus through the **Gravure Association of America (GAA)**. GAA provides consultative assistance, publishes a wide range of technical materials related to all phases of gravure production, has worked to establish industry standards, supplies technical aids, and has a tradition of collegial efforts to educate printers and to disseminate information on gravure printing. Much of the information contained in this chapter was compiled through the courtesy and cooperation of the GAA. Individuals interested in using GAA's services or in becoming affiliated with the organization should write to the Gravure Association of America, 1200A Scottsville Road, Rochester, New York 14624.

Basic Gravure Concepts

Gravure is so radically different in both concept and technique from other printing processes that it is important to first review a number of key ideas. With these concepts in place we can move to descriptions of cylinder preparation and presswork.

Methods of Cylinder Preparation

There are four basic methods of gravure cylinder preparation:

- Diffusion etch
- Direct transfer
- Electromechanical process
- Laser cutting

Diffusion-Etch Process

In the **diffusion-etch process** (figure 14.4), a special mask is prepared by first exposing it through a special gravure screen and then through a film positive of the printing image onto a light-sensitive base. The mask is then applied to a copper gravure cylinder and is developed on the cylinder. After development, the mask is thick in the nonimage areas of the cylinder and very thin where the image will carry ink. The cylinder and mask are then placed in an acid bath. The acid bath penetrates the thin areas of the mask and eats or etches away the copper of the cylinder. The final step of diffusion etch is to remove the mask and apply a thin layer of chrome over the entire cylinder by an electroplating process. (See the Copper Plating and Polishing section of this chapter). The purpose of the chrome is to extend the life of the surface areas.

Direct-Transfer Process

The second method of cylinder preparation is called **direct transfer**. The main difference between diffusion etch and direct transfer is the way in which the cylinder mask is exposed. In direct transfer, a light-sensitive mask is sprayed or applied over the cylinder surface. The mask is exposed by directing light through a halftone positive as it moves past the cylinder, which turns at the same rate that the positive moves (figure 14.5). The final steps of developing, etching, and chrome electroplating are the same as in the diffusion-etch technique.

Electromechanical Process

This direct digital process has essentially replaced chemical engraving as the most preva-

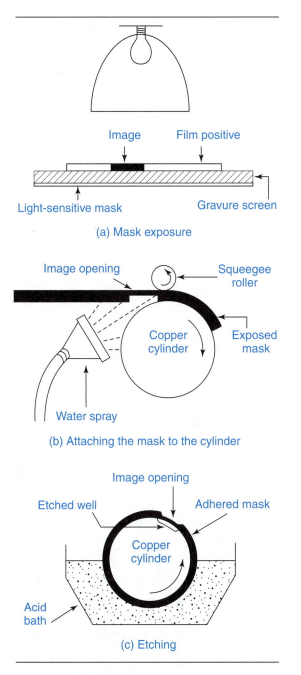

(a) Mask exposure

(b) Attaching the mask to the cylinder

(c) Etching

Figure 14.4 Cylinder preparation: Diffusion etch. The three main steps in the conventional gravure process are mask exposure (a), attaching the mask to the cylinder (b), and etching (c).

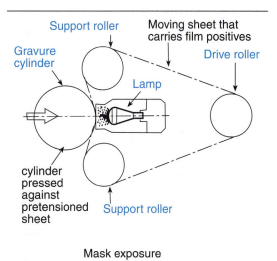

Mask exposure

Figure 14.5 Cylinder preparation: Direct transfer. In the direct-transfer process, the light-sensitive mask is exposed by passing light through a halftone positive as it moves in contact with the rotating cylinder.
Courtesy of Southern Gravure Service.

lent method of cylinder engraving. In this **electromechanical process**, a clean copper cylinder is mounted in a special engraving machine. The artwork and copy to be engraved are scanned by an optical device that uses photodiodes to receive the image, which is then transformed into digital data. This digitized information is translated to the motion of an engraving head, typically a diamond stylus that cuts into the surface of the cylinder as it rotates (figure 14.6). A diamond stylus can vibrate at approximately 5,000 cells per second. After cutting, the cylinder is chrome electroplates and made ready for the press.

One computer-driven approach to engraving large-format cylinders has been the HelioKlischograph, developed by Hell Gravure Systems. This electromechanical engraving machine can be driven from film mounted on a scanner or directly from computer files.

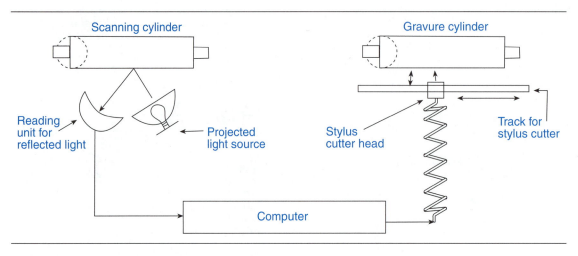

Figure 14.6 **Diagram of the electromechanical process.** The cylinder is etched by using a diamond stylus in the electromechanical process.

Hell has continued to improve the capabilities of its HelioKlischographs, with current machines capable of working as part of a fully automated workflow with up to 16 simultaneous engraving channels.

Laser-Cutting Process

The fourth technique of gravure cylinder preparation is called **laser cutting**. In this process, a series of small holes, or wells, is etched chemically over the entire surface of a clean copper cylinder. The wells are then filled with a plastic material until the cylinder again has a smooth, uniform surface. Like the electromechanical method, the original copy is scanned by a beam of light. The laser cutting process, however, uses the narrow beam of a laser to blast away or remove parts of the plastic from individual wells rather than a diamond tool to cut way metal. In the final step of laser cutting, the cylinder can then be sprayed with a special electrolyte and electroplates with chrome.

Direct laser engraving is not that widely used yet, but is gaining attention. Advance-

ments such as a copper alloy developed by the Daetwyler Corporation has proved much more successful at being digitally engraved by laser than ordinary copper cylinders. The LaserStar, by Daetwyler, engraves data processes in an open TIFF format and has dual engraving heads that allow for speeds of up to 140,000 cells per second (figure 14.7). As laser engraving does not involve parts to be worn down, such as the diamond stylus used in electromechanical engraving, it eliminates certain multichannel ribbon variances that could occur.

Of the four cylinder preparation processes, diffusion etch is the oldest and now, along with the direct-transfer process, the least used in the industry. Recent advances with the laser process point to changes in the future that may revolutionize gravure cylinder preparation. Currently, direct digital electromechanical engraving accounts for the vast majority of cylinder-making in the United States (figure 14.8). It is a proven cost-effective way to engrave cylinders and, coupled with a fully automatic workflow, is making gravure

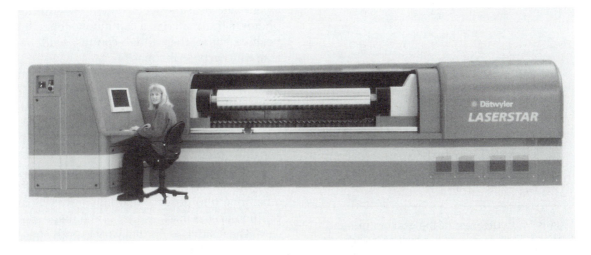

Figure 14.7 A high-speed laser engraver.
Courtesy of Max Daetwyler, Inc.

competitive with other shorter-run processes (figure 14.9).

Well Formation

Gravure transfers ink from the small wells that are etched or cut into the surface of the cylinder (figure 14.9). On the press, the cylinder rotates through a fountain of ink. The ink is wiped from the surface of the cylinder by a doctor blade. The cuplike shape of each well holds ink in place as the cylinder turns past the doctor blade. The formation of perfect wells is the main goal of the gravure engraver. There are several important ideas to understand about gravure wells.

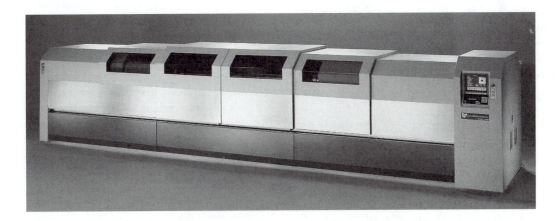

Figure 14.8 An electromechanical publication engraver with extensive automatic controls.
Courtesy of Max Daetwyler, Inc.

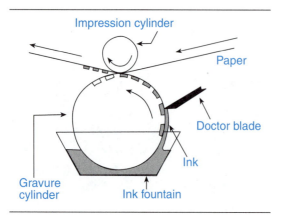

Figure 14.9 Diagram of the gravure printing process. Etched wells in the printing cylinder pick up ink from the fountain. The excess ink is wiped from the surface of the cylinder by the doctor blade before the ink is applied to the press sheet.

Every **gravure well** has four variables (figure 14.10):

■ Depth

■ Bottom

■ Opening

■ Bridge

The depth of the well is measured from the bottom of the well to the top surface of the cylinder. The opening is the distance across the well. The **bridge** is the surface of the cylinder between wells. The doctor blade rises against well bridges as it scrapes ink from the cylinder.

Within the diffusion-etch technique are two basic types of well design:

■ Conventional gravure

■ Lateral hard-dot process

In the **conventional gravure** design, every well on a cylinder has exactly the same opening size (figure 14.11a). The amount of ink to be transferred to the paper is controlled only

by the depth of the well. When reproducing photographic material, a continuous-tone film positive, rather than a high-contrast halftone, is used to expose the mask.

The second major type of well design with diffusion etch is called the **lateral hard-dot process** (sometimes called **halftone gravure design**). Two separate film positives are used to expose the mask with the lateral hard-dot process. The first is a continuous-tone film positive, as with conventional gravure. A second exposure is then made with a halftone film positive that falls in the same position on the mask as that of the first exposure. The result is wells that vary in both opening size and depth (figure 14.11b).

The direct-transfer method of cylinder preparation produces yet another well design. A single halftone positive is used to expose the mask in this process. The dot formation in the halftone defines the opening size of each well (figure 14.11c). The depth of each well is the same, however.

Electromechanical well formation is a bit different from diffusion etch or direct transfer.

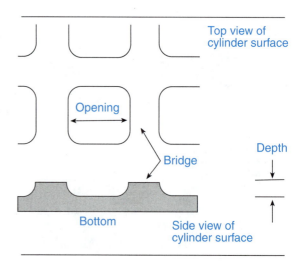

Figure 14.10 Diagram of gravure cylinder wells. A gravure well has four variables: depth, bottom, opening, and bridge.

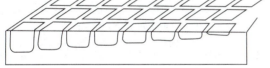

(a) Conventional gravure

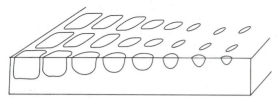

(b) Lateral hard dot

Varying cell opening size
uniform depth of cells

(c) Direct transfer

Figure 14.11   Three examples of gravure wells. (a) Conventional gravure wells vary in depth, but all have the same opening size. (b) Lateral hard-dot wells vary in both depth and opening. (c) Direct-contact wells vary in opening size, but all have the same depth.
Courtesy of the Southern Gravure Service.

In the electromechanical process, each gravure well is created by the action of a diamond stylus as it pushes into the soft copper surface of the cylinder (figure 14.12). A direct relationship exists between the depth of the cut and the well opening size. As the stylus pushes

deeper into the cylinder, it increases the opening of the well. This action influences the volume of ink that the well can carry. In photographs, shadow area wells are much deeper than highlight wells.

Film Positives

Most artwork is delivered to the gravure engraver in the form of film positives. The characteristics of film images used by gravure are somewhat different from those used in other

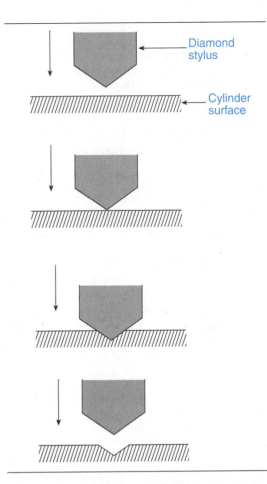

Figure 14.12   Cutting a cylinder surface. In the electromechanical engraving process, wells are cut in the cylinder as a diamond stylus moves into and out of the copper.

printing methods, however. The main difference is the image density range (see chapter 4 for a review of densitometry). Wells are etched or cut in proportion to the density of the corresponding area on the film positive.

There is a minimum well depth that holds ink during the gravure printing process. If the well is too shallow, the actions of the doctor blade and the rapidly spinning cylinder can actually pull ink from the well. Film positives must therefore be prepared with a minimum density so that each well is deep enough to hold ink.

For continuous-tone images, the GAA recommends a density range of 0.30 to 1.65. This means that the highlight areas of the positive should have a transmission density of 0.30 and a shadow reading of 1.65. The difference between the two measurements produces a BDR of 1.35, which is acceptable to commercial photographers yet still exceeds the range of most halftone negatives used in lithography.

Line images, such as type, ink, or line borders, are also supplied in film positive form. Line image density should be near the 1.65 shadow area density of continuous-tone images. Film positives are often supplied to the engraver with both continuous-tone and line images on the same piece of film. The most common approach is to first prepare each type of image separately in negative form, and then to make several contact exposures on a new sheet of film to create one film positive.

Cylinder Construction and Preparation

The quality of the final gravure image depends first on the construction of the cylinder. Almost all cylinder cores are made from steel tubing. Some packaging printers prefer extruded, or shaped, aluminum cores because they are much lighter, less expensive, and eas-

ier to ship than steel. A few companies use solid copper cylinders, but steel remains the most popular core material.

A steel cylinder is used when printing with adhesives or other corrosive materials. In most gravure printing, however, a thin coating of copper is plated over the steel core of the cylinder to carry the image. Copper is easier to etch than steel and can be replaced easily when the job is finished.

Cylinder Design

There are five important parts to identify on a gravure cylinder (figure 14.13).

- Axis
- Shaft
- Diameter
- Circumference
- Face length

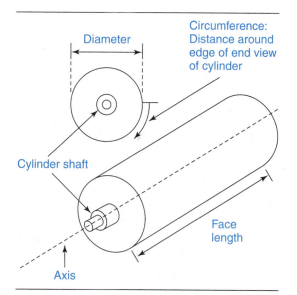

Figure 14.13 **Parts of a gravure cylinder.** The most commonly identified parts of a gravure cylinder are axis, shaft, diameter, circumference, and face length.

The axis is the invisible line that passes through the center of the length of the cylinder. The cylinder shaft is the bearing surface as the cylinder rotates in the press. If you look at the end view of a cylinder, the shaft appears as a circle. The diameter is the distance across the circle, through the center of the shaft. The circumference is the distance around the edge of the end view. The face length is the distance from one end of the cylinder to the other, along the length of the cylinder.

The face length of the cylinder limits the width of paper to be printed. The circumference limits the size of the image. One rotation of the cylinder around its circumference is called one **impression**. Continuous images can be etched on a cylinder without a seam so the design is repeated without a break. Wallpaper designs are commonly printed by gravure.

Gravure cylinders are built using many different sizes. The face length is always the same for each press to match the press sheet size but varies in diameter and circumference to closely match the cut-off size of the specific job. There are two basic cylinder designs (figure 14.14).

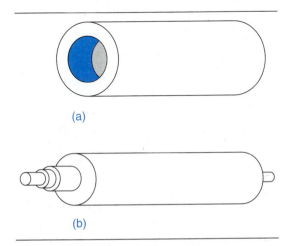

(a)

(b)

Figure 14.14 Two forms of gravure cylinders.
There are two basic forms of cylinder construction: mandrel (a) and integral shaft (b).

■ Mandrel

■ Integral shaft

A mandrel cylinder (sometimes called a sleeve or cone cylinder) is designed with a removable shaft. Most holes are tapered so that the shaft can be pressed into place and then removed easily.

In the integral shaft design, the shaft is mounted permanently on the cylinder. The cylinder is formed first, and then the shaft is either pressed or shrunk into place. The shaft is attached permanently by welding and remains in place for the life of the cylinder.

Integral shaft cylinders are more expensive than mandrel cylinders but are generally considered to produce high-quality images. This is because they produce greater support across the length of the cylinder during press runs than hollow mandrel cylinders.

Balancing the Cylinder

When a cylinder (or any round object) rotates at extremely high speeds, vibration can be a problem. That is why automobile tires must be carefully balanced before use to prevent undue wear or poor steering control. A major concern with gravure printing is vibration caused by an unbalanced cylinder (figure 14.15a). A great deal of fibration can bounce the cylinder against the doctor blade and result in a poor image. Vibration can also damage the press. There are two types of cylinder imbalance: static and dynamic.

Static imbalance occurs when the cylinder is not perfectly round or has different densities within a cross section (figure 14.15b). Static imbalance can result from such defects as air holes, impurities in the steel core, or improper copper plating and polishing (see following section).

Dynamic imbalance occurs when the cylinder differs in density or balance from one end to the other (figure 14.15c). Dynamic imbalance is the greatest cause of cylinder vibra-

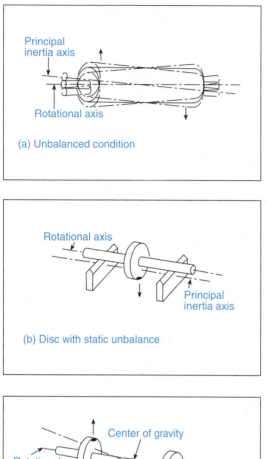

(a) Unbalanced condition

(b) Disc with static unbalance

(c) Discs realigned to cancel static unbalance cause dynamic or couple unbalance

Figure 14.15 **Examples of cylinder imbalance.**
Courtesy of Gravure Association of America.

tion at high press speeds. Both static and dynamic imbalance can be corrected by either reducing or adding weight to each end of the cylinder.

Copper Plating and Polishing

Electroplating is the process of transferring and bonding very small bits (called **ions**) of one type of metal to another type of metal. This process takes place in a special liquid **plating bath**. The ions are transferred as an electrical current passes through the bath. The longer the current flows, the more new metal that is plated to the cylinder.

The first step in the gravure electroplating process is to clean the surface of the cylinder thoroughly. The cylinder is cleaned by brushing or rubbing it with special cleaning compounds and then rinsing it with a powerful stream of hot water (figure 14.16). Some plants use special cleaning machines for this purpose. The goal is to remove all spots of grease, rust, or dirt so that a perfect coating of copper can be applied over the entire cylinder surface. Cylinder areas that will not be plated. such as the ends, can be coated with asphaltum or other staging materials, which covers and protects its clean surface.

To electroplate a cylinder, the cylinder is suspended in a curved tank and rotated through the plating bath (figure 14.17). The electrical current is allowed to flow from the copper anode (the plating metal) through the bath to the cylinder (base metal). Zinc sulfate, copper sulfate, or cyanide solutions are common plating-bath liquids. Six-thousandths of an inch (0.006 inch) to thirty-thousandths of an inch (0.030 inch) is the common thickness range for the copper layer on a gravure cylinder.

A **newage gauge** is a device used to test the hardness of copper. Copper hardness is measured by pushing a diamond point into the copper surface. The diagonal length of the opening created by the diamond point is measured and then compared with the amount of force required to push the diamond into the copper. The result is expressed in diamond point hardness (DPH). Most printers look for a DPH between 93 and 122.

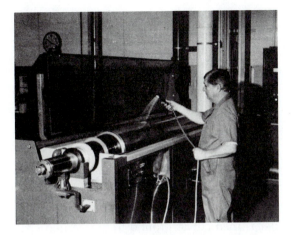

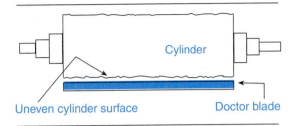

Figure 14.18 **Diagram of a doctor blade against an uneven cylinder.** If the cylinder is not uniform, the doctor blade will not be able to remove excess ink from the nonprinting surfaces.

Figure 14.16 **Cleaning the cylinder surface.** It is important to remove all spots of grease, rust, or dirt so that a perfect layer of copper can be applied to the cylinder surface.

The last step in constructing a gravure cylinder is to bring the diameter (and circumference) of the cylinder to the desired size and at the same time create a perfect printing sur-

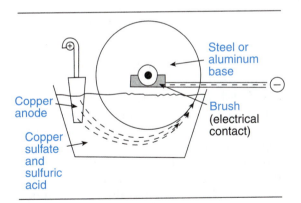

Figure 14.17 **Diagram of the electroplating process.** An electrical current passes from the copper anode through the plating solution to the steel or aluminum cylinder until the desired thickness of copper is plated on the cylinder. Courtesy of Southern Gravure Service.

face. The cylinder must not only be round and balanced perfectly, it must also be perfectly smooth and uniform across its length. If the cylinder is not uniform, the doctor blade will not be able to remove excess ink from the nonprinting surface (figure 14.18).

The newly plated cylinder is mounted in a lathe and prepared for final turning. Some plants use a diamond cutting tool to bring the cylinder into rough dimensions; they then use separate grinding stones to polish the cylinder's surface (figure 14.19). Other plants use specially designed precision machines that both cut and polish the cylinder at the same time. With these machines, cylinders can be cut within one ten-thousandth of an inch (0.0001 inch) of the desired size and surface. After the final turning, the cylinder is ready for image etching.

Reusing Cylinders

Gravure cylinders can be reused many times. One way to reuse a cylinder is to cut away the old image on a lathe. This involves removing only two-thousandths to three-thousandths of an inch of cylinder surface. The cylinder is then replated with copper and recut or reground to its original diameter.

Another way to reuse a cylinder is to simply dissolve the cylinder's chrome coating

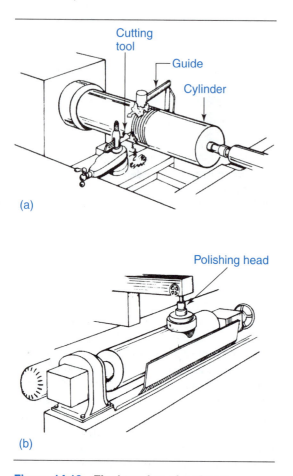

(a)

(b)

Figure 14.19 **Final turning of a plated cylinder.** (a) The cylinder is first cut to rough dimensions. (b) Then it is ground or polished to final size.
Courtesy of Southern Gravure Service.

(added as the final step in cylinder preparation to protect the soft copper on the press) and to then plate over the old image with new copper. The replating process fills the image areas above the original cylinder surface. Excess copper is then cut or ground away, and the cylinder is returned to the desired diameter size.

Ballard Shell Cylinders

The **ballard shell process** is a special technique used by some publication printers that allows easy removal of a copper layer after the cylinder has been printed. The cylinder is prepared in the usual manner, including copper plating, except that it is cut twelve-thousandths to fifteen-thousandths of an inch undersize in diameter. The undersized cylinder is coated with a special nickel separator solution and is returned to the copper plating bath. A second layer of copper is then plated onto the cylinder over the first layer. The cylinder is then cut or ground to the desired size, given an image etch, and printed.

The difference between most gravure cylinders and ballard shell cylinders is seen when the cylinder has been printed and is ready to receive another image. The second copper layer can be simply ripped off the ballard shell cylinder base. A knife is used to cut through the copper to the nickel separator layer, which allows the shell to be lifted away. The cylinder can then be cleaned, a new nickel separator solution can be applied, and another shell can be plated to receive the image.

Gravure Presswork

Almost all gravure printing is done on web-fed presses (figure 14.3). Paper or some other material (called a substrate) feeds from large rolls to the printing unit through an intricate system of tension and registration controls (figure 14.20). The paper then passes between the image cylinder and an impression cylinder. Some companies use offset gravure, but most transfer the image directly from the cylinder. After the paper leaves the printing unit, it might pass through a set of driers to set the ink, or it might follow an intricate set of rollers to dry by aerial oxidation and absorption. When the paper enters the delivery unit of the press, it might be slit (figure 14.21),

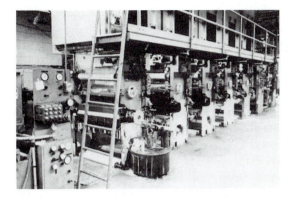

Figure 14.20   A printing unit of a web-fed press.
Courtesy of the Morrill Press.

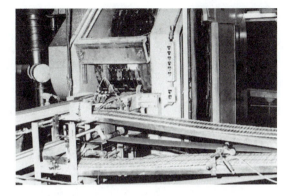

Figure 14.22   Folding unit of a web press.
Some jobs are cut into sheets and folded in line on the press.

cut into sheets and folded (figure 14.22), or rewound onto a roll for shipment to the customer (figure 14.23).

Many of the common concerns of gravure web-press operation are similar to others dealing with basic press design and operation. Special concerns of gravure inks are discussed in chapter 16. Some concerns, however, are unique to gravure press operation. The two main concerns of cylinder and doctor blade adjustment and impression rollers are examined here to complement the information presented in other chapters.

Cylinder and Doctor Blade Considerations

The function of the doctor blade is to wipe ink from the surface of the plate cylinder, leaving ink in only the recessed wells. A great deal of

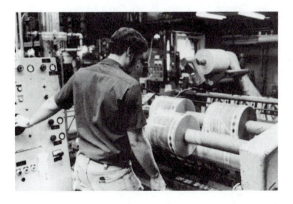

Figure 14.21   Slitting the printed paper. Some jobs require that the web be slit into smaller rolls at the delivery end of the press.
Courtesy of the Morrill Press.

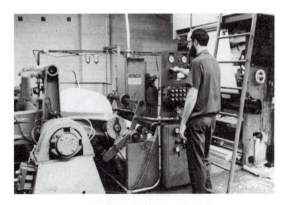

Figure 14.23   Rewinding printed paper. Some jobs are rewound onto a roll after printing.
Courtesy of the Morrill Press.

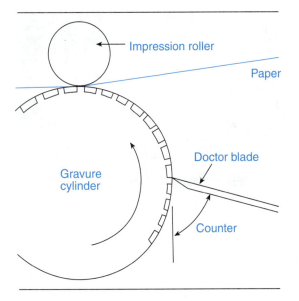

Figure 14.24 **Diagram showing the counter.** The counter is the angle between the doctor blade and the cylinder surface.

research has been done on materials, angles, and designs for doctor blades.

Several different materials are used for blades. The goal is to minimize blade wear and reduce heat generated by the rubbing of the blade against the turning cylinder. Plastic, stainless steel, bronze, and several other metals have been used with success. The most common blade material, however, is Swedish blue spring steel. Blades are usually between 0.006 inch and 0.007 inch thick. The blades must be relatively thin to reduce wear on the cylinder, but strong enough to wipe away ink.

Blade angle is another important consideration. The angle between the blade and the cylinder is called the **counter** (figure 14.24). There is much debate about the proper counter for the best image quality. The best counter depends on the method used to prepare the cylinder. For example, with electromechanically engraved cylinders, image quality decreases as the counter increases. Most angles

are set initially between 18 degrees and 20 degrees. After the blade is placed against the cylinder and production begins, however, the counter generally increases to around 45 degrees.

One way to set the blade angle is by using the reverse doctor principle. With this approach the doctor blade is set at a large enough angle to push the ink from the surface (figure 14.25).

Several different doctor blade designs are used by gravure printers (figure 14.26). The most popular are conventional and MDC/Ringier. Care must be taken to keep the conventional design sharp and uniform. Most printers hone the blade by hand with a special stone and then polish it with a rouge or emery paper to get a flawless edge while the MDC/Ringier design tends to self-sharpen. The MDC/Ringier design has a longer working life then the conventional form design and requires much less press downtime for blade cleaning and repair.

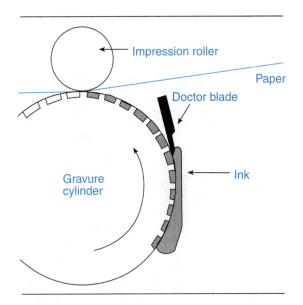

Figure 14.25 **Diagram showing a reverse doctor blade.** A reverse doctor blade pushes ink from the cylinder surface.

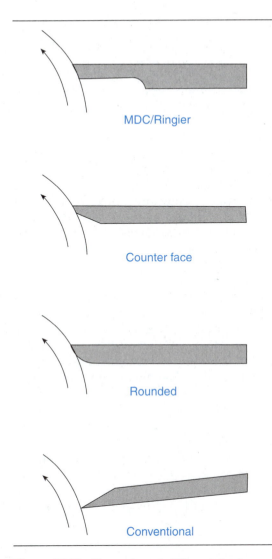

Figure 14.26 **Examples of different doctor blade designs**

The action of the doctor blade against the cylinder is of special concern. The blade rides against the cylinder with pressure. Pressure is necessary so that the ink does not creep under the blade as the cylinder turns. The most common method of holding the blade against the surface is by air pressure. The blade fits into a holder, which is mounted in turn in a special

pneumatic mechanism. Most printers use a pressure of one and a quarter pounds per inch across the cylinder length.

Most doctor blades are not stationary, however. As the cylinder rotates, the blade oscillates, or moves back and forth, parallel to the cylinder. This oscillating action works to remove pieces of lint or dirt that might otherwise be trapped between the cylinder and the blade. Dirt can nick the blade. Nicks allow a narrow bead of ink to pass to the cylinder surface. Nicks are major defects that can ruin the image or scratch the surface of the cylinder.

A **prewipe blade** is commonly used on high-speed presses to skim excess ink from the cylinder (figure 14.27). This device prevents a large quantity of ink from reaching the doctor

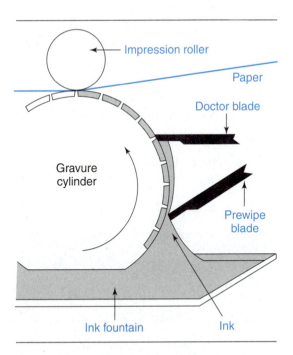

Figure 14.27 **Diagram of a gravure cylinder showing prewipe and doctor blades.** Most presses use prewipe blades to skim most of the ink from the cylinder before the cylinder reaches the doctor blade.

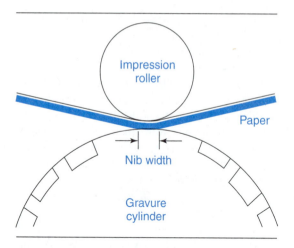

Figure 14.28 **Diagram showing the nib width.** The nib width is the area of the cylinder where the paper contacts the cylinder by the pressure of the impression roller.

blade and ensures that the thin metal blade wipes the cylinder surface perfectly clean.

Impression Rollers

Use of an impression roller is the second main difference between gravure presses and other web-fed machines. The purpose of the impression roller is to push the paper against the gravure cylinder to transfer ink from the image wells (figure 14.9). The major considera-

tions for impression rollers are coating and hardness, pressure, and electrostatic assist.

Coating and Hardness

Most impression rollers are formed from a steel core coated with rubber or a synthetic material, such as Du Pont's Neoprene. Rubber hardness is measured by a Shore durometer (discussed in chapter 13). Values are given in Shore A readings. Hardness increases as Shore A numbers get larger. Different types of paper or substrates require different degrees of hardness for the impression roller. Material such as cellophane might require 60 Shore A, but kraft paper or chipboard might need 90 Shore A.

Pressure

Ink transfers to the web by pressure of the impression roller. Pressure might vary from 50 pounds per linear inch (pli) to 200 pli. More pressure does not always give better image quality, however, The amount of pressure the operator sets is determined by previous tests for the kind of paper being printed. Whatever setting is selected, it is critical that uniform pressure is applied over the entire length of the cylinder.

The area of contact between the impression roller and the cylinder is called the **nib width**, or flat (figure 14.28). The amount of nib width is determined by the hardness of the

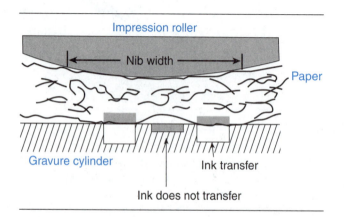

Figure 14.29 **Diagram showing inking on defective paper.** If defects in the paper prevent contact with the gravure cylinder, ink will not transfer.

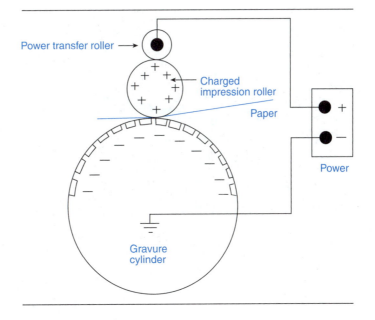

Figure 14.30 Diagram of electrostatic assist printing. Electrostatic assist printing charges the impression roller and the gravure cylinder so that the ink lifts electrostatically from the cylinder to the paper.

impression roller and the amount of pressure. The nib width is important because it is the area of image transfer to the paper or plastic web. The nib width is adjusted to give the best-quality image on the web stock.

Electrostatic Assist

A great advantage of the gravure process is that it allows high-quality images to be printed on low-grade papers. Problems do occur when the paper surface is coarse and imperfect, however. Ink transfers by direct contact. If a defect in the paper prevents that contact, then no image will transfer (figure 14.29). The Gravure Research Association (now part of the Gravure Association of America) designed and licensed a special device, called an **electrostatic assist**, to solve this problem and improve image transfer. With electrostatic assist printing, a power source is connected between the cylinder and the impression roller (figure 14.30). A conductive covering must be added to the impression roller, but the cover causes no special problems. An electric charge is cre-

ated behind the web, which forms an electrostatic field at the nib width. The charge pulls the ink around the edges of each well, which causes the ink to rise and transfer to the paper. Most presses are now equipped with electrostatic assist devices.

Trends in Gravure

Gravure printing presses are sophisticated devices that have a wide range of controls to ensure high image quality (figure 14.31). Technology has created rapid advances in press design and workflow. In 1997 the world's first 3.6-meter (11 ft 9 in.) wide gravure press was installed in Hamburg, Germany. According to Koenig and Bauer-Albert, a leading manufacturer of rotogravure presses: "The maximum speed achievable today with four pages around the cylinder circumference is 60,000 cylinder revolutions per hour. This is equivalent to a web speed of almost 3000 fpm. So, in a single second the press can print 615 sq ft of

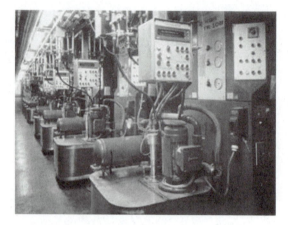

Figure 14.31   Print units of a 3.6-meter gravure press, operator side.
Courtesy of Koenig & Bauer-Albert.

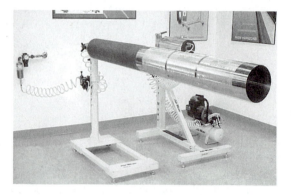

Figure 14.33   Lightweight gravure cylinder sleeve. Sleeve is on a cylinder mounting system.
Courtesy of Armotek Industries, Inc.

paper with four colors on both sides." (figure 14.32).

New cylinder technology is being developed to make the cylinders lighter and smaller. Different materials, including lightweight polymers, are being looked at to reduce the weight and difficulty of handling. Armoteck Corporation has developed a product called Fiberlyte that it claims reduces the weight of a cylinder by up to 80 percent, depending on size. Armotech has combined this with a new technology that uses lightweight disposable sleeves, which are then mounted on the cylinder (figure 14.33) The sleeves can be engraved remotely and then shipped at low cost to the printing or embossing plant.

The technological advances of the past decade, coupled with the fact that the gravure process offers high quality with a relatively simple printing process, will continue to make gravure printing one of the major printing processes in this country.

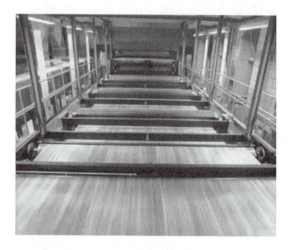

Figure 14.32   High-speed web.
Courtesy of Koenig & Bauer AG.

Key Terms

gravure
rotogravure
packaging printing
publication printing
specialty printing
Gravure Association of America
  (GAA)
diffusion-etch process
direct transfer
electromechanical process

laser cutting
gravure well
bridge
conventional gravure
lateral hard-dot process
halftone gravure design
impression
static imbalance
dynamic imbalance
electroplating

ion
plating bath
newage gauge
ballard shell process
counter
prewipe blade
nib width
electrostatic assist

Review Questions

1. What are the main characteristics of rotogravure printing?
2. List four characteristics of gravure that make it ideal for high-quality, long-run jobs.
3. What is the Gravure Association of America (GAA)?
4. List the four basic methods of gravure cylinder preparation.
5. What are the most commonly identified parts of a gravure cylinder?
6. What is the difference between static balance and dynamic balance?
7. What are the two basic forms of cylinder construction?
8. What is electroplating?
9. What is a newage gauge?
10. What is the ballard shell process?
11. What is the purpose of a doctor blade on a gravure press?
12. What is the difference between a conventional doctor blade design and a MDC/Ringier design?
13. What is the purpose of an impression roller in gravure press work?
14. What does electrostatic assist refer to in gravure press work?
15. What is the nib width on a gravure press?

15

Flexographic, Ink-Jet, and Digital Presses

Historical Background

All printing processes have been developed to meet a human need for information. Johann Gutenberg invented printing to meet Europe's increasing need for printed records in the late 1400s. His invention expanded the distribution of knowledge across all social classes. This expansion of knowledge quickly led to an increasing demand for more printed material. For centuries inventors and printers tried to find ways to set type and print images faster and faster. However, it took more than four hundred years before truly revolutionary changes occurred—the Linotype machine and the rotary relief press in the late nineteenth century. But revolutions also create demand, so the inventors kept looking for methods of producing printed information faster and faster.

In the 1950s, when the commercial phototypesetter was introduced, many felt that the device could set type faster than would ever be necessary. Within a few short years, however, the phototypesetter was outstripped by the offset lithographic process, which came to full acceptance in the late 1960s. And so it has gone throughout history. Each new technological innovation increases demand and leads to other, related innovations, which in turn produce more demand and spark the development of newer technologies.

The technological innovation that has probably had the greatest impact on the modern printing industry is the computer. Computers have made producing printed matter faster, easier, and more efficient than was ever thought possible. Printers use computers not only to set type but to control and to monitor almost every task in the printing plant. In addition, the computer has made a completely new type of printing, known as *on-demand* printing, possible. All traditional printing processes rely on a time-consuming and costly process that involves designing an image, generating camera-ready copy from which negatives are made, using the negatives to produce printing plates, and then using the plates to produce printed reproductions. The problem with this process is that producing the final copy requires a great deal of lead time. On-demand printing, in which copy is reproduced directly from computer memory without negatives or plates, reduces the lead time needed for printed matter from months to minutes.

The invention of plastic materials is another innovation that has had a profound effect on printing. Plastics have greatly expanded the type of printing substrates. Before the development of plastics, printers were called upon to print primarily on paper. Printing presses, inks, plates, and all developments in printing centered around a paper substrate. The development of cellophane in the 1930s represented a major breakthrough in the packaging industry. When used for food packaging, this material would keep foods fresh far longer than paper wrappers. The material was also easy to use because it would stretch and seal itself to the food surface and could be made clear so the customer could see the product inside the package. Above all, cellophane was inexpensive to produce, store, and handle. In all aspects of food packaging, cellophane provided the answer to the food processor's dreams. In all aspects, that is, except one: it was almost impossible to print on. Here, then, was a material that, in answering one need, created another. Aniline printing, which was introduced to this country in the early 1900s, rushed to meet this need. The aniline process, which today is known as flexography, provides the primary means for printing on plastic materials.

Will we ever have a printing process that can print on any material instantly? Perhaps, for as long as people can think, they will be creative. And as long as people create, they will produce a need for even more printing processes that will print at even greater speeds. This cycle of innovation leading to innovation is what makes technology so interesting. It guarantees a future for us all, not only as printers, but as members of the human race.

Objectives

After completing this chapter, you will be able to:

- Discuss the development of flexographic printing.
- Describe the major components of a flexographic press.
- Discuss the function of an anilox roll.
- Describe two-roll and three-roll flexographic inking systems.
- Explain how sheet and liquid photopolymer plates, and explain how rubber flexographic plates are made.
- Differentiate between a continuous spray printer and a drop-on-demand ink-jet printer.
- Discuss the major advantages of an ink-jet printer, and give an example of when an ink-jet printer would be used.
- Explain the difference between thermal ink-jet technology and piezoelectric ink-jet technology.
- Explain the terms *direct imaging press* and *digital toner-based printing*.
- Describe the operating principles of a direct imaging press and a digital toner-based printing system.
- Explain the term *direct imaging press*
- Describe the operating principles of a digital press.
- Outline the advantages digital printing has over every traditional printing method.
- Discuss the future implications and applications of digital presses to both consumers and the printing industry.

Introduction

This chapter introduces three printing processes not discussed anywhere else in this text. They are contained in one chapter, rather than as stand-alone sections, because few academic programs have facilities or equipment that allow access to and experimentation with them. The introductory nature of descriptions would result in short chapters when contrasted with the rest of the book. *Printing Technology* cannot ignore these processes and still be termed comprehensive—the three processes are simply too important.

Flexography, the first process discussed here, has long been a significant relief process used in the package printing industry. Over the past decade flexography has become increasingly sophisticated and is making inroads in some printing markets where offset technology has been the dominant printing process. Millions of images are produced each year by this method.

Ink-jet printing, the second process, is both a specialty printing process designed for relatively low quality printing of unique images at exceptionally high speeds and a process rapidly becoming a choice for proofing, both for FPO (for position only) and high-end contract work. The differentiating factor is whether it utilizes continuous ink-jet technology or a drop-on-demand system.

The third process discussed in this chapter is digital printing, both direct imaging presses and toner-based printing. Direct imaging presses combine the best of a conventional press while incorporating a digital workflow up until the imaging of the cylinders on press. First introduced in 1993, digital toner-based printing represents the second millennium revolution for the printing industry. The concept of a print run of one, unimaginable for a conventional press, is now possible because a digital printing system reimages the plate cylinder with each rotation.

Flexographic Printing

Flexography, commonly referred to as flexographic or flexo printing, is a rotary relief printing process in which the image carrier is a flexible rubber or photopolymer plate with raised image areas. This process was first introduced in the early 1900s. At that time it was called **aniline printing** because the inks were made from synthetic, organic aniline dyes.

A variety of packaging products, including foil, tissue, paper, paperboard, corrugated board, and plastic film, can be printed with flexo. In fact, flexographic printing owes its wide acceptance in the packaging industry to the invention of cellophane, which became popular in the 1930s because it proved ideal for food packaging. Cellophane cannot be printed with the offset process. Although it can be printed on with gravure, the cost of gravure cylinder production is so high that only extremely long press runs make cellophane printing economical.

Ironically, the flexo process, which is ideal for printing on cellophane food packaging, got off to a slow start in commercial printing because of the mistaken belief that aniline dyes were poisonous and that they would contaminate food products. Even though the United States government approved the use of aniline inks for food packaging in 1946, the name *aniline printing* still caused many package printers and food processors to reject the process. To overcome this problem, the aniline printing industry formally changed the name of the process to *flexographic printing* in 1952. Since this name change, flexography has grown to the point where it currently repre-

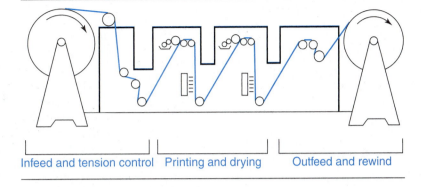

Figure 15.1 **Schematic of a typical web-fed outfeed and rewind flexographic printing press**

Infeed and tension control   Printing and drying   Outfeed and rewind

sents about 17 percent of the commercial printing market.

Components of a Flexographic Press

A flexographic press consists of three major units: the infeed, printing, and outfeed units (figure 15.1). As we discuss these units, it should become apparent that one of the greatest benefits of flexography is simplicity, from infeed to delivery.

Infeed Unit

The majority of flexographic printing is done on roll-fed materials such as film, foil, and laminates used for food, medical, and sanitary packaging materials. Sheet-fed flexo is also possible, and is the only practical solution for printing thicker materials such as corrugated board. As with other web systems (see chapter 11), the flexo infeed system consists of a roll stand with some type of tensioning device. The roll stand typically operates in conjunction with a dancer roll and brake to control web tension.

Sheet-fed flexographic infeed units are not far different from those found on sheet-fed offset presses, except that a sheet-fed flexo infeed system must be designed to feed heavier stock than is generally fed through an off-set press.

Printing Unit

The major advantage of flexographic printing lies in the printing unit, both in its simplicity and in its ability to deliver ink to a wide variety of substrates. Offset ink trains are designed to take relatively thick, viscous inks from an ink fountain and to spread them to thin consistencies by passing them through a number of distribution rollers and eventually to form rollers that ink the plate. Flexographic inks are much thinner than offset inks and require a much simpler inking system.

The heart of the flexo inking system is a roller with a cellular surface called the **anilox roll**. The process of manufacturing an anilox roll involves engraving a steel roller to form individual cells (from 10 to 550 cells per linear inch) on the roller surface. After the cells are formed on the steel roller, the roller is chrome plated or plasma coated with a ceramic material to protect it from corrosion and wear. The cells collect ink from the ink fountain and transfer it to the plate.

A great deal of research has gone into developing the structure, size, and number of

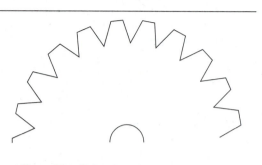

a. Pyramid cell structure

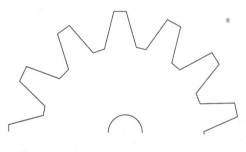

b. Quadrangular cell structure

Figure 15.2 **Cell structures.** (a) The pyramid cell structure has cells with sharply pointed bases. (b) The quadrangular structure produces cells with flat bases.

cells needed for particular printing applications. Two cells structures are commonly used. Under magnification, the **pyramid cell** structure appears as a number of inverted pyramids with sharply sloping walls that form cells which are pointed at their bases (figure 15.2a). The **quadrangular cell** structure appears as four-sided cavities with relatively straight walls that form cells which are relatively flat at their bases (figure 15.2b). The number, shape, and size of the cells required on the anilox roll depends on a variety of factors, including the type of ink to be used, the amount of ink to be transferred, the material to be printed on, the image to be printed, and whether the ink train is a three-roller or two-roller system.

Three-roller ink systems consist of an ink fountain roller, which is typically made of rubber, that passes ink to the anilox roll (figure 15.3). In these systems the fountain roller speed is kept constant but the anilox roll speed varies. As a result, the fountain roller not only passes ink to the anilox roll but it slips against it, wiping excess ink from the anilox roll. Therefore, ink metering is established in a three-roller ink system by controlling the rotating speed of the anilox roll.

Two-roller ink systems have no fountain roller. Instead, the anilox roll turns in the ink fountain directly and a steel doctor blade

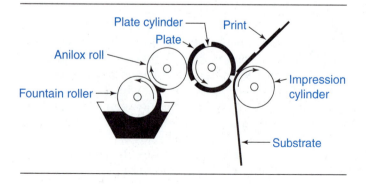

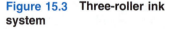

Figure 15.3 **Three-roller ink system**

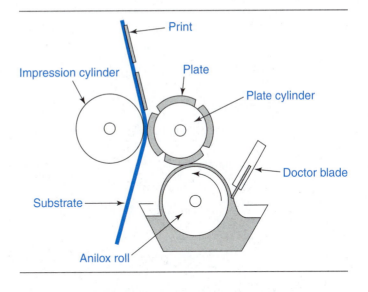

Figure 15.4 **Two-roller ink system**

is used to remove excess ink from the anilox roll (figure 15.4). The doctor blade is positioned parallel to and set at a 30-degree angle to the surface of the anilox roll. The doctor blade arrangement provides more precise and consistent ink metering, but it tends to produce more wear on the anilox roll than the three-roller system. This excess wear is compensated for to some extent by using quadrangular cells on the anilox rollers. Because quadrangular cells are square rather than pointed at their bases, they can tolerate more wear without significant reduction in cell capacity than can the pyramid-shaped cells used on three-roller systems (figure 15.5).

The plate cylinder is designed to hold the flexible flexographic plate through an adhesive. Unlike offset plates, flexographic plate size varies with the job to be printed. Generally, several repeat images are printed in succession from several plates mounted on the same cylinder. Thus, the size of the plate cylinder is chosen to match the repeated image size. That is, if the image to be printed is 6 inches, a 12-inch plate cylinder can be used to print

two repeated images. However, a 10-inch plate cylinder could not be used to print a 6-inch job. Because the plate cylinder must be changed to match the plate, and the anilox roll must also match the job, flexo presses are designed so that the plate cylinder and ink train can be removed easily and installed as a unit in the press each time a new job is run.

Many flexographic presses are configured with several printing units in a line so that four or more colors can be printed in one pass through the press. Drying units are located between each color head to dry the substrate before the next color is applied. Changing jobs on this type of flexographic press requires removing and replacing the printing units for each color. These replacements take time, but the lost time is compensated for because the new plates are mounted and proofed off press, which reduces on-press, make-ready time.

Pressure between the polished metal impression cylinder and the plate is adjusted to deliver what is termed a *kiss impression*. Because the film and laminate materials often

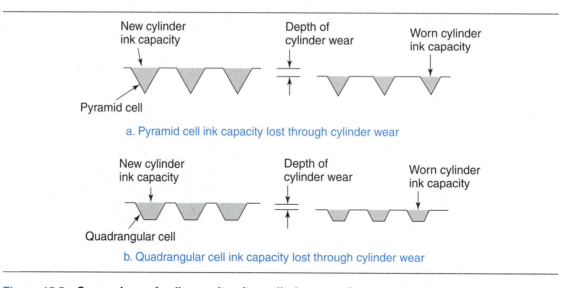

a. Pyramid cell ink capacity lost through cylinder wear

b. Quadrangular cell ink capacity lost through cylinder wear

Figure 15.5 Comparison of cell capacity after cylinder wear. Because of their shape, the ink capacity of quadrangular cells, which are wider at their bases than pyramid cells, contain more ink in their bases and are less affected by cylinder wear at the cells' surface.

printed with flexo are thin, and because the plate and image areas are flexible, the lightest possible impression pressure needed to transfer the image must be used in flexography. If the pressure is too great, it causes the image to spread and impedes quality. Far too much impression damages the plate or the substrate being printed.

Outfeed Unit

Outfeed units vary considerably with the type of work being printed. Many outfeed units consist only of a rewinder, which rewinds the substrate into a roll for later processing. A rewinder might be used for foil-laminated, printed candy bar wrappers, for example. After rewinding, the roll of printed wrappers is sent from the flexo plant to the candy manufacturer. There the roll is remounted and fed into the manufacturing line where each wrapper is filled with a candy bar, sealed, and placed in a carton. Often flexo presses are de-

signed to complement the manufacturing production line so that printing and packaging can be done as one continuous operation. Similarly, a sheet-fed flexo press for printing corrugated board may be configured to complement a converting machine that turns the printed board into folded cartons.

It is difficult to check for proper image register on substrates that are rewound for further processing. Stopping the press to check for register would destroy the image quality on the part of the web that was stopped in the printing unit(s). One approach to checking register on a moving web is to pass the web vertically before a large magnifying glass. The web is illuminated by a strobe light that flashes in time with the speed of the press. Synchronizing the strobe light with the press speed makes the image appear to be stationary in front of the magnifying glass. With this technique, the press operator is able to view register at web speed, and to make appropriate adjustments without shutting down the press.

Flexographic Plates

Flexographic plate composition must match to some extent the type of ink to be used and to the substrate to be printed. Both rubber and photopolymer plates are used.

Rubber Plates

Natural and synthetic **rubber plates** were the first type of flexo plates developed, and they are still used for some applications. The process of producing a rubber plate is not far different from the process used to produce photoengravings used in the hot type letterpress process (figure 15.6). A sheet of metal

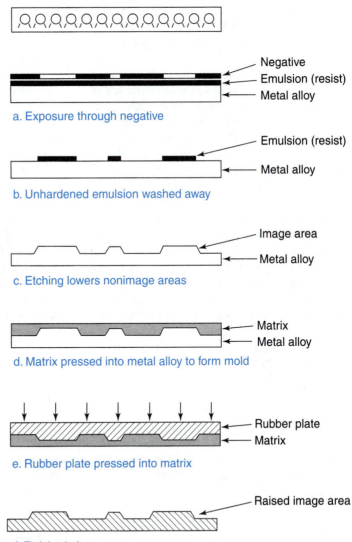

a. Exposure through negative

b. Unhardened emulsion washed away

c. Etching lowers nonimage areas

d. Matrix pressed into metal alloy to form mold

e. Rubber plate pressed into matrix

f. Finished plate

Figure 15.6 **Steps in producing a rubber plate**

alloy coated with a light-sensitive emulsion is first placed in a specially designed vacuum frame. The emulsion is not only light-sensitive, it is also an acid resist.

A negative is placed over the emulsion and light is passed through the negative. The acid resist hardens where light strikes the emulsion (image areas). During processing, the unhardened resist in the nonimage areas is washed away, leaving hardened resist only on the image areas. The metal alloy is then etched, which lowers the nonimage areas and leaves the image areas raised. The remaining resist is washed off.

The completed engraving is then moved to a molding press where a matrix (mold) of the engraving is made by pressing matrix material against the engraving with controlled heat and pressure. The matrix material sinks into the metal engraving to form the mold. The rubber plate is made from the matrix by pressing a rubber sheet into the matrix, again under controlled heat and pressure. Preformed sheets for rubber plates are available in a variety of thicknesses. The thickness depends on the job to be printed and the press to be used.

The major disadvantage of rubber plates is that they are more costly to make than photopolymer plates. Also, because they are made from an engraving, any plate problems identified during proofing must be corrected by remaking the engraving, which further increases the expense of the process.

Photopolymer Plates

Photopolymer plates eliminate many of the disadvantages of rubber plates. These plates are made from light-sensitive polymers (plastics) that are hardened by ultraviolet light. Photopolymer plates are made from both sheet and liquid materials.

Sheet photopolymer plates are supplied in a variety of thicknesses for specific applications. These plates are cut to the required size and placed in an ultraviolet light exposure unit (figure 15.7). One side of the plate is com-

pletely exposed to ultraviolet light to harden or cure the base of the plate. The plate is then turned over, a negative of the job is mounted over the uncured side, and the plate is again exposed to ultraviolet light. This hardens the plate in the image areas. The plate is then processed to remove the unhardened photopolymer from the nonimage areas, which lowers the plate surface in these nonimage areas. After processing, the plate is dried and given a postexposure dose of ultraviolet light to cure the whole plate.

Liquid photopolymer plates are made in a special ultraviolet light exposure unit. In this process, a clear plastic protective cover film is mounted over a negative transparency which is placed emulsion side up on the exposure unit (figure 15.8a). A layer of liquid photopolymer is then deposited by a motorized carriage over the transparency and cover film. The carriage deposits the liquid evenly over the cover film and controls the thickness of the deposit. While the carriage deposits the liquid, it also places a substrate sheet over the liquid (figure 15.8b).

The substrate sheet is specially coated on one side to bond with the liquid photopolymer and to serve as the back of the plate after exposure. Exposure is made first on the substrate side of plate. This exposure hardens a thin base layer of the liquid photopolymer and causes it to adhere to the plate substrate. A second exposure through the negative forms the image on the plate (figure 15.8c). As with sheet materials, the image areas are hardened by this exposure. The nonimage areas, however, remain liquid. Processing removes unwanted liquid in the nonimage areas to leave raised image areas. A postexposure is then made to cure the whole plate (figure 15.8d).

Flexographic Presses

Three basic configurations are used in flexography. The **stack press** was the first type of press designed and is used for multicolor printing (figure 15.9). It consists of color sta-

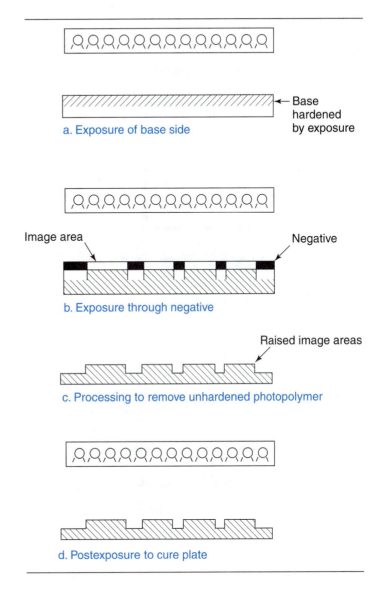

a. Exposure of base side

← Base
hardened
by exposure

Image area   Negative

b. Exposure through negative

Raised image areas

c. Processing to remove unhardened photopolymer

d. Postexposure to cure plate

Figure 15.7   Steps in producing a sheet photopolymer plate

tions that are stacked vertically. A stack press can include two to eight separate color stations, with each station having its own inking rollers, plate cylinder, and impression cylinder. The main advantage of this configuration is the ability to reverse the web easily to allow for both sides of the substrate to be printed. One drawback is trying to maintain correct register due to the fact that the web is not supported between the printing stations, but this can be avoided by staying with thicker papers and heavier-gauge materials that have less stretch.

A **central impression press** uses a large-diameter common impression cylinder that the web travels around from one station to the

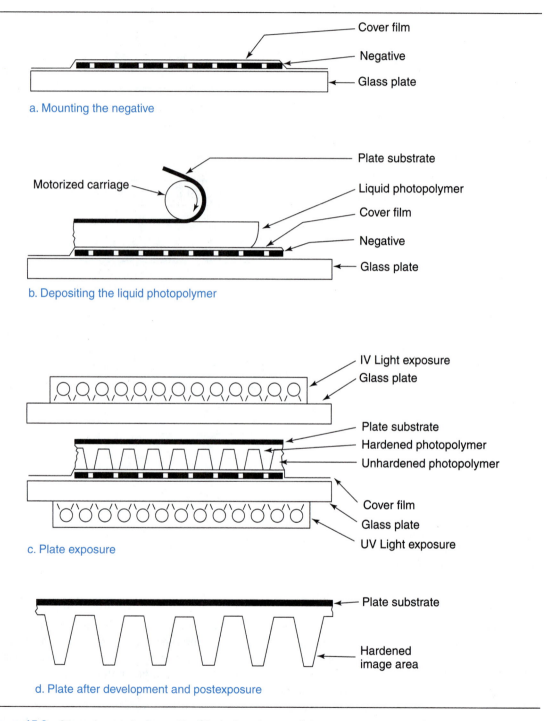

a. Mounting the negative

b. Depositing the liquid photopolymer

c. Plate exposure

d. Plate after development and postexposure

Figure 15.8 **Steps in producing a liquid photopolymer plate**

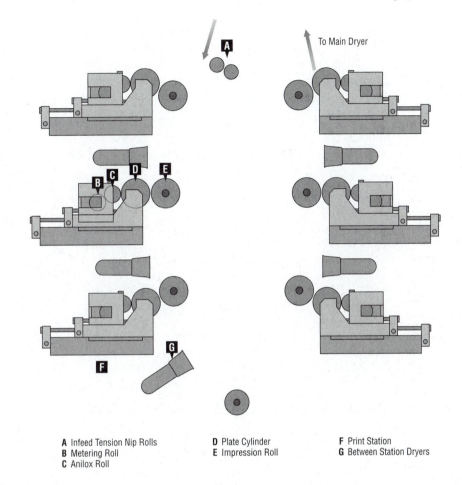

To Main Dryer

A Infeed Tension Nip Rolls
B Metering Roll
C Anilox Roll

D Plate Cylinder
E Impression Roll

F Print Station
G Between Station Dryers

Figure 15.9 Stack press.
Courtesy of Flexographic Technical Association.

next (figure 15.10). Registration is maintained better with this type of press configuration, but reversing the web is more difficult. Accurate registration, due to the fact that the web is supported between stations, allows for printing on substrates such as stretchable plastic film.

In-line presses are the third type of multicolor press (figure 15.11). Separate print stations are mounted in a horizontal line form front to back. Tension control devices are used to maintain tight register, because the distance the web travels between print stations can cause stretch. A variety of widths can be printed in this configuration, and reversing can be done through the use of turning bars to turn over the web.

The Future of Flexography

For years flexography had the reputation of producing relatively low-quality printed im-

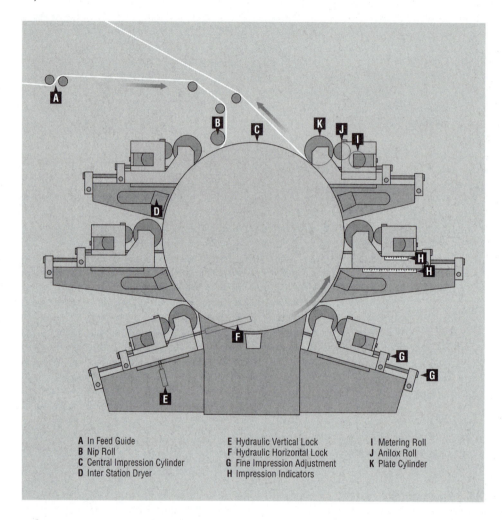

A In Feed Guide
B Nip Roll
C Central Impression Cylinder
D Inter Station Dryer

E Hydraulic Vertical Lock
F Hydraulic Horizontal Lock
G Fine Impression Adjustment
H Impression Indicators

I Metering Roll
J Anilox Roll
K Plate Cylinder

Figure 15.10   Central impression press.
Courtesy of Flexographic Technical Association.

ages, suitable only for package printing on nontraditional substrates such as foil and corrugated board. With the developments in inks and plates that are taking place today, this reputation is rapidly changing to where flexography is now being used increasingly for halftone work, critical line work, and four-color printing on paper stock (plate R).

When compared to offset printing, flexographic printing offers two major advan-

tages: long-run capabilities and relatively low waste during make-ready. Flexo can be used for press runs exceeding 5 million impressions. The flexible plate wears very little during a press run because of the low pressure used for impression. Also, all make-ready is done off press; this eliminates waste because the plate is proofed and produces quality copy after a few impressions once it is mounted on the press. Further, ink and water balance does

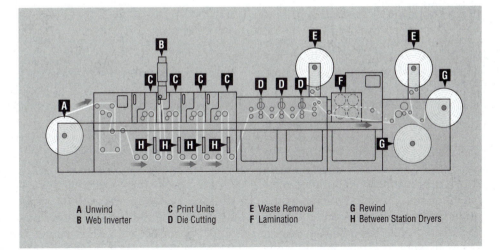

Figure 15.11 In-line press.
Courtesy of Flexographic Technical Association.

not have to be achieved as it does in offset lith-ography. As a result, press start up is quicker and, once the ink metering system is adjusted, image quality remains constant throughout the press run.

Another development that has created a dramatic upsurge in the interest in flexogra-phy is the digital imaging of the plates. Laser imaging permits the printing of very small dots, which had traditionally been a challenge for flexography. With finer dots and resolu-tions, finer halftone screens and finer image quality can be attained. The sleeve technology that is developing in gravure printing (refer to chapter 14) is also being used in flexography. This allows for faster press speeds and the po-tential for better registration than imaging flat sheet material.

One other reason the future of flexogra-phy is bright is because it is suitable for print-ing with water-based inks as well as solvent-based inks. Solvent-based inks have long been used for quality printing because they produce excellent color fidelity and dry quickly. These qualities make solvent-based inks extremely

suitable for four-color process printing on coated papers. The major disadvantage of these inks, however, is that during drying the evaporating solvent pollutes the environment.

Over the last several years, the United States government has established environ-mental pollution guidelines that have forced many printers to install complex and expen-sive fume recovery systems. Water-based inks, which do not pollute the environment, elimi-nate this need. As a result, flexography is be-ing used increasingly for color printing on a variety of papers, particularly for comic books and newspaper printing. Flexography was first used to print a newspaper in 1986. Since then there have been tremendous gains, with 36 American newspapers and 14 European newspapers using the process as of the end of 1999. Flexography produces clean sharp colors, and the water-based instant-dry ink does not rub off on the reader's hands as do solvent-based inks. As environmental controls become more stringent, and as research con-tinues in flexographic plates, ink, and register systems, the move toward flexo will continue.

Ink-Jet Printing

Ink-jet printing produces an image by directing individual tiny drops of ink, which are given an electrical charge, from an orifice (opening) through a small air gap to a printing surface (figure 15.12). This is a nonimpact process and can be used to print on a variety of substrates, including corrugated board, plastics, fabric, and paper. Ink-jet printing was originally used in personalizing direct-mail pieces. This has been traditionally known as direct mail merging; it occurs when a computer inserts database information into personalized printed pieces. This process has become extremely sophisticated and is now referred to as **variable data printing (VDP).** With VDP it is possible to create completely customized documents for individual recipients.

All ink-jet system processes rely on computer input to form a dot-matrix image that is made up of individual drops of ink. The major difference between ink-jet systems is whether the ink spray is *continuous* or *drop-on-demand*.

Continuous Ink-jet Technology

In **continuous ink-jet technology,** each ink orifice sprays ink drops toward the printing surface continuously. When the ink drops leave the orifice, they are subjected to electric charges that vary in strength based on digitized computer information. The electrical charges of various strengths deflect the ink drops from a straight path and move them in the appropriate directions to produce the desired dot-matrix image. Drops not needed in the matrix are given a charge that deflects them into the ink recycling system.

Commonly used in the packaging industry, continuous ink-jet technology, pioneered by Videojet Systems International, is able to print information, such as date and time, serialized numbers, and characters in any directions, in single or numerous lines and in a variety of sizes and can count how many

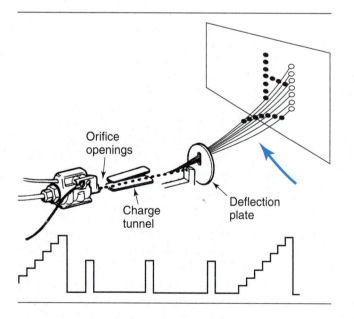

Orifice
openings

Charge
tunnel

Deflection
plate

Figure 15.12 Continuous ink-jet printing

times they print at speeds up to 1,200 feet per minute. This type of ink-jet printing works by continuously emitting a small stream of ink through a single ink orifice. When liquid is forced through a small orifice at high speed, it tends to break into a spray containing drops of various sizes. To control drop size and direction, the ink is given a frequency by a vibrating crystal. This frequency regulates the size, shape, and spacing of the emitted drops.

A variation on continuous ink-jet technology uses an **array**, rather than a single orifice (figure 15.13). Like regular continuous ink-jet technology, this is a noncontact form of printing in which the ink is given a frequency by a vibrating crystal. In an array, 100 to 200 nozzles can generate over 15 million droplets of ink per second, which allows for high-resolution images and flexibility in image creation (figure 15.14). Over 50,000 characters per second can be produced with an orifice array; only about 13,000 characters per second can be produced with a single orifice system.

Drop-on-Demand Systems

In a **drop-on-demand system** the printer produces a drop from the ink orifice only when the drop is needed to form the matrix image. The ink drops are given a frequency in a manner similar to that used for continuous drops. There are two main approaches to drop-on-demand ink-jet technology: thermal (bubble) and piezoelectric technology (figure 15.15).

Thermal Ink-jet Technology

Thermal ink-jet or bubble-jet technology uses heat to force small drops of ink out at high speed onto the substrate. This is accomplished by applying an electrical current to small resistors built into the nozzle. The ink is heated within the nozzle, causing it to vaporize locally and then form a bubble, which provides the force to eject the ink from the nozzle.

Piezoelectric Ink-jet Technology

Piezoelectric ink jet uses electrical impulses based on digitized information to cause individual drops to be squeezed out of the ink ori-

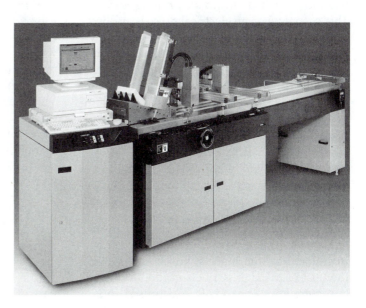

Figure 15.13 **A continuous ink-jet imaging system utilizing array technology.**
Courtesy of Marconi Data Systems, Inc.

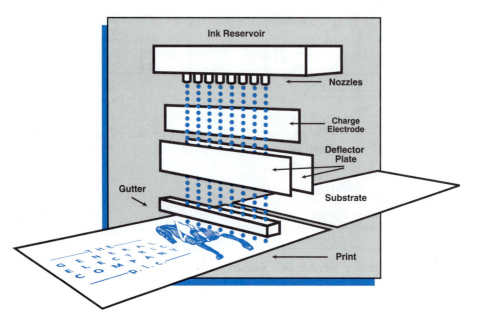

Figure 15.14 **Continuous ink-jet array.** This technology can produce high-resolution images at line speeds of up to 1,200 feet per minute.
Courtesy of Marconi Data Systems, Inc.

fice and propelled toward the printing surface. This occurs when an electrical pulse is applied to a piezo crystal, causing it to contract slightly and force the ink onto the substrate. Drop-on-demand units have the advantage of being less complicated than continuous-spray systems, because they do not require a dot deflection system to place needed dots or remove unwanted drops. They are also more economical, because ink is provided only where it is needed to form the image (figure 15.16).

Ink-jet Applications

Continuous ink-jet technology has proved invaluable in packaging by providing bar codes, manufacturer information, postal codes, and the host of tracking symbols needed to maintain complex databases. It is also used in labeling and for high-volume direct-mail im-

printing. Piezoelectric has become the choice for high-end proofers in the printing workflow, as in the Agfa Sherpa proofer series, which provides large-format, six-color contract quality proofs (figure 15.17). With a wider color gamut than a traditional press, acceptable contract color is achievable with the correct color profiles and calibration. And, as fewer customers demand to see halftone dots in their proofs, this technology will most likely continue to replace high-end, expensive halftone dot proofers.

Drop-on demand has grown from a slow process able to print only low-resolution images to a high-quality, high-resolution image technology capable of providing acceptable proofs to customers. This has also been helped by the development of color profiles that are part of current operating systems (or can be added on) and better color management. Ink-

The difference between thermal ink-jet printers and piezoelectric ink-jet printers is in how the ink is expelled. In a thermal ink-jet printer, resistors built into the nozzle heat up when an electrical charge is applied, which heats up ink in the reservoir, causing a bubble to form. The bubble displaces the ink and forces it onto the paper. In a piezoelectric ink-jet printer, a small electrical current makes an integrated piezo crystal contract, forcing ink from the nozzle.

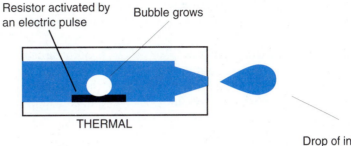

THERMAL

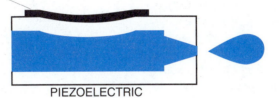

PIEZOELECTRIC

Figure 15.15 **Comparison of thermal and piezoelectric ink-jet technology**

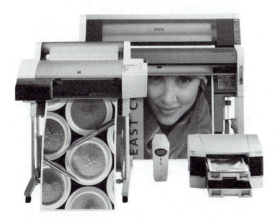

Figure 15.16 **Drop-on-demand ink-jet printers come in a variety of formats.**
Courtesy of Epson America, Inc.

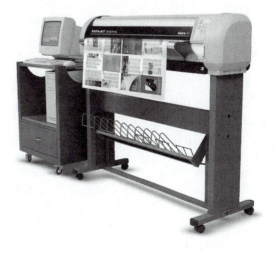

Figure 15.17 **A large format ink-jet proofer.**
Courtesy of Agfa Corporation.

jet printers have become relatively inexpensive and are increasingly being used by customers prior to submitting their work to the printer. In addition, low-end ink-jet printers are invariably bundled with PC purchases now, further ensuring the continued use of this technology.

Ink-jet printers are used extensively in check printing operations. Large corporations produce thousands of pay-roll checks every week. Each has a different name and dollar amount. Ink-jet printing is ideally suited to this application. Check blanks with the company name and bank identification information are preprinted as continuous, perforated rolls or sheets by offset printing. The variable information (name, address, and amount) is added by running the preprinted checks through an ink-jet printer.

One final advantage of ink-jet printing is that the process is nonimpact, which means the image carrier is not forced against the printing substrate. This feature makes it possible to print with ink jet on almost any surface, regardless of surface texture, shape, or pressure resistance. Ink-jet printing can place an image on a plastic container or bubble package (or even an egg yolk) as easily and as quickly as it can on paper, a textured surface such as sandpaper, or a curved surface such as a pill or capsule.

Digital Printing

Digital printing has revolutionized the printing industry. It has changed the production cycle and drastically shortened the turnaround time of a job. There are two basic approaches to digital printing: direct imaging or hybrid presses and digital toner-based printing.

Direct Imaging Presses
Direct imaging presses are presses with a digital front end and a conventional ink-based printing unit. Plates are imaged on press from digital data received by networking, essentially incorporating a computer-to-plate (C-T-P) unit within the press. There are several advantages to this type of press over a conventional press:

- Because the plate cassette is mounted on the press prior to imaging, there are almost no registration problems.
- The system significantly reduces press make-ready time.
- The plate often uses waterless technology, which is more stable and allows greater ink densities than water-based lithography.
- Material costs are competitive with traditional systems, but the process saves as much as 60 percent in labor costs.

Plate Exposure
Heidelberg is one of the leaders in direct imaging (DI) presses. The Heidelberg QuickMaster DI is a 13 by 19 inch format press that combines the best of direct imaging technology with offset technology (figure 15.18). It utilizes polyester plates created by Presstek that are imaged through an **ablation** process. The top silicon layer is vaporized by lasers, which expose the ink-receptive base layer. Plates are fed off a supply roll within the cylinder with material sufficient for 35 consecutive print jobs. All four plates are imaged simultaneously and in perfect register in six minutes at a resolution of 1,270 dpi. The plates are also able to be imaged at 2,540 dpi, sufficient for a 200-lpi screen. The waterless ink technology used supports high ink densities and is equipped with 12 ink rollers to provide a deep and even inking of solid areas (figure 15.19).

The new Speedmaster 74 DI press, a 20 by 29 inch format (four up) DI press, is equipped with automatic plate loading, with

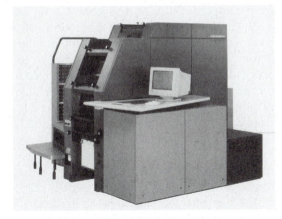

imaging of Presstek PEARLgold™ plates at 2,400 dpi in under three and a half minutes (figure 15.20). It uses Creo Squarespot© thermal imaging technology, which allows simultaneous imaging of plates in up to six printing units.

The main limitations of a direct imaging press is that duplex printing can be done only by the operator running the sheets through again with new plates and that once a plate is etched it cannot be altered. Although this technology does not allow for true variable data printing (VDP), certain types of versioning can be done by printing color shells that can then run through a digital printer for personalization. Direct imaging presses are gaining in acceptance due to the fact that the back end is

Imaging process
Digitally driven laser beams etch small depressions into specially treated silicon plates, not unlike the gravure process. Waterless ink flows into the depressions to create the image area while silicon protects the nonimage areas. Once etched, plates cannot be altered, making customization impractical.

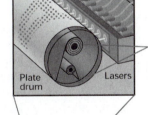

Plate drum

Lasers

Automated platemaking and cleanup
Material for 35 plates is stored on cassettes inside the unit. Used plates are wound onto other rollers. Blanket cleanup is also automated.

Paper path
Paper and other substrates stay on the large impression cylinder. This reduces the chance of shifting or misregistration, although trapping is still necessary.

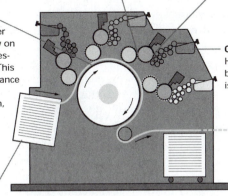

Colors
High ink density is possible because the SWOP ink is absorbed by the paper.

Single-sided printing
Only one side can be printed at a time. For duplex printing, the operator must run sheets through again, with new plates.

Input
Various substrates including paper are sheet-fed. Maximum sheet size is 18 1/8" x 13 3/8".

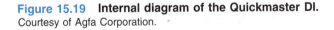

Figure 15.19 **Internal diagram of the Quickmaster DI.**
Courtesy of Agfa Corporation.

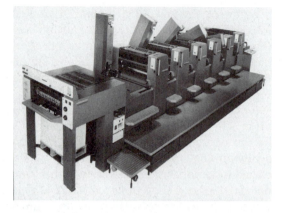

Figure 15.20 **A high-end digital imaging press capable of 15,000 sheets per hour.**
Courtesy of Heidelberg USA, Inc.

truly an offset press and provides quality output measurable against completely conventional presses, yet with a far faster turn-around time and less manual labor. There are predictions that by the year 2005 purchase of direct imaging presses may outnumber those of conventional presses.

Digital Toner Based Printing

Digital toner-based printing has truly caused a revolution in printing. Originally introduced in 1993, it has allowed "full-color pages to be printed directly or remotely from digital page data with the ability to vary the information at every cylinder revolution."[1] (Landa-Indigo) Four-color jobs can now be turned around in hours, rather than days or weeks, and print runs of one are now possible.

Press Configuration

Different vendors have different solutions, but the two basic digital print imaging technologies used are **laser electrophotographic** and **LED electrophotographic**. Digital printers

1. Mr. Benny Landa, Chairman and Chief Executive Officer of Indigo Group.

from companies such as Xerox and Canon use a digitally driven laser beam that reflects off a rotating prism to charge parts of the imaging drum. Toner powder is then attracted to the charged parts and subsequently transferred to the paper. Indigo, a manufacturer of digital printing presses, uses a liquid ink called ElectroInk rather than a dry toner (figure 15.21). Charged ink is injected at the plate, adhering to any area with an opposite charge. This plate transfers the image to a blanket, which in turn transfers it to the substrate. When the ElectroInk contacts the substrate, it hardens instantly and peels from the blanket completely. This offers two major advantages. First, because the ink dries upon contact with the paper, dimensional stability is guaranteed. Most offset inks dry on the paper by absorption or **aerial oxidation,** which introduces moisture into the sheet or leaves a wet ink layer (see chapter 16). When dimensional stability is assured, more accurate color is possible.

The second primary advantage, which is also true for LED (light-emitting diode) electrophotographic imaging, is that no residual ink remains on the blanket after each rotation. In contrast, conventional ink splits between the paper and blanket and leaves a residue. The lack of residual ink also helps eliminate dot gain. Because unused ink does not build up on the blanket, halftone dot size is assured.

Current imaging technology in the Indigo UltraStream™ uses 12 laser beams to image the photo-imaging plate and can operate at 240 feet per minute. Whereas the printing engine in conventional offset prints just one color, the UltraStream print engine prints all colors, with multiple engines multiplying throughput. The UltraStream is a cut-sheet seven-color press capable of 180 lpi.

Xeikon, one of the leading manufacturers of digital printing presses, both under their name and as an original equipment manufacturer for other vendors, has sheet-fed and web-fed press products. Xeikon utilizes an LED-array-based dry toner electrophotogra-

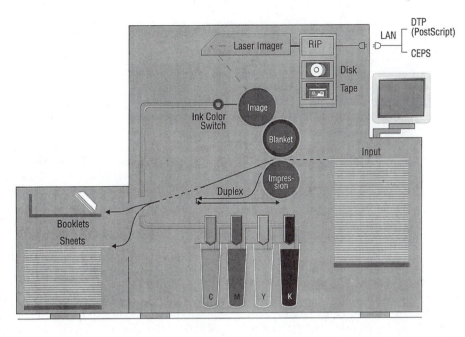

Figure 15.21 **Schematic of an Indigo digital toner-based press.** This system uses a liquid ink instead of a dry toner.
Courtesy of Indigo America, Inc.

phy (figure 15.22). The LED array exposes the charged photoconductor drum to different levels of light, creating conductive areas on the drum. Toner particles adhere to the charged area, forming the image that will be trans-ferred to the drum. Their sheet-fed solution, the CSP 320 D, uses one-pass-duplex technology that prints both sides of the substrate simultaneously, resulting in accurate back-to-front registration. Sheet size ranges from 8.5

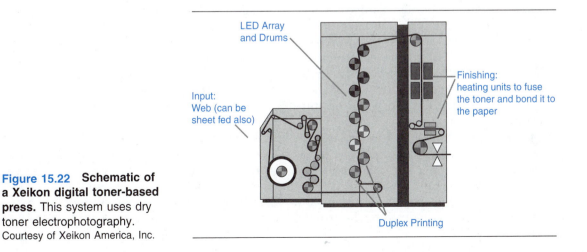

Figure 15.22 **Schematic of a Xeikon digital toner-based press.** This system uses dry toner electrophotography.
Courtesy of Xeikon America, Inc.

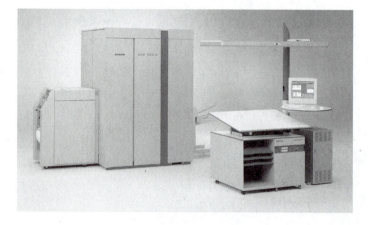

Figure 15.23   Digital toner-based press. This is a sheet fed unit capable of over 900 8.5 by 11 inch full-color duplex impressions per hour.
Courtesy of Xeikon America, Inc.

by 11 inches up to 12.6 by 18.5 inches on a variety of standard substrates, with speeds of up to 960 A4 (8.5 by 11 inches) full-color duplex impressions an hour. The CSP 320 D can achieve image quality equivalent to 2,400 dpi with a variety of screenings up to 175 lpi (figure 15.23).

Implications of Direct Digital Presses

Before Gutenberg, there was **demand-based publishing.** In demand-based publishing, if people wanted and could afford books they looked for ones to purchase or paid scribes to copy them. Gutenberg created **market-based publishing.** Gutenberg's invention created a situation where the printer decided what to print, prepared many copies, and then sought to convince the market it wanted the product.

For the past 500 years there have been few opportunities for individuals to participate in a demand-based information environment. Someone else decided what to reproduce and distribute.

The introduction of DTP in 1984 was the first step toward individual control and access to focused information. The reality of a true digital press in 1993 took the next step toward these goals, and will continue to transform both the graphic arts industry and our daily lives.

Personalized Magazines and Other Information Pieces

Every home receives hundreds of pounds of magazines and newspapers each year. Much of this material goes unread. There are probably parts of the daily newspaper you do not read. Even special interest magazines, such as *Mac-World, Sports Illustrated*, or the *Worm Runner's Journal*, contain articles of little or no interest to the subscriber. All of these unread, and unwanted, pages come as part of a total package, clutter our homes, and must be discarded.

Digital presses can be used to personalize every publication that comes to your home. Advertisers that sell products in your interest areas can purchase advertising space in your exclusive magazine or newspaper.

In the office community database management can be used to create one-of-a-kind reports, reference manuals, and information books for every employee.

Elimination of Traditional Bookstores

Bookstores sell books. They are everywhere when you walk in the door. Book lovers revel in the environment. However, even the most ardent book lover does not need 200 copies of the same book—one copy suffices.

Large bookstores are large because they need to shelve many copies of every title. If you do not come in and make a purchase then that storage space is wasted. Bookstores of the future may shelve only one sample copy of a work and print a fresh copy on a digital press when you have made your decision to purchase. Personalized information can be included in the copy in the process.

No Out-of-Print Books

Publishers only print and promote books that they can sell. If, after the first year of publication, the buying population of a book dwindles, then the publisher stops printing and promoting that book. The book then becomes out of print and is only available through libraries, used bookstores, or from a friend.

With digital presses a book will never go out of print. Computer archives can store digital information and anyone can order one or many copies of any book, no matter its current status.

Mass Marketing Replaced by Personalized Marketing

Mass marketing involves sending millions of pieces of mail to millions of individuals with the hope of selling an idea, service, or product to one or two percent of those individuals. Organizations like the Publisher's Clearinghouse have used ink-jet printing to customize direct mail solicitations with considerable success because individuals are more likely to open and read items that contain their names.

Indigo's founder, Benny Landa, offered an image of a customer who wishes to promote two or three dozen out of several thousand company products. However, there is no point to offering lawnmowers to apartment dwellers or diapers to pensioners. The smart company wants to customize individual color fliers so that each consumer sees only products he or she might actually buy. With a direct digital press, every consumer can receive a different catalog. It is now possible to deliver custom catalogs containing items the seller knows matches each buyer's personal interest.

In this example, the customer could program the digital press to deliver custom catalogs containing items it knows match your personal interests. Image databases could also be used to place your photograph next to the motorcycle, car, yacht, or pogo stick the customer wants you to buy.

Virtual Elimination of Warehousing

Traditional printing relies upon economies of scale. Companies order tens of thousands of copies of books, brochures, technical booklets, reference sheets, promotional items, and training manuals and store them for future use. The cost of warehouse space can be considerable, however.

All print storage space can be replaced by a digital press, computer memory, and a lot of blank paper. When a document is needed it can be simply ordered, printed, and delivered. Demand printing becomes a reality in this way.

Low-cost Access to Quality Color

According to the Xerox Corporation, their newest digital printer, which they refer to as a digital press, has achieved the low operating cost (service plus consumables) of less than 10 cents per page. This will allow retailers to sell copies for close to 50 cents a page, which is thought by some to be the point at which the market demand for color documents will truly take off.

Anyone with a computer and the right software can afford to prepare and create professional looking documents for personal use with digital printers. Small to medium business can print a variety of short-run promotional pieces at competitive prices and not have to store excess inventory. The ability to personalize a document with every revolution of the drum is already changing the face of advertising today.

Digital printing will have a significant impact on your life and career in printing.

Key Terms

flexography
aniline printing
anilox roll
pyramid cell
quadrangular cell
three-roller ink system
two-roller ink system
rubber plate
photopolymer plates
sheet photopolymer

liquid photopolymer
stack press
central impression press
in-line press
ink-jet printing
variable data printing (VDP)
continuous ink-jet technology
array
drop-on-demand system
thermal ink jet

piezoelectric ink jet
direct imaging press
ablation
digital toner-based printing
laser electrophotographic
LED electrophotographic
aerial oxidation
demand-based publishing
market-based publishing

Review Questions

1. What type of products are printed primarily with flexography?

2. What are the major components of a flexographic press?

3. What is the purpose of the anilox roll? Why does it have surface cells?

4. What is the difference between the pyramid cell structure and the quadrangular cell structure?

5. Why is the quadrangular cell structure used on ink systems that require a doctor blade?

6. How are rubber flexographic plates made?

7. Describe the processes for producing a sheet photopolymer plate and a liquid photopolymer plate.

8. Describe the three different flexographic press configurations.

9. What is the difference between continuous ink-jet printing and drop-on-demand ink-jet printing?

10. What is the difference between thermal ink-jet printing and piezoelectric ink-jet printing?

11. Explain the difference between a direct imaging press and digital toner-based printing.

12. What advantages does a digital toner-based press have over traditional printing methods?

16

Paper and Ink

Historical Background

Throughout the history of printing, the demand for paper has increased constantly. The paper industry has evolved to meet this growing demand. It is the craft of early papermakers that allows us to hold Gutenberg's first Bible today, 500 years after the sheets left his press.

The first paperlike material, called *papyrus*, was invented by the Egyptians about five thousand years ago. This paper was made from the papyrus plant, which grew along the banks of the Nile River. To make the paper the pith, or center of the plant, was first cut into strips. These strips were then glued together in thin, crosswise layers to form sheets. After pressing and drying, the sheets were ready to use. Papyrus sheets are still readable after more than five millennia.

The first truly modern paper was invented in China by Ts'si Lun in A.D. 105. Lun first shredded cloth fibers into a special hot-water solution. The resulting fiber solution was then poured into a frame covered with a loosely woven cloth screen. The water in the solution drained through the cloth, leaving fine, interwoven fibers on the screen. The frame was then placed in the sun to dry. Any remaining water evaporated from the fibers, resulting in paper.

Lun later created *laid papers* by immersing the frame in the fiber solution and gently raising the frame to the surface. This laid technique produced a better quality paper than did the earlier method. The laid process was used to produce all paper until around 1800.

The first automated process was developed in 1798 in the paper mill of M. Didot, member of a famous printing-publishing family, in Essonnes, France. Nicolas Louis Robert, a superintendent in Didot's mill, developed the idea of making paper by pouring the fiber solution onto a continuously moving wire belt. After the water drained through the belt, the paper was passed between felt-covered rollers. The machine worked very well and, with time for improvements, would have been a commercial success. However, the French Revolution and several lawsuits with Didot prevented Robert from reaching that goal.

In 1801 an associate of the Didot family, John Gamble, joined the Fourdrinier brothers in a partnership to develop Robert's idea in England. By 1807 they had designed and constructed the first fully automated, continuous papermaking machine.

In this process the fiber solution, called *stuff*, was deposited from a special box onto a finely woven copper wire belt. The belt moved both forward and side to side. The belt's copper web was 54 inches wide and 31 feet long. The full length of the machine, including driers, was almost 1000 feet. It took seven workers to operate and could produce a continuous roll of paper at the rate of more than 600 feet an hour.

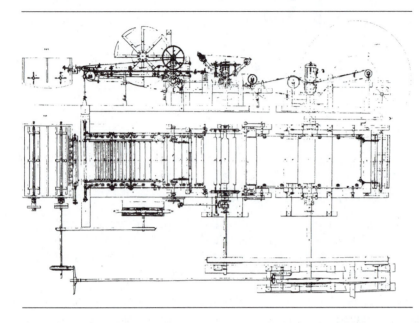

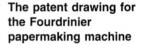

The patent drawing for the Fourdrinier papermaking machine

The papermaking machine operated better than expected and created great excitement. At long last, here was a way to meet the ever growing demand for printing papers. Like so many other creative people, the men who perfected one of the greatest contributions to modern printing died in poverty. The Fourdriniers lost a fortune attempting to market their device. Although by 1860 thousands of tons of paper were being produced on auto-mated machines all over the world, none of the papermaking pioneers ever benefited financially from the effort.

While many refinements and improvements have been made, the basic design of the 1807 machine is still used today to produce all paper. The machine is called a Fourdrinier in honor of the brothers and the partnership that gave the world the supply of paper it needed.

Objectives

After completing this chapter, you will be able to:

- Recall the basic papermaking process.
- Define six paper characteristics: bulk, opacity, finish, coated versus noncoated, reflectance, and grain.
- Classify paper into four common groups and recognize the characteristics of each.
- Recognize and define common paper terms such as ream, M weight, substance weight, and equivalent weight.
- Calculate press sheet cuts from standard paper sizes.

■ List and define the properties of ink, including viscosity, tack, and drying time.

■ List the common groups of ingredients of printing ink, including pigment, vehicle, and additives.

■ Describe the characteristics of lithographic, screen printing, letterpress, flexographic, and gravure inks.

■ Recognize the importance of color standards and accurate ink specifications.

■ List the five major components of ultraviolet-curing inks.

Introduction

Two of the most important ingredients for the printing processes are ink and paper. Traditionally printing consisted of images set in dense black ink on white paper. For many years, the problems of creating the ink and paper were so troublesome and time consuming that no one bothered to use different colors.

Today, however, the printer and the printing customer are faced with another problem. There are so many different kinds of paper—with different colors, textures, finishes, thicknesses, and weights—that it is hard to choose among them. So many different kinds of ink, each formulated for a specific process, problem, or paper, are available in any color of the spectrum that the printer is hard-pressed to understand even a fraction of the possible choices.

The purpose of this chapter is to organize the information on paper and ink into an understandable form. It is divided into two sections. The first section deals with paper; the second section deals with ink. Each section classifies materials and examines ideas that are important for a novice printer to understand.

Section 1: Paper

Introduction to Paper

The printed paper you are now reading and the sheets that form this book are made from cellulose fibers. Cellulose is the basic component of trees. By chopping wood into very small chips and then cooking them in a water mixture, the cellulose fibers can be released and used for papermaking. Wood fibers are filled with tree sap and bonding agents called **lignin**, which must be bleached or removed before making a sheet of printing paper. The brown sack you put your purchases in at the grocery store shows the color of unbleached wood fibers.

Historically, the bleaching process to remove lignin made papermaking among the most environmentally polluting industries in the world. Today, strict recycling of wastewater, efficient filtration devices, and water purification systems have drastically reduced environmental damage done by the industry.

Almost all industrial printing paper is made from a combination of softwoods (from

Georgia and South Carolina) and hardwoods (from Canada). The different characteristics of these woods together produce strong, durable paper.

Although wood is the most common source of cellulose fibers for papermaking, any cellulose fibers can be used. Cotton was once used widely for this purpose in the United States. The primary fiber source was cotton rags. Even today we use the term *rag content* to describe the percentage of cotton fibers in a sheet of paper. Cotton does not have lignin and therefore does not require the use of intense acids in the bleaching process. Any trace of acid in paper reduces its permanency, causes brittleness, and can create *acid burns* in the paper years after production. In some areas of the United States, legal documents must be typed or printed on 100 percent rag paper by law to ensure that they will survive at least

100 years. The sheets Gutenberg used to print his Bible in 1452 are still in good condition more than 500 years later. They were made from linen rags, without acid.

One fascinating application of the fact that any cellulose-based material can be used to make paper is a current project by the Levi Straus company. The company is converting waste from the manufacture of blue jeans to produce a specialty paper popular with contemporary graphic designers. *Blue jean paper* is exceptionally strong, permanent, and distinctive, and it is also very printable.

Papermaking

Early papermaking involved first preparing a *slurry* that was made from cellulose fibers suspended in water. The slurry was as much as 95 percent water and five percent fibers. A fine-meshed screen would then be dipped into

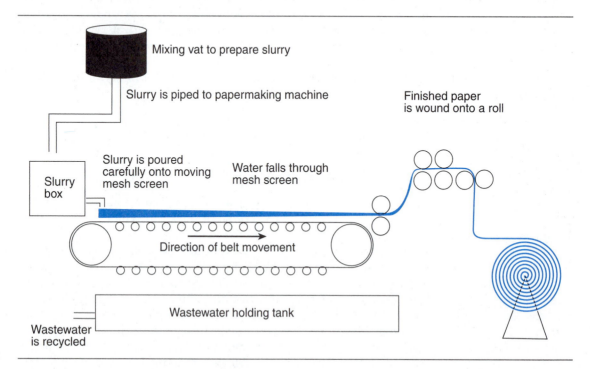

Figure 16.1   **Schematic of the Fourdrinier machine**

the slurry. Water would fall through the screen, leaving interwoven fibers on the screen. The fibers would be dried and ironed to produce paper.

Papermaking technology was revolutionized by the invention of the Fourdrinier machine in the nineteenth century. Automatic papermaking vastly increased the supply of material for the growing printing industry.

The Fourdrinier follows the same basic techniques as the hand papermaking process just described (figure 16.1). The slurry is prepared in a large mixing vat. Dyes and chemical additives are mixed with the slurry to give different characteristics to the finished paper. The slurry is then piped to the machine and poured carefully onto a moving mesh screen. The screen both moves forward and jogs from side to side. The side-to-side movement shakes the majority of fibers so they are parallel and point in the direction of the belt's movement (figure 16.2). The direction of the fibers defines paper grain (see the following Paper Characteristics section). The side-to-side motion also hastens the fall of water through the screen.

Enough water has been removed from the slurry at the end of the belt so the fiber sheet can be lifted free. The web of new paper is then passed through a variety of rollers to impart different characteristics. Some rollers are heated to further remove moisture. Others polish the paper or add a *watermark*, or design. Special textures such as a linen or parchment finish can even be embossed into the still soft sheet. Finally, the paper is wound onto a large roll for future use.

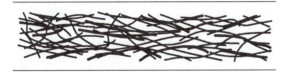

Figure 16.2 Magnified cross section of paper showing intertwined cellulose fibers

Paper Characteristics

Papermaking technology can deliver a nearly unlimited array of characteristics for use by the printing industry. Some characteristics are natural consequences of the process; others are added intentionally or are controlled to meet customers' needs. This section reviews six primary paper characteristics (figure 16.3).

Grain

Paper **grain** results from cellulose fibers aligning in the direction of the continuous screen's movement in a papermaking machine. Grain is determined easily. To determine grain, dampen a small sheet of paper. The sheet curls parallel to the grain direction (figure 16.4).

Paper grain is an important issue on the offset press. Lithography introduces water to the printing process. However, most paper is not dimensionally stable, which means it changes size with changes in temperature and humidity (changes in the presence of moisture). The larger the sheet, the greater the change in size.

Also, paper does not change size uniformly with exposure to moisture. It changes more *with the grain* (parallel to the grain) than it does *against the grain* (perpendicular to the grain). Therefore, it is often important with four-color printing to know the grain direction and feed the paper so it changes the least in size with repeated wettings. Papermakers identify grain direction for this reason (figure 16.5).

Grain long means that the grain is parallel to the long dimension of the sheet. **Grain short** means that the grain is parallel to the short dimension of the sheet. If the sheet is perfectly square, the paper carton or package indicates grain direction.

Grain is also important in the bindery. Paper folds easily with the grain, but it folds poorly against the grain. Try folding a sheet of paper in two right angle directions. One way gives a clean fold, the other breaks the grains

Bulk

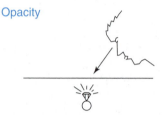

Refers to thickness of the sheet

Opacity

Refers to the ability to see (or rather, not see)
through the sheet

Finish

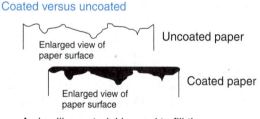

Refers to the texture or surface of the sheet

Coated versus uncoated

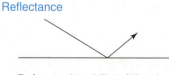

Uncoated paper

Coated paper

A clay-like material is used to fill the
porous, irregular surface of the sheet

Reflectance

Refers to the ability of the sheet to
reflect light

**Figure 16.3 Pictograms of five paper
characteristics**

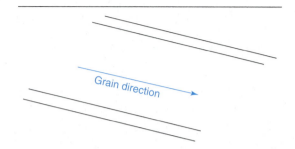

**Figure 16.4 Paper sheets curl parallel to the
grain direction**

and delivers a ragged edge. When folding
thick sheets against the grain, it is often necessary to **score**, or line indent, the sheet to get
a clean fold. This adds another operation to
the job and therefore increases cost.

Bulk

Bulk refers to the thickness of the sheet, not
its weight. It is possible to have two sheets that
weigh the same but have different thicknesses.
Think of bulk as pumping air between the cellulose fibers. Add more air and the paper becomes thicker or bulkier.

Bulk is measured in *points*. These points
differ from the points used to measure type
size, however. One point of bulk equals
1/1000th of an inch. Therefore, a 10-point paper is 0.010 inch thick ($10 \times 0.001 = 0.010$).
Common bulks are 8, 10, and 11 points.

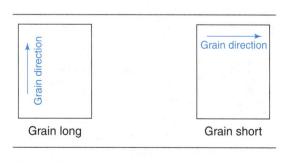

Grain long   Grain short

Figure 16.5 Grain direction

Opacity

Opacity refers to the ability of light to pass through a sheet, or it is the ability to see through a sheet. High opacity means it is difficult to see through the sheet. Low opacity means it is easy to see through the sheet.

When printing on both sides of a sheet of paper, high opacity is very important because we only want to see an image on one side. The image on the other side of the sheet should not interfere with readability. Hold your morning newspaper up to the light and try reading an article. You will see that most newsprint has low opacity.

Finish

In general, **finish** refers to the texture or surface of the sheet. Finish is usually applied after the wet paper leaves the moving wire screen on the Fourdrinier papermaking machine. Rollers, with patterns cut into the surface, can transfer nearly any finish to the wet material.

A smooth, hard surface is ideal for most industrial printing processes. Heated rollers can be used to achieve this type of surface. The terms *calendered* and *supercalendered* are used to describe an exceptionally hard, smooth, and printable finish.

Coated versus Noncoated

A microscopic view of paper shows a surface that is filled with much irregularity (figure 16.2). The intertwined cellulose fibers create peaks and valleys, a lot like a moonscape. When ink is applied to a plain sheet of paper, several problems can occur:

- Ink can absorb into the paper like a sponge. This results in *dot gain* when printing halftones—the dot actually grows in size.

- There can appear to be density variation. Ink is thick in the valleys and thin over the peaks.

- The sheet can actually change size in the process of absorbing wet ink then drying.

Calendering helps smooth the peaks and valleys of the paper. However, the ideal solution is to coat the paper surface with a claylike material to create **coated paper**. The clay fills the valleys of the paper and produces a nearly flat, nonabsorbent surface. Ink then dries on the surface by aerial oxidation, not by absorption. This means that the dot size is reproduced from the plate and sheet stability is retained. Coated papers are ideal for multicolor printing.

Reflectance

The term **reflectance** describes the ability of a sheet of paper to reflect light. Remember that process color printing acts like a series of light filters. We see certain colors because light passes through the translucent ink and is then reflected. With four-color process work, the higher the reflectance of a sheet, the more vivid and accurate the color image.

Reflectance can be controlled by changing the degree of bleaching of the original cellulose fibers, adding chemicals to the slurry, calendering, and altering the coating formulation.

Recycled Paper

There has been increasing attention given to the issue of recycled paper. Concern is not focused on papermaking as a polluting process; that is generally under control. The real motivation behind recycling paper is America's diminishing landfill capacity. Nearly 41 percent of America's solid waste is paper and paperboard. The United States Environmental Protection Agency (EPA) estimates that unless drastic changes are made in paper recycling, the nation's landfills could close by the end of this century.

The response to this concern has been profound and substantive. Manufacturers and consumers have shifted their attention to this problem. The major issue is the use of preconsumer or postconsumer waste materials.

Preconsumer paper waste includes anything that was used to manufacture consumer products but was not actually sold. Examples are paper waste from making cartons or packages and portions cut from the edges of finished press sheets. Preconsumer paper waste also includes items from a wholesaler's unused inventory. These are generally out-of-date products that were never sold. **Postconsumer paper waste** products are generally considered anything that is sold to paper users that would normally end up in landfills.

Most recycling in this decade has been of preconsumer waste. Postconsumer paper recycling has been almost exclusively in the area of newsprint. However, newspapers are made from low-grade paper and represent only a small fraction of our total paper consumption.

Recycling Definitions

The EPA has created a number of definitions of materials within the recycling process. Three important definitions are mill broke, recovered materials, and wastepaper.

Mill Broke

Paper waste that is generated in the paper mill before completing the papermaking process is called **mill broke**. This includes slurry and cut-off from the continuous wire screen on the Fourdrinier machine. All of this material is generally returned to the pulping process and is excluded from the list of recovered materials.

Recovered Materials

Recovered materials are a broad category that includes used postconsumer materials from retailers, office buildings, and homes. Examples of recovered materials are old newspapers, magazines, mixed wastepaper, and general fibrous wastes that enter and are collected from municipal and solid waste facilities, wastes generated after the papermaking and printing processes, and materials from obsolete inventories. Also included in this category are fibrous by-products of harvesting, manufacturing, and woodcutting processes. The latter examples could include flax, straw, forest residues, waste rope, and fibers recovered from waste water.

Wastepaper

The **wastepaper** category is similar to the recovered materials category in that it includes postconsumer waste such as old newspapers, corrugated boxes, bindery trimmings, and paper from obsolete or outdated copies of printed pieces in a company's inventories. However, wastepaper does not consider fibrous by-products of harvesting, manufacturing, or woodcutting processes.

Identifying Recycled or Recyclable Products

An absolute and universally accepted definition of *recycled paper product* has yet to emerge. Mill broke is not considered recycled material, but does a product have to be made from 100 percent wastepaper to be called recycled? In response to public and corporate interest, some products with as little as 10 percent postconsumer material are labeled recycled by the manufacturer. General EPA guidelines recommend a minimum of 50 percent wastepaper for printing and writing papers. However, these guidelines are not strictly followed.

The American Paper Institute has created symbols to assist consumers in identifying environmentally conscious products (figure 16.6). However, it is up to the manufacturer to determine if a product is recycled or recyclable. For example, Canada's EcoLogo symbol can only be used on paper products that

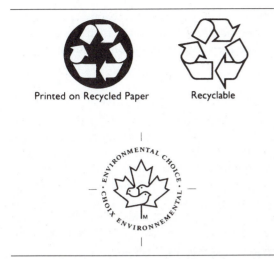

Figure 16.6 Environmental symbols. The top left symbol may be used in the United States on products and packages made from recycled paper. The top right image can be used in the United States on paper products that can be expected to be recycled. The EcoLogo (bottom) is used in Canada to indicate the paper meets requirements of the Office of Environmental Choice and the Canadian Standards Association.

contain more than 50 percent recycled paper and at least 10 percent postconsumer fiber.

Reclaiming Paper Materials

In order to be reused, paper must be returned to a clean, pure, cellulose fiber condition. The process of creating new paper from used paper involves de-inking, bleaching, and sludge disposal.

De-Inking

De-inking is a chemical and mechanical process that removes all additives from printed paper. These additives might include inks, fillers, clays, and metal materials such as foil, staples, or binders. There are two basic de-inking methods: washing and flotation.

The initial step for both de-inking methods is to chop the used paper into small pieces and blend them in a water mixture. The mixture is then filtered to remove metal and other impurities.

The washing de-inking method uses strong chemical detergents in a series of steps. It is much like the stages a washing machine follows in your home. The first bath contains the strongest chemicals. The mixture is then filtered and rinsed, and a weaker detergent is used for the next step. The sequence continues until the desired degree of cleanliness is reached.

The flotation de-inking method uses chemicals that cause inks and other noncellulose materials to float to the surface of the mixture. The undesirable materials are skimmed off while the mixture is stirred continually.

Some paper recycling companies use a combination of these two methods. Whatever method is used, the goal is to reduce the mixture to cellulose fibers suspended in a water slurry.

Bleaching

After the wastepaper is de-inked, it must be bleached because consumers want a bright, clean sheet of paper. Some papers are colored during the papermaking process. Ink on printed sheets that dry by absorption actually stains the cellulose fibers because it enters the fibers themselves. The de-inking process also tends to stain the fibers and discolors the water slurry mixture. Bleaching removes this stain and returns the cellulose to a pure white state.

The most effective bleaches are chlorine based. However, chlorine is a significant polluter. Discarding the chlorine could actually offset the benefits of recycling the paper. However, effective nonchlorine bleaches, such as sodium hydrosulphite, are being developed that reduce peripheral environmental impact.

Even though bleaching wastepaper is a major challenge, it should be recognized that virgin paper pulp must also be bleached to remove lignin. Most experts agree that bleaching de-inked fiber requires significantly fewer chemicals than bleaching virgin pulp.

Another solution to the bleaching waste challenge is to avoid bleaching all recycled fibers to pure white. Products such as newsletters, announcements, or newspapers that carry information with an extremely short use-life, do not have to be perfectly white.

Sludge Disposal

The by-product of the de-inking process is sludge. Sludge is composed of a variety of contaminants, fillers, and inks. Anything that is not cellulose fiber becomes sludge. Depending upon the type process, the type of paper, and the ink coverage, from 10 to 30 percent of wastepaper becomes sludge.

Under the EPA standards for ink manufacturing, air emissions, and water effluents, de-inking sludge is generally considered to be a nontoxic process. All sludge must be tested, however, and if a sample reaches a certain toxic level, it must be buried in a controlled landfill for hazardous materials.

Nontoxic sludge is disposed of in a variety of ways. Some sludge is placed in private or public landfills. Some manufacturers burn sludge to provide electrical power for the de-inking process. Others sell sludge as a raw material for other manufacturing processes, such as making molded nursery pots. Polycoatings reclaimed from the sludge of polycoated paper can be used to make new polyethylene products. They are sometimes used to cover a sheet to protect it from moisture or to give an extremely glossy finish.

The move to recycle postconsumer, high-grade printing and writing paper depends upon two factors. The first is the paper industry's production capacity to de-ink and return fibers to a clean state. The second is consumer demand. Both factors must increase radically before recycled paper becomes standard.

Classifying Paper

There are literally thousands of different papers available to the designer and to the printer. Every different paper manufacturer creates its own list of names and labels of its proprietary lines or products. Such a list can be confusing and mystifying for both new and experienced professionals. That there is no universally accepted method to categorize all papers adds to the difficulty.

However, one workable way that is emerging is to classify all papers under one of the following five headings: book, writing, cover, bristol, and an "other" category (table 16.1).

Book paper is the most common type of paper found in the industry. It is used as a gen-

Table 16.1. One way to classify types of paper

Book Papers	Bristol Papers
Offset	Tag
Opaque	Index
Converting	Post card
Writing Papers	**Other**
Bond	Groundwood
Duplicator	(newsprint)
Mimeograph	Lightweights
Ledger	Special purpose
Tracing	
Cover Papers	
General purpose cover	
Duplex	

eral purpose material for such things as catalogs, brochures, direct mail, and books. This classification includes *offset sheets* used in almost every plant in the country.

Writing paper is generally a high-quality material that was originally associated with correspondence and record keeping. Today it includes a wide range of qualities and uses such as stationery, inexpensive reproduction (such as for the ditto or mimeograph processes), and tracing or drawing.

Cover paper is commonly used for the outside covers of brochures or pamphlets and is generally thicker than both book and writing papers. Its common applications are booklets, manuals, directories, and announcements.

Bristol papers are stiff, heavy materials that are used widely for such things as business cards, programs, menus, file folders, and inexpensive booklet covers.

The "other" category is a holding bin for any paper that cannot be classified under the first four headings. Common examples are newsprint, lightweight materials such as onionskin, and items that meet a special purpose such as no carbon required (NCR) paper.

Basis Weight

All papers within each category are further classified (and sold) according to weight. The system is called basis weight. **Basis weight** is the weight in pounds of one **ream** (500 sheets) of the basic sheet size of a particular paper type. Unfortunately, all paper types do not use the same basic sheet size to determine weight (figure 16.7). The basic sheet sizes of the four common paper classifications are:

- Book paper: 25 inches $\times$ 38 inches
- Writing paper: 17 inches $\times$ 22 inches
- Cover paper: 20 inches $\times$ 26 inches
- Bristol: $22\frac{1}{2}$ inches $\times$ $28\frac{1}{2}$ inches

Most papers are available in a variety of basis weights. For example, the most common weights for uncoated book papers are basis 40, 45, 50, 70, and 80. One ream of basis 40 book paper measures 25 inches by 38 inches and weighs 40 pounds. A basis 80 book paper has the same dimensions as 40 book paper, but one ream weighs 80 pounds. Within each category of paper (such as book paper), then, the greater the basis weight, the heavier the sheet. It is not

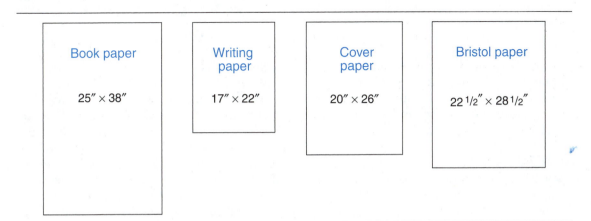

Book paper

25" × 38"

Writing paper

17" × 22"

Cover paper

20" × 26"

Bristol paper

22 1/2" × 28 1/2"

Figure 16.7 Basic sheet sizes

Table 16.2.   Regular sizes for book papers and corresponding equivalent M weights

Basis weights	40	45	50	60	70	80	90	100	120
Sizes (in inches)				Equivalent M Weights (in pounds)					
17 × 22	31	35	39	47	55	63	71	79	94
17⅛ × 22½	33	37	41	50	58	66	75	83	99
19 × 25	40	45	50	60	70	80	90	100	120
22½ × 29	55	62	69	82	96	110	124	137	165
22½ × 35	66	75	83	99	116	113	149	166	199
23 × 29	56	63	70	84	98	112	126	140	169
23 × 35	68	76	85	102	119	136	153	169	203
24 × 36	72	82	90	100	128	146	164	182	218
25 × 38	80	90	100	120	140	160	180	200	240
26 × 40	88	98	110	132	154	176	198	218	262
28 × 42	100	112	124	148	174	198	222	248	298
28 × 44	104	116	130	156	182	208	234	260	312
30½ × 41	106	118	132	158	184	210	236	264	316
32 × 44	118	134	148	178	208	238	266	296	356
33 × 44	122	138	152	184	214	244	276	306	366
35 × 45	132	150	166	198	232	266	298	332	398
35 × 46	136	152	170	204	238	272	306	338	406
36 × 48	146	164	182	218	254	292	328	364	436
38 × 50	160	180	200	240	280	320	360	400	480
38 × 52	166	188	208	250	292	332	374	416	500
41 × 54	186	210	234	280	326	372	420	466	560
41 × 61	210	236	264	316	368	422	474	526	632
42 × 58	206	230	256	308	358	410	462	512	616
44 × 64	238	266	296	356	414	474	534	592	712
44 × 66	244	276	306	366	428	490	550	612	734
46 × 69	268	300	334	400	468	534	602	668	802
52 × 76	332	374	416	500	582	666	748	832	998

possible, however, to make the same generalization between different categories of paper (such as comparing book paper to cover paper) because the sizes of the sheets being weighed are not the same.

M Weight

Sometimes basis weight is converted to **M weight**, which is the weight of 1,000 sheets (rather than 500 sheets) of the basic sheet size of a particular paper type. A paper's M weight is twice its basis weight. The M weight is used merely as a convenience for paper calculation.

Regular Sizes

Although the basic size of book paper is 25 inches by 38 inches, other sizes are available to the printer. If the order is large enough, the printer can specify the required size to the manufacturer. In order to meet the needs of small jobs, local paper suppliers generally stock a variety of sizes within each paper type. These common sizes are called **regular sizes**. The left column in table 16.2 shows some regular sizes for book papers. Regular sizes are also stocked in each of the common basis weights.

Table 16.3. Regular sizes for writing papers and corresponding equivalent M weights

| Sizes (In Inches) | Substance Weights | | | | | | | | |
	13	16	20	24	28	32	36	40	44
	Equivalent M Weights (In Pounds)								
8½ × 11	6.50	8	10	12	Sizes and weights normally				
8½ × 14	8.25	10.18	12.72	15.26	used for business papers—				
11 × 27	13	16	20	24	often called "cut sizes"				
16 × 21	23	29	36	43	50	57	65	72	79
17 × 22	26	32	40	48	56	64	72	80	88
17		41	51	61	71	81	92	102	112
18 × 23	29	35	44	53	62	71	80	89	97
18 × 46	58	70	88	106	124	142	160	178	194
19 × 24	32	39	49	59	68	78	88	98	107
19 × 48	64	78	98	118	136	156	176	196	214
20 × 28	39	48	60	72	84	96	108	120	132
21 × 32	46	58	72	86	100	114	130	144	158
22 × 34	52	64	80	96	112	128	144	160	176
23 × 36	58	70	88	106	124	142	160	178	194
24 × 38	64	78	98	118	136	156	176	196	214
28 × 34	66	82	102	122	142	162	184	204	224
34 × 44	104	128	160	192	224	256	288	320	352

Equivalent Weights

As mentioned earlier, a paper's M weight is twice its basis weight. Printers and paper manufacturers use table 16.3 to determine **equivalent weights** for regular sizes of book papers. For example, locate the basic sheet size for book paper (25 inches × 38 inches) in table 16.3. Notice that the M weight for basis 40 is 80 pounds. One ream (500 sheets) weighs 40 pounds, so two reams (1,000 sheets) weigh 80 pounds. The M weight is 80 pounds. Now find the 38 inch × 50 inch regular sheet size (which is double the basic sheet size of 25 inches × 38 inches) and find the equivalent weight of 160 pounds. One thousand sheets of 38 inch × 50 inch basis 40 book paper have an equivalent M weight of 160 pounds.

There are two general exceptions to this vocabulary of papers when dealing with the four main paper types. Some Bristol and cover papers are described not in terms of weight but rather in terms of points (see the Paper Characteristics section earlier in this chapter). One point is one one-thousandth of an inch. Therefore, an 11-point Bristol is 0.011 inch think (11 × 0.001 = 0.011). Common thicknesses or bulks are 8, 10, and 11 points. Most Bristols and covers, however, are classified by the more common basis weight designation.

The second general exception deals with writing papers. Although in this category the term *substance weight* is used instead of *basis weight*, the terms mean the same thing. **Substance weight** is the weight in pounds of one ream of the basic sheet size (17 inch × 22 inch) of one particular type of writing paper. Table 16.3 shows some equivalent M weights of a list of regular sizes of writing papers.

When printers buy paper for a job, they order it from the supplier according to total pounds, type, and basis weight.

Determining Paper Needs

Even though paper is sold by the weight, when printers work on the press they deal with sheets, not pounds. Printers calculate the number of sheets needed to produce a job, and then deal with the paper merchant to determine weight and price.

Not every job uses regular size press sheets that are obtained easily from the paper supplier. Most printers stock only a few sizes of each paper type and then cut them to meet the needs of individual jobs. Others purchase

the most efficient regular sizes to match the size of existing presses and gang several jobs together on a single press sheet. In either case, the printer is faced with the task of calculating the most efficient method of cutting smaller pieces from available stock sizes.

To illustrate the process, consider this example: A printer must cut a press sheet size of 8½ inches × 11 inches from a stock sheet that measures 28 inches × 34 inches. What is the maximum number of sheets that can be cut from the larger piece? Figure 16.8 shows the two common ways of solving the problem.

On the left side of figure 16.8, the width and the length of the sheet are divided by the width and length of the press sheet, respectively. The two answers are then multiplied to show that nine sheets can be cut this way. The

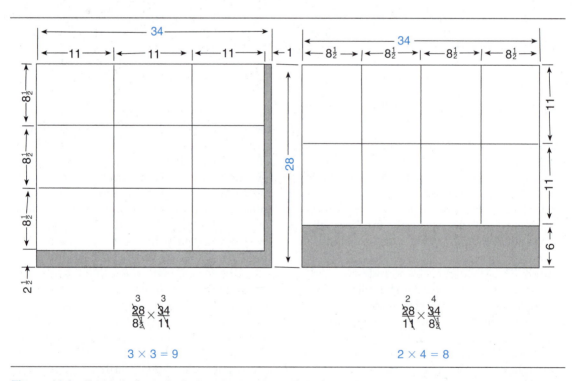

Figure 16.8 Example for calculating the number of sheets to be cut from a stock sheet by dividing or by drawing

same result can be obtained by simply drawing a picture of the stock sheet and blocking out the maximum number of press sheets.

On the right side of figure 16.8, the width and length of the stock sheet are divided by the length and width of the press sheet, respectively. The two answers are then multiplied to show that eight sheets can be cut this way. The printer, however, would probably cut the paper the first way to obtain nine press sheets to gain the maximum number of press sheets from the stock sheet.

This procedure of dividing corresponding dimensions and then dividing alternating dimensions of the stock and press sheets is rather straightforward, but paper calculations are not always this simple. Drawing a picture of the calculations can make the process easier and often can show where additional gains in numbers of sheets can be made. Individuals new to paper calculations should both draw a diagram and work the math computations to ensure accuracy.

Diagrams are very important. Sometimes careful observation can increase efficiency and

profits for a printing company. Drawing and working with the placement of press sheets on the stock sheet in figure 16.8 reveals that the stock sheet can actually be cut to obtain ten sheets instead of nine (figure 16.9). It is necessary, however, to tell the paper cutter the sequence of cuts.

Nonstandard Cuts

This process of manipulating the positions and order of cuts to gain an additional sheet is called making a **nonstandard cut** or a dutch cut. In an era when paper and other material can account for more than half the cost of a job, a nonstandard cut can often mean the difference between profit and loss.

Spoilage

A very important consideration when calculating the paper needs of a specific job is spoilage. All printing processes require some start up to get the press feeding properly and the press sheets printing at proper ink density. This process is called **make-ready**. Rarely does

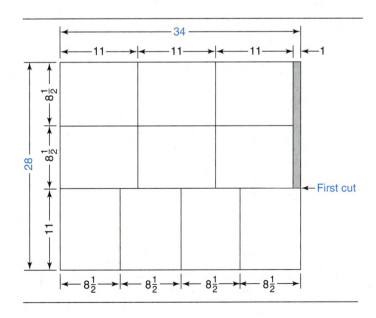

Figure 16.9 Example of a nonstandard cut. It is necessary to specify the sequence of cuts to be made by the paper cutter when a nonstandard sequence is to be followed.

Table 16.4.   Paper spoilage allowances (percentages represent press size sheets, not impressions)

Lithographic	1,000	2,500	5,000	10,000	25,000 and over
Single-Color Equipment					
One color, one side	8%	6%	5%	4%	3%
One color, work-and-turn or work-and-tumble	13%	10%	8%	6%	5%
Each additional color (per side)	5%	4%	3%	2%	2%
Two-Color Equipment					
Two colors, one side	—	—	5%	4%	3%
Two colors, two sides or work-and-turn	—	—	8%	6%	5%
Each additional two colors (per side)	—	—	3%	2%	2%
Four-Color Equipment					
Four colors, one side only	—	—	—	6%	5%
Four colors, two sides or work-and-turn	—	—	—	8%	7%
Bindery Spoilage					
Folding, stitching, trimming	4%	3%	3%	2%	2%
Cutting, punching, or drilling	2%	2%	2%	2%	2%
Varnishing and gumming	7%	5%	4%	3%	3%

The figures above do not include waste sheets used to run up color, as it is assumed that waste stock is used for this purpose.

Use the next higher percentage for the following papers:

1. Coated papers when plant does not run coateds.
2. Papers that caliper 0.0025 and less
3. Difficult papers such as foil, cloth, and plastic

Letterpress	1,000	2,500	5,000	10,000	25,000 and over
Single-Color Equipment					
One color, one side	7%	5%	4%	3%	3%
One color, two sides or work-and-turn	13%	9%	7%	5%	5%
Each additional color (per side)	6%	4%	3%	2%	2%
Two-Color Equipment					
Two colors, one side	—	—	4%	3%	2%
Two colors, two sides or work-and-turn	—	—	7%	5%	5%
Each additional two colors (per side)	—	—	3%	2%	2%
Four-Color Equipment					
Four colors, one side	—	—	—	6%	5%
Four colors, two sides or work-and-turn	—	—	—	8%	4%
Bindery Spoilage					
Folding, stitching, trimming	4%	3%	3%	2%	2%
Cutting, punching, or drilling	2%	2%	2%	2%	2%
Varnishing and gumming	7%	5%	4%	3%	3%

These paper spoilage allowance charts have been reproduced through the courtesy of the "Printing Industries of Metropolitan New York" and demonstrate how paper spoilage is calculated by printers belonging to this association.

a job not have some spoilage because of something as frustrating as a machine jam-up or as foolish as spilled coffee on a finished pile. It is necessary, then, to give the press or bindery operators more sheets than the job actually requires to allow for startup and printing problems. These extra sheets are called the **spoilage allowance**.

Table 16.4 shows a typical spoilage allowance chart that an estimator might use to calculate the average number of wasted sheets for different types of jobs. For example, if 5,000 copies that have two colors on one side are to be run on two-color equipment, the operator must begin the run with 5 percent more press sheets than the job requires or $(5,000 \times 0.05) + 5,000 = 5,250$ press sheets.

Sample Paper Estimating Problem

To tie the ideas presented so far together, let us consider a sample problem of paper estimating.

A printer has been asked to bid on a job that requires 15,000 copies of a two-color poster to measure 9 inches × 12 inches. The printer has a basis 60 book paper in a 25 inch × 38 inch regular sheet size left over from a previous job. The printer has only a single-color lithographic press and wants to run the job in the 9 inch × 12 inch size. How many pounds of paper must be purchased to run the job?

How many press sheets must be given to the press operator?

The printer must deliver 15,000 sheets to the customer, plus a 6 percent spoilage allowance (4 percent for the first pass through the press plus 2 percent for the second pass) of 900 sheets. Most make-ready problems occur with the first pass, therefore the spoilage allowance is reduced for subsequent passes.

$$15,000 \times 0.06 = 900$$
$$15,000 + 900 = 15,900$$

1. A total of 15,900 press sheets must be given to the press operator to ensure the customer gets 15,000 good sheets.

2. How many basic sheets are needed in order to cut 15,900 press sheets (figure 16.10)?

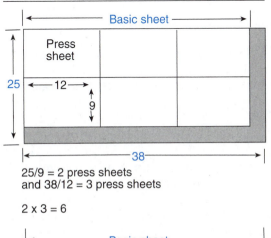

25/9 = 2 press sheets
and 38/12 = 3 press sheets

2 x 3 = 6

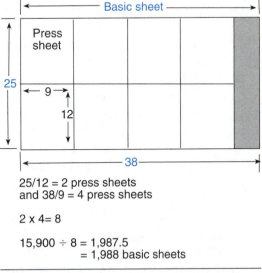

25/12 = 2 press sheets
and 38/9 = 4 press sheets

2 x 4= 8

15,900 ÷ 8 = 1,987.5
= 1,988 basic sheets

Figure 16.10 Calculations to determine the number of basic sheets needed to cut 15,900 press sheets

If eight press sheets can be cut from each stock sheet, then

$$15,900 \div 8 = 1,987.5$$

Because partial sheets cannot be bought, however, we must always go to the next full sheet. The number of regular sheets then is 1,988.

3. How much does 1,988 sheets of basis 60, 25 inch × 38 inch book paper weigh in pounds?

Referring to table 16.2, the equivalent M weight is 120 pounds per 1,000 sheets. We therefore need 1.988 M (1,000 sheets) or 1,988 ÷ 1,000 = 1.988

$$120 \times 1.988 = 238.56$$

To bid the job, the printer must determine the purchase cost of 238.56 pounds of book paper, basis 60, measuring 25 inches × 38 inches.

The task of calculating paper needs can become more complex than in this example, but the basic procedures are always the same.

1. Determine the spoilage allowance and find the total number of press sheets to run the job.
2. Calculate the most efficient method of cutting the stock sheets and determine the required number of stock sheets.
3. Find the total weight by referring to the paper's equivalent M weight.

Determining the Price of Paper

It is sometimes necessary to refer to a manufacturer's or distributor's price schedule to estimate the cost of the paper for the job without contacting a salesperson. Table 16.5 shows a typical tearsheet from a price catalog. (The prices here are samples only and do not represent current paper costs.) It is important that the estimator have an understanding of price differences according to the quantity of paper ordered. It is often economical to buy more paper than is needed for the specific job. Consider an example.

Assume that we need 1,100 sheets of 25 inches × 38 inches for a job we are to print. The line from Table 16.5 that interests us most is

	16 Ctns	4 Ctns	1 Ctn	less Ctn
25 × 38	41.10	44.16	50.52	75.78

Just as with most industrial or consumer products, the more we buy, the less the unit cost. If the supplier has to split open a carton to meet our needs, we pay more because of handling and the storage of the unused portion.

This is basis 60 paper, so the weight is 120 M (120 pounds per 1,000 sheets). There are 1,200 sheets per carton. We require 1,100, so we will figure the split-carton price. If the price is $75.78 per M, the cost per pound is $0.6315 ($75.78 divided by 120 pounds per M). The 1,100 sheets we need weigh 132 pounds (120 pounds per M × 1.1M). The cost of 1,100 sheets when purchased from a broken carton is $83.36 (132 pounds × $0.6315 per pound).

A quick glance at the carton price, however, shows that the price of an unbroken carton is over $30 less and we would get 100 more sheets if we bought a full box. The estimator must be aware of such price differentials and must spend time to calculate potential differences.

Table 16.5. A sample tear sheet from a paper catalog

Adams Brilliant Book

Shown in Sample Book number two.

Processes-- Offset and Letterpress
Color-- White
Finish-- Vellum and Coral
Packed-- Unsealed in Cartons
Basic Size-- 25 x 38

BA	Size, M Wt	G	Per Ctn	16 Ctns	4 Ctns	1 Ctn	Less Ctn
				Per 1,000 sheets			
Vellum Finish							
50	17.5x22.5- 41M	L	3600	14.04	15.09	17.26	25.89
50	23 x 35 - 85M	L	1800	29.11	31.28	35.79	53.68
50	38 x 50 - 200M	L	800	68.50	73.60	84.20	126.30
60	17.5x22.5- 40M	L	3200	17.13	18.40	21.05	31.58
60	19 x 25 - 60M	L	2400	20.55	22.08	25.26	37.89
60	23 x 29 - 84M	L	1800	28.77	30.91	35.36	53.05
60	23 x 35 - 102M	L	1500	34.94	37.54	42.94	64.41
60	25 x 38 - 120M	L	1200	41.10	44.16	50.52	75.78
70	17.5x22.5- 58M	L	2400	19.87	21.34	24.42	36.63
70	19 x 25 - 70M	L	2000	23.98	25.76	29.47	44.21
70	23 x 29 - 98M	L	1600	33.57	36.06	41.26	61.89
70	23 x 35 - 119M	L	1200	40.76	43.79	50.10	75.15
70	25 x 38 - 140M	L	1000	47.95	51.52	58.94	88.41
70	35 x 45 - 232M	L	600	79.46	85.38	97.67	146.51
80	23 x 35 - 136M	L	1100	46.58	50.05	57.26	85.88
80	25 x 38 - 160M	L	1000	54.80	58.88	67.36	101.04
80	35 x 45 - 266M	L	600	91.11	97.89	111.99	167.98
Coral Finish							
70	17.5x22.5- 58M	L	2400	21.66	23.26	26.59	39.90
70	19 x 25 - 70M	L	2000	26.15	28.07	32.10	48.16
70	23 x 35 - 119M	L	1200	50.80	54.54	62.36	93.57
70	25 x 38 - 140M	L	1000	52.29	56.14	65.19	97.64

Section 2: Ink

Ink forms the images you see as words and pictures in this book. Whatever the printing process, ink transfers to the paper in the shape of the lines on the image carrier.

Not all ink images, however, are transferred to paper. Although paper is the most common printing material, many other surfaces, such as metal foils, sheet laminates, plastics, and even wood veneers, are used. Because surfaces other than paper are also used to receive ink, they are given a special term. A **substrate** is any base material used in printing processes that receives an image transferred from a printing plate. The term *substrate* will be used throughout the rest of this chapter.

Properties of Ink

Three properties of ink that control the ease and quality of image transfer are viscosity, tack, and drying quality.

Viscosity

The term **viscosity** is used to describe the *body* of ink accurately. Some inks are thick and heavy (offset and letterpress inks), and some are fluid and light (flexographic and gravure inks). Viscosity, or resistance to flow, can be measured and is a term that is accepted universally in the printing industry.

Tack

Tack, or stickiness, is a property of ink that must be controlled in order to transfer images and deliver the sheet through the press. Tack can cause paper, especially coated paper, to adhere to the blanket of an offset press. Ink that is excessively tacky may also pick the surface of the paper and cause misfeeding. (Recall that *to pick* means to lift or tear small pieces of the paper's surface.) Tack increases when one color is printed over another. When printing multicolor and process color work, decrease the amount of tack on successive runs by adding a reducer. The first run should have the most tack. Each successive run should be printed with ink of less tack.

Drying Quality

The final, and extremely important, property of ink is its drying quality. There are two stages in the ink drying process. First, ink should **set** or stick to the paper instantly. When ink on the press sheet is set, it can be handled without smearing. If ink does not set when it is stacked in the delivery side of a press, the image will transfer to the bottom of the next sheet. This transfer of wet ink from sheet to sheet is called **set-off**.

The second stage in the drying process is called **hardening**. When ink has hardened, the vehicle (or solvent) has solidified completely on the paper surface and will not transfer. The time it takes for liquid ink to harden to a solid state is called the **drying time**.

Most natural or synthetic inks that contain a drying oil set and harden by a chemical process called **oxidation**. To oxidize is to combine with oxygen. When the oxygen of the air combines with the ink's drying oil, the vehicle of the ink changes from a liquid to a solid.

When an ink is printed on an absorbent substrate, drying results from a physical process called penetration. When ink dries by **penetration**, most of the vehicle of the ink absorbs into the substrate. The ink vehicle is not changed to a solid state in this drying process. As a result, inks that rely heavily on drying by penetration are not popular because the ink never hardens. Ink usually transfers to the hands when handling work printed with penetrating drying ink.

Some inks dry by **evaporation**. Resinous and other film-forming solutions in the ink vehicle pass off as vapor during the drying process. Drying by evaporation is much like drying by penetration. The volatile solutions disappear (by evaporating instead of penetrating), leaving an ink film on the surface of the substrate.

Ingredients in Ink

All printing inks are made from three basic ingredients: pigment, vehicle, and special additives. The **pigment** is the dry particles that give color to ink. The **vehicle** is the fluid that carries the pigment and causes it to adhere to the substrate. **Additives** are compounds that control ink characteristics such as tack, workability, and drying quality.

Pigments

The same basic pigments are used to produce all inks for the various printing processes. To some degree the pigment type determines whether the ink will be transparent or opaque. It also determines image permanency when exposed to various solvents such as water, oil, alcohol, and acid. Pigments are divided into four basic groups: black, white, inorganic color, and organic color pigments.

Black Pigments

Black pigments are produced by burning natural gas and oil onto a collecting device. The by-products from the burning process are called *thermal* black and *furnace* black. Furnace black, the most popular pigment, is made from oil in a continuous furnace. Sometimes furnace black is combined with thermal black, which is made from natural gas. Each type of black pigment has unique properties. The pigments are used individually or mixed to produce the best pigment for the specified printing process.

White Pigments

White pigments are subdivided into two groups: opaque pigments and transparent pigments. White ink containing *opaque* pigments (through which light cannot pass) is used when transferring an image to cover a substrate or when overprinting another color. Opaque whites are also used for mixing with other inks to lighten the color or hue.

Transparent white pigments (through which light can pass) are used to allow the background material or ink to be seen. Transparent whites are used to reduce the color strength of another ink, to produce a tint of another color, and to extend or add to some of the more costly materials in the ink's formula. Transparent pigments are often referred to as *extenders* or *extender bases*.

Organic Pigments

Organic pigments are derived from living organisms. All organic pigments contain carbon and hydrogen, and most are made from petroleum; however, coal, wood, animal fats, and vegetable oils are also used in organic pigment manufacture. The major advantages organic pigments have over inorganic pigments is that organic pigments provide a wider selection of colors and tend to be richer in color, brighter, more transparent, and purer. These qualities are important, particularly for four-color process printing.

Inorganic Pigments

Inorganic pigments are chemical compounds that are typically formed by precipitation. When inorganic pigments are formed, chemical solutions are mixed together and a chemical reaction takes place that produces an insoluble pigment (one that cannot be broken into the primary chemicals from which it was formed). The insoluble pigment is then allowed to precipitate (settle) and is filtered out of the mixture and dried. Eventual pigment color is determined by the proportions of the chemicals in solution. Cadmium yellow, for example, may contain the chemical cadmium sulfide in a compound with zinc sulfide. Inks made with inorganic pigments are less expensive to produce than those made with organic pigments. Although inorganic inks have good opacity, they lack some of the positive qualities of organic pigment inks, such as transparency.

Vehicles

The printing process and drying system determine the vehicle used in the manufacturing process. The vehicle of an ink is the liquid portion that holds and carries the pigment. The vehicle also provides workability and drying properties and binds the pigment to the substrate after the ink has dried.

Each vehicle used in the manufacture of ink has a slightly different composition. Nondrying vehicles used in newspaper and comic book production are made from penetrating oils such as petroleum and rosin. Resins are added to the oil base to control tack and flow.

Most letterpress and offset inks dry by oxidation. Linseed oil and litho varnish are the most widely used drying vehicles for these inks. The way in which the oil and varnish are *cooked* or prepared determines the viscosity of the final ink.

Gravure inks for paper consist of hydrocarbon solvents mixed with gums and resins. This combination causes rapid evaporation with or without heat. Naturally, the evaporation rate increases with the use of heat. Plastic, glassine, foil, and board links are made with lacquer solvents and resins.

Alcohol and other fast-evaporating solvents that are combined with resins or gums are used to produce flexographic inks. Flexographic and gravure printing are capable of imaging many substrates. The substrate's surface characteristics determine the final ingredients of the vehicle.

Screen printing inks dry by evaporation and oxidation. Therefore, a solvent-resin vehicle is used in their manufacture.

Offset and letterpress *heat-set inks* are made from varnishes or soaps and hydrocarbon resins dissolved in petroleum solvents.

"*Quick-setting inks*" used for offset and letterpress consist of resin, oil, and solvent. During the drying process the solvent is absorbed by the substrate, leaving an ink film of resin and oil that dries by oxidation.

Additives

Additives are added to ink during the manufacturing process, and some are added in the press room to give the ink special characteristics. Additives can reduce ink if it is too stiff. They can make ink less tacky or shorten its drying time. Additives should not be used carelessly, however. Many inks are ready to use and in normal situations will image best as they are. When you use additives, be sure they are compatible with the ink's vehicle. The following list identifies major additives and describes their uses:

- *Reducers*: Varnishes, solvents, oils, or waxy or greasy compounds that reduce the tack or stickiness of ink. They also aid ink penetration and setting.

- *Driers*: Metallic salts added to inks to speed oxidation and drying of the oil vehicle. Cobalt, manganese, and lead are commonly used metallic salts. Cobalt is the most effective drier.

- *Binding varnish*: A viscous varnish used to toughen dried ink film. Can increase image sharpness, resist emulsification, eliminate chalking, and improve drying. Emulsification occurs in offset lithography when excessive fountain solution mixes with the ink. The result of emulsification is an ink that actually appears to break down and becomes greasy looking.

- *Waxes*: Usually cooked into the vehicle during the manufacturing process. Can be added to the ink later in the process. Paraffin wax, beeswax, carnauba wax, microcrystalline, ozokerite, and polyethylene are commonly used waxes. Wax helps prevent set-off and sheet sticking. Wax also *shortens* the ink; that is, it limits the ink's ability to stretch or web.

- *Antiskinning agents*: Prevent ink on ink rollers from forming a skin and drying on the press. If these agents are used excessively, the ink will not dry on the paper.

- *Cornstarch*: Can be used to add body to a thin ink. Also helps prevent set-off.

Calculating Ink Usage

A challenge for every printer when estimating the price of a job is to determine ink costs. For short-run jobs, ink expense is minimal and the

Table 16.6. Ink mileage chart

Grade of Stock	Black	Purple	Haven Blue	Sky Blue	Kelly Green	Yellow Lake	Opaque Orange	Fire Red	Antique Red	Opaque Base	White
Enamel	360	320	330	330	200	275	250	300	250	310	250
Litho coated	300	300	280	300	175	240	180	240	200	265	200
Label	240	250	250	220	155	190	160	190	165	195	165
Dull coated	205	200	200	205	120	160	130	170	140	190	140
Newsprint	150	155	150	140	160	110	140	130	105	110	104
Antique finish	135	120	130	120	140	95	115	110	90	95	90
Machine finish	180	170	180	170	180	100	140	130	125	120	120

The numbers indicate the approximate number of thousand square inches of area that one pound of offset litho ink will cover on a standard sheet-fed press.

cost is often ignored in final calculations. This approach is shortsighted, however, because ink costs then come out of profits.

Ink mileage charts are available for every ink type manufactured (table 16.6). They typically show the number of thousand square inches of area that can be covered by one pound of ink. Of course, coverage varies by printing process and type of paper or substrate. In practice, a ruler is used to measure area.

Figure 16.11 shows a layout for a job about to be printed. The order is for 50,000 final posters, printed in black on newsprint. It makes no difference when calculating ink coverage that the job will be run four-up. Whether the job is ganged or run one final sheet at a time, the same number of ink inches will be printed.

Estimating the actual square inches of coverage is not an exact science. The inexact nature of this problem is compounded with the use of tints. Does a 10 inch × 10 inch area with a 50 percent tint count as 100 square inches of coverage (10 × 10) or 50 square inches [(10 × 10) ÷ 2]? The answer is actually nearer 50 than 100. In any calculations, esti-

mated coverage is determined by the experience of the craftperson.

Returning to figure 16.11, the estimator judged that the job covered 10 square ink inches per poster.

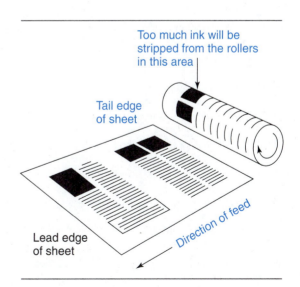

Figure 16.11 A job layout evaluated for ink coverage

10 square ink inches $\times$ 50,000 posters
= 500,000 square ink inches

From table 16.6 we see that this ink delivers approximately 150,000 square inches of coverage per pound on newsprint.

500,000 square ink inches $\div$
150,000 square inches of coverage per
pound = 3.3 pounds of ink

The job will require 3.3 pounds of ink, but the cost will probably be priced to an even 4 pounds because most ink is purchased by the even pound.

    This procedure is simplified in many automated estimating systems or programs. The estimator is asked to classify the job as light, medium, or heavy ink coverage. The program then includes ink costs in its calculation based upon historical averages.

Ink Specifications and Standards

It is generally ink that forms the images we read as words, the dots we see as pictures, or the lines we interpret as drawings. Sometimes, images are created by die cutting or embossing, but most of the time it is ink. The ability to specify and match ink color is fundamental to communication between the designer and printer. This section introduces the language and system of specifying inks.

The PANTONE Matching System®

The **PANTONE Matching System**® is a method nearly universally accepted for specifying and mixing colors. This system is often called the *PMS system*, but this term is not legally associated with the Pantone Corporation.

Table 16.7. The PANTONE matching system®

Item	Features
PANTONE Matching System 1000	International reference for selecting, specifying, and matching printed colors
PANTONE Color Formula Guide 1000	Displays corresponding printing ink formulas for each color
PANTONE Color Specifier 1000	Provides perforated tear-out chips that can be used for quality control
PANTONE Process Color System	Digitally created, provides more than 3,000 color effects, with process tint values
PANTONE Process Color Imaging Guide	Pairs a solid PANTONE Color beside its closest PANTONE process color simulation that can be achieved on a computer monitor, output device, or printing press
PANTONE Color Reference Guides	Displays metallics, pastels, black colors and effects, color tints, color and black combinations, two-color combinations, and PANTONE Colors for film and foil
PANTONE by Letraset Graphic Artists' Materials	Offers an array of markers, color papers, transfer materials, and transparent film that can be used by graphic designers to prepare compositions that reflect accurate PANTONE Colors

It is unusual in this text to identify or refer by name to specific proprietary products or services. The PANTONE Matching System® is mentioned specifically in this chapter because of its profound, unique, and far-reaching impact and use. Table 16.7 summarizes the range of PANTONE products that are used by the printing industry.

Lawrence Herbert originated the PANTONE system in 1956 in an attempt to systematize what was then a chaotic, ill-defined, and unorganized approach to specifying printing ink colors. Every printer had individual color samples. If a customer changed printers, new color specifications were necessary. Herbert conceived of labeling colors by number and providing swatch book samples of standard colors (figure 16.12). Herbert's concept also included standard formulas to duplicate the sample colors on the printing press (figure 16.13). While the PANTONE system is today's common, accepted method of color specification, in 1956 it was a revolution.

Using the PANTONE system, artists and customers select any of the more than 500 hues from a swatch book. The printer can then mix the desired color by using the swatch number and referring to a formula guide. The formula guide gives the formula for making the color.

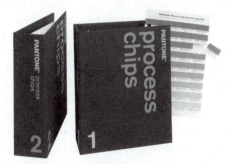

Figure 16.12 PANTONE® process chips. The books provide color samples that can be used to identify, by number, an ink color desired for a 4-color printing job.
(Courtesy of Pantone, Inc.)

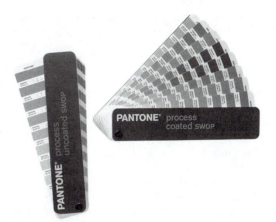

Figure 16.13 PANTONE® process guide coated SWOP. The guides provide corresponding ink formulas, or mixing directions, to duplicate the sample colors on coated and uncoated stocks on the printing press.
(Courtesy of Pantone, Inc.)

It identifies the basic colors involved and indicates how much of each color to mix together. The ten basic colors in the PANTONE Matching System® are rhodamine red, purple, reflex blue, yellow, warm red, rubine red, process blue, green, black, and transparent white.

Today the PANTONE Matching System® is not only used for printing color control. It is applied in the fashion industry for fabric colors, in the interior design field for paint and textile colors, and in the computer field for specifying colors on color terminals across all computer-aided-design (CAD) applications.

Lithographic Inks

There are many ink formulations to serve lithographic printers. Table 16.8 charts various ink formulations for different presses and substrates. Lithographic inks are used on sheet-fed presses and on web-fed presses. A variety of ink vehicles are required because of the dif-

Table 16.8. Lithographic inks and substrates

Lithographic Inks	
Sheet-fed presses	Web-fed presses
Substrates	*Substrates*
Paper	Mostly paper
Foil	
Film	
Thin metal	
Ink Vehicle Class	*Ink Vehicle Class*
Oxidative—Natural or synthetic drying oils	Oxidative—Drying oil varnish
Penetrating—Soluble resins, hydrocarbon oils and solvents, drying and semidrying oils and varnishes	Penetrating—Hydrocarbons, oils and solvents, soluble resins
Quick Set—Hard soluble resin, hydrocarbon oils and solvents, minimal drying oils and plasticizers	Heat Set—Hydrocarbon solvents, hard soluble resins, drying oil varnishes, and plasticizers
UV Curing—High reactive, cross-linking proprietary systems that dry by UV radiation	UV Curing—Highly reactive, cross-linking proprietary systems that dry by UV radiation
Gloss—Drying oils, very hard resins, minimal hydrocarbon solvents	Thermal Curing—Dry by applying heat and using special cross-linking catalysts

ferences between sheet feeding and web feeding and because of the many substrates on which the printer must transfer images.

The viscosity of lithographic ink varies according to the vehicle and the pigment formulation. Some inks appear fluid, while others are stiff and viscous. An ink that appears stiff does not necessarily require an additive such as a reducer. Some inks are *thixotropic*, which means they become stiff and heavy when left standing in their containers. Thixotropic ink is conditioned and milled by the ink train of the press before it reaches the printing unit. As a result, it is not as stiff and as heavy when it reaches the substrate as it was when it came from the can. The thixotropic phenomenon is typical in rubber-base ink formulations.

Rubber-Base Offset Ink

Rubber-base ink is a heavy formulation that gives quick setting and quick drying on both coated and uncoated paper. Rubber-base ink

is a good all-purpose offset and letterpress ink; it can remain on the press for long periods without forming a skin of dried ink. It is also compatible with aquamatic or conventional dampening systems (see chapter 11).

Rubber-base ink can be left on the press and still stay usable overnight. After standing overnight, the ink on the rollers might appear to be setting or stiffening, however. To overcome this problem, leave a heavy ink film on the rollers by simply placing extra ink on the large oscillating roller and running the press. When restarting the press after the long shutdown, let the press idle. If the press is aquamatic, remove the dampening solution. If the press is overinked slightly, **sheet off** the excess ink by manually feeding scrap sheets of paper in and out of the ink train. The paper will collect the excess ink and bring the ink train to a normally inked condition.

Rubber-base ink works well with aquamatic dampening systems in which the ink and water travel on the same rollers because of its high tack and viscosity. When inking up the press, use just enough ink to cover the ink rollers and run low on the dampening solution. Then increase both ink and water to achieve the desired density. Do not overink and/or overdampen. It is also important to keep the pH (acid content) of the fountain solution between 4.5 and 5.5. The pH factor keeps the nonimage area of the plate clean. Using additives with rubber-base inks is not recommended under normal conditions.

Nonporous Ink

Van Son's Tough Tex is an example of an ink with a nonporous formulated vehicle. Nonporous ink is suited for plastic-coated or metallic types of papers because it dries by oxidation rather than by absorption. It is important not to overdampen this ink. Because the substrate is nonporous, the fountain solution remains in the ink. Excessively dampened ink will not dry or set and will smear easily or set-off to the adjacent sheet. To prevent set-off, do not allow a large pile of paper to accumulate in the stacker and use small amounts of spray powder. An acid level of less than 4.5 will also retard drying. Ink additives are not recommended with this ink formulation.

Quick-Set Ink

Quick-setting, low-tack ink is formulated with the color and process printer in mind. Quick-set ink is usually available in a full range of process colors that will trap in any sequence. **Trapping** refers to the degree of ink transfer onto wet or dry ink films already on the substrate. Successful trapping depends on the relative tack and thickness of the ink films applied. Quick-set ink usually has very good drying qualities. It also produces accurate color and is scuff and rub resistant.

Additives for Lithographic Ink

The five ink characteristics that can be controlled with ink additives are tack, flow or lay,

drying quality, body, and scuff resistance. The following list identifies major lithographic ink additives and describes their effects and uses:

- *Smooth lith*: A liquid that controls lay and set-off. Smooth lith also reduces tack, which prevents picking. Because smooth lith is a colorless solution, it does not change the hue of the ink. It also aids in the drying process. Use approximately one capful per pound of ink. If you are using small amounts of ink, add smooth lith with an eyedropper.

- *Reducing compound*: Cuts the tack of ink without changing its body. This compound is used to alter the ink's viscosity. About ½ ounce of reducer to each pound of ink is a starting recommendation (a heaping tablespoon is approximately ½ ounce).

- *#00, #0 Litho varnish*: A thin-bodied compound that reduces the ink's body rapidly. Use approximately ¼ ounce of varnish to each pound of ink (a teaspoon is about ¼ ounce).

- *#1 Litho varnish*: Reduces tack and body. It is used as a lay compound and prevents picking.

- *#2, #3, #4, and #5 Litho varnishes*: Increase ink flow without changing the ink's body. Use about ¼ ounce of varnish to each pound of ink.

- *Overprint varnish*: A gloss finish used to print over already printed ink. Also used as an additive to help prevent chalking on coated paper. When overprinting with varnish, use it directly from the can. When using overprint varnish as an additive to prevent chalking, add 1½ ounces to each pound of ink.

- *Cobalt drier, concentrated drier, and three-way drier*: Basic types of driers. Cobalt and some concentrated driers

Table 16.9.   Troubleshooting lithographic ink problems

Problem	Cause	Cure
Set-off in delivery pile	Acid fountain solution	Test pH; keep between 4.5 and 5.5
	Overinking	Adjust fountain roller speed or fountain keys
	Not enough drier	Add three-way or cobalt drier
	Ink not penetrating paper	Add smooth lith or #00 varnish
	Too much paper in delivery pile	Remove small piles from press
	Paper pile being squeezed before ink sets	Handle with care
	Using wrong ink	Consult literature, manufacturer, or vendor
Scumming or tinting	Bad plate	Make a new one
	Overinking/underdampening	Adjust ink/water balance
	Incorrect pH	Keep pH between 4.5 and 5.5
	Too much drier	Change ink; use less drier
	Dirty molleton or dampening sleeve	Change cover or sleeve
	Soft ink	Add binding base, body gum, and aqua varnish
Slow ink drying	Incorrect pH—too acid	Test pH; keep between 4.5 and 5.5
	Bad ink/stock combination	Check with your paper or ink vendor
	Too little drier	Add drier
	Acid paper	Use different grade
Chalking	Too little drier	Add three-way or cobalt drier
	Wrong ink used	Overprint with varnish
	Ink vehicle penetrated too quickly	Add body gum or binding base
Hickies	Dust from cutting paper	Jog and wind paper before printing
	General dirt and dust	Clean, vacuum, and sweep press and press area
	Dried ink particles	Do not place drier or skinned ink into ink fountain
Scratching and scuffing	Overinked	Adjust ink fountain roller or keys
	Too little drier	Add drier concentrate or cobalt
	Wrong ink used	Overprint with varnish
	Ink not resistant enough	Add wax compound or scuff-proof drier

are recommended for jobs that will be cut or folded soon after printing. These driers should not be used for process colors or inks that will be overprinted. Some concentrated driers are rub proof. They are excellent for package printing where rough handling is anticipated. The ink's body can be built up with additives such as luster binding base, aqua varnish, and body gum.

■ *Luster binding base*: Builds viscosity, gives ink a luster finish, and makes ink more water repellent. Mix about 1½ ounces of binding base to each pound of ink.

■ *Aqua varnish*: Builds body and tack of ink. Works well for inks used in aquamatic types of presses. Aids the ink in repelling water and helps prevent emulsification (ink breakdown). Use approximately ¼ ounce of aqua varnish to each pound of ink.

■ *Body gum*: A heavy varnish that increases the ink's body, tack, and water repellency. Use ¼ ounce of body gum for each pound of ink.

■ *Gloss varnish and wax compound*: Increase the ink's resistance to scratching and scuffing. Gloss varnish gives ink a bright finish and helps prevent chalking on coated papers. Use about ½ to 2 ounces of gloss varnish to each pound of ink, depending on the ink's color strength. In addition to improving scratch resistance, wax compound also reduces tack and picking. It should not be used when ink is to be overprinted. This additive is good for package or label printing. Use about ¼ to 1 once of wax compound to each pound of ink.

Troubleshooting Lithographic Ink Problems

Many problems that occur on press are ink related. Set-off, scumming, slow drying, chalking, hickies, and scuffing are just a few. There is seldom one cause for each problem. Table 16.9 outlines common problems and their possible solutions.

Screen Printing Inks

Inks for screen printing are available in a rainbow of colors. Each type of screen printing ink has a binder suited to a specific class of substrate. Screen inks are formulated to be short and buttery for sharp squeegee transfer. These ink solvents should not evaporate rapidly. Rapid solvent evaporation would cause screen clogging during the printing process. Table 16.10 lists the many types of ink and substrates available to the screen printer.

Table 16.10. Screen printing inks and substrates

Ink Types	Substrates
Water soluble	Paper
Lacquer	Cardboard
Plastics	Textiles
Enamels	Wood
Metallic	Metals and foil
Ceramic	Glass
Electrical conducting	Lacquer-coated fabrics
Etching	Masonite
Luminescent	All plastics
Fluorescent	

Poster Ink

Inks whose end use is to produce point-of-purchase (PoP) displays, posters, wallpaper, outdoor billboards, greeting cards, and packaging materials are classified as poster inks. The following list identifies major poster inks and their uses:

■ *Flat poster ink*: Recommended for printing on paper and board stocks. Dries by solvent evaporation in about 20 minutes or can be force dried with special driers in seconds. Produces a flat finish and is used for displays, posters, and wallpaper.

■ *Satin poster ink and halftone colors*: Recommended for printing on paper and cardboard displays. Dries by solvent evaporation in about 20 to 30 minutes or can be force dried in seconds. Are used to print PoP displays, posters, outdoor billboards, greeting cards, and packaging materials. Standard colors are opaque; halftone colors are transparent.

■ *Gloss poster inks*: Produce a hard gloss finish and are formulated for paper and board stocks. Are used to print PoP displays, posters, greeting cards, corrugated displays, and packaging materials. Dry by evaporation in about 15 to 20 minutes or can be force dried in seconds.

- *Economy poster inks*: Much like flat poster ink series but lack the outdoor durability of flat poster ink. Made for supermarket and chain store applications. Dry to a flat finish in about 20 to 30 minutes by evaporation or can be force dried in seconds.

- *24-Sheet poster ink*: Formulated mainly for outdoor use. Are waterproof and flexible and can withstand finishing processes such as die cutting, creasing, and folding. Recommended for posters, outdoor displays, sign cloth, and bumper stickers. Dry by evaporation in about 20 to 30 minutes or can be force dried.

Enamel Ink

Enamels are inks that flow to a smooth coat and usually dry to a glossy appearance slowly. Because enamels penetrate the substrate less than do poster inks and dry mainly by oxidation, their drying times are much longer. Enamel inks include gloss enamel (normal and fast dry), synthetic gloss enamel, and halftone enamel.

Gloss Enamel

Gloss enamels are used to image substrates such as wood, metal, glass, paper, cardboard, and fiber drums. They are also used as an adhesive base for flocking or beads in a variety of decorative products. Normal gloss enamels dry by oxidation and should be allowed to stand overnight. In addition to the substrates listed for gloss enamel, fast-dry gloss enamels are commonly used to image polyethylene bottles and lacquer-coated fabrics. This formulation will air dry in approximately 60 min-

utes or it can be cured (dry and usable) in about five minutes at 180°F (82°C).

Synthetic Gloss Enamels

Synthetic gloss enamels have high durability and are excellent outdoor inks. The synthetic vehicle adheres to a wide variety of surfaces. These enamels are great for imaging metal, wood, masonite, glass, anodized aluminum, some types of plastics, novelty toys, synthetic decals, and packaging containers. They dry by oxidation in 4 to 6 hours or can be cured at 180°F (82°C) in about 30 minutes.

Halftone Enamels

Halftone enamels are formulated to give the special hues required for halftone process work. They are made to be durable under outdoor conditions. Halftone enamels are used on the same substrates as synthetic gloss enamels. Halftone vehicles dry to a satin finish (instead of a gloss finish) in 4 to 6 hours or can be cured in 30 minutes at 180°F (82°C). All halftone enamels are transparent inks.

Lacquer Ink

There are basically two types of lacquer inks:

- A general industrial lacquer ink that can produce a gloss or flat, hard finish with excellent adhesion to a wide variety of finishes

- A lacquer ink specifically formulated for making decals or printing on a specific substrate

Industrial Lacquer Ink

Industrial lacquer inks have numerous applications where chemical and abrasion resistance is important. They are used to image enamel, baked-urea or melamine-coated metal parts, and many polyester finishes. Because of their high opacity, lacquer inks are also popular for printing on dark-colored book cover stock. In addition, they are used to image lacquer and pyroxylin surfaces, many plastics (cellulose acetate, cellulose acetate butyrate, acrylics, nitrocellulose, ethyl cellulose) and many polyesters. Wood, paper, and foils can also be imaged with lacquers. Lacquer ink dries by solvent evaporation in about 30 minutes or can be jet dried in seconds. It can be cured for 10 minutes at 250°F (93°C) for industrial applications.

Decal Lacquers

Decal lacquers are made for printing decalcomanias. **Decalcomania** is the process of transferring designs from a specially printed substrate to another surface. Decalcomanias can also be printed on any surface where a flexible lacquer ink is needed. Consult the manufacturer's literature on printing procedures. Decal lacquer dries by solvent evaporation in one to two hours.

Printing on Plastic

Because so many plastics are being manufactured, a complete line of special inks is needed by screen printers. Plastic materials are either thermoplastic or thermosetting. A **thermoplastic** material is one that can be reformed. A **thermosetting** plastic cannot be reformed once it has been formed and cured. Table 16.11 lists several thermoplastic and thermosetting materials and some of their uses. Inks used to print on plastic include acrylic lacquer, vinyl, mylar, and epoxy resin inks.

Acrylic Lacquer Inks

Acrylic lacquer inks are general purpose formulations for imaging thermoplastic substrates such as acrylics; cellulose butyrate; styrene; vinyl; and acrylontile, butadiene, and styrene (ABS). They are used to image vacuum-formed products; in fact, adhesion and gloss are improved by vacuum forming.

Table 16.11. Screen printing inks, plastic substrates, and uses

Screen Printing Inks	
Print on Thermoplastic Substrates	**For End Use**
Acrylontile, butadiene, and styrene (ABS)	Safety helmets, automotive components, refrigerator parts, and radio cases
Acrylics	Outdoor signs
Cellulose acetate	Packaging, toys, book cover laminations, lampshades, and toothbrush handles
Cellulose acetate butyrate	Outdoor signs and packaging materials
Polyethylene	Cosmetic packaging
Polypropylene	Housewares, medicine cups, luggage, and toothpaste and bottle caps
Polystyrene	Construction, insulation, packaging, signs, displays, and refrigerator liners
Vinyl	PVC bottles, book covers, decorative tiles, and building components
Print on Thermosetting Substrates	
Melamine and urea	Cosmetic packaging and electrical components
Phenolics	Electronics and appliance industry (excellent insulators)

Acrylic laquer inks dry by solvent evaporation in about 30 minutes, or they can be force dried.

Vinyl Inks

Vinyl inks are naturally formulated for both rigid and flexible vinyl substrates. These include novelties, inflatables, wall coverings, and book covers. They dry by evaporation in approximately 30 minutes, or they can be force dried. The ink vehicles can be formulated to produce a flat, fluorescent, or gloss finish. Gloss vinyl inks can be vacuum formed.

Mylar Inks

Mylar inks are formulated to image untreated mylar and other polyester films. They dry by solvent evaporation in about 30 minutes, or they can be force dried.

Epoxy Resin Inks

Epoxy resin inks are formulated for difficult to print surfaces such as phenolics, polyesters, melamines, silicones, and nonferrous metals and glass. Epoxy inks dry by a chemical process called **polymerization** and require a catalyst prior to use. Once the catalyst is added properly, the ink must stand for approximately 30 minutes. This period of time allows the catalyst to become part of the solution and to activate the polymerization process. The polymerization drying process takes approximately two to three hours and about 10 days for maximum adhesion and chemical resistance. The ink can be cured in 30 minutes at 180°F, in 10 minutes at 250°F, or in four minutes at 350°F. Epoxy inks that require no catalyst must be cured or baked and are not recommended for outdoor use. They are used on thermosetting plastic, glass, and ceramics. They dry to a flat finish and must be baked at 400°F for three minutes or at 350°F for seven minutes. This type of epoxy ink is very suitable for nomenclature printing on circuit boards that must be soldered.

Resist Inks

Resist inks include alkali removable resist, solvent removable resist, vinyl plating resist, and solder resist inks.

Alkali Removable Resist Inks

Alkali removable resist inks are ideal for print-and-etch boards. They are less expensive than solvent removable resist inks (see following) and can reproduce fine lines. They cure from between 250°F to 265°F (120°C to 130°C) in about three or four minutes. Air drying takes about four or five hours. Alkali removable ink can be removed from the print-and-etch board after etching with a one to four percent solution of sodium hydroxide.

Solvent Removable Resist Ink

Only black solvent removable resist ink is formulated for plating etch-resistant operations such as circuit boards or nameplates. It has excellent adhesion and printability and resists acids such as ferric chloride, ammonium persulphate, and other common etchants. Removable etch resist ink air dries in 30 minutes or can be dried in five minutes at 200°F (93°C).

Vinyl Plating Resist Inks

Vinyl plating resist inks are also formulated for plating or etch resist operations. They air dry in approximately 30 minutes or in 10 minutes at 200°F (93°C). They can be removed after etching with trichlorethylene or xylol.

Plating Resist Inks

Plating resist inks are formulated specifically for plating operations. These inks are recommended for long plating cycles. Curing takes about 30 minutes at 200°F (93°C). The resist can be removed from the substrate with trichlorethylene or xylol.

Solder Resist Ink

Solder resist inks are alkyd melamine formulations for printing on copper or copper-treated coatings. Solder resist inks cure in 20 minutes at 250°F (140°C), in 10 minutes at 300°F (150°C), or in five minutes at 350°F (160°C).

Textile Ink

The three basic inks available to the textile printer are standard textile, plastisol, and dye inks.

Standard Textile Inks

Standard textile inks are formulated for cotton and other nonsynthetic fabrics. Ease of application makes these the most widely used inks for natural fabrics. They dry to a flat finish in about 45 minutes or can be cured in five minutes at 275°F (135°C).

Plastisol Inks

Plastisol textile inks are formulated for woven or knitted cotton and some synthetic fabrics. These inks can be printed directly onto the fabric or onto a coated release paper. When printing directly onto the fabric, cure for three minutes at 300°F (150°C). When printing onto release paper, cure for one and a half to two minutes at 225° to 250°F (107° to 120°C). Images on release paper can be transferred to fabric with an iron or a heat transfer machine. Be sure to allow the release paper and fabric to cool before peeling away the paper backing.

Dye Inks

Dye textile inks are water-in-oil concentrated pigments that must be mixed with a clear extender. The proportions of water and oil in the mixture determine the color strength. These inks are used to image cotton, rayon, linen, some nylon, and other synthetic blends. Dye textile inks dry in three minutes at 300°F (150°C) and in five minutes at 250°F (120°C). Water-soluble stencil material cannot be used with dyes because of their water content. For best results use knife-cut lacquer or a direct emulsion when preparing the stencil.

Letterpress Inks

Letterpress was once the major printing process in the industry. Much of what is known about ink today was discovered for the letterpress process. Although letterpress is gradually being replaced by other processes, it is still used to produce newspapers, magazines, packaging, and some commercial printing.

Some letterpress inks are much like offset inks. They are viscous, tacky compositions that dry mainly by oxidation. Letterpress inks include job, quick-set, gloss, moisture-set, and rotary inks.

Job Ink

Job inks are standard items in most shops. They must be formulated to be compatible with a wide variety of presses and papers. By using additives, the characteristics of job inks can be altered to be short-bodied for platen press work, to flow well on faster automatic presses, or to set properly on different papers. In many shops, a rubber-base offset ink is a common job ink for both general printing on platen letterpresses and on small duplicator machines.

Quick-Set Ink

Quick-set inks are used when it is necessary to print another run or another color immediately or to subject the substrate to finishing operations. Quick-set inks are used mostly on coated papers and boards. The ink vehicle is a resin-oil combination that dries by a combination of oxidation, absorption, and coagulation. When printed, the oil penetrates the stock and leaves the heavy material on the surface to dry by oxidation and coagulation (thickening).

Gloss Ink

Gloss inks are made of synthetic resins (modified phenolic and alkyd) and drying oils that do not penetrate the substrate as other inks do. This resistance to penetration produces the ink's high gloss. Gloss ink combined with a paper that resists penetration produces the best ink finish. Because gloss ink does not penetrate the substrate rapidly, it must dry mainly by oxidation and coagulation.

Moisture-Set Ink

Moisture-set inks are used mainly in printing food packaging. Because they are free of odor, moisture-set inks are used to print wrappers, containers, cups, and packaging materials. The ink vehicle is a water-insoluble binder dissolved in a water-receptive solution. The ink sets as the water-insoluble binder adheres to the paper when the water-receptive solvent is exposed to humidity. Atmospheric humidity or moisture in the stock might be sufficient to cause setting on some substrates.

Rotary Ink

Rotary inks are used mainly to print newspapers, magazines, and books. These types of publications require different substrates. Book papers range from soft to hard and are coated or uncoated. Rotary inks for book printing flow well and are quick setting to be compatible with these substrates. Magazines are usually printed on coated or calendered paper, which often requires a quick-drying, heat-set ink. Heat-set inks are composed of synthetic resins dissolved in a hydrocarbon solvent. Presses using heat-set inks must be equipped with a heating unit, cooling rollers, and an exhaust system.

Flexographic Inks

Flexography is a relief process much like rotary letterpress. This economical process is now printing a variety of substrates with a fast-drying, volatile ink. *Flexo printing* is used commonly to transfer an image to plastic films for laminating packaging, glassine, tissue, kraft, and many other paper stocks. It is also a popular process for printing wrapping paper, box coverings, folding cartons, and containers.

Flexographic ink is formulated with alcohols and/or esters and a variety of other solvents. Plasticizers and waxes are used to make the ink flexible and rub resistant. These volatile ingredients cause the ink to dry extremely rapidly by evaporation.

Water-base inks are also used to print paper, board, kraft, and corrugated substrates. There are many different water-base vehicles, including ammonia and casein. However, water-base inks are limited to absorbent stocks rather than nonabsorbent materials such as foil or plastic because they dry slowly and have low gloss. Water-base inks are popular because they are easy to use and are inexpensive.

Gravure Inks

Gravure printing uses two major kinds of ink: publications and packaging. Both inks are available in a full range of colors and properties. Publications ink basically consists of modified resins, pigments, and hydrocarbon solvents. Most packaging ink is formulated with nitrocellulose and various modifiers.

Because of the increased popularity of gravure printing on a variety of substrates, ink making and ink classification has become confusing. Many resins and solvents are used to make the gravure ink, and most are not compatible or cannot be mixed together. In order to know which solvents can be used with the inks purchased, a major ink supplier initiated the classification of various types of inks by using letters. In this system, all inks of a single type (a single letter) are compatible. Types of inks are identified by letters as follows:

■ A-type inks are low-cost aliphatic hydrocarbons

■ B-type inks use resins and aromatic hydrocarbons

■ C-type inks are made up of modified nitrocellulose and an ester class of solvent

■ D-type inks consist basically of a polyamide resin and alcohol

■ E-type inks are based on binders thinned with alcohols

■ T-type inks consist of modified chlorinated rubber reduced with aromatic hydrocarbons

■ W-type inks use water and sometimes alcohol as a reducing solvent

This method of classification indicates which solvents should be used to obtain the proper viscosity. When you are mixing ink, examine the technical data sheets carefully because ink suppliers frequently use trade names rather than type classifications.

Ultraviolet-Curing Inks

Ultraviolet-curing inks, or UV inks, are used mainly in specialty printing such as cosmetic packaging and metal decoration, screen printing, and flexography (especially on corrugated board). It is part of a technology referred to as **energy curing** and refers to inks that are cured or hardened by radiant energy or high-energy concentrated electron beams (referred to as EB curing). The drying process in conventional ink involves the evaporation of the ink vehicle, leaving behind the solids, which form the ink film on the substrate. In UV inks, all the components of the ink remain, but are chemi-

Table 16.12.   Solvent versus ultraviolet-curing ink

Solvent Evaporative Ink	RESINS
	PIGMENT
	SOLVENT
	ADDITIVES
UV Curable Ink	OLIGOMER
	MONOMER
	PIGMENT
	ADDITIVES
	PHOTOINITIATOR

cally transformed when exposed to ultraviolet radiation.

There are five major components of UV inks. As in conventional inks, there are pigments and additives. In addition, there are **monomers**, which are simple lightweight chemicals similar to solvents that determine the surface characteristics of the ink; **oligomers**, which are the resin providing the body and binding properties of the ink; and **photoinitiators**, which are the chemicals that react to the radiation and start the actual curing reaction (table 16.12)

The advantages of UV inks are significant, allowing for reduced downtime, because UV inks will not dry on press rollers, and the elimination of drying racks, because inks dry instantaneously when cured. These inks are highly durable and resistant to abrasion, which permits their usage in harsh environments and where chemical resistance is required. Their use is increasing because they do not emit toxic gases and **VOCs** (volatile organic compounds), as do heat-set inks using solvents. They can be used in nearly every printing process, on nearly every substrate, and on sheet-fed or web presses.

Key Terms

lignin
grain
grain long
grain short
score
bulk
opacity
finish
coated paper
reflectance
preconsumer paper waste
postconsumer paper waste
mill broke
recovered materials
wastepaper
de-inking
book paper
writing paper
cover paper

Bristol paper
basis weight
ream
M weight
regular sizes
equivalent weight
substance weight
nonstandard cut
make-ready
spoilage allowance
substrate
viscosity
tack
set
set-off
hardening
drying time
oxidation
penetration

evaporation
pigment
vehicle
additives
PANTONE Matching System®
sheet off
trapping
decalcomania
thermoplastic
thermosetting
polymerization
ultraviolet-curing inks
energy curing
monomers
oligomers
photoinitiators
VOCs

Review Questions

1. What is grain?

2. What is bulk?

3. What is opacity?

4. What is reflectance?

5. What is the purpose of de-inking in the paper recycling process?

6. What are the five basic main paper types?

7. What is basis weight?

8. What is M weight?

9. Why is spoilage always considered when calculating paper needs?

10. Define the word *substrate*.

11. Describe how the PANTONE Matching System® is used.

12. List at least four factors that slow the ink-drying process.

13. Define *polymerization*.

14. Differentiate between an inorganic pigment and an organic ink pigment.

15. Define ultraviolet-curing inks.

16. What are the three components of UV inks that differ from conventional inks?

17

Finishing Operations

Around A.D. 800, Charlemagne, the Frankish king who ruled from A.D. 742 to A.D. 814, ordered every abbot, bishop, and count to permanently employ a scribe who would reproduce books by hand and write in only roman letters. The books that the scribes lettered were to be bound and stored in special rooms called *scriptoriums*, which later evolved into what we know today as libraries.

Binding the finished pages of the books was nearly as important as copying. It was felt that just as each page of a manuscript needed to be decorated, so too did the case that held the pages together. The more valuable works were often encased in bindings of precious metal such as gold and silver. These books were sculptured works of art. They were often so cumbersome that special lecterns were built

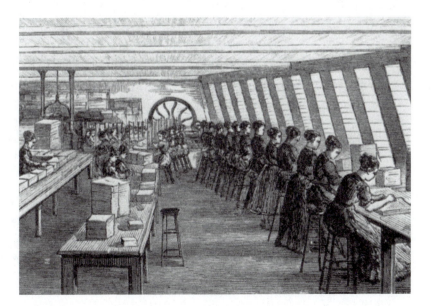

An industrial binding operation from around 1880

just to hold them while they were being read. There is even a recorded instance when a reader accidently dropped a well-bound, sculptured book and was seriously injured. He almost had to have his leg amputated.

By the 1400s, bookbinding had grown into a profession with several special subdivisions. The person who sewed the pages and built the cover was called the *forwarder*. The binding was then passed to a *finisher* who ornamented the cover. When a book was destined for a great deal of use, hog skin was frequently used as its binding. If it was to be a more expensive, carefully handled volume, calf or goat skin was often the binding choice. Large, inexpensive works were often bound in thin planks of wood.

The process of binding books remained a slow, specialized craft until the eighteenth century. The illustration shows one part of an industrial binding operation from around 1880. Several activities are taking place in this room. The women at the right are hand folding press sheets that will become signatures. Each is us-

ing an *ever-in-hand paper folder*, which today we would call a bone knife, to crease each edge as a fold is made. The two rows of tables to the left hold the folded signatures, which are piled in the sequence they will appear in the finished book. The women gather the book together as they walk down the rows, picking up one signature from each pile. After the signatures are gathered, three holes are punched through the edge of each one by the *stabbing machine*. The women seated in front of the large power wheel to the back are all involved with hand sewing the signatures together by passing thread through the punched holes. On the floor below, the sewed books are trimmed, glue is applied to the backs, and covers are put in place.

The bindery of 1880 may look a bit crude to us today, but it was a big step beyond the tedious book work of five hundred years before. The work that took months to complete in 1400 took only days in 1880. The same job can be done today in only a few minutes.

Objectives

After completing this chapter, you will be able to:

- Define the term *finishing operations*
- List the steps in safely operating an industrial paper cutter and identify machine parts, safety steps, size adjustment, and actual cutting.
- Describe the basic folding devices and differentiate between knife folders and buckle folders.
- List and define the common assembling processes, including gathering, collating, and inserting.
- Describe and explain the advantages of in-line finishing.
- List and define the common binding processes, including adhesive binding, side binding, saddle binding, self covers, soft covers, and casebound covers
- Describe several uses of demographic binding.
- Recall that finishing is not the final step in printing production, but is followed by packaging, shipping, and billing.

Introduction

Few printing jobs are delivered to the customer in the form in which they leave the printing press. Some work, such as simple business forms or posters, requires no additional handling other than boxing or wrapping. However, the vast majority of printed products require some sort of additional processing to meet the job requirements. The operations performed after the job has left the press are called **finishing**. Sometimes the term *postpress* is used.

A printer might do all the work on a complex book job through the press, and then hire another company to do the binding. Because of the specialized nature of some finishing operations, and the high cost of equipment, some companies offer bindery services to other printers. Recall from chapter 1 these types of companies are called **trade shops**. Most organizations, however, have a small section in the plant that does common finishing operations.

Larger companies that handle repetitive types of jobs, such as book printing, might actually attach finishing equipment to the press to create a continuous operation. This is called **in-line finishing**.

The most common finishing operations are cutting, folding, assembling, and binding. Techniques such as embossing, perforating, scoring, and die cutting were discussed in chapter 2, and are also classified as finishing procedures. Finishing operations do not follow any certain order or sequence in a job and are not necessarily all performed on the same job (although it is possible). The following sections examine some basic techniques within each of the four common operations. Because paper is the most widely used printing receiver, the discussions are restricted to devices and techniques used to finish paper materials.

Cutting

The Basic Cutting Device

The basic paper-cutting device used in the printing industry is called a **guillotine cutter**, or simply a paper cutter (figure 17.1). Guillotine cutters are manufactured in all sizes and degrees of sophistication. The size of the cutter is defined by the widest cut that it can make. Its sophistication is defined by the speed with which it can be set up and take a cut.

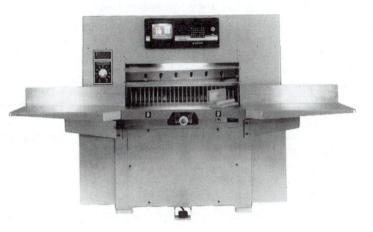

Figure 17.1 An industrial paper cutter.
Courtesy of AM International, Inc.

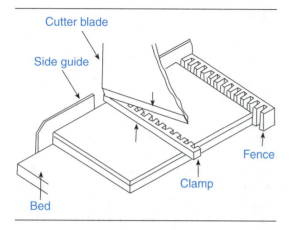

Figure 17.2   Diagram of a guillotine cutter.
The blade of a guillotine cutter moves down and across to cut the paper pile.

The bed of the guillotine cutter is a flat table that holds the paper pile. The back guide, or fence, is movable and is usually calibrated with some measurement system that tells the operator the distance of the guide from the cutter blade (figure 17.2). The side guides are stationary and are always at perfect right angles to the edge of the bed. The clamp is a metal bar that can be lowered into contact with the paper pile before a cut is made. Its purpose is to compress the pile to remove air and to keep the paper from shifting during the cut. The cutter blade itself is usually mounted up away from the operator's view and hands. When activated, the blade moves down and across to cut the pile in one motion.

The simplest sort of guillotine cutter is called a **lever cutter**. The lever cutter obtains its power from the strength of its operator. The operator moves a long lever that is linked directly to the cutter blade. The most common cutting device is a power cutter, which automatically makes the cut at the operator's command. An electric motor, which operates

a hydraulic pump, delivers the cutting action and the necessary power.

Moving paper onto and off of the bed of the guillotine cutter is the most fatiguing part of the paper cutter's job—one ream of paper can weigh 200 ponds and several tons of paper are usually cut in one day. Many devices are equipped with air film tables that work to reduce the operator's fatigue. With an air film table, the paper is supported by a blanket of air that escapes from small openings in the table. The air allows any size of paper pile to be moved easily over an almost frictionless surface (figure 17.3).

One of the most time-consuming actions when making a series of different cuts is resetting the fence, which controls the size of cut to be made. Automatic spacing devices can be programmed to remember the order and setting for as many as 20 different cuts. As the operator removes a pile, the machine readjusts the fence and is ready for the next cut by the time the new pile is in place. Some cutters can split the fence into three sections and then con-

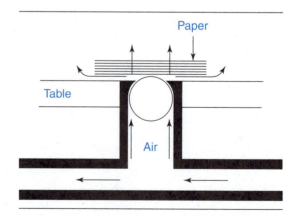

Figure 17.3   Side view of an air film table. A sketch of the side view of an air film table shows one of the table's small openings that releases air onto the table surface.

trol each position independently so that three different lengths can be cut with one motion of the cutter blade.

Cutting Safety

The guillotine cutter is named after the infamous guillotine that so efficient removed heads in times past. Today's guillotine cutter is intended to cut only paper. Like its ancestor, however, the guillotine cutter will cut easily almost anything placed in its path.

Today's paper cutters require an operator to use both hands to activate the cutter blade. Early machines had no such safety feature. As a result, many operators lost fingers or hands. No cutting device is foolproof, so it should be a standard procedure to keep hands away from the blade and blade path at all times. It is also a wise practice never to place anything but paper on the bed of a cutter. A steel rule or paper gauge can damage the cutter by chipping the blade's cutting edge. This requires resharpening the blade.

Operating a Paper Cutter

Paper cutting is a critical operation. The time and effort that go into every job can be made useless by one sloppy cut. The fence and side guide of a paper cutter function similarly to the side guide and headstop of a printing press. If the pile is in contact with both guides on the cutter, the sheet will be cut square and to the proper length.

Every job delivered to the paper cutter should have a cutting layout attached to the pile (figure 17.4). The **cutting layout** is generally one sheet of the job that has been ruled to show the location and order of the cuts. Sequence may not seem important at first, but if the cutting layout is not followed faithfully, some part of the main sheet will be damaged and the job will have to be done over.

The first step in operating a paper cutter is to determine the length of the first cut from the cutting layout and adjust the fence to that

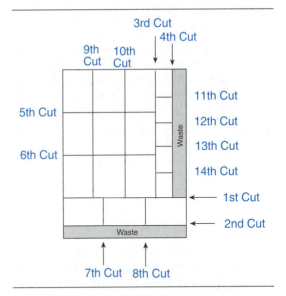

Figure 17.4 Sample cutting diagram

dimension. Place a paper pile on the cutter table and seat it carefully against both the fence and the side guide. Activate whatever control system the machine uses and make the cut. Remove the scrap paper and pull the cut pile free. The scrap paper is generally compacted and sold back to the paper mill to be recycled (figure 17.5). This type of paper by-

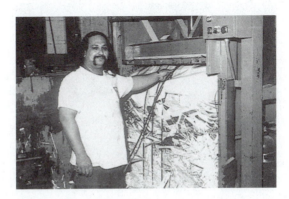

Figure 17.5 A typical packing device used to bind scrap into bales

product would be considered preconsumer waste.

If the job is large and the cutter is not equipped with automatic spacing, the same cut would be repeated for the entire pile. Then the fence would be adjusted for the next cut, and the entire pile would be cut again. If automatic spacing is used, the cutter goes to the next cutting position at the operator's command.

Folding

The Basic Folding Devices

The most basic folding device is called a **bone folder**. Printers have used it for hundreds of years to do hand folding. The process is simple. The printer registers one edge of the sheet with the other and then slides the bone folder across the seam of the paper to make a smooth crease (figure 17.6). Bone folders are used today only for very small, limited-run jobs. Nearly all industrial folding is now done by high-speed machines. The two common industrial folding devices are knife folders and buckle folders.

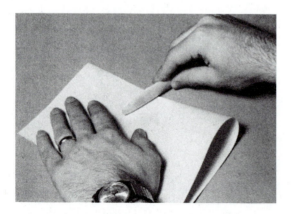

Figure 17.6   Example of a bone folder.
Courtesy of SUCO Learning Resources and R. Kampas.

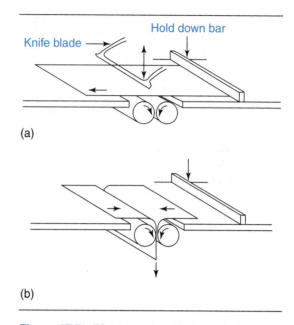

(a)

(b)

Figure 17.7   Diagram of knife folder operation

Knife Folders

Knife folders operate by means of a thin knife blade that forces a sheet of paper between two rotating rollers. The action takes place in two steps. First the sheet is carried into the knife folder and comes to rest at a fold gauge (figure 17.7a). Just as in a press, the sheet is positioned by means of a moving side guide. Next the knife blade is lowered between the two rotating rollers until the knurled (ridged) surfaces of the rollers catch the sheet, crease it, and pass it out of the way so the next sheet can be moved into register (figure 17.7b). If sets of rollers and knives are stacked one over the other, many folds can be made on the same sheet as the piece travels from one level to the next.

Buckle Folders

Buckle folders also pass the sheet between two rotating rollers (figure 17.8). The sheet in this system, however, is directed a bit differently. Instead of a knife or some other object

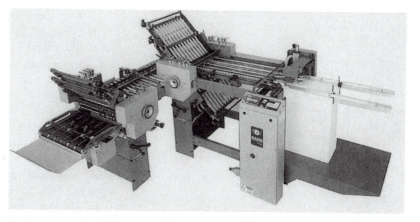

contacting the paper and causing the crease, the sheet is made to buckle or curve and passes of its own accord into the rollers. The sheet is passed between two folding plates by a drive roller until the sheet gauge is reached. The gap between the folding plates is so slight that the paper can only pass through the opening between the rollers. As the sheet hits the sheet gauge, the drive roller continues to move the sheet, which buckles directly over the folding rollers and passes through the two rollers to be creased and carried to the next level.

Sequence of Folds

Two important terms must be understood when discussing the sequence of folds. They are "right-angle folds" and "parallel folds." Figure 17.9a shows a traditional formal fold, called a **French fold**, that is frequently used in the production of greeting cards. To make a French fold, first fold a sheet across its length. Then make a second fold at a right angle to the first across the sheet's width. A French fold is a **right-angle fold** because it has at least one fold that is at a right angle to the others. Figure 17.9b illustrates an **accordion fold** that is commonly used in the preparation of road maps. An accordion fold can be made in a number of ways, but each fold is always par-

allel to every other crease. This is therefore called a **parallel fold**.

Ideally, all parallel folds should be made with the crease running in the same direction as (parallel to) the grain of the paper. Great stresses are involved with folding, and grain direction should be considered whenever possible (figure 17.10).

Some folding products result from using either right-angle folds or parallel folds or a combination of the two. The sequence of folds is important and must be considered throughout the printing process.

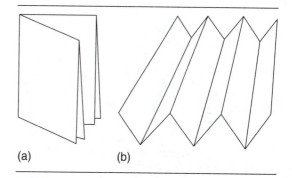

(a)   (b)

Figure 17.9 **Examples of French and accordion folds.** A French fold (a) is often used for greeting cards. An accordion fold (b) is often used for road maps.

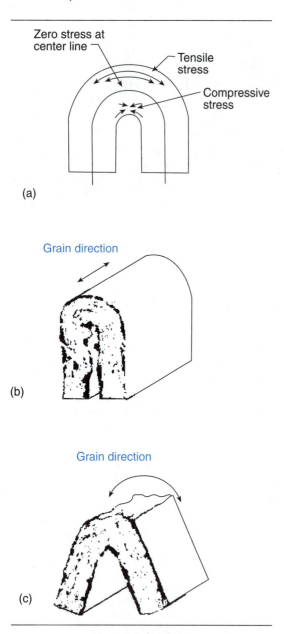

(a)

(b)

(c)

Figure 17.10   **Diagram showing areas of stress in folding (a). Fibers bend easily with the grain (b), but tend to break because of the stresses when folding against the grain (c).** Courtesy of Mead Paper.

The ideas of signature, work-and-turn imposition, and work-and-tumble imposition were discussed in chapter 6. When laying out for imposition, the order of folds in the bindery room dictates the position of each paper or form on the press sheet. Figure 17.11 shows four different ways that one sheet can be folded to produce a 16-page signature. It also shows the page layouts for one side of the sheet. If the job is laid out for one sequence of folds but another sequence is actually used, the final result will be unusable.

The sequence of folds is so important that the stripper always calls the bindery for a sample before starting to work on a job. The sample is a blank signature that has been folded on the piece of equipment and in the same sequence that will be used on the final press sheets. This blank signature is used to prepare the *dummy*, which shows page number positions and head and foot orientation. If the stripper makes an error in imposition, then the entire job will have to be redone. It is critical to understand that planning on nearly every job starts at the bindery and moves back to prepress. If cannot happen any other way.

Special Letterpress Applications

As discussed in chapter 2, the letterpress printing accounted for almost all the printing in the world for over 400 years. Although other printing processes have replaced it today, many specialty applications are still performed with a relief press. Some use no ink to create an image and others contribute to the final image design. Some of the possible operations are perforating, creasing, embossing, die cutting, hot foil stamping, and numbering. These specialty operations help letterpress to continue to play an active role in modern printing technology.

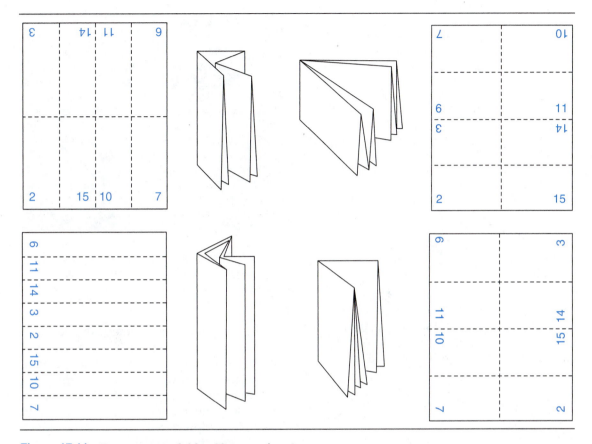

Figure 17.11   Four ways to fold a 16-page signature

Perforating is commonly required in jobs where portions of a piece are to be removed by the consumer (such as a ticket with a removable stub). In the perforating process, a series of very short slits are cut in the stock paper, leaving only a small bridge of paper in place. A perforating rule is a strip (generally about two points thick) of hardened steel that is made up of a series of equally spaced teeth. The teeth are driven through the stock by the motion of the press.

Creasing is a process that uses a solid strip of hardened steel to crush the grain of the paper to create a straight line for folding. The process is also referred to as *scoring*. A ragged or cracked fold can occur when the printer tries to fold a heavy paper or when the job requires that the sheet be folded against the grain of the paper (see chapter 16).

Embossing is a process that creates a three-dimensional image by placing a sheet of paper between a concave and convex (sometimes called female and male) set of dies (figure 17.12). The concave die is usually made of $\frac{3}{16}$- or $\frac{1}{4}$-inch brass and is mounted on a metal plate so that the topmost surface is type-high.

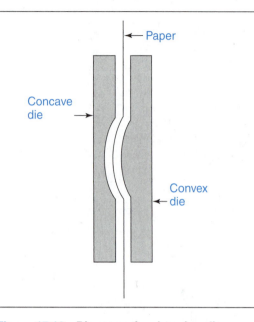

Figure 17.12 **Diagram of embossing dies.**
Embossing creates a three-dimensional image
between a convex and concave set of dies.

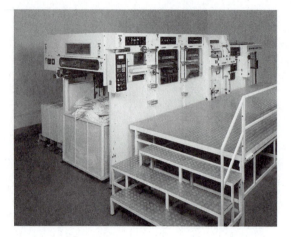

Figure 17.13 **Die cutter.** A modern commercial
die cutter capable of speeds of up to 8,000
impressions per hour.
Courtesy of MAN Roland.

The convex die is usually formed from the concave die, which has been mounted in a chase
and placed on the press.

Die cutting is a process that uses a ra-
zor-sharp steel rule to cut or punch various
shapes (typically irregular) in press sheets. It
is possible for the printer to produce basic die
forms, but complicated designs should be prepared by commercial firms that are tooled-up
to work with the hard steel rule (figure 17.13).

Hot foil stamping is a form of specialty
printing that uses the platen press to its full
advantage. In this process, the relief type form
is locked into a special chase which can be
heated while on the press. The ink rollers are
removed from the press and replaced with a
device that holds a plastic ribbon in front of
the type form. The ribbon is available in a variety of metallic colors, including gold and silver. As an impression is made, the heated type
combined with the pressure of the press during impression causes the metallic color from
the ribbon to be transferred to the press sheet.
Hot foil stamping is often used on greeting
cards, business cards, and book covers.

Numbering is a process that is used to
print a sequential number on each press sheet.
The pressure produced during each impression causes the numbering machine to advance to and print each sequential number.
Rate tickets are one example of a job that can
be numbered, printed, and perforated with the
relief process.

Assembling

Understanding Assembling Terms

Assembling is a term that is generally used to
describe several similar operations that have
the same final goal. Before a printed product
can be bound, the separate pieces must be
brought together into a single unit. For a hard-
back book, also called casebound, that unit
might be made up of ten 16-page signatures;
for a NCR forms job, the unit might be only
two sheets. Whatever the size of the unit, as-

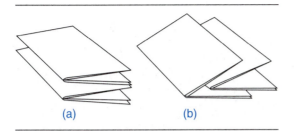

(a)   (b)

Figure 17.14 Two ways of assembling signatures. (a) Gathered signatures are placed next to each other. (b) Inserted signatures are placed one within another.

sembling generally includes gathering, collating, and inserting.

Gathering is the process of assembling signatures by placing one next to the other (figure 17.14a). Gathering is commonly used to prepare books whose page thickness will be greater than $\frac{3}{8}$ inch (0.95 cm).

Collating once meant checking the sequence of pages before a book was bound, but now it means gathering individual sheets instead of signatures.

Inserting is combining signatures by placing one within another (figure 17.14b). Inserting can be done for pieces whose final page thickness will be less than $\frac{1}{2}$ inch (1.27 cm).

Basic Assembling Techniques

Assembling procedures are either manual, semiautomatic, or totally automatic.

Manual Assembly

Manual assembly is exactly what the term implies. Piles of sheets or signatures are laid out on a table, and workers pick up one piece from each stack and gather, collate, or insert them to form bindery units. Equipment is available that improves this process a bit by moving the piles on a circulator table by a stationary worker. The process is still slow and clumsy, however. Manual assembly is reserved for ei-

ther extremely small jobs or for work so poorly planned that it cannot be assembled in any other way. Nearly all contemporary industrial assembly is done with semiautomatic or automatic equipment.

Semiautomatic Assembly

Semiautomatic assembly machines require no human interaction except to pile the sheets or signatures in the feeding units. In semiautomatic inserting, a moving chain passes in front of feeding stations. At each station an operator opens a signature and places it on the moving conveyor at *saddlebar* (figure 17.15). The number of stations at the machine is the same as the number of signatures making up the unit or book. By the time each saddlebar has moved past every station, an entire unit has been inserted or assembled and a saddle pin pushes the unit off the machine. The assembled unit can then be moved in line with a bindery unit for fastening or it can be stacked for storage and later binding. Little gathering or collating is done with semiautomatic equipment, but it uses the same general principle as inserting.

Automatic Assembly

Automatic assembling machines also use a conveyer device that moves past feeding stations. However, a machine instead of a person delivers the sheet or signature (figure 17.16). Almost all automatic systems are in line with bindery equipment so that assembly and fastening are accomplished at the same time.

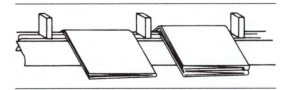

Figure 17.15 Diagram of open signatures placed at saddlebars on a conveyor

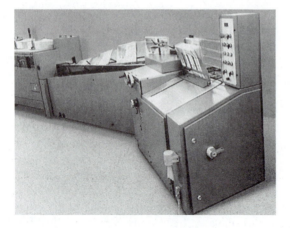

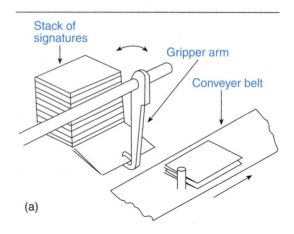

Stack of
signatures

Gripper arm

Conveyer belt

(a)

Figure 17.16   Automatic gathering during assembly.
Courtesy of Muller Martini Corporation.

Two designs of feeding mechanisms are used on automatic gathering devices (figure 17.17). Both designs allow for continuous loading of signatures because pieces are delivered from the bottom of the stack. With the swinging arm device, a vacuum sucker foot lowers one signature into position to be received by a gripper arm. The arm, with signature in hand, swings over the conveyer system and drops the piece into place on the belt. The rotary design uses the same suction system, but a rotating wheel with gripper fingers removes the signature and delivers it to the moving chain. With each rotation, the rotary device can gather two signatures and is therefore considered faster than the swinging arm mechanism.

Automatic collating equipment is similar in design to gathering machines, except that feeding is generally done from the top of the pile, as with most automatic printing presses. Even though the machine must be stopped to load the feeding units, the device is nearly as efficient as continuous devices because many single sheets can be placed in the same area that only a few large signatures would take up.

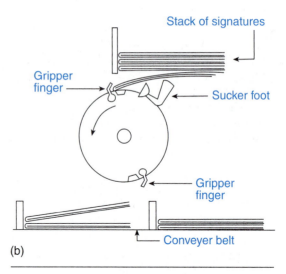

Stack of signatures

Gripper
finger

Sucker foot

Gripper
finger

Conveyer belt

(b)

Figure 17.17   Two types of feeder mechanisms used on automatic gathering machines. (a) A swinging arm mechanism and suction action are used to move signatures onto a conveyer belt, or (b) a rotating wheel with gripper fingers does the same.

Automatic inserting devices also operate with a moving belt and receive individual units from a stack feeder (figure 17.18). Many automatic inserting units are part of a closed system of operations that extends from the composition room through plate preparation

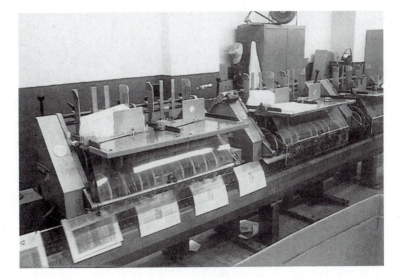

Figure 17.18 Perfect binding machine

and press and past assembly to fastening, trimming, labeling for mailing, and even bundling of piles by zip code order. Magazines such as *Time* and *Newsweek*, with editions of sometimes one million copies and little allowance for production time, require accurate planning, speed, accuracy, and a tightly controlled closed system of production. High-speed inserting is done by a combination of vacuum and grippers that removes the signature, opens it, and places it in the proper sequence with the other signatures in the job.

Binding

It is difficult to categorize neatly all the methods used by the printing industry to fasten the assembled unit into its final form. The type of cover used on a printed piece is often confused with the actual method of attaching the pages. Sheets or signatures can be fastened by using such techniques as adhesive, side, or saddle binding. The fastened pages can be covered with self-covers, soft covers, or casebound covers. The following sections describe the most common binding methods and covers.

Adhesive Binding

The simplest form of **adhesive binding**, called **padding**, is found on the edge of the common notepad. In the adhesive binding process, a pile of paper is clamped together in a press and a liquid glue is painted or brushed along one edge. The most common gluing material is applied cold and is water soluble while in a liquid state, but becomes insoluble in water after it dries. Individual sheets can be easily removed by puffing them away from the padding compound.

The popular paperback or pocket book is an example of an adhesive binding technique called **perfect binding** or **patent binding**. The perfect fastening process is generally completely automatic (figure 17.19). If signatures rather than individual sheets are combined, the folded edge is trimmed and roughened to provide a greater gripping surface. The liquid adhesive (generally hot) is then applied, and a gauzelike material called **crash** is sometimes embedded in the pasty spine to provide additional strength.

Adhesive binding offers many advantages in both book and magazine publishing.

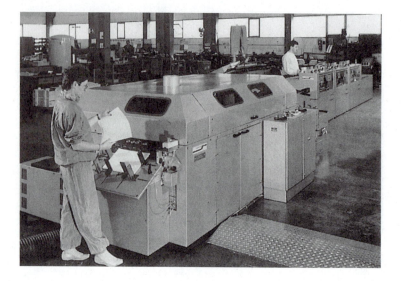

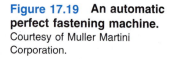

Figure 17.19 **An automatic perfect fastening machine.** Courtesy of Muller Martini Corporation.

Not only is the process relatively fast and inexpensive, but it can be used to combine a number of different printing substrates in the same publication. In addition to the printed signatures used for most of the publication, special signatures or single pieces of paper, printed plastic sheets, and other printed substrates can be added to the publication. Paper of different thicknesses and different finishes may also be added without affecting the binding process.

Side Binding

A common office stapler is probably the most familiar device used for **side binding**. With this technique, the fastening device is passed through a pile at a right angle to the page surface. In addition to the wire staple, side binding can be accomplished by mechanical binding, looseleaf binding, or side-sewn binding.

Mechanical Binding

Mechanical binding is a process that is usually permanent and does not allow for adding sheets. One of the most common mechanical binders is a wire that resembles a spring coil.

The wire runs through round holes that have been punched or drilled through the sheets and cover. The coil is generally inserted by hand into the first several holes of the book. Then the worker pushes the wire against a rotating rubber wheel that spins the device on the rest of the way.

Looseleaf Binding

Looseleaf binding devices are considered permanent, but they allow for the removal and addition of pages. The casebound, three-ring binder is one popular looseleaf item, but they come in many other forms. An increasingly popular device is a plastic comb binder (figure 17.20). With this system, a special device is used to punch the holes, and another device expands the plastic clips so the pages can be inserted on the prongs of the clips. The binder can be opened later to add sheets or it can be removed completely and used to fasten another unit.

Side-Sewn Binding

One pattern for side sewing a book is shown in figure 17.21. With hand sewing, the pile is

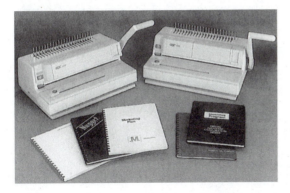

Figure 17.20 **A hand-operated plastic punch and binder.**
Courtesy of Plastic Binding Corporation.

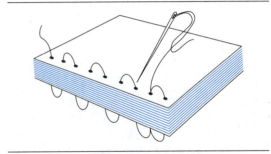

Figure 17.21 **Diagram of hand side sewing of a book**

first drilled (always an odd number of holes) and them clamped in place so the individual pages will not shift. A needle and thread is passed in and out of each hole from one end of the book to the other and then back again to the last hole, where the thread is tied. Automatic equipment has been designed that produces a side-sewn book rapidly and accurately, although with a different thread pattern than the hand technique (figure 17.22). The main drawback to side-sewn or wire-stapled

side binding is that the book does not lie flat when open.

Saddle Binding

Saddle binding is the process of fastening one or more signatures along the folded or backbone edge of the unit. The term comes from the fact that a signature held open at the fold resembles—with some imagination—the shape of a horse's saddle.

Popular news magazines are fastened by saddle wire stitching. With large editions, the stitching is done automatically in line with the

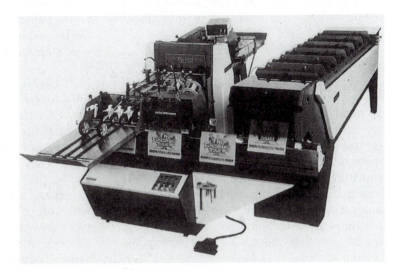

Figure 17.22 **An automatic side-sewing device.**
Courtesy of Rosback Company.

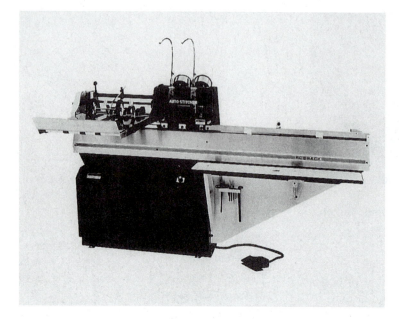

Figure 17.23 A semiautomatic saddle-stitching device.
Courtesy of Rosback Company.

inserting of signatures. Saddle wire stitching can also be done by hand with large staple machines. It can be performed semiautomatically: the operator merely places the signature over a support, the wire is driven through the edge, the wire is crimped, and the signature is delivered (figure 17.23). This method of wire fastening is generally restricted to thicknesses of less than $\frac{1}{2}$ inch (1.27 cm).

Smyth sewing is commonly considered the highest-quality fastening technique in the world today. Sometimes called *center-fold sewing*, the process produces a book that will lie nearly flat when open. Nearly all Smyth-sewn books are produced on semiautomatic or completely automatic equipment. Semiautomatic devices require an operator to open each signature and place it on a conveyer belt that moves it to the sewing mechanism and combines it with the rest of the book. Automatic machines are usually in line with a gathering mechanism that delivers a single unit to the sewing device.

Self-Covers

Self-covers are produced from the same material as the body of the book and generally carry part of the message of the book. Newspapers and some news magazines have self-covers. No special techniques are required to assemble or attach the cover to the body of the work. Self-covers are generally restricted to the less expensive binding techniques, such as wire staple, side binding, or saddle fastening.

Soft Covers

Soft covers are made from paper or paper fiber material with greater substance than the material used for the body of the book. Soft covers rarely carry part of the message of the piece. They are intended to attract attention and to provide slight, temporary protection. Paperback books are one example of books with soft covers. Soft covers can be glued in place, as with perfect binding, or they can be attached by stitching or sewing. The covers are generally cut flush with the pages of the book.

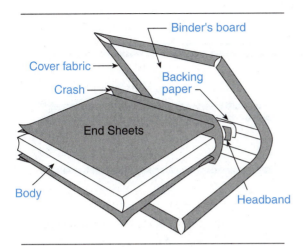

Figure 17.24 **The anatomy of a casebound book**

Casebound Covers

A **casebound cover** is a rigid cover that is generally associated with high-quality bookbinding. The covers are produced separately from the rest of the book and are formed from a thick fiber board glued to leather, cloth, or some form of moisture-resistant, impregnated paper (figure 17.24). A casebound cover ex-

tends over the edge of the body of the book by perhaps $\frac{1}{8}$ inch (0.32 cm). This *turn-in* provides additional protection for the closed pages.

In order to casebind a book, several operations called *forwarding* are necessary. All forwarding can be completed on automatic equipment. First, the signatures are trimmed, generally by using a three-knife device that cuts the three open sides of the signature in a single motion (figure 17.25). The back or fastened edge of the book is then rounded. Rounding gives the book an attractive appearance and keeps the pages within the turn-in of the cover (figure 17.26). Next the edges of the signature are backed. The purpose of backing is to make the rounding operation permanent and to provide a ridge for the casebound cover. Backing is accomplished by clamping the rounded book in place and mushrooming out the fastened edges of the signatures (figure 17.27). Next the book goes through a *lining-up* process, which consists of gluing a layer of crash and strips of paper called *backing paper* to the backed edges of the signatures. The crash and backing paper are later glued to the case and provide additional support for the book. A headband is a deco-

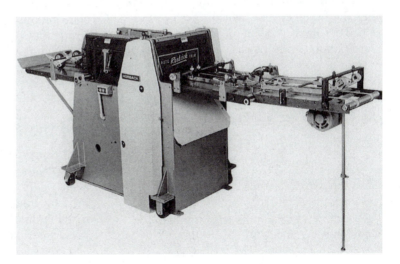

Figure 17.25 **A three-knife trimming machine.**
Courtesy of Rosback Company.

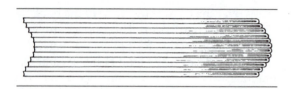

Figure 17.26 **Rounded signatures of a book**

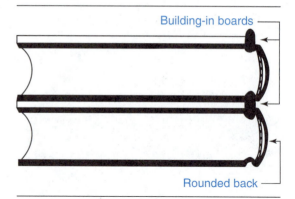

Figure 17.28 **Diagram of the use of traditional building-in boards**

rative tape that can be attached to the head and tail of the back of the book to give a pleasing appearance. The headband is not always attached, however.

The case itself is made from two pieces of thick binder's board glued to the covering cloth. The cloth can be printed before gluing to the board or it can be printed afterward by such processes as relief hot stamping or screen printing. The binder's board is cut so that it extends over the body of the book by at least $\frac{1}{8}$ inch (0.32 cm) on each open edge and misses the backed ridge by the same distance. The cloth is cut large enough so that it covers one side of both boards completely and extends around the edges by at least $\frac{1}{2}$ inch (1.27 cm) (see figure 17.24). The positions of the two boards on the cloth are critical and must be controlled carefully. Automatic equipment exists that cuts both the board and the cloth and joins the two pieces in their proper positions.

The final process of joining the forwarded book with the case is called *casing in*.

In this process, the two parts of the case are attached by two sheets called **end sheets** (see figure 17.24). End sheets can be the outside leaves of the first and last signatures, or they can be special pieces that were joined to the pages during the assembling and fastening operations.

To case in a book, the end sheets are coated with glue, the case is positioned on the end sheets, and pressure is applied. The pressure must be maintained until the adhesive is dry. This was traditionally accomplished by stacking the books between special *building-in boards* (figure 17.28). This technique has been replaced gradually by special heat-setting adhesives that dry in a matter of seconds once the end sheets contact the case.

In-Line Finishing

Traditionally, the postpress operations of collating, gathering, binding, and finishing have been costly, labor-intensive operations handled by trade shops with specialized equipment. In-line finishing equipment links postpress operations directly to the press room.

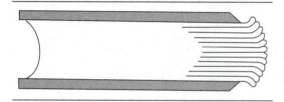

Figure 17.27 **Backing the edges of the signatures**

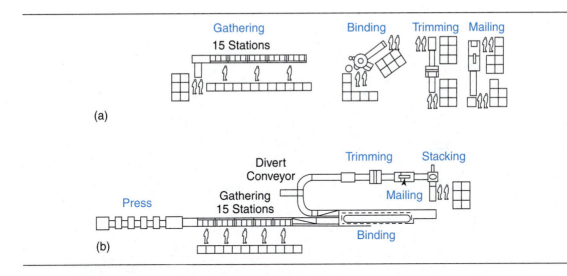

Figure 17.29 **Off-line finishing compared to in-line finishing.** An off-line finishing operation (a) may require as many as four operators and seventeen helpers to produce 2,000 to 4,000 finished units per hour. In contrast, an in-line operation (b), in which all finishing devices are connected and operate automatically, can require as few as three operators and eight helpers to produce 8,000 to 14,000 units per hour.

The sheet or web moves directly from the delivery end of the press into the binding unit.

In-line finishing reduces the amount of labor required and speeds the finishing process. Figure 17.29 shows plant diagrams for both in-line and off-line finishing systems. The configuration in figure 17.29a illustrates an off-line design: The job is first printed, the press sheets are next moved physically to another room for assembly, then the sheets are moved to the trimming or other finishing operations, and finally they are carted to packaging or the mail room. The layout in figure 17.29b links all operations: As each individual form is printed and dried, it travels directly to an assembly unit, then to trimming, and leaves the system in boxes, ready for delivery (figure 17.30). With in-line operations a sheet of paper enters the system at one end and exits at the other as a finished product (figure 17.31).

Demographic Binding

The sophistication and intensity of competition for consumer attention has created a relatively new area of direct-mail and publication marketing. The term for this new area is **demographic binding**.

At the heart of many in-line finishing operations is a computer that not only controls the printing finishing equipment but contains information that personalizes each product element for a particular individual.

Say a manufacturer has a product that would appeal to the following very narrow part of the American population:

- Spanish speaking
- College educated
- Interested in coin collecting

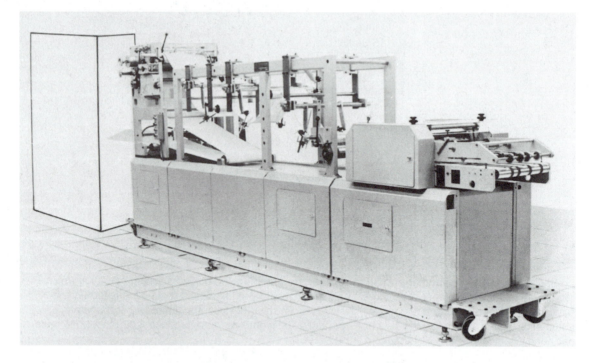

Figure 17.30 **In-line finishing system.** This in-line finisher is designed to be rolled into place and set up at the outfeed side of the press. The machine can fold, cut, trim, glue, slit, score, perforate, and stack in one continuous operation. Additional folders can be added as modular units to produce multiple folds. Stacked items can be delivered directly to additional in-line equipment for further finishing and addressing. Courtesy of Custom-Bilt Machinery, Inc.

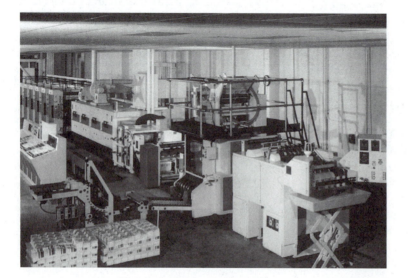

Figure 17.31 **In-line finishing.** This is a six-color web offset press equipped with an in-line folder, trimmer, and stitcher. Note the computer console that controls the operation. Courtesy of Rockwell Graphic Systems, Rockwell International Corporation.

- Over 35 years of age
- Annual income above $40,000

These descriptors are called *demographics*, which simply means characteristics of a population of people. There are companies that specialize in selling mailing lists across any number of demographic characteristics. With demographic binding, the computer can be used to link mailing information to a label or ink-jet printer that addresses each publication in zip code order.

Another application of demographic binding is selective assembly. Say a magazine has five signatures. The last signature could be designed so its contains the same editorial content (articles or news pieces) as the original signature but different advertisements. In other words, the last signature might be printed in three different ways: one for the eastern part of the United States, one for the Midwest, and another for the western portion of the country. During finishing, the computer then selectively assembles final copies based on address information. Thus, it is possible for local advertisers to place ads in a national magazine such as *People* and have their information appear only in the magazines received by customers within their selling area. Magazines delivered to Chicago, for example, will contain advertisements for Chicago merchants; those magazines delivered to New York will advertise New York merchants.

Even greater personalization is possible. Surely every adult in America has received some form of sweepstake promotion announcing in print that he or she just won a million dollars. Ink-jet technology, and the new digital presses (see chapter 15), can merge demographic information directly in the printed piece—not just on a mailing label. Add further digital imaging technology to the mix (see chapter 5) and full-color pictures of the recipient on direct mail pieces will soon be commonplace.

Demographic binding meets advertisers' and publishers' demands for the illusion of personalized attention and, because products are addressed in zip code order, allows printed products to qualify for lower postal rates.

Packaging and Shipping

Those new to the printing industry think the finishing process is over after all finishing operations are complete. Even the term *finishing* on the surface suggests that everything is done. In reality, there are at least two more steps: packaging and shipping and sending the customer a bill. Billing is discussed in chapter 18.

The customer specifies the end use of a printed job. Some jobs must be packed in cartons for either shipping or storage. For example, *Printing Technology* is produced in sets of 5,000 units. The books are packed in cartons of 16 books and shipped to a distribution plant in Florence, Kentucky. As orders arrive at the plant, labels are placed on the cartons and the cartons are shipped to a bookstore. For single-copy sales, a carton is opened and one book is placed in a mailing envelope. Most books,

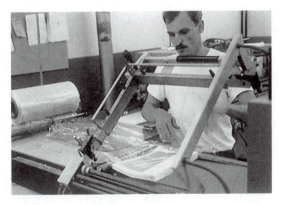

Figure 17.32 Shrink wrapper

however, leave the bindery in boxes for later distribution and are not delivered to readers individually.

Magazines, on the other hand, leave the bindery individually addressed for consumer delivery. Some plants that specialize in magazine or periodical printing have direct links to mailing organizations, such as the United States Postal Service or alternative delivery companies. Pieces are addressed, sorted, given the appropriate indicia, and bagged according to geographic area. **Indicia** are similar to stamps in that they indicate that postage or delivery charges have been paid. They are printed on the piece directly and indicate an account number to which mailing is charged.

A very popular packaging method is shrink wrapping (figure 17.32). Individual items, or a set of several items, is inserted in a thin polymer film. The wrap is then cut, and the entire package is heated. The polymer is heat-sensitive and shrinks when warmed. The result is a strong, nearly weightless package.

Key Terms

finishing
trade shop
in-line finishing
guillotine cutter
lever cutter
cutting layout
bone folder
knife folder
buckle folder
French fold
right-angle fold
accordion fold
parallel fold

perforating
creasing
scoring
embossing
die cutting
hot foil stamping
numbering
assembling
gathering
collating
inserting
adhesive binding
padding

perfect binding
patent binding
crash
side binding
saddle binding
self-cover
soft cover
casebound cover
end sheets
demographic binding
indicia

Review Questions

1. What are the most common finishing operations?

2. How is the size of a guillotine paper cutter defined?

3. Differentiate between the operation of a knife folder and that of a buckle folder.

4. What do the terms *right-angle fold* and *parallel fold* mean?

5. What do the terms *creasing, perforating, embossing, die cutting, hot foil stamping,* and *numbering* mean?

6. What are the differences between gathering, collating, and inserting?

7. What does the term *perfect binding* mean?

8. Give three examples of side binding.

9. What is the process of saddle binding?

10. Explain the differences between self-covers, soft covers, and casebound covers.

11. What does the term *forwarding* describe?

12. Describe a typical in-line finishing operation.

13. What are some uses of demographic binding?

14. Why is finishing *not* the last step in the printing process?

18

The Business of Printing

Historical Background

Printing has made many contributions to our written and spoken language. Before printers, spelling and punctuation were inconsistent. When books were hand written by medieval scribes, words, sentences, and even paragraphs could be run together on the whim of the scribe. These words and sentences could become very difficult to read. Spaces between words, commas, periods, and other marks were invented by early printers to act as signals to the reader. There are many examples of print-ers' language in conversation today. Two examples are the terms *uppercase* and *lowercase* to describe capital letters and small letters in our alphabet, respectively.

One of the early places to store pieces of foundry type was in a set of individual bins called a *news case* (see illustration). Two news cases were necessary to store a complete alphabet. There was one case for the minuscule, or small, letters and another for the majuscule, or capital, letters. In practice, the printer placed the

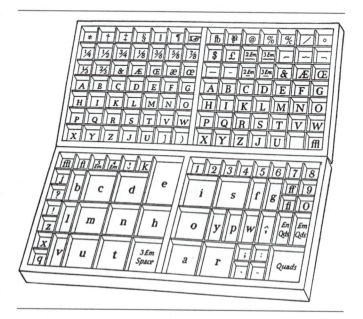

One of two news cases necessary to store a complete alphabet.
Courtesy of Mackenzie and Harris, Inc.

case holding the capital letters above the case containing the small letters.

When the master printer wanted a certain letter, he would call out to his *devil* (a worker with less status than an apprentice) "Get me a *C* from the upper case." When he was trying to save time he would shout, "Get me an uppercase *C*." This is how the terms *uppercase* and *lowercase* were born.

These terms have been accepted as the nicknames for the capital and small characters in our alphabet and are a direct result of the language of the early relief printers.

Objectives

After completing this chapter, you will be able to:

- Explain how estimates are determined for the length of time required to complete a task and how to use a unit/time standards form.

- Explain how fixed costs are identified and determined in production costs.

- Explain the two methods used in job costing.

- Outline the basic job estimating process.

- Discuss how a job work order is used to direct a job through scheduling and production control.

- Describe the major components of an automated data collection and information management system.

- Describe three approaches to e-management by the Internet.

Introduction

Printing is an exciting industry. Few other enterprises attract such devotion, commitment, and enthusiasm from its participants. The expression "I've got printer's ink in my blood" expresses the special relationship between worker and craft. The printing craft, the process of translating ideas into physical forms that can be communicated to millions of other people, is so appealing that printers often lose sight of the true aim of their business. In America, the purpose of commercial organizations is to make profits.

What is profit? In the simplest terms, profit is the numeric difference between what it costs to perform a task or service and what the customer pays. However, as with most things in life, profit is usually not that simple. Sometimes it is difficult to anticipate all costs associated with a task.

Say you are hired by a neighbor to spend two days digging post holes for a new fence. You work 8 hours the first day and are paid $5 per hour. You have a $40 profit. Your neighbor then asks you to bring a spade the second day. You buy a spade for $19.20. At the end of the second day, your profit is now only $40 − $19.20, or $20.80. Obviously, having to buy the spade decreased your profits. You now own the spade, however.

If you can find other jobs digging post holes with the spade, your profit will go up. Say you are able to obtain 10 days of work with another neighbor. You can spread out the cost of the spade over those 10 days ($19.20 ÷ 10 = $1.92). If you charge $1.92 of the spade against your profit for each day, then your *net profit* each day is $40 − $1.92, or $38.08.

What you have done is to amortize the cost of your spade over the entire digging job. If you had many more digging jobs, then the daily cost of the tool would go down, and your profit would continue to go up. **Amortization** is the process of distributing equipment costs across time periods or jobs. The term **depreciation** is often used with amortization interchangeably, but depreciation more accurately refers to annual decreasing value because of amortization.

The previous scenario is easy to understand. However, what if you had to buy a shovel on the third day of work, a special set of wire cutters on the fourth, replace worn gloves on the sixth, and buy a hammer on the eighth? The process of amortization and determining profit could then require more thought.

Managing a printing company profitably is even more complex than this. The company must earn a profit or it will go out of business.

This chapter introduces basic concepts in four key areas:

- Determining real printing costs
- Job estimating and job costing
- Production planning
- e-management

Determining Real Printing Costs

There are three major **cost centers** in any manufacturing operation:

- Human labor
- Fixed costs (equipment and facilities)
- Raw materials

The most critical cost center is human labor. Included in this first category are all the people who work in the company—salespeople, estimators, accountants, managers, clerical staff—not just craftspeople.

Fixed costs include items for which there would be expenses whether the company printed one job or 10,000 jobs in a year. The physical space the organization occupies must be leased or provided for by monthly mortgage payments. The space must be heated or cooled, it must have lights, and it must have normal utilities. Most people think of presses as normal printing equipment, but literally hundreds of other tools, such as storage cabinets, telephones, computers, printers, desks, and wastebaskets, must all be in place and ready to use when an order arrives. Even if no job comes in the front door, the expenses for the equipment and facilities remain.

Raw materials are obvious needs. Ink and paper have been the foundation of printing for more than 500 years. However, other supplies—chemicals, rags, razor blades, pencils, and even toilet paper—are part of running a company. In addition to raw materials, outside materials or services purchased to complete a job must be considered, such as embossing, specialty die cuts, or even additional illustrations and image acquisition. Paper and ink cost estimates were introduced in detail in chapter 16. As a result this cost center is not discussed here.

It would be easy if a company could perform a job, measure the amount of time it took, and then bill the customer. Unfortunately, few orders come in with the direction "just bill me." Clients want to know the cost before the job is performed. This prediction is called a **job estimate** or a bid.

Therefore, every company must know how long it takes to perform a specific task. Without information on time and cost standards, it is impossible to predict the cost of a job accurately. A bid would be either so low that the company loses money or so high that a competitor gets the job.

Determining the Cost of Human Labor

A variety of techniques are used by the printing industry to determine labor standards. The complexity or simplicity of the procedures depends on the size and diversity of the business. A small *"quick-print"* company that uses only one sheet size sold in units of 100 will have one standard—a set amount of dollars per 100 sheets. A large job shop, on the other hand, might need to determine labor standards for as many as 1,000 different operations. Let us consider the procedures that a medium-sized job shop might use to determine labor costs. In this case, medium sized means from 30 to 50 employees and gross annual sales around $4 million.

Figure 18.1 shows a typical form used in any department of the plant to determine unit/time standards. The department supervisor maintains this form for each operation or piece of equipment. Some supervisors record every job; others select only a random sample of each week's work to be entered on the form. In either instance, an entry is simply the average time needed to complete a specified number of units for a specific operation.

Standards Sheet

Thomas E. Schildgen & Associates, Inc.

Description		Department		Equipment		Unit Quantity	
Labor		Press		GTO		1,000 sheets	

Entry	Date	Employee	Units	Total Hours	
1	7/9	Mike Wick	5	1.13	0.23
2	7/9	Will Romano	7	1.44	0.21
3	7/10	Joe Metcalf	2	0.88	0.44
4	7/10	Mike Wick	4	0.82	0.21
5	7/10	Bill Mulvey	10	2.1	0.21
6	7/11	Phil age	5	0.98	0.20
7	7/11	Mike Wick	2	0.9	0.45
8	7/11	Doug Clayton	6	1.3	0.22
9	7/11	Will Romano	5	1.2	0.24

Total   2.39

Total (2.39   ) ÷ No. Entries (9   ) =   0.27

Standard for this Sample = .27 hrs / M

Figure 18.1   A typical unit/time standards form

The example in figure 18.1 is concerned with determining the average time to print 1,000 sheets of paper in the press section on a GTO press. On July 9, Mike Wick ran 5,000 sheets in 1.13 hours. The *unit quantity* in this case is 1,000 sheets, so Wick ran 5 units (5,000 ÷ 1,000 = 5). This run averaged 0.23 hours per unit (1.13 hours ÷ 5 units = 0.23 hours per unit). The supervisor took a random sample of work on the GTO press for six different press operators across several shifts and several days and recorded them on the form. In each case the average time per unit (1,000 sheets), or the target unit quantity, was determined.

Industry has found it more convenient to record time in decimal units instead of hours, minutes, and seconds. It is far simpler to multiply $12.00 per hour times 1.13 rather than 1 hour, 7 minutes, and 48 seconds. The number 1.13 is a decimal equivalent of 1 hour, 7 minutes, and 48 seconds.

The arithmetic to determine a decimal equivalent is easy to follow:

1. Convert 48 seconds to minutes:

   48 seconds/60 seconds in 1 minute = 0.8 minute

2. Convert minutes to hours:

   a. 7 minutes + 0.8 minute = 7.8 minutes
   b. 7.8 minutes/60 minutes in an hour = 0.13 hour

3. Combine all units:

   1 hour + 0.13 hour (7 minutes and 48 seconds) = 1.13 hours

When the supervisor determined the labor standards sheet was full in figure 18.1, the *average hours per unit* column was totaled (2.39) and that total was divided by the number of

entries (9) to give the standard time needed to print 1,000 sheets (0.27 hours).

When a request for an estimate comes in that calls for 7,500 sheets to be printed on the GTO, the estimator uses this labor standard to determine how long it will take to print the job:

7,500 sheets = 7.5 units (7,500 ÷ 1,000)
7.5 units × 0.27 hour per unit = 2.025 hours

Multiply 2.025 by the hourly rate to get the press labor cost for the job.

This procedure can be duplicated in each department of the company. A master list can then be compiled for the estimator to use when preparing any job bid (figure 18.2). Some companies keep track of production standards continually and update their master lists weekly. Others merely spot-check their standards monthly or quarterly.

Computer-based management and estimating systems typically have applications that capture and update labor standards continually. When the press operator logs a job number into the press controls, the information is recorded in memory. When the job is done and logged off, the time is recorded in program memory automatically. These systems are discussed in greater detail later in this chapter.

Some printing companies keep no standards. They rely upon average industry standards provided through publications such as the *Franklin Printing Catalog.* These publications suggest what to charge for different types of jobs. However, without plant-specific performance standards no organization can truly know if it is maximizing profits or losing money on jobs.

Determining Fixed Costs

In any business there are expenses that are difficult to determine when completing a job estimate. How many paper clips should be

Standard Labor Unit per Quantity		
Thomas E. Schildgen & Associates, Inc.		
Preliminary	Job Set-up	.10 hour
	Preflight	.20 hour
Assembly	Image/color editing	
	average	.40 hour
	difficult	.70 hour
	Page Layout/editing	.05 hour/p
Output	Color Proof	
	Digital FPO	.10 hour/p
	Digital Contract	.20 hour/p
	Conventional Contract	.30 hour/p
	Film	
	Average	.25 hour/p
	Difficult	.35 hour/p
	Imposition	.20 hour/p
	Plate	
	Conventional	.30 hour/p
	CTP	.10 hour/p
Press, GTO	Single-color job	
	Make-ready	.42 hour
	1000 sheets	.20 hour
	Each additional color	
	Spot Color, 1000 sheets	.20 hour
	Process Color, 1000 sheets	.30 hour
	Wash-up per additional color	.35 hour
Finishing	Single fold	
	11 × 17 or less, 1000 sheets	.24 hour
	Double fold	
	11 × 17 or less, 1000 sheets	.38 hour

Figure 18.2   Part of a master list used by estimators to prepare job bids

charged to that job? What was the cost of the electricity used to run an extra shift to finish the job? How much water was used to wash the press operators' hands at the end of the day, and what job should be charged? When considered individually these items are small. But when summed over the span of a year, they become significant. They are expenses that must somehow be included in the final charge for each job.

Per Hour Cost Factor Technique

One technique of distributing fixed costs across many jobs is to add a fixed factor to each productive hour spent on every job. Determining that fixed amount is a bit involved, but it is a fairly accurate method of accounting for the difficult to measure expenses of any business. Much of the preparatory data collection needed here is also necessary for other techniques, such as adding an overhead factor to each job (see the following section).

Consider figure 18.3, a floor plan of Print, Inc. This is a typical, although imaginary, medium-sized printing company. By reviewing previous years' bills, it was determined that the company has a fixed annual building cost of $46,800.

If this were a start-up company, the figures needed to calculate this cost could be projected easily from the following documents and sources:

- Annual lease contact
- Maintenance contract with an outside organization
- An insurance agent who can provide an accurate estimate of annual insurance costs.
- City or town officials who know the building's exact assessed valuation and annual taxes
- Utility and telephone companies that provide base cost estimates

There are 15,600 square feet in the Print, Inc., building. To determine annual fixed costs per square foot, divide $46,800 by 15,600; it will cost Print, Inc. $3.00 per square foot each year to operate the building.

By measuring the square feet of every building section it is possible to assign a portion of fixed annual costs to each area of the building. Refer to the first three columns of table 18.1a. Each department is listed with its square feet (S.F.). To determine the figures for the Fixed Building Costs by Department column, multiply the S.F. by Department column by the "Fixed Costs per S.F."

Another cost that is difficult to apportion to each job is equipment expense (remember the spade story). Somehow the cost of the presses, platemakers, scanners and all the other equipment must be paid for. Their combined cost is so great that no single job could cover it, however. Annual depreciation is arrived at by dividing the total cost for each piece of equipment by the number of years it should be productive. Table 18.2 shows annual depreciation for two units in the press department. The equipment manufacturers (and the Internal Revenue Service) have determined that with proper maintenance and service these two presses will each last 10 years. Their purchase prices are then divided by 10 to determine the annual cost that must be covered so that at the end of the life of each press a new press can be purchased.

The fourth column in table 18.1a lists equipment depreciation for each department. These figures were determined in the same manner as with the two presses in table 18.2. These amounts are then added to the fixed building cost in the third column. The resulting sums represent the amount that must be charged, throughout the entire year, for work done in each department (last column).

Table 18.1 shows two sets of numbers, (a) (b). We have just reviewed table 18.1a to determine the Total Fixed Costs per Department

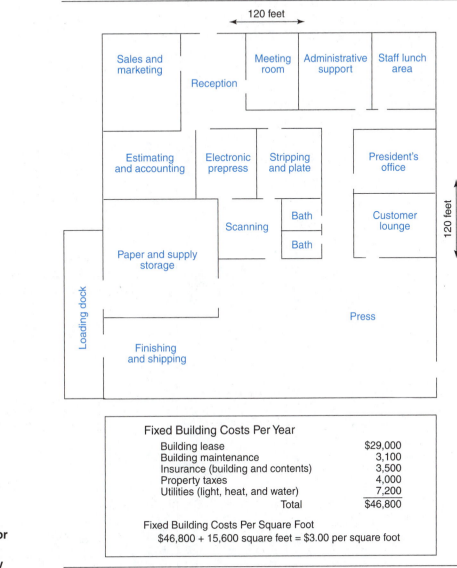

Figure 18.3 **Floor plan of a typical printing company**

per Year. The second table (table 18.1b) looks at determining an hourly charge. Notice that the first column in table 18.1b duplicates the last column in table 18.1a.

In table 18.3 the total number of available productive hours per worker per year has been calculated. In table 18.4 the number from table 18.3 has been multiplied by the number of employees in each department to determine the total productive hours each year. Those figures have been transferred to the second column of table 18.1. If the Total Fixed Costs per Department per Year are divided by the Total Productive Hours per Year, Hourly

Table 18.1. Fixed cost factor per production hour

(a)

Department	Square Feet Department	×	Fixed cost per Square Foot ($)	=	Fixed Building Costs by Department	+	Equipment Depreciation by Department	=	Total Fixed Costs per Department per Year
All administration	6,100	×	3.00	=	$18,300	+	$ 4,000	=	$23,300
Electronic prepress	800	×	3.00	=	2,400	+	10,000	=	12,400
Stripping and plate	800	×	3.00	=	2,400	+	2,800	=	5,200
Scanning	400	×	3.00	=	1,200	+	6,000	=	7,200
Press	6,200	×	3.00	=	18,600	+	25,800	=	44,400
Finishing and ship	1,300	×	3.00	=	3,900	+	4,000	=	7,900
Total	15,600				$46,800		$52,600		$99,400

(b)

Department	Total Fixed Costs per Department per Year	÷	Total Production Hours per Year	=	Hourly Fixed Costs ($)	+	Fixed Administrative Factor ($)	=	Fixed Cost Factor per Production Hour ($)
All administration	$23,000	÷	11,520	=	2.00	+	0.40	=	
Electronic prepress	12,400	÷	9,600	=	1.29	+	0.40	=	1.69
Stripping and plate	5,200	÷	3,840	=	1.35	+	0.40	=	1.75
Scanning	7,200	÷	3,840	=	1.87	+	0.40	=	2.27
Press	44,400	÷	17,280	=	2.57	+	0.40	=	2.97
Finishing and ship	7,900	÷	7,680	=	1.03	+	0.40	=	1.43
Total	$99,400		53,760						

Table 18.2. Depreciation, press section

	Purchase Price	Depreciation Life	Annual Depreciation
Press 1	$200,000	10	$20,000
Press 2	$ 58,000	10	$ 5,800
			$25,800

Fixed Costs have been determined (third column of table 18.1b).

A difficulty arises with the hourly fixed cost for the administrative department. It is not possible to identify how much office time was devoted to each job. Also, time is spent estimating jobs that the company does not get, and that cost must be absorbed somewhere in the operation. Much office time is either non-productive or is not associated with particular jobs.

To solve this problem, the fixed office cost is divided equally among all the other departments. In this case, $2.00 was divided by 5 (the number of remaining departments) to determine a fixed administrative factor. Therefore, $0.40 of Fixed Administrative Factor is added to the Hourly Fixed Cost for each department to determine a Fixed Cost Factor per Production Hour for each department of production (last column of table 18.1b). These amounts are then added to the base labor costs

Table 18.3. Productive hours per year, per person

Total scheduled plant work hours
52 weeks × 40 hours/week = 2,080 hours

Paid, Nonproductive Time	Hours
2 weeks paid vacation	80
10 paid holidays	80
10 paid sick days	80
Company meetings	10
Total	250
Scheduled work hours	2,080
Nonproductive time	250
Total productive work hours	1,830

per department. In other words, if a finishing and shipping worker earns $9.37 per hour, for costing purposes the new charge becomes $10.80 ($9.37 + $1.43, which comes from the last column in table 18.1b). For a job that requires 10 hours of finishing and shipping work, the estimator will calculate costs in this area as 10 hours × $10.80 or $108.00.

Overhead Charge per Job Technique

Another technique to distribute fixed operating costs across many jobs is to determine a fix percentage charge. This is called **overhead**.

Refer to the upper right column in table 18.1a called Total Fixed Costs per Department

Table 18.4. Productive work hour calculation

Department	Number of Employees	×	Productive Hours/Year	=	Total Productive Hours/Year
All administration	6	×	1,920	=	11,520
Electronic prepress	5	×	1,920	=	9,600
Stripping and plate	2	×	1,920	=	3,840
Scanning	2	×	1,920	=	3,840
Press	9	×	1,920	=	17,280
Finishing and ship	4	×	1,920	=	7,680
Total	28				53,760

per year. Look at the total, $99,400. This figure represents total building expenses and equipment depreciation for one year.

Say that Print, Inc., projected $3,000,000 in total sales for the coming year. Divide $99,400 by $3,000,000; the result is 0.0331. Convert 0.0331 to a percentage by multiplying by 100 to get 3.31%. Round this percentage for simplification and the figure becomes 3.3%. This is the overhead figure.

To determine the cost for a particular job, the estimator first determines and then sums all labor and material expenses. That total is then multiplied by 3.3%, the overhead figure. Say labor and materials sum to $2,210.00. 3.3 percent of $2,210 is $72.93 ($2,210 × 0.033). The new estimate becomes $2,282.93 ($2,210.00 + $72.93).

In America the purpose of commercial organizations is to make a profit. Print, Inc., should not submit a bid of $2,282.93 because it would yield no profit. That bid simply covers the cost of doing business and completing the work. The bid submitted should be higher. The last step in the estimating process, then, is to multiply the total estimated cost of the job by the target profit percentage. The target profit percentage varies from company to company. The estimated cost plus the profit amount becomes the job bid amount.

The previous discussion is only a brief introduction to costing techniques. In actual practice, the procedures are much more complex and involve a great number of other factors. Refer to the bibliography of this text for sources that provide more detailed coverage of this topic.

Job Estimating

Each company uses estimating procedures that work best for its type of organization. As mentioned previously, there are published pricing guides, such as the *Franklin Printing Catalog*, that give *average* costs for nearly all operations or products of a typical printing company. Computer-based applications are available that require the estimator to enter job specific information into a computer terminal. Estimated costs then display and can be printed in a variety of forms.

The Basic Estimating Process

Some companies prepare price schedules for items they work with frequently to avoid estimating every job. Whatever the method—computer application, pencil and paper, or published guide—certain procedures are always followed to obtain a final job estimate. There are eight basic steps for making any estimate. Some might expand or reduce the number of steps by combining or separating items, but the basic process is always the same.

1. Obtain accurate specifications.
2. Plan the job sequence.
3. Determine material needs and convert to standard units.
4. Determine time needed for each task.
5. Determine labor costs.
6. Determine fixed costs.
7. Sum costs and add profit.
8. Prepare formal bid contract.

When predicting the cost of a job, it is important to have all information about what the customer wants or expects. It is the job of the sales personnel to obtain all job specifications and to ensure that the company meets the job requirements within the final formal job estimate.

It is impossible to estimate printing costs without knowing how the job will be produced. It is necessary to outline the sequence of operations so time and material requirements can be determined easily. If an opera-

Table 18.5. Cost summary detail

Labor	Hours	Cost	Sell	
Setup	0.40	$57.46	$76.13	1 Setup
Make-ready	1.00	143.64	190.32	4 Make-ready
Sheetfed Press Run	0.95	137.12	181.68	7,000 sheet, 7,333 impressions/hour
Wash-up, Unit 4	0.80	114.91	152.26	4 wash-up
Total	3.15	$453.13	$600.39	

tion is forgotten or estimated incorrectly, the cost of that operation must come out of the profits. Customers will not pay more than the contracted bid price unless, of course, they contract for extra services after accepting the bid.

Once the sequence of operations has been determined, determining the quantities of materials needed for each task is simple. These quantities are then converted to unit amounts. The estimator can calculate the amount of time necessary to complete each operation from the standard units (see figure 18.2). Labor costs, which are usually paid on a per hour basis, are then determined for each operation. Fixed costs, or overhead, which are usually based on the time needed for each task, are then added. An example of calculating a specific cost center charge is reflected in a detail taken from the cost summary report shown in figure 18.8. If we look at the underlying calculations for the cost of labor in the press category, we see that specific procedures are taken into account to calculate the total (table 18.5). For example, press setup is measured at 0.40-hour units for a total cost of $57.46. With markup, the selling price is $76.13 for press setup on the 32-page promotional booklet. This cost is one of many included in the final number for labor under the category of presses in the cost summary. The final sum of all the proposed costs (labor and materials and any outside services), with any additional markup determined by the company, comprises the selling price.

As a last step, the estimator usually prepares a formal bid that acts as a binding contract for the company. The formal bid states that the company will print a specific job for the stated amount. The customer commonly has a fixed number of days to accept the bid before the contact offer becomes void. Most estimating today is done with either proprietary or vendor-supplied estimating software and will be discussed in a following section.

Production Planning

Before any job can go into production, it is necessary to carry the preliminary work done with the estimate a bit further. Jobs do not automatically flow through the shop. Every job requires continual planning, guidance, and follow-up. The following list outlines the typical steps involved in implementing printing production:

1. Prepare a production work order from the estimate request sheet and the estimate.
2. Determine in-house availability of materials and order if necessary.
3. Prepare a detailed job schedule.
4. Merge a detailed schedule into production control schedule.
5. Coordinate materials with the job's arrival in each department.
6. Put the job into production.

7. Check quality control and production as necessary.

8. Reschedule as necessary.

9. Remove the job from the production control schedule and send all records to accounting.

To follow through with the previous example, let us assume that the Sanders brochure that was bid in the previous section was awarded to Liedtke Graphics.

The Job Ticket

After a customer has accepted a bid and any legal contacts have been signed, the production manager takes control of the job. The first step is to transfer the information from the estimate request and the estimate request sheet to a **job ticket** or a production work order (figure 18.4a and b). At this point the job is assigned a job ticket number. This is an internal reference used by the company to refer to a specific job. The job ticket is the road map that charts the job through all the production steps. It is used by the production control department to check on the progress of a job. It also notifies the accounting department to prepare an invoice. Most job tickets operate electronically today and utilize real-time data collection. This allows the production path of a job to be charted easily, because each employee's record of working on the job is recorded electronically at his individual workstation. The job ticket can also serve as a means of updating the labor standards sheet (see figure 18.1).

At the same time that the job ticket is completed, inventory control staff must check to determine if all the required materials are on hand and are not reserved for another job. If the materials are in storage, they are reserved. If the supplies are not available in house, they are ordered and information about the expected delivery date is sent to the people responsible for job scheduling.

Job Scheduling and Production Control

Job scheduling and production control is a problem of coordinating the most efficient combination of materials, machines, and time. This responsibility is typically assigned to the scheduling department, sometimes called production control. In small organizations this function may be only a part-time job for one individual. Large corporations, however, may have a dozen or more people assigned to the task full time.

A skillful production manager schedules jobs in a sequence that requires minimum machine changes. For example, if four jobs will be run on one press next Tuesday—two with black ink, one with yellow, and another with red—it is wise to schedule the yellow job first, then the red job, and then the two black. The lightest colors should be run first (which makes roller cleanup easier), and the two black runs should be paired together. Likewise, jobs with the same sheet sizes should be scheduled back to back.

The first step in the orderly scheduling of individual jobs is to prepare a detailed **job schedule** sheet (figure 18.5). Again, the operations are listed in sequence and the number of hours estimated in each section are identified.

Any job schedule is really only hypothetical. If the company had only one job, with each department waiting to perform its task, then the schedule would be real. However, this situation is not realistic. No company could survive with only one small job each day. In reality, each job must be merged with many others also flowing through the production sequence.

The frustration of production control is that jobs do not always conform to the esti-

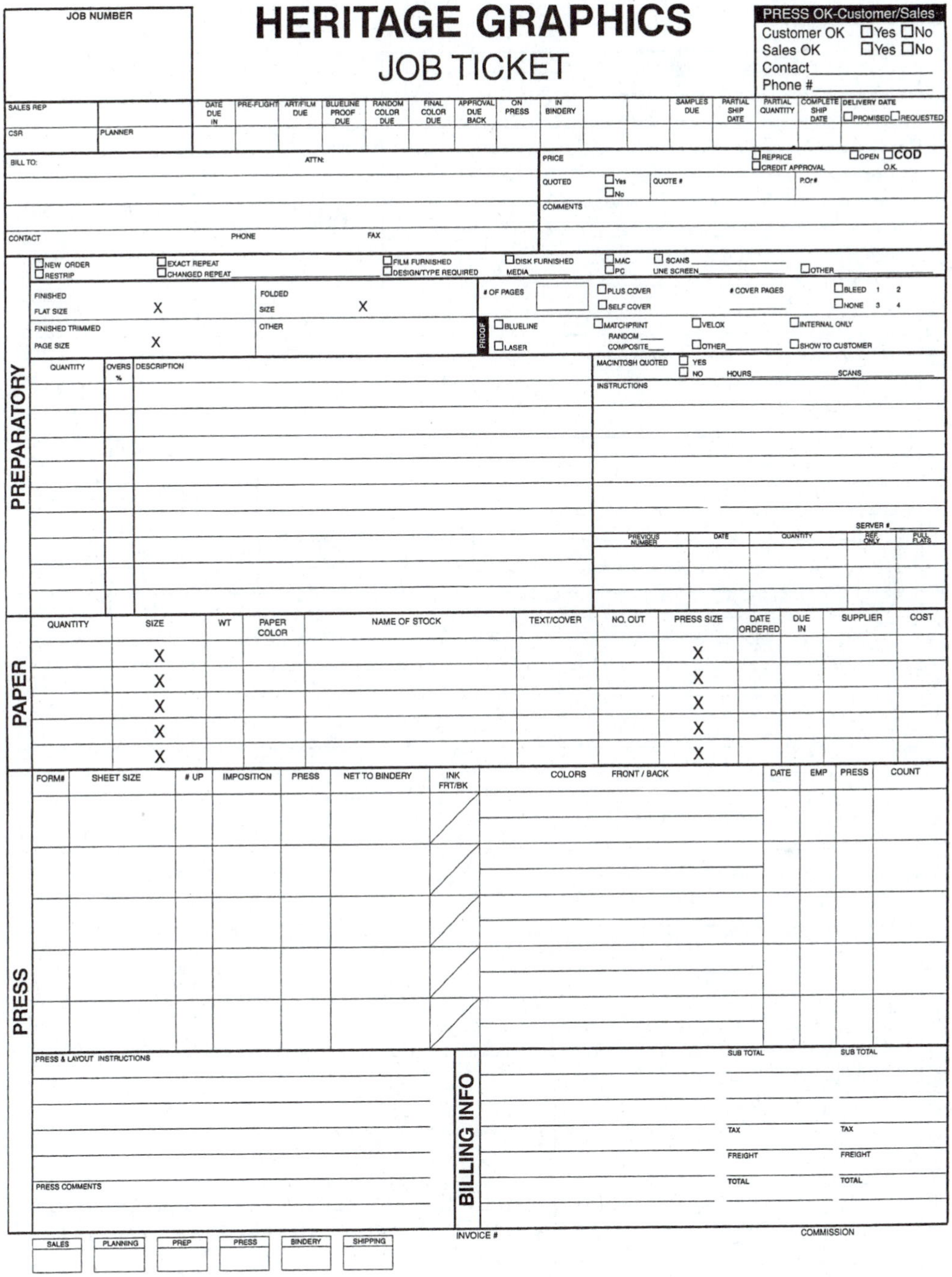

HERITAGE GRAPHICS
JOB TICKET

JOB NUMBER

PRESS OK-Customer/Sales
Customer OK ☐Yes ☐No
Sales OK ☐Yes ☐No
Contact_____
Phone #_____

SALES REP			DATE DUE IN	PRE-FLIGHT	ART/FILM DUE	BLUELINE PROOF DUE	RANDOM COLOR DUE	FINAL COLOR DUE	APPROVAL DUE BACK	ON PRESS	IN BINDERY			SAMPLES DUE	PARTIAL SHIP DATE	PARTIAL QUANTITY	COMPLETE SHIP DATE	DELIVERY DATE
CSR		PLANNER																☐PROMISED ☐REQUESTED

BILL TO: ATTN: **PRICE**   ☐REPRICE   ☐OPEN ☐COD O.K.
☐CREDIT APPROVAL

QUOTED ☐Yes ☐No   QUOTE #   P.O.#

COMMENTS

CONTACT   PHONE   FAX

☐NEW ORDER ☐RESTRIP   ☐EXACT REPEAT ☐CHANGED REPEAT   ☐FILM FURNISHED ☐DESIGN/TYPE REQUIRED   ☐DISK FURNISHED   MEDIA   ☐MAC ☐PC   ☐SCANS_____ LINE SCREEN   ☐OTHER_____

PREPARATORY

| FINISHED FLAT SIZE | X | FOLDED SIZE | X | # OF PAGES | | ☐PLUS COVER ☐SELF COVER | # COVER PAGES | ☐BLEED 1 2 ☐NONE 3 4 |
| FINISHED TRIMMED PAGE SIZE | X | OTHER | | PROOF ☐BLUELINE ☐LASER | | ☐MATCHPRINT RANDOM_____ COMPOSITE_____ | ☐VELOX ☐OTHER | ☐INTERNAL ONLY ☐SHOW TO CUSTOMER |

MACINTOSH QUOTED ☐YES ☐NO   HOURS_____   SCANS_____

INSTRUCTIONS

QUANTITY	OVERS %	DESCRIPTION

SERVER #_____

PREVIOUS NUMBER	DATE	QUANTITY	REF. ONLY	FULL FLATS

PAPER

QUANTITY	SIZE	WT	PAPER COLOR	NAME OF STOCK	TEXT/COVER	NO. OUT	PRESS SIZE	DATE ORDERED	DUE IN	SUPPLIER	COST
	X						X				
	X						X				
	X						X				
	X						X				
	X						X				

PRESS

FORM#	SHEET SIZE	# UP	IMPOSITION	PRESS	NET TO BINDERY	INK FRT/BK	COLORS FRONT / BACK		DATE	EMP	PRESS	COUNT

PRESS & LAYOUT INSTRUCTIONS

PRESS COMMENTS

BILLING INFO

	SUB TOTAL	SUB TOTAL
TAX		
FREIGHT		
TOTAL		

INVOICE #   COMMISSION

SALES	PLANNING	PREP	PRESS	BINDERY	SHIPPING

(a)

Figure 18.4 **Job ticket.**
Courtesy of Heritage Graphics.

JOB #

BINDERY

☐ DELIVER FLAT PRESS SHEETS   ☐ TRIM TO SIZE   TRIM SIZE_____ X _____

☐ FOLD TO_____ X _____   ☐ RIGHT ANGLE ☐ PARALLEL ☐ ACCORDION ☐ GATE ☐ OTHER_____

☐ WIRE-O ☐ SPIRAL WIRE ☐ PLASTIC COIL   COLOR_____

☐ SADDLE STITCH # OF STITCHES ____ TRIM SIZE _____ X _____ BIND ON _____ " SIDE

☐ PERFECT BIND ☐ SIDE STITCH   TRIM SIZE _____ X _____ BIND ON _____ " SIDE

☐ PAPER BAND #_____ ☐ SHRINKWRAP #_____ ☐ KRAFT WRAP #_____ ☐ BOX   ☐ PLAIN ☐ PRINTED

☐ PAD IN #_____ POSITION_____ ☐ DRILL # HOLES_____ POSITION_____ SIZE HOLE_____

☐ COLLATE # PC _____ ☐ NUMBERING START _____ END _____ COLOR INK _____

HAND BINDERY (Description) _____

SPECIAL BINDERY INST. (Labeling, Boxing, Etc.) _____

BINDERY COMMENTS _____

LETTERPRESS / FINISHING

☐ DIE CUT   ☐ EMBOSS ☐ REGULAR DIE   ☐ FOIL
          ☐ SCULPTURED DIE   COLOR_____

☐ SCORE   ☐ PERFORATE TYPE_____

POCKETS ☐ GLUED # ____ SIZE ____ ☐ B.C.SLITS # ____
        ☐ NOT GLUED # ____ SIZE ____ ☐ B.C.SLITS # ____

ADDITIONAL FINISHING_____

FINAL COUNT

OUTSIDE VENDORS
1_____
2_____
3_____
4_____
5_____

DISK / ARTWORK

☐ RETURN TO CUSTOMER
   ☐ WITH SHIPMENT
   ☐ SEPARATE FROM SHIPMENT
   ☐ RETURN WITH SAMPLES

☐ RETURN TO SALES REP.

☐ FILE AT HERITAGE GRAPHICS

☐ _____

SAMPLES

| QUANTITY | PACKING INST. | SHIP VIA | QUANTITY | PACKING INST. | SHIP VIA |

SHIP WITH: ☐ DISK ☐ ART ☐ DUMMY'S ☐ LASERS ☐ OTHER

ATTENTION OF

COMPANY

ADDRESS

CITY, STATE, ZIP

SHIP WITH: ☐ DISK ☐ ART ☐ DUMMY'S ☐ LASERS ☐ OTHER

ATTENTION OF

COMPANY

ADDRESS

CITY, STATE, ZIP

OF SAMPLES FOR

SALES_____

CSR_____

TICKET_____

SAMPLE ROOM_____

PULLED BY_____

SHIPPING

SHIP TO

ADDRESS

CITY, STATE, ZIP

ATTENTION OF

QUANTITY

SHIP VIA   ☐ PREPAID ☐ COLLECT

SHIP TO

ADDRESS

CITY, STATE, ZIP

ATTENTION OF

QUANTITY

SHIP VIA   ☐ PREPAID ☐ COLLECT

DELIVERY

DATE	#PER PKG.	# PACKAGES	# CARTONS	TOTAL QUANTITY	SHIP VIA	WAYBILL NUMBER	PARTIAL-COMPLETE	FREIGHT COST	TOTAL SHIPPED TO CUSTOMER	INVENTORY

OUTSIDE PURCHASES

VENDOR	P.O. NUMBER	DESCRIPTION	PRICE

NOTES

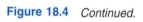
(b)

Figure 18.4 *Continued.*

mated time. Perhaps a computer crashes, or a file becomes corrupted. Paper might jam in the press, and 30 minutes are wasted removing the scrap. Materials might not arrive in the department on schedule, and time is wasted checking on the delay. A delay at one point in the schedule is felt throughout the shop. It is therefore necessary to alter and adjust the flow of jobs continually to make up for time gains or losses.

The challenge of production control is to merge each individual job diagram into the

---

Ironwood Litho
Scheduling Report
Job Scheduled Detailed by Number   Today: Mon 6/18 09:41

Selection
JOB STATUS: Production jobs
Task Status : S, U, D, H
Job # : 6000

6000   promo booklet   Cust: 1050 ASU
              Sales: 8 Randy Peck   Planner: 55 D. Cipolla
              Booked 6/15   Due: 7/6
              Planned Ship: 6/28   priority
              Quantity 1000   Job Status - Scheduled

St	SJ	DEPT		HRS	START	END
S	1	110	Scanning	1.3	700 06/18	06/18
S	2	153	Macintosh	5.5	0 06/18	06/18
S	2	153	Imagesetter	10.7	700 06/19	06/19
S	2	340	Strip/Film/Proof	3.9	700 06/20	06/20
		347	Strip/Proof/Out	0.0	0 06/20	
		348	Strip/Proof/Back	0.0	0 06/21	
S	2	351	Platemaking	4.2	06/21	06/21
S	1	420	5/C Press	6.7	600 06/22	1242 06/22
S	2	415	2/Color Press	18.0	700 06/22	06/23
S	1	616	Cutters	2.0	0 06/25	06/25
S	2	631	Folders	19.4	0 06/25	06/26
S	1	620	Die Cutter	7.4	1200 6/26	06/26
S	99	677	Mueller Autosticher	5.2	700 6/27	06/27
S	99	690	Shrinkwrap	3.3	0 6/27	06/27
S		904	FINAL SHIP	0	6/28	

Figure 18.5 Sample job schedule.
Courtesy of Ironwood Lithographers.

overall shop schedule. The goal is to match time blocks efficiently with available personnel; materials; and common sizes, colors, or types of jobs. The production manager prepares detailed production control schedules for each day's work well in advance. With a job scheduled as far as a week in advance, it is possible to coordinate the materials required in each department as the job flows through the shop.

If there are delays, the production manager must make adjustments. It is also the production manager's task to know the stage of each job at almost every moment in the day. When customers call and want to know how their material is progressing, it is important to be able to give them immediate and accurate answers. Information is critical. If there are problems, the department supervisor must inform production control immediately.

When the job has reached the last production step and is waiting to be picked up or is on its way to the customer, all records are sent through the production control office to the accounting or billing office. The job is removed from the production control schedule, and any materials that are to be stored, such as the original paste-up copy, negatives, or printing plates, are filed and new jobs enter the system. A bill is sent to the customer and payment is received.

Job Costing

An important part of creating a profitable company is determining if what you are charging is actually accurate or are you absorbing cost overrun errors that could be prevented. **Job costing** is the process of comparing your estimated production times and costs to what the actual production costs and times are. Job costing helps to increase profits by discovering where discrepancies might be from what you have estimated to what actually occurred. Perhaps a company consistently ends up doing lengthier preflighting for customers than

had been estimated for. By determining the time actually spent, costs can be adjusted or information provided to customers so they can prepare more appropriate files in the future to decrease preflight time.

There are two ways to approach job costing. It can be done prior to or after invoicing. If done prior to invoicing, it is possible to adjust your invoice to more accurately reflect time and production costs. But care must be taken if the reasons for overrun are not your customer's responsibility. If the extra costs are due to approved and agreed on author's alterations, additional charges are acceptable. But if it is because internal evaluation of specific production processes and time need are incorrect, then job costing can be done after invoicing, because the company will absorb the charges. Job costing is an important feedback mechanism for a company and allows for correct estimation of actual chargeable hours and production schedules. Although printing facilities are extremely busy places, new computer management systems help to reduce the time it takes to properly job cost a job.

Computer-Based Management Tools

The development of computer-based management tools is a natural outgrowth of the entrance of the computer into almost every phase of printing operations. For years, larger printing firms have been using computer-based **management information systems (MIS)** software to compare and assess business data. For the most part, true MIS systems were only available to the largest printing firms capable of making considerable investments in computer hardware and software. But now MIS systems that manage everything from job tracking to data collection are not only available for reasonable costs to small and mid-sized firms, but on-line management, coordination, and print procurement are available through the Internet and accessible anywhere. We will discuss the new paradigm of print management in a later section of this chapter.

Estimating Software

Estimating software takes the process of estimating and elevates it to a new level of efficiency by tying it to active databases and plant data collection. The estimate becomes the starting point for an electronic job jacket that can follow the job through the entire production process through to invoicing. The software can either handle complete estimating built from the specific budgeted hourly rates entered by the printing facility based on their production processes, or it can be price estimating software that is based on a predetermined pricing template, such as the Franklin Estimating System mentioned earlier.

printCafe Logic estimating software is one example of computer-based estimating software. The user enters the appropriate information into the dialogue boxes, and the software generates the estimate detail and cost summary report from which the company can generate its own customer quote. In the request for estimate shown in figure 18.6, the customer is requesting a quote for 10,000, 15,000 and 25,000 copies of a 32-page promotional booklet. In this case the sales person delivers a handwritten quote to the estimating department (although many companies may have their sales force create the original request for quote in digital format on a portable computer). The estimator then enters these data into the printCafe Logic estimating software, which has already been set up to reflect the different pricing schedules that the company has established. The different parameters of the job, such as layout and type of press it is intended for, are all included in the fields of the software (figure 18.7). On the same computer, software from various other suppliers,

such as paper companies, may be present and available for quick access to adjust a quote accordingly.

The cost summary report not only provides the company with the material costs of the job, but also the all-inclusive costs (costs plus value) and the total estimate with the targeted selling price (overall mark-up applied to the all inclusive cost) (figure 18.8). This price can be adjusted by management, but it gives a suggested price along with the value-added dollars of the estimate. *Value added* refers to the amount the value (in dollars) of the product increase due to manufacturing and service components separate from material costs and other directly chargeable costs. In its simplest form, it refers to the dollars generated by services and processes inside the facility apart from material costs and outside plant costs. The final step is to add on the desired mark-up or profit margin that has been determined either by management policy or on a per job basis. This information is then provided to the customer as the final estimate for the job (figure 18.9).

As truly digital workflows become more prevalent, computer management of jobs, production, estimating, and invoicing will become more and more critical to the makeup of a profitable printing facility.

Information Gathering

At the heart of any MIS system is the accurate and timely gathering of information. Traditionally, information on inventory, job status, operating costs, and other expenses related to a specific job was gathered at the end of a shift, a workday, or a work week. Such information proved valuable in assessing expenses and in isolating high-expense areas, but it was historical—all information was collected only after the job was printed. As a result, it was not useful for correcting problems as they occurred. **Automated data collection (ADC)** is a response to this problem. With ADC, data is

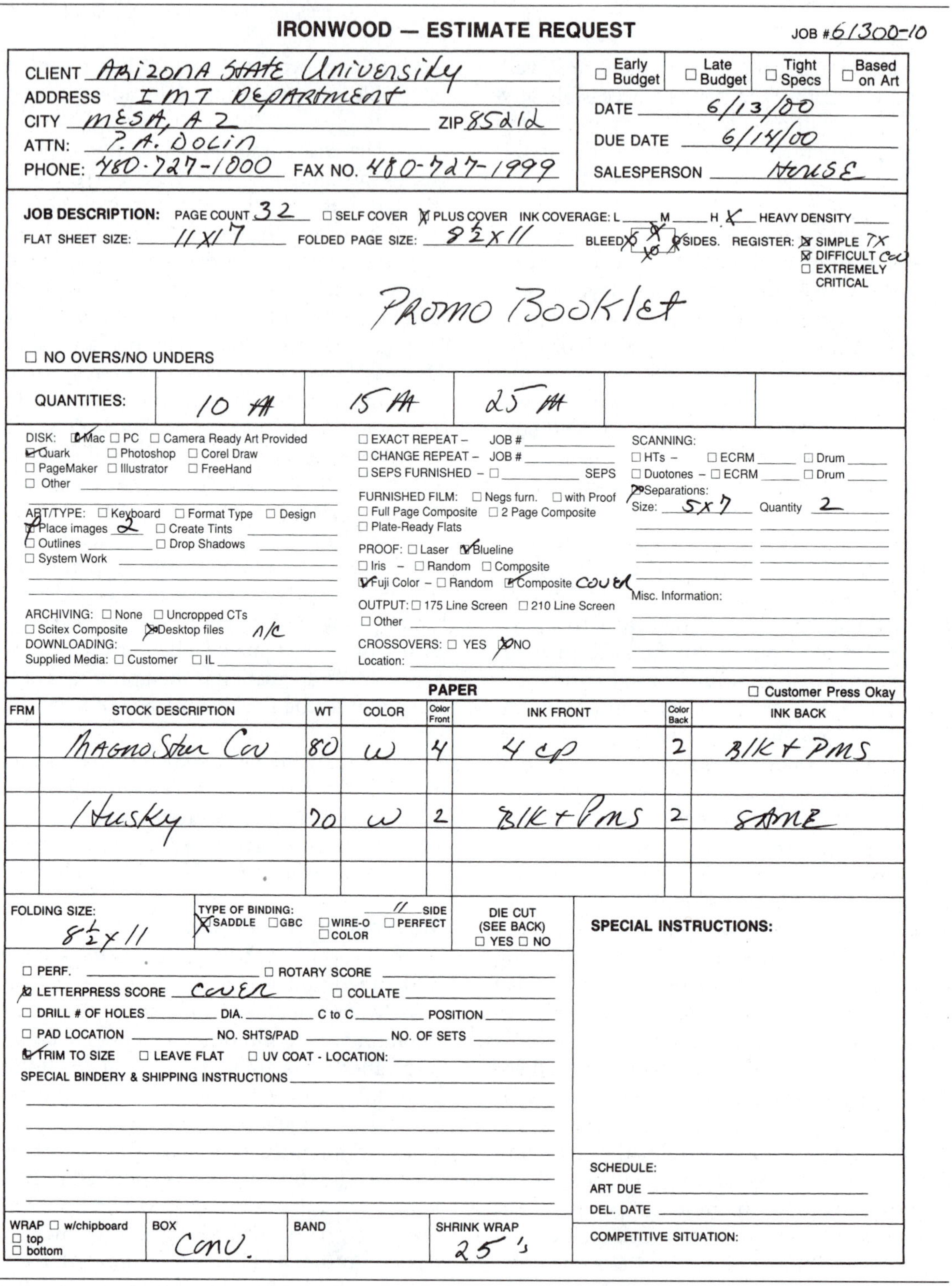

IRONWOOD — ESTIMATE REQUEST JOB # 61300-10

CLIENT _Arizona State University_

ADDRESS _IMT Department_

CITY _Mesa, AZ_ ZIP _85212_

ATTN: _P.A. Dolin_

PHONE: _480-727-1000_ FAX NO. _480-727-1999_

	Early ☐ Budget	Late ☐ Budget	Tight ☐ Specs	Based ☐ on Art

DATE _6/13/00_

DUE DATE _6/14/00_

SALESPERSON _House_

JOB DESCRIPTION: PAGE COUNT _32_ ☐ SELF COVER ☒ PLUS COVER INK COVERAGE: L ___ M ___ H ☒ HEAVY DENSITY ____

FLAT SHEET SIZE: _11 x 17_ FOLDED PAGE SIZE: _8½ x 11_ BLEED ☒/☒ ☒ SIDES. REGISTER: ☒ SIMPLE _7x_ ☒ DIFFICULT _cov_ ☐ EXTREMELY CRITICAL

Promo Booklet

☐ NO OVERS/NO UNDERS

QUANTITIES: | _10 M_ | _15 M_ | _25 M_ | | |

DISK: ☒ Mac ☐ PC ☐ Camera Ready Art Provided
☒ Quark ☐ Photoshop ☐ Corel Draw
☐ PageMaker ☐ Illustrator ☐ FreeHand
☐ Other _____

ART/TYPE: ☐ Keyboard ☐ Format Type ☐ Design
☒ Place images _2_ ☐ Create Tints _____
☐ Outlines _____ ☐ Drop Shadows _____
☐ System Work _____

ARCHIVING: ☐ None ☐ Uncropped CTs
☐ Scitex Composite ☒ Desktop files _n/c_
DOWNLOADING: _____
Supplied Media: ☐ Customer ☐ IL _____

☐ EXACT REPEAT – JOB # _____
☐ CHANGE REPEAT – JOB # _____
☐ SEPS FURNISHED – ☐ _____ SEPS
FURNISHED FILM: ☐ Negs furn. ☐ with Proof
☐ Full Page Composite ☐ 2 Page Composite
☐ Plate-Ready Flats
PROOF: ☐ Laser ☒ Blueline
☐ Iris – ☐ Random ☐ Composite
☒ Fuji Color – ☐ Random ☒ Composite _cover_
OUTPUT: ☐ 175 Line Screen ☐ 210 Line Screen
☐ Other _____
CROSSOVERS: ☐ YES ☒ NO
Location: _____

SCANNING:
☐ HTs – ☐ ECRM _____ ☐ Drum
☐ Duotones – ☐ ECRM _____ ☐ Drum
☒ Separations:
Size: _5 x 7_ Quantity _2_

Misc. Information:

PAPER ☐ Customer Press Okay

FRM	STOCK DESCRIPTION	WT	COLOR	Color Front	INK FRONT	Color Back	INK BACK
	Magno Star Cov	80	W	4	4 cp	2	Blk + PMS
	Husky	70	W	2	Blk + PMS	2	Same

FOLDING SIZE: _8½ x 11_

TYPE OF BINDING: ☒ SADDLE ☐ GBC ☐ WIRE-O ☐ PERFECT ☐ COLOR _11_ SIDE

DIE CUT (SEE BACK) ☐ YES ☐ NO

SPECIAL INSTRUCTIONS:

☐ PERF. _____ ☐ ROTARY SCORE _____
☒ LETTERPRESS SCORE _cover_ ☐ COLLATE _____
☐ DRILL # OF HOLES _____ DIA. _____ C to C _____ POSITION _____
☐ PAD LOCATION _____ NO. SHTS/PAD _____ NO. OF SETS _____
☒ TRIM TO SIZE ☐ LEAVE FLAT ☐ UV COAT - LOCATION: _____
SPECIAL BINDERY & SHIPPING INSTRUCTIONS _____

SCHEDULE:
ART DUE _____
DEL. DATE _____

WRAP ☐ w/chipboard ☐ top ☐ bottom
BOX _Conv._
BAND
SHRINK WRAP _25's_

COMPETITIVE SITUATION:

Figure 18.6 Estimate request.
Courtesy of Ironwood Lithographers.

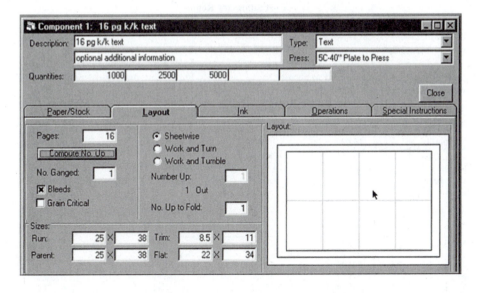

Figure 18.7 **Estimating software.** This window deals with layout considerations that affect pricing. Courtesy of printCafe Logic.

collected through computer input as soon as it is known, rather than at the end of a specific time frame. This "real time" collection of data greatly enhances the plant's ability to assess the status of any particular operation and correct problems as they occur.

There are many approaches to ADC. One approach by printCafe Logic has been to connect all facets of a facility through their DMI© (Direct Machine Interface) automatic, real-time, digital data collection technology. While jobs are running, information from equipment is collected automatically without any operator action and connected to other parts of the information system for accurate and timely information collection. Everything from estimating to prepress production, press operation, bindery, and on through to shipping can be monitored and collected (figure 18.10). These data are used to track job status dynamically, provide feedback to scheduling systems, identify operational problems, and maintain waste and spoilage control.

printCafe, the parent company of printCafe Logic, provides software applications for many crucial business processes, some of which are the following:

- Estimating
- Job costing, sales analysis
- Job tracking and tickets
- Scheduling
- Purchasing
- Inventory
- Shipping
- Invoicing
- Printer branded web sites

The primary advantage of a computer-based ADC/MIS system is that whatever information is known about a particular job is available immediately. Thus, the customer service representative, in response to a customer's question, can look up the status of any

Cost Summary Report

Estimate No: 362521   **Promo Booklet; 32pg+cover**

Est Date: 06/13/2000	*** DRAFT ***	**By:** Michael
Issued No:	**Stds Ver:** ironwood	**Sales Rep:** House (49)
Configuration: Saddlestitch; s/wrap 25's; box/del		**For:** Arizona State University (0)
Trim Size: 8.5 x 11		**Contact:**
		Phone:
		Fax:

Quantity:	10,000	15,000	25,000
Cost:	8,201.78	10,345.04	14,645.27
Sell:	10,364.88	13,238.80	18,990.01
Addl 1000s:	684.14	647.69	613.41

Labor	10,000	15,000	25,000
Digital Pre-press	1,213.49	1,213.49	1,213.49
Stripping	252.43	252.43	252.43
Proofing	202.20	202.20	202.20
Platemaking	318.99	318.99	318.99
Presses	1,806.94	2,239.76	3,143.80
Letterpress	179.94	243.39	376.64
Cutting	54.87	71.79	105.62
Folding	690.60	962.20	1,505.39
Large Machine Bindery	339.18	435.70	628.77
Packing	77.46	112.45	181.95
Total Labor	5,136.10	6,052.40	7,929.28

Materials	10,000	15,000	25,000
	72.82	72.82	72.82
Stripping	19.19	19.19	19.19
Proofing	57.76	57.76	57.76
Platemaking	92.00	92.00	92.00
Packing	81.15	122.00	202.60
Paper	2,278.17	3,253.82	5,080.14
Ink	464.57	675.03	1,096.92
Total Material	3,065.66	4,292.62	6,621.43

****** Cover - 4cp/blk+pms**

Component No: 1

Details: 4 pages Cover, As 1-4 Pages, Run 2 up, SW, 2 out of press sheet, 1 up to Fold
Folded Trim size: 8.5 x 11   Flat size: 17 x 11   Run size: 20 x 26 (Bleeds)

Stock   80# MagnoStar cvr   MCC: 1000
    Stock Type: Cover, coated   BWT/GSM: 80.00   MWT: 160
    Price: $71.00 $/Cwt (Q1) ; $71.00 $/Cwt (Q2); $71.00 $/Cwt (Q3)
    Order Sheet Size: 20 x 26

	10,000	15,000	25,000
Net Sheets	5,182	7,556	12,578
Spoilage	1,818	1,944	2,172
Gross Sheets	7,000	9,500	14,750
Gross Lbs	1,120.00	1,520.00	2,360.00
Percent Spoilage	35.1%	25.7%	17.3%

Estimate No: 362521	**Promo Booklet; 32pg+cover**	**Cost Sum: Page 1**

Figure 18.8   **Page 1 of a 3 page printCafe Logic cost summary report.**
Courtesy of Ironwood Lithographers.

QUOTATION / PURCHASE ORDER

To: Arizona State University
Dept. of Information and
Management Technology
Mesa, AZ 85212

Date: _____ 06/13/00

Quote Number: _____ 362521

Subject to standard terms and conditions which appear on the back hereof, we quote as follows:

Description	Promo Booklet, 32 Page plus Cover, 8-1/2 x 11
Paper Stock	Cover: 80# Magno Star Cover Text: 70# Husky Offset
Copy and Artwork	MAC disk furnished; 2 - 5x7 scans Please note: Flats are stored for 3 years, then recycled, unless otherwise requested.
Ink Colors	Cover: 4 color process over Black + PMS Text: Black + PMS, 2 sides
Binding	Saddle-stitch on 11" side
Remarks	
Packaging & Delivery	Shrinkwrap in 25's and box Includes 1 local delivery. Additional deliveries or drop shipments, will be charged at prevailing rates.
Quantity and Prices	10,000 Qty 15,000 Qty 25,000 Qty ----------- ----------- ------------- $10,365.00 $13,239.00 $18,990.00 The above quote is based on a schedule of ___15___ working days from receipt of all final art.

Special Instructions:
All estimates are subject to
adjustments for the cost of paper
at the time the job is submitted.

Credit Terms:

THIS QUOTATION IS SUBJECT TO REVIEW OF
FINISHED ART AND AVAILABILITY/PRICE OF PAPER
AT TIME OF ORDER.

This order becomes a binding contract, subject to the terms and conditions
hereof, when accepted by acknowledgment or commencement of performance.
No change in specifications, variation or revision of this order, or the quantities
and prices herein, shall be valid unless in writing and signed by Buyer.

If any such change causes an increase or decrease in the cost of, or time required
for performance of, any part of the work under this order, an equitable
adjustment shall be made in the contract price and/or delivery schedule. Above
prices do not include sales tax unless otherwise indicated.

Purchase Order Authorized by: _____
Please sign this form to place order. (After signing you may copy for your files.)

Quote Presented by: _____
asu.613   Ironwood Lithographers

ILIRONWOOD LITHOGRAPHERS, INC. 455 S. 52nd Street, Tempe, AZ 85281, (480) 829-7700

Figure 18.9 Final quotation.
Courtesy of Ironwood Lithographers.

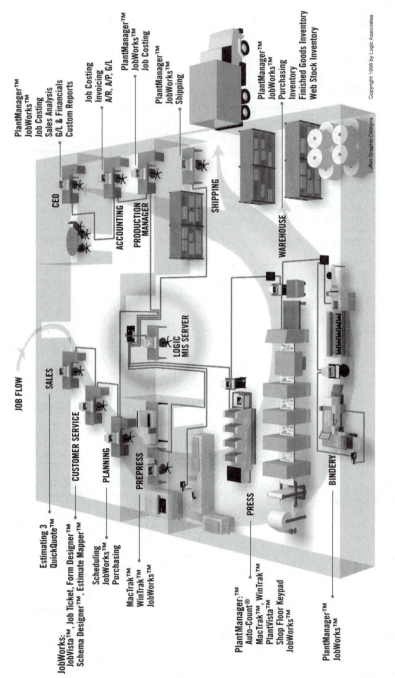

JOB FLOW

SALES

CUSTOMER SERVICE

PLANNING

PREPRESS

LOGIC MIS SERVER

CEO

ACCOUNTING

PRODUCTION MANAGER

SHIPPING

WAREHOUSE

PRESS

BINDERY

PlantManager™
JobWorks™
Job Costing
Sales Analysis
G/L & Financials
Custom Reports

Job Costing
Invoicing
A/R, A/P, G/L

PlantManager™
JobWorks™
Job Costing

PlantManager™
JobWorks™
Shipping

PlantManager™
JobWorks™
Purchasing
Inventory
Finished Goods Inventory
Web Stock Inventory

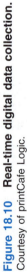

Copyright 1998 by Logic Associates

Lufkin Graphic Designs

JobWorks:
JobVista™, Job Ticket, Form Designer™
Schema Designer™, Estimate Mapper™

Estimating 3
QuickQuote™

Scheduling
JobWorks™
Purchasing

MacTrak™
WinTrak™
JobWorks™

PlantManager:™
Auto-Count®
MacTrak™ WinTrak™
PlantVista™
Shop Floor Keypad
JobWorks™

PlantManager™
JobWorks™

Figure 18.10 **Real-time digital data collection.**
Courtesy of printCafe Logic.

458

printing job instantly on the computer screen and tell the customer how far the job has progressed through the plant, whether there have been any delays, and when the job will be delivered.

The ADC/MIS systems also greatly reduce the amount of paperwork to be done by workers at each individual workstation. With an ADC/MIS system, operators at each workstation must only enter data on the computer and check it on the screen rather than write all information out longhand on a form or on the job jacket. This makes data entry faster and more accurate.

This entire shift to digital production being integrated with digital management of the process and business is referred to as **computer-integrated manufacturing** (discussed in chapter 11). It is a necessary approach in the printing environment of today, which is characterized by lower prices, quality service, and the need for extremely fast turnaround.

E-Management

Along with the digital revolution changing the way that we publish and produce communication pieces, the Internet has changed the way that we connect to others, whether customers or suppliers. **E-management** has become a fact of life. As customers become more technologically savvy, they are demanding that the services that they interact with be able to accommodate this new business model. This new model has a business sharing files and data among different locations and businesses, tracking production remotely, and connecting suppliers and customers 24 hours a day, 7 days a week. Location is no longer critical, but fast digital access is. The old paradigm was print and distribute; the facility printed the job and shipped it to where it needed to go. Now the approach can be to distribute and print, because the files can be sent to multiple sites at the same time, reducing shipping costs and providing faster turnaround.

There are several ways that the Internet is becoming part of the way printers do business today. Although not pervasive in the industry yet, the following approaches are gaining momentum and proving beneficial to those willing to invest in these methods.

E-Hubs

The main function of an **e-hub** is to facilitate the flow of information and work materials between the print buyer and the print vendor. The hub itself may or may not promote a product, but its main function is to provide a forum and conduit through which jobs and proofs can be transferred, orders tracked, services located, and even buyer–seller transactions conducted. The interface for all these functions is a Web site with both open and password protected access. An example of a successful e-hub company is Noosh (figure 18.11), which provides a service called Noosh.com that they promote in the following way:

> Noosh.com is the Internet-based communications and collaboration service that dramatically improves the process of buying, selling and managing print. The noosh.com service, powered by Live Jobs collaborative technology, helps print buyers and their printers work more productively together to create superior end-products by creating a centralized online workspace where everyone involved on a project can work together effectively and more efficiently.

Their service provides on-line estimating, job quoting, real-time order status reports, and product delivery information. Many companies are vying to provide the print industry these services. printCafe is a company that provides an on-line environment for buyers, printers, and suppliers. Their approach involves different levels of service, with access to a variety of proprietary tools, applications, and technologies. Their stated goal is to preserve and enhance printer and supplier brand

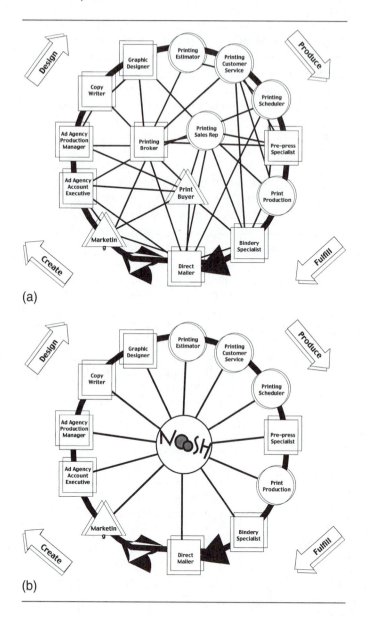

(a)

(b)

Figure 18.11 The concept of an e-hub company. Noosh depicts the work flow as (a) decentralized to begin with and then (b) centralized and streamlined with the implementation of an e-hub.
Courtesy of Noosh, Inc.

identity by "connecting print buyers, printers and suppliers and automating the printing process by integration of a new Web-based print procurement platform with [their] existing advanced suite of print design, specification, manufacturing, distribution and supply chain management enterprise software applications." They supply services that include proprietary tools, applications, and technologies that facilitate digital solutions by software and through the Internet. Services offered include estimating and job tracking software, online collaborative tools, and Web sites designed for print procurement.

The main attraction can be seen in the fact that printers themselves do not have to spend capital and time developing the infrastructure for online collaborations themselves, but can participate through membership.

Auction Sites

Internet **auction sites** for the printing industry can be as simple as online databases for suppliers with links to listed sites or as complex as online submission and distribution to member vendors. This frees smaller customers from being confined to their geographical region in searching out the best services. These sites tend to focus on quick-printing facilities and area also a good way for printers to sell excess press time. Sites such as Printbuyer.com allow a customer to submit an estimate request to numerous companies through an online request for quote process. This process is not necessarily used for large and complex printing jobs, but can be an excellent way to get simple flyers, brochures, and stationary printed.

StoreFront

Storefront sites refer to Web sites that have one printer providing accessible interface for customers to purchase their services. They can range from simple quick-print sites to complex ones that have multiple levels of access depending on the transactions to be done. Some are entirely Internet based. They may access and utilize facilities around the country, but the company itself maintains its business presence only on the Internet. Others combine a substantial physical presence while also promoting online access. Sir Speedy is a global corporation consisting of over 1,100 locations in 23 countries that offers one-stop print procurement for regular and business consumers regardless of location through their Web-based ordering system (figure 18.12). Through their Web site, customers can request a quote,

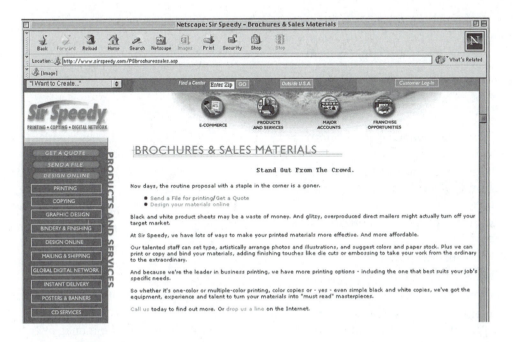

Figure 18.12 Storefront Web site.
Courtesy of Sir Speedy, Inc.

transmit files, and even design custom pieces such as letterhead, business cards, and envelopes. Sir Speedy offers collaborative services with other associated businesses that offer Web site design, proprietary file transfer networks and even billing services. This new approach to service allows customer access 7 days a week, 24 hours a day. As with so many industries, the Internet has changed the way that business must now operate in the new millennium to remain successful and profitable.

The Future

The 1990s saw incredible changes in the actual process of printing, primarily in the areas of prepress. The new challenge for the industry in the 21st century has to do with how business is conducted. How information is managed, tracked, and distributed, from the client's jobs to actual print facility operations, will determine the profitable plants of this decade and beyond.

Key Terms

amortization
depreciation
cost center
job estimate
Franklin Printing Catalog
overhead
job ticket
job scheduling and production
   control

job schedule
job costing
estimating software
management of information
   systems (MIS)
automated data collection
   (ADC)
computer-integrated
   manufacturing

e-management
e-hub
auction site
storefront site

Review Questions

1. What is the advantage of a uniform price schedule?

2. Why is reviewing the sequence of operations an important part of the estimating process?

3. What is the purpose of a production work order?

4. What is job scheduling?

5. What is a production control schedule?

6. Convert 4.70 hours to hours and minutes.

7. Explain why timely and accurate record keeping by production workers is important to accurate estimating.

8. What is a unit/time standards form?

9. Explain how fixed costs are identified and added to production costs.

10. List the eight steps of the estimating process.

11. What is the function of a work order?

12. What is the purpose of production scheduling?

13. What are the two approaches to job costing?

14. What are some of the features provided by estimating software?

15. What is meant by e-management?

16. Discuss the differences between an e-hub, an auction site, and a storefront site.

19

Customer-Defined Quality Management

Historical Background

W. Edwards Deming is considered the father or the *quality movement*. Born on a Wyoming homestead in 1900, Deming earned his undergraduate degree from the University of Wyoming and went on to complete a Ph.D. in Physics from Yale University in 1924.

During his undergraduate years Deming worked at General Electric's infamous Hawthorne plant in Chicago. More than forty-six thousand people worked at the plant to build telephone equipment. Of those, fifty-two hundred were assigned to the inspection department. Workers were paid by the unit and were docked for every piece that failed inspection. This experience influenced Dr. Deming's ideas about the failures of postproduction inspection. It was critically important to ensure consistency in manufacturing so every product would function as required. Without consistency there was no dependability.

While working for the Department of Agriculture in 1927 Deming met Walter A. Shewhart, a statistician for Bell Laboratories. Shewhart developed *statistical control*, which later became the foundation for Deming's quality approach.

Statistical control examined random variation and established limits—highs and lows—that indicates when a process was out of control.

Deming's previous experience with sampling and quality control prompted the United States government to hire him to teach statistical control methods to World War II manufacturers. Following the war, however, Deming's ideas fell out of favor. Corporations felt his approach was unnecessary, expensive, and time consuming.

In 1949, Deming was asked to assist with Japan's redevelopment. His initial work involved sampling data for housing, employment, and food production and consumption.

Japanese industrial leaders began to listen to Deming's ideas and adopted his quality methods nearly universally. The Japanese government credits Deming with the model that transformed Japanese production. Japan's highest, most coveted industrial recognition award is now called the *Deming Medal*.

Deming died in 1993. He never used the term *total quality management*. Others developed the term and ascribed it to him.

Objectives

After completing this chapter you will be able to:

- Define quality in terms of the customer's context or use, time requirement, and measure of success.
- Recall key terms, including continuous quality improvement, *total quality management*, and *total responsiveness management*.
- Explain the meaning of the term *Kizan*.
- Recall the purpose of ISO 9000 Standards Registration.
- Outline the motivation for customer-defined quality management

- Define the customer in terms of external and internal clients.
- Recognize the cost of failure.
- Recognize the principles of customer-defined quality management.
- Outline a typical total quality management implementation process.
- Recognize four statistical process control tools, including histograms, Pareto charts, cause and effect charts, and control charts.
- Outline a six-step problem solving process.
- Recall three team roles, including leader, scribe, and timekeeper.
- Name several effective team behaviors.

Introduction

The term *quality* is meaningless. It carries no meaning for several reasons, but it is meaningless primarily because it is applied to every situation. Television and newspaper advertisements announce "if you are looking for true quality, then buy. . . ." Soda containers are called jumbo rather than large. Society's use of the superlative communicates nothing. When a word like *quality* is overused, it loses definition.

Just what is a quality printed product? Consider two products:

Product 1. Will Romano is marketing manager for a medium-size manufacturing company that specializes in oil refinery pumps. The national distributors meeting is scheduled for 9:00 A.M. tomorrow. The company president has just announced a price reduction and wants the new information put in

the briefing package that will be given to each of the 150 distributors at the meeting.

The briefing package is a thick, three-ring binder; one section of the binder contains the old price list. The cartons of binders are waiting at the hotel. At 4:00 P.M. Romano updates the price list on his computer and prints out the three-page list. He rushes to a local print shop and asks for 200 copies of each of the three pages.

Using an electrostatic copier, the printer copies the pages on the same paper used in the binder, drills three holes in all 600 sheets, and delivers the job to Romano while he waits. Rushing to the hotel, Romano's staff quickly replaces the old list with the new one. At 9:00 A.M. the meeting goes off without a hitch and no one notices any difference in the price section. The president is very pleased.

Product 2. Ray Davis is vice president of advertising for a nationally based travel agency. The agency wants to promote winter vacations in the Bahamas. The promotion vehicle will be a full-color brochure used as a direct mail piece to 300,000 high-income households.

Davis works with the agency's advertising department to design the piece. The final design involves four-color process photographs. Undercolor removal (UCR) is used to enhance the images. An 80-pound coated offset paper is the base. A separate varnish coat is added to each photo during printing to make the image appear to "jump off the page." The fold lines are prescored for especially crisp edges.

The entire production, from concept to product, takes three months and hundreds of hours, but meets the September 15 mail date target. The campaign is a huge success and Davis is given a free vacation in the Bahamas.

Does scenario 1 or 2 deliver a higher quality product? The answer is "yes." They are both high-quality printed products. They both have specific context, focused use, and time limits, and they were judged successful.

Defining Quality

Only these elements give meaning to the concept of quality.

Context or Use

The customer has a specific context for every job brought to the printer. That context might be a problem or a goal. The job might be critical to a company's continued success, or it might be only a small element of continuing operations. The purpose of the job might be to inform, persuade, sell, motivate, or entertain. Whatever the motivation of the job, the customer defines what is important and judges the printed product in that context.

Time

Every job has a time limit. It is a rare customer who says, "Print it when you get a chance." Nearly every job must meet a deadline that is defined by the customer. A price list delivered an hour late to an important meeting has no value. A brochure mailed a month outside a selling window is also worthless.

Measure of Successful Use

After the printed product is delivered and used it is evaluated. Did the national distributors find the new price list useful and effective in selling more oil pumps? Did individuals respond to the direct mail campaign and purchase vacation packages to the Bahamas? Every customer knows how to measure the success of the printed piece. If the intent was met, then the product has great value; if the intent was not met, then the product has no merit.

The point is this: Quality is a term that has different meaning for every printing job. Quality depends upon context, time, and the measure of successful use. Quality is defined by the customer, not by print materials, ink density, or elaborate technical preparations (figure 19.1).

Customer-Defined Quality

American industry has given attention to customer-defined quality over the last several decades. Several popular terms have emerged that describe the process of making each manufacturing or service step responsive to the customer's needs or expectations. At least three terms have emerged in the popular printing industry vocabulary:

- **Continuous quality improvement (CQI)**
- **Total quality management (TQM)**
- **Total responsiveness management (TRM)**

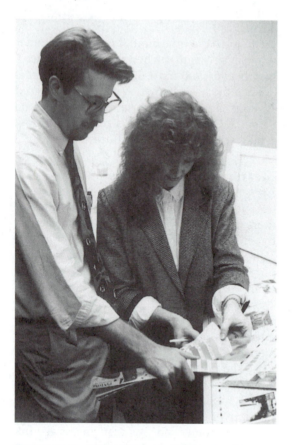

Figure 19.1 **The customer defines quality.**
The definition of quality is based upon context, time, and the measure of successful use.

This chapter is intended to provide an overview of the process of responding to customers' needs and expectations. Language is an important part of this process. The word "process," rather than "project," is used purposefully. "Process" is broad, ongoing, and denotes a permanent commitment. "Project" is a narrow, typically one-time event, and it is something that can be accomplished and then forgotten.

Although the concept of customer-defined quality was developed in the United States during World War II, the Japanese corporations used the term **Kizan** (pronounced "Key-Zan") to describe the continuous improvement effort. Kizan means that the capacity for improvement is endless. Incremental improvement is the key to success. The customer has more information than anyone. There is no limit to continually making small improvements and thereby improving customer satisfaction.

The drive for customer-defined quality is an attitude. It requires ongoing attention, absolute commitment, and specific behaviors. Continuous customer-defined improvement is a process. That process is transforming the American printing industry rapidly.

ISO 9000 Standards Registration

One measure of commitment to customer-defined quality is international **ISO 9000 standards registration**. The International Organization for Standardization (ISO) was founded in 1946 to establish international standards that would communicate clear, process-based operations. Its purpose is to facilitate the global exchange of products and services. Today ISO has more than ninety member countries. The American National Standards Institute (ANSI) is America's representative in ISO.

In 1987, ISO published five standards dealing with what it termed the *quality system*:

- *ISO 9000*

  Quality Management and Quality Assurance Standards—Guidelines for Selection and Use

- *ISO 9001*

  Quality Systems—Model for Quality Assurance in Design/Development, Production, Installation, and Servicing

- *ISO 9002*

  Quality Systems—Model for Quality Assurance in Production and Installation

■ *ISO 9003*

Quality Systems—Model for Quality Assurance in Final Inspection and Test

■ *ISO 9004*

Quality Management and Quality System Elements—Guidelines

These standards outline expectations for the process, management structure, and materials that produce consistent and predictable products to specifications provided by a customer.

There are five steps in the ISO 9000 standards registration process:

1. Company commitment to pursue registration
2. Evaluate current organization and procedures against ISO standards
3. Develop a compliance plan that transforms all elements of the company and ensures that all appropriate ISO standards are met
4. Implement the compliance plan
5. Conduct a registration audit (typically, a third-party, ISO-certified auditor examines the plan and its conformance to specifications)

Of course, the company must continue the commitment and actions that will maintain registration.

For those manufacturing companies that market and deliver products globally, ISO registration is critical. Pharmaceuticals, aircraft, and machine tools are prime examples of these products. Few America-based printing companies supply printed work for consumption in Europe or Asia. However, many printers provide print support for organizations that are international players. If a corporation has earned ISO registration, then all suppliers to that organization must also conform to ISO standards.

Apart from the actual registration, ISO standards are one method the graphic arts industry is using to become more customer-defined quality oriented.

Motivation for a Customer-Defined Quality Orientation

The discussion of how and who defines quality can be viewed as academic in companies faced with the realities of day-to-day operation. Even successful companies wonder why they should change what they are doing. A common response is "Printing is such a competitive business. There is so little time to spare. Why should I start a new project that will interfere with my job?"

It is exactly the competitive environment that motivates successful printers to embrace a customer-defined attitude.

Printing is a manufacturing process. However, it differs from almost all other manufacturing industries in that it produces custom-made products. Customers do not select four-color brochures for their product lines off of the rack in a department store. Print consumers place orders when they have needs that are specific to their organizations. There is perhaps a more direct relationship between the manufacturer and the customer in printing than in any other industry.

This close relationship, linked with a competitive environment, is moving successful printers to embrace a customer-defined attitude.

Technology Levels the Playing Field

This textbook is about print technology. Every chapter, except this one, deals with print organization, preparation, planning, prediction, or tools and materials. In reality, the equip-

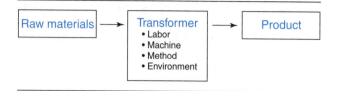

Figure 19.2 **Elements of a manufacturing process**

ment used by one company differs little from the equipment in another. Every company has access to the same paper, ink, film, and solvents that support the technology.

Progressive managers ask the question, then "Why does a customer chose my company over my competitor to print a job?" The conclusion in nearly every case is not related to technology. The answer is in the attitude, commitment, and behaviors of individual employees as they perform each step in the process of delivering a final product. The understandings and efforts of individual employees to produce customer-defined quality establishes and maintains the reputation of any organization.

The accelerating technical sophistication of print tools have made this reality even more apparent. Companies face an endless, ever increasing array of new and better equipment to purchase. This sophistication forces companies to recognize that the only true difference in the product they offer is meeting or exceeding customer expectations.

Defining a Manufacturing Process

Figure 19.2 outlines a simple view of how products are manufactured. Raw materials first enter the system. In printing these are typically paper, ink, film, and chemicals. The raw materials are transformed by a process that involves skilled craftspeople, equipment, transformation techniques (such as stripping and platemaking), and the work facility. The result is a product.

Figure 19.3 shows a more traditional view of what actually happens during manufacture. The process takes place (materials → transformer → product). Customer service keeps the client informed as the process develops. At the end of the process the product is inspected. The question is asked, "Does the product meet specifications?" If the answer is yes, the product is delivered to the customer. If the answer is no, the product is scrapped and redone.

Increasingly, companies are finding this approach flawed. It is good that defective or bad workmanship is discovered before it

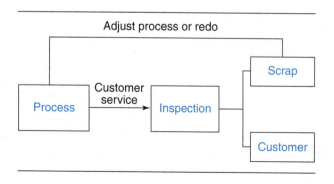

Figure 19.3 **The traditional production control system**

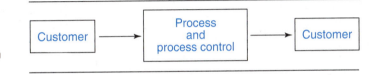

Figure 19.4 **A new control system model**

reaches the customer. However, two costs interfere with profits. The first is the cost of having a separate function that inspects the product. The second is the cost of waste associated with doing a job over. The cost of failure and the cost of preparing to catch failure are simply too high.

A more effective, productive view is shown in figure 19.4. It starts and ends with the customer. First, the customer defines expectations. The process and control of the process conform to those expectations. Every step is devoted to meeting job requirements. The customer also defines the control system. The key to this system is the skill, attitude, and attention of each employee in the company.

Some experts suggest that the traditional approach, which involves quality control after the process is finished, costs American business $60 billion a year. When this figure is translated to the printing industry, it means that a company might increase its annual profit by 4 to 10 percent.

Increased customer loyalty and increased profits mean continued job security. Moreover, nearly everyone who has been involved with a company that has moved to this new view of customer-defined quality feels an increased sense of self-worth, job satisfaction, and sense of purpose.

A New Definition of Customer

The traditional definition of customer is "someone who hires us to do a job." However, in this new environment, that definition has several meanings.

Differing View of the Printing Process

This book presents a comprehensive view of printing production. A schematic of the production view of printing is presented in figure 19.5. It is a relatively accurate overview of the steps involved in the production of a printed job through most contemporary graphic arts companies.

However, not everyone has this same view. For example, figure 19.6 shows how the general manager or company president might see the printing process. This process begins

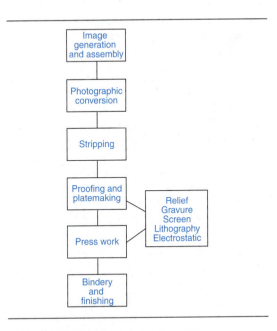

Figure 19.5 **Workflow as viewed by production.**
Courtesy of Gorelick & Associates.

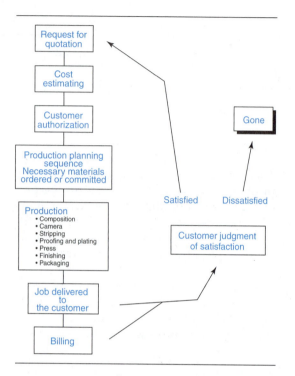

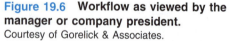

Figure 19.6   Workflow as viewed by the manager or company president.
Courtesy of Gorelick & Associates.

tomer is not concerned with how a job is produced. The client is concerned only with the product.

The customer is not impressed with technical equipment—only with the final product. It makes sense, then, that every printing company should be more concerned with its customer's view of the process rather than with its equipment.

Defining Customers

It is critical that the last three figures are understood. Where you stand in the printing process influences how you see it. This understanding has developed several definitions of customer.

The idea of internal and external customers has gained wide acceptance. External

with a job estimate. An estimate is produced and the client makes a decision. The company devotes significant resources to a sales force to bring new work to the organization. Once the customer gives authorization, production planning is the next step. Then the production step take place. Next the job is delivered to the customer, and finally, a bill or invoice is sent. External to the process is the customer's evaluation. If the customer is satisfied, then another job might be given. If the customer is not satisfied, however, then no more work will appear.

Figure 19.7 shows yet another view of the printing process. This is how the customer sees the process. It differs radically from the two previous diagrams. The entire planning and production sequence is invisible. The cus-

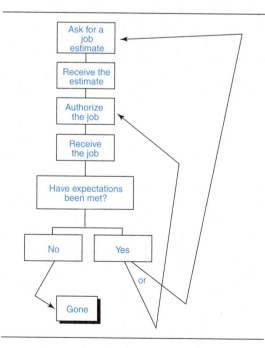

Figure 19.7   Workflow as viewed by the customer.
Courtesy of Gorelick & Associates.

customers are obvious. They are the people who place the orders and use the printed products. External customers pay the invoices.

There is at least one other external customer. Say you are printing labels that will be glued to a prescription drug bottle. Information on the label can mean life or death to a patient. Is the patient who takes the drug also your customer? The answer is yes. End users also have a role in defining quality and must be considered.

The idea of customer-defined quality is made even more powerful when internal customers are defined and listened to. An internal customer is anyone who follows you in the manufacturing or service sequence.

Say a stripper is working on a complex multicolor job on the light table. The stripper's responsibility is to deliver a quality job to the platemaker, to the press room, to the bindery. The person at each next step is the stripper's internal customer. If the stripper makes a mistake on registration marks or trim lines, then it is highly probable that someone after will not be able to perform his or her job properly. The stripper has a responsibility to both the customer who ordered the job and to the partners who are producing it.

Everyone inside a company is both a supplier and customer to someone else. The accounting department cannot send invoices on time if their coworkers do not provide them with accurate, timely information. Therefore, people in the accounting department are customers. On the other hand, the president wants a weekly and monthly summary of accounts payable and accounts receivable. Accounting then becomes a supplier of information to the president.

This approach also makes the concept of customer-defined quality a bit more personal. A process photographer working in the darkroom might feel somewhat removed from the external customer. However, the photographer will deliver her product to the stripping department, where it will be tested on the press. If the photographer does not produce exactly what is required, she will learn rapidly of the extra effort needed by the stripping department to compensate. The photographer will learn to serve her internal customer.

The Cost of Failure

Yet another motivation for adopting a customer-defined quality management program is the cost of failure. Look again at figure 19.3. When a job is scrapped or redone the company must absorb the additional costs of materials and labor. Moreover, redoing a job bounces a new job out of sequence and delays profitable work.

Say a customer rejects a run of 10,000 four-color brochures because the registration is off. The company must redo the job. Consider the associated additional costs:

■ The job must be returned to the stripping department. Flats must be disassembled and restripped.

■ New plates must be made.

■ New paper, ink, and chemicals must be used.

■ The production schedule must be interrupted and work in progress is delayed at every step in the process.

■ Time to produce the job is more than doubled because each operation has to be repeated once.

■ After the job is reworked, the jobs that were delayed may require overtime to complete.

After the job is redone, it is also highly probable the customer will take future work to some other company. Every salesperson knows it is far easier and less expense to keep an existing client than it is to solicit a new one. Failure has long-term implications.

By some estimates, the cost of failure represents 12 percent of all gross revenues and affects the printing industry's profit margin by 4 percent.

The Principles of Customer-Defined Quality Management

The anecdote for this chapter introduced W. Edwards Deming who is considered the founder of the world quality movement. Deming developed 14 points as the foundation and guiding principles for his ideas. These 14 points are fundamental understandings for any organization that wishes to implement customer-defined quality management.

- **Create consistency of purpose for improvement of product and service.**
  Deming says organizational purpose must change. Profit cannot be the goal. Profit is the result of a larger purpose—staying in business; providing jobs through innovation, research, and constant improvement; developing a reputation for exceptional customer satisfaction.

- **Adopt a new philosophy.**
  We can no longer accept poor workmanship, sullen service, and defective materials as the norm. This attitude prevents improved quality, productivity, customer satisfaction, and worker motivation. Deming speaks of the need for a new religion that rejects mistakes and negativism.

- **Cease to depend on postinspection to ensure quality.**
  American companies have traditionally relied upon product inspection as it comes off the production line—after the possibility of control or intervention. Failed results are either discarded or reworked. Quality must be built into the process using customer-based criteria. Inferior products should never reach the end of the line.

- **Cease awarding business on the basis of price.**
  Companies that buy supplies and products from the low bidder are not involved with the process. The new decision formula = customer-defined quality + perceived value + confidence in the supplier + delivery + price.

- **Improve constantly and forever the system of production and service.**
  Improvement is not an event—it is a continuous process. Production workers can only deliver a small portion of potential improvement. Management has the greatest responsibility. However, improvement must be a fundamental attitude shared by all.

- **Institute training.**
  Everyone must know his or her job. It is the company's responsibility to provide sufficient training and accurate instructions. If a job is not defined clearly it cannot be performed.

- **Institute supervision**
  The function of supervision is problem solving, not worker watching or enforcement. The supervisor uses statistical tools to identify, evaluate, and control customer-based quality problems. The measure of successful supervision is not quantity.

- **Drive out fear.**
  Few employees ask questions out of fear—fear of ridicule, fear of job loss, fear of revealing they do not know a specific job task. The result is lack of attention to customer desires, economic loss to the company, and inferior or unacceptable products.

■ **Break down barriers between staff areas.**
Functional work areas often feel in competition with other departments or, at best, reveal in placing blame for errors on other units. The entire organization must see itself as a team, seeking to anticipate and solve production problems that interfere with customer satisfaction.

■ **Eliminate slogans, exhortations, and posters for the workforce.**
These things to not work.

■ **Eliminate numerical quotas.**
Quotas look only to numbers, not process, product quality, or customer expectations. They are the surest way to ensure inefficiency, a cult of fear, increased costs, and product problems.

■ **Remove barriers to pride of workmanship.**
Individuals fundamentally want to do a good job. Some barriers are misguided supervisors, inexact directions, poor equipment and tools, and inferior or defective materials.

■ **Institute a vigorous program of education and retraining.**
A fundamental shift in philosophy, attitude, and behaviors requires education and retraining. Everyone in the organization must embrace the philosophy, realign attitudes, and alter behaviors. The customer is the primary teacher.

■ **Take action to accomplish the transformation.**
Seminars, discussion groups, reading volumes on philosophy and new ideas, and even great resolve cause no change. Top leadership must develop and implement a comprehensive plan that will transform the entire organization.

Other Voices but Similar Principles

Deming is not the only individual who has added to the definition of customer-defined quality. Joseph M. Juran followed Deming to Japan and has had at least the same influence on industrial organizations there. In the United States two decades later Philip B. Crosby introduced the ideas of *zero defects* and *conformance to quality*. Scores of others have added their voices to the process.

Books have been written by and about these individuals. Although there are differences between them, it is more important to recognize their similarities. Five concepts emerge as a common foundation for customer-defined quality management.

■ Commit to quality improvement throughout your entire organization.

■ Attack the system rather than the employee.

■ Strip down the work process to find and eliminate problems that prevent quality—whether production or service.

■ Identify your customer, internal or external, and satisfy that customer's requirements in the work process or in the finished product.

■ Eliminate waste, instill pride and teamwork, and create an atmosphere for continued and permanent quality improvement.

Some have referred to these ideas as "a blinding flash of the obvious."

The Typical TQM Process

Companies with a seemingly endless stream of problems, that are perhaps on the brink of failure, sometimes look to the TQM process as a solution. All experience, however, shows that TQM is not a solution to profound problems. The process is most effective when implemented in already strong organizations. It allows good companies to become better.

Immediate results are rarely found. Again, in reports from experienced companies, it takes 12 to 24 months before fundamental change takes place.

Organizations that have completed transformation to customer-defined quality management report four fundamental implementation steps: commitment, steering committee, training, and teams.

Commitment

The TQM process begins with a commitment at the highest level of the organization. Unless the president or CEO is actively committed and involved then the transformation process is doomed to failure.

This means that the top company officer is a partner with the entire organization in defining goals, helps outline and implement actions, does not interfere with team processes even if they appear to be taking too long, and does not allow a crisis to delay or prevent any meeting or scheduled activity. It also means the top company officer accepts the conclusions or recommendations of the team if there is a rational, information-based problem-oriented solution.

Steering Committee

Action truly begins when a steering committee is formed. Employees from across the entire organization are invited to participate. The committee is commonly composed of six to eight individuals, including the president, managers and supervisors, production workers, and office or support staff. Members are chosen based on a history of involvement with the company, openness to new ideas, evidence of wanting to do a good job, a commitment to the client, and a desire to improve the system.

The steering committee directs implementation of the transformation process. It identifies initial problems, develops an implementation plan, coordinates training, forms and charges teams, serves as a model, monitors progress, and supports and encourages everyone in the organization.

Logistically, the steering committee meets more frequently during the initial, proactive stage, perhaps several times a week, and moves into a responsive, supportive mode with less frequent meetings as the process gains momentum and acceptance.

In accepting a position on the steering committee, members also accept the responsibility to read, study, and learn about the process before the rest of the organization. Committee members must be prepared to answer questions and provide leadership. Both skills only come from knowledge and information.

Membership of the steering committee might change over time, but the committee as a body will continue forever as a functioning, critical part of the organization.

Training

Making a verbal commitment and forming a steering committee is only the beginning. Alone they are not sufficient to transform the organization. All participants must be given the tools to act.

Training includes at least the following elements:

- Belief in the company's commitment to the process
- Introduction to the vocabulary of customer-defined quality management
- Understanding that the process is based in precedence and success
- Successful team behaviors
- Decision making and problem-solving techniques
- Basic statistical methods
- An implementation model

Training might be delivered by the steering committee or by a firm outside of the company that specializes in such training.

Teams

The heart of the TQM process is the formation and action of individual teams. Teams might be cross-functional; that is, they may be made up of members from different departments in the company. Or, they might be all of the members of one department.

Whatever the composition, a team is charged with solving a problem. The team members follow a process (see next section). They gather information. They test solutions. They recommend action.

Most importantly, as both team members and individuals, employees are given license to change the way things have "always been done." They focus on internal and external customers. The following sections introduce basic statistical tools and the problem-solving process typically used by teams.

Statistical Process Control

A problem that cannot be quantified is difficult to solve. **Statistical process control (SPC)** describes the body of techniques that measure the elements of a manufacturing process that lend themselves to quantification. The goal of SPC is to describe numerically what is happening at any point in a process.

Detailed explanation of SPC is beyond the scope of this book. It is, however, possible to introduce a few basic tools used in SPC: histogram, Pareto chart, cause and effect chart, and control chart.

Histogram

A **histogram** shows the history of what has happened at one point in a process (figure 19.8). Histograms are frequency distributions.

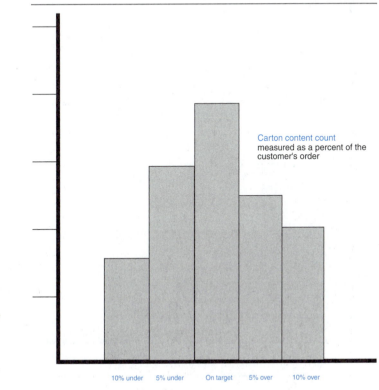

Carton content count measured as a percent of the customer's order

10% under   5% under   On target   5% over   10% over

Figure 19.8 Example of a histogram. Contents of cartons were packed in the bindery. The number of final pieces for each job was measured against the customer's order, and the number was converted to a percentage. The graph plots individual results for many jobs across a defined time period.
Courtesy of Gorelick & Associates.

This means that they show how often an event takes place. Data is sorted into numerical categories that are usually presented in the form of a bar graph.

In figure 19.8 a company was concerned with how accurately the customer's job was delivered in terms of count. If an order was for 5,000 pieces, the company wanted to know how many were actually delivered. For one week a team counted the number of pieces for each job. Each count was then converted to a percentage.

If the order was for 6,000 pieces and 5,790 pieces were delivered, the job was 3.5 percent under what was specified on the order $(6,000 - 5,790 = 210; 210 \div 6,000 = 0.035; 0.035 = 3.5$ percent). On a tally sheet, a tick mark was made under the "5% under" category. At the end of the week all marks under each category were summed and the results were displayed on a histograph.

Histograms cannot reveal what the process is going to do next, but it can report what has been done in the past. Knowing what has happened helps in understanding the process and is a first step toward controlling the process.

Pareto Charts

A **Pareto chart** is another form of frequency distribution (figure 19.9). Histograms typically examine variation in a focused part of the process, such as piece count accuracy, density consistency, or job readiness. Pareto charts generally look at frequency across a larger section of the process.

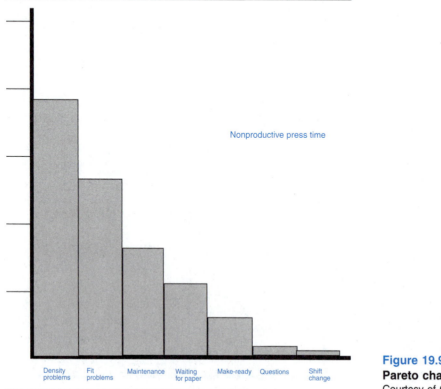

Nonproductive press time

Density problems — Fit problems — Maintenance — Waiting for paper — Make-ready — Questions — Shift change

Figure 19.9 Example of a Pareto chart.
Courtesy of Gorelick & Associates.

Figure 19.9 was created in response to a company's concern about the high number of nonchargeable or nonproductive hours on one press. For one week team members counted each time the press stopped and noted why. This Pareto chart was created to display the count within each category in a bar chart. The categories are arranged from most frequent to least frequent.

The value of this type of chart is that it quickly shows what is the most vital or most important problem. It also shows items that are trivial and are not worth immediately addressing. Using figure 19.9 a team might quickly make the decision to find solutions for press control—density and fit or registration problems.

Cause and Effect

A **cause and effect chart** is a tool used to outline all elements of a process or problems (figure 19.10). It is sometimes call a *fishbone chart* because it looks somewhat like the skeleton of a large fish. Once a problem has been defined, a cause and effect chart can be used by the team to examine causes or potential causes.

All processes using this tool involve six elements. Consider how we might complete a cause and effect chart for operating an offset lithographic press:

■ **Environment**
the press room

■ **Equipment**
press   densitometer
paper wedges   job proof

■ **Material**
plates   paper
ink   fountain solution
solvent

■ **Measurement**
density readings   sheet count
registration marks

■ **Methods**
make-ready   press run

■ **Operators**
senior press operator   helper

Examining all details of a process allows a team to consider problem sources and how changes might be made.

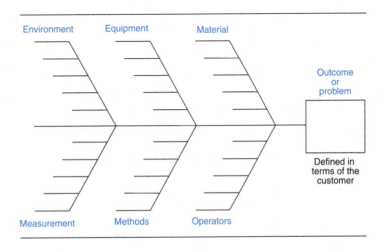

Figure 19.10 Cause and effect or fishbone charts are used to define each element in a process

Control Charts

A **control chart** is a visual tool used to examine variation in a repeating process (figure 19.11). A control chart is based on the principle of random probability.

Random probability refers to the likelihood of an event happening. What is the probability of getting heads when you flip a coin? The answer is 50 percent because flipping a coin has an equal chance of landing on one side as it does on another. This idea also applies to rolling dice. What is the probability of rolling a 5 with one die? The answer is 1 out of 9 or 11.1 percent.

If you flipped a coin 100 times and it came up heads 75 times and tails 25 times, then you would suspect something was not right. Some influence moved the process out of control—one side of the coin was weighted probably.

Control charts use this idea to examine whether something is "not right" about the process. Is some influence, outside of what we would normally expect, affecting the result? Control charts also establish normal limits of variation.

We might measure press ink density about every 100 sheets. Say we consistently read densities about 1.4 (the range is from 1.28 to 1.52). Suddenly we read 1.12. We would expect variation a few points on either side of the average, but 1.12 is beyond what is expected normally. Something influences the

process. Clearly, the operator must intervene and remove or adjust the influence to get the density "back into control."

Control charts can be developed by teams to look at specific problem areas. However, data is nearly always collected by the individual worker. In established TQM organizations, the operator is monitoring data continually. When the process goes out of control he or she is empowered to stop and adjust the process.

The example of measuring press density is a simple one. There are many formulas that can be used to create control charts for even the most complex processes. Individuals or teams interested in these more advanced tools should refer to a text on statistical process control.

The Problem-Solving Process

Teams deal with problems and processes. Most teams use a six-step problem-solving process (figure 19.12).

Identify the Problem

The steering committee or the team itself usually identifies the problem. Awareness comes from external feedback—from the customer or one of the company's suppliers—and from internal sources—colleagues or personal observation.

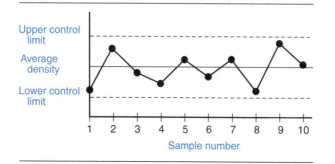

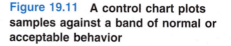

Figure 19.11 A control chart plots samples against a band of normal or acceptable behavior

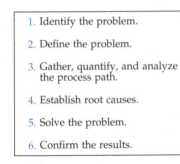

1. Identify the problem.

2. Define the problem.

3. Gather, quantify, and analyze the process path.

4. Establish root causes.

5. Solve the problem.

6. Confirm the results.

Figure 19.12 The six problem-solving steps.
Courtesy of Gorelick & Associates.

External customers might complain that it takes too long to prepare an estimate, that density is always too low, that job orders are always short of the specified number, or that invoices do not arrive in a timely fashion.

Internal customers might complain that there are too many plate remakes, that paper is always late arriving at the press, that information flow to production planning is too slow, or that there is always a backlog in the camera department.

Teams must be able to write down the problem because if it cannot be written then it cannot be identified.

Define the Problem

There is a difference between identifying the problem and defining it. "The company is not making enough money" is an identifiable problem. However, that is not the definition of the problem. Perhaps there are not enough jobs and the workforce is idle most of the time. Or perhaps estimates submitted to clients never cover actual job costs.

Recall the problem identified in figure 19.9—too much nonchargeable or nonproductive press time. Information from the Pareto chart suggests that the primary problem should be defined as lack of press control with density and registration.

In this step, the team must define the problem succinctly by answering the questions "what," "how," "why," and "when." Concrete definition leads to examining the process discussed in the next step.

Gather, Quantify, and Analyze the Process Path

Information must be collected and analyzed. The SPC tools, such as histograms or control charts, are used to describe the process. Decisions can only be made based upon data. A basic information set is the foundation for the next step—establishing causes.

Establish Root Causes

Cause and effect charts are put to good use at this point. Using the information that has been gathered, and a complete cause and effect chart, what are the possible root or basic causes of the problem?

The team might move back to the previous step and focus further data gathering and analysis upon one element, such as materials or method. Information is again the key.

Solve the Problem

At some point the team decides it has gathered enough information and has a possible solution to the problem. In practice, there might be several ideas that sum to a set of recommended changes.

Confirm the Results

The solutions must be tested. Again, information is collected and the process is examined. Has the problem disappeared? Is the process effectively back in control? If it is, then the team considers others problems or disbands. If it is not, then the process begins again with step two, defining the problem.

Group Processes

It should be apparent from the previous discussion that at the heart of this transformation process are employee teams. Success is measured in terms of individual team performance and accomplishments. The point is to empower individuals who control the system to make decisions about how to do their jobs better. If people take pride in meeting customers' expectations then the entire organization is transformed.

It is important to take a moment to discuss how groups or teams perform most effectively.

Teamwork Requirements

A team is a group of individuals who come together to solve a problem. Each individual can make a difference in the outcome of the problem. Everyone is accountable for performance. Everyone shares one mission or purpose.

To be successful, TQM teams must be well organized and well directed. Typically, teams meet once each week for 1 to 2 hours. With so little time, team meetings must be focused, efficient, and productive. To that end, most teams select individuals to fill several important roles:

■ **Leader**
Every meeting must have an agenda. The leader ensures that all discussion stays focused and on track. The leader also assigns tasks identified by the team that will take place outside the meeting.

■ **Scribe**
It is important that accurate records about what took place at each meeting are maintained. The scribe takes notes and writes a summary after the meeting. The minutes are read by the steering committee so members are informed of progress. The minutes are also used by the team to recall previous decisions and action.

■ **Timekeeper**
Time is critical. The team often decides to limit discussion on a specific agenda item. The timekeeper monitors progress and reminds the team where it is in the dialogue.

The team must make difficult decisions sometimes. Every member must emotionally and intellectually buy into the process that is taking place. If one member is disruptive or does not contribute to the process, then the team can ask the steering committee for a replacement.

Effective Team Behaviors

There is a wealth of information on effective team behaviors. Team training must be part of the education process developed and directed by the steering committee. Four key characteristics emerge as fundamental to team success:

■ **Full participation**
This means both physical and mental participation. The leader must be especially sensitive to drawing every member into discussion. Individuals must encourage each other by acknowledging each others' ideas and worth.

■ **Lack of dominance or peer pressure**
No one may be allowed to dominate the discussion, ideas, or processes. Unless there is full participation, free exchange of ideas, and the shared belief everyone was part of the solution, then nothing will change.

■ **Listening**
Sometimes individuals are so anxious to speak that they do not hear what others are saying. A good listening

technique is for the leader to ask someone to summarize what someone else said. The exchange of ideas means everyone hears and considers.

- **Consensus decisions**
  This is the most difficult, but most powerful and effective, team behavior.

Everyone should agree before action is taken. The behavior takes time. It involves give and take and negotiation. When this technique is achieved, however, everyone is committed.

Key Terms

Continuous quality improvement (CQI)
Total quality management (TQM)
Total responsiveness management (TRM)

Kizan
ISO 9000 standards registration
statistical process control (SPC)
histogram

Pareto chart
cause and effect chart
control chart

Review Questions

1. Who was W. Edwards Deming and what was his role in customer-defined quality management?
2. How does the customer define quality in terms of context, time, and measure of success?
3. What does *Kizan* mean?
4. What is ISO 9000 standards registration?
5. Contrast how the customer and a press operator might view the printing process.
6. What is an internal customer?
7. Why did Deming urge the elimination of postinspection?
8. What are the five common concepts of customer-defined quality management?
9. What are the four typical TQM implementation steps?
10. What is the difference between a histogram and a Pareto chart?
11. What are the six steps in a problem-solving process?
12. What is the difference between identifying a problem and defining a problem?
13. What is the function of a team scribe?

Appendix A

Color Temperature

Color temperature is a term used often by both printers and photographers but without accurate understanding. Light sources are often classified according to color temperature (Table A.1), which makes people think that temperature is a primary concern for all photography—but it is not. Color temperature is not a concern in black-and-white process photography, but it is of paramount importance in color work, whether original photography or color separation.

Color temperature is a measure of the sum color effect of the visible light emitted by any source. The blue end of the visible spectrum is rated as having a higher color temperature than the red end. Color temperature is defined theoretically by heating a perfect radiator of energy or *black body*. As the temperature increases, the color of the body changes. Each color of the visible spectrum is then assigned a temperature that corresponds to the temperature of the black body for that color. Color temperature is measured in Kelvins (K), which are derived by adding 273 to the temperature in degrees Celsius (°C). Color temperature is not such an unusual idea. For centuries blacksmiths judged temperature visually by the color a piece of metal displayed as it was heated.

It is important to realize that color temperature describes only the visual appearance of a light source and does not necessarily describe its photographic effect. Both tungsten and fluorescent light sources might be rated at the same color temperature, but because they differ in spectral emissions, they might produce totally different results on a piece of film.

Table A.1. Color temperature of various light sources

Light Source	Color Temperature
Clear blue sky	15,000°K to 30,000°K
Sun	5,100°K
Partly cloudy sky	8,000°K to 10,000°K
Fluorescent lights, daylight	6,500°K
Pulsed xenon	6,000°K
Quartz-iodine (high level)	3,400°K
Carbon arcs, white flame cored	5,000°K
Incandescent, 100-watt	3,000°K

Source: *Handbook of Tables for Applied Engineering Science*, CRC, 1970.

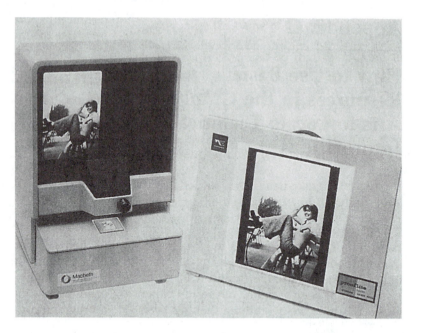

Figure A.1 Color transparency viewers.
Courtesy of Kollmorgen Corp., Macbeth Color and Photometry Division

Most color films are balanced for a particular color temperature. In other words, they are designed to record images accurately under certain color conditions. If a film is rated around 5000K, it should faithfully record color balance as viewed under natural sunlight. If film is rated around 3000K, it is designed to be used under artificial incandescent light, as found in the average home.

Graphic arts films are rarely identified as being balanced for a particular color temperature. However, when working with color originals, the graphic arts photographer has to be certain that the reflected light that reaches the film is describing the color balance of the copy being reproduced faithfully. For that reason the industry has even adopted a color temperature standard for viewing and judging color proofing and printing (5000K) to ensure consistent human color perception. Figure A.1 is an example of a standard viewing device. It ensures that each transparency viewed is illuminated with a light source used throughout the industry.

Finding Information Resources in the Graphic Arts

There is more information on print and the graphic arts than any single book, reference manual, or individual could hold. This book is intended to be a contemporary, comprehensive review of printing technology. However, because of its breadth, it is impossible to treat any single topic in exhaustive detail. In other words, behind every chapter or section is a vast array of information that was not discussed.

In some ways this appendix may be the most important portion of this entire book. There is an old Chinese saying: "Give a man a fish and he eats for a day; teach a man to fish and he eats for a lifetime." The purpose of this section is to outline the procedures and resources available to help you find information beyond what is covered in this book.

Strategy One

To begin any search, you must first get an idea of how much information is available on the topic. To do this, you need a quick overview. Any basic printing textbook (such as this one) is a good start. Read the chapter that contains your topic, and make notes on key terms. These key terms are called *descriptors*. Also, work to gain a snapshot understanding of the issues or questions.

Use the index to determine if your key terms are used anywhere else in the text. See how they are used and if they appear in another context that might be related to the topic. Then review the bibliography. A *bibliography* is a list of books that describe a body of information. Each entry in a bibliography is called a *citation*. A citation contains enough information to locate the work. Typical information is author's name, book title, publisher's name and city, and date of last publication. Some citations also include the number of pages in the text. Identify citations that appear appropriate to your topic.

Another way to find an overview of a subject is to use one of the encyclopedialike books on printing. *The Lithographers Manual*, published by the Graphic Arts Technical Foundation, is one example. It is updated every five or six years and is a very technical treatment of every area of lithography. Another example is *The Gravure Industry*, published by the Gravure Association of America. Use the index to locate your descriptors. Then review the information in the book. Again, the purpose is to gain a good overview of issues and to identify other, more specific references.

Strategy Two

The next step is to locate the books described in your citations. Many printers have them in their personal libraries. Companies often purchase books on an ongoing basis from professional associations in order to maintain a reference collection.

Individuals seeking information do not typically have access to such resources. The best source is a public library. Large libraries purchase books across many topics. Good collections of printing books are typically held by better libraries. Another possibility might be the library of a university, community college, or technical institute with a program in printing. Even small libraries can be resources because they often have borrowing privileges from larger libraries. The system is called "interlibrary loans."

You can also locate additional information by looking in the library's card catalog. Many libraries have moved to electronic catalogues, but whether the catalog is paper or electronic, the problem is to link your key terms with the subject headings used by the library. Most large libraries use the same subject headings as the Library of Congress in Washington, D.C. Here are some useful headings from that system:

- Printing

  Used for general books about the whole industry

- Printing, practical

  Used for books that are about technical aspects

- Lithography

  Used for books concerned primarily with lithography for artists

- Offset Printing

  Used for books that are about technical aspects of industrial lithography

- Screen Process Printing

  Used for books that are about technical aspects of industrial screen printing

- Serigraphy

  Used for books about screen printing for artists

You might also find information under:

- Advertising Layout and Typography
- Book Industries and Trade
- Color Printing
- Color Separation
- Chromolithography
- Desktop Publishing
- Electrostatic Printing
- Flexography
- Handpress
- Intaglio Printing
- Map Printing
- Newspaper Layout and Typography
- Paper—Printing Properties
- Photolithography
- Printing Industry
- Proofreading
- Type and Type Founding
- Typesetting

If at any time you are having trouble finding what you need, be sure to ask a librarian for help. That is what librarians are there for.

Strategy Three

There are over two hundred magazines concerned with printing and the graphic arts in one form or another. Sitting down and thumbing through many issues of magazines is the most inefficient way to find information, however. An index is a list of all the articles in a number of different magazines or journals. All the titles of articles that relate to that same subject are grouped together with the name of the publication, date, and page number included for each one. Most indexes are compiled so that by looking in one book you will find everything under a subject heading that was published in a single year.

The *Business Periodicals Index* indexes *Graphic Arts Monthly* and *American Printer* (as well as a few other magazines concerned with publishing) and can lead you to some technical information quickly. Many indexes also include an *abstract*. An abstract is a short summary of the article so you can tell whether it will help you without actually reading the entire article.

Most indexes are *online*, meaning that they can be accessed and searched using a computer. Systems vary, but each library will provide instructions on use.

Strategy Four

In additional to using an index to find specific information, you can use the most common magazines to keep up with what is currently happening in your field. You should read the summaries at the front of each publication regularly and then read the complete articles if you have time. Some trade magazines are free. The following is a list of the most common printing trade publications. You may write or fax to ask for subscription information.

American Printer
20 N. Wacker Dr.
Chicago, IL 60606-3298
Tel: 312-726-2802
Fax: 312-726-3091
http://www.americanprinter.com/

Graphic Arts Monthly
249 W. 17th St.
New York, NY 10011
Tel: 800-637-6089
Fax: 212-463-6530
http://www.gammag.com/

Printing Impressions
401 North Broad St.
Philadelphia, PA 19108
Tel: 215-238-5300
Fax: 215-238-5457
http://www.napco.com/pi/pi1.html

Publishers Weekly
249 W. 17th St.
New York, NY 10011
Tel: 800-842-1669
Fax: 212-463-6631
http://www.publishersweekly.com/

U & l c International Typeface Corporation
866 Second Ave.
New York, NY 10017
Tel: 212-371-0699
Fax: 212-752-4752
http://www.itcfonts.com/itc/home.html

Computer Publishing Magazine
Pacific Magazine Group
513 Wilshire Blvd., Suite 344
Santa Monica, CA 90401
Tel: 213-455-1414
Fax: 213-393-5222
http://www.cpg.com/

Gravure Association of America
1200-A Scottsville Rd.
Rochester, NY 14624
Tel: 716-436-2150
Fax: 716-436-7689
http://www.gaa.org/

Web Techniques
CMP Media
600 Harrison St.
San Francisco CA 94107
Tel: 415-905-2200
http://www.webtechniques.com

Publishing & Production Executive
401 N. Broad St.
Philadelphia PA 19108
Tel: 215-238-5300
Fax: 215-238-5457
http://www.ppe-online.com

Electronic Publishing
PennWell-Advanced Technology
98 Spit Brook Rd.
Nashua NH 03062-5737
Tel: 603-891-9166
Fax: 603-891-0539
http://www.electronic-publishing.com

PEI (Photo Electronic Imaging)
229 Peachtree St. NE St. 2200
International Tower, Atlanta GA 30303
Tel: 404-522-8600
Fax: 404-614-6405
http://www.peimag.com

AGFA Monotype
200 Ballardval St.
Wilmington, MA 01887-1069
Tel: 978-657-5600
http://www.monotype.com/index.html

Publish
462 Boston St.
Topsfield, MA 01983-1232
Tel: 978-887-7900
Fax: 978-887-6117
http://www.publish.com/

Strategy Five

In addition to libraries and publications, technical and professional associations provide a good source of information on the graphic arts. There are associations associated with nearly every aspect of the industry. The following is only a partial list that focuses on national associations. Many states and most major cities also have local associations or clubs.

All these associations provide information to people interested in the area of the industry represented by their membership. Many publish books, newsletters, and other educational materials. Most offer educational membership at a reduced cost to students and teachers in the graphic arts.

Association membership can be an important part of your career. Often the people you meet through an association remain friends for a lifetime, broaden your perspective, and increase your opportunities for advancement.

National Printing Equipment Suppliers (NPES)
1899 Preston White Dr.
Reston, VA 22091-4367
Tel: 703-264-7200
Fax: 703-620-0994
http://www.npes.org/

Screen Printing Association International
10015 Main St.
Fairfax, VA 22031
Tel: 703-385-1335
Fax: 703-273-0456
http://www.sgia.org

Printimage International
401 North Michigan Ave
Chicago, IL 60611
Tel: 312-644-6610
Fax: 312-321-6869
http://www.napl.org

International Association of Printing House Craftsmen
7042 Brooklyn Blvd.
Minneapolis, MN 55429-1370
Tel: 800-446-4274
Fax: 800-733-4274
http://www.iaphc.org/

Graphic Arts Technical Foundation
200 Deer Run Road
Sewickley, PA 15143-2600
Tel: 412-741-6860
Fax: 412-741-2311
http://www.gatf.org/

International Prepress Association
7200 France Ave., South
Edina, MN 55435-4302
Tel: 612-896-1808
Fax: 612-896-0181
http://www.ipa.org/

*Flexographic Technical
Association/Flexographic Technical
Foundation*
900 Marconi Ave.
Ronkonkima, NY 11779-7212
Tel: 516-737-6026
Fax: 516-737-6813
http://www.flexography.org/

*Research & Engineering Council of the
Graphic Arts Industry*
Box 639
Chadds Ford, PA 19317
Tel: 215-388-7394
Fax: 215-388-2708
http://www.recouncil.org/

Tag & Label Manufacturers Institute
1700 First Ave., South
Iowa City, IA 52240
Tel: 319-337-8247
Fax: 319-337-8271
http://www.tlmi.com/

Printing Industries of America
100 Daingerfield Rd.
Alexandria, VA 22314
Tel: 703-519-8192
Fax: 703-548-3227
http://www.printing.org/

National Newspaper Association
1627 K St., NW
Washington, DC 20006
Tel: 202-466-7200
Fax: 202-331-1403
http://www.nna.org/

National Paper Trade Association
111 Great Neck Rd.
Great Neck, NY 11021
Tel: 516-829-3070
Fax: 516-829-3074
http://www.gonpta.com/

Paper Industry Management Association
2400 East Oakto St.
Arlington Heights, IL 60005
Tel: 708-956-0250
Fax: 708-956-0520
http://www.pima-online.org/

Newspaper Association of America
11600 Sunrise Valley Dr.
Reston, VA 22091
Tel: 703-648-1000
Fax: 703-620-4557
http://www.naa.org/

Direct Marketing Association
11 West 42nd St.
New York, NY 10036-8096
Tel: 212-768-7277
Fax: 212-768-4546
http://www.the-dma.org/

*Engraved Stationery Manufacturers
Association, Inc.*
305 Plus Park Blvd.
Nashville, TN 37217
Tel: 615-366-1094
Fax: 615-366-4192
http://www.iega.org

Fibre Box Association
2850 Golf Rd.
Rolling Meadows, IL 60008
Tel: 708-364-9600
Fax: 708-364-9639
http://www.fibrebox.org/Modularity
Standard/Default.asp

International Press Association
222 South Jefferson, Suite 200
Chicago, IL 60661
Tel: 312-441-9017
Fax: 312-441-9019
http://www.hrdi.org

Magazine Publishers Association
919 Third Ave.
New York, NY 10022
Tel: 212-752-0055
Fax: 212-888-4217
http://www.magazine.org

American Business Press Association
675 Third Ave, Suite 415
New York, NY 10017
Tel: 212-661-6360
Fax: 212-370-0736
http://www.americanbusinessmedia.com

American Institute of the Graphic Arts
164 Fifth Ave.
New York, NY 10010
Tel: 212-807-1990
Fax: 212-807-1799
http://www.aiga.org

Association of American Publishers
71 Fifth Ave.
New York, NY 10003-3004
Tel: 212-255-0200
Fax: 212-255-7007
http://www.publishers.org

Binding Industries of America (PIA Special
Interest Group)
70 E. Lake St.
Chicago, IL 60601
Tel: 312-372-7606
Fax: 312-704-5025
http://www.bindingindustries.org

Business Forms Management Association
316 SW Washington, Suite 7110
Portland, OR 97204
Tel: 503-227-3393
Fax: 503-274-7667
http://www.bfma.org/~bfma

Digital Graphics Association
408 Eighth Ave., Suite 10-4
New York, NY 10001-1816
Tel: 212-629-3232
Fax: 212-465-2012
http://www.bindernet.com/dga.html

Digital Printing & Imaging Association
10015 Main St.
Fairfax, VA 22031
Tel: 703-385-1339
Fax: 703-359-1336
http://www.dpia.org

Document Management Industries
Association
433 E. Monroe Ave.
Alexandria, VA 22301
Tel: 703-836-6225
http://www.emia.org

Education Council of the Graphic Arts
Industry
1899 Preston White Dr.
Reston, VA 22091
Tel: 703-648-1768
Fax: 703-620-0994
http://www.emia.org./

Graph Comm Central
Virginia Tech
Technology Education Program—Mark
Sanders
College of Human Resources and
Education
144 Smyth Hall
Blacksburg, VA 24061-0432
Tel 540-231-8173
Fax: 540-231-4188
http://TechEd.vt.edu/GCC

Graphic Communications Council
(formerly the *Graphic Arts Education and
Research Foundation*)
1899 Preston White Dr.
Reston, VA 22091-1367
Tel: 703-264-7200
Fax: 703-620-0994
http://www.npes.org/

International Digital Imaging Association
84 Park Ave.
Flemington, NJ 08822
Tel: 908-782-4635
Fax: 908-782-4671
http://pwr.com/idia

International Prepress Association
7200 France Ave., S, Suite 327
Edina, MN 55435
Tel: 612-896-1908
Fax: 612-896-0181
http://www.ipa.org

*National Association of Printers &
Lithographers*
780 Palisade Ave.
Teaneck, NJ 07666
Tel: 201-342-0700
Fax: 201-692-0286
http://www.napl.org

Graphic Communications Council
(formerly the *National Scholarship Trust
Fund*) *(GATF)*
200 Deer Run Rd.
Sewickley, PA 15143-2600
Tel: 412-741-6860
Fax: 412-741-2311
http://www.gatf.org

Society of Publication Designers
60 East 42nd St., Suite 721
New York, NY 10165-0051
Tel: 212-983-8585
Fax: 212-983-6043
http://spd.org

Technical Association of the Graphic Arts
68 Lomb Memorial Dr.
Rochester, NY 14623
Tel: 716-475-5593
Fax: 716-475-7052
http://www.webelectric.com/

Women in Production
347 Fifth Ave., Suite 1406
New York, NY 10016
Tel: 212-481-7793
Fax: 212-481-7969
http://www.wip.org

XPLOR International
The Electronic Document Systems
Association
24238 Hawthorn Blvd.
Torrance, CA 90505-6505
Tel: 310-373-3633
Fax: 310-375-4240
http://www.xplor.org

Gravure Association of America (GAA)
1200-A Scottsville Road
Rochester, NY 14624
Tel: 716-436-2150
Fax: 716-436-7689
http://www.gaa.org

Health and Safety Issues

A safe and healthy workplace is important not only to the well-being of the worker, but also to the bottom line of the company. According to OSHA (the federal Occupational Safety and Health Administration), "every year over 6,000 Americans die from workplace injuries, an estimated 50,000 people die from illnesses caused by workplace chemical exposure, and 6 million people suffer nonfatal workplace injuries." Clearly, health and safety issues need to be addressed in printing facilities. Chemical and machine hazards comprise the major categories to be concerned with. Chemical hazards can include solvents, plate- and film-processing solutions, ink mists, and toxic dusts. Machine hazards can involve concerns such as improperly guarded equipment, faulty hydraulics, and lockout devices (an energy-isolating device) not in the proper safe position. In addition, there are ergonomic issues concerning the proper physical adaptation of the job requirements to the worker. One well-known hazard is carpal tunnel syndrome, which can result from incorrect keyboard and arm positioning along with constant repetitive keyboarding.

This topic is a large one with a multitude of specific rules and regulations applying to the printing industry. It is not within the scope of this book to address all the concerns and approaches of a comprehensive health and safety program. Note that OSHA maintains an excellent Web site that provides access to current standards and directives, along with manuals, statistics, and current OSHA events.

Contact Information

U. S. Department of Labor
Occupational Safety and Health
Administration
Office of Public Affairs, Room N3647
200 Constitution Avenue
Washington, DC 20210
(202) 693-1999
www.osha-sic.gov

Glossary

Accordion fold. Several folds made parallel to each other.

Actinic light. Any light that exposes light-sensitive emulsions.

Actinic output. Energy that activates or hardens light-sensitive coatings; consists of shorter wavelengths of visible spectrum.

Additive primary colors. Colors that make up white light; red, blue, and green are the additive primary colors.

Additive plate. Presensitized lithographic plate on which ink-receptive coating must be added to exposed area during processing.

Additives. Compounds that control such ink characteristics as tack, workability, and drying time.

Adhesive binding. Glue fastening of printed sheets or signatures.

Agitation. Flow of solution back and forth over film during chemical processing.

Alphanumeric code. A unique code made of numbers and letters for all uppercase and lowercase letters, numbers, as well as some common punctuation and symbols.

Amortization. The process of distributing equipment costs across time periods or jobs.

Aniline printing. An early term for flexography. See *Flexography*.

Anilox roll. An inking roller used on a flexographic press with a cellular surface.

Antihalation dye. Dye that is generally coated on back of most transparent-based film to absorb light that passes through emulsion and base during exposure.

Aperture. Opening through which light passes in the lens of a camera.

Area array. In a digital camera, a set of CCDs arranged in a block to capture an entire image at once, rather than line by line.

Ascender. Any portion of a letter that extends above the x-height.

ASCII (pronounced "as-key"). An alpha-numeric code used in telecommunication.

Asphaltum. Tarlike material used as an acid resist in gravure printing.

Assembling. Finishing operations that bring all elements of a printing job together into final form; common assembling operations are gathering, collating, and inserting.

Balance. Equilibrium of the visual images on a sheet.

Ballard shell process. Special technique used by many gravure publication printers for easy removal of copper layer after cylinder has been printed.

Basic density range (BDR). Range of detail produced from halftone screen by main exposure.

Basic exposure. Camera aperture and shutter speed combination that produces a quality film image of normal line copy with standardized chemical processing.

Basic sheet size. Basis from which all paper weights are determined by the manufacturer; differs for each of the four paper classifications:

book paper (25 inches × 38 inches), writing paper (17 inches × 22 inches), cover paper (20 inches × 26 inches), and Bristol paper (22 inches × 28 inches).

Basis weight. Weight in pounds of one ream (500 sheets) of the basic sheet size of a particular paper type.

Baumé. Density scale used by Antoine Baumé, a French chemist, in graduating his hydrometers.

Bézier curves. A smooth, mathematically defined curve or line consisting of two endpoints (anchors) and two control points.

Bimetal plate. Plate manufactured with two dissimilar metals; one forms the ink-receptive image and the other forms the solution-receptive area.

Binary system. Numbering system in which all numbers consist of only two digits, 0 and 1.

Bit depth (color depth). The number of colors that can be displayed, which is a function of the amount of bits used to describe each screen pixel.

Blanket cylinder. Part of a rotary press that transfers the image from the plate cylinder to the press sheet.

Bleed. Extension of a printing design over the edge of a sheet.

Blueline flat method. Special method of preparing a flat as part of one multiflat registration system; blueline flat carries all important detail, including register marks.

Blueprint paper. Inexpensive photomechanical proofing material; is exposed through the flat on a platemaker, developed in water, fixed in photographic hypo, and then washed to remove fixer stains.

Blue-sensitive material. Photographic material that reacts to the blue part of white-light exposure.

Body-height. Distance from the base line to the top of a lowercase letter *x* in a given font; varies depending on alphabet design; also known as *x-height*.

Bone folder. Most common type of hand folding device; consists of a long, narrow blade of bone or plastic.

Book paper. Most common type of paper found in the printing industry; available in a wide range of grades and noted for easy printability.

Bridge. Surface of a gravure cylinder between wells.

Bristol paper. Stiff, heavy material used for business cards, programs, file folders, inexpensive booklet covers, and the like.

Buckle folder. Paper-folding machine that operates by forcing a sheet between two rollers and causing it to curve.

Byte. Unit consisting of 8 bits. The amount of memory needed to store a single character.

Cab. Special film mask used in gravure printing; is punched and marked to be used as a guide for stripping negatives prior to making a gravure cylinder.

Cache memory. High-speed memory that stores data and instructions that the central processing unit is likely to need quickly.

Calendering. Papermaking process that passes paper between rollers to smooth or polish the paper surface.

California job case. Most popular case for holding foundry type; contains all characters in a single drawer.

Camera-ready copy. Finished paste-up used to create the images of the final job.

Cause and effect chart. A tool used to outline all elements of a process or problem.

Casebound cover. Rigid cover generally associated with high-quality bookbinding.

CCD (charge-coupled device). A technology characterized by the use of an array of light-sensitive elements that translates analog signals into digital information. Common in scanners and digital cameras.

Center lines. Lines drawn on a paste-up in light-blue pencil to represent the center of each dimension of the illustration board.

Central processing unit (CPU). The computer's primary processing hardware.

Chain gripper delivery. Press delivery unit technique in which sheets are pulled onto the delivery stack by a mechanical system.

Characteristic curve. Visual interpretation of a light-sensitive material's exposure/density relationship.

CIP3 (Consortium for Integrating Prepress, Press, and Prepress). An organization working to create formats for digital files that can be generated in prepress and used to set up press and finishing devices.

Clip art. Art supplied in camera-ready form; copyright given with purchase; available from a number of companies that specialize in providing art to printers.

Closed shop. Shop that requires craftspeople to joint a union to maintain employment.

Coated paper. Paper with an added layer of pigment bonded to the original paper fiber surface to smooth the rough surface texture.

Cold-type composition. Preparation of any printing form intended to be reproduced photographically.

Collating. Finishing operation in which individual printed sheets are assembled into the correct sequence.

Collodion. Viscous solution of cellulose nitrates, ether, and alcohol used to coat photographic plates.

Colloid. Any substance in a certain state of fine division.

Color sensitivity. Chemical change response of a particular silver halide emulsion to an area of the visible electromagnetic spectrum.

Color temperature. Measure of the sum color effect of the visible light emitted by any source.

Commercial printing. Type of printing in which nearly any sort of printing job is accepted.

Complementary flats. Two or more flats stripped so that each can be exposed singly to a plate but still have each image appear in correct position on the final printed sheet.

Composition. Process of assembling symbols (whether letters or drawings) in the position defined on the rough layout during image design.

Comprehensive. Artist's rendering that attempts to duplicate the appearance of the final product.

Computer-to-plate. Workflow process in which files are output directly to plates rather than outputting to film first.

Control chart. A visual tool used to examine variation in a repeating process.

Continuous quality improvement (CQI). Process of making each manufacturing or service step responsive to the customer's needs or expectations.

Continuous sheet-feeding system. A press that adds sheets to the feeding system without stopping the press in the middle of a run.

Continuous-tone photograph or copy. Image created from many different tones or shades and reproduced through photography.

Continuous-tone photography. Process of recording images of differing density on pieces of film; continuous-tone negatives show varying shades of grey or different hues of color.

Contract proof. A proof produced by the printer prior to running the job on press. It represents the agreed on appearance of the final printed product between the printer and the customer and normally is signed off by the customer.

Contrast. Noticeable difference between adjacent parts in tone and color.

Control strip. Piece of film used in automatic film processing to gauge the activity level of solutions in the machine; several times a day the photographer sends a pre-exposed control strip through the machine and then examines the processed piece to determine whether machine adjustments need to be made.

Conventional gravure. Method of preparing gravure cylinders that delivers well openings of the same opening size.

Copy. Words to be included on the rough layout; final pasteup; or, in some situations, the final press sheet.

Copyboard. Part of a process camera that opens to hold material to be photographed (the copy) during exposure.

Copy density range (CDR). Difference between the lightest highlight and the darkest shadow of a photograph or continuous-tone copy.

Counter. In gravure printing, angle between the doctor blade and the cylinder; in relief printing, sunken area just below the printing surface of foundry type.

Counting keyboard. Operator-controlled keyboard that requires end-of-line decisions as copy is being typed.

Cover paper. Relatively thick paper commonly used for outside covers of brochures or pamphlets.

Crash. Gauzelike material that is sometimes embedded in the perfect binding adhesive to increase strength.

Creasing. Process of crushing paper grain with a hardened steel strip to create a straight line for folding.

Cross-media. Taking digital content and sending it to a variety of output solutions, including print, the Internet, and CD.

Ctn weight. Weight in pounds of one carton (ctn) of paper.

Cursor. A blinking line or rectangle on a computer screen that marks the next point of data entry.

Cutting layout. Drawing that shows how a pile of paper is to be cut by the paper cutter.

Cylinder line. Area of a printing plate that marks the portion of masking sheet used to clamp the plate to the plate cylinder; always marked on the flat before stripping pieces of film.

Dampening sleeves. Thin fiber tubes that are slightly larger in diameter than the water form roller when dry; when moistened, they shrink to form a seamless cover.

Dark printer. One of the halftones used to make a duotone; usually printed with the use of black or another dark color; often contains the lower middle tones to shadow detail of the continuous-tone original.

Database. A collection of related data organized with a specific structure.

DCS. A PostScript file format used with raster art to save specific color information into separate files.

Default parameters. Parameters supplied by the computer when the operator fails to provide them.

Delivery unit. Unit on a printing press that moves the printed sheet from the printing unit to a pile or roll.

Densitometry. Measurement of transmitted or reflected light with precision instruments expressed in numbers.

Density. Ability of a photographic image to absorb or transmit light.

Depreciation. Financial technique of spreading the cost of major purchases, such as equipment or a building, over several years.

Descender. Any portion of a letter that extends below the base line.

Design. Process of creating images and page layouts for printing production.

Desktop publishing. The process of assembling pages on a desktop computer. The term is increasingly being replaced with the broader term *digital prepress*.

Developer. Chemical bath used to make the image on a light-sensitive emulsion visible and useful to the printer; some developers are used in the darkroom to process line film; others are used in proofing, platemaking, stencil preparation in screen printing, and some areas of masking in gravure.

Diaphragm. Device that adjusts the aperture, or opening size, in the camera lens.

Diazo paper. Light-sensitive material developed by exposing to ammonia fumes; also, a material used in one of the proofing processes.

Die cutting. Finished technique used to cut paper to shape.

Digital photography. Using a digital camera to digitize (or convert) an image into digital data as it is being taken.

Digital toner-based press. A press that accepts digital files with no interim plate making. It is characterized by the ability to reimage an image carrier for each impression.

Direct imaging press. A press with a digital front that includes imaging plates on press and a conventional ink on paper backend.

Direct/indirect process. Method of photographic, screen printing stencil preparation in which stencil emulsion is applied to clean screen from precoated base sheet; when dry, the base is removed and the stencil is exposed and developed directly on fabric; see also *Photographic stencils*.

Direct process. Method of photographic, screen printing stencil preparation in which stencil emulsion is applied wet to screen fabric, dried, and then exposed and developed; see also *Photographic stencils*.

Direct screen color separation. Color separation method that produces a color-separated halftone negative in a single step.

Dominance. Design characteristic that describes the most visually striking portion of a design.

Dot area meter. Transmission or reflection densitometer designed to display actual dot sizes.

Double-dot black duotone. Reproduction of a continuous-tone original made by printing two halftones, both with black ink; its purpose, when compared with a halftone, is to improve quality in tone reproduction.

dpi (dots per inch). A measure of the resolution of a computer monitor, scanner, or printing device. The resolution is determined by how many dots can fit in a linear inch. Also referred to as *pixels per inch* (ppi).

Drafting board. Hard, flat surface with at least one perfectly straight edge that is used to hold the board during paste-up.

Drum scanner. A high-end optical scanning device used to convert an image to digital information.

Drying time. Time it takes for something to dry or for liquid ink to harden.

Dry offset. Printing process that combines relief and offset technology; in dry offset, a right-reading relief plate prints onto an intermediate blanket cylinder and produces a wrong-reading image, and the wrong-reading image is then transferred to paper as a right-reading image.

DSL (Digital Subscriber Lines). A sophisticated modulation scheme that allows for digital voice and data transmission over copper wiring.

Ductor rollers. Any press roller that moves ink or water from the foundation to the distribution rollers.

Dummy. Blank sheet of paper folded in the same manner as the final job and marked with page numbers and heads; when unfolded, can be used to show page and copy positions during pasteup or imposition.

Duotone. Reproduction of a continuous-tone image that consists of two halftones printed in register; adds color and quality to the image.

Duplicating film. A film designed to produce either duplicate film negatives from original negatives or duplicate film positives from original positives.

Duplicator. Any offset lithographic machine that makes copies and can feed a maximum sheet size of 11 inches by 17 inches.

Dynamic imbalance. Defect in the cylinder balance on a press such that the cylinder differs in density or balance from one end to the other.

Dynamic range. The gamut of tones is displayed and expressed as the difference between the area of maximum density (darkest or shadow areas) and the area of minimum density (lightest or highlight areas). Also referred to as the *density range*.

Electric-eye mark. Mark added to the gravure cylinder as an image to be read by special electronic eyes to monitor registration.

Electromechanical engraving. Method of producing a relief plate by cutting an image into a material with a device that is electrically controlled.

Electromechanical process. Technique used in gravure printing to place an image on a gravure cylinder by cutting into the metal surface of the cylinder with a diamond stylus.

Electroplating. Process of transferring very small bits (called ions) of one type of metal to another type of metal.

Electrostatic assist. Device licensed by the Gravure Association of America that pulls ink from the cylinder wells in gravure printing by using an electronic charge.

Electrostatic transfer plate. Transfer plate produced by electrical charges that cause a resin powder to form on the image area; the powder is then fused and forms the ink-receptive area of the plate.

Electrotypes. High-quality duplicate relief plates made by producing a mold from an original form; the final printing plate, which is made from silver and copper or nickel, is then produced in the mold by an electrochemical exchange.

E-management. The management of business through the Internet, including both the procurement and selling of products and services to businesses and the retail market.

Embossing. Finishing operation that produces a relief image by pressing paper between special dies.

Em quad. Basic unit of type composition; physical size varies with the size of type being set (for 12-point type, an em quad measures 12 points × 12 points; for 36-point type, it measures 36 points × 36 points).

Emulsified. Condition in which something has become pastelike from contact with a highly acidic substance.

Emulsion. Coating over a base material that carries the light-sensitive chemicals in photography; the emulsions in mechanical masking film and hand-cut stencil material are not light sensitive.

En quad. Unit of type composition whose physical size varies with the size of type being set; two en quads placed together equal the size of the em quad for that size of type.

End sheets. The two inside sheets that hold the casebound cover to the body of the book.

EPS (encapsulated PostScript). A PostScript file format used for saving vector or raster images that includes a optional preview file.

Equivalent weight. Weight, in points, of one ream of regular size paper; see *Regular sizes.*

Etch resist. See *Staging solution.*

Ethernet. The most common network protocol; it requires computers to take turns sending data.

Evaporation. Conversion that occurs when a liquid combines with oxygen in the air and passes from the solution as a vapor.

Exacto knife. Commercial cutting tool with interchangeable blades.

Excess density. Density difference after the basic density range of the screen is subtracted from the copy density range (CDR).

Fake color. One-color reproduction printed on a colored sheet.

Fake duotone. Halftone printed over a block of colored tint or a solid block of color.

Feathering. Tendency of ink on a rough, porous surface to spread.

Feeding unit. A unit on a printing press that moves paper (or some other substrata) from a pile or roll to the registration unit.

File. A related set of computer data or program instructions that has been given a name.

Fillet. Internal curve that is part of a character in alphabet design.

Filmboard. Part of a process camera that opens to hold the film during exposure; a vacuum base usually holds the film firmly in place.

Film speed. Number assigned to light-sensitive materials that indicates sensitivity to light; large numbers (like 400) indicate high sensitivity; low numbers (like 6 or 12) indicate low sensitivity.

Final layout. See *Mechanical*.

Finish. Texture of paper.

Finishing. Operations performed after the job has left the press; common finishing operations are cutting, folding, binding, and packaging.

Fit. Relationship of images both to the paper and, if multicolors, to each other; often confused with the term *registration*, which refers to position of the press sheet in the press.

Fixing bath. Acid solution that removes all unexposed emulsion in film processing; the third step in processing which follows the developer and stop-bath; also called fixer.

Flare. Exposure problem caused by uncontrolled reflection of stray light passing through the camera's lens.

Flat. Assembled masking sheet with attached pieces of film; the product of the stripping operation.

Flatbed cylinder press. Press designed so that the sheet rolls into contact with the type form as a cylinder moves across the press.

Flexography. A rotary relief printing process in which the image carrier is a flexible rubber or photopolymer plate.

Focal length. Distance from center of lens to filmboard when lens is focused at infinity.

Focusing. Process of adjusting the lens so light reflected from the object or copy is sharp and clear on the film.

Fold lines. Lines drawn on a pasteup in light-blue pencil that represent where the final job is to be folded; small black lines are sometimes drawn at the edge of the sheet to be printed and used as guides for the bindery.

Font. A set of all characters in a typeface, which is made up of all the alphanumerics, punctuation marks, and special characters of the specific typeface.

Form. Grouping of symbols, letters, numbers, and spaces that make up a job or a complete segment of a job (such as one page set to be printed in a book).

Formal balance. Design characteristic in which images of identical weight are placed on each side of an invisible center line.

Form rollers. Any press rollers that contact the plate.

Fountain. Unit that holds a pool of ink or water and controls the amount of ink or water passed to the inking unit on a press.

Four-color process printing. Technique using cyan, magenta, yellow, and black process inks to reproduce images as they would appear in a color photograph.

FPO (for position only). Low-resolution files used for digital positioning.

Franklin Printing Catalog. Privately published pricing guide for printers to use to determine average costs for nearly all operations or products.

French fold. Traditional paper fold made by first creasing and folding a sheet along its length and then making a second fold at a right angle to the first, across the width.

Frisket. Sheet of paper placed between two grippers to hold a press sheet while an impression is made; the form prints through an opening made in the frisket.

f/stop system. Mathematically based way of measuring aperture size in the lens of a camera; f/stop numbers predict the amount of light that passes through any lens; moving from one f/stop number to the next either doubles or halves the amount of light.

Furniture. Any line-spacing material that is thicker or larger than 24 points; used primarily in relief printing.

Furniture-within-furniture technique. Method of arranging furniture around a relief form when the form is of standard furniture dimension.

Gathering. Finishing operation that involves assembling signatures by placing one next to the other.

GIF (CompuServe graphics interchange format). A bitmapped color graphics file format using lossless compression, used on the Internet, but not suitable for high-end printing.

Gigabyte. Approximately 1 billion bytes, or 1,024 megabytes.

Glaze. Buildup on rubber rollers or blanket that prevents proper adhesion and distribution of ink.

Graining. Mechanical or chemical process of roughing a plate's surface; ensures quality emulsion adhesion and aids in holding solution in the nonimage area during the press run.

Grain long. Condition in which the majority of paper fibers run parallel to the long dimension of the sheet.

Grain short. Condition in which the majority of paper fibers run parallel to the short dimension of the sheet.

Graphic images. Images formed from lines.

Gravity delivery. Process in which sheets simply fall into place on the press delivery stack.

Gravure. Industrial intaglio printing in which an image is transferred from a sunken surface.

Gravure well. Sunken portion of a gravure cylinder that holds ink during printing.

Gray-scale image. Continuous-tone picture of shades of gray used by graphic arts photographers to gauge exposure and development during chemical processing; also known as *step tablet* or *step wedge*.

Grippers. Mechanical fingers that pull a sheet through the printing unit of a press.

Gripper margin. Area of paper held by mechanical fingers that pull the sheet through the printing unit of the press.

Guillotine cutter. Device used to trim paper sheets; has a long-handled knife hinged to a large preprinted board which can be used to accurately measure the size of each cut.

Halftone gravure design. See *Lateral hard-dot process.*

Halftone or conversion. Process of breaking continuous-tone images into high-contrast dots of varying shapes and sizes so they can be reproduced on a printing press.

Hard disk. A magnetic storage system used for computer data storage.

Hardening. Stage in ink drying when vehicle has solidified completely on paper surface and will not transfer.

Headstop. Mechanical gate that stops the paper on the registration unit of a press just before the gripper fingers pull the sheet through the printing unit.

Hickey. Defect on the press sheet caused by small particles of ink or paper attached to the plate or blanket.

Highlight area. Lighter parts of a continuous-tone image or its halftone reproduction.

Histogram. A visual frequency distribution that shows the history of what has happened at one point in a process. Data is sorted into numerical categories that are usually presented in the form of a bar graph.

Horizontal process camera. Type of darkroom camera that has a long, stationary bed; film end is usually in the darkroom, and lights and lens protrude through a wall into a normally lighted room.

Hot-type composition. Preparation of any printing form used to transfer multiple images from a raised surface; examples include Linotype, Ludlow type, foundry type, and wooden type.

HTML (Hypertext mark-up language). The most common fixed language for interchange of hypertext between a World Wide Web client and server. It is also used to import pictures, video, and other codes into the Web page being viewed.

Hypo. Fixing bath of sodium thiosulfate.

Illustration board. Smooth, thick paper material used in pasteup to hold all job elements.

Image assembly. Second step in the printing process; involves bringing all pieces of a job into final form as it will appear on the product delivered to the customer.

Image carrier preparation. Fourth step in the printing process; involves photographically recording the image to be reproduced on an image carrier (or plate).

Image conversion. Third step in the printing process; involves creating a transparent film image of a job from the image assembly step.

Image design. First step in the printing process; involves conceptual creation of a job and approval by the customer.

Image guidelines. Lines used in pasteup to position artwork and composition on illustration board; are drawn in light-blue pencil and are not reproduced as a film image.

Imagesetter. A device used to digitally expose film for printing processes.

Image transfer. Fifth step in the printing process; involves transfer of the image onto the final job material (often paper).

Imposing stone. Metal surface on which letterpress forms are arranged and locked into a chase or metal frame.

Imposition. Placement of images in position so they will be in desired locations on the final printed sheet.

Impression. Single sheet of paper passed through a printing press; is measured by one rotation of the plate cylinder.

Impression cylinder. Part of a rotary press that presses the press sheet against the blanket cylinder.

Incident light. Light that illuminates, strikes, or falls on a surface.

India ink. Special type of very black ink used for high-quality layout.

Indirect process. Method of photographic, screen printing, stencil preparation in which stencil is exposed and developed on a support base and then mounted on the screen; see also *Photographic stencils.*

Indirect relief. Process that involves transferring ink immediately from a relief form to a rubber-covered cylinder and then onto the paper; often called dry offset printing.

Indirect screen color separation. Color separation method that first produces a continuous-tone separation negative; requires additional steps to produce color-separated halftone negatives.

Informal balance. Design characteristic in which images are placed on a page so that their visual weights balance on each side of an invisible center line.

Ink-jet printing. A printing process that produces an image by directing individual drops of ink from an opening, through a small air gap, and to a printing surface.

Ink proofs. Press sheets printed on special proof presses using the ink and paper of the final job; are extremely expensive and usually reserved only for high-quality or long-run jobs.

Ink train. Area from ink fountain to ink form rollers.

Ink viscosity. Measure of ink's resistance to flow.

In-plant printing. Any operation that is owned by and serves the needs of a single company or corporation.

Input. A computer term used to describe entering information (data) into computer memory.

Inserting. Finishing operation that involves placing one signature within another.

Instant image proof paper. Proofing material that creates an image when exposed to light; does not require special equipment or chemicals.

Intaglio printing. Transferring an image from a sunken surface.

ISDN (Integrated Services Digital Network). A system of digital phone connections that allows voice and data to be transmitted simultaneously.

ISO 9000 standards registration. Established by the International Organization for Standardization (ISO) establishes international standards to communicate clear process-based operations and facilitate the global exchange of products and services; ISO 9000 registration is one measure of commitment to customer-defined quality.

Job costing. The process of comparing your estimated production times and costs to what the actual production costs and times are.

Job estimate. Document submitted to printing customers that specifies the cost of producing a particular job.

Job schedule. Schedule prepared for each printing job as it passes through each production step; shows how long each step should take and the order of its movement through the shop.

Job scheduling and production control. Section of most printing companies that directs the movement of every printing job through the plant.

JPEG (joint photographics expert group). A file format using lossy compression. Commonly used to display photographic images on the Internet, but not suitable for high-end printing.

Justification. Technique of setting straight composition in which the first and last letters of each line of type fall in vertical columns.

Kilobyte. Approximately 1,024 bytes.

Kizan. A Japanese term that describes the never ending effort for incremental improvement and customer satisfaction.

Knife folder. Paper-folding machine that operates using a thin knife blade to force a sheet of paper between two rotating rollers.

LAN (local-area network). Network of computers located physically near each other that allows shared access to common resources.

Laser cutting. Process used in gravure printing to transfer an image to a gravure cylinder by means of a laser that cuts small wells into a plastic surface on the cylinder; the finished plastic surface is then chrome plated.

Laser printer. A computer-driven output device that uses electrophotography to create images on paper.

Latent image. Invisible change made in film emulsion by exposure to light; development makes latent image visible to the human eye.

Lateral hard-dot process. Type of well design used in gravure printing in which a cylinder is exposed by using two separate film positives: continuous-tone and halftone.

Lateral reverse. Changing a right-reading sheet of film to a wrong-reading one.

Lead. Thin line-spacing material used in hot type composition; is lower than type high and is generally 2 points thick.

Lead edge. Portion of a sheet that enters the printing press first; for sheet-fed automatic presses, the gripper margin is the lead edge.

Lens. Element of a camera through which light passes and is focused on the film.

Letterpress. Process that prints from a raised or relief surface.

Lever cutter. Hand-operated guillotine paper cutter.

Ligature. Two or more connected letters on the same type body.

Light integrator. Means of controlling film exposure by measuring the quantity of light that passes through the lens using a photoelectric cell.

Light table. Special device with a frosted glass surface and a light that projects up through the glass for viewing and working with film negatives and positives.

Line photography. Process of recording high-contrast images on pieces of film; line negatives are either clear in the image areas or solid black in the nonimage areas.

Line art. Any image made only from lines, such as type and clear inked drawings.

Linen tester. Magnifying glass used for visual inspection.

Lithography. Transfer of an image from a flat surface by chemistry.

Live form. Any form waiting to be printed.

Lockup. Process of holding a relief form in a frame or chase.

Logic board. The main circuit board that contains the central processing unit, memory chips, and other hardware used in the operation of the computer. Also known as a *motherboard*.

Logo. Unique design created to cause visual recognition or a product, service, or company.

Logotype. Two or more letters not connected but still cast on the same type body in relief printing.

Lossless compression. A data compression technique that does not result in data loss when compressed and expanded.

Lossy compression. A data compression algorithm that causes loss of data while file size is being reduced.

Lowercase. Letters in the alphabet that are not capitals.

Make-ready. All preparation from mounting the image carrier (plate, cylinder, typeform, stencil) on the press to obtain an acceptable image on the press sheet.

Mask. Any material that blocks the passage of light; is used in pasteup, stripping, and platemaking; is generally cut by hand and positioned over an image; photomechanical masks used in color separation are produced in the darkroom.

Masking. Continuous-tone photographic image that is used mainly to correct color and compress tonal range of a color original in process color photography.

Masking sheets. Special pieces of paper or plastic that block the passage of actinic light; are used most commonly in the stripping operation.

Master flat. In multiflat registration, the flat with the most detail.

Master plate. In gravure printing, a frame with register pins that hold the film positives in correct printing position during exposure to the cylinder masking material.

Mechanical. Board holding all elements of composition and artwork that meet job specifications and are of sufficient quality to be reproduced photographically; also called a *pasteup*, final layout, or camera-ready copy.

Medium. Channel of communication; mass media are radio, television, newspapers, and magazines.

Megabyte. Approximately 1 million bytes or 1,024 kilobytes.

Microcomputer. A small, general purpose computer with the ability to accept a wide variety of software and additional components to increase power; much smaller and less powerful than a mainframe and not dedicated like a minicomputer; also called a *personal computer* or a *PC*.

Middle tone area. Intermediate tones between highlights and shadows.

Moiré pattern. Undesirable image produced when two different or randomly positioned screen patterns (or dots) overprint.

Molleton covers. Thin cloth tubes that slip over water form rollers.

Monofilament screens. Fabrics made from threads composed of a single fiber strand, such as nylon.

Multifilament screens. Fabrics made from threads composed of many different fibers, such as silk.

M weight. Weight of 1,000 sheets of paper rather than of a ream (500 sheets).

Mylar sheet. Clear or frosted stable-base plastic material commonly used for overlays in paste-up.

Negative-acting plate. Plate formulated to produce a positive image from a flat containing negatives.

Network. A system of interconnected computers that communicate with one and another and share common resources such as applications, data, and hardware components.

Newage gauge. Gauge used to test hardness of copper.

News case. Container formerly used to store foundry type; upper case held capital letters and lower case held small characters.

Nib width. Area of contact between impression rollers and plate (or image) cylinder on any rotary press.

Nonstandard cut. In paper cutting, manipulation of positions and order of cuts to gain an additional sheet; always produces press sheets with different grain direction.

Occasional. One of the six type styles; includes all typefaces that do not fit one of the other five styles; also known as novelty, decorative, and other typeface.

Optical character recognition (OCR) system. Optical scanning device that converts, stores, and/or outputs composition from special typewritten information.

Off-contact printing. Screen printing in which screen and stencil are slightly raised from printing material; stencil touches stock only while squeegee passes over screen.

Offset press. Press design in which an image is transferred from a plate to a rubber blanket that moves the image to the press sheet; offset principle allows plates to be right reading and generally gives a better-quality image than do direct transfers.

Offset lithographic press. Any machine that can feed sheets larger than 11 inches × 17 inches.

Offset paper. Paper intended for use on an offset lithographic press; surface is generally smooth and somewhat resistant to moisture.

On-contact printing. Screen printing in which screen and stencil contact material throughout ink transfer.

Opaque. Liquid used to paint out pinholes on film negatives; also used as adjective meaning "not transparent or translucent under normal viewing."

Opaque color proofs. Proofs used to check multicolor jobs by adhering, exposing, and developing each successive color emulsion on a special solid-base sheet.

Open shop. Shop that does not require craftspeople to join a union to maintain employment.

OPI (open prepress interface). A system invented by Aldus in which low-resolution images replace the original high-resolution images during page assembly. The high-resolution images are brought back into the layout prior to output.

Optical center. Point on a sheet that the human eye looks to first and perceives as the center; is slightly above true, or mathematical, center.

Orthochromatic material. Photographic material that is sensitive to all wavelengths of the visible spectrum except red.

Oscillating distribution rollers. Press rollers in ink and water systems that cause distribution by both rotation and movement back and forth.

Overcoating. Protective coating placed on most transparent-based film to protect film emulsion from grease and dirt.

Overhead. Cost of operating a business without considering cost of materials or labor; typically includes cost of maintaining work space and equipment depreciation.

Overlay sheet. Sheet often used in pasteup to carry images for a second color; clear or frosted plastic overlay sheet is hinged over the first color and carries artwork and composition for the second.

Oxidation. Process of combining with oxygen; in aerial oxidation, a solution or ink combines with oxygen in the air to evaporate.

Packets. A small block of data that is transmitted over a network. Along with a destination header, it contains the actual data (known as a *frame*) to be sent.

Panchromatic material. Photographic material that is sensitive to all visible wavelengths of light and some invisible wavelengths.

Pantone Matching System®. Widely accepted method for specifying and mixing colors from a numbering system listed in a swatch book.

Paper lines. Lines drawn on pasteup board to show final size of printed piece after it is trimmed; are measured from center lines and are usually drawn in light-blue pencil.

Pareto chart. Another form of frequency distribution that displays categories from the most to least frequent.

Patent binding. See *Perfect binding*.

PDF (portable document format). The open de facto standard for electronic document distribution. Adobe PDF is a universal file format that preserves all the fonts, formatting, colors, and graphics of any source document, regardless of the application and platform used to create it.

Penetration. Drying of ink by absorption into a substrate (usually paper),

Perfect binding. Common adhesive binding technique to glue signatures into a book, usually a paperback; also known as *patent binding*.

Perfecting press. Press that prints on both sides of the stock (paper) as it passes through the press.

Perforating. Finishing operation in which slits are cut into stock so a portion can be torn away.

Photoelectric densitometer. Instrument that produces density readings by means of a cell or vacuum tube whose electrical properties are modified by the action of light.

Photoengraving. Relief form made by photochemical process; after being exposed through laterally reversed negative, nonimage portion of plate is acid etched, allowing image area to stand out in relief.

Photographic stencils. Screen printing stencils produced using a thick, light-sensitive, gelatin-based emulsion that is exposed and developed either on a supporting film or directly on the screen itself; the three types of stencils include direct, indirect, and direct/indirect stencils.

Photomechanical proofs. Proofs that use light-sensitive emulsions to check image position and quality of stripped flats; are usually exposed through the flat on a standard platemaking device.

Photopolymer plates. Plates formed by bonding a light-reactive polymer plastic to a film or metal base; polymer emulsion hardens upon ultraviolet exposure and unexposed areas are washed away to leave image area in relief.

Photostat. Photographic copy of a portion of a pasteup; images are sometimes enlarged or reduced and then positioned on the board as a photostat; also called a *stat*.

Phototypesetting. Cold-type composition process that creates images by projecting light through a negative and a lens and from mirrors onto light-sensitive material.

pH scale. Measure of a liquid's acidity; numeric scale is from 0 (very acid) to 14 (very alkaline, or a base); midpoint, 7, is considered neutral.

Pica. Unit of measurement used by printers to measure linear dimensions; 6 picas equal approximately 1 inch; 1 pica is divided into 12 points.

Picking. Offset press problem identified by small particles of paper torn from each press sheet and fed back into the inking system.

Pigment. Dry particles that give color to printing ink.

Pilefeeding. Method of stacking paper in feeder end of press and then operating press so that individual sheets are moved from top of pile to registration unit.

Pinholes. Small openings in film emulsion that pass light; are caused by dust in the air during camera exposure, a dirty copyboard, or, sometimes, acidic action in the fixing bath; must be painted out with opaque in the stripping operation.

Pixel. A dot or picture element in a computer scanned image; also one element in computer image resolution.

Plate cylinder. Part of a rotary press that holds the printing form or plate.

Platemaker. Any machine with an intensive light source and some system to hold the flat against the printing plate; light source is used to expose the film image on the plate; most platemakers use a vacuum board with a glass cover to hold the flat and plate.

Platen press. Traditional design used almost exclusively for relief printing; type form is locked into place and moves into contact with a hard, flat surface (called a platen) that holds the paper.

Plates. Thin, flexible aluminum sheets for lithographic printing; can be purchased uncoated and then sensitized at the printing plant or obtained presensitized and ready for exposure and processing; specific characteristics vary depending on end use.

Platesetter. A device used to digitally expose plates for the printing process.

Plating bath. Solution used for electroplating.

Point. Unit of measurement used by printers to measure type size and leading (space between lines); 12 points equal 1 pica; 72 points equal 1 inch.

Polymerization. Chemical process for drying epoxy inks.

Positive-acting plate. Plate formulated to produce a positive image from a flat containing positives.

Posterization. High-contrast reproduction of a continuous-tone image; usually consists of two, three, or four tones and is reproduced in one, two, or three colors.

PostScript. A page-description language developed by Adobe Systems. It has become a de facto standard for high-end imaging.

Preflight. A procedure for checking digital files before they go to press (or any media) in order to catch errors that may result in slowed down or incorrect workflow.

Prepress. Prepress is a term that describes the technological changes that have transformed traditional copy preparation steps prior to reaching the printing press. In general, it refers to computer applications of full-page composition, color separation, and color proofing.

Prepunched tab strip method. Strips of film punched with holes and used to hold flat in place over pins attached to light table.

Pressboard. Hard, heavy sheet used as packing material when dressing a platen press.

Prewipe blade. Blade sometimes used in gravure printing to skim excess ink from cylinder.

Primary plates. Relief plates intended for use as printing surfaces; capable of producing duplicate plates.

Printing. The process of manufacturing multiple copies of graphic images.

Printing processes. Relief, intaglio, screen, and lithographic printing.

Process camera. Large device used by graphic arts photographers to record film images; can enlarge or reduce images from the copy's original size and can be used to expose all types of film.

Process color. Use of ink with a translucent base that allows for creation of many colors by overprinting only four (cyan, magenta, yellow, and black).

Process color photography. Photographic reproduction of color originals by manipulation of light, filters, film, and chemistry.

Proof. A copy of what is intended to be printed that is used for checking for errors such as typos or layout problems and for verifying color. It can be created from film or digitally.

Profile. The specific characteristics of a particular output device against a standard target.

Proportion. Design characteristic concerned with size relationship of both sheet size and image placement.

Proportionally spaced composition. Composition made up of characters that occupy horizontal space in proportion to their size.

Proportion scale. Device used to determine percentage of enlargement or reduction for piece of copy.

Protocol. A set of rules and procedures that determines how a computer system receives and transmits data.

Publishing. Category of printing services that prepare and distribute materials such as books, magazines, and newspapers.

Punch and register pin method. Method of multiflat registration in which holes are punched in the tail of the flat or in strips of scrap film taped to the flat; the punched holes fit over metal pins taped to light table surface and cause the flat to fall in correct position.

Quadding out. Filling a line of type with spacing material after all characters have been set in a composing stick.

Quality printing. Has different meaning for every printing job; judgment of quality depends upon context, time, and the measure of successful use.

Quick. Early term for a skilled compositor (especially foundry type composition).

Quick printing. Printing operation characterized by rapid service, small organizational size, and limited format of printed product.

RAID (redundant array of inexpensive disks). A group of hard drives that appears as a single logical storage unit or drive.

Random-access memory (RAM). Temporary, or volatile, memory that stores data and programs while they are being used.

Rapid access. A process of preparing a film image using an emulsion and developer that allows for wide latitude in skill to produce an acceptable film image.

Raster image. An image defined by a grid of pixels, also referred to as a *bitmap image*. Most common format for photographic images.

Raster image processor (RIP). Converts Post-Script and raster data to machine bitmaps that an output device such as an imagesetter or platesetter can process.

Rational tangent screening (RT screening). The angle of screen rotation in terms of discrete numbers on a reference grid of horizontal and vertical image spots.

Read-only memory (ROM). A permanent, or nonvolatile, memory chip used to store instructions and data, including the computer's start-up instructions.

Ream. Five hundred sheets of paper.

Reflectance. Measure of ability of a surface or material to reflect light.

Reflection densitometer. Meter that measures light reflected from a surface.

Register marks. Targets applied to the pasteup board and used in stripping, platemaking, and on the press to ensure that multicolor images fit together in perfect register.

Registration unit. Unit on a printing press that ensures that sheets are held in the same position each time an impression is made.

Reglets. Thin pieces of wood used to fill small spaces and protect larger furniture from quoin damage during lockup.

Regular sizes. Sizes other than basic sheet size in which paper is commonly cut and stocked by paper suppliers.

Related industries. Category of printing services that includes raw material manufacturers (ink, paper, plates, chemicals), manufacturers of equipment, and suppliers that distribute goods or services to printers.

Relief printing. Transferring an image from a raised surface.

Removable storage. Any media used for information storage that can be removed from the computer and transported physically.

Reproduction proof. Proof taken from hot type composition; can be reproduced photographically.

Resist. Material that blocks or retards the action of some chemical.

Resolution. The amount of pixels used (on screen) to describe an image, or the amount of dots per inch used to describe an image on an output device. Higher-resolution images contain more information and produce finer detail.

Resolution dependent. A file based on raster or bitmap information that is composed of a specific amount of pixels that can be output at one optimum resolution.

Resolution independent. A file based on vector information that can be output at the highest resolution that the output device is capable of.

Right-angle fold. Any fold that is at a 90-degree angle from one or more other folds.

Right reading. Visual organization of copy (or film) from left to right so that it can be read normally; see *Wrong reading*.

Rollup. Technique used to cover an area on a gravure cylinder for re-etching.

Roman. One of the six type styles; is characterized by variation in stroke and by use of serifs.

Rotary press. Press formed from two cylinders, one holding the type form and the other acting as an impression cylinder to push the stock against the form; as the cylinders rotate, a sheet is inserted so an image is placed on the piece.

Rotating distribution rollers. Press rollers in ink and water systems that cause distribution by rolling against each other; see *Oscillating distribution rollers*.

Rotogravure. Printing by the gravure process from a round cylinder.

Rough layout. Detailed expansion of thumbnail sketch that carries all printing information necessary for any printer to produce final reproduction.

Saddle binding. Technique or fastening one or more signatures along the folded or backbone edge of a unit.

Safelight. Fixture used in the darkroom that allows the photographer to see, but not expose, film; color and intensity of safelight vary with type of film used.

Sans serif. One of the six type styles; is characterized by vertical letter stress, uniform strokes, and absence of serifs.

Scanner. An input device used to transform an image into digital data (flatbed or drum scanner or digital camera).

Scoring. Finishing operation that creases paper so it can be folded easily.

Screen angle. The angles used to align color halftone screens.

Screen mesh count. Measure of the number of openings per unit measure.

Screen printing. Transferring an image by allowing ink to pass through an opening or stencil.

Screen ruling. Number of dots per inch produced by a halftone screen or a screen tint.

Screen tint. Solid line screen capable of producing evenly spaced dots and of representing tone values of 3 to 97 percent in various fine rulings.

Script. One of the six type styles; is characterized by a design that attempts to duplicate feeling of free-form handwriting.

Scumming. Offset press condition in which non-image areas of the plate accept ink.

Self-cover. Cover produced from the same material as the body of the book.

Sensitivity guide. Transparent gray scale often stripped into a flat to be used as a means of gauging plate exposure; also used in one method of direct color separation.

Sensitometer. An instrument that exposes a step tablet or grey scale onto light-sensitive materials.

Series. Variations within a family of type; common series are bold, extra bold, condensed, thin, expanded, and italic.

Serifs. One of three variables in alphabet design; refers to small strokes that project from top or bottom of main character strokes.

Set. Ability of ink to stick to paper; properly set ink can be handled without smearing.

Set-off. Transfer of excess ink from one sheet to another when press is overinked.

Set width. Distance across nick or belly side of foundry type.

Shadow area. Darker parts of a continuous-tone image or its halftone reproduction.

Shaft. Center support of a press cylinder.

Sheet-fed press. Press that prints on individual pieces of paper rather than on paper from a roll.

Sheet off. Process of removing excess ink from ink rollers by carefully hand rolling a sheet of paper through the ink system and then removing it.

Sheet separators. Elements used in the press feeder unit to ensure that only one sheet is fed into the registration unit at a time.

Sheetwise imposition. Arrangement in which a single printing plate is used to print on one side of a sheet to produce one printed product with each pass through the press.

Shore durometer. Device to measure rubber hardness in units called "durometers"; the lower the rating, the softer the rubber.

Short-stop. See *Stop-bath.*

Shutter. Mechanism that controls the passage of light through the camera lens by opening and closing the aperture.

Shutter speed. Length of time the camera lens allows light to pass to the film; is adjusted by use of a shutter.

Side binding. Technique of fastening pages or signatures by passing the fastening device through the pile at a right angle to the page surface.

Signature imposition. Process of passing a single sheet through the press and then folding and trimming it to form a portion of a book or magazine.

Slug. Thick line-spacing material used in hot-type composition; is lower than type high and is generally 6 points thick.

Slur. Condition in which an image is inconsistent in density and appears to be unsharp or bluffed; is usually caused by platen press roller condition or adjustment.

Soft cover. Book cover made from paper or paper fiber material with greater substance than that used for the body of the book but with much less substance than binder's board.

Soft proof. A proof that is displayed on a computer monitor.

Software. Collection of electronic instructions that direct the CPU to carry out specific tasks.

Special-purpose binding. Printing operation that accepts orders for only one type of product, such as forms work, legal printing, or labels.

Spectral highlight. White portion of a photograph with no detail, such as bright, shiny reflection from a metal object.

Spoilage allowance. Extra sheets delivered to the press to allow for inevitable waste and to ensure that required number of products are delivered to the customer.

Spot color. Ink the printer purchases or mixes to order for a specific job.

Spot plater. Machine used to build up the metal in small areas on a gravure cylinder.

Square serif. One of the six type styles; is characterized by uniform strokes and serif shapes without fillets or rounds.

Squeegee. Device used to force ink through the stencil opening in screen printing; also used in platemaking.

Stable-base sheet. Sheet that does not change size with changes in temperature.

Staging. Process of covering bare metal in gravure printing.

Staging solution. Solution used as a resist in the etching process; prevents dots or tones from being etched.

Stat. See *Photostat.*

Static eliminator. Piece of copper tinsel mounted in delivery unit to remove static electric charge that makes it difficult to stack individual sheets of paper.

Static imbalance. Defect in cylinder balance on a press that occurs when a cylinder is not perfectly round or has different densities within a cross section.

Stencil. Type of mask that passes ink in the image areas and blocks ink passage in nonimage areas.

Step tablet. See *Gray scale.*

Step wedge. See *Gray scale.*

Stereotyping. Process of producing a duplicate relief plate by casting molten metal into a mold (or mat) made from an original lockup.

Stochastic screening. Also known as *frequency modulated* or *FM screening;* this screening varies the frequency of the spacing and keeps the dot size fixed.

Stone proof. Proof taken from a form in hot type composition without using a machine.

Stop-bath. Slightly acidic solution used to halt development in film processing; is sometimes called the *short-stop.*

Stream feeder. Press element that overlaps sheets on the registration table; allows registration unit to operate at a slower rate than the printing unit and gives better image fit.

Stress. One of three variables in alphabet design; refers to distribution of visual heaviness or slant of the character.

Stripping. Process of assembling pieces of film containing images that will be carried on the same printing plate and securing them on a masking sheet that will hold them in their appropriate printing positions during the platemaking process.

Stroke. One of three variables in alphabet design; refers to thickness of lines that actually form each character.

Subjective balance. Design characteristic in which images are placed on white space in such a way as to create a feeling of stability.

Substance weight. Weight in pounds of one ream of the basic sheet size (17 inches × 22 inches) of one particular type of writing paper.

Substrate. Any base material used in printing processes to receive an image transferred from a printing plate; common substrates are paper, foil, fabric, and plastic sheet.

Subtractive plate. Presensitized lithographic plate with ink-receptive coating applied by the manufacturer; nonimage area is removed during processing.

Subtractive primary colors. Colors formed when any two additional primary colors of light are mixed; subtractive colors are yellow, magenta, and cyan; yellow is the additive mixture of red and green light; magenta is the additive mixture of red and blue light; cyan is the additive mixture of blue and green light.

Successive sheet-feeding system. Most common form of press-feeding system; feeding unit picks up one sheet each time the printing unit prints one impression.

Sucker feet. Elements used in the press feeding unit to pick up individual sheets and place them in the registration unit.

T-1 line. A high-speed communication line supporting digital transmission with a bandwidth of 1.544 Mbps.

Tack. Characteristic of ink that allows it to stick to the substrate (usually paper).

TCP/IP (Transmission Control Protocol/Internet Protocol). A set of commands and timing specifications that allows computers to communicate with each other. It is the standard communication protocol of the Internet.

Telecommunication. A method of sending data from one computer to another over telephone lines or by satellite.

Terabyte. Approximately 1 trillion bytes, or 1,024 gigabytes.

Text. One of the six type styles; is characterized by a design that attempts to recreate the feeling of medieval scribes.

Thermoplastic. Condition in which a material is capable of being heated and reformed after hardening and curing.

Thermosetting. Condition in which a material is not capable of being reformed after hardening and curing.

Three-cylinder principle. Most common configuration for most offset lithographic presses; the three cylinders are plate, blanket, and impression.

Thumbnail sketch. Small, quick pencil renderings that show size relationships of type, line drawings, and white space; the first step in the design process.

TIFF (tagged image file format). Standard file format commonly used to save raster images.

Tinting. Offset press problem identified by slight discoloration over entire nonimage area, almost like a sprayed mist.

Tones. Values of white, black, or color.

Tooth. Roughening of the threads of monofilament screen fabrics to increase the stencil's ability to hold on to the fabric; is applied prior to mounting a stencil.

Topology. The physical configuration of a network.

Total quality management (TQM). Process of making each manufacturing or service step responsive to the customer's needs or expectations.

Trade shops. Printing operation that provides services only to other printers.

Transfer lithographic plate. Plate formed from a light-sensitive coating on an intermediate carrier; after exposure, an image is transferred from the intermediate carrier to the printing plate.

Transmission densitometer. Meter that measures light passing through a material.

Transmittance. Measure of the ability of a material to pass light.

Transparent-based image. Any image carried on a base that passes light; transparent-based sheets can be seen through.

Transparent color proofs. Proofs used to check multicolor jobs; each color is carried on a transparent plastic sheet, and all sheets are positioned over each other to give the illusion of the final multicolor job.

Trapping. Method of compensating for misregister when printing successive images and colors on press.

Triangle. Instrument used to draw right-angle lines with a T-square; is also available in a variety of angles, such as 30, 45, and 60 degrees.

T-square. Instrument used to draw parallel lines.

Tusche. Lithographic drawing or painting material of the same nature as lithographic ink.

Tusche-and-glue. Artist's method of preparing a screen printing stencil by drawing directly on the screen fabric with lithographic tusche and then blocking out nonimage areas with a water-based glue material.

Two-cylinder principle. Offset lithographic duplicator configuration that combines the plate and impression functions to form a main cylinder with twice the circumference of a separate blanket cylinder.

Typeface. Alphabet design used in a printing job.

Type family. Unique combination of stroke, stress, and serif created and named by a typographer; is generally made up of many different series.

Type specifications. Directions written on rough layout that informs compositor about alphabet style, series, size, and amount of leading or space between lines.

Type style. Grouping of alphabet designs; the six main type styles are roman, sans serif, square serif, text, script, and occasional.

Typographer. Craftsperson who designs typefaces.

Uncoated paper. Paper is made up merely of raw interlocking paper fibers; see *Coated paper*.

Underlay. Piece of tissue or paper pasted under the form in areas light in impression.

Unity. Design characteristic concerned with how all elements of a job fit together as a whole.

Uppercase. Capital letters in the alphabet.

Variable data printing. Printing that enables different data to be printed on successive pages. A unique characteristic of digital printing.

Vector image. An image in which the elements are represented by mathematical equations. Typically used for illustrations.

Vehicle. Fluid that carries ink pigment and causes printing ink to adhere to paper or some other substrate.

Vertical process camera. Type of darkroom camera that is contained entirely in the darkroom; is a self-contained unit that takes up little space because the filmboard, lens, and copyboard are parallel to each other in a vertical line.

Vignetted screen pattern. Pattern made up of gradually tapering density and found in halftone screens; produces the variety of dots found in a typical halftone reproduction.

Viscosity. See *Ink viscosity*.

Visual densitometer. Instrument that helps the operator to measure density by visual comparison.

Waterless printing. A printing process that utilizes a special silicone-rubber-coated printing plate and special inks instead of the traditional water or dampening system (formerly called *dryography*).

WAN (wide-area network). A computer network in which two or more LANs are connected across a wide geographical area.

Web-fed press. Press that prints on a roll of paper.

Wedge spectrogram. Visual representation of a film's reaction to light across the visible spectrum.

Wet-on-wet printing. Printing of one color directly over another without waiting for the ink to dry.

Window. Clear, open area on a piece of film created on the pasteup by mounting a sheet of black or red material in the desired window location.

Work-and-tumble imposition. Printing on both sides of a sheet, with the tail becoming the lead edge for the second color by turning the pile for the second pass through the press.

Work-and-turn imposition. Printing on both sides of a sheet, with the same lead edge for both passes through the press.

Workflow. The process and path that a job takes through the production process from start to finish.

Work order. Production control device that carries all information about a particular printing job as it passes through each step of manufacturing.

Workstation. A fast, powerful microcomputer used for scientific, graphic, and other complex applications.

Writing paper. High-quality paper originally associated with correspondence and record keeping; is considered the finest classification of paper, except for some specialty items.

Wrong reading. Backward visual organization of copy (or film) from right to left; see *Right reading*.

WYSIWYG (pronounced "Wizzy-wig"). "What you see is what you get."

x-height. Distance from the base line to the top of a lowercase letter *x* in a given font; varies depending on the particular design; also known as *body height*.

XML (Extensible mark-up language). A universal format for structured documents and data on the World Wide Web that is more comprehensive and robust than HTML, allowing for customizable features.

XY technology. A scanning technology that allows high-resolution scans anywhere on the scanning bed with maximum uniform quality and sharpness.

Zeroing. Setting or calibrating a densitometer to a known value.

Bibliography

Abe, T.; Dove, D. B.; and Heinzl, J. *Printing Technologies for Images, Gray Scale, & Color.* Bellingham, WA: SPIE, International Society for Optical Engineering, 1991.

Adams, J. Michael. *Graphic Arts Processes.* Teaneck, NJ: National Association of Printers & Lithographers, 1994.

Adams, J. Michael.; Faux, David D.; and Rieber, Lloyd J. *Printing Technology 4/E.* Albany, NY: Delmar Publishers, 1994.

Adams, Richard M.; and Romano, Frank. *Computer-to-Plate: Automating the Printing Industry.* Sweickley, PA: Graphic Arts Technical Foundation, 1996.

Aldrich-Ruenzel, Nancy (Ed.). *Designer's Guide to Print Production: A Step-by-Step Publishing Book.* New York, NY: Watson-Guptill Publications, Inc., 1990.

Aldrich-Ruenzel, Nancy (Ed.). *Designer's Guide to Typography: A Step-by-Step Publishing Book.* New York, NY: Watson-Guptill Publications, Inc., 1991.

American Printer. November 1999–July 2000. Overland Parks, KS: Intertec Publishing Corporation.

Ames, Steven E. *Elements of Newspaper Design.* Westport, CT: Greenwood Publishing Group, Inc., 1989.

Apicella, Vincent; Pomeranz, Joanna; and Wiatt, Nancy. *The Concise Guide to Type Identification.* Blue Ridge Summit, PA: TAB Books, 1990.

Baker, Kim, *Professional Publishing with Quark-Xpress for the Macintosh: High-Level Design & Power.* New York, NY: Random House, Inc., 1993.

Banister, Manly. *Practical Lithographic Printmaking.* New York, NY: Dover Publications, Inc., 1987.

Banks, W. H. (Ed.). *Advances in Printing Science & Technology.* Elkins Park, PA: Franklin Book Co., Inc.

Banzhaf, Robert A. *Screen Process Printing.* Westerville, OH: Glencoe, 1983.

Barnard, Michael. *Introduction to Print Buying.* New York, NY: Van Nostrand Reinhold, 1991.

Baudin, Fernand. *How Typography Works: And Why It Is Important.* Blue Ridge Summit, PA: TAB Books, 1989.

Beach, Mark and Cowden, Steve (Illustrator). *Graphically Speaking: An Illustrated Guide to the Working Language of Design & Printing.* Manzanita, OR: Coast to Coast Books, 1992.

Beach, Mark; Shepro, Steve; and Russon, Ken. *Getting It Printed: How to Work with Printers & Graphic Arts Services to Assure Quality, Stay on Schedule & Control Cost.* Manzanita, OR: Coast to Coast Books, 1986.

Beechick, Al. *Resource Manual for Typesetting with Your Computer.* Pollock Pines, CA: Arrow Press, 1986.

Benton, Randi and Balcer, Mary S. *The Official Print Shop Handbook: Ideas, Tips & Designs for Home, School & Professional Use.* Foreword by Doug Carlston. New York, NY: Bantam Books, Inc., 1987.

Bergsland, David. *Printing in a Digital World.* Albany, NY: Delmar Publishers, 1997.

Bivins, Thomas H. and Ryan, William E. *How to Produce Creative Publications: Traditional Techniques & Computer Applications.* Lincolnwood, IL: NTC Pub Group, 1992.

Blatner, David; Fleishman, Glenn; and Roth, Steve. *Real World Scanning and Halftones: The Definitive Guide to Scanning and Halftones from the*

Desktop, 2/E. Berkley, CA: Peachpit Press, 1998.

The Blueprint Dictionary of Printing & Publishing. New York, NY: Van Nostrand Reinhold, 1991.

Blum, Mike. *Understanding & Evaluating Desktop Publishing Systems: A How To Guide from Graphic Services Publications.* Arroyo Grande, CA: Graphic Services Publications, 1992.

Bold, Mary (Ed.). *Publishing in the Classroom: Sourcebook for the Teacher as Publishing Consultant.* Arlington, TX: Bold Productions, 1992.

Book, Albert C. *Fundamentals of Copy & Layout: A Manual.* Lincolnwood, IL: NTC Pub Group, 1990.

Borowsky, Irvin J. *Opportunities in Printing Careers.* Lincolnwood, IL: NTC Pub Group, 1991.

Brady, Philip. *Using Type Right.* Cincinnati, OH: North Light Books, 1988.

Bridgewater, Peter and Woods, Gerald. *Halftone Effects: A Complete Visual Guide to Enhancing & Transforming Halftone Images.* San Francisco, CA: Chronicle Books, 1993.

Brier, David (Ed.). *Typographic Design.* New York, NY: Madison Square Press, 1992.

Bringhurst, Robert. *Elements of Typographic Style.* Point Roberts, WA: Hartley & Marks, Inc., 1992.

Bristow, Nicholas. *Screenprinting: Design & Technique.* North Pomfret, VT: Trafalgar Square, 1991.

Busche, Don and Keefe, Nick. *Desktop Publishing Using PageMaker on the IBM-PC.* Englewood Cliffs, NJ: Prentice Hall, 1991.

Byers, Steve. *Linotype Type Library.* New York, NY: Bantam Books, Inc., 1993.

Carter, Rob; Meggs, Phil; and Day, Benjamin R., II. *Typographic Design: Form & Communication.* New York, NY: Van Nostrand Reinhold, 1985.

Chapman, Gillean. *Making Books: A Step-by-Step Guide to Your Own Publishing.* Boston, MA: Houghton Mifflin, 1992.

Clarke, Joe. *Control Without Confusion: Trouble Shooting Screen Printed Process Color.* Cincinnati, OH: Signs of the Times Publishing Co., 1987.

Clifton, Merritt. *The Samisdat Method: A Do-It-Yourself Guide to Offset Printing.* Shushan, NY: Samisdat, 1990.

Cogoli. *Photo Offset Fundamentals.* New York, NY: Macmillan Publishing Co., 1986.

Collier, David. *Collier's Rules for Desktop Design & Typography.* Redding, MA: Addison-Wesley Publishing Co., 1991.

Collier, David and Cotton, Bob. *Basic Desktop Design & Layout.* Cincinnati, OH: North Light Books, 1989.

Collin, P. H. *Dictionary of Printing & Publishing.* Kinderhook, NY: i.b.d., Ltd., 1989.

The Color Guide and Glossary: Communication, Measurement, and Control for Digital Imaging and Graphic Arts [Handbook]. Grandville, MI: X-Rite, Inc., 1996.

Cost Study on Web Presses. Teaneck, NJ: National Association of Printers and Lithographers, 1990.

Craig, James. *Production for the Graphic Designer.* New York, NY: Watson-Guptill, Inc., 1990.

Crouse, David B. and Schneider, Robert J., Jr. *Web Offset Press Operating.* Pittsburgh, PA: Graphic Arts Technical Foundation, 1989.

Current, Ira. *Photographic Color Printing: Theory & Technique.* Stoneham, MA: Focal Pr, 1987.

Curtin, Dennis P. *Desktop Publishing with WordPerfect 5.1–5.25 Bk-Disk Package.* Englewood Cliffs, NJ: Prentice Hall, 1991.

Day, David. *Trouble with Fonts: The Font Answer Book.* Carmel, IN: Alpha Books, 1993.

Deaton, Donald B. (Ed). *Glossary of Printing Terms.* Research Triangle Park, NC: AATCC, 1991.

Dennis, Ervin A. *Lithographic Technology.* New York, NY: Macmillan Publishing Co., 1980.

Dennis, Ervin A. *Lithographic Technology.* New York, NY: Macmillan Publishing Co., 1986.

Desktop Publishing: Design Basics. New York, NY: Van Nostrand Reinhold, 1991.

Destree, Thomas M. (Ed.). *Lithographers Manual.* Pittsburgh, PA: Graphic Arts Technical Foundation, 1994.

Duff, Jon M. *Introduction to Desktop Publishing.* Englewood Cliffs, NJ: Prentice Hall, 1989.

Durbin, Harold. *Interactive Page Layout Comparison Charts, 1992.* Easton, PA: Durbin Assocs., 1992.

Eakins, Jan. *Desktop Publishing! Using Page-Maker 3.0-IBM Ps-2 Version with DeskDisc.* New York, NY: McGraw-Hill, Inc., 1990.

Easy Way to Tone B&W Prints. Kingston, NY: Embee Pr., 1988.

Eckhardt, Robert. *Publish Tips & Techniques.* New York, NY: Bantam Books, 1991.

Eckstein, Helene W. *Color in the 21st Century: A Practical Guide for Graphic Designers, Photographers, Printers, Separators, & Anyone Involved in Color Printing.* New York, NY: Watson-Guptill Publications, Inc., 1991.

Eldred, Nelson R.; Scarlett, Terry; and Stevenson, Deborah L. (Ed.); O'Toole, Mary A. (Illustrator) *What the Printer Should Know about Ink.* Introduction by Thomas M. Destree. Pittsburgh, PA: Graphic Arts Technical Foundation, 1990.

Electronic Publishing, September 1999–July 2000. South Sheridan, OK: PenWell Corporation.

Field, Gary G. and Destree, Thomas M. (Ed.); O'Toole, Mary A. (Illustrator). *Tone & Color Correction.* Pittsburgh, PA: Graphic Arts Technical Foundation, 1991.

Field, Gary G. *Color and Its Reproduction.* Pittsburgh, PA: Graphic Arts Technical Foundation, 1988.

Field, Gary G. and Mertz, Ann (Ed.). *Color Scanning & Imaging Systems.* Pittsburgh, PA: Graphic Arts Technical Foundation, 1990.

Flick, Ernest W. *Printing Ink Formulations.* Park Ridge, NJ: Noyes, 1985.

From Design to Distribution in the Digital Age: A Guide to Print Media Production [Handbook]. Randolph, MA: Agfa Educational Publishing, Agfa Inc., 1999.

GATF World: Magazine of the Graphic Arts Technical Foundation. November/December 1999, January/February 2000, March/April 2000. Sweickley, PA: Graphic Arts Technical Foundation.

Gaynor, J. (Ed.). *Hard Copy & Printing Materials, Media, & Processes.* Bellingham, WA: SPIE, International Society for Optical Engineering, 1990.

Geis, A. John and Stevenson, Deborah L. (Ed.); O'Toole, Mary A. (Illustrator). *Printing Plant Layout & Facility Design Handbook.* Pittsburgh, PA: Graphic Arts Technical Foundation, 1991.

Geist, A. John; Addy, Paul L.; and Destree, Thomas M. (Ed.). *Materials Handling for the Printer.* Pittsburgh, PA: Graphic Arts Technical Foundation, 1993.

Glossary of Reprography & Non-Impact Printing Terms for the Paper & Printing Industries: Technical Association of Pulp and Paper Industries. 1990.

Glover, Gary. *Clip Art Scanning & Enhancement.* Blue Ridge Summit, PA: TAB Books, 1993.

Goldberg, Ron. *Digital Typography: Practical Advice for Getting the Type You Want When You Want It.* San Diego, CA: Windsor Professional Information, 2000.

Green, Merrill. *A Practical Guide to Screen Printing.* Chicago, IL: The Advance Group, 1984.

Groff, Pamela; Jorgensen, George; Lavi, Abrahim; and Mooney, Dillon. *Lithographic Press Operator's Handbook.* Pittsburgh, PA: Graphic Arts Technical Foundation, 1988.

Hargrave, Sally and Berkemeyer, Kathy M. (Ed.). *Desktop Publishing with WordPerfect.* Addison, IL: FlipTrack OneOnOne Computer Training, 1990.

Hart, Thomas L. and Everhart, Nancy. *Instant Pagemaker Handbook.* Englewood, CO: Libraries Unlimited, Inc., 1992.

Herod, Thomas D. and Trainor, Diane (Ed.). *Environmental Compliance in the Printing Industry.* Woodstock, VT: Compliance Technologies, 1991.

Hinderliter, Hal. *Understanding Digital Imposition.* Sweickley, PA: Graphic Arts Technical Foundation, 1998.

Hird, Kenneth. *Introduction to Photo-Offset Lithography.* New York, NY: Bennett Publishing Co., 1981.

Hoff, Samuel B. *Screen Printing: A Contemporary Approach.* Albany, NY: Delmar Publishers, 1997.

Holman, R. and Oldring, P. (Ed.). *UV & EB Curing Formulations for Printing Inks, Coatings & Paint.* Port Washington, NY: Scholium International, Inc., 1988.

Holt, Roger W. and Millman, Jack H. *A Methodology for Measurement of Publications Quality.* Redding, MA: Addison-Wesley Publishing Co., 1992.

Holtzschue, Linda; and Noriega, Edward. *Design Fundamentals for the Digital Age.* New York, NY: Van Nostrand Reinhold, 1997.

Hulburt, Allen, *Layout.* New York, NY: Watson-Guptill Publications, Inc., 1989.

Hunt, Larry. *Larry Hunt's Keys to Successful Quick Printing.* Burnham Ln, FL: Larry Hunt, 1988.

An Introduction to Computer-to-Plate Printing [Handbook]. Randolph, MA: Agfa Educational Publishing, Agfa Inc., 1999.

An Introduction to Digital Color Printing [Handbook]. Randolph, MA: Agfa Educational Publishing, Agfa, Inc., 1999.

Japan Typography Staff. *Applied Typography.* Carson, CA: Books Nippan, 1993.

Jinno, Yoh. *Color Communication: How to Get the Most Out of Printers.* Chestnut Ridge, NY: Jinno International, 1989.

Jinno, Yoh. *Creative Process Color Chart.* Chestnut Ridge, NY: Jinno International, 1990.

Jinno, Yoh. *Printing Production Workbook.* Chestnut Ridge, NY: Jinno International, 1990.

Johnson, Jerome L. *Principles of Nonimpact Printing.* Irvine, CA: Palatino Press, 1992.

Johnson, Lois M.; Stinnett, Hester; and Naples, Marie (Ed.); Denick, David and Johnson, Lois M. (Photographers). *Water-Based Inks: A Screenprinting Manual for Studio & Classroom.* Philadelphia, PA: University of Arts Press, 1990.

Kagy, Frederick, D. and Adams, J. Michael. *Graphic Arts Photography.* Albany, NY: Delmar Publishers, 1983.

Karsnitz, John R. *Graphic Arts Technology.* Albany, NY: Delmar Publishers, 1984.

Karsnitz, John. *Graphic Communication Technology.* Albany, NY: Delmar Publishers, 1992.

Kieper, Michael L. *The Illustrated Handbook of Desktop Publishing & Typesetting.* Blue Ridge Summit, PA: Tab Books, 1987.

Kieran, Michael. *Understanding Desktop Color.* Berkley, CA: Peachpit Press, 1994.

King, Jean. *Designer's Guide to PostScript Text Type.* New York, NY: Van Nostrand Reinhold, 1993.

Kleper, Michael L. *The Illustrated Dictionary of Typographic Communication.* Rochester, NY: Technical & Educational Center of the Graphic Arts, Rochester Institute of Technology, 1983.

Kleper, Michael L. *The Illustrated Dictionary of Typographic Communication.* Pittsford, NY: Graphic Dimensions, 1983.

Kosloff, Albert. *Photographic Screen Printing.* Cincinnati, OH: Signs of the Times Publishing Co., 1987.

Krasucki, Cheryl A. *The Art of Professional Typography—Mac Style.* Norfolk, VA: TypograMac Publishing, 1990.

LaBuz, Ronald. *Typography & Typesetting.* New York, NY: Van Nostrand Reinhold, 1987.

Lampe, Harold C. *Paper Complaint Handbook.* Alexandria, VA: Printing Industries of America, Inc., 1988.

Lawson, Alexander S. *Anatomy of a Typeface.* Boston, MA: David R. Godine Publisher, Inc., 1990.

Leach, Robert. *The Printing Ink Manual.* New York, NY: Van Nostrand Reinhold, 1988.

Magee, Babette. *Screen Printing Primer.* Pittsburgh, PA: Graphic Arts Technical Foundation, 1985.

Mantus, Roberta. *Design Guidelines for Desktop Publishing.* Albany, NY: Delmar Publishers, 1992.

McMurtrie, Douglas C. *The Book: Story of Printing & Bookmaking.* New York, NY: Dorset Press, 1990.

Misanchuk, Earl R. *Preparing Instructional Text: Document Design Using Desktop Publishing.* Englewood Cliffs, NJ: Educational Technology Publications, Inc., 1992.

Molla, Rafiqul K. *Electronic Color Separation.* Introduction by Michael Bruno. Charleston, WV: R.K. Printing & Publishing Co., 1988.

Morgenstern, Steve. *No-Sweat Desktop Publishing: A Guide from Home Office Computing Magazine.* New York, NY: AMACOM, 1992.

Mort, J. *The Anatomy of Xerography: Its Invention & Evolution.* Jefferson, NC: McFarland & Co., Inc., Publishers, 1989.

Mott, W. S. *Printing Four Color Process on a Duplicator or Small Press: A How to Guide from Graphic Services Publications.* Arroyo Grande, CA: Graphic Services Publications, 1992.

Mulvihill, Donna C. *Flexography Printer.* Pittsburgh, PA: Graphic Arts Technical Foundation, 1985.

Munro, Kathy. *Bringing Typesetting In-House.* New York, NY: Van Nostrand Reinhold, 1991.

Myers, R. and Harris, M. *Aspects of Printing.* Detroit, MI: Omnigraphics, Inc., 1988.

Nothmann, Gerhard A. and Destree, Thomas M. (Ed.); O'Toole, Mary A. (Illustrator). *Nonimpact Printing.* Pittsburgh, PA: Graphic Arts Technical Foundation, 1989.

Offset Printing Communication Guide System Series. Chestnut Ridge, NY: Jinno International, 1990.

O'Quinn, Donnie; and LeClair, Matt. *Digital Prepress Complete.* Indianapolis, IN: Hayden Books, 1996.

Pantone Book of Color. Moonachie, NJ: Pantone Inc., 1992.

Pantone Color Formula Guide 1000. Moonachie, NJ: Pantone Inc., 1992.

Pantone Color Tint Selector 1000. Moonachie, NJ: Pantone Inc., 1992.

Pantone Library of Color. Moonachie, NJ: Pantone Inc., 1992.

Pantone Process Color Imaging Guide 1000. Moonachie, NJ: Pantone Inc., 1992.

Perfect, Christopher. *The Complete Typographer.* Englewood Cliffs, NJ: Prentice Hall, 1992.

Perfect, Christopher and Rookledge, Gordon. *Rookledge's International Typefinder.* Preface by Adrian Frutiger. Wakefield, RI: Moyer Bell, 1991.

Phil's Photo Staff (Ed.). *A Typeface Sourcebook.* Rockport, MA: Rockport Publishers, 1990.

Pickens, Judy E. *The Copy-to-Press Handbook: Preparing Words & Art for Print.* New York, NY: John Wiley & Sons, Inc., 1985.

Plate Mounting on the Offset Press. Pittsburgh, PA: Graphic Arts Technical Foundation, 1985.

Pocket Glossary of Printing, Binding & Paper Terms. New York, NY: Van Nostrand Reinhold, 1991.

The Print & Production Manual Practical Kit. New York, NY: Van Nostrand Reinhold, 1991.

The Print & Production Manual. New York, NY: Van Nostrand Reinhold, 1991.

Print's Best Letterheads & Business Cards, 1990. Portland, OR: R.C. Publications, 1990.

Printing with a Small Lithographic Offset Press. Pittsburgh, PA: Graphic Arts Technical Foundation, 1985.

Prust, Z. A. *Photo-Offset Lithography.* South Holland, IL: Goodheart-Wilcox Co., 1977.

Publish. January 2000–July 2000. Topsfield, MA: Publish Media.

A Review of Current Imaging Technologies Affecting Major Print Markets [Handbook]. Menasha, WI: Banta Corporation, 1999.

Richardson, Kristin K. (Ed.). *Total Quality Management in the Printing & Publishing Industry.* Alexandria, VA: Graphic Communications Association, 1992.

Richmond, Wendy. *Design & Technology.* New York, NY: Van Nostrand Reinhold, 1990.

Rimmer, Steve. *Graphic File Toolkit: Converting & Using Graphic Files.* Redding, MA: Addison-Wesley Publishing Co., 1992.

Ritchie, Ward. *The Mystique of Printing: A Half Century of Books Designed by Ward Ritchie.* Foreword by Lawrence C. Powell. Sacramento, CA: California State Library Foundation, 1984.

Romano, Frank J. *PDF & Printing Workflow.* Upper Saddle River, NJ: Prentice Hall PTR, 1999.

Romano, Frank J. *Professional Prepress, Printing, and Publishing.* Upper Saddle River, NJ: Prentice Hall, 1999.

Romano, Frank. *The Typencyclopedia: A User's Guide to Better Typography.* New Providence, NJ: Bowker R.R.A. Reed Reference Publishing Company, 1984.

Romano, Frank J.; and Romano, Richard M. *The GATF Encyclopedia of Graphic Communications.* Pittsburgh, PA: GATF Press, 1998.

Rosen, Arnold. *Desktop Publishing: Applications & Exercises.* Fort Worth, TX: Dryden Pr, 1988.

Rosen, Ben. *Digital Type Specimens: The Designer's Computer Type Book.* New York, NY: Van Nostrand Reinhold, 1990.

Rosen, Ben. *Type & Typography: The Designer's Type Book.* New York, NY: Van Nostrand Reinhold, 1989.

Ross, Shirley. *Learning to Print: Level Two.* Los Angeles, CA: Price Stern Sloan, Inc., 1992.

Rudman, Jack. *Offset Lithography.* Syosset, NY: National Learning Corp., 1991.

Ruggles, Philip K. *Printing Estimating,* 4/E, Albany, NY: Delmar Publishers, 1996.

Safe Handling of Materials in the Printing Industry. Lanham, MD: UNIPUB, Division of Kraus Limited, 1988.

Saltman, David and Forsythe, Nina. *Lithography Primer.* Pittsburgh, PA: Graphic Arts Technical Foundation, 1986.

Sassoon, Rosemary. *Computers & Typography.* Allentown, PA: Cromland, Inc., 1993.

Scaling Copy. Pittsburgh, PA: Graphic Arts Technical Foundation, 1985.

Schneider, Robert J., Jr. (Ed.). *Solving Sheetfed Offset Press Problems.* Pittsburgh, PA: Graphic Arts Technical Foundation, 1993.

Schneider, Robert J., Jr. (Ed.) and O'Toole, Alice (Illustrator). *Solving Web Offset Press Problems.* Introduction by Thomas M. Destree. Pittsburgh, PA: Graphic Arts Technical Foundation, 1990.

Schneider, Robert J., Jr. *Aligning & Adjusting Cylinders on the Sheetfed Offset Press.* Pittsburgh, PA: Graphic Arts Technical Foundation, 1990.

Schneider, Robert J., Jr. *Direct-Screen Color Separation Instructor's Guide.* Pittsburgh, PA: Graphic Arts Technical Foundation, 1989.

Schneider, Robert J., Jr. *Direct-Screen Color Separation.* Pittsburgh, PA: Graphic Arts Technical Foundation, 1989.

Schneider, Robert J., Jr. *Make Ready on the Sheetfed Offset Press.* Pittsburgh, PA: Graphic Arts Technical Foundation, 1990.

Schneider, Robert J., Jr. *Operating the Dampening System on a Sheetfed Offset Press.* Pittsburgh, PA: Graphic Arts Technical Foundation, 1990.

Schneider, Robert J., Jr. *Operating the Inking System on the Sheetfed Offset Press.* Pittsburgh, PA: Graphics Arts Technical Foundation, 1990.

Schneider, Robert J., Jr. *Paper Estimating.* Pittsburgh, PA: Graphic Arts Technical Foundation, 1990.

Schneider, Robert. *Layout Preparation & Markup.* Pittsburgh, PA: Graphic Arts Technical Foundation, 1987.

Screen Printing. Pittsburgh, PA: Graphic Arts Technical Foundation, 1988.

The Secrets of Color Management [Handbook]. Randolph, MA: Agfa Educational Publishing, Agfa Inc., 1997.

Seidman, Michael. *From Printout to Published.* New York, NY: Carroll & Graf Publishers, 1992.

Sharma, M. K. (Ed.). *Surface Phenomena & Additives in Water-Based Coatings & Printing Technology.* New York, NY: Plenum Publishing Corp., 1992.

Sharma, M. K. and Micale, F. J. (Ed.). *Surface Phenomena & Fine Particles in Water-Based Coatings & Printing Technology.* New York, NY: Plenum Publishing Corp., 1990.

Shushan, Ronnie and Wright, Don (Ed.). *Desktop Publishing by Design: Aldus PageMaker Edition.* Redmond, WA: Microsoft Park, 1991.

Silver, Gerald A. *Professional Printing Estimating.* Encino, CA: Editorial Enterprises, 1991.

Smith, Keith A. *Structure of the Visual Book.* Buffalo, NY: Sigma Foundation, Inc., 1993.

Smith, Robert C. *Basic Graphic Design.* Englewood Cliffs, NJ: Prentice-Hall, 1992.

Sosinsky, Barrie. *Beyond the Desktop: Tools & Technology for Computer Publishing.* New York, NY: Bantam Books, Inc., 1991.

Southworth, Miles F. *Color Separation Techniques.* Livonia, NY: Graphic Arts Publishing, Inc., 1989.

Southworth, Miles. *Pocket Guide to Color Reproduction Communication & Control.* 3rd ed., Livonia, NY: Graphic Arts Publishing, Inc., 1989.

Spring, Michael B. *Electronic Printing & Publishing.* New York, NY: Marcel Dekker, Inc., 1991.

Stephens, John. *Screen Process Printing: A Practical Guide.* New York, NY: Van Nostrand Reinhold, 1991.

Stone, Bernard and Eckstein, Arthur. *Preparing Art for Printing.* New York, NY: Van Nostrand Reinhold, 1983.

Stone, Summer and Wu, Brian. *On Stone: The Art & Use of Typography on the Personal Computer.* San Francisco, CA: Chronicle Books, 1991.

Stopke, Judy; Staley, Chip; and McClaran, Jeanne L. (Ed.). *An Eye for Type.* Ann Arbor, MI: Promotional Perspectives, Inc., 1992.

Sutton, James and Bartram, Alan. *Typefaces for Books.* Franklin, NY: New Amsterdam Books, 1990.

Swerdlow, Robert M. *The Step-By-Step Guide to Photo-Offset Lithography.* Englewood Cliffs, NJ: Prentice Hall, 1982.

Swerdlow, Robert M. *The Step-by-Step Guide to Screen Process Printing.* Englewood Cliffs, NJ: Prentice Hall, 1985.

Swiftwater, George A. *Small Press Publishing Techniques: Desktop (Word) Publishing.* Round Rock, TX: Homer W. Parker, 1989.

Test Images for Printing. Compiled by Pamela Groff and Frank Kanonik. Pittsburgh, PA: Graphic Arts Technical Foundation, 1990.

Van Milligen, Jane and Gray, Bill. *Tips on Layout & Design.* Blue Ridge Summit, PA: TAB Books, 1992.

Virkus, Robert. *Quark Prepress: Desktop Production for Graphics Professionals.* New York, NY: John Wiley & Sons, Inc., 1993.

Waste & Spoilage in the Printing Industry: Web Press Edition. Teaneck, NJ: National Association of Printers and Lithographers, 1987.

Webb, Richard C. *Screen Printing Production Management.* Cincinnati, OH: Signs of the Times Publishing Co., 1989.

West, Suzanne. *Working with Style.* New York, NY: Watson-Guptill Publications, Inc., 1990.

Westerfield, Wiley. *Desktop Publishing Teletypesetting: A Resource Guide to Electronic Publishing.* San Diego, CA: Westerfield Enterprises, Inc., 1987.

White, Alex. *How to Spec Type.* Introduction by Jan White. New York, NY: Watson-Guptill Publications, Inc., 1987.

White, Jan V. *Color for the Electronic Age.* New York, NY: Watson-Guptill Publications, Inc., 1990.

Wilkinson, Judith. *Designing & Producing Artwork.* New York, NY: Intermediate Technology Development Group of North America, 1985.

Wilkinson, Judith. *Planning the Project.* New York, NY: Intermediate Technology Development Group of North America, 1985.

Wilkinson, Judith. *Printing Processes.* New York, NY: Intermediate Technology Development Group of North America, 1985.

Will-Harris, Daniel. *Desktop Publishing with Style: A Complete Guide to Design Techniques & New Technology for the IBM PC & Compatibles.* Introduction by Peter A. McWilliams. South Bend, IN: And Books, 1987.

Williams, Roger L. *Paper & Ink Relationships.* Introduction by David G. Vequist. Nappanee, IN: Practical Printing Management, 1986.

Williams, Thomas A. *How to Save Money on Printing.* Plantation, FL: Venture Pr., 1991.

Worcester, Robert L. and Pugsley, Anna (Illustrator). *In Print: How to Plan, Purchase, & Produce Print.* Bloomingdale, IL: Media Assocs. International, Inc., 1989.

Working with Prepress and Printing Suppliers [Handbook]. Randolph, MA: Agfa Educational Publishing, Agfa Inc., 1994.

Selected Bibliography
Customer-Defined
Quality Management

Barker, Joel A. *Future Edge: Discovering the New Rules of Success.* New York: Morrow, 1992.

Bennis, Warren. *On Becoming a Leader.* Redding, MA: Addison-Wesley, 1990.

Bennis, Warren. *Why Leaders Can't Lead: The Unconscious Conspiracy Continues.* San Francisco: Jossey-Bass, 1990.

Butman, John. *Flying Fox: A Business Adventure in Teams and Teamwork.* New York: American Management Association, 1993.

Byham, William C. and Cox, Jeff. *Zapp! The Lightning of Empowerment.* New York: Fawcett Columbine, 1988.

Cocheu, Ted. *Making Quality Happen: How Training Can Turn Strategy into Real Improvement.* San Francisco: Jossey-Bass, 1993.

Cribbin, James J. *Leadership: Strategies for Organizational Effectiveness.* New York: AMACOM, 1984.

Crosby, Philip B. *Quality is Free: The Art of Making Quality Certain.* New York: McGraw-Hill, 1979.

Crosby, Philip B. *The Art of Getting Your Own Sweet Way.* New York: McGraw-Hill, 2nd ed. 1981.

Crosby, Philip B. *Quality Without Tears: The Art of Hassle-Free Management.* New York: McGraw-Hill, 1984.

Deming, W. Edwards. *Out of Crisis.* Cambridge, MA: MIT Center for Advanced Engineering Study, c1986.

Deming, W. Edwards. *Quality, Productivity and Competitive Position.* Cambridge, MA: MIT Center for Advanced Engineering Study, c1982.

Denton, D. Keith. *Quality Service.* Houston: Gulf Publishing Company, 1989.

Drucker, Peter F. *Managing for the Future: The Nineteen Nineties & Beyond.* New York: NAL-Dutton, 1992.

Drucker, Peter F. *Managing in Turbulent Times.* New York: Harper-Collins, 1985.

Guest, Robert H. et al. *Organizational Change Through Effective Leadership* (2nd ed.). Englewood Cliffs, NJ: Prentice-Hall, 1986.

Griffiths, David N. *Implementing Quality: With a Customer Focus.* Milwaukee: American Society for Quality Control, 1990.

Juran, Joseph M. *The Corporate Director.* New York, American Management Association, 1966.

Juran, Joseph M. *Juran on Planning for Quality.* New York: Free Press; London: Collier Macmillan, c1987.

Juran, Joseph M. *Juran on Quality by Design: The New Steps for Planning Quality into Goods and Services.* New York: Free Press; Toronto; Maxwell Macmillan Canada; New York: Maxwell Macmillan International, c1992.

Juran, Joseph M. *Juran's Quality Control Handbook.* New York: McGraw-Hill, c1988.

Juran, Joseph M. *Quality Planning and Analysis, from Product Development through Usage.* New York: McGraw-Hill, 1970.

Juran, Joseph M. *Juran on Planning for Quality.* New York: Free Press, 1987.

McLagan, Patricia and O'Brien, Michael. *Designshop: Customer-Focused Instructional Design.* San Diego: Pfeiffer & Co., 1992.

Pascale, Richard T. *Managing on the Edge: How the Smartest Companies Use Conflict to Stay Ahead.*

New York: Touchtone Books, Simon & Schuster Trade, 1992.

Peters, Thomas J. *In Search of Excellence: Lessons from America's Best-Run Companies.* New York: Harper & Row, c1982.

Peters, Thomas J. *Liberation Management: Necessary Disorganization for the Nanosecond Nineties.* New York: A.A. Knopf, 1992.

Peters, Thomas J. *A Passion for Excellence: The Leadership Difference.* New York: Random House, c1985.

Peters, Thomas J. *Thriving on Chaos: Handbook for a Management Revolution.* New York: Knopf; Distributed by Random House, 1987.

Peters, Thomas J. and Waterman, Robert H., Jr. *In Search of Excellence.* New York: Warner Books, 1993.

Prichett, Price and Pound, Ron. *Team Reconstruction: High Velocity Moves for Repairing Work Groups Rocked by Change.* Dallas, TX: Prichett Assoc., 1992.

Quinn, Robert E. et al. *Becoming a Master Manager: A Competency Framework.* Thompson, Michael P. and McGrath, Michael R. (Ed.) New York: Wiley, 1990.

Reid, Peter C. *Well Made in America: Lessons from Harley-Davison on Being the Best.* New York: McGraw-Hill, 1992.

Ryan, Kathleen D. and Oestreich, Daniel K. *Driving Fear Out of the Workplace: How to Overcome the Invisible Barriers to Quality, Productivity, & Innovation.* San Francisco: Jossey-Bass, 1993.

Wellins, Richard S. et al. *Empowered Teams: Creating Self-Directed Work Groups That Improve Quality, Productivity, & Participation.* San Francisco: Jossey-Bass, 1991.

Withers, Ric. *Digital Workflow: Implementing Cost-Effective Print-Based Automation.* San Diego, CA: Windsor Professional Information, 2000.

Zemke, Ron and Bell, Chip R. *Service Wisdom: Creating & Maintaining the Customer Service Edge.* Minneapolis: Lakewood Publications, 1989.

Zemke, Ron and Schaff, Dick. *Service Edge: One Hundred One Companies That Profit from Customer Care.* New York: NAL-Dutton, 1990.

Index